# A History of Herat

Edinburgh Studies in Classical Islamic History and Culture
Series Editor: Carole Hillenbrand

Titles in the series include:

*The Body in Arabic Love Poetry: The 'Udhri Tradition* Jokha Alharthi

*Arabian Drugs in Early Medieval Mediterranean Medicine* Zohar Amar and Efraim Lev

*Towards a History of Libraries in Yemen* Hassan Ansari and Sabine Schmidtke

*The Abbasid Caliphate of Cairo, 1261–1517: Out of the Shadows* Mustafa Banister

*The Medieval Western Maghrib: Cities, Patronage and Power* Amira K. Bennison

*Christian Monastic Life in Early Islam* Bradley Bowman

*Keeping the Peace in Premodern Islam: Diplomacy under the Mamluk Sultanate, 1250–1517* Malika Dekkiche

*Queens, Concubines and Eunuchs in Medieval Islam* Taef El-Azhari

*Islamic Political Thought in the Mamluk Period* Mohamad El Merheb

*The Kharijites in Early Islamic Historical Tradition: Heroes and Villains* Hannah-Lena Hagemann

*Classical Islam: Collected Essays* Carole Hillenbrand

*Islam and the Crusades: Collected Essays* Carole Hillenbrand

*The Medieval Turks: Collected Essays* Carole Hillenbrand

*The Books of Burhān al-Dīn: Literacy and Book Ownership in Mamluk Jerusalem* Said Aljoumani and Konrad Hirschler

*Medieval Damascus: Plurality and Diversity in an Arabic Library – The Ashrafiya Library Catalogue* Konrad Hirschler

*A Monument to Medieval Syrian Book Culture: The Library of Ibn ʿAbd al-Hādī* Konrad Hirschler

*The Popularisation of Sufism in Ayyubid and Mamluk Egypt: State and Society, 1173–1325* Nathan Hofer

*Defining Anthropomorphism: The Challenge of Islamic Traditionalism* Livnat Holtzman

*Making Mongol History: Rashid al-Din and the Jamiʿ al-Tawarikh* Stefan Kamola

*Lyrics of Life: Sa'di on Love, Cosmopolitanism and Care of the Self* Fatemeh Keshavarz

*Art, Allegory and The Rise of Shiism In Iran, 1487–1565* Chad Kia

*The Administration of Justice in Medieval Egypt: From the 7th to the 12th Century* Yaacov Lev

*Zoroastrians in Early Islamic History: Accommodation and Memory* Andrew D. Magnusson

*A History of Herat: From Chingiz Khan to Tamerlane* Shivan Mahendrarajah

*The Queen of Sheba's Gift: A History of the True Balsam of Matarea* Marcus Milwright

*Ruling from a Red Canopy: Political Authority in the Medieval Islamic World, From Anatolia to South Asia* Colin P. Mitchell

*Islam, Christianity and the Realms of the Miraculous: A Comparative Exploration* Ian Richard Netton

*The Poetics of Spiritual Instruction: Farid al-Din 'Attar and Persian Sufi Didacticism* Austin O'Malley

*Sacred Place and Sacred Time in the Medieval Islamic Middle East: An Historical Perspective* Daniella Talmon-Heller

*Conquered Populations in Early Islam: Non-Arabs, Slaves and the Sons of Slave Mothers* Elizabeth Urban

edinburghuniversitypress.com/series/escihc

# A History of Herat

## From Chingiz Khan to Tamerlane

Shivan Mahendrarajah

EDINBURGH
University Press

Edinburgh University Press is one of the leading university presses in the UK. We publish academic books and journals in our selected subject areas across the humanities and social sciences, combining cutting-edge scholarship with high editorial and production values to produce academic works of lasting importance. For more information visit our website: edinburghuniversitypress.com



Edinburgh University Press Ltd
The Tun—Holyrood Road
12 (2f) Jackson's Entry
Edinburgh EH8 8PJ

First published in hardback by Edinburgh University Press 2022

Typeset in 11/15 Adobe Garamond by
Cheshire Typesetting Ltd, Cuddington, Cheshire

A CIP record for this book is available from the British Library

ISBN 978 1 4744 9934 7 (hardback)
ISBN 978 1 4744 9935 4 (paperback)
ISBN 978 1 4744 9936 1 (webready PDF)
ISBN 978 1 4744 9937 8 (epub)

# Contents

## PART TWO  Social, Economic, and Cultural Renewal in Herat

# Illustrations

## Maps



## Figures

## Tables

# Abbreviations

| | |
|---|---|
| *ABC* | *Afghan Boundary Commission* |
| *ANS* | *American Numismatic Society* (*http://numismatics.org/*) |
| *BSOAS* | *Bulletin of the School of Oriental and African Studies* |
| *CAJ* | *Central Asiatic Journal* |
| *CHI* | *Cambridge History of Iran* |
| *Dihkhuda* | *Lughatnamah-yi Dihkhuda* |
| *EIr* | *Encyclopædia Iranica* |
| *EI²* | *Encyclopedia of Islam* (2nd ed.) |
| *EI³* | *Encyclopedia of Islam* (3rd ed.) |
| *EQ* | *Encyclopaedia of the Qur'an* |
| *HJAS* | *Harvard Journal of Asiatic Studies* |
| *IJMES* | *International Journal of Middle East Studies* |
| *JAH* | *Journal of Asian History* |
| *JAOS* | *Journal of the American Oriental Society* |
| *JESHO* | *Journal of the Economic and Social History of the Orient* |
| *JRAS* | *Journal of the Royal Asiatic Society* |
| *PIHC* | *Proceedings of the Indian History Congress* |
| *Toyo Bunko* | *Memoirs of the Research Department of the Toyo Bunko* |
| *ZDMG* | *Zeitschrift der Deutschen Morgenländischen Gesellschaft* |

# Note on Transliteration

The *IJMES* systems for Arabic and Persian are followed. Macrons (*ā*/*ī*/*ū*) and diacritics (*ḍ*/*ḥ*/*s̱*/*ṣ*/*ṭ*/*z̤*/*ż*/*ẓ*) are used; *ayn* (ʿ) and *hamza* (ʾ) represent letters of the alphabet. The letter *waw* is rendered (*w*); diphthongs are (*aw*) and (*ay*); the doubled final form of vowel *ī* is (*-iyy*). Spelling follows options in dictionaries by Hans Wehr and Francis Steingass. Arabic, Turkish, Persian, and Mongol words accepted into English and in Webster's or OED are not transliterated; hence ulama, darwish, waqf, etc.

# Acknowledgments

The genesis of this book is from my time with Professor Richard W. Bulliet at Columbia University, where the importance of Iranian and Islamic local histories was emphasized. Bulliet implanted in me an interest in Shaykh al-Islam Ahmad of Jam, the subject of my first book, *The Sufi Saint of Jam*; and in the Kartid dynasty, which is central to *A History of Herat*. Professor David Morgan[†] was an immense source of inspiration and encouragement for both monographs. I am indebted to both scholars.

I am irredeemably indebted to Geoffrey Khan (Department of Middle Eastern Studies, University of Cambridge); Tony Street (Divinity Faculty, Cambridge); and Jürgen Paul (Der Martin-Luther-Universität Halle-Wittenberg), for their support and manifold acts of kindness over the years. Heartfelt thanks go to faculty and staff at the University of St Andrews, especially Ali Ansari, Andrew Peacock, and Tim Greenwood.

Jürgen Paul, Thomas Barfield, Robert McChesney, and Michael Hope read drafts and offered valuable comments and corrections. Apart from saving me from howlers, the readers forced me to re-evaluate many aspects, such as presentation, arguments, and conclusions. Stephen Album and Bahram ʿAlaʾ al-Dini shared with me their insuperable expertise on Islamic numismatics. I am grateful to each for his assistance. Errors of fact or interpretation that persist despite their diligent efforts are my sole responsibility.

I benefited from bibliographic sources and insights from Kamyar Abedi, Denise Aigle, Viola Allegranzi, Rohullah Amin Mojadiddi, Saqib Baburi, Warwick Ball, Hamid-Riza Ghelichkhani, Norman Hammond, Peter Jackson, Timothy May, Andrew Peacock, Cameron Petrie, Jawan Shir

[†] Died 23 October 2019.

Rasikh, Maria Subtelny, Mehran Toosizadeh, and Neguin Yavari. Thomas Urban and the *Ancient Herat* project are thanked for supplying Figure 10.4, their depiction of the Kartid Wall. Jolyon Leslie and *Aga Khan Trust for Culture* are thanked for supplying schematics of Herat's citadel, one of which is used here as Figure 10.2. Jürgen Paul translated for me sections of Natalia Tumanovich's *Gerat*—a history of Herat in Russian—for which I am very grateful.

I am especially grateful to those individuals who secured copies of documents when libraries were offering limited services during the pandemic: Denise Aigle, Saqib Baburi, Warwick Ball, Tom Barfield, Peter Jackson, Geoffrey Khan, Timothy May, Parviz Mohebbi, Stephen Pow, Jawan Shir Rasikh, Annika Schmeding, Maria Szuppe, Zahra Talaee (Mashhad), and Abdul Wafa Waheed (Kabul). Thank you.

In Herat, I received assistance from Ghulam Haydar Kabiri Harawi,[†] and Behzad and Behzood Hakkak, of Herat University; and Davood Moradian and Shahin Mardin of *Afghanistan Institute for Strategic Studies* (AISS). I am grateful to each of them. Staff at the *American Institute of Afghanistan Studies* (AIAS) in Kabul are thanked for facilitating many sojourns in Kabul, Mazar-i Sharif, and Herat. Special thanks go to Dr. Rohullah Amin Mojadiddi, former Director of AIAS/Kabul, for being a superb friend.

The *Ministry of Foreign Affairs* of the I.R. of Iran facilitated many research visits to Iran. MFA's embassies in London and Colombo; and the *Iranian Cultural Center and Library* in Colombo, are cordially thanked for their manifold courtesies.

*British Institute of Persian Studies* (BIPS), *British Academy, Royal Historical Society, Gibb Memorial Trust, E.G. Browne Memorial Research Fund*, and *Soudavar Fund for Persian Studies*, are thanked for financing my intellectual pursuits. BIPS and British Academy are acknowledged for funding research toward this book. AIAS is thanked for the *John F. Richards Fellowship* that went toward research for this book.

† Deceased (n.d.).

*To my nephew,*
*Amrit,*
*with love*

Map 1 Greater Iran and its neighbors.

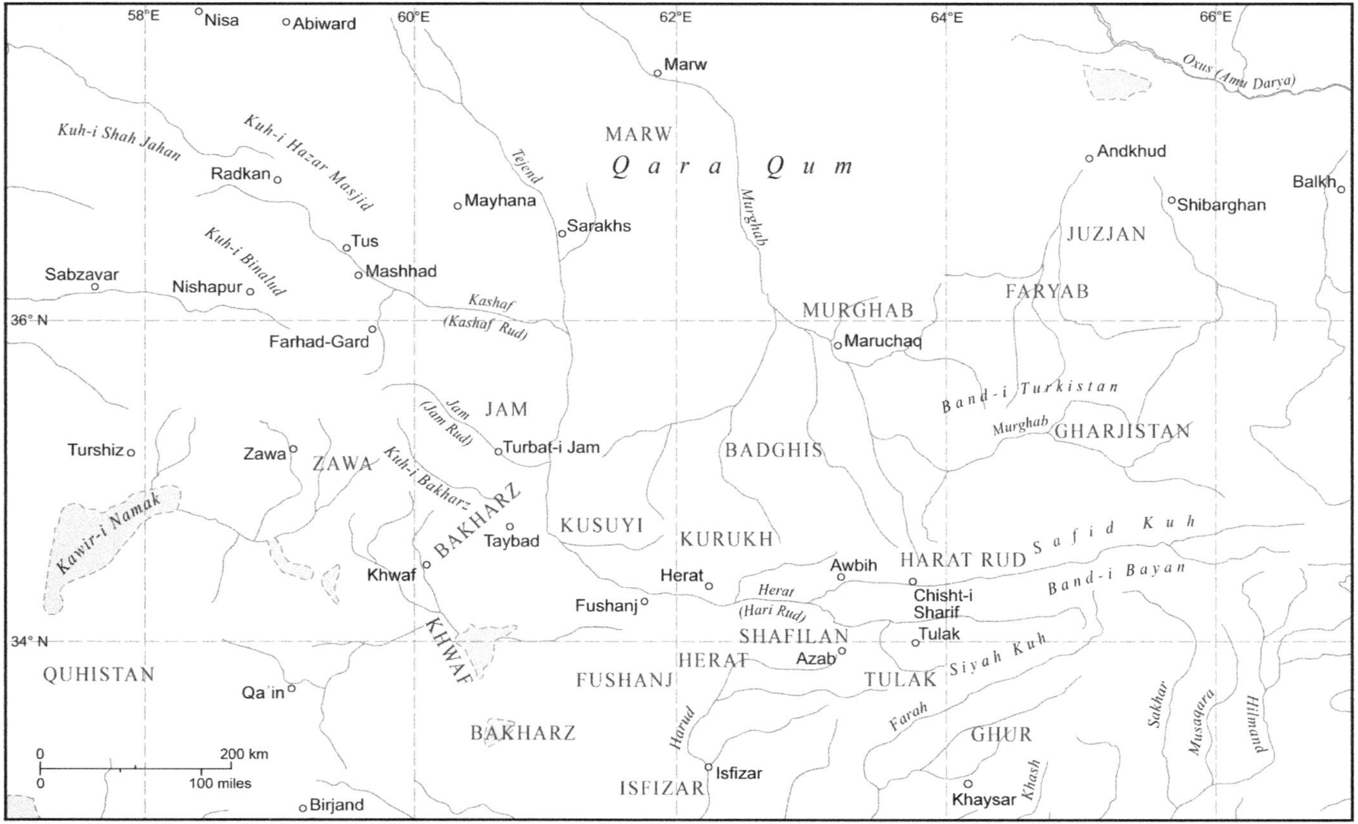


Map 2 Herat and its surroundings.

# Introduction

*Consider this World an Ocean, [and] Khurasan an Oyster within [it]*
*And the City of Herat, the Pearl in its Midst*[1]

This is a history of Herat, a storied city of the medieval Islamic east. Herat has since fallen on hard times, a consequence of Iran's loss of Herat in 1857 pursuant to a treaty imposed on its hapless Qajar shahs (r. 1796–1925) by British imperialists. Herat—the *Pearl of Khurasan*—an Iranian (Tajik) metropolis and epicenter of Islamic learning and ethos, has been trapped inside an alien body.[2]

This Persian city was savaged by Chingiz Khan in 1222,[3] but revitalized by his progeny and an autochthonous Tajik dynasty, the Kartids (1245–1381), which originated in the Ghūr mountains of eastern Persia. Chingiz Khan's grandson and heir, Grand Qaʾan Möngke (r. 1251–58), fostered the Kartid dynasty through his appointment in 649/1251 of Shams al-Dīn Muḥammad Kart as the ruler of Herat, its dependencies, and territories. Kartid domains stretched from Jām, Bākharz, and Khʷāf in the west, to the Oxus, Sīstān, Balūchistān, Indus (*shaṭṭ-i Sind*), and border with India (*ḥadd-i Hind*).

Why Herat? Why not Balkh? Why care about Mongol rejuvenation endeavors at Herat? Why study the history of a medieval Tajik dynasty?

Firstly, it was the Mongols and their Persian advisors that selected Herat for rejuvenation instead of Khurasan's other major cities: Balkh, Marw, or

[1] This epigram appears in manifold medieval Persian texts, including Sayf al-Harawī's *Tarīkhnāmah-yi Harāt*, Ḥamd-Allāh Mustawfī's *Nuzhat al-Qulūb*, Ḥāfiẓ-i Abrū's *Jughrāfiyā*, and Ghiyāth al-Dīn Khʷāndamīr's *Ḥabīb al-siyar*.

[2] "Pearl of Khurasan" is borrowed from Charlie Gammell, *The Pearl of Khorasan* (London: Hurst, 2016), a delightful survey of Herat's history from the Mongols to modern times.

[3] "Persia" is employed except when referring to the modern state.

Nishapur. The Kartids were funded and installed by the Mongols to advance imperial agendas. Herat and the Kartids were, in effect, pre-selected for historians.

Secondly, as Charles Tilly observed, "the wielders of coercion find themselves obliged to administer the lands, goods, and people they acquire; they become involved in extraction of resources, distribution of goods, services, and income, and adjudication of disputes."[4] The Mongol Empire's administration of conquered lands and extraction of resources have been analyzed from the perspectives of the Empire, most notably, by the late Thomas Allsen, in *Mongol Imperialism*. An objective here is to analyze the roles of the city of Herat, its agricultural environs, and eastern Khurasan *within* the Mongol Empire. This is principally a *local history* of a significant Muslim-majority Persian metropolis.

## Historical Approaches

Richard Bulliet expressed "deep dissatisfaction" with the manner of relating Islamic history. The "history of Islam as commonly narrated," he insists, "leads in the wrong direction." This is because "[t]he story of Islam has always privileged the view from the center."[5] This center being the imperial capital (Damascus, Baghdad, Cairo, Istanbul); the empires of the Umayyads, ʿAbbasids, Mamluks, or Ottomans. Local history should *supplement* imperial history. Bulliet's rationale:

> Where the view from the center starts with a political institution, watches it expand mightily, and then observes its dissolution, the view from the edge does the opposite. *It starts with individuals and small communities scattered over a vast and poorly integrated realm*, speaking over a dozen different languages, and *steeped in religious and cultural traditions of great diversity*. From this unpromising start, an impressive measure of social, institutional, and doctrinal cohesion slowly emerges [...].[6]

[4] Charles Tilly, *Coercion, Capital, and European States, AD 990–1990* (Cambridge, MA: Basil Blackwell, 1990), 20.

[5] R.W. Bulliet, *Islam: The View from the Edge* (New York: Columbia University Press, 1994), 4.

[6] Ibid., 8–9 (emphasis added).

Charles Melville's viewpoint complements Bulliet's rationale:

> The history of Iran is still told very much in terms of events on center-stage. A common enough lament: the intrigues at court, the deeds—edifying or otherwise—of the ruler and his entourage, the marching of armies and squashing of revolts, the rise and fall of dynasties, these seem to be the main stuff of history. When recognized for what it is, the tossing of waves, we blame the sources for the fact that we can't see below the stormy surface [...]. *The regions of Iran tend to come into focus only when they are, in fact, briefly transformed into centers.*[7]

The city of Herat is the "pearl"; however, the pearl cannot be truly esteemed without appreciating the "oyster," Khurasan, within which it was nurtured. This is a *local* history with respect to Herat and its *districts* (sgl. *bulūk*); and a *regional* history with respect to the *provinces* (sgl. *wilāyat*) of Herat's Khurasanian cradle. This approach is in accord with Jean Aubin's advice that town and country be studied together.

> This tendency in Persian to not distinguish between the territory, limited or vast, and its dominant locality, prompts us to situate the study of the urban aspect within the framework of the historic territorial divisions. The spatial unit to be observed is not that delineated by the city walls or their surrounding belt of suburbs: the agglomeration [= city of Herat] cannot be dissociated from its territory [= Khurasan].[8]

## Structure and Themes of the Book

The book is in two distinct parts: military-political history in Part One; social and economic history in Part Two. Part One provides the context for Part Two. I have endeavored to cross-reference events and dates from Part One in Part Two, but must avoid repetition.

Part One is divided into three periods (615–76/1218–78, 677–729/1278–1329, 729–83/1329–81). Each period has a prolegomenon. Key themes are highlighted below.

[7] C.P. Melville, "Persian Local Histories: Views from the Wings," *Iranian Studies* 33/1 (2000): 7–14, 7 (emphasis added).

[8] Jean Aubin, "Elements for the Study of Urban Agglomerations in Medieval Iran," In *Cities of Medieval Iran*, eds David Durand-Guedy, et al. (Leiden: Brill, 2020), 27–38, 31.

*Part One: Military and Political Affairs*

Chapters One and Two (years 615/1218 to 676/1278). How eastern Persia—lands congruent with eastern Iran and most of Afghanistan—came to suffer the wrath of the Mongols. Included is Table 1.1, "A Chronological Guide to the Mongol Invasions of Khurasan and Transoxiana, 615/1218 to 619/1222."

Chapter Two. Shams al-Dīn Kart's stewardship was undermined by the political machinations of Chinggisid factions; and his absences from Herat campaigning against the Ilkhanate's enemies, including the Golden Horde. His legacy is a rudimentary state, bound together by a mosaic of loyalists (sgl. *banda*; pl. *bandagān*).

Chapters Three and Four (years 677/1278 to 729/1329). Unfolded is the Roving Bandit[9] v. Stationary Bandit thesis.[10] Economists, principally, Professor Mancur Olson,[11] developed St Augustine's observation on how bands of brigands occupied lands and adopted "the name of a kingdom." The Mongols, who had hitherto thrived on *portable wealth* (gold, livestock, slaves) acquired by *violent theft* (rob and run), realized they stood to profit from the rejuvenation of Herat. The Mongol Empire switched to *gentle theft* (also called taxation). The Mongols became stationary bandits. The Empire needed conscripts for further expansion. Kartids supplied the Mongols with thousands of conscripts.

Chapter Four. Fakhr al-Dīn Kart was a willful man who precipitated sieges of Herat, and earned the enmity of Öljeitü, who as Il-Khan, "devoted much time to fighting with the Kart dynasty of Herat" (Michael Hope's words). But rebuilding of Herat commenced during this turbulent period. Ghiyāth al-Dīn Kart replaced his brother as Herat's ruler. He had to contend for years with Öljeitü's distrust of Kartids; machinations by Ilkhanid amirs against the Kartids and Öljeitü; and migrations from Transoxiana and Chaghataid raids in Khurasan. Included is Table 4.1, "Chaghataid-Ilkhanid

[9] *Roving Bandits*: Bands that despoil and depart (e.g., *early* Vikings and Mongols).

[10] *Stationary Bandits*: Autocrats that develop an economy that they ruined; establish a monopoly on theft; deliver *public goods* (e.g., security, property rights); and create for themselves revenue streams through taxation (e.g., *later* Vikings and Mongols).

[11] "Obituary: Mancur Olson," *The Economist* (7 March 1998).

Struggles for Supremacy in Khurasan: Key Events, 706/1306 to 720/1320." But with this behind him, and Öljeitü dead and a friendly Il-Khan (Abū Saʿīd) and his regent (Amir Chupan) in Tabriz, Ghiyāth al-Dīn's last decade in office was one of the best for Heratis.

Chapters Five and Six (years 729/1329 to 783/1381). The Kartid state transitioned from Ilkhanid client to independent Persian kingdom. The death of Abū Saʿīd accelerated the unraveling of the Ilkhanate. Muʿizz al-Dīn Kart declared a sultanate and reached for the mantle of *Pādishāh-i Islām*—the idealized Tajik Padishah.

The Sarbadar polity emerged in Nishapur Quarter from the chaos that followed Abū Saʿīd's death. They aligned with a "Sufi" shaykh with Shiʿi tendencies. Sarbadars and their Shiʿi allies marched on Herat in 743/1342 but were defeated by the Kartids. Muʿizz al-Dīn and ʿAlī Muʾayyad, the terminal Sarbadar leader, instituted détente and demarcated boundaries between their adjoining kingdoms.

Muʿizz al-Dīn's favored son and heir, Ghiyāth al-Dīn (Pīr ʿAlī), terminated the Sarbadarid-Kartid détente; secured a fatwa from ulama and brought sectarian conflict to Nishapur Quarter. Table 6.1, "Kartid-Sarbadarid Campaigns in the Nishapur Quarter, 773/1371–72 to 783/1381," summarizes the campaigns and social/political impacts.

Temür/Tamerlane, who had consolidated his kingdom and was planning fresh conquests, perceived this abysmal state of affairs. Notables (*ashrāf wa aʿyān*) of Khurasan became fearful of Temür's wrath should Pīr ʿAlī resist his armies as planned. Led by the Kartid vizier, Muʿīn al-Dīn Jāmī, they secretly communicated with Temür to negotiate a soft landing for Herat, its peoples, and themselves.

Thus expired the Kartid dynasty in 783/1381.

*Part Two: Social and Economic Affairs*

Chapters Seven and Eight address efforts to revitalize hydrological systems and galvanize agricultural production. Grand Qaʾan Ögödei (r. 1229–41) took steps, *c.* 634/1236f., to rejuvenate Herat. Canals supplying the inner city with potable water were refurbished and re-opened. Revivification endeavors were impacted by struggles between agents of Chinggisid shareholders. But cooperation was also recorded. The 638/1240–41 census enumerated *c.* 6,900 persons in Herat, and with the re-opening of canals, people "from Khurasan and Turkistan" started migrating to Herat.

Determined revitalization efforts by the Ilkhanate had to await the accession of Maḥmūd Ghāzān (r. 1295–1304). The Il-Khan and vizier, Rashīd al-Dīn, recognized that "there has never been a realm more devastated than this one [Persia]"; and amended, inter alia, land-tenure laws, rates, and modes of taxation. Ilkhanid fiscal-legal reforms inverted the paradigm that had persisted in post-Mongol Khurasan: fear of opaque and fluid fiscal-legal policies. Haphazard policies, and fraught political circumstances, had hindered investments in irrigation systems and fallow lands. Reforms transformed the investment climate: from one where fear of unknowable phenomena (i.e., *immeasurable uncertainties*) dominated, to one where *measurable uncertainties* persisted. A *measurable uncertainty* is a *manageable risk* (i.e., potential for profit/loss can be evaluated).[12]

Ghiyāth al-Dīn Kart and son, Muʿizz al-Dīn, engaged in revitalization endeavors. Muʿizz al-Dīn devised a system for water distribution: water-managers, water-control devices, dams, and barrages diverted water from primary to secondary and tertiary channels, thence to farms. Kartids delegated to Islamic institutions (mosques, shrines, hospices) of Herat and vicinities responsibilities for revitalization and administration of hydrological and agricultural holdings. These agro- and hydro-managers consequently became affluent and powerful. In 906/1511, when the Timurid era expired, Sufi or ʿAlid institutions in Jām, Balkh, Herat, and Mashhad were prominent landlords, waterlords, and agricultural producers. Appendix Two, "Land and Water Use," summarizes the water resources and agricultural products of Herat Quarter.

The rebuilding of Herat is the focus of Chapters Nine and Ten. Development inside Herat began in earnest under Fakhr al-Dīn, who defied Mongol proscriptions on construction in Herat. His brother, Ghiyāth al-Dīn Kart, flush with tax-exemptions, cash, and plunder following victories over Chaghataids and their allies, invested in construction projects. Charitable and commercial construction projects are itemized in Appendix Three, "Urban Development in the Kartid Period."

[12] Conceptualizations on risk and uncertainty are by Frank Knight. "Dr. Frank Knight, Economist, Dies," *New York Times*, 21 April 1972.

Fakhr al-Dīn Kart constructed and/or re-constructed the fortifications of Herat, including walls, bastions, gates, and citadel. Chapter Ten is on (a) Herat's fortifications; and (b) defensive postures. The Kartid's kingdom's network of known strongholds is in Table 10.1, "The fortified landscape of the Kartid realm."

Islamic activities thrived. Benefactors sponsored Sufi hospices (*khānaqāh*) and seminaries (madrasa). Promotion of Sufism and Islamic scholarship; the establishment or re-introduction of ranks and offices like Shaykh al-Islam, *qāḍī al-quḍāt*, *Ṣadr*/*Ṣadr al-Sharīʿa*, and *muḥtasib*, contributed to Herat's rejuvenation.

The thesis propounded is that Herat enjoyed socio-economic recovery. It has been argued that post-Mongol Persia had suffered socio-economic decline, which may be true for regions of Persia, but not for Herat. Arguments in Appendix Four, "Settlements and Population," are that *decline* with respect to Herat is an *assumption*—a bridge built on shaky pillars. Herat under the Timurids witnessed a grand epoch for artistic, literary, intellectual, and Sufi expressions. The splendor of Timurid Herat would not have been possible without the Kartids.

## Note on Sources

An indispensable source for the study of post-Mongol Herat is Sayf al-Harawī's *History of Herat*,[13] which suffers from the "defects" that Melville mentioned: the palace-oriented nature of historical writing. Sayf al-Harawī was commissioned by Kartids and focuses on them, but his history is partly a contemporaneous narrative on Mongol and Kartid Herat. Sayfī's prolixity is irksome; but jewels of socio-economic information are interspersed in *Tarīkhnāmah*. Regrettably, Sayfī expired at an inopportune moment (for this writer): just when Herat began flowering under Kartid rule.

All was not lost. Ḥāfiẓ-i Abrū, a boon-companion (*nidām*) to Temür and informed insider who chronicled the Timurids, picks up Sayfī's baton in

[13] Sayf al-Harawī, *Tarīkhnāmah-yi Harāt*, ed. Ghulām-Riżā Ṭabāṭabāʾi-Majd (Tehran: Intishārāt-i Asāṭīr, 1383/2004); idem, *Tarīkhnāmah-yi Harāt*, ed. Muḥammad Zubayr al-Ṣiddīqī (Calcutta: Baptist Mission Press, 1944). The Tehran edition is used here.

*History of the Kart Kings.*[14] Ḥāfiẓ-i Abrū is perceptive but taciturn; the social-economic data that historians crave is sparse. His writings do not compensate for the lack of contemporaneous reports, from Sayfī's death (*c.* 1322) to late Kartid Herat. A miscellany of historical sources allow for a reasonable reconstruction of the circumstances and characteristics of the rejuvenation of Herat and its environs.

## Note on Terminology: People and Places

The toponyms,[15] hydronyms (bodies of water), hodonyms (streets and such), ethnonyms (or exonyms), and cognomina used by Sayfī are specific.[16] He categorizes, for instance, the composition of the Kartid troops involved in specific campaigns: Harawī (demonym for denizens of Herat), Balūchī, Ghūrī, Sijzī (from Sīstān), Mongol, Nikudari, Afghan,[17] Khalaj, etc.[18] Sayfī and Ḥāfiẓ-i Abrū follow the custom of identifying a person's *balad* (town, district) or *waṭan* (homeland) at micro-level.[19] To illustrate, instead of a macro-*nisba* (e.g. "Khurāsānī"), the *nisba* may be given as "Mābīzhan-Ābādī Khʷāfī": so-and-so from Mābīzhan-Ābād village (Ar. *qarya*; Per. *dīh*), Khʷāf province (*wilāyat*), the kingdom of Khurasan (*mamlakat-i Khurāsān*). This practice persists in Afghanistan and Iran; hence *nisbas* signifying birthplace or domicile (e.g. Aḥmadābādī, Jāmī, Panjshīrī). A person's *waṭan* could be their *manteqa* (*minṭaqah*), a social and geographical zone to which their social

[14] Ḥāfiẓ-i Abrū, *Tārīkh-i salāṭīn-i Kart*, ed. Mīr-Hāshim Muḥaddis̱ (Tehran: Markaz-i pizhūhishī-i mīrās̱-i maktūb, 1389/2010).

[15] See, generally, "Toponymy," *Encyclopaedia Britannica* (online); Jan Tent, "Approaches to Research in Toponymy," *Names* 63/2 (2015):65–74.

[16] On *nisba* (cognomen), see Annemarie Schimmel, *Islamic Names* (Edinburgh: Edinburgh University Press, 1989), 10–12.

[17] Afghan (*awghān*): ethnonym synonymous with Pashtun/Pathan: Indic peoples from the Sulayman Mountains (now Pakistan) that speak Pashtu, an Indo-Iranian language. Pashtuns migrated west into Persian geographical, political, and cultural spaces. See, e.g., Donald Wilber, *Afghanistan* (New Haven: HRAF Press, 1962), 39–44.

[18] Pierre Oberling, "Khalaj," *EIr*, 15:363–64. The Khalaj are Central Asian Turkic peoples. Some Khalaj/Khalji became Ghilzai/Ghilji (Pashtuns). See Muḥammad b. Najīb Bakrān, *Jahān-nāmah*, ed. M.A. Riyāhī (Tehran: Ibn Sina, 1342/1963), 73; Anon., *Ḥudūd al-ʿĀlam*, ed. and tr. Vladimir Minorsky (Cambridge: E.J.W. Gibb Memorial Trust, 1937 [1982 reprint]), 348; Wilber, *Afghanistan*, 42–43.

[19] On terms, see Roy Mottahedeh, "Medieval Lexicography on Arabic and Persian terms for City and Countryside," In Durand-Guedy, et al. (eds), *Medieval Iran*, pp. 465–78.

identities are fused.[20] *Manteqas* are ubiquitous across Afghanistan and eastern Iran. Boundaries of *manteqas* are known to residents,[21] but are usually not delineated on political and/or administrative maps.[22]

A toponym utilized by Sayfī or Ḥāfiẓ-i Abrū is integral to one or more nation-states: Jām, Bākharz and Khʷāf are in Iran; Sīstān is divided between Afghanistan and Iran; Balūchistān is shared by Iran, Afghanistan, and Pakistan. Toponyms change.

Afghanistan, "land of the Afghans," is a creation of British imperialism. It meant something different in Sayfī's time. *Afghānistān* as used by Sayfī refers,[23] approximately, to a tract from Ghazni to Qandahar, which encompassed fertile lands along the Tarnak and Arghandab rivers; and east/southeast to the Sulayman Mountains (see Map 1).[24] It is incorrect to say that Sayfī "uses the designation of Afghānistān in contradistinction to Khurāsān,"[25] which implies equality in territory and significance that did not exist.[26] Möngke's patent itemized territories awarded to the Kartids. *Afghānistān* is one of the twenty-one named provinces (*wilāyāt*) subject to Herat's authority (Chapter Two).

Sayfī limits his use of *macro*-toponyms like Khurasan and Turkistan.[27] Instead, he utilizes *micro*-toponyms: villages, towns, districts.[28] Most of the

[20] Bernt Glatzer, "War and Boundaries in Afghanistan: Significance and Relativity of Local and Social Boundaries," *Die Welt des Islams* 41/3 (2001):379–99, esp. 380–81; Thomas Barfield, *Afghanistan* (Princeton: Princeton University Press, 2010), 19.

[21] While walking with a friend at Turbat-i Jām, he casually said, "we are now in Maʿd-Ābād," the ancient village subsumed by Turbat-i Jām. There were no visible markers.

[22] A reconstruction of *manteqa* boundaries in the Hazarajat is in Alessandro Monsutti, *War and Migration: Social Networks and Economic Strategies of the Hazaras of Afghanistan* (New York: Routledge, 2005), 69–99 and Figures 4–5.

[23] Henceforth, *Afghānistān* will refer to the Kartid era region; Afghanistan, the country demarcated by nineteenth- and twentieth-century British imperialists, and Joseph Stalin.

[24] On *Afghānistān*, see Vartan Gregorian, *The Emergence of Modern Afghanistan* (Stanford, CA: Stanford University Press, 1969), 29.

[25] Christine Noelle-Karimi, *The Pearl in its Midst: Herat and the Mapping of Khurasan (15th–19th centuries)* (Vienna: Österreichischen Akademie der Wissenschaften, 2014), 297. In 2021, *Encyclopædia Iranica* published a multi-author article of 73,253 words on Khurasan. It offers keen social and political analyses (see bibliography).

[26] Khurasan was the "essential core" of *Īrān-zamīn* to certain pre-Mongol writers. In the post-Mongol age, other regions also enjoyed prominence as evinced by their statuses in geographies and histories. *Afghānistān* is not one of them. Charles Melville, "The Mongol and Timurid Periods, 1250–1500," in *Persian Historiography*, ed. C.P. Melville (London: I.B. Tauris, 2012), pp. 155–208, esp. 162–76.

[27] Macro- and micro-toponym have precise uses in onomastics. My usage is limited to the dichotomy of "large geographical space" v. "small geographical space."

[28] On semantic evolution of nouns for city and district, see Aubin, "Urban," 30–31.

micro-toponyms that he supplies are integral constituents of the "land of Iran" or "Greater Iran" (*Īrān-zamīn* or *Īrānshahr*),[29] like Balkh, Bust, Farāh, Herat, Kabul, Marw, and Zābul;[30] or micro-toponyms that abutted historical *Īrānshahr*, like Ghazni[31] and *Afghānistān*. Afghan is an ethnonym in medieval texts;[32] but *Afghānistān* does not materialize until the post-Mongol era.[33] Sayfī is *possibly* the first to mention *Afghānistān*. *Afghānistān* was a micro-toponym that became a macro-toponym because of imperialistic interventions.[34]

We turn to how Herat met ruin: an act of avarice perpetrated in Central Asia by an underling of the Khwārazm-Shāh, the Turkic potentate of Central Asia and Khurasan, which mobilized Chingiz Khan's vengeful armies.

[29] *Īrānshahr*: see Touraj Daryaee, *Sasanian Persia* (London: I.B. Tauris, 2009), 2–6.

[30] See Touraj Daryaee, *Šahrestānīhā i Ērānšahr [Cities of Iranshahr]* (Costa Mesa, CA: Mazda, 2002), esp. 17–21 (regions and cities of Iran); Anon., *Ḥudūd*, §§ 23–24.

[31] Anon./Minorsky, *Ḥudūd*, § 24, ¶ 9 (Ghazni once belonged to India).

[32] Ibid., § 10, ¶¶ 48, 50; Muhammad al-Utbi, *Kitab-i Yamini*, tr. James Reynolds (London: Oriental Translation Fund, 1858), 467–71. See also Gregorian, *Afghanistan*, 29–30.

[33] *Afghānistān* is not in *Ḥudūd al-ʿĀlam* (completed *c.* AH 372/AD 982); nor in Bakrān, *Jahān-nāmah* (completed shortly before the Mongol invasions).

[34] Afghanistan emerged in the past 150 years. Ahmad Shah Durrani (d. 1772), so-called father of Afghanistan, did not use the label Afghanistan: he was Shah of Khurasan. See Sayed Mousavi, *The Hazaras of Afghanistan* (Richmond: Curzon, 1998), 2–5.

# PART I

# IMPERIAL AND LOCAL HISTORIES: MONGOLS AND KARTS

# Prolegomenon
# The Early Period: 615–76/1218–78

Herat lay prostrate before the Mongol corps that had crossed the Oxus into Persia. Inhabitants of Herat and its environs had more than an inkling of the horrors that awaited them: the Mongols' reputation for barbarism, rapine, enslavement, and mass murder had preceded their vanguards. Indeed, Mongols relied on tales of horror to spur capitulations. Balkh, Bukhara, Marw, Nishapur, and Samarqand lay ravaged. Herat was besieged (twice) and suffered terribly. Herat remained desolated for years (Chapter One).

Immediate successors of Chingiz Khan took steps to revitalize Herat (Chapter Two). But Herat was a prize in Chinggisid internecine struggles for supremacy, with factions vying for influence. Möngke created the Kart dynasty to advance the Mongol Empire's aspirations for order and administration in Khurasan. Shams al-Dīn Kart's stewardship was undermined by the political machinations of Chinggisid factions; and his absences from Herat campaigning against the Ilkhanate's enemies, including the Golden Horde.

Shams al-Dīn Kart was assigned vast tracts in Möngke's patent, but had to negotiate and fashion alliances with local lords in those region. If they failed to become his bondsman (sgl. *banda*; pl. *bandagān*), he fought them. His spent years battling recalcitrant local lords in Khurasan, *Afghānistān*, and Sīstān, and the Golden Horde; but left to his heirs a rudimentary state bound together by a mosaic of *bandagān*.

# 1

# Mongol Invasions of Khurasan

## Khurasan before the Mongols

Khurasan was governed by the Khʷārazm-Shāhs,[1] an ancient regnal title adopted by the sovereign of Khʷārazm—the Achaemenid satrapy of Khorezmia: Central Asian lands east of the Caspian. Since the Black Sands (*Qara-Qum*) desert occupies space between the Caspian Sea and the Oxus River (*Amū Daryā, Jayhūn*), and the Red Sands (*Qizil-Qum*) desert does the same between the Aral Sea and Jaxartes River (*Syr Daryā, Sayhūn*), settlements tended to be located along the banks of the Oxus and Jaxartes.[2]

Khʷārazm-Shāhs acquired territories from the fragmented empire of the Great Seljuqs of Persia (r. 431–552/1040–1157) and the Ghurids—the Shansabānī dynasty from the highlands of eastern Persia (r. from before *c.* 401/1011 to *c.* 610/1213).[3] They wrested Transoxiana from the Qara Khitai/Xi Liao (r.*c.* 1141–1218), a dynasty straddling China and the Islamic world.[4] The Khʷārazm-Shāh and Chingiz Khan had,[5] in effect, divided the territories of the Qara Khitai between themselves. The Khʷārazm-Shāh's domains at the cusp of the 615/1218 Mongol invasions were extensive and wealthy, and

[1] The silent *w* in *khw* is in superscript; hence Khʷārazm: "Khorezm"; anglicized Khorezmian. Khorezmian is used instead of the clunky Khʷārazmian.

[2] The geography of Turkic and Mongol Central Asia is adroitly described in Svat Soucek, *Inner Asia* (Cambridge: Cambridge University Press, 2000), 1–29.

[3] C.E. Bosworth, "Ghurids," *EIr*, 10:586–90.

[4] Michal Biran, *The Empire of the Qara Khitai in Eurasian History* (Cambridge: Cambridge University Press, 2005).

[5] On the title, "Chingiz Khan," see Peter Jackson, *The Mongols and the Islamic World* (London: Yale University Press, 2017), 64.

linguistically and ethnically heterogeneous. His realm included Bukhara and Samarqand, and Balkh, Herat, Marw, and Nishapur in Khurasan.

Sultan ʿAlāʾ al-Dīn (Abū al-Fatḥ) Muḥammad (r. 596–617/1200–21), the penultimate Khʷārazm-Shāh, incurred the wrath of Chingiz Khan (d. 1227) through gross provocations. In 615/1218, a merchant caravan from Mongolia to the "Silk Road" oasis town of Utrār (east of the Jaxartes, 195 km/121 miles northwest of Tashkent), was plundered and the merchants massacred by a Khorezmian governor.[6] ʿAlāʾ al-Dīn's culpability is uncertain. Rather than apologizing to Chingiz Khan and executing his subordinate, ʿAlāʾ al-Dīn exacerbated the crisis by executing a Mongol ambassador, and shaving the beards of two ambassadors to humiliate them, thereby affronting Chingiz Khan.[7] The breach of the steppe tradition of the inviolability of envoys terminated Chingiz's quest for a diplomatic solution.[8] He had shown remarkable restraint, but was pushed into war by ʿAlāʾ al-Dīn Khʷārazm-Shāh.[9]

## The Mongol Irruptions

Chingiz Khan mobilized his armies in 615/1218. After consolidating his control in Mongolia, from *c.* 1205 he had followed the nomadic practice of attacking Chinese states. In 1216, he turned west to subjugate the Qara Khitai. It is likely that Chingiz, although sixty years old when the events at Utrār unfolded, would eventually have sought to conquer the territories of the Khʷārazm-Shāh: their states abutted. Chingiz Khan's attentions, however, were turned to the Muslim lands prematurely, fueled by rage. He was not just seeking plunder or tribute, with the incorporation of the Khʷārazm-Shāh's empire into the Mongol empire as his objective: revenge dominated his agendas. Although incensed, Chingiz Khan did not allow his anger to cloud his judgment. He strategized and meticulously planned his

6 For a fresh interpretation of the Utrār crisis, see ibid., 72–75.

7 See Minhāj al-Dīn Jūzjānī, *Ṭabaqāt-i Nāṣirī*, tr. H.G. Raverty, 2 vols (London: Gilbert & Rivington, 1881), 2:966–68; ʿAlaʾ al-Dīn ʿAta-Malik Juvainī, *The History of the World-Conqueror*, tr. J.A. Boyle, 2 vols (Manchester: Manchester University Press, 1958), 1:78–81; Muḥammad b. Aḥmad Nasawī, tr. Mujtabá Mīnuwī, *Sīrat-i Jalāl al-Dīn Mīnkubirnī* (Tehran: Bungāh-i tarjumah wa nashr-i kitāb, 1344/1965), 50–52; V.V. Barthold, *Turkestan Down to the Mongol Invasion* (Cambridge: E.J.W. Gibb Memorial Trust, 4th ed., 1977), 397–99.

8 Michal Biran, *Chinggis Khan* (Oxford: Oneworld, 2007), 55.

9 Paul Ratchnevsky, *Genghis Khan* (Oxford: Blackwell, 2003), 119–34.

campaigns: he gathered troops and sappers (particularly Chinese skilled in siege warfare);[10] and trained his divisions and organized logistics.[11] Chingiz held a hunt in summer 616/1219 that served to train men and horses, and generated stocks of dried meat.[12] He designated his third son, Ögödei (d. 1241), as political heir,[13] which momentarily abated feuding among the fraternal lineages.

In 616/1219,[14] the Mongol armies marched on Utrār. It was captured in 616/1220 (February or March); the governor and Utrār's inhabitants were massacred.[15] Meanwhile, Chingiz Khan had dispatched his eldest son, Jochi (d.*c.* 1225), with an army to subjugate the cities along the northern Jaxartes. A smaller division was dispatched to the Ferghana Valley to do likewise.[16] Even before Utrār fell, Chingiz Khan and youngest son, Tolui (d. 1232), had advanced with the primary corps toward Bukhara and Samarqand, cities on the Zarafshan River, which flows through the Zarafshan Valley located at the southern extremity of the Qizil-Qum. Guided by a renegade Khorezmian scout, Mongols traversed the Qizil-Qum and materialized to the north of Bukhara, frightening the Khorezmian garrison. Units fled but were pursued and massacred. Bukhara surrendered, Dhū al-Ḥijja 616/February 1220,

[10] On Chinese warfare techniques and the Mongols' acquisition of Chinese techniques and technologies, see Ch'i-Ch'ing Hsiao, *The Military Establishment of the Yuan Dynasty* (London and Cambridge, MA: Harvard University Press, 1978), 12, 133 n.79 ("The Mongols mainly relied upon Chinese and later Moslems to manufacture and operate siege machines"); Ratchnevsky, *Genghis*, 131, 173–74 (Mongols possibly employed Muslim siege specialists); Thomas Allsen, "The Circulation of Military Technology in the Mongolian Empire," in Nicolo Di Cosmo, ed. *Warfare in Inner Asian History (500–1800)* (Leiden: Brill, 2002), 265–93; Peter Purton, *A History of the Late Medieval Siege, 1200–1500* (Woodbridge: Boydell, 2010), 2–6, 9–10; Joseph Needham and R. Yates, *Science and Civilization in China* (Cambridge: Cambridge University Press, 2002), 5.6:198, 218–26 (vol. 5, pt. 6; part 7 is 5.7).

[11] Mongol armies were organized in a decimal system: 10s, 100s, 1,000s. A *tümen* is nominally 10,000. Timothy May, *The Mongol Art of War* (Barnesly, UK: Pen & Sword, 2007), 27–41, at 31. Units are designated by position: left-wing (*je'ün ghar*), center (*töb, qol*), right-wing (*barghun ghar*); situated as vanguard, center, rearguard (ibid., figure, p. 37).

[12] On the hunt as military conditioning, see Thomas Allsen, *The Royal Hunt in Eurasian History* (Philadelphia: University of Pennsylvania Press, 2006), esp. 209–32; on care of the army and logistics, see May, *Mongol Art*, 58–68.

[13] Biran, *Chinggis*, 55–56.

[14] The campaign probably commenced in early autumn. Mongols favored fighting in winter and recuperating in summer.

[15] Juvainī/Boyle, *World-Conqueror*, 1:81–86; Jūzjānī/Raverty, *Nāṣirī*, 2:968–71; Barthold, *Turkestan*, 406, 412.

[16] Barthold, *Turkestan*, 406–07.

when elders elected to open the gates. Isolated pockets of resistance were suppressed.[17]

Mongols marched thence to Samarqand. They were reinforced by troops from Utrār led by Ögödei, and Chingiz Khan's second son, Chaghatai (d. 1242). Samarqand capitulated, Muḥarram 617/March 1220, after a brief siege.[18] A general massacre (*qatl-i ʿāmm*)—wanton pillaging, raping, slaying—was not commanded at Bukhara or Samarqand. Both cities were looted; and levies (*ḥashar*) of townsmen were extracted to advance before Mongol soldiers. Craftsmen and artisans, girls and young women, were enslaved. Bukhara fell to flames in the rampage. Samarqand was despoiled and fortifications leveled.

ʿAlāʾ al-Dīn Khʷārazm-Shāh, ensconced in Balkh when Samarqand surrendered, had maintained a large elite army in Samarqand, but which he had failed to deploy to the field or to command effectively.[19] With news of Samarqand's fall, amidst rumblings of dissent in the Khorezmian army, ʿAlāʾ al-Dīn fled thence to Nishapur, arriving in Safar 617/April 1220. Chingiz Khan, with summer 617/1220 nearing, moved his division to the highlands near Samarqand. He dispatched a three *tümen* strike force commanded by generals (*noyan*) Jebe (d.*c.* 1223) and Sübedei (d. 1243), to pursue ʿAlāʾ al-Dīn.[20] Thus commenced the pursuit of ʿAlāʾ al-Dīn across Persia to the Iraq border, thence north to Āẕarbayjān. The sultan found shelter on an island in the Caspian, where he died in winter 617/1220–21. Jebe and Sübedei exited Āẕarbayjān, traversing up the western Caspian Sea route to Central Asia through the Qipchaq Steppe.[21]

[17] Ibid., 409–11.

[18] Ibid., 411–14.

[19] Critics have accused him of pusillanimity and stupidity, but as Barthold observed, the Khʷārazm-Shāh had "inimical relations" with his generals; he needed a military "as docile" as that commanded by Chingiz Khan. If the sultan's "generals had worked in harmony," the outcome could have been different. Barthold, *Turkestan*, 405. The truth of Barthold's insight becomes manifest when measured against the ferocity of the resistance in Herat, Bamiyān, Ghūr, Gharjistān, Ṭāliqān, and other locales in eastern Persia.

[20] Juvainī/Boyle, *World-Conqueror*, 1:142–49; Jūzjānī/Raverty, *Nāṣirī*, 2:987–92; cf. Rashīd al-Dīn Faẓl-Allāh, *Jāmiʿ al-tawārīkh*, in *Classical Writings of the Medieval Islamic World*, ed. and tr. Wheeler Thackston, 3 vols (London: I.B. Tauris, 2012), 3:176–77 (date given for Jebe's and Sübedei's expedition is 618/1221).

[21] A reconstruction of routes taken by Jebe and Sübedei is in Yuri Bregel, *An Historical Atlas of Central Asia* (Leiden: Brill, 2003), Map 18. Further on the mission, see Stephen Pow, "The last campaign and death of Jebe Noyan," *JRAS* 27/1 (2017):31–51, esp. 37–38.

In general, the three *tümen* (nominally 30,000-man) expeditionary force commanded by Jebe and Sübedei did not molest the inhabitants of the districts they entered during the pursuit; however, some cities, like Āmul (on the Oxus), Adkhān/Radkān, Fūshanj, Isfarāyn, and Khabūshān, were attacked because the Mongols had experienced resistance or slights. In cities like Balkh, Nishapur, Jām, Ṭūs, and Juwayn, where submission had been tendered, the expeditionary army demanded comestibles and fodder, appointed overseers (*shaḥna*),[22] settled small garrisons, and resumed their chase.

*Shaḥnas* in early Mongol Persia represented the Khan. Their ill-treatment, coupled with resistance by Jalāl al-Dīn Mengübirtī (d. 628/1231, Kurdistan), the Khʷārazm-Shāh's son and heir, was to prove catastrophic for the peoples of Khurasan. ʿAlāʾ al-Dīn ʿAṭāʾ-Malik Juwaynī (1226–83),[23] a historian, and an official with the "Toluids" (the branch descending from Chingiz Khan's son, Tolui), is not a neutral narrator: his tone and prose are manifestly panegyrical. But Juwaynī does not sanitize Mongol violence.[24] Regarding the Transoxiana campaign, he emphasizes that Chingiz Khan had not "caused a river of blood to flow"; the capture of Samarqand and Bukhara had not led "to the extreme of a general massacre."[25] Despite localized resistance and sporadic rebellions—including the murder of a *shaḥna* and an envoy—Juwaynī's assessment is accurate:[26] the peoples of Transoxiana were punished less harshly than the peoples of Khurasan.[27]

The division commanded by Jochi had traversed northwest along the Jaxartes and captured tracts to the north and east of the Aral Sea, although total subjugation was not realized immediately.[28] Jebe and Sübedei were still pursuing the Khʷārazm-Shāh in Persia. The Transoxiana phase of the

22 On overseers (*dārūġachī, dārūġa, basqaq, shaḥna*), see Timothy May, *The Mongol Empire* (Edinburgh: Edinburgh University Press, 2018), 82–84, 88–91 and his notes (especially to titles by Istaván Vásáry and Donald Ostrowski); Jackson, *Mongols*, 107–111.

23 On this family, see George Lane, *Early Mongol Rule in Thirteenth-Century Iran* (London: Routledge Curzon, 2003), 177–212.

24 Mongols are vilified in literature, but romanticized Alexander of Macedon, on his eastern campaigns, raped, massacred, deported, and enslaved people; looted and wrecked cultural heritages. Historian Arrian (d.*c.* AD 160) emphasized Alexander's "body count."

25 Juvainī/Boyle, *World-Conqueror*, 1:96; see also Jackson, *Mongols*, 157.

26 Juvainī/Boyle, *World-Conqueror*, 1:96–97 (punishments of towns in Iraq and Persia).

27 This topic has been exquisitely treated in Jackson, *Mongols*, 153ff.

28 Juvainī/Boyle, *World-Conqueror*, 1:86–91; Constantin d'Ohsson, *Histoire des Mongols* (Amsterdam: Frederik Muller, 1852), 1:221–24.

campaign was nearing its terminus. The division commanded by Chingiz Khan summered at Nakhshab/Qarshi.[29] Mongol armies,[30] meanwhile, prepared for the next campaign: the invasion of Persia.

## The Mongols in Persia

### *Balkh*

In Autumn 617/1220, Chingiz Khan's army advanced from Nakhshab toward Tirmiz, a populous and thriving entrepôt on the north bank of the Oxus. Tirmiz was invested; the citadel fell. Tirmiz was razed and its denizens were massacred. Following a pause along the embankments of the Oxus in Winter 617/1220–21, presumably to prepare for the fording, Chingiz Khan crossed the Oxus. In the taxonomy of the epoch, Khurasan comprised four "quarters" (*rubʿ*), with each *rubʿ* led administratively and culturally by the capital city that lent the quarter its name: Balkh, Marw, Nishapur, and Herat.[31]

Balkh, at the cusp of annihilation, enjoyed bounteous intellectual and architectural legacies. The *dārūġa* installed by Jebe and Sübedei was murdered. Balkh capitulated Dhū al-Ḥijja 617/February 1221 after a thirty-seven day siege.[32] Balkh, after being spared initially, was pillaged, devastated, and inhabitants massacred because Mengübirtī was "riding his horse on to the field of rebellion and contumacy."[33] Balkh never did regain its glory, but enjoyed efflorescence under Timurids (1381–1506) and Shaybanids (10th/16th century). It is a charming town, home to the resplendent shrine of Khʷajah Abu Nasr Parsa. Balkh is now overshadowed by Mazar-i Sharif ("the Noble Shrine"), which professes to hold the blessed sepulcher of Hazrat Imam ʿAli b. Abi Talib (d. 40/661).

[29] Qarshi or Nakhshab: oasis at 1,227 ft/374 m, *c.* 83 miles/134 km southwest of Samarqand. It became a summer pasture for Mongols.

[30] Determining the size of the Mongol armies has vexed scholars; but generally admitted as 100,000 to 130,000 Mongol "regulars" at the peak of Chingiz Khan's career. Recruits, allies, and levies swelled Mongol ranks. John Masson Smith, "Mongol Manpower and Persian Population," *JESHO* 18 (1975):271–99; David Morgan, "The Mongol Armies in Persia," *Der Islam* 56/1 (1979):81–96; May, *Mongol Art*, 27–31.

[31] On the four *rubʿ* and the primary towns in each quarter, see Ḥamd-Allāh Mustawfī, *Nuzhat al-Qulūb*, ed. Guy Le Strange (London: Luzac & Co., 1915), 147–59; idem, tr. Guy Le Strange (London: Luzac & Co., 1919), 146–56; Guy Le Strange, *The Lands of the Eastern Caliphate* (New York: Barnes & Noble, 1966), 382–432.

[32] al-Harawī, *Harāt*, 87.

[33] Juvainī/Boyle, *World-Conqueror*, 1:130. See also Jackson, *Mongols*, 159 and n.47.

At this juncture, the division commanded by Chingiz Khan diminishes in interest for our narrative. After Balkh, Chingiz Khan, learning of fierce resistance at Fort Naṣr-Kūh in Ṭāliqān,[34] decided to personally support the besiegers.[35] The Khan, however, had to hastily disengage and join the hunt for Mengübirtī: in late Spring/early Summer 618/1221, three *tümens* of reinforcements for a defeated vanguard were themselves defeated at Parwān[36] by Turkic and Ghurid forces commanded by Mengübirtī.[37] Chingiz, after delegating to officers the siege of Naṣr-Kūh, marched on Ghazni, suffered resistance at Gurzuwān (west of Ghūr) that delayed him a month,[38] and detoured east to Bamiyan.[39] Chingiz Khan was responsible for the carnage at Bamiyan (late Summer/early Autumn 618/1221), vengeance (sources allege) for a grandson killed at Bamiyan.[40] Pressured by the Khan's division,[41] Mengübirtī retreated over the River Indus (Shawwāl 618/ November 1221).[42] After spending summer 619/1222 in the pastures of Baghlān,[43] Chingiz Khan re-crossed the Oxus in Autumn 619/1222. He would not return to Persia.

[34] Ṭāliqān: Jūzjānī/Raverty, *Nāṣirī*, 2:1,008, n.5; V.V. Barthold, *An Historical Geography of Iran*, tr. Svat Soucek (Princeton: Princeton University Press, 1984), 35–37; Le Strange, *Lands*, 423–24. Ṭāliqān was in the Murghāb basin, equidistant from Marw al-Rūd (near Murghāb), and Dawlat-Ābād (Fāryāb). On the Ṭāliqān situated east of Qunduz, see Ludwig Adamec (ed.), *Historical and Political Gazetteer of Afghanistan*, 6 vols (Graz: Akademische Druck und Verlagsanstalt, 1972–1985), 1:176–77.

[35] On Naṣr-Kūh receiving the attention of Chingiz, see Juvainī/Boyle, *World-Conqueror*, 1: 131–32; Jūzjānī/Raverty, *Nāṣirī*, 2:1008–12; Barthold, *Turkestan*, 439.

[36] Parwān: Barthold, *Geography*, 23; Adamec, *Gazetteer*, 6:639.

[37] On Mengübirtī's rallying of Khorezmian loyalists in Ghazni, and the Battle of Parwān, see Juvainī/Boyle, *World-Conqueror*, 2:404–07; Jūzjānī/Raverty, *Nāṣirī*, 2:1016–21; Nasawī/ Mīnuwī (tr.), *Mīnkubirnī*, 106–09; see also Barthold, *Turkestan*, 441–42; Jackson, *Mongols*, 80, 88.

[38] Juvainī/Boyle, *World-Conqueror*, 1:132. Jūzjānī/Raverty, *Nāṣirī*, 2:1,003: Gurzuwān had a citadel. Sayfī names Gurzuwān (Jurziwān/Jurzuwān) as a dependency of Herat. al-Harawī, *Harāt*, 619; Barthold, *Turkestan*, 443–44 (on the events). On the toponym, see Barthold, *Geography*, 32; Le Strange, *Lands*, 424.

[39] Juvainī/Boyle, *World-Conqueror*, 1:132–33; Barthold, *Turkestan*, 443–44.

[40] Ratchnevsky, *Genghis*, 161–64.

[41] On the battle, see Nasawī/Mīnuwī (tr.), *Mīnkubirnī*, 110–12.

[42] Mengübirtī remained in India until 620/1223 then returned to Persia. See Peter Jackson, "Jalāl al-Dīn, the Mongols, and the Khwarazmian Conquest of the Panjāb and Sind," *Iran* 29 (1990):45–54. He died an ignominous death in 628/1231 at the hands of Kurdish bandits.

[43] Barthold, *Turkestan*, 454–55.

In Ṣafar 618/April 1221, after a siege of four to six months, armies commanded by Jochi, Ögödei, and Chaghatai seized Urganch, Khʷārazm's capital. The population was massacred after the usual levies. The three brothers had been disunited in purpose, which forced Chingiz Khan to appoint Ögödei as their supreme commander. The siege of Ṭāliqān was underway when Urganch fell.[44] The brothers, although quarrelsome, united to divide the booty: they "shared the people of the cities among all three of them but did not give Činggis Qa'an a share," thus infuriating their father.[45] Reports, assuredly exaggerated by narrators with each retelling, and rumor-mongering, of Mengübirtī's actual or chimerical successes against hitherto "invincible" Mongol armies, inspired scattered rebellions and spawned the murders of Mongol overseers. The murders had terrible consequences for the peoples of Khurasan.

*Marw*

Tolui, "a daring soldier," in René Grousset's romanticizing words, "dreaming only of conquests,"[46] unleashed his armies across Khurasan, in part to squash scattered rebellions that had manifested as news or rumors of Mengübirtī's real or imagined triumphs reached Persian ears. Chingiz Khan had invested Ṭāliqān citadel when the Balkh phase of operations concluded. The Khan's division was apportioned (at Ṭāliqān): "a large army" was allotted to Tolui;[47] another was tasked with suppressing Mengübirtī's insurgency.[48] Tolui's expedition (*c.* 80,000 men) decamped for Marw, the first Khurasanian quarter to be targeted afresh, in Dhū al-Ḥijja 617 or Muḥarram 618/late February–March 1221.

44 Ibid., 433–37. Igor de Rachewiltz, *The Secret History of the Mongols* [*Yüan ch'ao pi-shih* or *Mongqol-un niuča to(b)ča'an*], 3 vols (Leiden: Brill, 2004–13), § 260.

45 de Rachewiltz, *Secret History*, § 260.

46 René Grousset, *Empire of the Steppes* (New Brunswick, NJ: Rutgers University Press, 1970), 255.

47 Juvainī/Boyle, *World-Conqueror*, 1:131–32, 1:150–52; Jūzjānī/Raverty, *Nāṣirī*, 2:1,027, n.8 (Tolui at Ṭāliqān; Chingiz Khan's allocations to Tolui's army); cf. Rashīd al-Dīn/Thackston, *Jāmi'*, 3:180 (Tolui dispatched in Autumn 617/1220).

48 Juvainī/Boyle, *World-Conqueror*, 1:133.

Tolui completed his mission in three months.[49] Settlements in each *rub*ʿ were to be systematically reduced, and inhabitants deported or exterminated. The Nishapur Quarter contained a surfeit of burgs and village agglomerations, foremost being Abīward, Isfarāyn, Jājaram, Juwayn, Mashhad-Ṭūs, Nisā, Radkān, Sabzavār, and Sarakhs.[50] Herat Quarter had towns and dependencies like Bākharz, Jām, Fūshanj, Khʷāf, Kūsūyi, and Zāwa (in the west); Isfizār and Mālān (to the south); Bādghīs, Kurūkh, Murghāb (north/northeast); settlements in Ghūr and Gharjistān (east), and along the Herat River Valley (the largest being Awbih).[51]

The (now-late) Khʷārazm-Shāh's governor at Marw decided to resist. Tolui spent several days surveying Marw's defenses before launching his attack. The siege lasted three weeks, with high casualties on both sides. An *imām* was sent outside to parley with Tolui, who honored him. The *imām* returned to Marw. Lulled by Tolui's offer of clemency, Marw's governor emerged with a retinue. Tolui demanded 400,000 dinars in ransom and promised him safe conduct. The governor identified 400 notables to be held hostage until the ransom was paid; but when the notables came outside, they were seized and subjected to tortures (to extract payment). Although the ransom was paid, governor and retinue were slaughtered. Tolui ordered the destruction of Marw and the annihilation of its peoples. The task behind him, he turned to Nishapur.[52]

### *Nishapur*

Jebe and Sübedei had passed through Nishapur, *c.* Rabīʿ I 617/May–June 1220. They had summoned local dignitaries, including the city's

[49] al-Harawī, *Harāt*, 91: Tolui's departure given as Rabīʿ I 618/May 1221. This is late. See, e.g., Juvainī/Boyle, *World-Conqueror*, 1:160: 1 Muḥarram 618/25 February 1221 for Tolui being at Marw, i.e., he had departed in late Dhū al-Ḥijja 617/February 1221. See de Rachewiltz, *Secret History*, § 258: Tolui ordered to Iru (Herat), Isebür (Nishapur), and other Khurasanian towns; cf. § 259: Tolui's return after attacking settlements along the Hari Rud.

[50] On the Nishapur Quarter, see Le Strange, *Lands*, 382–96.

[51] On the Herat Quarter, see ibid., 407–19. Bākharz, Jām, Khʷāf, and Zāwa are often listed by geographers as within Quhistān region. See ibid., 352–63.

[52] al-Harawī, *Harāt*, 92–95; cf. Juvainī/Boyle, *World-Conqueror*, 1:160–63 (different rendition).

Shaykh al-Islam, shown them a letter in Uighur (presumably a *pāʾīza*),[53] demanded provisions and fodder, rustled livestock, and left.[54] Jebe and Sübedei could not have subjugated and garrisoned every burg they entered because their mobile force was not equipped for siege warfare and occupation; moreover, Jebe and Sübedei often divided their forces by sweeping in different directions (a tactic to protect their flanks and rear). The pair relied instead on terror and the Mongols' fearsome reputation to prevent settlements to their rear from rebelling. If burghers see Mongols less frequently, Juwaynī noted in colorful terms, they are tempted to rebel;[55] hence the dispatch of Toquchar Bahadur (d. 617/1220) to protect Sübedei's and Jebe's rear, suppress rebellions, and pave the path for the principal Mongol corps.[56]

Toquchar's army reached Nishapur around Ramaḍān 617/November 1220.[57] Sayfī's report of the circumstances leading to Toquchar's death at Nishapur states that Sübedei and Jebe were present: they had wanted to pursue the shah, but Toquchar had been willful and advanced on Nishapur to steal livestock.[58] Sayfī is confused: Toquchar's disobedience of Chingiz Khan's orders was in the Year of the Hare (1219), an act for which he could have been executed but was only demoted.[59] The circumstance of Toquchar's death is unclear; the consequences, however, are clear. An imperial decree (*yarlīgh*) was issued: Nishapurians' effrontery had to be punished; henceforth, no creature was to live in Nishapur and the city itself was to be effaced from the earth.[60]

Before addressing Tolui's attack on Nishapur, his arsenal is examined.

[53] Chinese: *pʾai-tzu*; Mongolian: *gerege*: a "tablet of authority" carried by envoys (*ilchī*). This practice has eastern origins. Tablets were of gold, silver, or wood, with engravings. David Morgan, *The Mongols* (Oxford: Blackwell, 2d ed., 2007), 90–94 and Plate 4.3.

[54] Juvainī/Boyle, *World-Conqueror*, 1:172–73.

[55] Ibid., 1:173: "When for some time the passing of Mongol armies had been less frequent [. . .], the demon of temptation laid an egg in the brains of mankind."

[56] Chingiz deployed Toquchar as Sübedei's rearguard in the "Year of the Hare" (616/1219). de Rachewiltz, *Secret History*, § 257: "He sent Jebe as vanguard. He sent Sübeʾetei in support of Jebe and sent Toqučar in support of Sübeʾetei." Jebe + Sübedei + Toquchar = vanguard + middle + rearguard. On Mongol formations, see May, *Mongol Art*, 37.

[57] Juvainī/Boyle, *World-Conqueror*, 1:174 (date of arrival).

[58] al-Harawī, *Harāt*, 97.

[59] See de Rachewiltz, *Secret History*, § 257; on Toquchar, see *Secret History*, 2:940–41, 1031.

[60] al-Harawī, *Harāt*, 96.

The arsenal according to Sayfī:[61] 3,000 siege crossbows (*charkh-andāz*);[62] 100 *manjanīq*[63] *wa ʿarrāda*;[64] 1,000 scaffolds (*kharak*);[65] 4,000 ladders (*nardubān*);[66] 1,700 naphtha-hurlers (*naft-andāz*).[67] They brought 2,500 *kharwār*s of stone for use as projectiles.[68]

Quantities and classes of armaments offered by Sayfī are not dispositive,[69] but are useful in appreciating, inter alia, the differences between a mobile expeditionary force (like Jebe's and Sübedei's) and a siege army.[70] The former rarely possesses siege equipment and artillery, whereas the latter marches ponderously. Since *manjanīq wa ʿarrāda* must first be stripped for transport, then re-assembled and repaired before deployment, army engineers expend time re-assembling and preparing the equipment.

[61] al-Harawī, *Harāt*, 98. I thank Timothy May for his assistance in unpacking details on the weapons. Mistakes remain my responsibility. On definitions of arcuballistae and ballistae, and development of torsion and non-torsion artillery, see E.W. Marsden, *Greek and Roman Artillery: Historical Development* (Oxford: Clarendon, 1969), *et passim*. On crossbow types, see Needham, *Science*, 5.6:120–78, 187–99; George Lane, *The Mongols in Iran: Quṭb al-Dīn Shīrāzī's Akhbār-i Moghūlān* (New York: Routledge, 2018), 78–79.

[62] *Charkh-andāz*: rendered as "shooters of fiery arrows worked by a wheel." Jūzjānī/Raverty, *Ṭabaqāt-i Nāṣirī*, 2:1,191, n.1; not challenged by Needham, 5.6:219; cf. Kate Raphael, "Mongol Siege Warfare on the Banks of the Euphrates and the Question of Gunpowder (1260–1312)," *JRAS* 19/3 (2009):355–70, 361 ("hurled round catapult stones").

[63] *Manjanīq* (*manganon, manganikon*): terms for "pole-framed trebuchet," but broadly refers to "any model of trebuchet." Paul Chevedden, "The Invention of the Counterweight Trebuchet: A Study in Cultural Diffusion," *Dumbarton Oaks Papers* 54 (2000): 71–116, 79.

[64] *ʿArrāda*: "comes from a nearly identical Aramaic form, which is a direct translation of the Greek *onagros* ('wild ass')." Semantic shifts led to confusion in understanding. W.T.S. Tarver, "The Traction Trebuchet: A Reconstruction of an Early Medieval Siege Engine," *Technology and Culture* 36/1 (1995):136–67, 144. See also Needham, *Science*, 5.6:184–240.

[65] *Kharak*: "little donkey." Not the *onager* (see *onagros*, above). Engineers erected scaffolds (*kharak*) to shield sappers and fighters from weapons launched from battlements.

[66] *Nardubān*: On ladder types, see Needham, *Science*, 5.6:446–55.

[67] *Naft-andāz*: Needham, *Science*, 5.7:73ff.; Jackson, *Mongols*, 88–89, 136–38, nn.79–81, 129–130.

[68] al-Harawī, *Harāt*, 98. One *kharwār* ≈ 297 kg/653.40 lb (equivalent to one "ass-load"). If the statement is accepted literally, Tolui's army hauled 742,500 kg/1,633,500 lb of stones.

[69] Cf. Juvainī/Boyle, *World-Conqueror*, 1:176 (quantities of weapons are different). Further on Mongol armaments (albeit for the era that began with Hülegü's 653/1255 entry to Persia), see Jackson, *Mongols*, 136–38 and nn.75–88.

[70] A siege army epitomizes *combined arms warfare*: "the cooperation and combination of different military units (such as infantry, artillery, and cavalry) in a military operation." Timothy May, "Military Integration in Mongol Warfare: The development of Combined Arms Warfare in the Mongol Empire," *Acta Mongolica* (2019):41–51.

*Naft-andāz* requires qualification.[71] Persian primary sources use *naft* in a manner that subsumes other implications for *naft*; for example, gunpowder usage. "[T]here is evidence from Chinese sources that at Bukhara [...] the invading Mongol armies deployed incendiary devices based on gunpowder."[72] Chinese technology had advanced such that "[c]atapults capable of throwing fire-bombs to a considerable distance were in use in China by the mid-eleventh century."[73] Technologies would have progressed by the early thirteenth century; and techniques will have improved through battlefield experiences between 1218 and 1222 when Mongols were fighting in Central Asia and Persia. The employment of gunpowder at Balkh, Marw, Nishapur, and Herat cannot be shown, but the possibility of gunpowder usage exists. However, since the second siege of Herat lasted six to eight months, gunpowder devices, if used, did not generate "shock and awe" (to adopt a modern military colloquialism), shorten the siege, or compel capitulation.

Ballistae and mangonels of miscellaneous technical categories, "primitive" weapons in modern terms, were deadly when employed by professionals.[74] As Peter Jackson noted, Chinese technologies and techniques had advanced significantly: "the striking-range of Chinese siege engines had undergone a threefold increase in the twelfth-century [...]."[75] A florid description of the power of siege engines, albeit from AD 67—*c.* 1,153 years before more sophisticated weapons were employed by Mongols—comes from Flavius Josephus, on the Roman siege of Jotapata by Vespasian (d. 79), later Emperor of Rome (r. AD 69–79):

71 *Naft* (naphtha) is often termed "Greek fire," but chemical-based incendiaries of sundry types have been in use since antiquity. J.R. Partington, *A History of Greek Fire and Gunpowder* (Baltimore: Johns Hopkins University Press, 1999), 1–41.

72 Jackson, *Mongols*, 89.

73 S.G. Haw, "The Mongol Empire: the first 'gunpowder empire'?," *JRAS* 23/3 (2013):441–69, 445; L.C. Goodrich and Feng Chia-sheng, "The Early Development of Firearms in China," *Isis* 36/2 (1946):114–23; Wang Ling, "On the invention and use of Gunpowder and Firearms in China," *Isis* 37/3 (1947):160–78; John M. Smith, "Mongol Warfare with Chinese Weapons: Catapults—and Rockets?," in V.P. Nikonorov (ed.), *Tsentral'naia Aziia ot Akhemenidov do Timuridov* (St Petersburg: In-t istorii material'noĭ kul'tury RAN, 2005), pp. 320–22.

74 On ranges and effects of artillery, see Marsden, *Greek*, 86–98. "[A]ncient artillery, when operated by skillful hands, could achieve a high standard of accuracy right up to maximum effective range." Ibid., 94.

75 Jackson, *Mongols*, 88.

> [F]or the force with which these engines threw stones and darts made them hurt several at a time, and the violent noise of the stones that were cast by the engines was so great, that they carried away the pinnacles of the wall, and broke off the corners of the towers [...] his head was carried away by such a stone, and his skull was flung as far as three furlongs.[76]

Artillery is powerful and terrifying, but artillery by "itself cannot win battles or take cities. [In every instance] the final blow must be delivered by infantry and cavalry."[77] Thus so at Nishapur.

Tolui launched his offensive in Ṣafar 618/March–April 1221.[78] Nishapur's governor, Sharaf al-Dīn Amīr Majlis (depicted as cocksure but courageous), emplaced 12,000 archers at each of the four gates (meaning, the parapets along the battlements).[79] After eight days of intense fighting, with heavy casualties on both sides, Nishapur's governor sent the city's *qāḍī*, Mawlānā Rukn al-Dīn ʿAlī b. Ibrahīm al-Marghīsī, out to parley with Tolui. The noble Mawlānā did not return. The next day, besiegers launched their offensive, concentrating the power of mangonels and naphtha-throwers (on one sector).[80] Scaffold teams advanced. Sappers filled in (sections) of the trench (*khandaq*). Dawn broke and battle cries pierced the air as 10,000 "bloodthirsty" (*khūn-khʷār*) warriors surged inside Nishapur through seventy breaches (sgl. *sūrākh*) in the ramparts (*dīwār-i bārū*).[81]

*Dīwār-i bārū* is built atop the mound. Breaches were struck along the battlements (top of the *dīwār-i bārū*). This section reflects crenels and merlons, and is weaker than the wall's base. Infantrymen advanced to the "pinnacle of the battlements" (*shurufāt-i bārū*), that is, they scaled the mound ("assault

76 Flavius Josephus, *The Wars of the Jews*, tr. William Whiston (n.p., n.d.; [London: J.M. Dent, 1928?]), Book 3, Chapter 7, § 23.

77 Marsden, *Greek*, 99.

78 al-Harawī, *Harāt*, 98: Thursday, "middle of (*muntaṣaf*) Rabīʿ II" = 16 Rabīʿ II 618/9 June 1221. The date is precise but probably late.

79 The citadel had two gates and the city had four. On the pre-Mongol city and fortress, see Richard Bulliet, "Medieval Nishapur: A Topographic and Demographic Reconstruction," *Studia Iranica* 5 (1976):67–89, esp. 73, 85–86.

80 Sayfī does not specify concentration of fire, but focusing artillery strikes is common military practice; moreover, fire concentration was a Mongol tactic. They used signals and banners to direct artillerymen. May, *Mongol Art*, 72.

81 al-Harawī, *Harāt*, 99.

by escalade") using the 4,000 ladders, and entered Nishapur through the (seventy-plus) breaches.[82]

Mongols advanced to the city center. Women, children, elderly, the infirm—hitherto sheltered by Nishapur's walls and from the impacts of enemy projectiles—were suddenly trapped in the middle and at the mercy of the Mongols. Nishapur's governor and warriors (*mubārizān wa ṣafdarān*) fought "like angry lions" in the bazaar and streets and alleys of the four quarters, and dispatched Mongols hither-and-thither. The governor fell, disheartening his men. Mongols counterattacked from two sides and Nishapur was captured. Toquchar's wife allegedly arrived with 10,000 cavalry to inflict punishment for her husband's death.[83] Irrespective of whether the wife's presence is fact or fable—it is a topos in my opinion—Nishapurians "quaffed from the goblet of martyrdom" (*jām-i shahādat mī nūshīd-and*). The city's citadel, ramparts, and edifices were demolished.[84]

Tolui's armies, like a swarm of temporarily satiated desert locusts, swept through the plains to Herat via Bādghīs district (where he besieged a citadel),[85] and pillaged towns, notably, Herat's satellites of Fūshanj (first) and Kūsūyi (second),[86] before settling outside the defensive circumvallations of Herat.

## The Sieges of Herat

### *The First Siege*

The *first* Mongol attack on Herat is easier to describe than to satisfactorily date. The city fell to Tolui in early Rabīʿ II 618/25 May to 22 June 1221, following a siege of ten days. The surrender (by my estimation) was in the early part of Summer 618/1221: according to the *Secret History*, Chingiz Khan commanded Tolui thusly: "The weather has become warm. The other troops must set up camp too. You come and join Us."[87] When Tolui received the order, he had already

[82] Ibid. *Shurufāt-i bārū*: merlons or pinnacle.

[83] Ibid.; Juvainī/Boyle, *World-Conqueror*, 1:177 (that she is the daughter of Chingiz Khan).

[84] al-Harawī, *Harāt*, 99–101. Fields and city were allegedly flooded.

[85] Ibid., 102–103. Say, ten days to survey, prepare, invest, and reduce Bādghīs?

[86] al-Harawī, *Harāt*, 104–105. Investing and reducing forts and settlements in Fūshanj and Kūsūyi probably consumed another ten to fifteen days (see Table 1.1, *infra*).

[87] de Rachewiltz, *Secret History*, § 259.

> captured the cities of Iru [Herat], Isebür [Nishapur] and others, had destroyed the city of Sisten [Sīstān] and was just destroying the city of Čuqčeren. [After Tolui had] destroyed the city of Čuqčeren [he] pitch[ed] camp and joined Činggis Qan.[88]

Tolui had received his orders *c.* Dhū al-Ḥijja 617/February 1221;[89] and apparently completed his assigned tasks within three months.[90] Therefore the first surrender of Herat was *early* in Rabīʿ II 618 (meaning end of May/early June 1221).

The *first* siege of Herat commenced in late Rabīʿ I or early Rabīʿ II, 618/May 1221, after Tolui destroyed Nishapur; then reduced, first, smaller burgs in the Nishapur Quarter; next in the Herat Quarter (such as Kūsūyi and Fūshanj). The reconstruction of the two sieges of Herat is muddied by Jūzjānī's confusion,[91] and Juwaynī's muteness.[92] In writing his history, Sayf al-Harawī utilized oral reports from interlocutors in Herat, and textual sources, which included Jūzjānī and Juwaynī. The histories are silent on Herat's interactions with Jebe and Sübedei: we do not know whether a *shaḥna* had been appointed, and if so, whether the man had been molested or murdered.

Tolui's army camped at a meadow between Herat's southern entryway and the Hari Rud.[93] An emissary (*ilchī*), Zanbür, was sent into Herat to command city notables to appear before Tolui and assuage the wrath of the world-burner (*sakhaṭ-i jahān-sūz*). *Malik* Shams al-Dīn Muḥammad Jūzjānī, a potentate loyal to Mengübirtī, elected to "rouse the believers to

88 Ibid. "Čuqčeren" is "Chakhcharān," a synonym for the Hari Rud. Ḥāfiẓ-i Abrū, *Jughrāfiyā-yi Ḥāfiẓ-i Abrū*, 3 vols, ed. Ṣādiq Sajjādī (Tehran: Mīrāṣ-i maktūb, 1375–78/1997–99), 1:166–67; Le Strange, *Eastern*, 408. "City of Čuqčeren" presumably refers to some luckless settlement along the Hari Rud.

89 Juvainī/Boyle, *World-Conqueror*, 1:131–32, 1:150–52 (Tolui received orders and troops after Balkh fell); see also Jūzjānī/Raverty, *Nāṣirī*, 2:1,031, n.8 (continuation of note on 2:1,027, last paragraph: Tolui was dispatched in February 1221).

90 Juvainī/Boyle, *World-Conqueror*, 1:152: "in two or three months Toli [Tolui] subjugated cities [...]"; see also Jūzjānī/Raverty, *Nāṣirī*, 2:1,036–37, n.1 (Raverty's rendition).

91 Jūzjānī/Raverty, *Nāṣirī*, 2:1,038, 2:1,048–51. Raverty noted Jūzjānī's "complete confusion" regarding the details of the first and second sieges (ibid., 2:1,038 n.5).

92 Juwaynī devotes chapters to the sieges of Marw and Nishapur, but not the sieges of Herat. On the omission, see Juvainī/Boyle, *World-Conqueror*, 1:151, n.5 (Boyle's comments).

93 al-Harawī, *Harāt*, 106. The location of the meadow (*Marghzār-i bashūrān*) is not known. The tract north of Mālān Bridge (*Pul-i Mālān*) was a staging zone for besiegers. The northside of the bridge is *c.* 5.2 km from Herat's southern gateway.

fight" (Q8:65). Zanbür was killed. Tolui was enraged. Vengeful Mongols, instructed to spare no Tajik, surrounded Herat like a "black cloud." Heratis pummeled the besiegers for seven days, with both sides suffering high losses. The *malik* was killed on day eight, which cracked open the door to factionalism: one bloc wanted to keep fighting; whereas another wanted to submit. The histories become murkier at this critical juncture. Herat capitulated. Young women were enslaved. The killing spree lasted for one day, until Tolui halted it after *namāz khuftan* (night prayer).[94]

Sayfi reports Jūzjānī's claim of 600,000 killed in each of Herat's four quarters (for a total, by Jūzjānī's reckoning, of 2,400,000 dead).[95] The figures by Jūzjānī for dead, enslaved, and survivors are not acceptable. Tolui evidently spared Herat from the depredations that had characterized the surrenders of Marw and Nishapur. Herat was not pulverized nor was the *qatl-i ʿāmm* commanded. The Timurid era historian, Mīrkhʷānd, harmonized conflicting reports. He asserts that apart from the massacre of Mengübirtī's partisans (*c.* 12,000 men), "the rest of the people came to no harm whatsoever."[96] A topos is that Tolui had fancied Herat and its salubrious climate, and desired to spare it a grisly fate. Tolui trotted out to the Firūzābād Gate, halted by the trench, and addressed the peoples of Herat (in Mongolian? Persian? Turkic?), calling for submission, which was subsequently tendered.[97] Since Herat was fortified and resisted the second siege for six to eight months, it is all but certain that the surrender was negotiated, possibly by the socio-economic bloc represented by ʿIzz al-Din Muqaddam al-Harawī (d. 636/1238–39). He was subsequently deported to Turkistan.[98] Ögödei returned him to Herat in 635/1237 to help revitalize the city (see Part Two).

Tolui had pragmatic reasons for sparing Herat: it would have taken him weeks to reduce such a large city; and he had other towns and villages scattered

[94] al-Harawī, *Harāt*, 106–09. Seven is a popular number in the Qurʾan and has cosmological connotations. Tolui (allegedly) flooded Nishapur for seven days (ibid., 100).

[95] Jūzjānī multiplies by four the 600,000 (alleged) deaths in one quarter, to reach 2.4 million. Jūzjānī/Raverty, *Nāṣirī*, 2:1038. All figures (casualties, troop strengths, captives, etc.) must be taken *cum grano salis*.

[96] Muḥammad b. Khāwandshāh b. Maḥmūd Mīrkhʷānd, *Tārīkh-i rawżat al-ṣafā fi sīrat al-anbiyāʾ wa al-mulūk wa al-khulafāʾ*, 15 vols, ed. Jamshīd Kiyānfar (Tehran: Intishārāt-i Asāṭīr, 1380/2001), 3,880 (vol. 5 of 1339/1960 edition. See bibliography).

[97] Ibid.; al-Harawī, *Harāt*, 110; Jūzjānī/Raverty, *Nāṣirī*, 2:1036–37, n.1.

[98] al-Harawī, *Harāt*, 110; Mīrkhʷānd, *Rawżat*, 3,880.

about Khurasan and Sīstān to assault before returning to Chingiz Khan and their summer pastures (as his father had commanded him). Tolui appointed Abū Bakr Marjakī as governor (*malik*) of Herat, and coupled him with a Mongol *shaḥna* named Mangitaï.[99] If Mīrkhʷānd is accurate, Tolui went from Herat to Ṭāliqān (to assist the besiegers),[100] before re-joining his father.[101]

*The Second Siege*

After Tolui departed, the *malik* and *shaḥna* (Abū Bakr Marjakī and Mangitaï) repaired Herat's gates and attended to public works. Heratis went about their business.[102] Abū Bakr and Mangitaï were, however, murdered. What may be surmised from the sundry reports is that Mengübirtī's triumph at Parwān;[103] and resistance in Ghūr and Gharjistān (namely, citadels at Kālawīn, Fīwār, and Fīrūzkūh),[104] had energized Mengübirtī's partisans. The siege of Fort Naṣr-Kūh (Ṭāliqān) exemplifies the Mongols' travails in the mountainous regions of eastern Persia. Sayf al-Harawī, however, de-emphasizes Parwān as causation for rebellion in Herat. He points to defenders at Kālawīn who had joined with Khorezmian partisans inside Herat, and who were fabricating weapons, like javelins and shields (*darʿ wa rimāḥ*).[105] Meanwhile, Mongol units, including units based in/near Herat, surged to Kālawīn to assist comrades.[106] This presumably left Herat less well-defended and encouraged insurrection. Marjakī and Mangitaï were slain in this febrile milieu. Mubāriz al-Dīn Sabzavārī, erstwhile castellan of Fort Fīrūzkūh,[107] assumed the governorship of Herat; and Fakhr al-Dīn ʿAbd al-Raḥman ʿIbrānī (the Hebrew?) became chief (*raʾīs*) of the province.[108]

99 al-Harawī, *Harāt*, 110.
100 Mīrkhʷānd, *Rawżat*, 3,880.
101 See Table 1.1, *infra*.
102 al-Harawī, *Harāt*, 111.
103 Jūzjānī/Raverty, *Nāṣirī*, 2:1042: when news of Mengübirtī's victories "reached all the cities of Khurasan, in every city and town wherever [*shaḥnas*] were stationed, the people thereof [rebelled and] dispatched the whole of them to hell [...]."
104 On resistance at citadels, see al-Harawī, *Harāt*, 112; Barthold, *Turkestan*, 438–39; on the locations of the aforenamed citadels, see Le Strange, *Lands*, 417.
105 al-Harawī, *Harāt*, 112: vowelled *darʿ* by editor; Steingass has *dirʿ*.
106 al-Harawī, *Harāt*, 111–13; see also Mīrkhʷānd, *Rawżat*, 3,882–83.
107 On Sabzavārī's appointment by Mengübirtī, see Jūzjānī/Raverty, *Nāṣirī*, 1:285.
108 On *raʾīs*, see Jürgen Paul, "Local Lords or Rural Notables: Some Remarks on the *raʾīs* in Twelfth Century Eastern Iran," in *Medieval Central Asia and the Persianate World*, eds A.C.S. Peacock and D.G. Tor (London: I.B. Tauris, 2015), 174–209.

Chingiz Khan was enraged: "The dead have come alive. This time, their heads must be separated from their bodies; all residents of Herat must perish."[109] Tolui bore the brunt of his father's wrath for having spared Herat.[110] *Noyan* Elǰigidei,[111] with a formidable army of 80,000 men, was dispatched from Ghaznīn/Ghazni. He encamped in the southern environs of Herat, Shawwāl 618/November 1221. Elǰigidei allowed himself about a month to prepare the siege; and awaited the arrival of reinforcements (*c.* 50,000 men) dispatched from both sides of the Oxus. Herat's defenders prepared for a protracted siege, and pledged to each other to avoid factionalism and fight to the end.

Elǰigidei surrounded Herat, arrayed troops and armaments, and launched the first attack from four directions. Offensives continued for more than six months. Around Jumādá I 619/June–July 1222, Herat was low on provisions; inevitably, divisions materialized among the beleaguered. The Mongols utilized a panoply of weapons (*manjanīq wa ʿarrāda*) to strike breaches (sgl. *sūrākh*) in the walls (*dīwār-i bārah*); deployed sappers that advanced under the protection of scaffolds (*kharak*) to tunnel beneath (the embankment) and weaken towers (*burj wa bārah*).[112] Four hundred Mongols died when a fifty *gaz* section of the embankment collapsed.[113] Repeated strikes from mangonels and sapping breached the defenses. In June/July, Herat fell. The *qatl-i ʿāmm* was commanded. Buildings, homes, ramparts, and towers were leveled, the trench filled in. Killing, burning, and razing continued for seven days.[114] Elǰigidei decamped for Kālawīn. In line with Mongol "standard operating procedures," he ordered squadrons to double back to Herat to extirpate survivors emerging from hiding.

[109] al-Harawī, *Harāt*, 114.

[110] Mīrkhʷānd, *Rawżat*, 3,883.

[111] "Elǰigidei" in de Rachewiltz, *Secret History*, §§ 229, 275, 278.

[112] Herat's Kartid era fortifications are in Chapter Ten. During the two Mongol sieges there was probably an earthen embankment, *c.* 40–60′ in height, circumvallating inner Herat; the glacis inclined, say, 40–45°. A trench (wet or dry) circumvallated the mound's base. Curtain walls and towers were erected on the embankment's crown.

[113] *Gaz* is said to be the *zirāʿ*/*dhirāʿ* (Ar.), where 1 *zirāʿ* is *c.* 1 m/1 yd. But *gaz* is also said to be one cubit (*c.* 18″), however, estimates of *gaz* have ranged from 24″ to 40″ across time and space. Units are not quantified by me.

[114] al-Harawī, *Harāt*, 115–18; Mīrkhʷānd, *Rawżat*, 3,883–85 (Mīrkhʷānd claims Herat captured in Jumādá II 619/July–August 1222).

The desolation of Herat was almost complete. It is impossible to appraise the extent of the structural damage. Given the size of the walled city and putative extents of suburbs, it is unlikely that Herat was completely flattened. Elǰigidei had ordered the destruction of major edifices, but the Congregational Mosque (*masjid-i jāmiʿ*) survived. Central features of the defenses were demolished, but a stump of the citadel apparently survived.[115]

Historical memory did not favor Elǰigidei, upon whom Heratis bestowed the epithet, *laʿīn*: "Elǰigidei, the Accursed."

[115] al-Harawī, *Harāt*, 118. Explained in Chapter Ten, § 2 "The Historical Evidence."

*Table 1.1 A Chronological Guide to the Mongol Invasions of Khurasan and Transoxiana, 615/1218 to 619/1222*

| Year | Event | Comments |
|---|---|---|
| 615/1218 | Mongol caravan to Utrār attacked | Diplomacy rebuffed by Khʷārazm-Shāh (cf. Jackson, *Mongols*, 72–75) |
| 615/1218–19 | Mongols prepare for the upcoming conflict | Ögödei designated Chingiz Khan's political heir |
| 616/1219 | • Ögödei and Chaghatai march on Utrār<br>• Jochi to northern Jaxartes<br>• Smaller division to the Ferghana Valley<br>• Chingiz and Tolui march on Bukhara and Samarqand | Utrār falls in 616/1220 (*c.* March?) |
| Dhū al-Ḥijja 616/ February 1220 | Bukhara falls | *c.* mid-February 1220 (Barthold, *Turkestan*, 410). No general massacre (*qatl-i ʿāmm*) |
| Muḥarram 617/ March 1220 | Samarqand falls | *c.* mid-March 1220 (Barthold, *Turkestan*, 413). No *qatl-i ʿāmm* |
| Spring 617/1220 | Jebe and Sübedei begin their pursuit of the Khʷārazm-Shāh | Toquchar led the 3rd *tümen* as rearguard. He did the same for Sübedei in 615–16/1219 See *Secret History*, § 257 |
| Rabīʿ I 617/June 1220 | Jebe and Sübedei at Nishapur | Notables summoned, *pāʾiza* shown; provisions demanded; city not attacked. Juwaynī's date: 1 Rabīʿ I 617/6 June 1220 |
| Summer 617/1220 | Chingiz Khan at Nakhshab/Qarshi | Oasis southwest of Samarqand |
| Autumn 617/1220 | Chingiz Khan decamps Nakhshab and marches on Tirmiz | Tirmiz falls, *c.* Ramaḍān 617/ November–December 1220 Chingiz Khan pauses, briefly |
| Ramaḍān 617/ November 1220 | Toquchar Bahadur arrives in Nishapur; he is killed in action | Toquchar was rearguard |
| Winter 617/1220–21 | Chingiz Khan crosses the Oxus into Persia | Besieges Balkh |

*Table 1.1* (*Continued*)

| Year | Event | Comments |
|---|---|---|
| <u>Dh</u>ū al-Ḥijja 617/ February 1221 | Balkh falls (to Chingiz Khan) | Balkh besieged for 37 days (al-Harawī, *Harāt*, 87). City initially spared the *qatl-i ʿāmm*, but massacre ordered after acts of rebellion |
| <u>Dh</u>ū al-Ḥijja 617/ February 1221 | Chingiz Khan turns from Balkh to the conquest of Ṭāliqān | Fierce defense of Fort Naṣr-Kūh caught Chingiz Khan's attention. Long siege (*c.* 7–8 months). |
| <u>Dh</u>ū al-Ḥijja 617/February 1221 (or possibly in early Muḥarram 618/February– March 1221) | Tolui received orders and allocated forces at/near Ṭāliqān | Juvainī 1:131–32, 1:150–52; Jūzjānī, 2:1,027, n.8; cf. *Jāmiʿ al-tawārīkh*, 3:180, 3:273 (dates the event to Autumn 617/1220) |
| Late Muḥarram 618/ March 1221 | Marw falls (to Tolui) | Preparations and siege consumed *c.* 30 days (al-Harawī, *Harāt*, 92–95). *Qatl-i ʿāmm* ordered |
| Ṣafar 618/April 1221 | Nishapur falls (to Tolui) | City is said to have fallen 15 Ṣafar 618/10 April 1221. *Qatl-i ʿāmm* ordered |
| April 1221 | Urganch falls (to armies led by Jochi, Ögödei, and Chaghatai) | Ögödei was supremo (*Secret History*, §§ 258, 260) |
| Ṣafar–Rabīʿ I 618/ April–May 1221 | Fort in Bādghīs besieged; then citadels in Fūshanj and Kūsūyi (by Tolui, en route to Herat) | After Nishapur. These attacks consumed *c.* 20–25 days (estimated), based on al-Harawī, *Harāt*, 102–103 (Bādghīs), 104–105 (Kūsūyi, etc.) |
| Late Rabīʿ I, possibly early Rabīʿ II 618/late May or early June 1221 | First siege of Herat (falls to Tolui) | Short siege, *c.* 10 days (estimated from report in al-Harawī, *Harāt*, 106–110). Almost certainly a negotiated surrender |
| Rabīʿ II or Jumādá I 618/ June or July 1221 | Tolui re-joined Chingiz Khan for summer hiatus (possibly after assisting with the capture of Ṭāliqān) | Tolui received orders and forces, <u>Dh</u>ū al-Ḥijja 617/February 1221. Tasks completed in *c.* 3 months. |

| | | |
|---|---|---|
| Early Summer 618/1221 | Mongols defeated by Mengübirtī at Parwān | Parwān happened between first and second siege of Herat (cf. al-Harawī, *Harāt*, 112) |
| Early Summer 618/1221 | Chingiz Khan's division quits Ṭāliqān for Ghazni (Mengübirtī's appanage) to pressure Mengübirtī | Chingiz delegated command of Ṭāliqān siege and turned to assist *after* the defeat at Parwān |
| Summer 618/1221 | Chingiz Khan's division faces resistance at Gurzuwān/Jurziwān (west of Ghūr), then detours to Bamiyan | Delay due to resistance at Gurzuwān. Why detour if Mengübirtī was Chingiz's focus? To remain in the cooler mountains for summer? |
| Late Summer or Early Autumn 618/1221 | Rapine and carnage at Bamiyan by Chingiz Khan's division | Purportedly revenge for the death of Chingiz Khan's grandson (son of Chaghatai) at Bamiyan |
| Autumn 618/1221 | Battle at the Indus; Mengübirtī retreats to India | Dated to Shawwāl 618/November 1221 |
| Late Summer or early Autumn | Murders of Mongol appointees at Herat, *malik* Abū Bakr Marjakī and *shaḥna* Mangitaï | Chingiz Khan is enraged: "This time […] all residents of Herat must perish" |
| Shawwāl 618/ November 1221 | Elǰigidei and large siege army settle outside Herat | He awaits additional forces and equipment. The city was then not blockaded (i.e., still porous) |
| *c.* November–December 1221 | Second siege of Herat | City was probably sealed by now |
| Jumādá I 619/ June–July 1222 | Herat falls | *c.* 6–8 month siege. Herat is low on provisions; there is factionalism. Elǰigidei ravages Herat |
| Autumn 619/1222 | Chingiz Khan leaves Persia | Chingiz Khan had been in Baghlān for summer, and during the siege and ruin of Herat |

# 2

# Mongol Imperial Policies and Herat

## Chinggisid Fault Lines

Herat became a prize in Chinggisid internecine struggles for supremacy. Chingiz Khan had designated Ögödei as political heir. There were other legitimate contenders: Chingiz's brother, Temüge Otchigin, "on the basis of the seniority principle was best qualified to succeed" him.[1] Another was Chingiz's oldest son, Jochi, albeit of dubious birth: he was conceived around when his mother, Börte, was held captive by Chingiz Khan's enemies. Chaghatai disrespected Jochi as a "bastard"; they even "engaged in fisticuffs."[2] Tolui's and Ögödei's views of Jochi are less certain. Chingiz accepted Jochi as his son and bequeathed to him a proportionate inheritance. But Jochi predeceased him (d.*c.* 1225).

In Chingiz Khan's bequests, Jochi was appointed chief of the hunt, a pastime and training regimen for steppe warriors. Chaghatai was designated the keeper of Mongol laws (*yasa*); Tolui, "the command and organization of troops and the equipment of armies"; and Ögödei, administrator of empire.[3] To each according to his talents was their father's logic.[4] Chaghatai accepted the selection of Ögödei but not Tolui. Consequent to his father's death, Tolui, the youngest, and therefore the "hearth-prince" (*otchigin*)—guardian of the ancestral heartlands—ruled as regent.

[1] Peter Jackson, "The Dissolution of the Mongol Empire," *CAJ* 22/3 (1978):186–244, 197.

[2] May, *Mongol Empire*, 69: "'How can we let ourselves be ruled by this bastard offspring of the Merkit?'"

[3] Juvainī/Boyle, *World-Conqueror*, 1:40.

[4] On the contenders' personalities, see May, *Mongol Empire*, 69–70.

Tolui convened the congress (*quriltai*) that confirmed Ögödei.[5] Despite any private objections held by Tolui, since Ögödei had been designated by Chingiz, Mongol notables would have not permitted deviation. When Ögödei died (1241), Temüge Otchigin tried to seize the throne but failed. Ögödei's empress, Töregene (r. 1242–46; d. 1246) ruled as regent during the interregnum.[6] Töregene's and Ögödei's son, Güyük (r. 1246–48) was enthroned after more political theater. He and Jochi's son, Batu (d. 654/1256), were estranged. Batu exercised dilatory tactics to prevent the *quriltai* that would elect Güyük.[7] Toluids bided. Their opportunity emerged with Güyük's death in 1248. Möngke (r. 1251–58), Tolui's son, was crowned at the 1251 *quriltai*, following a two-year interregnum in which Güyük's wife, Oghul-Qaimish, ruled.[8]

Chinggisid fault lines outlined above were exacerbated by the senior Chinggisids' interpretations of their patrimony's relationship to the Mongol Empire. Each of Chingiz Khan's sons had received a territorial appanage (*yurt*) with an accompanying *ulus* (specified tribes and peoples). Each prince received a dowry (*injü*) for the upkeep of his court and for other expenses, funded in part from the tax revenues of the conquered territories of China, "Turkistan" (Caucasus to Xinjiang), and Persia.[9] In the original dispensation, Jochi, being the eldest, received in accordance with tradition, lands farthest from the hearth ("as far in that direction as the hoof of Tartar horse had penetrated"): the Qipchaq Steppe and north Caucasia; and following their conquests (after Chingiz Khan's death), Rus, and lower Volga; whereas Tolui inherited eastern Mongolia (the hearthlands); Chaghatai received western Turkistan (from Uighuristan to Transoxiana); and Ögödei received western Mongolia.[10] Chingiz Khan's brothers, and petit royals received appanages or shares (*qubi*). Conquered lands, in theory, were to be jointly administered

[5] Ibid., 94–97; cf. Barthold, *Turkestan*, 463 (Tolui's reluctance to convene *quriltai*).

[6] On this remarkable woman and the political difficulties with which she had to contend, see Anne Broadbridge, *Women and the Making of the Mongol Empire* (Cambridge: Cambridge University Press, 2018), 164–94; see also Jackson, *Mongols*, 100–101.

[7] May, *Mongol Empire*, 123; Jackson, "Dissolution," 198–99.

[8] Broadbridge, *Women*, 195–224; May, *Mongol Empire*, 132–35; Jackson, *Mongols*, 101.

[9] Grousset, *Empire*, 253.

[10] Juvainī/Boyle, *World-Conqueror*, 1:42–43; Thomas Allsen, "Sharing out the Empire: Apportioned Lands under the Mongols," in *Nomads in the Sedentary World*, eds Anatoly Khazanov and André Wink (Richmond: Curzon, 2001), 172–90, esp. 172–73. See also, Jackson, *Mongols*, 101–06.

by Chingiz Khan's legatees for the benefit of every rights-holder. Chingiz Khan's successor was *primus inter pares*.

China and Persia were not in any princely appanage and treated as joint property. On the allotment of lands in Persia, Juwaynī writes: "the census of the provinces having been completed [in 1257], the World-Emperor [Möngke] apportioned them all amongst his kinsmen and brothers."[11] Jūzjānī describes Batu's access rights to his Persian holdings: "Out of every country [region] of Iran which fell under the jurisdiction of the Mongols, he [Batu] had a specified assignment, and his factors [agents] were placed over such portions as had been allotted him."[12] The arrangement to jointly manage common assets appears to have lasted to the reign of Güyük (d. 1248). The roots of the tension that would divide the empire did not emerge from Chingiz Khan's distribution of appanages or their precise borders, but "over access to and control of apportioned lands."[13]

### *The Jochids Establish Dominance in Herat*

Early Mongol rule in Khurasan was chaotic. The region was anarchic. "Rebels and Turks would appear on every side and cast confusion amongst the people; [...] scum and rabble [...] would gain the upper hand so that an area which had been pacified and subdued would relapse into chaos because of these troubles and disturbances"; furthermore, two of ʿAlāʾ al-Dīn Khʷārazm-Shāh's former amirs were waging a guerrilla campaign against the Mongols, and making "raids on Nishapur and its dependencies."[14] In 630/1232f., Ögödei appointed Chin-Temür (d. 633/1235f.) as governor of Khurasan. Ögödei had been pleased with Chin-Temür.[15] He, with Ögödei's favor and decree (*yarlīgh*) in hand, appointed Sharaf al-Dīn al-Khʷārazmī as vizier;[16] Körgüz (d.*c.* 1242), as fiscal administrator and tax collector;[17] and

[11] Juvainī/Boyle, *World-Conqueror*, 2:523; Thomas Allsen, *Culture and Conquest in Mongol Eurasia* (Cambridge: Cambridge University Press, 2001), 48.

[12] Jūzjānī/Raverty, *Nāṣirī*, 2:1,172.

[13] Allsen, "Sharing," 173.

[14] Juvainī/Boyle, *World-Conqueror*, 2:483. On Mongol operations to subjugate the region, see Timothy May, "The Ilkhanate and Afghanistan," in *New Approaches to Ilkhanid History*, eds T. May, et al. (Leiden: Brill, 2020), pp. 272–320, esp. 276–81.

[15] Juvainī/Boyle, *World-Conqueror*, 2:486–87.

[16] Ibid., 2:487; on vizier Khʷārazmī, see Lane, *Mongol Rule*, 40, 184.

[17] Juvainī/Boyle, *World-Conqueror*, 2:483; on Körgüz, see Lane, *Mongol Rule*, 40, 61, 64, 181; Broadbridge, *Women*, 173–74, 176.

Bahā᾿ al-Dīn Juwaynī (the historian's father) as the Chief Minister (*ṣāḥib-dīwān*).[18] Death found Chin-Temür before fortune did. His decease gave Batu the freedom to co-opt Chin-Temür's subordinates, appoint his own henchmen, and subvert Ögödei's agenda.

Batu exercised his right to appoint agents in apportioned territories. Sharaf al-Dīn al-Khʷārazmī's initial appointment had been to represent Batu's interests (but under Chin-Temür's supervision). Unlike the princelings that frequently tried to involve themselves in imperial business, Batu had influence where it mattered: "all the Grandees and Leaders of the Mughal forces were obedient unto" him.[19] Elǰigidei had been Jochi's representative in Khurasan; he remained a regional commander under Batu. Batu's appointment of Majd al-Dīn Kālyūnī as the *malik* of Herat (*c.* 638/1240–41),[20] with the power to terminate Ögödei's appointee, was intended to advance Jochid claims to Persia, which "had never been explicit [but] had long been implicit."[21] Batu's administrators included Körgüz and Sharaf al-Dīn al-Khʷārazmī. They were Batu's "eyes and ears" in Herat; more significantly, they embodied the tip of the Jochid spear into Khurasan.[22]

### *Chaghataids Covet Herat*

Ögödei made three appointments to administration at Herat. A *shaḥna*, Kharlugh;[23] a *bitikchī*, Sūkū;[24] and Shams al-Dīn Muḥammad (n.d.) b. ʿIzz al-Dīn Muqaddam Harawī.[25] The trio arrived in Herat in 637/1239f. Appointments by different Chinggisid factions were bound to generate friction; Kālyūnī's arrogance inflamed the situation. Kālyūnī "openly gave preferential treatment to the representatives from Batu over those on business from the Qa᾿an."[26] Kālyūnī, when not disrespecting Ögödeids, was disrespecting Chaghataids (namely, their chief, Yesü Möngke; r. 1246–51). Chaghataids had also desired roles in administering Herat. Yesü Möngke, therefore, sent

18 Juvainī/Boyle, *World-Conqueror*, 2:487; on the Juwaynīs, see Lane, *Mongol Rule*, 177–212.
19 Jūzjānī/Raverty, *Nāṣirī*, 2:1,172.
20 al-Harawī, *Harāt*, 159; on Kālyūnī in Herat, see Lane, *Mongol Rule*, 153–56.
21 Lane, *Mongol Rule*, 40.
22 On Chinggisid rivalries in Khurasan, see May, "Ilkhanate."
23 On Kharligh/Kharlugh, see Lane, *Mongol Rule*, 153–54, 167.
24 al-Harawī, *Harāt*, 152–53. *Bitikchī*: secretary-registrar in financial administration.
25 On Muḥammad b. ʿIzz al-Dīn, see Lane, *Mongol Rule*, 153.
26 Ibid., 154.

a *bitikchī* to Herat in 639/1241f., but Kālyūnī seized his decree and ejected him from the city. Kālyūnī became entrenched in Herat. He lavished favors on Batu's envoys but was less than welcoming of Ögödei's envoys, including Arghūn Aqa (d. 1275), *basqaq* for Khurasan.[27] Kālyūnī was unafraid of snubbing Ögödeids and Chaghataids, but his arrogance ultimately cost him his life (d.*c.* 640/1241f.).[28]

*Toluids Seek Control of Herat*

The Toluids had waited for their chance. It arrived with the elevation of Möngke (r. 1251–58), son of Tolui, to the rank of Grand Qaʾan.

Möngke's election was to seminally alter imperial dynamics and politics.[29] Hitherto, fiscal and political administration in the Mongol Empire had been chaotic. Chinggisid princes and petit royals issued *pāʾīza*s and *yarlīgh*s hither-and-yon, and injected parochial interests into imperial business. Yesü Möngke's and Batu's maneuverings typify the problem. Tax collectors, like Körgüz and Sharaf al-Dīn al-Khʷārazmī, were rapacious (Khʷārazmī acquired a hyperbolic reputation for vileness).[30] Arghūn Aqa arrived in Khurasan in 1247, tasked by Töregene with ordering imperial affairs;[31] however, Arghūn, by George Lane's estimation, was ineffective.[32] He failed to sack Khʷārazmī or to re-organize administration.

Enter now Möngke's solution, which coincided with Toluid ambitions to fold China and Persia into their domains. This was Shams al-Dīn Muḥammad Kart (r. 643–76/1245–78), maternal nephew of Rukn al-Dīn Muḥammad Marghanī (d. 643/1245),[33] castellan of Fort Khaysār, Ghūr.[34]

[27] al-Harawī, *Harāt*, 164; Lane, *Mongol Rule*, 154.

[28] On Kālyūnī's execution, see Lane, *Mongol Rule*, 63. Faṣīḥ Khʷāfī, *Mujmal-i Faṣīḥī*, ed. Muḥsin Nājī Naṣrābādī, 3 vols (Tehran: Intishārāt-i Asāṭīr, 1386/2007f.), 794.

[29] Thomas Allsen, *Mongol Imperialism: the Policies of the Grand Qan Möngke in China, Russia, and the Islamic Lands, 1251–1259* (Berkeley: University of California Press, 1987).

[30] Juvainī/Boyle, *World-Conqueror*, 2:525ff, esp. 533–46.

[31] Broadbridge, *Women*, 176–77.

[32] George Lane, "Arghun Aqa: Mongol Bureaucrat," *Iranian Studies* 32/4 (1999):459–82, esp. 482 (Lane's assessment of the *basqaq*'s competence).

[33] Genealogy established by Lawrence G. Potter, "The Kart Dynasty of Herat: Religion and Politics in Medieval Iran." (Ph.D. diss., Columbia University, 1992), 32–37.

[34] Khaysār: see ibid., 62–66; al-Harawī, *Harāt*, 183–84; Muʿīn al-Dīn Zamchī Isfizārī, *Rawżāt al-jannāt fī awṣāf-i madīnat-i Harāt*, ed. Muḥammad Kāẓim Imām, 2 vols (Tehran: Dānishgāh-i Tihrān, 1338/1959), 1:357–58; Le Strange, *Lands*, 410; Barthold, *Geography*, 54; ʿAtīq-Allāh Pizhwāk, *Ghūriyān* ([Kabul]: Anjuman-i tārīkh-i Afghānistān, 1345/1967), 27–32.

Chingiz Khan had not wanted to besiege Khaysār; he offered Marghanī a *yarlīgh* for continued rule over Ghūr in exchange for service. Marghanī accepted.[35] The date of their encounter was *c.* 618/1221, when the Mongols were facing stiff resistance at Ṭāliqān, Kālawīn, Fīwār, and Fīrūzkūh (Ghūr's capital). Rukn al-Dīn Marghanī faithfully served his Mongol overlords for more than twenty years. Following his death,[36] Shams al-Dīn Muḥammad Kart was confirmed in his stead.

Shams al-Dīn established the "House of Kart" (*Āl-i Kart*), which ruled from Herat until the city was surrendered to Tamerlane (Temür) in 783/1381. Shams al-Dīn received a fresh patent from Möngke in 649/1251 that vastly expanded the provinces under his aegis, along with substantial funds: "seed money" for his embryonic polity, such that it could "establish itself on a firm basis." Kartids were "a creation of the Mongols."[37] This assessment should not, however, detract from the *Iraniyyat* ("Iranian-ness") of the Kartids.

## The Kartids

*Āl-i Kart* were originally from Ghūr and of ethnic Persian (Tājīk) stock. Later Kartids acquired Turkic and Mongol blood through marriages.[38] The progenitors of the Kartids had served the Shansabānī dynasty (Ghurids) in various capacities, primarily as castellans.[39] Kartids later claimed descent from the Seljuq sultan, Sanjar (r. 511–52/1118–57), a Turkic king idealized by Turk and Tajik alike:

> The pride of Sanjar's family are you,
> A scion of Alexander's kingdom are you.[40]

[35] al-Harawī, *Harāt*, 186 (purported text of *yarlīgh*); Ḥāfiẓ-i Abrū, *Kart*, 4–5; Isfizārī, *Rawżāt*, 1:359 (abridged version of *yarlīgh* proffered by al-Harawī).

[36] Faṣīḥ, *Mujmal*, 796.

[37] Allsen, *Mongol Imperialism*, 71.

[38] See Potter, "Kart Dynasty," 145.

[39] Muḥammad Ismāʿīl Mablagh Gharjistānī, "Farmānrawāʾān-i Khaysār [The Castellans of Khaysār]," *Āryānā* No. 182 (1336/1957f.):29–36. See also ʿAbd al-Ḥayy Ḥabībī, "Taʿdīl dar nasab-nāmah-yi Āl-i Kart [Adjustment to the genealogy of the House of Kart]," *Āryānā* No. 68 (1327/1948):1–8.

[40] Mīrkhʷānd, *Rawżat*, 3,686; Ghiyāth al-Dīn Khʷāndamīr, *Ḥabīb al-siyar*, ed. Muḥammad Dabīr Siyāqī, 4 vols (Tehran: Intishārāt-i markazī khayyam pīrūz, 1333/1954), 3:367. Translation is by Thackston in Ghiyāth al-Dīn Khʷāndamīr, *Ḥabīb al-siyar*, tr. Wheeler Thackston, 2 vols (Cambridge, MA: Sources of Oriental Languages and Literatures, 1994), 213.

Historians of the period did not supply the short vowels (*a, i, u*); just the consonants (*k-r-t*). They knew the correct enunciation and assumed their readers did. One proffer on enunciation is "Kurt," from a 725/1325 text.[41] The correct enunciation was established by Lawrence Potter, who supplies this quote from Shaykh al-Islam Saʿd al-Dīn Masʿūd b. ʿUmar b. ʿAbdallāh Taftāzānī (722–93/1322–90), a contemporary of later Kartids: "'Kart with *fatḥ* on *kāf* and *sokuns* on *re* and final *te* is a title or *laqab* relating to grandeur (*taʿẓīm*) in their traditions.'"[42] Taftāzānī's explanation, in a book on rhetoric (*balāgha*) completed in Herat in Ṣafar 748/May 1347, and dedicated to the reigning Kartid, "al-Sulṭān al-Ghāzī al-Mujāhid fī sabīl ʾillāh, Muʿizz al-Ḥaqq wa al-Dunyā wa al-Dīn, Ghiyāth al-Islām wa al-Muslimīn, Abū al-Ḥusayn Muḥammad Kart," is unequivocal.[43]

Shams al-Dīn Kart's territories at his accession (i.e., after Rukn al-Dīn's death) were confined to Ghūr and its environs. His realm did *not* include Herat and its vicinities. In the early years, Shams al-Dīn had served in the Mongol armies during their eastern campaigns: Multān, the Delhi Sultanate's (1206–1389) northwestern bastion, was besieged in 644/1246f. by a Mongol amir, Sali Noyan,[44] and Shams al-Dīn Kart. The latter negotiated with Multān's Shaykh al-Islām Bahāʾ al-Dīn Zakariyya (d. 664/1265f.);[45] the siege was lifted for a ransom of 100,000 dinars. Meanwhile, an army led by Sali Noyan had departed from Multān during the talks and laid siege to Lahore. They were joined by Shams al-Dīn. In like manner, the Kartid campaigned in India and *Afghānistān* until Möngke's accession.[46]

41 Lola Dodkhudoeva, "Translating and copying in pre-Timurid Herat: A Persian translation of the *Iḥyaʾ ʿulūm al-dīn*, 725–726/1325," in *Écrit et culture en Asie centrale et dans le monde turco-iranien Xe-XIXe siècles*, eds F. Richard and Maria Szuppe (Paris: Studia Iranica Cahier 40, 2010), pp. 165–93, at 176–77.

42 Potter, "Kart Dynasty," 31–32.

43 Saʿd al-Dīn Masʿūd Taftāzānī, *al-Muṭawwal* (Delhi: Kutub-khānah-i Rashīdīyya, n.d.), 9. On the title, see Carl Brockelmann, *History of the Arabic Written Tradition*, tr. Joep Lameer, 2 vols, 3 supp. vols (Leiden: Brill, 2017–19), 2:278–80 (biography no. 2, title no. 7).

44 On Sali Noyan and Indian campaigns, see Peter Jackson, *The Delhi Sultanate* (Cambridge: Cambridge University Press, 1999), 107–08, 111.

45 Faṣīḥ, *Mujmal*, 820 (biographical death notice).

46 al-Harawī, *Harāt*, 192–95. Further on Shams al-Dīn's early years of service to the Mongols, see Lane, *Mongol Rule*, 155–61.

*Möngke: Rooting the Kartids at Herat*

Güyük's death in 1248 set in motion a fresh round of succession intrigues. Möngke was enthroned in Rabīʿ II 649/July 1251,[47] after "a bloody *coup d'état*, organized by Batu [...] in collaboration with the Toluids." Ögödeids and Chaghataids were purged; henceforth, the Grand Khanate remained "a perquisite of the house of Tolui."[48] Shams al-Dīn Kart was at the Mongol court and supported the Toluids; he had battled Güyük's forces for Möngke. Having convinced the Grand Qaʾan of his fealty by these actions, and following an interview, an investiture ceremony was convened in 649/1251, at which Shams al-Dīn Kart received his *yarlīgh* and aforementioned seed money.[49]

The *yarlīgh*'s preamble makes manifest the imperative of redeveloping devastated territories, specifically, the reconstruction of Herat (*bih kār-i ʿimārat-i shahr-i Harāt*), the paramount city in Khurasan (*muʿẓam-tarīn bilād-i Khurāsān*). *Malik*s and *shaḥna*s were to strive toward this objective.[50] Shams al-Dīn Kart was granted:[51]

> Dominion of the city of Herat (*bih-mulkī-yi shahr-i Harāt*) and [its] protection (*ḥimayat*); and [Herat's] dependencies (*tawābiʿ-i uw*):[52] Jām, Bākharz, Kūsūyi, Kharih [Kurūkh], Fūshanj, Āzāb, Tūlak, Ghūr, Fīrūzkūh, Gharjistān, Murghāb, Fāryāb, and Marjuq [Marūchāq], to the River Oxus (*āb-i āmūyī*); Isfizār, Farāh, Sijistān [Sīstān], Tikīnābād [near Qandahār],

[47] Juvainī/Boyle, *World-Conqueror*, 2:567; cf. al-Harawī, *Harāt*, 196ff. Sayfī narrates events under 645/1247–48; but for Möngke's reign, al-Harawī's dates deviate by several years. See explanation in Allsen, *Mongol Imperialism*, 133.

[48] Morgan, *Mongols*, 104.

[49] al-Harawī, *Harāt*, 200–05; Isfizārī, *Rawżāt*, 1:409–11; Allsen, *Mongol Imperialism*, 70–71. See also, Lane, *Mongol Rule*, 161–63.

[50] al-Harawī, *Harāt*, 201–02; cf. Isfizārī, *Rawżāt*, 1:410.

[51] al-Harawī, *Harāt*, 202–03. Itemization of locales (*balad*, pl. *bilād*; *tābi*, pl. *tawābiʿ*) reflects Sayfī's utilization of *micro*-toponyms, which are reproduced in the order presented by him. For insightful analyses of the geography, see Anon./Minorsky, *Ḥudūd al-ʿĀlam*, et passim; Dorothea Krawulsky, *Ḫorāsān zur Timuridenzeit* [*Tārīkh-i Ḥāfiẓ-i Abrū: Bakhsh-i jughrāfiyā-yi Khurāsān*], 2 vols (Wiesbaden: Ludwig Reichert, 1982–84), *et passim*; Le Strange, *Lands*, 352–63 (on Quhistān), 404–06 (Murghāb & Marūchāq), 407–19 (Herat Quarter), 420–32 (Balkh Quarter); Barthold, *Historical Geography*, 35–46 (Marw & Murghāb), 47–63 (Herat & Herat River Valley), 64–86 (regions south of Herat; Sīstān & Balūchistān, including Tikīnābād).

[52] On Herat's dependencies as understood today, see Noelle-Karimi, *Pearl*, 30–40.

> Kābul, Tirāh, Bustistān [Bust]; and *Afghānistān* [see Maps 1, 3], to the Indus (*shaṭṭ-i Sind*) and border with India (*ḥadd-i Hind*).[53]

Shams al-Dīn Kart had suzerainty over the extent of the provinces itemized above (*zimām-i ḥall wa ʿaqd wa qabẓ wa basṭ-i īn wilāyāt-i maẕkūra*). He had to ensure the prosperity and habitability of these territories (*īn mawāẓiʿ rā ābādān gardānad*).

These are extensive territories, encompassing sections of eastern Iran and nearly the entirety of Afghanistan, and into Pakistan, Turkmenistan, and Uzbekistan. The award did not, however, equate with *control* of territory. Shams al-Dīn spent the next two decades folding the itemized territories into his dominion through conquest (where necessary), and by concomitantly developing an extensive network of loyalists (pl. *bandagān*) who helped stabilize the Kartid polity, and extend his writ into towns, villages, and hamlets.

Shams al-Dīn Kart, with his *yarlīgh*, three golden *pāʾīza*s, dinars, gifts, and military gear (*ālat-i ḥarb*), decamped for Khurasan. He remained at Bādghīs, a Mongol cantonment,[54] for twenty days. Thence to Fūshanj for pilgrimage (*ziyārat*) at a minor shrine (Ribāṭ-i Pay); thence to Turbat-i Jām for two days of pilgrimage at the sepulcher of Shaykh al-Islām Aḥmad-i Jām (d. 536/1141).[55] This was his primary destination.

The Kartid's visit to Turbat-i Jām is significant: progeny of Aḥmad of Jām married with the Kartids (by 702/1302f.), uniting spiritual and temporal royalty. Shams al-Dīn Kart was buried near Aḥmad-i Jām's tumulus.[56] The Kartid was grateful for God's grace, which he ascribed to the spiritual intercession of Aḥmad. His pilgrimage heralded the beginning of the

[53] Sind v. Hind: Sind was considered Muslim territory but Hind (India) was not; hence the subtle distinction in the decree. On *ḥadd*, see R.W. Brauer, "Boundaries and frontiers in medieval Muslim geography," *Transactions of the American Philosophical Society* 85/6 (1995):1–73, 12–13.

[54] Bādghīs: see Le Strange, *Lands*, 412–15; Krawulsky, *Ḫorāsān*, 1:31–32, 2:29–30. Bādghīs had abundant waters, good pastures, and air. Bādghīs is not listed in Möngke's diploma because it had become a Mongol cantonment. On Bādghīs, see R.G. Kempiners, "The Struggle for Khurasan: Aspects of Political, Military, and Socio-economic Interaction in the Early 8th/14th Century." (Ph.D. diss., University of Chicago, 1985), 46–48.

[55] Shivan Mahendrarajah, *The Sufi Saint of Jam: History, Religion, and Politics of a Sunni Shrine in Shiʿi Iran* (Cambridge: Cambridge University Press, 2021), 43, 152.

[56] Ibid., 162 and n.74.

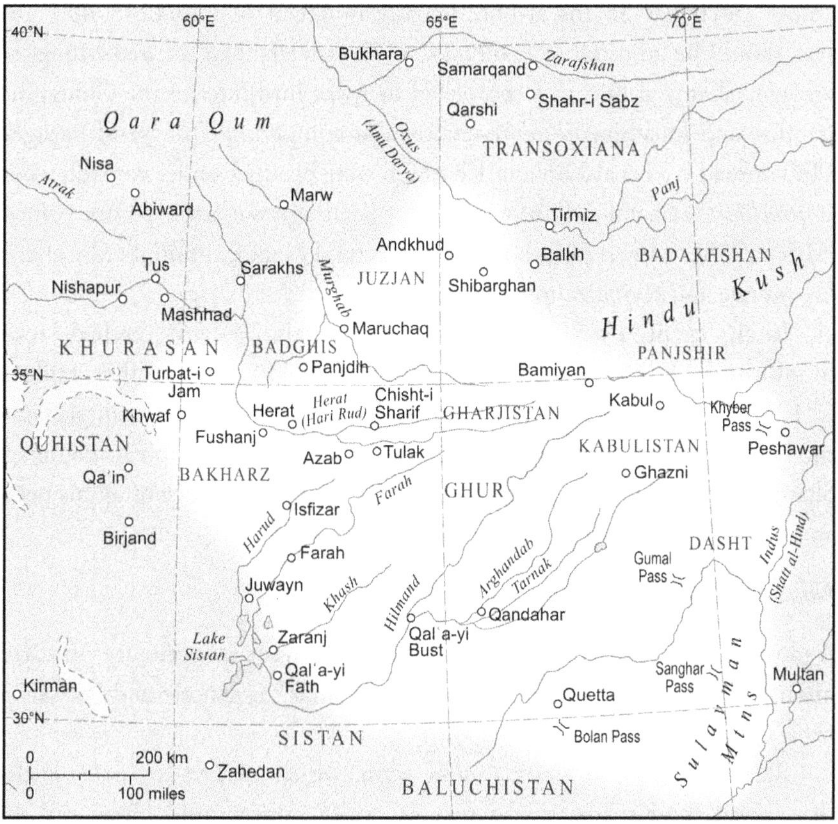


Map 3 Kartid domains itemized in Möngke's 1251 decree. Follows on map in Potter, "Kart Dynasty," p. 57, with amendations.

engagement of the Sufis of Jām in Kartid and Herati affairs: they shaped Kartid policies, but also abetted Tamerlane in dethroning the Kartids in 783/1381. In any event, following his pilgrimage, he quit Jām for Ṭūs, the headquarters of the Mongol viceroy, Arghūn Aqa, who awarded him supplemental funds.[57]

The chronological sequence of political happenings in and about Herat are jumbled at this point. Sayf al-Harawī's chronology, beginning *c.* 645/1247–48 (with Narrative 26), is suspect for the next several

[57] al-Harawī, *Harāt*, 204–05.

years.[58] Sayfī has Shams al-Dīn arriving in Herat in 646/1248–49;[59] the year should be adjusted to *c.* 649/1251–52 (after he had secured Möngke's *yarlīgh*). Shams al-Dīn was compelled to wade into internecine Chinggisid politics, and to subjugate representatives of competing Chinggisid lineages. Muḥammad b. ʿIzz al-Dīn and Kharlugh were brought under control, while a *bitikchī* (one Sharaf al-Dīn) was killed.[60] Kharlugh was removed from office, *c.* 657/1258f.[61] The political intrigues unsettled Heratis, undoubtedly affecting morale and revitalization efforts.

In any event, a new age was dawning in Persia: envoys reached Herat to inform the Kartid of the impending arrival of Möngke's brother, Hülegü (r. 1256–65), the new overlord (*īl-khān*) of Persia. Hülegü had grim plans for the Ismaʿilis (the "Assassins" of lore), and the ʿAbbasid caliph in Baghdad. Shams al-Dīn Kart hurried to "welcome the King in advance of all his peers and equals."[62] It was Shawwāl 653/November 1255.

## *Notes on* Malik *and* Banda

A gloss on *malik*, the title utilized by Kartid dynasts, is necessary. *Malik* is often given as "king" or "vassal king," but "*malik*" is generic and "vassal" is from European history.

*Malik* (pl. *mulūk*) was a generic term, which applied to "petty lords" that served the Kartids. Sayfī writes of *mulūk* from around Herat and the provinces of Bākharz, Gharjistān, Ghūr, Isfizār, Jām, Jurziwān, and Khʷāf traveling to Herat to acknowledge their tributary (*kharāj-guzārī*) status to the reigning Kartid *malik*, Fakhr al-Dīn Kart (d. 706/1307).[63] *Malik*, obviously, had gradations in meaning.

58 See Allsen, *Mongol Imperialism*, 133.

59 Ibid., 210 (at Herat); Ḥāfiẓ-i Abrū, *Kart*, 12 (reproduces al-Harawī's date).

60 al-Harawī, *Harāt*, 217; Faṣīḥ, *Mujmal*, 799. Their dates are probably incorrect.

61 Faṣīḥ, *Mujmal*, 810–11.

62 Juvainī/Boyle, *World-Conqueror*, 2:612–13 and n.30; Lane, *Mongol Rule*, 163. Also in Rashīd al-Dīn/Thackston, *Jāmiʿ*, 3:341; Faṣīḥ, *Mujmal*, 806. The Kartid appointed Arasī Shāh Ināltikīn as his viceroy for Sīstān and went to greet Hülegü. See Anon., *Tārīkh-i Sīstān*, ed. Malik al-Shuʿarāʾ Muḥammad Taqī Bahār (Tehran: Intishārāt-i Muʿīn, 1381/2002 [reprint of 1314/1935 ed.]), 368 (Ṣafar 653/March–April 1255). Pagination in this edition varies from the 1314/1935 edition. On this history, see C.E. Bosworth, "Sistan and its Local Histories," *Iranian Studies* 33/1 (2000):31–43, esp. 34–39.

63 al-Harawī, *Harāt*, 453.

A Kart *malik* is a *banda*,[64] loyal subordinate/servant of the Grand Qa'an, to whom he owes service (*khidma*) and fidelity (*wafā'*);[65] for instance, military service. Shams al-Dīn Kart loyally served the Mongol Empire in this capacity. The Kartid realm (in Shams al-Dīn's lifetime) provided the Empire with seven *tümens* of warriors,[66] and tax revenues.[67] The relationship between *malik* and Qa'an includes *mutual obligations* and *mutual loyalties*: the Qa'an owes his *banda* (the Kart *malik*) *khidma* and *wafā'*. Service and fidelity implicate, inter alia, provision by the Qa'an of *tangible* and *intangible* benefits pursuant to circumstances and/or mutual agreement; for example, funds, armaments, and troops.[68]

The founding of the Ilkhanate (in 1256) altered the direct relationship of Qa'an and *banda*. The Kart *malik* became the *banda* of the *īl-khān*—himself subservient (in theory) to the Qa'an. How the introduction of an intermediary (*īl-khān*) affected the compact between Grand Qa'an and Kart *malik* is unclear, especially in the later history of the Mongol Empire, when political connections between the Ilkhanid capital (Tabriz) and the Mongol capital (Qaraqorum) frayed, but had yet to decouple.

Kart *maliks* had *bandagān* (sgl. *banda*) and referred to them as *bandagān* in official documents.[69] Their *bandagān* were "petty lords": loyal servants of the Kartids. Relations between *bandagān* and Kartid *maliks* entailed *mutual loyalties* and *mutual obligations*.

Persian political thought on the status and obligations of *bandagān* is not novel. In Old Persian, a *bandaka* (pl. *bandakā*) is a "nobleman 'bound' to the king in a relationship which, though subordinate, was freely accepted and probably sealed with an oath."[70] The Persian King of Kings (*Shāhanshāh*)

64 *Banda*; pl. *bandagān*: bondman, servant; *bandagī*: bondage, servitude; *bandagī kardan*: to render service.

65 This discussion was shaped by the superlative analyses of Jürgen Paul in "*Khidma* in the Social History of pre-Mongol Iran," *JESHO* 54 (2014):392–422.

66 al-Harawī, *Harāt*, 221; Allsen, *Mongol Imperialism*, 205. Areas beyond the Kartid realm, Ṭūs, Nishapur, Isfahan, Kāshān, and Qum, also supplied *tümens*.

67 Allsen, *Mongol Imperialism*, 166–67 (taxation and Khurasan's finances).

68 A Mongol *tümen* was attached to the Kartids, but for how long, and its roles, are lacunae. The *yarlīgh*, *pā'izas*, cash, arms, and gifts are examples of tangible benefits and proofs of authority from Qa'an to *bandagān*. Arghūn Aqa's award of cash is an example of a tangible benefit from an agent of the Qa'an to one of the Qa'an's *bandagān*.

69 Kartid documents preserved in *Farā'id-i Ghiyāṣī* (the title is fully identified in Chapter Four).

70 W. Eilers and C. Herrenschmidt, "Banda," *EIr*, 3:682–85: *bandak*, *bandag*, and *bandaka* had the meaning of "'henchman, (loyal) servant, vassal,' but not 'slave'."

viewed his satraps as *bandaka*: dutiful servants.[71] Āl-i Kart originated from aristocratic political stock and acquired royal rank. Their *bandagān*, too, were men of high political and/or social pedigree who were compelled—by arms or circumstance—to subordinate themselves to the Kartids. Select Kartid *bandagān* chafed at their "lowly" status and rebelled (as we shall discover).

*Jochid-Toluid Politics and the Kartids*

Möngke's election as Qa'an shifted control from Ögödei's lineage to Tolui's, which "represented a political coup of the first order."[72] The Ögödeids had lost the internecine war and hundreds of Ögödeids were killed. The Chaghataids had backed the Ögödeids and suffered for it, but as subsequent events were to prove, their setbacks were not irreversible. The Jochids ("Golden Horde") had supported Möngke's faction. They had a strong footing on Persia's northwest (the Caucasus) and northeast (east of the Caspian, from the Qipchaq Steppe to Khʷārazm). In due course, the Jochids would be targeted by the Toluids. Batu's death, *c.* 1256, dissolved the Jochid-Toluid compact. The geographical epicenter of Jochid-Ilkhanid tensions would *later* become western Persia, chiefly in Āẕarbayjān,[73] where the Golden Horde and the Ilkhanate (based at Tabriz) faced one another. In the interim, Herat, where Batu had had agents (for instance, Elǰigidei, Körgüz, al-Khʷārazmī), became a Jochid-Toluid flashpoint as Shams al-Dīn Kart tried to assert control over his capital. Persia was still joint imperial property as reflected in the composition of Hülegü's armies crossing into Persia in 653/1255. Despite the civil war, there were significant contributions by the Chaghataids and Jochids, but evidently no Ögödeid representation.[74]

The Il-Khan[75] was expected to administer common imperial assets (Anatolia, Persia, and Iraq) for the benefit of all stakeholders. The Toluid

[71] See, e.g., Robin Lane Fox, *Alexander the Great* (New York: Penguin, 1986), 95–96. *Bandaka* is used consistently by Darius I in the sense given. See Rüdiger Schmitt, *The Bisitun Inscriptions of Darius the Great* (London: Corpus Inscriptionum Iranicarum, 1991), *et passim*; but see n.19, where the editor insists: "*bandaka* [...] does not mean, as it has commonly been interpreted in the past, 'subject, servant', but rather 'vassal, (feudal) tenant'." Two European concepts—*vassal* and *feudal*—are being used to "explain" a Persian concept.

[72] Jackson, "Dissolution," 186.

[73] Ibid., 208ff.

[74] Ibid., 220–21.

[75] On the title *īl-khān*, see Jackson, *Mongols*, 139 and nn.90 and 93.

brothers (minus, later, Arigh-Böke) eventually incorporated the Ilkhanate into their family's portfolio.[76] The issue—debated by scholars of the Mongol Empire—on whether the Toluids had intended to incorporate Persia, and then China, need not detain us.[77] The focus here is on Shams al-Dīn's implementation of the Toluid writ—Möngke's and Hülegü's agenda(s)—at Herat. George Lane was the first to discern that Shams al-Dīn was an Ilkhanid loyalist and willing participant in Chinggisid politics.[78] Irrespective of whether the Toluids had secret plans to seize Persia or not, Shams al-Dīn Kart helped deliver the Kartid realm to the Toluids; moreover, by fighting the Golden Horde, he helped secure the Ilkhanate's western frontier.

Shams al-Dīn Kart, almost certainly acting under Hülegü's instructions, initiated a decisive break with previous practices; for instance, by refusing relatively minor demands on Herat's *dīwān* by pro-Jochid amirs.[79] Three amirs in the service of Jījagāy (Batu's man in Bādghīs), had pursuant to custom (*bar ʿadāt maʿhūd*) been entitled to remounts (*ulāgh*; also *ulāq*), tents (*khayma*), and funds (*wujūh*), which Kharlugh and Muḥammad b. ʿIzz al-Dīn had paid (ten steeds; two tents; 300 fine dinars (*dīnār-i ʿadalī*)). Shams al-Dīn Kart, however, on being presented with the demand, thundered "henceforth you will not receive a thing from Herat's treasury!" (*min baʿd, shumā rā az dīwān-i Harāt chīzī na-kh$^{w}$āhad rasīd*).[80] The aggrieved scurried to complain to Jījagāy, who dispatched an emissary to Batu. The Jochid's reaction was predictable: he wanted Shams al-Dīn's head, but Hülegü stood by the Kartid.

What this report reveals is that Shams al-Dīn was confident of Hülegü's protection. He was surely acting on instructions from Möngke and Hülegü to implement Kartid-Toluid sovereignty in Herat, and to thwart Jochid ambitions. Denying access to Herat's revenues was a clear signal to the Jochids. The denial of such a paltry amount—the payment of which would not have

[76] Möngke's brother, Qubilai, founded the Yüan dynasty (r. 1271–1368). The Yüan (at its apogee) included China, Manchuria, Mongolia, Tibet, Korea, and parts of Turkistan and Southeast Asia. Toluids came to control two wealthy civilizations.

[77] On Hülegü's commission, see the thoughtful discussion in Jackson, *Mongols*, 138–42.

[78] Lane, *Mongol Rule*, 167–68.

[79] al-Harawī, *Harāt*, 260–61 (narrative # 39). Date is uncertain (*c.* 653/1255f.?).

[80] al-Harawī, *Harāt*, 260. See also Jackson, "Dissolution," 222.

dented Herat's finances—was to provoke a reaction and to demonstrate to the Jochids that Herat was under new management.

After Batu died (654/1256),[81] the Jochids were led briefly by two successors, before the accession of Berke Khan (r. 1257–66), Batu's brother. Berke was a dogmatic convert to Islam and a resolute foe of the Ilkhanate. He was incensed by Hülegü's 656/1258 attack on Baghdad and execution of the ʿAbbasid caliph. As time passed, with the consolidation of rich lands under Toluid control, the Jochids became uneasy. As Lane explained, "there was genuine apprehension at the sudden expansion of the lands under the direct control of the three Tuluid brothers, Möngke, Hülegü, and Qubilai."[82] Simmering hostilities between the Ilkhanate and Golden Horde erupted into open conflict in 660/1262. Before this, Ilkhanids and Jochids had been engaged in proxy wars. In 659/1260f., one Tāj al-Dīn Kurd had sought Berke's support in recovering a town lost to Kartids. Berke was not reticent about arming Kurd and thereby provoking the Kartids and Ilkhanids. Kurd seized the town and executed the Kartid garrison.[83] The Toluid-Jochid shadow war eventually morphed into open war.[84] The factions that had allied with the primary contenders were compelled to declare their support, which provided indispensable clarity: everyone had to pick a team.

Möngke died in 1258. Brothers Arigh-Böke (d. 664/1265–66)[85] and Qubilai vied for the crown. Although Qubilai Qaʾan (r. 1260–94) triumphed, Toluid harmony evaporated.[86] Hülegü died in 663/1265 and was succeeded by his eldest son, Abāqā (r. 663–79/1265–81). Shams al-Dīn joined Abāqā in 665/1267 to campaign against the Golden Horde, which was threatening Ilkhanid control of Āẕarbayjān.[87] In George Lane's estimation, Shams al-Dīn was an Ilkhanid partisan: "[t]here is no hint here that there was any coercion involved in Shams al-Dīn's participation [...]."[88]

81 Faṣīḥ, *Mujmal*, 807.
82 Lane, *Mongol Rule*, 39.
83 al-Harawī, *Harāt*, 293–96; see also Lane, *Mongol Rule*, 165.
84 Lane, *Mongol Rule*, 77, 165–66.
85 On Arigh-Böke's death, see Faṣīḥ, *Mujmal*, 820.
86 On this succession struggle, see Jackson, "Dissolution," 227–30; Lane, *Mongol Rule*, 72–73.
87 al-Harawī, *Harāt*, 316–24; Ḥāfiẓ-i Abrū, *Kart*, 40–43.
88 Lane, *Mongol Rule*, 168.

*Abāqā and the Kartids*

Shams al-Dīn returned to Herat with a new imperial decree, armaments, and prizes. He had to confront a fresh threat: Barāq (r. 1266–71), khan of the Chaghatai, who crossed the Oxus in 668/1269f. and menaced Khurasan. Barāq was "a willing lackey dancing to the drums of his eastern cousin,"[89] Qaidu (1236–1301), one of Ögödei's grandsons seeking to regain his patrimony.[90] Barāq's armies were poised to devastate Bukhara and Samarqand when wiser counsel prevailed. His armies, however, once they set foot in Persia, murdered and pillaged from Badakhshān to Nishapur. Barāq was warned against pillaging Herat lest he alienate Shams al-Dīn (then entrenched in the family bolt-hole at Khaysār). The Kartid's intentions now become murky. He could have hunkered inside the fort until Abāqā's armies reached Khurasan, and sallied to merge the Kartid and Ilkhanid armies. Instead, he received Barāq's envoys and traveled to his camp, where he was feted. Barāq offered him dominion over Khurasan. He was "apparently impervious to the Kart king's true feelings," and made demands of him. When news of Abāqā's approach reached Herat, the city's gates slammed shut to Barāq. On 1 Dhū al-Ḥijja 668/22 July 1270 the Ilkhanid and Chaghataid armies faced each other near Herat. Barāq was defeated and retreated beyond the Oxus.[91]

It is possible the Kartid was playing for time until the Ilkhanid armies arrived. In the interim, he had interceded on behalf of Heratis to curb excesses by the Chaghataids, who had little more than rapine on their minds. George Lane, referencing the Ilkhanid vizier's (Rashīd al-Dīn's) evaluation of Shams al-Dīn Kart, writes: "he was an extremely canny and shrewd man and he understood the inherent fragility of Baraq's fortunes."[92] Shams al-Dīn's actions, perhaps being a little too clever, could be interpreted as betrayal

[89] Ibid., 78–79.

[90] On Qaidu and Barāq, see Michal Biran, *Qaidu and the Rise of the Independent Mongol State in Central Asia* (Richmond: Curzon, 1997), 30–32.

[91] al-Harawī, *Harāt*, 328–51; Ḥāfiẓ-i Abrū, *Kart*, 43–58; Barāq's invasion is analyzed in Lane, *Mongol Rule*, 78–95 (quote, see p. 86); see also Michal Biran, "The Battle for Herat (1270): A case of inter-Mongol warfare," in Nicolo Di Cosmo, ed., *Warfare in Inner Asian History (500–1800)* (Leiden: Brill, 2002), 175–219.

[92] Lane, *Mongol Rule*, 86.

of the Il-Khan and Qa'an, which is what happened. Shams al-Dīn fled to Khaysār and did not emerge for years. He had to be cunningly lured from his redoubt so he could be murdered.[93]

The Ilkhanids were incensed that the Ilkhanid-Chaghataid war had drained them of blood and treasure. Abāqā—irate and impetuous—blamed the victim:[94] because Herat was fertile, irrigated, and wealthy, it attracted invaders. Therefore Herat must be obliterated and its population deported.[95] In early 669/Autumn 1270, Mongol troops rampaged within Herat. A saner mind prevailed, to wit, the *ṣāḥib-dīwān*, Shams al-Dīn Juwaynī (d. 684/1285). Rapine—the preferred method of payment for troops—was halted. Sayfī's explanation is that Herat was spared because it was shielded by a surfeit of saints, and the spiritual and sepulchral edifices erected in their honor.[96] A plausible explanation is that the *ṣāḥib-dīwān* had made a pragmatic argument for sparing Herat and harnessing the region's revenues and resources. This is the reasoning that had undergirded Ögödei's revivification project (see Chapter Seven). A Herati notable, Bulabān (r. 669–70/1270–71), was installed as *malik* in the fugitive Kartid's stead. He was instructed to motivate Heratis to engage with agricultural production and reconstruction.

## Shams al-Dīn Kart's Legacy

Shams al-Dīn Kart, before he fled to Khaysār, had to bring his extensive but nominal domains under his authority. His efforts to rebuild Herat's infrastructure and revivify the economy were haphazard for a multiplicity of reasons, such as campaigning on behalf of the Ilkhanate.[97] He also spent two decades crisscrossing the regions itemized in Möngke *yarlīgh* subjugating recalcitrant local lords (where necessary);[98] and consolidating his realm by weaving a network of alliances with loyalists (*bandagān*). It was this *shifting*

93 This fateful episode has been elucidated in ibid., 172–75.
94 Ibid., 175: Abāqā "suffered fearsome attacks of alcohol-induced paranoia."
95 al-Harawī, *Harāt*, 352–55. See also Mīrkhʷānd, *Rawżat*, 3,690.
96 al-Harawī, *Harāt*, 353.
97 Lane, *Mongol Rule*, 167–68 (on his campaigns).
98 Independent confirmation of resistance to Shams al-Dīn when he first tried to impose his will on Sīstān's ruler in 653/1255f., is in Anon./Bahār (ed.), *Sīstān*, 368–70; Anon., *The Tārīkh-e Sīstān*, tr. Milton Gold (Rome: Istituto italiano per il Medio ed Estremo Oriente, 1976), 324–26. This history is explicated and evaluated by Lane, *Mongol Rule*, 155–76.

network of alliances that held the Kartid kingdom together until Temür's invasions.

It was not necessary for Shams al-Dīn Kart (or later Kartids) to control every square inch of the realm in order to efficiently administer and extract. Thomas Barfield articulated the "Swiss cheese" model of governance that had prevailed in Turko-Persian states.[99] Here, rulers elect to dominate the "cheesy bits": best agricultural lands (irrigated or near waters), good pastures, and economic centers. However, the "holes" (dry farmed regions, mountain, steppe, and desert) were of lower economic value. If people residing in the holes proved to be disruptive, punitive expeditions were mounted. Kartids found it expedient to dominate economically significant regions but not marginal lands.

Paradoxically, Shams al-Dīn Kart's exile at Khaysār, 669–74/1270–75, proved to be productive. He dominated the territories from Ghūr, east toward Ghazni and the Indus. His son, Malik Tark (n.d.),[100] was appointed *locum tenens* at Herat with the sanction of Abāqā's brother, Tübshin (n.d.). Tark was favorably received by Heratis. Shams al-Dīn's writ again extended into Herat. "He received copies of all correspondence and met with and advised and directed all the functionaries and notables of the city."[101] Tübshin pretended to support Shams al-Dīn, but plotted with Abāqā to lure the Kartid from his lair to slay him. Shams al-Dīn was persuaded by Abāqā's promises to leave Khaysār and travel to Tabriz, the Ilkhanid capital. Assisting Abāqā in the subterfuge were *ṣāḥib-diwān* Shams al-Dīn Juwaynī, and his son, Bahā' al-Dīn (d. 678/1279).[102] Shams al-Dīn Kart died *c.* 15 Shaʿbān 676/11 January 1278 after eating poisoned watermelon. His corpse was conveyed to Turbat-i Jām for interment beside Shaykh al-Islām Aḥmad-i Jām (d. 536/1141).[103]

Shams al-Dīn Muḥammad Kart bequeathed to his successors a contiguous kingdom whose contours, from *c.* 676/1278 to 783/1381, remained virtually unchanged. The nascent state was held together by a

[99] Barfield, *Afghanistan*, 67–71.
[100] Nothing further is known about this son.
[101] Lane, *Mongol Rule*, 172.
[102] Details are in al-Harawī, *Harāt*, 362–81; Rashīd al-Dīn/Thackston, *Jāmiʿ*, 3:382–83; Mīrkhʷānd, *Rawżat*, 3,692–94; Lane, *Mongol Rule*, 172–76.
[103] Ḥāfiẓ-i Abrū, *Kart*, 72; Isfizārī, *Rawżāt*, 1:422. Mahendrarajah, *Sufi Saint*, 162.

mosaic of *bandagān* and skeletal administrative structure. His "legacy to his successors was [...] the concept of a Kurt [Kart] state, centered at Herat."[104] The Kartid state (post-Shams al-Dīn), protected *Iranshahr*'s eastern frontiers, which were subject to military incursions and migrations by Turco-Mongol peoples of Central Asia. Kartids hindered the inflows of peoples from Transoxiana. Ultimately, the Chaghataid dam ruptured with Temür's invasion of Khurasan in 782/1380.

Kartids sustained and propagated Persian and Islamic heritages during the Mongol chapter of *Iranshahr*'s history.[105]

[104] Kempiners, "Khurasan," 48.
[105] See, e.g., Potter, "Kart Dynasty," 8–11, 157–66, 168–69.

# Prolegomenon
# The Middle Period: 677–729/1278–1329

This period of Ilkhanid-Kartid control at Herat began inauspiciously. It ended with the Ilkhanate nearing dissolution; the Kartid state politically and financially ascendant; and the economy of Herat flourishing.

Political, social, and economic conditions in Khurasan (generally), and in Herat (specifically), were impacted by events beyond Kartid control: Jochid-Toluid, Chaghataid-Toluid, Chaghataid-Ögödeid, and Chaghataid-Jochid hostilities on Persia's frontiers. The Ilkhanid center (Tabriz) and the Mongol imperial center (Qaraqorum) were not focused on Herat. The Chaghataid-Ögödeid alliance under Qaidu challenged Qubilai Qa'an in Mongolia and Uighuristan in 1268, 1275, 1286, and 1290.[1] The Ilkhanate was pressured by the Golden Horde in the northwest in 1288 and 1290.[2] The Golden Horde, under the leadership of Berke Khan (r. 1257–66), had allied with the Mamluk Sultanate of Egypt and Syria (r. 1250–1517). Mamluks and Ilkhanids battled in the west, from 1260,[3] until a peace accord was instituted in 1323. Shaken loose in the Ilkhanid-Jochid, Ilkhanid-Ögödeid, and Ilkhanid-Chaghataid struggles were consortia that became principal actors in Khurasan: (1) Jawni-Qurban, (2) Nikudaris, (3) Qaraunas.

*Conflict Ecosystem* is a concept that emerged with the Pentagon's misadventures in the Middle East.[4] It may prove helpful toward visualizing the *shifting* complex of *competing* or *cooperating* elements that constitute a

[1] Allsen, *Culture*, 35; Biran, *Qaidu*, 37ff.
[2] Allsen, *Culture*, 35.
[3] See Reuven Amitai-Preiss, *Mongols and Mamluks: The Mamluk-Īlkhānid War, 1260–1281* (Cambridge: Cambridge University Press, 1995).
[4] The concept is credited to Lt-Col (Dr) D.J. Kilcullen, Australian Armed Forces.

specific conflict. Elements within this ecosystem included the Jawni-Qurban, Nikudaris, and Qaraunas (Chapter Three).

The *Roving Bandit v. Stationary Bandit* concept, about how predators settle and establish nascent polities that become the *kernel of government*, is also articulated in Chapter Three.

The administration of Herat and its surroundings was in disarray with the death of the first Kartid. Shams al-Dīn's son, Rukn al-Dīn (r. 677–705/1278–1305), was installed by Abāqā as successor. He took the regnal name, Shams al-Dīn Kihīn ("the Younger").[5] He was an absent king who preferred the safety of the Kartids' Ghurid homestead, Fort Khaysār, to administering his domains from Herat (Chapter Three).

Fakhr al-Dīn Kart was installed at Herat by Nawrūz (d. 696/1297), a Mongol amir who became instrumental in the accession of Il-Khan Maḥmūd Ghāzān. The Nawruzid-Kartid union, which had fused two headstrong men, was dissolved (Chapters Three and Four). Fakhr al-Dīn defied the Mongols, leading to two sieges of Herat. However, earnest rebuilding in Herat began on his watch. His brother, Ghiyāth al-Dīn Kart replaced him. He had to contend with migrations from beyond the Oxus and raids by a Chaghataid princeling. The final decade of Ghiyāth al-Dīn's reign brought prosperity to Herat and its environs (Chapter Four).

[5] al-Harawī, *Harāt*, 382ff.; Isfizārī, *Rawżāt*, 1:424f. Muḥammad Ismāʿīl Mablagh Gharjistānī, "Shams al-Dīn Muḥammad wa Shams al-Dīn Kihīn," *Āryānā* No. 191 (1336/1957f.):33–35.

# 3

# Turmoil in Herat and Khurasan

## The Political, Military, and Social Environments

Charles Melville observed how historians see the "tossing of waves" but not "below the stormy surface."[1] An imperfect approach to perceiving processes transpiring below the surface—currents and counter-currents—is through conceptualization.

No two conflicts are identical. The Prussian theorist Carl von Clausewitz showed that the *nature* of war is eternal (unchanging).[2] It is only the *character* of war that changes.[3] There are *select* factors common to virtually every conflict (ancient, medieval, or modern): multiple political and/or military factions; oppositional politics; conflicting religions and ideologies; symbiosis (mutualism, commensalism, parasitism, amensalism); and external interference (for example, by foreign powers).

### *Aspects to Consider*

A "simple" battle where two antagonist blocs faced each other across a battlefield was not the norm in post-Mongol Khurasan. The region experienced invasions, rebellions, sieges; migrations of peoples and livestock; slave raiding and pillaging of town and country. Khurasan was anarchic; hence Ögödei's appointment of Chin-Temür to implement law and order; Möngke's support for Shams al-Dīn Kart's attempts to implement order. The period from

[1] See Introduction.

[2] Carl von Clausewitz, *On War*, trs and eds Michael Howard and Peter Paret (Princeton: Princeton University Press, 1976), 75–123.

[3] The character of war is in flux. It is shaped by, inter alia, new doctrines and technologies. In the Mongol age, for example, technological advances in catapult designs and chemical-based incendiaries changed the conduct of warfare.

*c.* 677/1278 to *c.* 720/1320 was characterized by protracted *low-intensity conflict*[4] (e.g., civil strife, banditry), interrupted by sporadic episodes of tranquility or eruptions of *high-intensity conflict.* Examples of intermittent but intense violence include predatory raids on Herat, and sieges of Herat by Ilkhanid expeditions.

Just as vultures and hyenas follow a lion's kill and hover for scraps, foragers and predators follow in the wake of armies to sift through plundered settlements. Squatters settle in villages, farms, and pastures, and claim ownership of dwellings, shops, windmills, watermills, irrigation channels (*jūy, kārīz*), and other immovable assets. Watermills (*jūy ṭāḥūna*), windmills (*āsyābi bādī*), and subterranean channels (*qanāt, kārīz*), even if partially wrecked, may be valuable assets. By acquiring properties that belong to others, squatters create the bases for future conflict with other claimants, including the rightful owners. The nineteenth-century Pashtun colonization of Khurasan,[5] for instance, was a cause of twentieth-century conflicts in northern Afghanistan.[6] Certain Ilkhanid fiscal-legal reforms were necessary to settle ambiguities over ownership of lands and waters (see Chapter Eight). Disputes over water rights persisted into the late Kartid era, compelling governmental action (ibid.).

Protracted conflicts involve myriads of stakeholders—armies, tribes, clans, ethnic-linguistic groupings, brigands, peasants, nomads, pastoralists, landlords, waterlords, ulama, Sufis, and so on—that shift and shape *collective* and *individual* choices.

If a conflict attracts outsiders—foreign powers, mercenaries, arms dealers, religious fanatics, political ideologues, looters, slavers, and so on—it could become a catastrophic war. This is manifest in modern conflicts in Iraq, Syria, and Yemen, and also in the Kartid-Sarbadarid war (Chapter Six), which attracted foreign forces from Fars, Mazandaran, and Transoxiana. Extremist Shiʿi militants (*ghulāt*) were armed by a (Sunni) Kartid ruler and unleashed on the Twelver Shiʿa Sarbadarid state at Sabzavar, predictably exacerbating the war and wreaking havoc in the Nishapur Quarter.

4 See definitions in Frank Kitson, *Low Intensity Operations* (London: Faber & Faber, 1971), 1–9.

5 See, e.g., Nancy Lindisfarne-Tapper, "The advent of Pashtūn '*Māldārs*' in north-western Afghanistan," *BSOAS* 36/1 (1973):55–79.

6 See, e.g., Liz Alden Wily, "The battle over pastures: The hidden war in Afghanistan," *Revue des mondes musulmans et de la Méditerranée* 133 (2013):95–113.

Ideologies are intangible factors that mold conflicts: (1) religion (Buddhist, Shaman, Christian, Sunni, Shiʿa, Zoroastrian); (2) Islamic laws (*shariʿa*) v. Mongol "laws and customs" (*yasāq wa yusūn*); (3) steppe warrior ethos adapting to Perso-Islamic sedentary civilization; "civilized" Perso-Islamic peoples adapting to "barbaric" steppe peoples. As the Mongols converted to Islam and embraced Persian cultural tenets, tensions between the laws and customs of the steppe, and the laws of Islam and customs of Persia, collided.[7] One dialectic explicated below (on *Roving Bandit v. Stationary Bandit*) divided the Mongols: *Settle & Rule v. Plunder & Leave*.[8] Ghāzān's purported speech to Mongol amirs uncovers this tension: "If you insult the *raʿiyyat*, take their oxen and seed, and trample their crops into the ground, what will you do in the future?"[9]

Conflicts originating in (1) ecological anomalies—unusual cold, warm, wet, or dry spells;[10] (2) famine and pestilence; (3) land and water rights—may become intractable.

Refugees generate conflict with locals by competing for resources (housing, water, pastures, farmlands, comestibles, sanitation, and employment). Sedentary and nomadic Khurasanians, for instance, opposed refugee inflows from Transoxiana.[11] Il-Khan Öljeitü (r. 703–16/1304–16) allowed Chinggisid political refugees to migrate to Khurasan, sparking a crisis for the Ilkhanate. One "refugee," Yasaʾur (d. 720/1320), ran amok in Khurasan and Sīstān for five years. This protracted conflict was resolved by Abū Saʿīd (r. 716–36/1316–35) b. Öljeitü, Kartids, and Kebek (r. 1318–26), khan of the Chaghataids (Chapter Four).

[7] See, e.g., Reuven Amitai-Preiss "Ghazan, Islam and Mongol tradition: A view from the Mamlūk sultanate," *BSOAS* 59/1 (1996):1–10; Michael Hope, *Power, Politics, and Tradition in the Mongol Empire and the Īlkhānate of Iran* (Oxford: Oxford University Press, 2016), 128 n.218. See also David Morgan, "The 'Great *yāsā* of Chingiz Khān' and Mongol Law in the Īlkhānate," *BSOAS* 49/1 (1986):163–76.

[8] See hypothesis in Kazuhide Kato, "Kebek and Yasawr: the Establishment of the Chaghatai Khanate," *Toyo Bunko* 49 (1991):97–118, 98.

[9] I.P. Petrushevsky [Petrushevskiĭ], "The Socio-Economic Conditions of Iran under the Il-Khans," in *CHI* 5:483–537, 494.

[10] I do not wish to wade into debates on *Medieval Warm Periods* and *Little Ice Ages*, but if these climate phenomena had manifested in Khurasan and Transoxiana, they will have adversely impacted on humans and livestock; and disrupted migratory and farming patterns.

[11] See, e.g., Kempiners, "Khurasan," 110.

Common trends or factors in medieval or modern conflicts lead us to the conflict ecosystem concept. A conflict ecosystem is not unlike an ecological system. A biological ecosystem thrives within a geographical area, where biotic (living) and abiotic (non-living) elements interact as a *system*. External factors (e.g., climate, topography) shape and control the system. Biotic components form clusters and symbiotic relationships emerge. Every conflict ecosystem has discrete elements (intangible and tangible): myriads of "organisms," some definable, some indefinable. External factors shift and shape the conflict ecosystem; its configuration morphs as organisms enter or exit. Like biological organisms, a conflict ecosystem's biotic elements *evolve* or *adapt*. No two conflict ecosystems will be alike due to the multiplicity of effable and ineffable variables.

*Theory to Reality*

A Kartid ruler must identify and manage the fluid ecosystem in which he operated. Shams al-Dīn Kart the Younger could not manage his environment and sought refuge in the Kartids' Ghurid homestead, Fort Khaysār. On the other hand, his son Fakhr al-Dīn Kart, ably managed—truly dominated—his environment.

The sources make manifest that aspects identified—symbiosis, clustering, shifting allegiances, and conflicting ideologies—shaped social, political, and military environments. However, not every active "organism" is identified; and if mentioned, there is no edifying commentary. Case in point: Nikudars and Qaraunas.[12]

References are found in Sayfī's history to Afghan (Pashtun), Balūch, Ghurid, Khalaj, and Sīstānī contingents serving in (or with) the Kartid army, but little is given about their roles in local politics. Pashtuns were probably involved in Herat's politics, but their roles pass unrecorded, whereas Pashtun involvement in the political-military affairs of Fars and Kirman is found in the *History of the Muzaffarids*.[13] Nikudaris included predatory bands; but Nikudaris also served with (or in) the Kartid army. Were there "good" Nikudaris and "bad" Nikudaris? Or did Nikudari clusters switch sides?

[12] On both consortia, see May, "Ilkhanate," 285–91.

[13] See Maḥmūd Kutbī, *Tārīkh-i Āl-i Muẓaffar*, ed. ʿAbd al-Ḥusayn Nawāʾi (Tehran: Amīr Kabīr, 1364/1985).

Three influential political consortia are contextualized below.

*Jawni-Qurban*

Jawni-Qurban (*je'ün-i qurbān*; "Three Percenters") were a "tribe" created through the assignment of every three (*je'ün*) per hundred (*qurbān*) soldiers from assorted peoples. The Jawni-Qurban's ruling clan—progeny of the *basqaq*, Arghūn Aqa (d. 673/1275)—were influential in Khurasan from the inception of the Jawni-Qurban (*c.* 1297), and reached the zenith of political power and control of territory in Khurasan with the death in 736/1335 of the last Il-Khan. Temür curbed their power in the late 8th/14th century.[14] The relationship between the Jawni-Qurban and Kartids, to utilize a cliché, was "complicated," but serves to describe a relationship where the Kartids helped the Mongols execute Nawrūz (d. 696/1297) b. Arghūn Aqa (d. 673/1275), yet Nawrūz's son (or nephew), Arghūn-Shāh (d. 743/1343 or 746/1345f.), and Arghūn-Shāh's son, Muḥammad Bīk (d. 774/1373), maintained mutually profitable liaisons, including a marital bond, with the Kartids.

*Nikudars and Qaraunas*

Nikudari (Negüderi) and Qaraunas ("mixed breeds")[15] are appellations utilized interchangeably and indiscriminately in sources; however, Hirotoshi Shimo has established that Nikudaris and Qaraunas are separate consortia.[16] Marco Polo describes "Caraunas" that he encountered near Kirman, *c.* 1270, as:

> a most cruel & wicked race and robbers who go scouring the land & doing great harm. And why are they called Caraunas, which means to say as much as [...] mongrels in our tongue? Because long ago their mothers were Indian and their fathers Tartars [...] and their king is called Negodar.[17]

[14] James Reid, "The Je'ün-i Qurbān Oirat Clan in the Fourteenth Century," *JAH* 18/2 (1984): 189–200; Jürgen Paul, "Zerfall und Bestehen: Die Ǧaun-i qurban im 14. Jahrhundert," *Asiatische Studien/Études Asiatiques* 65/3 (2011):695–733.

[15] Gunnar Jarring, "A Note on *Qarauna*," *Orientalia Suecana* 40 (1991):146–48; Jean Aubin, "L'ethnogénèse des Qaraunas," *Turcica* 1 (1969):65–94.

[16] Hirotoshi Shimo, "The Qarāūnās in the Historical Materials of the Īlkhanate," *Toyo Bunko* 35 (1977):131–81.

[17] Marco Polo, *The Descriptions of the World*, trs A.C. Moule and P. Pelliot, 2 vols (London: Routledge, 1938), 1:122; cf. idem, *The Book of Ser Marco Polo* [hereafter *Travels*], tr. Henry Yule, 2 vols (London: John Murray, 1871), 1:92–93. For a historiography of Polo's book, see Peter Jackson, "Marco Polo and His 'Travels'," *BSOAS* 61/1 (1998):82–101.

Marco Polo's confounding of Nikudaris and Qaraunas is understandable: both terms are in the primary sources, and Nikudaris and Qaraunas shared geography and pastimes—like brigandage. Sayf al-Harawī never uses Qaraunas—just Nikudari. A report by Rashīd al-Dīn makes manifest that Qaraunas and Nikudaris were distinct consortia:

> In Shaʿbān 698/May 1299, a 1,000 man unit of Qaraunas living near Ṭārum, led by Būqā, deserted (*bih-gurīkhtand*). They took the road to Iraq that passed Yazd and Kirman, pillaging (*tārāj*) along the way. At Bibīnīgāw, they joined forces (*paywastand*) with the Nikudaris.[18]

Nikudaris originated under Chaghataid command, *c.* 1279. Nikudar was one of the Golden Horde's generals in Berke's time; he possibly served with Hülegü's expedition into Persia. The Nikudaris were later directed by a chieftain appointed by the Chaghataid khan, Du'a (r. 1282–1307), son of Barāq (r. 1266–71).[19]

Qaraunas "were originally a body of troops, directly attached to Ābāqā [...] After the death of Ābāqā, they cooperated with his son, Arghūn [...] [*c.* 1295] it was decided that this 10,000 strong corps [should] come under the command of [Baidu]."[20] Qaraunas were active in both Iraqs. There were another 10,000 Qaraunas in Khurasan, *c.* 1272, under Nawrūz or Hindū Bītikchī. The Qaraunas corps of Khurasan was distinct from the corps attached to the Il-Khan. The Qaraunas *tümen* of Khurasan splintered (between 694/1295 and 703/1304), but acknowledged Ghāzān's authority.[21]

## Herat's Socio-economic Gains Unravel

The above conceptualization on the opaque conflict ecosystem, and discourses on the Jawni-Qurban, Nikudaris, and Qaraunas, may help in understanding how fragile socio-economic gains in Herat unraveled. Jawni-Qurban, Nikudaris, and Qaraunas were leading actors in the undermining of Kartid rule. It also did not help Heratis that their sovereign, Shams al-Dīn

[18] Rashīd al-Dīn, *Kitāb-i tārīkh-i mubārak-i Ghāzānī: dāstān-i Ghāzān Khān*, ed. Karl Jahn (Ābādān: Nashr-i pursish, 1388/2009 [reprint of 1940 Luzac ed.]), 123; Shimo, "Qarāūnās," 161. On Ṭārum (in Fars), see Le Strange, *Lands*, 291–92.

[19] Shimo, "Qarāūnās," 160–63.

[20] Ibid., 136.

[21] Ibid., 148, 155.

Muḥammad Kart the Younger, was absent from Herat at crucial moments, most notably, when Herat was pillaged (repeatedly) by Nikudaris.

*Shams al-Din Kart "the Absent"*

Shams al-Dīn Kihīn (d. 12 Ṣafar 705/3 September 1305) was appointed *locum tenens* by his father before he set out on his fateful journey to Tabriz. The Younger was confirmed in office by Abāqā, *c.* 677/1278, following an interview at his *urdu* where he had to convince him that he was not "disloyal" (like his father). He decamped for Herat with a *yarlīgh*, *pā ʾīza*, robe of honor (*khilʿat-i fākhira*), and presents.[22] Abāqā's interest, if any, in the revivification of Herat cannot be assessed. He had, after all, refused to permit construction inside Herat, and sought to raze Herat. The Younger, in any case, was not the man for the hard task of rebuilding. He reigned from 677/1278 to 705/1305 but did not rule: he spent the majority of the years from Dhū al-Ḥijja 680 or Muḥarram 681/April–May 1282 to Ṣafar 705/September 1305 at Khaysār. His flight was precipitated by the death of Abāqā on 20 Dhū al-Ḥijja 680/1 April 1282. Shams al-Dīn feared that he would become a casualty of Chinggisid internecine struggles. He ensured that Kartid redoubts were held by trusted castellans (*kūtwāl*) and governors (*ḥāris*);[23] and he encouraged *raʿāyā*[24] to continue with their economic activities.[25] Thusly did Sham al-Dīn secure his environment. Farmers and pastoral nomads would have kept Fort Khaysār supplied with foodstuffs and materiel.

Arghūn (r. 1284–91), Abāqā's son, acceded to the throne after a fleeting reign by Tegüder (1281–84),[26] one of Hülegü's sons and Arghūn's rival. Pillars of the former regime, such as the Juwaynī family—historian, ʿAlaʾ al-Dīn ʿAṭāʾ-Malik; vizier, Shams al-Dīn—were hounded by rivals, and following Tegüder's execution and Arghūn's enthronement, found themselves on the losing side.[27] While judging it prudent to remain at Khaysār, Shams

[22] al-Harawī, *Harāt*, 386; Ḥāfiẓ-i Abrū, *Kart*, 73; Isfizārī, *Rawżāt*, 1:425–26.

[23] *Kūtwāl* (or *kutwāl*): on Ghaznavid adoption of an Indian term, see Abuʾl-Fazl Beyhaqi, *The History of Beyhaqi*, tr. C.E. Bosworth, rev. M. Ashtiany, 3 vols (Boston: Ilex, 2011), 3:13 n.40.

[24] *Raʿāyā*: sedentary classes: peasants, artisans, craftsmen, merchants.

[25] al-Harawī, *Harāt*, 389; Ḥāfiẓ-i Abrū, *Kart*, 73.

[26] Peter Jackson, "Aḥmad Takūdār," *EIr*, 1:661–62; Hope, *Power*, 125–34.

[27] On the Juwaynī clan, see Lane, *Mongol Rule*, 177–212; on the campaign against the Juwaynī bureaucrats, see Hope, *Power*, 119–134.

al-Dīn Kihīn appointed his son, ʿAlāʾ al-Dīn (r.*c.* 682–87/1283–88), in 682/1283f. as *locum tenens* at Herat. In 683/1284f., when Arghūn visited Herat before traveling to Bādghīs, thence to Sarakhs, the Kartid did not leave Khaysār to greet his liege-lord and secure a fresh patent. Instead, ʿAlaʾ al-Dīn greeted Arghūn and secured for his father the patent, golden tablet of authority (*pāʾīza-i zar*), and robe of honor.[28]

Shams al-Dīn Kart (II) had astutely judged prevailing fissures and factions.[29] Arghūn was a compromise choice;[30] tensions between the Ilkhanid crown and its military hierarchy generated strife, 1284–95;[31] and Herat was situated between two active tectonic plates: the quasi-Toluid Ilkhanate and Chinggisid rivals in Transoxiana. Further imperiling his position was involvement in the execution of a Qaraunas amir, Hindū Noyan (d. 685/1287f.). Hindū murdered Tay-Temür (an amir who had served Arghūn). Tay-Temür's allies pursued Hindū, who sought asylum at Khaysār in *c.* 685/1287f. After hesitating, briefly, Shams al-Dīn seized Hindū Noyan and dispatched him to Arghūn. This act of fealty was acknowledged by the Il-Khan with gifts,[32] but it spawned a feud between Qaraunas and Kartids.[33]

### *Nikudaris Raid Herat*

Allies of Hindū Noyan disparaged the Kartid to the Il-Khan. As tensions emerged between Il-Khan and *malik*, ʿAlāʾ al-Dīn Kart quit Herat for Ghūr, leaving Herat politically rudderless. Rumors proliferated and people became unsettled. In 687/1288, into the midst of this simmering discontent plunged the Nikudaris: raiding first the Mālān region (south of the city of Herat), plundering, and enslaving. They entered Herat from several directions; sacked, killed, and enslaved.[34] Other militias, notably a refractory Mongol

[28] al-Harawī, *Harāt*, 397; Ḥāfiẓ-i Abrū, *Kart*, 75.

[29] On these fissures, see Hope, *Power*, esp. 111ff.

[30] See May, *Mongol Empire*, 235–36.

[31] Hope, *Power*, 135–59.

[32] al-Harawī, *Harāt*, 398–401; Faṣīḥ, *Mujmal*, 844 and 846.

[33] Michael Hope, "Some Notes on Revenge and Justice in the Mongol Empire and the Īl-Khānate of Iran," *JAOS* 136/3 (2016):551–66, esp. 555.

[34] The enslaved were taken to the *Garmsīr* (dry, hot region; warm country; cf. *Sardsīr*: wet, cold region). al-Harawī, *Harāt*, 402: he means the Sīstān-Hilmand region. See, e.g., Barthold, *Geography*, 73–75. For observations made during a journey from Sind to Persia, see H.W. Bellew,

*noyan*, seized the moment and joined in the rapine. Major Herati militia leaders fled the city.[35] They were followed by denizens of all social ranks. Sayf al-Harawī, our chronicler, was then six years old (b.*c.* 681/1281f.):[36] recounts he of the streams of the starved and harried fleeing Herat for Ghūr, Gharjistān, Khʷāf,[37] Isfizār,[38] and Jām.[39]

### *Amir Nawrūz and Nikudaris Join Forces*

The Nikudaris returned in 688/1289 to plunder Herat. Nikudaris were allied with Nawrūz (d. 696/1297) b. Arghūn Aqa, a formidable Ilkhanid amir considered (by the Il-Khan) to be "in rebellion." Nawrūz would become integral to a pivotal change in Kartid, Persian, and Islamic histories; but first, we should explain how he came to be associated with the despoliation of Herat.

Nawrūz was a scion of the Oirat ruling "clan" (*oboq*) of Jawni-Qurban.[40] Arghūn's young son, Ghāzān, was appointed viceroy of Khurasan, with Nawrūz as his *atabeg* (Turkish: father-tutor). Alliances were fluid: an ally of today was the rebel of tomorrow, and vice versa. Nawrūz exemplified this reality. Between early 688/1289 and early 694/late 1294 Nawrūz was in rebellion.[41] Arghūn died in Rabīʿ I 690/March 1291 and was succeeded by his brother, Geikhatu (r. 1291–95), the viceroy of Anatolia. Uncle and nephew became rivals. Ghāzān's chance emerged with Geikhatu's execution in Jumādá II 694/April 1295 following the revolt of Hülegü's grandson, Baidu (r. 694/1295).[42]

The Nikudari raid on Herat occurred about the time that Nawrūz had Ghāzān and his army on the backfoot. Ghāzān had spent winter 687/1288–89 in Marw. Nawrūz broke away from him around January/February

*Record of the March of the Mission to Seistan* (Calcutta: Foreign Department Press, 1873), 21–70, esp. 52–54 (on the "hot tract" called "Gurmsel").

35 The names are in al-Harawī, *Harāt*, 402.

36 al-Harawī, *Harāt*, 402–04; Isfizārī, *Rawżāt*, 1:427–28; Faṣīḥ, *Mujmal*, 847.

37 Khʷāf: see Krawulsky, *Ḫorāsān*, 1:37, 2:34–35; Le Strange, *Lands*, 357–58.

38 Isfizār: see Krawulsky, *Ḫorāsān*, 1:35–36, 2:33; Le Strange, *Lands*, 340, 412, 431.

39 Jām: see Krawulsky, *Ḫorāsān*, 1:40–41, 2:36–37; Ibrāhīm Zanganah, *Sarzamīn-i Jām wa rijāl-ān* [*Jām Region and its Eminent Men*] (Turbat-i Jām: Intishārāt-i Shaykh al-Islām Aḥmad-i Jām, 1384/2006); Le Strange, *Lands*, 356–57; Mahendrarajah, *Sufi Saint*, 93–98.

40 Reid, "Je'ün-i Qurbān," 190.

41 Michael Hope, "The 'Nawrūz King': the rebellion of Amir Nawrūz in Khurasan (688–694/1289–94) and its implications for the Ilkhan polity at the end of the thirteenth century," *BSOAS* 78/3 (2015):451–73.

42 On Baidu, see Patrick Wing, *EI3*, "Bāydū," 2015–04, pp. 52–54.

1289. In Rabīʿ I 688/March–April 1289, Ghāzān decamped to the Sarakhs area, heading toward Ṭūs and Radkān.[43] He directed Nawrūz to join him at his camp by the Kashaf River. On 27 Rabīʿ I 688/20 April 1289, Nawrūz attacked the camp and Ghāzān took flight toward Nishapur.[44] Nawrūz clashed with Ilkhanid forces on 15 Rabīʿ II 688/8 May 1289 near Radkān and was again victorious. Two days before the second battle, Qaraunas bands had attacked Nawrūz's camp, forcing Nawrūz to protect his people and property. "[H]e sent his tents and retainers (*mutaʿalliq-ān*) to Herat" while he pursued the Ilkhanid army. Having overestimated his position, Nawrūz was unprepared for strong resistance and was forced to turn back at Jām.[45]

Returning to the impending sack of Herat, it appears that Nawrūz's confederate, Amir Yājī,[46] a Nikudari,[47] was marching on Herat at Nawrūz's request (*Amīr Yājī bā sipāh-i girān bih istidʿāʾ-yi Amīr Nawrūz badān ṭarf āmad*).[48] Perhaps he was escorting Nawrūz's "tents and retainers"? The degree of coordination between Yājī and Nawrūz, and the sequence of events, may only be surmised. It is likely the raid on Herat took place after the second rout of Ghāzān, but before the height of the summer: this is when Ghāzān was "camped at the gates of Herat next to the Mālān Bridge."[49]

Shams al-Dīn Kihīn dispatched a mandate (*mithāl*) from Khaysār to Herat with an emissary. The directive, addressed to his deputies and functionaries (*nawwāb wa ʿummāl*), proclaimed that a sizeable army under Yajī was marching on Herat. "Every effort must be made to please him. No delay or dereliction is permitted. His intention is to move the army into Khurasan [read: he will bypass Herat]; and most of us think that he will not molest the people of Herat." Nevertheless, the *malik* cautioned them not to blindly trust

[43] Radkān: see Krawulsky, *Ḫorāsān*, 1:84–96, 2:59–61; Le Strange, *Lands*, 393–94.

[44] Rashīd al-Dīn/Thackston, *Jāmiʿ*, 3:420. The Kashaf Rud flows southeast from Radkān into the Hari Rud.

[45] Rashīd al-Dīn/Thackston, *Jāmiʿ*, 3:422; Rashīd al-Dīn/Jahn, *Ghāzān*, 21; ʿAbdallāh b. Fażlallāh Waṣṣāf, *Taḥrīr-i tārīkh-i Waṣṣāf*, ed. ʿAbd al-Muḥammad Āyatī (Tehran: Pizhūhishgāh-i ʿulūm-i insānī wa muṭālaʿāt-i farhangī, 1383/2004), 177.

[46] Ḥāfiẓ-i Abrū, *Kart*, 78 (identified as Abāchī b. Qunqūrdāʾī).

[47] Cf. Aubin, "Qaraunas," 88 (Amīr Yājī is identified as Qaraunas).

[48] al-Harawī, *Harāt*, 405.

[49] Rashīd al-Dīn/Thackston, *Jāmiʿ*, 3:422; Rashīd al-Dīn/Jahn, *Ghāzān*, 22. Mālān Bridge is *c.* 5.2 km from Herat's south gate (see Chapter One, n.93).

the estimate, and to barricade themselves inside citadels.[50] Shaykh al-Islam Quṭb al-Dīn Chishtī (n.d.) of the Chishtiyya Sufis, sent a missive to Herat: "the people of Herat must not fight Amir Yājī [but should] close the city's gates to his army."[51] That Herat was relatively defenseless (at the moment) is manifest from subsequent events.

Yājī did not immediately attack Herat. He surveilled the city; on the fourth day, his men went around beating drums and declaring: "Amir Yājī has proclaimed that everyone must come outside the city at [the time of] the sunset prayer (*namāz-i shām*)." Sayfī does not elucidate whether people complied or not, but the rapine began on the fifth day. Many Heratis were captured by the Nikudaris for enslavement, while "a contingent of retainers of Amir Nawrūz (*qawmī az muta'alliq-ān-i Amīr Nawrūz*) and another [amir?] seized the rest of the people." Children were separated from their mothers; terrible cruelties and abuses were inflicted on Heratis. Not satisfied with the wanton slaughter within the city's limits, Yājī sent cavalry after Heratis who had fled; refugees that were captured were killed. Yājī and his men quit Herat with plunder that included captive Heratis.[52]

Sayf al-Harawī's descriptions of Herat in the aftermath of the Nikudari raids include aspects that appear hyperbolic. Herat was deserted, writes Sayfī, with barely 100 survivors. In wards where there had been one hundred *kadkhudās*,[53] two to five survived. Hidden grain stores and well-water sustained survivors. Nobody ventured out at night. Herat was deserted for one year. Khurasanians hunkered in redoubts while the struggle between Nawrūz and the Ilkhanate unfolded.[54]

### *Amir Nawrūz and Ghāzān Khan*

Nawrūz had crossed the Oxus to seek help from Qaidu. Nawrūz was "lent" an army, commanded by a Chaghataid princeling, Yasa'ur (d. 720/1320),

[50] al-Harawī, *Harāt*, 405. It is unclear to which citadels he refers. There is mention of "Ḥiṣār-i Ikhtiyār al-Dīn"; a Timurid era copyist's interpolation? Repeated in Ḥāfiẓ-i Abrū, *Kart*, 78. The citadel was rebuilt in 699/1299–1300 and acquired the appellation later.

[51] al-Harawī, *Harāt*, 405. Eljigidei destroyed city gates. It is unclear what replaced them.

[52] al-Harawī, *Harāt*, 405–06; Ḥāfiẓ-i Abrū, *Kart*, 78; Faṣīḥ, *Mujmal*, 847.

[53] *Kadkhudā*: see Beyhaqi/Bosworth, *History*, 3:17–18 n.64 (Bosworth's edifying note).

[54] al-Harawī, *Harāt*, 407–08; Ḥāfiẓ-i Abrū, *Kart*, 78.

and accompanied by minor Ögödeid royals.[55] Nawrūz's return to Khurasan in 691/1291 coincided with Arghūn's death. Major cities like Nishapur and Ṭūs, and their dependent villages, were ravaged, with many killed, wounded, or enslaved. Viceroy Ghāzān was unable to restore Ilkhanid authority in Khurasan. Ghāzān, and his father, Arghūn, had stronger alliances in the west (both Iraqs—Arab Iraq and Persian Iraq; and Āẕarbayjān) than they did in Khurasan. On the other hand, Nawrūz was a prominent lord of Khurasan, and had cultivated a network of alliances with amirs, lords, and dynasts of Khurasan—including Shams al-Dīn Kihīn. Nawrūz became the master of Khurasan. Vizier Rashīd al-Dīn, commissioned by Il-Khan Ghāzān to write *Jāmiʿ al-tawārīkh* (*Compendium of Chronicles*), does not highlight his master's loss of Khurasan during his viceroyship. Nawrūz retained independent control of Khurasan until 694/1295, when Ghāzān became Il-Khan with Nawrūz's assistance. Tensions emerged between the Il-Khan and the "kingmaker," Nawrūz (I shall elaborate later).

Herat specifically, and Khurasan generally, were caught between the Ilkhanid anvil and the Nawrūzid hammer. Khurasanians suffered terribly. Deprivations and sufferings were exacerbated by opportunistic slave raiding by Nikudaris and Qaraunas. The Qaraunas included bands loyal to the Ilkhanate, like the group stationed at Jām.[56] Another group of Qaraunas commanded by Danishmand Bahadur—a man fated to die as a consequence of a spectacular act of Kartid treachery—entered Juwayn and "wrought havoc."[57] Nawrūz led the Jawni-Qurban, but also commanded Qaraunas detachments. Ilkhanid troops were not without blame, although Rashīd al-Dīn glosses over such embarrasments: Fūshanj was, for instance, plundered, ostensibly because its inhabitants had refused demands for provisions. By 691/1291, famine, or near-famine conditions, persisted in Khurasan, where "a hundred maunds of grain could not be purchased for a hundred dinars."[58] Hyperbolic, possibly, but indicative of dire socio-economic conditions.

55 Rashīd al-Dīn/Thackston, *Jāmiʿ*, 3:423–24; Waṣṣāf, *Taḥrīr*, 177; Mīrkhwānd, *Rawżat*, 4, 201–02; Biran, *Qaidu*, 57–59; Hope, "Nawrūz," 460.

56 Rashīd al-Dīn/Thackston, *Jāmiʿ*, 3:422.

57 Ibid., 3:423.

58 Ibid., 3:426.

## The Kartid-Nawruzid Union: Another Start for Herat

The general thrust of events leading to the revivification of socio-economic activity in Herat in the aftermath of the aforementioned attacks, as narrated by Sayf al-Harawī and Ḥāfiẓ-i Abrū—who frequently follows Sayfī but adds fresh information, too—is acceptable; however the chronology and certain statements by Sayfī and Ḥāfiẓ-i Abrū are suspect. For example, Ḥāfiẓ-i Abrū claims that with the death of Arghūn in 690/1291, Ghāzān took his place, and appointed Nawrūz as viceroy for Khurasan with a mandate to revivify Herat.[59] His account is an abstract of Sayfī's narrative, which includes an extract of an *Āl tamghā* by Nawrūz.[60] Reports in Waṣṣāf and Mīrkhʷānd help correct certain deficiencies.

The context for Nawrūz's endeavors at administration and revitalization of Herat and its environs, as Michael Hope has persuasively argued, is that "Nawrūz realized from a very early stage that his political survival depended on the revenues of these towns, which led him to take a close interest in their administration and wellbeing."[61] If we strip away from al-Harawī's and Ḥāfiẓ-i Abrū's reports claims of Ilkhanid involvement in Khurasan's affairs, we discover this pith: Nawrūz ruled *independently* from *c.* 690/1291 to 694/1295. In 694/1295, he allied with Ghāzān and helped him to secure the throne.

Nawrūz wrote in 690–91/1291–92 to Shams al-Dīn Kihīn (then still at Khaysār). Nawrūz requested (apparently demanded) his presence in Herat to oversee the revivification of the region.[62] The Kartid demurred, *c.* 691–92/1292.[63] As a consequence of the Kartid's refusal to perform his obligations, Nīkī Bāwarchī was appointed *shaḥna* of Herat (on him, see Chapter Seven). But Nawrūz did not end his search for a Kartid to situate at Herat. He turned to Fakhr al-Dīn Muḥammad Kart, son of

[59] Ḥāfiẓ-i Abrū, *Kart*, 78. Nawrūz was in rebellion for about four years. Ghāzān did not accede to the Ilkhanid throne until 694/1295.

[60] al-Harawī, *Harāt*, 409. *Āl tamghā* (Turkish: "red seal"), "term for the supreme seal of the Mongol Il-Khans of Iran. The term also meant 'document with a red seal'." See F. Doerfer, "Āl tamghā," *EIr*, 1:766–68. On changes to the Ilkhanid *tamghā* with Ghāzān's conversion to Islam, see Hope, *Power*, 158–59.

[61] Hope, "Nawrūz," 457.

[62] al-Harawī, *Harāt*, 411; Ḥāfiẓ-i Abrū, *Kart*, 79; Faṣīḥ, *Mujmal*, 853 (under AH 691).

[63] al-Harawī, *Harāt*, 409, 412–14; Ḥāfiẓ-i Abrū, *Kart*, 79–81; Faṣīḥ, *Mujmal*, 854 (AH 692).

Shams al-Dīn the Younger. He sought his appointment as the *malik*'s *locum tenens*. Father and son were estranged; Fakhr al-Dīn was languishing in Fort Khaysār's gaol. Fakhr al-Dīn was an excellent warrior, a qualification desired by Nawrūz. Shams al-Dīn the Younger, uneasy about the formation of a political battery at Herat that included Fakhr al-Dīn *and* Nawrūz, refused Nawrūz's entreaties: he even accused his son of insanity. Nawruz dispatched shaykhs al-Islam Shihāb al-Dīn Ismāʿīl Jāmī (d.*c*. 738/1338) of Turbat-i Jām,[64] and Quṭb al-Dīn Chishtī (n.d.) of Chisht-i Sharīf,[65] to appeal to Shams al-Dīn. The *malik* relented and released his son in 693/1293–94.[66]

Fakhr al-Dīn Kart was tasked with the subjugation of Khʷāf and Farāh.[67] The Khʷāf campaign necessitated the capture of forts. Between the Khʷāf and Farāh campaigns, Fakhr al-Dīn was installed at Herat, having proved his martial skills and fealty to Nawrūz.[68] Fakhr al-Dīn also demonstrated his diplomatic prowess by persuading Nawrūz's erstwhile enemy, *malik* Ināltikīn of Farāh, to become a Kartid or Nawrūzid *banda*. The Fakhr al-Dīn-Nawrūz alliance included a marital union to seal the political union: Nawrūz's niece (a brother's daughter) married the Kartid in 694/1295.[69]

## Mongol Factionalism and the Kartids

The imperial (Ilkhanid) history of this period, from Geikhatu's death in April 1295 to Baidu's defeat and Ghāzān's accession in October 1295, has been vividly reported by Rashīd al-Dīn.[70] While the battle for the Ilkhanate occupied Nawrūz and Ghāzān, and unfolded in the west, Fakhr al-Dīn Kart had to secure the Ilkhanate's east. Nawrūz ruled independently until 694/1295, but his independence was now being threatened by Qaidu. Ürüng Temür, the man Nawrūz had installed as suzerain, defected to Qaidu with

64 On Shihāb al-Dīn Ismāʿīl Jāmī, see Mahendrarajah, *Sufi Saint*, 59–63, 143–48.

65 Quṭb al-Dīn Chishtī, see notice in, Gūyā ʿIttimādī, "Darbār-i mulūk-i Kart [The court of the Kart kings]" *Āryānā* No. 2/16 (1323/1944):46–54, 50.

66 al-Harawī, *Harāt*, 415–23; Ḥāfiẓ-i Abrū, *Kart*, 81–85; Faṣīḥ, *Mujmal*, 856 (AH 693). Fakhr al-Dīn did not govern independently until *c*. 694/1295.

67 Farāh: see Krawulsky, *Ḫorāsān*, 1:35–37, 2:33–34. Le Strange, *Lands*, 341, 351.

68 al-Harawī, *Harāt*, 424–25; Ḥāfiẓ-i Abrū, *Kart*, 85–86. The year given is 694/1295.

69 Waṣṣāf, *Taḥrīr*, 190–91; Faṣīḥ, *Mujmal*, 861.

70 Rashīd al-Dīn/Thackston, *Jāmiʿ*, 3:432–40; see also Hope, *Power*, 148–59.

his army, prompting (by Michal Biran's calculus), Nawrūz's entreaties to Ghāzān in 694/1294–95.[71]

*Ögödeid-Chaghataid Pressure in the East*

In early 694/1295 a joint force of Ögödeids and Chaghataids, commanded by the Chaghataid prince, Du'a (son of Barāq), invaded Khurasan, encouraged in part by Ghazan's distractions. Du'a was appointed by Qaidu, *c.* 1282, as chief of *ulus* Chaghatai. This served to cement Ögödeid-Chaghataid cooperation. He was "Qaidu's right-hand man."[72] Du'a settled in Mazandaran for eight months.[73] When he finally stirred his army, it was to march home, sacking, burning, and enslaving along the way. Towns in Mazandaran, and Abīward, Marw, Nisā,[74] and Sarakhs in Khurasan, were attacked.[75] Fūshanj and Kūsūyi were besieged; Kūsūyi did not fall but Fūshanj did. Besieger and besieged suffered heavy casualties. Countless wretches were enslaved by Du'a and hauled off to Transoxiana.[76]

Why did Du'a's army sit in Mazandaran for eight months, from *c.* March 1295 to *c.* October/November 1295? The region was favored as winter quarters (*qishlāq*), but is hardly comfortable as summer quarters (*aylāq*). It is, however, relatively neutral territory, away from Ghāzān's and Fakhr al-Dīn's forces and their network of allies. My sense is that Qaidu and Du'a had elected to watch the scrimmage for the Ilkhanid throne, and depending on outcome, make their move. Du'a had approached Fakhr al-Dīn and offered him dominion over Khurasan. The Kartid demurred.[77] Fakhr al-Dīn was astute. He had read the political-military landscape and decided that Nawrūz and Ghāzān would be successful; that his own fortunes rested with Nawrūz and Ghāzān—or perhaps just Ghāzān.

[71] Biran, *Qaidu*, 59. AH 694: from 21 November 1294 to 9 November 1295.
[72] Ibid., 33.
[73] He probably camped on the southeast littoral of the Caspian, in Gorgan (Jurjān).
[74] Nisā: see Le Strange, *Lands*, 377, 393–94, 429–30.
[75] al-Harawī, *Harāt*, 426; Ḥāfiẓ-i Abrū, *Kart*, 86.
[76] al-Harawī, *Harāt*, 432–40; Ḥāfiẓ-i Abrū, *Kart*, 88–92; Faṣīḥ, *Mujmal*, 863–64.
[77] al-Harawī, *Harāt*, 426–27; Ḥāfiẓ-i Abrū, *Kart*, 86–87.

## *Fakhr al-Dīn Kart and Ghāzān Khan*

At some point in 694/1295,[78] Fakhr al-Dīn had met with Ghāzān, who was evidently impressed by what he heard at the interview. Fakhr al-Dīn departed the meeting with the standard honors of investiture, 10,000 dinars, 1,000 (*hazāra*) Mongol troops, and a *yarlīgh* to govern (*mulkī*) and protect (*ḥimayat*) Herat.[79] Du'a and Qaidu, on realizing that Ghāzān had secured the Ilkhanid throne and had the backing of Mongol troops in Persia, decided to withdraw, but for Du'a to pillage eastern Persia on his journey to Transoxiana, in part to ruin Ghazan's kingdom, in part to benefit their polity's economy. Although Fakhr al-Dīn had yet to fortify Herat's defenses, as a consequence of the Ögödeid-Chaghataid army's costly clashes at Kūsūyi and Fūshanj, Du'a evidently considered it prudent to bypass Herat and transport his spoils into Transoxiana.

Fakhr al-Dīn Kart (r. 695–706/1295–1307) was in charge at Herat by 694–95/1295. He was probably there in 693 (December 1293 to November 1294), about a year earlier than the "official" date. The year, 694/1295, is central to Persian and Islamic histories: Ghāzān Khan converted to Islam.[80] This set in train events that transformed the relationship between the Mongol sovereign of Persia and his Muslim subjects: the alien Shamanist/Buddhist *khān* of the Central Asian steppes eventually became the Persianized (read: civilized) Muslim *sulṭān*. Of immediate relevance to the harried peoples of Persia is that Ghāzān's conversion *initiated* the gradual transition of the Ilkhanid state from an exploitative occupying force with little regard for the welfare of its subjects, to a Persian-Islamic state, which through its Persian bureaucrats, promulgated, inter alia, fiscal-legal reforms to alleviate onerous taxations and tedious regulations, and to foster agricultural and commercial activities.

[78] Sayfī reports the meeting under 695/10 November 1295 to 29 October 1296. It probably took place before Ghāzān traveled west to confront Baidu.

[79] al-Harawī, *Harāt*, 430–31; Ḥāfiẓ-i Abrū, *Kart*, 88.

[80] Charles Melville, "*Pādshāh-i Islām*: The Conversion of Sultan Maḥmūd Ghāzān Khān," in *Pembroke Papers* 1 (1990):159–77.

*Ghāzān's Journey from Pagan Il-Khan to Muslim Sultan*

Nawrūz had a central role in bringing Ghāzān to Islam. Five to six months before Geikhatu's death (d. 694/1295),[81] Nawrūz had set in motion the process of reconciliation with Ghāzān by dispatching emissaries to his court.[82] Ghāzān was warned by advisers that "mak[ing] peace with one's enemies is like having a serpent as a companion." Nevertheless, he cautiously agreed to meet with Nawrūz. Ghāzān traveled to the Sarakhs region; thence to a plain situated between Marw and Shibūrghān,[83] where, perched atop a hill, Ghāzān looked "down on the valley in amazement" at the vastness of Nawrūz's army and thought, "Nawrūz had might, power, and strength."[84] Suffice it to note that Ghāzān had the incentive to truce with Nawrūz. The latter begged for forgiveness and an alliance was born. Impelling Nawrūz's desire for a compact was the antagonism that he and Fakhr al-Dīn Kart faced in Khurasan from Nawrūz's former allies in Transoxiana. Nawrūz, stuck between two dynamic tectonic plates—the Ögödeid-Chaghataid union and the Ilkhanids—feared being squashed; hence the imperative for him to make peace with the Ilkhanids and alleviate the pressure he was currently experiencing. The Ögödeid-Chaghataid union's rupture with Nawrūz, and its despoliation of Khurasan (again), will be addressed momentarily.

Ghāzān was occupied suppressing opponents in Khurasan when news of Baidu's challenge reached him. He turned toward Āẕarbayjān to meet the challenge. Nawrūz's army would be indispensable to his cause. Nawrūz impressed upon him the urgency of securing the support of Turko-Mongols that had already converted to Islam. Nawrūz made the case that the throne can be captured by the Padishah of Islam. As David Morgan drolly put it, "Tabriz was worth a *shahada*." On 4 Shaʿbān 694/19 June 1295, Ghāzān converted to Islam before Sufi shaykh Ṣadr al-Dīn Ibrahīm Ḥammūya.

Baidu was executed on 23 Dẖū al-Qaʿda 694/4 October 1295. On the suspiciously auspicious day of "the Feast of the Sacrifice" (*ʿīd al-aḍḥa*), 10

[81] Geikhatu ran afoul of his amirs and died on 6 Jumādá II 694/23 April 1295.

[82] Rashīd al-Dīn/Thackston, *Jāmiʿ*, 3:429, 432. Emissaries were dispatched on 1 Muḥarram 694/21 November 1294.

[83] Shibūrghān: see Krawulsky, *Ḫorāsān*, 1:75–76; Barthold, *Geography*, 31.

[84] Rashīd al-Dīn/Thackston, *Jāmiʿ*, 3:430 (*c.* mid-Ṣafar 694/4–5 January 1295).

Dhū al-Ḥijja 694/21 October 1295,[85] sultan Maḥmūd (Ghāzān) khan took the Ilkhanid throne. The broader implications of Ghāzān's conversion shall not detain us.

Before returning to Nawrūz's and Fakhr al-Dīn's joint rule in Herat, the economic framework that fashioned the Kartid-Nawruzid union must be explained.

## Roving Bandits v. Stationary Bandits

Nawrūz's political rupture with the Ögödeid-Chaghataid faction was undergirded by economic rationale: one faction wanted to pillage and leave; one faction wanted to remain, develop the region's economy (that they had ruined), and "gently rob" subjects (that is, tax the *raʿāyā*). Nawrūz's ambition to develop Herat's economy gave birth to political union.

### *Economic Factors and Political Choices*

Nawrūz had installed Ürüng Temür (Per.: Awrang Timūr), a descendant of Ögödei, as the nominal Chinggisid suzerain of Khurasan. Nawrūz converted Ürüng Temür to Islam and gave a daughter to him in marriage.[86] Nawrūz ruled in his name, purportedly "to spread the Islamic faith" (*Islām rā shāyiʿ sāz-and*).[87] Nawrūz, by establishing himself as ruler over settled and nomadic peoples of a part of Khurasan, broke with his backers, the Ögödeid-Chaghataid union led by the Ögödeid, Qaidu. The primary reason for Nawrūz's rupture was identified by Michael Hope as "disagreements concerning the nature of their mission to Khurasan": Nawrūz wanted to rule Nishapur, but the union "simply wanted to raid the city's outskirts and did not see the value in imposing direct control over the town." They wanted "to gorge themselves on the loot of Khurasan before returning to their own patrimonies on the east bank of the Oxus River."[88] An apropos segue to the economics of raiding.

[85] Khʷāndamīr/Siyāqī (ed.), *Ḥabīb*, 3:145–46; Khʷāndamīr/Thackston (tr.), *Ḥabīb*, 1:82; cf. Rashīd al-Dīn/Thackston, *Jāmiʿ*, 3:440 (enthroned: 23 Dhū al-Ḥijja 694/3 November 1295); Ḥamd-Allāh Mustawfī, *Tārīkh-i guzīda*, 2 vols, ed. Muḥammad Rawshan (Tehran: Bunyad-i mawqūfāt-i Dr. Maḥmūd Afshār, 1394/2015), 2:532 (enthroned: 29 Dhū al-Ḥijja 694/9 November 1295).

[86] Biran, *Qaidu*, 58.

[87] Waṣṣāf, *Taḥrīr*, 178.

[88] Hope, "Nawrūz," 460–61.

*The Economics of Raiding*

Economists in the United States and Scandinavia were instrumental in developing concepts on why predators and predatory groups made individual or collective choices. Foremost among these intellectuals is the late Mancur Olson. However, modern economists were developing ideas propounded by St Augustine (on how predators settle and establish kingdoms), and Ibn Khaldun (on taxation and property law).[89]

An ancient supplication, the vulgar "Sword's Prayer," encapsulates the centrality of booty: "We should pray that our enemies be endowed with all good things except courage, so that their possessions will belong no longer to them, but to us by the sword."[90] Plunder was the catalyst for raiding lands near and far. Cicero (d. 43 BC) noted that, "the true sinew of war was 'endless streams of money'."[91] Acquisition of *portable wealth* mobilized predators of every stripe: Macedonians, Vikings, Mongols, Nikudars.

Since ancient times, the rules of war governing the treatment of the vanquished by the victor were harsh but simple: boys and girls were separated for ravishment and for the slave markets;[92] craftsmen and artisans, healthy men and women were enslaved and served their captors until they expired or were traded. The infirm and the elderly were massacred. Gold, silver, and jewels were looted; grain stocks plundered and livestock rustled; dwellings torched. The short- and long-term economic values to raiding are clear if we look beyond the images of raiders running berserk, raping and pillaging: acquisition of portable wealth: gold, silver, pearls, cereals, livestock, slaves; young women to bear children that replenish a predatory band's numbers, which tend to decline given its vocation.[93]

89 The titles: Mancur Olson, *The Logic of Collective Action: Public Goods and the Theory of Groups* (Cambridge: Harvard University Press, 1971), 1–65; idem, *Power and Prosperity* (New York: Basic, 2000), 6–13, 25–30; idem, "Dictatorship, democracy, and development," *American Political Science Review* 87/3 (1993):567–76; M.C. McGuire and Mancur Olson, "The economics of autocracy and majority rule: the invisible hand and the use of force," *Journal of Economic Literature* 34/1 (1996):72–96.

90 F.L. Holt, *The Treasures of Alexander the Great* (Oxford: Oxford University Press, 2016), 68.

91 J. Lacey, *Gold, Blood, and Power: Finance and War through the Ages* (Carlisle Barracks, PA: U.S. Army War College Press, 2015), ix, 66.

92 See David McNally, *Blood and Money: War, Slavery, Finance, and Empire* (Chicago: Haymarket, 2020), esp. Chapter 1. Slaves were equivalent to "heaps of coins."

93 Polygyny in Bedouin and Turkic cultures pre-dates Islam and had economic utility.

The economic utility of healthy slaves to slave traders, and the value of slave labor to slave owners, require no elaboration. Financial gain is not the sole or even the primary motivator for individuals to choose to become raiders: young men joined marauding bands to acquire bride wealth and *social capital*. The *act* of acquiring wealth may be as important as, or possibly more important than, the tangible wealth acquired.[94]

The motivation of groups is primarily for profit, although pursuit of the "collective good" can implicate non-financial factors. There will be rules that control the raiding band. Is it a closed-access or an open-access group, i.e., is the group "exclusive" or "inclusive"? If it is exclusive, what criteria determine membership? What is the formula for sharing the plunder? How does the band ensure that shirkers are not rewarded, unfairly reducing the economic share (dividend) of the band's toilers?

There will be tangible and intangible factors that determine the band's size and its internal dynamics. A group's size will determine its cohesiveness and effectiveness: smaller groups tend to be more cohesive, motivated, and efficient: "action taking" groups tend to be smaller than "non-action taking" groups.[95] It may benefit a band to become "exclusive" and reduce its size for the collective good; for example, if the available plunder is low, then the larger the group the smaller the dividend to each member. A band may elect to become "inclusive" (expand membership) to achieve a specific political objective that could not be achieved by a smaller band, and which will yield a higher profit per member.

*Roving Bandits*

Two critical concepts are introduced:[96] *roving bandit* and *stationary bandit*. The roving bandit is exemplified by mobile predatory bands of Nikudaris and Qaraunas, whose wealth is primarily derived from *violent* theft (raiding).

[94] See, e.g., S.P. Ashby, "What really caused the Viking Age? The social content of raiding and exploration," *Archaeological Dialogues* 22/1 (2015):89–106.

[95] Olson, *Logic*, 53.

[96] See Olson, "Dictatorship"; McGuire and Olson, "Economics"; Peter Kurrild-Klitgaard and Gert Tinggaard Svendsen, "Rational bandits: Plunder, public goods, and the Vikings," *Public Choice* 117 (2003):255–72; Andrew Young, "What does it take for a roving bandit to settle down?: Theory and an illustrative history of the Visigoths," *Public Choice* 168 (2016):75–102.

These bandits, like rapacious desert locusts, despoil and depart in search of fresh vegetation to strip.

Prevailing economic conditions, such as whether plunder is plentiful or scarce,[97] will determine the choices made by bands like Nikudaris and Qaraunas. In circumstances where the pickings are negligible, bands will splinter, each seeking to raid villages and hamlets for whatever they can seize. Predators will roam farther and farther from their usual zones of operation in search of prey. Bands may, under such circumstances, become competitors for dwindling resources—and turn on one another.

If, however, a specific target is expected to yield a valuable quantity of plunder, but that target can only be overwhelmed by a superior force, then it behooves competitors to confederate to achieve this objective. As Mancur Olson explained, the choice of "[w]hether a group behaves exclusively or inclusively [...] depends upon the nature of the objective the group seeks, not on any characteristics of the membership [...]."[98] I wrote earlier about how a "1,000 man unit of Qaraunas living near Ṭārum, led by Būqā, deserted [...]. At Bibīnī-gāw, they joined forces with the Nikudaris." This is possibly an example of rival groups allying for a limited (one-off) purpose. Once a coalition has achieved its objective, it will share the booty according to some pre-arranged formula; then the discrete components decouple and return to pursuing independent agendas.

If raiding is profitable, and there are no ethical or military constraints to raiding, then miscellaneous bands will enter the marketplace to engage in raiding. If marauding by manifold bands becomes commonplace, then anarchy will prevail as economic incentives for urban and rural dwellers to remain in their settlements, to continue to husband, farm, produce, create, trade, and invest, evaporate. The producers—landowners, pastoralists, peasants, traders, artisans, craftsmen—will flee to safer territories. This is precisely what happened with the Mongol invasions. When predators dominate and producers flee, there will be nothing left to plunder. The economic utility of

[97] Thomas Barfield, The *Perilous Frontier* (Cambridge, MA: Blackwell, 1989), 90–91: nomadic states were dependent on rich sedentary civilizations.

[98] Olson, *Logic*, 39.

raiding will approach zero.[99] An *inflexion point* has been reached. Predators have three choices. They can:

1. elect to withdraw to their homelands (if they can return) to enjoy the social and economic fruits of their recent raids (until the band's coffers have to be replenished and they are compelled to launch new raids);
2. to rove farther and farther from their "comfort zone" in search of new targets, which creates (for the band) uncertainties and hazards;
3. to remain in the region.

*Stationary Bandits*

There are sound economic reasons for a raider to choose to remain in a plundered region. A stationary bandit is someone who once was a roving bandit but has established political-military control of a region, and instituted within his domains a *monopoly on theft*. The stationary bandit fosters economic activities within his domains and extracts wealth from his subjects through *gentle theft* (taxation).

Nawrūz had discovered that the economic utility of raiding was at/near zero after Khurasan and Sīstān had been stripped in 687/1288, 688/1289, and 691/1291 by swarms of "locusts." Moreover, given his tenuous affiliation with the Ögödeid-Chaghataid union, he had incentive to settle in Khurasan, where he also had family. Nawrūz elected to develop commerce and agriculture in Khurasan and Sīstān, and profit from taxation. By "making himself a settled ruler with a given rate of tax theft, he leaves his victims with an incentive to produce"; and by "providing a peaceful order and other public goods, he makes his subjects more productive."[100]

## Stationary Bandits and Embryonic Government

Stationary bandits form the *kernel of government*. The Kartid-Nawruzid union is an instance of a roving bandit transforming into a stationary bandit.

99 Illustration of over-plundering is in Kurrild-Klitgaard and Svendsen, "Rational bandits," Fig. 1. Total costs of over-plundering include loss of life (to the band), for which surviving shareholders (including decedents' dependents) receive no economic benefit.

100 McGuire and Olson, "Economics," 72. See the pioneering study by Margaret Levi, "The Predatory Theory of Rule," *Politics & Society* 10/4 (1981):431–65.

St Augustine of Hippo's evaluation is fair, famous, and worth quoting at length:

> Justice being taken away, then, what are kingdoms but great robberies? For what are robberies themselves, but little kingdoms? The band itself is made up of men; it is ruled by the authority of a prince, it is knit together by the pact of the confederacy; the booty is divided by the law agreed on. If, by the admittance of abandoned men, this evil increases to such a degree that it holds places, fixes abodes, takes possession of cities, and subdues peoples, it assumes the more plainly the name of a kingdom, because the reality is now manifestly conferred on it, not by the removal of covetousness, but by the addition of impunity. Indeed, that was an apt and true reply which was given to Alexander the Great by a pirate who had been seized. For when that king had asked the man what he meant by keeping hostile possession of the sea, he answered with bold pride, "What thou meanest by seizing the whole earth; but because I do it with a petty ship, I am called a robber, whilst thou who dost it with a great fleet art styled emperor."[101]

Metamorphosis from raider to ruler is not uncommon. "Viking" (masc. *víkingr*; sea warrior; fem. *víking*: military maritime expedition), in the original sense (*c.* 790) applied to those who journeyed by sea to raid. It did not apply to Scandinavians that stayed home and engaged in peaceful occupations. "Viking" encompassed non-Scandinavians that engaged in raiding, just as "Mongol army" included non-Mongols. Scandinavian seaborne warriors raided the British Isles in the "First Viking Age"; their successors settled in the Isles in the "Second Viking Age." Outlooks of the marauders of Lindisfarne, AD 793, diverged from the outlooks of Britain's Scandinavian rulers displaced by the Normans in AD 1066.

Mongols were little different from Vikings: raiders that settled down, established kingdoms and morphed into developers of economies. Ögödei took the Mongol Empire's first (hesitant) steps in this direction, although it was Möngke who seminally transformed the Empire's approach.[102] At the local level (Herat), this metamorphosis is reflected in the establishment of a

[101] Aurelius Augustine, *City of God*, tr. M. Dods (New York: Modern Library, 2000), Book IV, Chap. 4.

[102] See May, *Mongol Empire*, 85, 151–56; Allsen, *Mongol Imperialism, et passim.*

kingdom (technically, emirate) by the erstwhile bandit, Nawrūz, with Fakhr al-Dīn Kart as his governor.[103]

## Nawrūz at Herat

Why would Khurasanians accept a man as vile as Nawrūz, recently responsible for cruelties and murders? Mancur Olson pondered, "why would warlords, who were stationary bandits continuously stealing from a given group of victims, be preferred, by those victims, to roving bandits who soon departed?"[104] His thesis is reformulated below.

Firstly, given a binary choice between anarchy and exploitative government, people find the latter imperfect but preferable. The crux of Augustine's evaluation is that without justice, the principal differences between brigandage and government lie in respective size and power. The priceless *public good* is *justice*—even of rudimentary type (namely, protection of property rights and enforcement of contracts).

Secondly, if Nawrūz extracts only one part of the incomes of society's productive elements, *ra ʿāyā* have incentives to produce knowing they will retain the balance: "The method of stealing, taxation or confiscation, depends on the time horizon. If the bandit expects to stay in control indefinitely, then it will be optimal for him to tax some [income and wealth] rather than confiscate everything [...]."[105] The key distinction between roving bandit and stationary bandit is that the former confiscates as much as he can in a rampage lasting hours/days; but the latter confiscates a little at a time over a longer period.

Thirdly, if Nawrūz establishes *security* (by curbing violence by predators other than himself) and establishes a *monopoly on theft*, producers will not fear theft by anyone (other than him), especially if he enforces laws that protect property: "A stationary bandit has, as the 'owner' of all wealth [in his realm], an incentive to establish a relatively peaceful order, i.e., one where nobody else can successfully challenge his position."[106]

103 To clarify sequencing: Nawrūz dominated swathes of Khurasan and Sīstān. Once Fakhr al-Dīn terminated the Kartid-Nawruzid union in 696/1297, Kartid rule at Herat resumed. Nawrūz's embryonic emirate was subsumed by the Kartid state.

104 Olson, "Democracy," 568.

105 Kurrild-Klitgaard and Svendsen, "Rational," 260.

106 Ibid., 260.

The three points are elucidated below:

*Anarchy or Exploitation?*

Marshal Feng Yü-hsiang (Feng Yuxiang; 1882–1948), a stationary bandit in China, was respected and favored by peasants because he provided security, funded public works, and insisted on fair dealings between his soldiers and peasants.[107]

Ismail Khan, a Tajik native of Isfizār,[108] and celebrated anti-Soviet *mujahidin* leader, became amir of Herat after the U.S.-led invasion. Khan, however, was branded a "warlord" by detractors in Kabul and Washington. Khan was siphoning tax revenues coveted by the kleptocrats of Kabul. He was not embezzling; he put the diverted funds to profitable use in his homeland. Khan provided Heratis with indispensable public goods when they needed it most: security, public works, and education for boys and girls. He was deposed in 2004 by Hamid Karzai, Ashraf Ghani, the U.S. Army, and the Bush White House.

Michael Metrinko,[109] Persian-speaker and retired State Department official, worked in Herat (2003 and 2004). He was interviewed by the U.S. Institute of Peace. On Ismail Khan and his provision of indispensable public goods, Metrinko said:

> Security was excellent in the area [...] Herat province and those provinces of western Afghanistan had plenty of money because Ismael Khan [...] was siphoning a great deal of money from customs revenues and putting it into projects in the city and in the province.[110]
>
> In Herat province, I've forgotten the exact percentage, but I think it's about 40 or 45% of all the students in Herat province are female. There are a huge number of girls going to school in Herat province. This was always encouraged by Ismael Khan. He encouraged us to build schools for girls. He encouraged other things for girls [...].[111]

[107] James Sheridan, *Chinese Warlord: the Career of Feng Yü-hsiang* (Stanford, CA: Stanford University Press, 1966), esp. 90–94, 283–94. Feng Yü-hsiang's public works were minor.

[108] Isfizār or Sabzavār-i Harāt; now Shindand: see Adamec, *Gazetteer*, 3:343–46.

[109] *Afghan Experience Project*, Interview #1 (22 March 2005; at https://tinyurl.com/Metrinko). Subjects are not identified, but the interviewee is Metrinko.

[110] Ibid., 5. There was a daily inflow of *c.* $160,000 (2003/04 dollars), *c.* $60 million/year, to the Herat customs house from the-then thriving trade between Herat and Iran.

[111] Ibid., 25–26.

> We never saw anything that resembled an opium field or an opium poppy field [in 2003]. We went to villages all over the province. When we would ask the villagers, they would laugh and say, "We don't dare do it [i.e., cultivate poppy]. Ismael Khan would kill us."[112]

Ismail Khan's anti-opium fervor has a parallel: "Feng embarked on a program to stamp out three vices: narcotics, gambling, and prostitution."[113] "Drugs returned to Herat in 2004 after the ouster of Ismael Khan, which may have been why he was ousted."[114]

Ismail Khan's "warlordism" was preferred by Heratis because he delivered public goods: safety, education for boys and girls, building projects; fostering a climate in which social and economic activities flourished. The gruff and grizzled "Lion of Herat"—exiled to Iran in 2021 by the Taliban—remains a respected figure in Afghanistan and Iran.

*Gentle Theft (or That Which We Call Taxation)*

The importance of low taxes for economic growth was articulated (a century after Nawrūz) by Ibn Khaldun (d. 1406): "taxation yields a large revenue from small assessments [when only the canonical taxes are levied];[115] [however] taxation yields a small revenue from large assessments" (namely, imposition of non-canonical taxes). "When tax assessments and imposts upon the subjects are low, the latter have the energy and the desire to do things." Ibn Khaldun argued that when the cumulative tax burden is onerous, economic activities decline; adding "the strongest incentive for cultural activity is to lower as much as possible the individual imposts levied [...]."[116] The *Laffer Curve* (an inverted "U" shape),[117] is rooted in Ibn Khaldun's ideas.[118]

[112] Ibid., 33–34.

[113] Sheridan, *Chinese Warlord*, 91.

[114] *Afghan Experience Project*, Interview #1, p.2.

[115] Land, charity, and poll taxes have "fixed limits that cannot be exceeded." Ibn Khaldun, *The Muqaddimah*, ed. Franz Rosenthal (Princeton: Princeton UP, 2005), 230.

[116] Ibid., 230–31; Ibn Khaldun, *The Muqaddimah*, 3 vols, ed. Franz Rosenthal (Princeton: Princeton University Press, 1958), 2:89–91 (Chap. 3, § 36); and Chap. 3, § 37.

[117] See, e.g., R. Hemming and J.A. Kay, "The Laffer Curve," *Fiscal Studies* 1/2 (1980):83–90; J.M. Buchanan and D.R. Lee, "Politics, Time, and the Laffer Curve," *Journal of Political Economy* 90/4 (1982):816–19.

[118] A.H. Mouhammed, "Ibn Khaldun and the neo-liberal model," *History of Economic Ideas* 12/3 (2004):85–109, 87.

Laffer shows that no revenue is derived at tax rates of 0% and 100%; but there exists an optimal rate between 0% and 100% that maximizes inflows. If, however, the tax rate is raised/lowered past the optimal rate, inflows decline.

Ibn Khaldun's and Arthur Laffer's concepts are integral to the thesis that economic growth is stimulated through low tax rates. Nawrūz established a monopoly on theft: "for two years, no person, Mongol or Muslim, shall harass or make demands of the people of Herat,"[119] but the tax rates applied by him are unknown.[120]

*Monopoly on Theft*

Ibn Khaldun expressed the logic undergirding property rights:

> Attacks on people's property remove the incentive to acquire and gain property [...]. When attacks on (property) are extensive [...], affecting all means of making a livelihood, business inactivity, too, becomes general [...]. When people no longer do business [...], and when they cease all gainful activity, the business of civilization slumps, and everything decays. People scatter everywhere in search of sustenance.[121]

## Plunder or Administer?

The above should suffice for the proffers articulated below. My foci are parochial. Applicability to the Mongol context—the Mongol Empire's transformation from "rob and run" to "stay and build"—awaits further explorations.[122]

1. There is economic utility to raiding, but raiding cannot be repeated often in one locale because survivors flee and socio-economic activities decline/

[119] Isfizārī, *Rawżāt*, 1:428; cf. al-Harawī, *Harāt*, 409.

[120] He stood to acquire higher profits in the long term through taxation than from plunder. See analysis by Kurrild-Klitgaard and Svendsen, "Rational," 259–60 (not specific to Nawrūz).

[121] Ibn Khaldun, *Muqaddimah*, 238; see also idem, *Muqaddimah*, 2:103–111 (Chap. 3, § 41; parentheses in the original; bracketed text is mine). Ibn Khaldun's insight is echoed by Hume, who argues there can be no property without a system of justice. David Hume, *A Treatise of Human Nature*, ed. L.A. Selby-Bigge (Oxford: Clarendon, 1888), 490ff.

[122] See also comments in Part One: "Reflections and Conclusions."

cease. The region must be re-populated and allowed time to prosper before it can be pillaged again.

2. A raider determined to remain a raider will have to roam farther and farther in search of fresh settlements to plunder. By traveling farther from home base, he is:
   (i) more distant from his safe haven(s) and vulnerable to counter-attack;
   (ii) he has longer distances over which to transport booty: his baggage train and live booty (livestock and humans) are vulnerable to (a) insider theft (Alexander also experienced this); (b) attack by other predatory bands;[123] and (c) attack by militias seeking to punish slavers/raiders, and free their enslaved countrymen;[124]
   (iii) if his booty includes humans, he has to clothe, feed, and transport them over longer distances.[125] The economic value of living assets (people and livestock) is *depreciated* by weather (cold, wet, snow, heat), famine, thirst, and (human and veterinary) disease; and *depleted* through their deaths.[126]
3. The economy will recover if a *roving bandit* becomes a *stationary bandit* and:
   (i) excludes other predators from his newly-founded kingdom;
   (ii) establishes a *monopoly on theft* (only he can steal from subjects); fosters economic growth by providing security (only he can harm subjects); and provides basic protections under law (enforcement of contracts, sales, rights to land and water);
   (iii) *limits taxation* to just one *part* of an individual's income, *raʿāyā* will return to the (de-populated) territory to engage in economic production.[127]

[123] On the logistics of transporting plunder and threats of attack (by *outsiders*) and theft (by *insiders*), see Holt, *Treasures*, 56–57, 86–88, 130, 137–41. See also D.W. Engels, *Alexander the Great and the Logistics of the Macedonian Army* (Berkeley: University of California Press, 1978).

[124] See, e.g., al-Harawī, *Harāt*, 649 (on Kebek crossing the Oxus in pursuit of raiders).

[125] Slaves represented a large share of Alexander's non-tax revenues. Holt, *Treasures*, 44–45, Fig. 3.1. Troops had to be paid and campaigns funded. Alexander appears to have followed his father's (Philip's) practice of selling slaves quickly. See, e.g., ibid., 42, 53, 57–58.

[126] Certain assets deplete with extraction (e.g., oil, gas). Humans and animals, replenishable by breeding, will be depleted or exhausted if the death rate exceeds the birth rate. Evidence for the proffer in ¶ 2 is in Chapter 4, § 4(ii): "Yasaʾur's Predicament."

[127] Möngke's installation of the Kartids was to implement some/all of the elements of ¶ 3.

To illustrate, in 638/1240–41, consequent to rudimentary revitalization efforts at the direction of Ögödei, the census showed Herat's population standing at *c.* 6,900 persons. Following re-openings of arterial waterways, people from "Khurasan and Turkistan" began migrating to Herat.[128] A census required the registration of persons, and was a prerequisite for taxation and conscription.[129] The population of the Kartid realm swelled such that Shams al-Dīn Kart (the Elder) was able to supply the Mongol Empire with seven *tümens* of conscripts.[130]

Returning to Nawrūz and his transitory union with Kartids, Nawrūz had discovered that the booty economy had inherent constraints. There was nothing left to plunder and survivors had escaped. His Chinggisid allies had no interest in ruling sedentary peoples. This was not the sole reason for the rupture: Nawrūz's arrogance generated enmity.[131] A "divorce" was mutually beneficial. That Nawrūz resuscitated the moribund economies of Herat Quarter and Sīstān can be demonstrated.[132]

[128] al-Harawī, *Harāt,* 159–63. See Chapter 7, §: "Ögödei's Initiatives."
[129] On the census, see Allsen, *Mongol Imperialism*, 130–31.
[130] Ibid., 205; al-Harawī, *Harāt,* 221.
[131] Hope, "Nawrūz," 461.
[132] See Chapter 7, §: "Nawrūz's Revitalization of Herat and Sīstān."

# 4

# Stability in Herat and Khurasan

## Reign of Fakhr al-Dīn Kart

We are back in Herat again, where Nawrūz's protégé, Fakhr al-Dīn Kart, was trying to repulse Nawrūz's erstwhile Ögödeid-Chaghataid allies. Fakhr al-Dīn battled the invaders, secured Ghāzān's support, and placed Herat on the road to social and economic renewal. The Kartid-Nawruzid union was working—until the arrangement no longer suited Fakhr al-Dīn and had to be dissolved.

### *Dissolving the Kartid-Nawruzid Union*

Fakhr al-Dīn Kart was to draw Herat to a fuller recovery from the despoilments of 687/1288 and 688/1289, but had to contend with the fallout from his decisions. In 696/1297, Nawrūz's uneasy alliance with Ghāzān sundered.[1] Nawrūz fled to Herat with an Ilkhanid army in pursuit. He was given refuge by Fakhr al-Dīn, which initiated the Kartid's first clash with Ghāzān.[2] Fakhr al-Dīn was indebted to Nawrūz (he had extricated him from his father's jail). Moreover, he was Nawrūz's brother's son-in-law, and possibly experienced pressure from the harem to grant Nawrūz sanctuary. Meanwhile, the Ilkhanid expedition besieged Herat. As the days passed, tensions flared between Kartid hosts and Nawruzid guests. Fakhr al-Dīn had second thoughts. An intervention by a distinguished Sufi shaykh afforded him an honorable way out of a perilous situation.

1 On Nawrūz's fall, see Hope, *Power*, 162–69.

2 al-Harawī, *Harāt*, 443–51; Ḥāfiẓ-i Abrū, *Kart*, 92–97; Faṣīḥ, *Mujmal*, 864–65 (under AH 696/1296f.); Rashīd al-Dīn/Thackston, *Jāmi'*, 3:445–47.

The commander of the Ilkhanid expeditionary force, Qutlugh-Shāh, enlisted the Shaykh al-Islam of Jām, Shihāb al-Dīn Ismāʿīl Jāmī (d.*c.* 738/1338), to mediate.[3] Jāmī had helped secure Fakhr al-Dīn's release; he was trusted—and the Kartid's in-law by *c.* 1300, possibly even by 1297.[4] He wrote to the *malik*, "[y]ou must do something to remedy this situation; otherwise Herat and the whole realm of Khurasan will be lost over this affair."[5] The letter was smuggled into Herat. Nawrūz and his retinue were seized and delivered to Qutlugh-Shāh. Nawrūz was executed on 23 Shawwāl 696/14 August 1297.

Since Fakhr al-Dīn had delivered Nawrūz to Qutlugh-Shāh, his "sin" of sheltering the fugitive was evidently forgiven by Ghāzān. The *malik* received a new *yarlīgh* confirming his status, and sumptuous (*fākhir*) gifts that included a *pāʾiza* and *Āl tamghā*.[6] Nawrūz's execution instilled fear (*khaʾif*) in Ilkhanid/Kartid *bandagān* (*mulūk wa umarā-yi Khurāsān*). *Mulūk* traveled to Herat from Bākharz, Gharjistān, Ghūr, Isfizār, Jām, Jurziwān, and Khʷāf to acknowledge their tributary status (*kharāj-guzārī*).[7] Pragmatism motivated the *bandagān*.[8] Nawrūz, a centripetal force, had pulled certain *malik*s and *amīr*s of Khurasan into his orbit. These lords realized that with Nawrūz dead, Fakhr al-Dīn was the Il-Khan's surrogate in the Herat Quarter; and the ultimate centripetal force. They hurried to tender their submission, hoping to curry favor and acquire any patronage being dispensed by Fakhr al-Dīn.

### *Öljeitü versus Fakhr al-Dīn (Round One)*

Fakhr al-Dīn's next transgression, in 698/1298f., was more serious. It contributed to the enmity that Ghāzān's brother and successor as Il-Khan,

3 On the obligations of *shaykhs al-Islām*, see Shivan Mahendrarajah, "The Shaykh al-Islam in Medieval Khurasan," *Afghanistan* 1/2 (2018):257–81, esp. 280; on Shaykh al-Islam Jāmī, see Mahendrarajah, *Sufi Saint*, 59–63, 143–48.

4 See Mahendrarajah, *Sufi Saint*, 62 and Figure A1.5 (Kart-Jāmī marital bonds).

5 Rashīd al-Dīn/Thackston, *Jāmiʿ*, 3:446; Rashīd al-Dīn/Jahn, *Ghāzān*, 113.

6 Faṣīḥ, *Mujmal*, 865 (AH 697/1297f.). He identifies the two items.

7 al-Harawī, *Harāt*, 452–53; Ḥāfiẓ-i Abrū, *Kart*, 96–97.

8 Select Kartid *bandagān* were refractory: Ināltikīn (of Farāh), Quṭb al-Dīn (Isfizār), Farrukhzād b. Quṭb al-Dīn (Tūlak), and Rukn al-Dīn (Āzāb), violated their duty of *wafāʾ* and *khidma* to Kartids and turned renegade when opportunities materialized (discussed below).

Öljeitü (r. 703–16/1304–16), had for Kartids. The feud originated with Öljeitü's humiliation by Fakhr al-Dīn. Consequently, Öljeitü "devoted much time to fighting with the Kart dynasty of Herat."[9] The feud emerged when Ghāzān dispatched Öljeitü to Herat at the head of an army because Fakhr al-Dīn had granted refuge to a Nikudari band.

The Nikudaris, around 3,000 strong, led by one Amir Būqā, had been confined to Iraq by Ghāzān. They quit Iraq without his permission, traveled to Quhistān, thence Herat, where Fakhr al-Dīn welcomed them. He gave each a horse, robe, weapon, and cereals; and pointed them toward Quhistān,[10] Sīstān,[11] Farāh, and Jurziwān, which the Nikudaris plundered.[12]

A charitable interpretation of these circumstances is that Fakhr al-Dīn was keeping Nikudaris away from Herat. The brigands could have pillaged Herat since its defenses were weak. Yet Nikudari rampages were confined to regions that—with the possible exception of Jurziwān—appear to have been outside Kartid control. Extending this point, it suggests that Fakhr al-Dīn used the Nikudaris to further his objectives: subjugation and punishment of recalcitrant provinces to his kingdom's south/southeast. He probably received a share of the booty: Fakhr al-Dīn was financially flush after the Nikudari raids; he spent extensively beginning in the following year, 699/1299–1300 (see Chapters Nine and Ten).

Öljeitü settled the Ilkhanid army in Nishapur and sent an emissary to Fakhr al-Dīn demanding that he hand over Būqā, et al. The *malik* honored the emissary and returned him to Öljeitü with the message that Būqā and his troopers had left Herat about a month earlier to "pillage *Afghānistān*"; but he, Fakhr al-Dīn Kart, remained a loyal servant of the Padishah. He promised to deliver the fugitives to the Padishah's army. Öljeitü did not trust him and mobilized the army, which settled by the Herat River (probably in the expanses south of the city) with siege equipment (mangonels, ballistae, scaffolds, ladders). Fakhr al-Dīn installed Harawī, Ghurid, Khalaj, Mongol, and

[9] Hope, *Power*, 15.
[10] Quhistān: see Barthold, *Geography*, 133–47.
[11] Sīstān and Balūchistān: see ibid., 64–86.
[12] al-Harawī, *Harāt*, 454–55; Ḥāfiẓ-i Abrū, *Kart*, 97–98. See also Mīrkhwānd, *Rawżat*, 4,226–27; Isfizārī, *Rawżāt*, 1:435.

Sijzī regiments at the gates and bolted to Fort Iskilchih (also called Amān Kūh),[13] a Kartid redoubt.[14]

The Mongols surrounded Iskilchih. Both sides went at it, with reported 2,000 dead and 3,000 wounded on the Mongol side (no figures are given for the Kartids). In the dark of night, Fakhr al-Dīn slipped out with a loyal retinue, made his way to Herat, and thence to Ghūr. Öljeitü switched his attention to Herat. The siege continued for eighteen days, with Mongol losses at 10,000. An impasse was reached. Öljeitü had been ordered to minimize civilian casualties; although headstrong, he probably did not want to launch any assault that led to catastrophe. Shihāb al-Dīn Ismāʿīl Jāmī came to the rescue. He parleyed with Öljeitü for a ceasefire. The shaykh noted that the offending parties had left Herat; Öljeitü was just harming third parties. They agreed that Heratis would pay a ransom of 100,000 dinars to compensate for Ilkhanid losses of blood and treasure. The following day, the shaykh's darwishes came to Herat to collect ransom contributions from notables, but only 30,000 dinars was collected, with the balance promised (Öljeitü was surely peeved). Öljeitü terminated the blockade and withdrew from Herat.[15]

The people rejoiced and gave thanks to God. Fakhr al-Dīn was delighted, too, and donated 4,000 dinars to the indigent and the infirm of Ghūr; thereafter, he quit Khaysār for Herat. He honored Herat's defenders. Peasants were exempted (*muʿāf wa musallam*) from the corvée, or possibly just taxes specific to sedentary peoples (pl. *qalān-āt*);[16] and *dīwān* taxes and tolls (pl. *ʿawāriż-āt*). Qurʾan readings were commanded, with blessings pronounced for ulama, sayyids, shaykhs (Sufis), and ascetics.[17] Fahkr al-Dīn's largesse reinforces my view that he had received shares of the plunder taken by Nikudaris.

[13] Iskilchih (southwest of Herat): location noted in Ḥāfiẓ-i Abrū, *Kart*, 186; distance of four *farsakhs* in Barthold, *Geography*, 54. Called Amkilchih in Mustawfī, *Nuzhat*, 152; Mustawfī/Le Strange (tr.), *Nuzhat*, 150.

[14] al-Harawī, *Harāt*, 456–57; Ḥāfiẓ-i Abrū, *Kart*, 98–99. See also Mīrkhwānd, *Rawżat*, 4,227–28; Isfizārī, *Rawżāt*, 1:436; Faṣīḥ, *Mujmal*, 867.

[15] al-Harawī, *Harāt*, 458–60; Ḥāfiẓ-i Abrū, *Kart*, 99–101. See also Mīrkhwānd, *Rawżat*, 4, 228–29; Isfizārī, *Rawżāt*, 1:436–37; Faṣīḥ, *Mujmal*, 867.

[16] *Qalān*: taxes specific to sedentary peoples. John Masson Smith, "Mongol and Nomadic Taxation," *HJAS* 30 (1970):46–85, esp. 52–60; cf. Ann Lambton, *Landlord and Peasant* (London: I.B. Tauris, 1991), 80–81 (corvée, forced labor, for agricultural or public works projects).

[17] al-Harawī, *Harāt*, 461; Ḥāfiẓ-i Abrū, *Kart*, 101.

### *Öljeitü versus Fakhr al-Dīn (Round Two)*

It was customary for *bandagān* to appear before a newly crowned Il-Khan and make perfunctory but respectful noises about fealty (*wafā'*) and service (*khidma*). The Il-Khan, in his turn, would shower the *bandagān* with royal favors and honors (*soyūrghāmīshī wa 'ināyat-i shāhanshāhī*). Öljeitü, following his accession in 703/1304, sent Fakhr al-Dīn a fresh *yarlīgh* and ceremonial robe through an emissary, and directed him to present himself in Tabriz.[18] Fakhr al-Dīn accepted the diploma and robe, honored the emissary and gave him 10,000 dinars, but refused to depart, claiming he could not leave Herat: "today, the pillars of the state and the notables of the Padishah's kingdom are Nawrūz's allies (*nawrūzī-ān-and*), and demand my blood [for Nawrūz's death]. In no matter small or large do I trust them."[19] He insisted that he remained faithful and dutiful to the Padishah.[20]

The following year, 704/1304f., was one of prosperity (*rafāhīyat*) and contentment (*firāgh al-bāl*) in Herat according to Sayfī, due to the "munificence and justice" of Fakhr al-Dīn Kart.[21] But a storm was brewing in Tabriz that would carry away the Kartid.

Öljeitü was infuriated by the snub: his interpretation was that "*malik* Fahkr al-Dīn drew his sword on me (*dar rūyi man tīgh kashīd*),"[22] but held fire—for now. A "peace treaty" concluded in 1304 by Chinggisid factions offered the Ilkhanate impermanent relief against the Golden Horde.[23] Qaidu's death in 701/1301 allowed Du'a to free himself from Ögödeid hegemony and begin switching control of Transoxiana to the Chaghataids.[24] Öljeitü, with his neighbors otherwise engaged, was free to deploy resources to campaigns in Gilan (in late 706/Spring 1307) and Herat.

Danishmand Bahadur—a Qaraunas amir—received command of a *tümen* for the Khurasan expedition. The Ilkhanid army settled in Nishapur. The Chief Justice (*qāḍī al-quḍāt*) of Herat, Mawlānā Wajīh al-Dīn Nasafī (one

18 al-Harawī, *Harāt*, 478–79.
19 Ibid., 479; cf. Ḥāfiẓ-i Abrū, *Kart*, 107.
20 The emissary delivered the rebuff to Öljeitü. Faṣīḥ, *Mujmal*, 881.
21 al-Harawī, *Harāt*, 480.
22 Ibid., 485.
23 Biran, *Qaidu*, 66; 71–72 and n.33.
24 Ibid., 72–80.

of Fakhr al-Dīn's appointees) asked for permission (on a pretext, perhaps) to leave Herat, and traveled to Nishapur. He sought out Danishmand, whom he advised on the best method of besieging Herat.[25]

Certain Kartid *bandagān* defected to Danishmand.[26] Three persistent burrs under the Kartids' saddles were Ināltikīn of Farāh,[27] his brother, Jalāl al-Dīn, and Quṭb al-Dīn of Isfizār.[28] Jalāl al-Dīn had been released from Nawrūz's custody in an accord between Fakhr al-Dīn Kart and Ināltikīn, where Ināltikīn had agreed to tender loyal service in exchange for Jalāl al-Dīn's freedom. Ināltikīn breached his covenant with Fakhr al-Dīn.[29]

Danishmand Bahadur, following the Chief Judge's advice, sealed off roads to Herat, blocking inflows of comestibles and outflows of people. Fakhr al-Dīn had rejected entreaties earlier. The armies clashed. Shaykh al-Islam Quṭb al-Dīn Chishtī was co-opted as mediator; a truce was reached whereby Fakhr al-Dīn was allowed to withdraw unmolested to Fort Iskilchih, leaving a deputy, Jalāl al-Dīn Muḥammad Sām, in command at Herat. Once the Kartid was safely ensconced in Iskilchih, Danishmand Bahadur entered Herat.

The rest of this scintillating story is one of Herat's best-known historical episodes. Danishmand Bahadur entered Herat citadel with perfidy on his mind,[30] but was masterfully outclassed by Muḥammad Sām in the department of perfidy. Once the Ilkhanid squadron, around 180 strong, was inside the bowels of the citadel, Ghurids pounced, slaying and severing heads. Floors and walls were bloodied, red like a "tulip-field" (*lālizār*). Hapless Shaykh al-Islam Chishtī was seen begging for the slaughter to be halted, but the Ghurid swordsmen ignored him. Once the butchering inside the citadel was concluded, Kartids sallied outside and slaughtered Mongols in the streets and alleys of Herat.[31]

25 al-Harawī, *Harāt*, 489.

26 The turncoats are identified in ibid., 488–89.

27 One *malik* Ināltikīn of Farāh is in the *History of Sistan* fighting Mongols in 622ff./1225ff. Anon./ Bahār (ed.), *Sīstān*, 365–66; see also Mīrkhʷānd, *Rawżat*, 3,681–82. The Kartid period Ināltikīn was descended from this noble family.

28 Ḥāfiẓ-i Abrū, *Ẕayl-i jāmiʿ al-tāwarīkh-i Rashīdī*, ed. Khān-Bābā Bayānī (Tehran: Anjumān-i āṣār-i millī, 2nd ed., 1350/1971), 78–79; al-Harawī, *Harāt*, 485–89.

29 al-Harawī, *Harāt*, 425.

30 This is the citadel *later* labeled Qalʿa-yi Ikhtiyār al-Dīn.

31 Ḥāfiẓ-i Abrū, *Rashīdī*, 79–92; al-Harawī, *Harāt*, 489–521; Isfizārī, *Rawżāt*, 1:442–53. A superb translation by Wheeler Thackston is in Khʷāndamīr/Thackston (tr.), *Habib*, 1:215–17. See also Gammell, *Pearl*, 41–43; May, "Ilkhanate," 306–07.

Fakhr al-Dīn remained at Iskilchih and denied involvement in the carnage inside the citadel, blaming it on Muḥammad Sām. His denial is belied by his deputy's actions after the massacre. Muḥammad Sām went up to the roof of the citadel (in Herat) and kindled a fire to signal Fakhr al-Dīn at Fort Iskilchih; the Kartid, on seeing the smoke, exclaimed satisfaction at the victory.[32] Condensing the later events,[33] Öljeitü was enraged further. He ordered Böjäi (d. 715/1315), son of Danishmand,[34] to lead a punitive expedition against Herat.

Herat was besieged from Shaʿbān 706/February 1307 to Dhū al-Ḥijja 706/late June 1307. People suffered terribly, initially from famine, then after vengeful Mongols entered the city. Muḥammad Sām and cohorts were executed.[35] Fakhr al-Dīn had died unexpectedly at Iskilchih in Shaʿbān 706/February 1307, purportedly from ill health.[36]

## The Reign of Ghiyāth al-Dīn Kart

The reign of Ghiyāth al-Dīn Muḥammad Kart (r. 707–29/1307–29) was immensely beneficial to the Kartids, their clients (particularly the Sufi shrine at Jām), and the peoples of Herat. But before we delve into these aspects, it behooves us to appreciate how Ghiyāth al-Dīn came to succeed his brother. The outline is this: Öljeitü, as a consequence of the rout of Danishmand's *tümen*, terminated Kartid rule, appointed Amir Yasāʾūl (d.*c.* 717/1317) as Ilkhanid plenipotentiary to Khurasan, and picked Danishmand's son, Böjäi, to command the army in Khurasan. Ghiyāth al-Dīn was in Öljeitü's court when Herat spiraled into turmoil consequent to Fakhr al-Dīn's and Muḥammad Sām's deeds. The Il-Khan pressed a *yarlīgh* into Ghiyāth al-Dīn's hand and dispatched him to Herat to restore rule and order.[37]

32 al-Harawī, *Harāt*, 515–16. Iskilchih therefore had line of sight to the Herat citadel.

33 Details are in Khʷāndamīr/Thackston (tr.), *Habib*, 1:217–18.

34 For Danishmand Bahadur's family tree, see Kempiners, "Struggle," 105, Figure 8. Böjäi, Muḥammad Duldāʾī b. Danishmand Bahadur, Mubārak-Shāh b. Böjäi, Abū Yazīd b. Böjäi, and Bayram-Shāh b. Duldāʾī, played key roles in later events.

35 Ḥāfiẓ-i Abrū, *Rashīdī*, 92–95; Ḥāfiẓ-i Abrū, *Kart*, 108–116; al-Harawī, *Harāt*, 522–27, 547–56.

36 al-Harawī, *Harāt*, 528–29. Fakhr al-Dīn ran a hedonistic court (wine, carnality, narcotics) and ingested cannabis. See Gammell, *Pearl*, 40–41. Sudden heart failure is a possibility.

37 For an account of his reign, see Muḥammad Ismāʿīl Mablagh Gharjistānī, "*Malik* Ghiyāth al-Dīn," *Āryānā* No. 193 (1337/1958f.):33–41.

*Ghiyāth al-Dīn at Öljeitü's Court (First Time)*

If, however, we look past the headline, it becomes clear that Ghiyāth al-Dīn's presence at the *urdu* was not fortuitous. He had contrived to be near the Il-Khan when his brother politically self-immolated. Their father, Shams al-Dīn Kihīn, died on 12 Ṣafar 705/3 September 1305.[38] Ghiyāth al-Dīn and ʿAlāʾ al-Dīn Kart (the middle son placed at Herat, *c.* 682–87/1283–88) battled for control of Khaysār and Shams al-Dīn Kihīn's treasury. Ghiyāth al-Dīn was advised to seek Öljeitü's support since the Il-Khan was dissatisfied with Fakhr al-Dīn. He departed via Herat for Öljeitü's court, then at Baghdad. En route, he met with Danishmand, who sought his assistance in settling the crisis. Ghiyāth al-Dīn was asked to counsel Fakhr al-Dīn. He agreed. His brother welcomed him with an embrace; officials greeted him respectfully. But Ghiyāth al-Dīn was not successful in defusing the looming calamity. The *malik*-in-waiting probably did not try too hard to negotiate a peace. Ghiyāth al-Dīn returned to Danishmand, who thanked him for his intercession, and prepared letters on his behalf for officials at the *urdu*.[39]

Ghiyāth al-Dīn traveled thence to Turbat-i Jam, where he remained for three days at the shrine of Shaykh al-Islam Aḥmad-i Jām. He was hosted by his Sufi preceptor and in-law, Shaykh al-Islam Jāmī. The Shaykh's oldest son was married to Ghiyāth al-Dīn's daughter.[40] Ghiyāth al-Dīn was at Jām to worship (*ziyārat*) at the blessed tomb of the Sufi saint of Jām and to acquire blessings (*baraka*). He received spiritual counsel from the Shaykh al-Islam, and definitely, political counsel, too. He left Jām for Mashhad, where he performed *ziyārat* at the ʿAlid shrine of Imam ʿAlī b. Mūsá al-Riżā (d. 202/818).[41]

Shihāb al-Dīn Ismāʿīl Jāmī (as discussed) had parleyed with Öljeitü and negotiated a ransom. The pair may have established a rapport. There is a story in a Jāmī hagiography of a later meeting between Jāmī and Öljeitü,[42] but whether it took place is unprovable. The Il-Khan had also granted the Shaykh

[38] al-Harawī, *Harāt*, 484; cf. Faṣīḥ, *Mujmal*, 882 (mistakenly entered under AH 704).
[39] al-Harawī, *Harāt*, 561–66; Ḥāfiẓ-i Abrū, *Kart*, 116–18.
[40] Mahendrarajah, *Sufi Saint*, 61–62, and Figure A1.5.
[41] al-Harawī, *Harāt*, 566; Ḥāfiẓ-i Abrū, *Kart*, 118.
[42] ʿAlī Būzjānī, *Rawżat al-riyāḥīn*, ed. Heshmat Moayyad (Tehran: Bungāh-i tarjuma wa nashr-i kitāb, 1345/1966), 100.

al-Islam an agricultural tract and hydrological system.[43] Jāmī, who helped free Fakhr al-Dīn from his father's jail and twice mediated sieges of Herat, was conspicuously absent in the negotiations that preceded Danishmand Bahadur's fateful entry into the citadel. Jāmī was therefore not tainted by involvement in the mediation that had led to an accord between Danishmand and Fakhr al-Dīn/Muḥammad Sām; an accord violated by Kartids. If blame or failure was perceived by the baleful Il-Khan, Quṭb al-Dīn Chishtī was the designated scapegoat. Participation by Chief Justice Wajīh al-Dīn Nasafī lends weight to my suspicion of machinations by prominent religious personalities at Jām and Herat to oust Fakhr al-Dīn. Shaykh al-Islam Jāmī doubtless wanted his in-law and Sufi acolyte seated on the Kartid throne.

Ghiyāth al-Dīn Kart pressed his case at Öljeitü's court. He had insisted (says Sayfī, who wrote his history in the reign of Ghiyāth al-Dīn—his patron), that he was his father's rightful legatee, a claim presented to Öljeitü. The Kartid had to overcome the odor attached to his family's name. Indeed, certain of Danishmand's people wanted Ghiyāth al-Dīn's head, but the letters penned by Danishmand saved him—and opened doors. Months passed, but once news of Böjäi's victory reached the *urdu*, Öljeitü's mood shifted in favor of Ghiyāth al-Dīn. In early 707/late 1307, Öljeitü executed a fresh diploma for Kartid dominion of Isfizār, Farāh, Sīstān, Ghūr, Gharjistān, and Jurziwān (the six specified provinces), to the Oxus and to the Indus.[44] Ghiyāth al-Dīn quit the Il-Khan's *urdu*. He sojourned at Jām for three days of spiritual counsel with Shaykh Jāmī and *ziyārat* with Aḥmad-i Jām—the "friend of God" (*walī Allāh*) whom he believed had enabled him to secure the throne at Herat.[45]

Ghiyāth al-Dīn circulated his diploma in the named regions, and demanded accounts from *bandagān* and tax-collectors in Isfizār, Farāh, and such. Ikhtiyār al-Dīn Muḥammad Hārūn, castellan of Fort Iskilchih, accepted Ghiyāth al-Dīn as the king and surrendered the fort, garrison, and treasury. He had refused to surrender the fort to Böjäi, claiming that he only acknowledged Ghiyāth al-Dīn's authority. This certainly won him the Kartids' respect. Herat's citadel, Qalʿa-yi Ikhtiyār al-Dīn, acquired its name

[43] A *yarlīgh* dated 29 Ṣafar 706/9 September 1306. See Mahendrarajah, *Sufi Saint*, 130–32.
[44] al-Harawī, *Harāt*, 571 (abstract of patent); Ḥāfiẓ-i Abrū, *Kart*, 120 (same).
[45] al-Harawī, *Harāt*, 566–71; Ḥāfiẓ-i Abrū, *Kart*, 118–120; Mahendrarajah, *Sufi Saint*, 61–62.

in his honor. Böjäi was displeased by the elevation of the Ghurid prince to *malik* because Ghurids had instigated the massacre of his father, Danishmand Bahadur, and his squadron. Böjäi went to Amir Yasāʾūl with his demands. The viceroy rejected them and ordered Böjäi to respect the Il-Khan's decision; he warned him against inflaming strife (*fitna*) in Herat.[46]

*Ghiyāth al-Dīn Kart: Undermined at Herat*

Lingering animosities in the Mongol camp, and the intrigues of putative candidates for Herat's throne, weakened Ghiyāth al-Dīn and hindered development in Herat. Around 709/1309f. the region had regained a degree of prosperity and rebuilding was underway. However, old nemeses (namely, Böjäi) resurfaced with new allies (namely, ʿAlāʾ al-Dīn Hindū; d. 722/1322f.). When Yasāʾūl, Hindū, and other Ilkhanid notables visited Herat, the *malik* tried to please them and win favor; he even gifted (*pīshkish*) large sums.[47] The group departed. Hindū, an Ilkhanid vizier,[48] was in cahoots with Böjäi and his brother, Muḥammad Duldāʾī (d.*c.* 715/1315). Hindū and Böjäi conferred and wrote to Öljeitü about what Hindū had allegedly witnessed on his visit. He claimed that Ghiyāth al-Dīn was like his brother, and plotting against the Il-Khan. He claimed the Kartid was revamping Herat's forts, turrets, and gates; fabricating arms, enlisting troops, and hoarding provisions.[49] Ghiyāth al-Dīn was just repairing towers, ramparts, and gateways that had been damaged by Böjäi's soldiers when Herat capitulated. The amplifications were intended to provoke Öljeitü.

Öljeitü was distrustful of the Kartids, but his response was not what Hindū and Böjäi had expected: a swift political—possibly literal—decapitation. Ghiyāth al-Dīn also expected a hard response and fled to Khaysār. Öljeitü, despite the intrigues of Böjäi's allies nested in his *urdu*, was not convinced. He summoned the Kartid to answer the indictments. Ghiyāth al-Dīn accepted,

46 al-Harawī, *Harāt*, 571–75; Ḥāfiẓ-i Abrū, *Kart*, 119–121.

47 Isfizārī, *Rawżāt*, 1:456. See Ann Lambton, "'*Pīshkash*': Present or Tribute?," *BSOAS* 57/1 (1994):145–58.

48 Hindū is identified as a vizier in Öljeitü's 706/1306 land-grant to Shaykh al-Islam Jāmī. Mahendrarajah, *Sufi Saint*, 130–31; on Hindū, see also Waṣṣāf, *Taḥrīr*, 151; Abū al-Qāsim ʿAbdallāh b. Muḥammad Qāshānī, *Tārīkh-i Ūljaytū*, ed. Mahīn Hambly (Tehran: Bungāh-i tarjuma wa nashr-i kitāb, 1348/1969), 154.

49 al-Harawī, *Harāt*, 582–84; Ḥāfiẓ-i Abrū, *Kart*, 121; Isfizārī, *Rawżāt*, 1:456–57.

but before journeying to the *urdu*,[50] he secured Herat. The Kartid erected barriers to ensure that if he were deposed, political transfer of Herat to a successor picked by Öljeitü would not be smooth. He nominated a young son, Shams al-Dīn Muḥammad (d.*c.* 730/1330), as his *locum tenens*, with Nāṣir al-Dīn ʿUbaydallāh in the vizierate (*wizārat*) and Shams al-Dīn ʿUmar Shāh Khʷāndazī[51] as his deputy (*rāh-i niyābat*). ʿAzīz al-Dīn Shihāb was appointed to the *dīwān*. Ikhtiyār al-Dīn was confirmed as castellan (therefore guardian of the treasury).[52] Khaysār and other Kartid strongholds in Ghūr, and Fort Iskilchih, were also presumably secured.

### *Ghiyāth al-Dīn at Öljeitü's Court (Second Time)*

In 711/1311 Ghiyāth al-Dīn Muḥammad began his journey to the Il-Khan's *urdu*. He doubtless had in mind the fate that had befallen the last Kartid recalled by an irate Il-Khan. That man, his grandfather Shams al-Dīn Muḥammad, had returned to Khurasan in a coffin. He sojourned with Shaykh al-Islam Jāmī at Turbat-i Jām,[53] securing spiritual and temporal guidance from his shaykh, and seeking blessings (*baraka*) from his intercessor before God, Shaykh al-Islam Aḥmad of Jām—the guardian of kings.[54]

Ghiyāth al-Dīn Kart's woes stem primarily from struggles between the Il-Khan and his amirs for control of the provinces. Ghāzān had secured firmer control of the provinces, but Öljeitü was unable to continue Ghāzān's "centralization" policies. Moreover, Öljeitü's conversion to Twelver Shiʿism presented his rivals, most prominently Amir Chūpān Suldus (d. 728/1327),[55] the excuse to oppose his policies on ostensibly religious grounds. Another oppositional wing were Mongol traditionalists disgusted with the creeping Islamization of the Ilkhanate. They demanded reversion "to the laws and

50 Öljeitü was in Sulṭāniyya when Ghiyāth al-Dīn left Herat (on 19 Rabīʿ I, 711/5 August 1311, according to al-Harawī, *Harāt*, 591), but may have transferred his *urdu* to Baghdad for the winter when the Kartid reached him. Charles Melville, "The Itineraries of Sultan Öljeitü, 1304–16," *Iran* 28 (1990):55–70, 65.

51 Khʷāndazī: possibly *khʷān-dār* (or *khʷān-sālār*, chief steward). *Dihkhuda* 7:10,042.

52 I have tried to harmonize reports in al-Harawī, *Harāt*, 584–90; Ḥāfiẓ-i Abrū, *Kart*, 122–23; Isfizārī, *Rawżāt*, 1:457–58; Faṣīḥ, *Mujmal*, 888.

53 al-Harawī, *Harāt*, 591–92; Ḥāfiẓ-i Abrū, *Kart*, 123; cf. Isfizārī, *Rawżāt*, 1:458.

54 On Aḥmad-i Jām, "patron saint of kings," see Mahendrarajah, *Sufi Saint*, 40–45.

55 Charles Melville, *The Fall of Amir Chupan and the Decline of the Ilkhanate, 1327–37: A Decade of Discord in Mongol Iran* (Bloomington, IN: RIIAS, 1999), 21 and n.51; Hope, *Power*, 188 and n.39.

customs (*yasāq wa yasūn*) of Chingiz Khan."[56] Öljeitü was losing power in Anatolia and Khurasan to his amirs.[57] Hindū's and Böjäi's allegations against Ghiyāth al-Dīn Kart were aimed at ousting the person who was protecting the Il-Khan's interests in Khurasan.

Böjäi and Muḥammad Duldāʾī did not ravage, destroy, and enslave, presumably because Herat was integral to the Il-Khan's realm; but instead resorted to "booty economy lite" tactics against Herat's peoples, namely, extorting the affluent and abusing the *raʿāyā* on the premise that they (Danishmand Bahadur's progeny) were "owed" for the misdeeds of Fakhr al-Dīn Kart and Muḥammad Sām. The Kartid's deputies were inclined to unleash their troops on the abusers, but notables counseled against provocations, lest they lead to escalations by their oppressors.[58]

Ghiyāth al-Dīn Kart, meanwhile, was a hostage in Öljeitü's itinerant *urdu*, albeit in a gilded cage. During his four years with the Il-Khan's court he encountered and befriended eminent members of the imperial household: viziers Rashīd al-Dīn Fażlallāh (d. 718/1318) and his son, Ghiyāth al-Dīn Muḥammad (d. 736/1336); Tāj al-Dīn ʿAlī Shāh Gīlānī Tabrīzī (d. 724/1324); Amir Chūpān (d. 728/1327); and Öljeitü's son and heir, Abū Saʿīd Bahādur Khān (r. 716–36/1316–35). Regrettably, Ghiyāth al-Dīn's chronicler, Sayfī, offers no details of his patron's interactions at Öljeitü's *urdu*. The Kartid's fate—which was not dire or he would have been slain—was seminally altered by the expansion of Chaghataid influence in Central Asia and its social and economic spillovers into Khurasan. The 1304 Mongol "peace treaty" (mentioned above) offered limited respite from Chinggisid rivalries. Qaidu's death initiated processes whereby political control of Transoxiana shifted to the Chaghataids,[59] resulting in flows of Ögödeid princelings, supporters, dependents, and *tümens* (including Qaraunas) into Khurasan. Öljeitü dispatched his son, Abū Saʿīd Bahādur Khān, to Khurasan with an army. The young prince was under the tutelage of his *atabeg*, Amir Siwinch (d. 717/1317). The inflows of humans and livestock tore Böjäi and Duldāʾī away from extorting Heratis. Both were killed in action. As pressures

[56] Qāshānī, *Ūljaytū*, 98; Hope, *Power*, 188.
[57] Hope, *Power*, 188–89.
[58] al-Harawī, *Harāt*, 601–02; Ḥāfiẓ-i Abrū, *Kart*, 124.
[59] Biran, *Qaidu*, 69–80.

against the Ilkhanate intensified on its eastern frontier, Öljeitü released Ghiyāth al-Dīn (in 715/1315) with a mandate to extinguish fires.

The narrative propounded by Sayfī of the circumstances leading to Ghiyāth al-Dīn's release is borderline hagiographical. Rashīd al-Dīn Fażlallāh and Tāj al-Dīn ʿAlī Shāh, Sayfī claims, had been in the "service" (*khidmat*) of Shaykh al-Islam Nūr al-Dīn ʿAbd al-Raḥman Isfarāyinī (d. 717/1317), who lived in Baghdad. When the viziers visited Isfarāyinī, he asked why Ghiyāth al-Dīn Kart, progeny of a noble family, a just (*ʿādil*) and able *malik*, a man that had faithfully served the padishah, was not granted a fresh *yarlīgh* and returned to Herat to abolish the oppression and injustice (*ḥayf wa taʿaddī*) gripping the east? More fluff follows, including an improbable speech by Öljeitü in praise of Ghiyāth al-Dīn.[60]

The likely scenario is that in late 714/early 1315, with the situation on the frontier deteriorating, Rashīd al-Dīn and/or Tāj al-Dīn ʿAlī Shāh had counseled Öljeitü to release the Kartid and to profitably employ his martial and political talents. The intercession of Shaykh al-Islam Isfarāyinī is doubtless accurate. ʿAlāʾ al-Dawla Simnānī (d. 735/1336) had contacted Isfarāyinī,[61] who asked the viziers to secure Ghiyāth al-Dīn's parole. Simnānī was in Shaykh al-Islam Jāmī's network. If the mass of correspondence (*inshāʾ*) in *Farāʾīd-i Ghiyāṡī*, to/from Jāmī centers of influence (Jām, Herat, Nishapur, Tirmiz, and Samarqand), to/from sultans, viziers, amirs, ulama, and sayyids (including members of Öljeitü's *dīwān*, e.g., complainant ʿAlāʾ al-Dīn Hindū), is indicative,[62] the Sufi social network was extensive, formidable, and capable of obtaining meaningful favors (*ʿināyat*) from the Ilkhanid court.

[60] al-Harawī, *Harāt*, 622–24; Ḥāfiẓ-i Abrū, *Kart*, 128–30. Shaykh Isfarāyinī was ʿAlāʾ al-Dawla Simnānī's "only true master." Jamal Elias, *The Throne Carrier of God* (Albany, NY: SUNY Press, 1985), 37–38. *Khidmat* in Sufi thought involves intricate relationships and obligations.

[61] Faṣīḥ, *Mujmal*, 891 and n.1; Faṣīḥ Khʷāfī, *Mujmal-i Faṣīḥī*, ed. Muḥammad Farrukh, 3 vols (Mashhad: Intishārāt-i bāstān, 1339/1960), 3:23: that Simnānī had interceded because Isfarāyinī was deceased. But Isfarāyinī died 3 Jumādá I 717/14 June 1317. See G.M. Martini, *ʿAlaʾ al-Dawla al-Simnani between spiritual authority and political power* (Leiden: Brill, 2018), 92, n.301. In short, both Isfarāyinī and Simnānī had interceded.

[62] Jalāl al-Dīn Yūsuf-i Ahl [Jāmī], *Farāʾīd-i Ghiyāṡī*, 2 vols, ed. Heshmat Moayyad (Tehran: Intishārāt-i bunyād-i farhang-i Īrān, vol. I, 1356/1977; vol. II, 1358/1979); idem, *Farāʾīd-i Ghiyāṡī* (Berlin: Staatsbibliothek zu Berlin, Ms. Orient. Fol.110); idem, *Farāʾīd-i Ghiyāṡī* (Tehran: Central Library, University of Tehran, 4756); idem, *Farāʾīd-i Ghiyāṡī* (Istanbul: Süleymaniye Kütüphanesi, Fatih 4012); idem, *Farāʾīd-i Ghiyāṡī* (Istanbul: Süleymaniye Kütüphanesi, Aya Sofya 4155).

Ghiyāth al-Dīn Kart was liberated in 715/1315. He received a new patent (*bih-tajdīd yarlīgh niwishtand*) that renewed Kartid sovereignty from Herat to *Afghānistān* and the Oxus (*khiṭṭa-yi Harāt rā tā iqṣā-yi Awghānistān wa ḥadd-i Āmūya badū mufawważ kard[and]*). Ghiyāth al-Dīn departed Baghdad with gifts, robes, and *pāʾizas*.[63] He sojourned again at Turbat-i Jām; three days of veneration of Aḥmad-i Jām (grateful, surely, that his life had been spared and Öljeitü's support renewed); and in *khidmat* to his spiritual guide, Shaykh al-Islam Shihāb al-Dīn Ismāʿīl Jāmī.[64] Ghiyāth al-Dīn was visited on day four by Shams al-Dīn Muḥammad Kart, Shams al-Dīn ʿUmar Shāh, and Herat's Chief Justice (*qāḍī al-quḍāt*), Ṣadr al-Dīn Khaysārī.[65] The *malik*'s principal appointees had remained faithful during his four-year absence. Kartid operatives of sundry classes (*ḥukkām wa ʿummāl wa ṣudūr*) visited him at Jām. On day five, he departed for Herat. The next five years presented Kartids with daunting challenges.

*Chaghataid Incursions: 715/1315 to 720/1320*

The influx of Turko-Mongol peoples from Chaghataid Transoxiana into the Iranian Plateau in the late 7th/13th and early 8th/14th centuries was a manifestation of an ancient problem in a fresh guise. For millennia, trickles and streams of peoples and their livestock had made the journey from their Central/Inner Asian homelands into the Plateau.

Turko-Mongol migrants seeped across the Oxus into Khurasan, perhaps with a sultan's permission to settle in a specific location, as with the Ghuzz (Oghuz). Roving bands arising from within migrant communities preyed on settled communities of Khurasan. The Ghuzz offer notorious examples of the negative effects of mass migrations: they sacked Nishapur on several occasions and ruined it in 556–57/1161–62 after bringing Seljuq sultan Sanjar (r. 511–52/1118–57) to his knees. Migrations, within limits, were not necessarily negatives for Khurasan's multifarious regional economies: sedentary peoples and nomads interacted and traded; they exchanged meats, dairy, and pelts for crafted goods, cereals, and vegetables. The social, economic, and

63 al-Harawī, *Harāt*, 626–27; Ḥāfiẓ-i Abrū, *Kart*, 130.

64 al-Harawī, *Harāt*, 630; Ḥāfiẓ-i Abrū, *Kart*, 131.

65 *Qāḍī al-quḍāt* of Kartid domains. Appointed by Ghiyāth al-Dīn in 714/1314f. and endorsed by Öljeitü. al-Harawī, *Harāt*, 617–21; Ḥāfiẓ-i Abrū, *Kart*, 128.

ecological implications of migrations into limited space cannot be properly treated here.[66] I focus mainly on the military-political challenges.

Possibly the first Chinggisid political refugees to the Ilkhanate as a consequence of the Chaghataid ascendancy arrived in early 706/late 1306, which included Ögödeids and one Qaraunas *tümen*. They were greeted by Yasāʾūl, Böjäi, and amirs Bīktūt (Bektūt) and Ramażān. Yasāʾūl allocated to each incoming princeling a pastureage, food, and forage as necessary and in accordance with his social-political station, and integrated his unit into the Ilkhanid military.[67] Migrants were not invariably welcomed: the chief of one cluster, for instance, was dragged before the Il-Khan and forced to convince him of his fealty.[68] Öljeitü, it would appear, regarded the migrants as a bulwark against Chaghataid expansion, but also appreciated that introducing armed bands into Khurasan, which then did not suffer from a dearth of militias, generated security problems.

Sayfī's attention was focused on Herat. He neglects to cover circumstances on the frontier until they spiraled out of control, *c.* 715/1315, which coincides with Ghiyāth al-Dīn's return to Herat. The confusing morass of military engagements in Khurasan between migrant clusters and Ilkhanid resisters cannot be unraveled in this space, but fortunately, an exposition is unnecessary: the task has been skillfully performed by Russell Kempiners.[69] In engagements preceding the Kartid's return, Ramażān was routed in 714/1314; Böjäi was killed in 715/1315. The Ilkhanid military was on the backfoot. A major Chaghataid player in Khurasan was Yasaʾur, who had entered the region *c.* 715/1315. His activities occupied the Kartids' attention for five years (see below).

The Kartid's position in 715/1315 was fragile. He had armed Chaghataids traversing the frontier; Mongol amirs—ostensibly defenders of the Ilkhanate—who were antagonistic toward him. These amirs were also likely to change direction faster than weathercocks. He had adversaries embedded at court: notables pledged fealty but there were resentments.

[66] But see Kempiners, "Struggle," 110, 122 (he raises excellent points for further research).

[67] Waṣṣāf, *Taḥrīr*, 265. Waṣṣāf uses "Qaraunas" and give the identities of the migrants. See also Qāshānī, *Ūljaytū*, 54.

[68] Waṣṣāf, *Taḥrīr*, 266–67 (events of 708/1308f.).

[69] Kempiners, "Struggle," esp. 68–97, 134–61.

To illustrate, Chief Justice Muḥammad b. ʿAlī Nuṣrat (n.d.) had been sacked by Ghiyāth al-Dīn around 714/1314f., and replaced by Qāḍī Ṣadr al-Dīn b. Fakhr al-Dīn Khaysārī (fl. 721/1321–22). The dismissal originated with a complaint by ulama that Qāḍī Nuṣrat was deficient in learning and applying the Shariʿa incorrectly.[70] The objections, in my opinion, were rooted in Herat's politics, not the judge's erudition. The losing faction concealed its antipathy, and would strike if an opportunity surfaced.[71] Lastly, although Quṭb al-Dīn Isfizārī and Ināltikīn Farāhī had professed fealty, they, too, prepared to pounce.

Table 4.1 itemizes crucial events impacting Ilkhanids and Kartids. The spectrum of the conflict ecosystem was in evidence from 706/1306 to 720/1320.

*Yasaʾur's migration to Khurasan*

Before delving into the political-social impacts of Yasaʾur's (d. Jumādá I 720/June 1320) activities in Khurasan, putative causes for the Chaghataid exodus from Transoxiana, and the Ilkhanate's welcome of Chaghataid refugees, are analyzed below.

R.G. Kempiners argued in favor of rivalries between two Chaghataid lines forcing Yasaʾur to leave Transoxiana: once control of *ulus* Chaghatai shifted to Esen-Buqa (r. 1310–18), Duʾa's son, migration to Khurasan became an attractive option.[72] Why the Ilkhanate permitted mass migration is unclear.[73] In my judgment, Öljeitü did not comprehend, firstly, the magnitude of the migrations: that once the sluice was opened a trickle would become a flood; secondly, that the infusion of enormous numbers of (sedentary and nomadic) Turko-Mongol peoples and livestock into Khurasan would generate political, social, economic, and ecological problems. Migrations were not the "normal" volume of seepage to be expected through porous borders. In this case, the scale of human and animal migrations into *fixed* space during a brief period (just a few years) had adverse impacts.[74]

70 al-Harawī, *Harāt*, 617–21; Ḥāfiẓ-i Abrū, *Kart*, 128.
71 Herat's religious politics were byzantine. Mawlānā Wajīh al-Dīn Nasafī (as noted) had advised Danishmand on blockading Herat.
72 Kempiners, "Khurasan," 77–80, 83–85, 97.
73 But see ibid., 111–16 (Kempiners's conclusions).
74 See ibid. 110 (earlier waves of émigrés were opposed to the new émigrés).

*Table 4.1 Chaghataid-Ilkhanid Struggles for Supremacy in Khurasan: Key Events, 706/1306 to 720/1320*

| Year | Event | Political/Military Impact | Social/Economic Impact |
|---|---|---|---|
| 706/1307 | Amir Yasāʾūl appointed Ilkhanid plenipotentiary to Khurasan | Kartid rule terminated consequent to the slaughter of Danishmand's troops | – |
| 706f./1307f. | Ögödeids, non-Ögödeids, Qaraunas "refugees" granted permission to settle south of the Oxus | More armed bands introduced into Khurasan, which did not suffer any dearth of armed bands | Yasāʾūl allocated to Ögödeid princelings, fodder, food, and pasturages |
| early 707/ late 1307 | Ghiyāth al-Dīn Kart appointed as new *malik* of Herat | Yasāʾūl remained a lingering menace (plenipotentiary status continued) | – |
| 711/1311f. | Ghiyāth al-Dīn re-called to Öljeitü's *urdu*; hostage for four years (from 711/1311f. to 715/1315) | Influence of ʿAlāʾ al-Dīn Hindū, Böjäi b. Danishmand, Muḥammad Duldāʾī b. Danishmand, et al., increased in Herat | Socio-economic progress in and around Herat was hindered; *raʿāyā* and *aʿyān* were abused and extorted by Mongol amirs |
| 711/1311f. | Abū Saʿīd Bahādur Khān sent to Khurasan with Amir Siwinch | – | – |
| 711–15/ 1311–15 | Hostilities flare between Ilkhanid forces and interlopers | Military conditions deteriorate on the frontier. Böjäi, et al., are killed | Tensions and clashes between Khurasanians (settled and nomadic) and the interlopers over resources and pastures |
| 715/1315 | Yasaʾur enters Khurasan | Pledged allegiance to Öljeitü, who allocated to Yasaʾur tracts around Bādghīs, Panjā (Panjdih?), Sarakhs | Yasaʾur arrived with 10,000 troops, dependents, live booty (humans and livestock), steeds, etc. Added social, ecological, economic pressures (see, e.g., Kempiners, "Struggle," 110, 120–22) |

| | | | |
|---|---|---|---|
| 715/1315 | Kebek pursues Yasaʾur over the Oxus to recover livestock and people captured as booty | Yasaʾur forced to move live booty from Fāryāb and Murghāb deeper into Khurasan (= nearer to Herat) | – |
| In Winter (715/1315–16?) | Extreme cold event (*yūt*) strikes in parts of Khurasan, killing livestock; famine (*qaḥṭ*) followed | – | Yasaʾur's booty (humans and animals) were impacted; *c.* 100,000 souls (allegedly) perished from cold, famine, and disease |
| 715/1315 | Öljeitü returns Ghiyāth al-Dīn to Herat with new patent (*yarlīgh*) | Ghiyāth al-Dīn's star is ascendant | – |
| 716/1316 | Öljeitü dies | Ghiyāth al-Dīn is free of Öljeitü; has friendly sultan and regent on his side | – |
| *c.* 716/1316 | Sultan Abū Saʿīd sends ʿ*ahd-nāmah* (covenant) to Yasaʾur | The sultan makes it clear that Yasaʾur is in Khurasan temporarily | – |
| *c.* 717/1317 | Amir Yasāʾūl's camp attacked; he is subsequently killed | Ghiyāth al-Dīn Kart is free of Yasāʾūl | Heratis are freed from Yasāʾūl and his financial exactions |
| 717/1317 | Yasaʾur enters Herat River Valley | Demands Kartid submission, but is rebuffed by Ghiyāth al-Dīn Kart | Yasaʾur plundered harvests; cereals are scarce; Chaghataids akin "plague of locusts" (*malakh*) |
| 718/1318 | Yasaʾur attacks Mazandaran | "Tipping point" reached. Abū Saʿīd & Chūpān "greenlight" hard response | – |
| 718/1318 | Yasaʾur is officially "in rebellion" (*bā mā yaghī shudi-and*) against the Ilkhanate | Amir Ḥusayn dispatched with army;<br>Golden Horde marches on Darband;<br>Ghiyāth al-Dīn Kart receive mandate to terminate threats in the east | – |
| *c.* Shawwāl 718/Dec.–Jan. 1318–19 | Yasaʾur demands Shaykh al-Islam Jāmī's presence or submission | Yasaʾur is rebuffed and furious;<br>*Lashkar* dispatched to Turbat-i Jām;<br>armed Sufis fight off Chaghataids | The Sufis, and by extension the denizens of Jām, rewarded for their loyalty |

*Table 4.1 (Continued)*

| Year | Event | Political/Military Impact | Social/Economic Impact |
|---|---|---|---|
| 718–19/1319 | Chaghataids on the backfoot | "no town or citadel [of Khurasan] had yielded [to Yasaʾur] and most of his army had perished [. . .]" | Yasaʾur in "roving bandit" status and confined to tracts from Hilmand River to Qandahar |
| Muḥarram 719/ Feb.–Mar. 1319 | First assault on Herat (led by Mubārak-Shāh b. Böjäi) | Failed (see Chapter Ten on fortifications) | – |
| 5 Rabīʿ I 719/26 April 1319 | Second assault on Herat (led by Bektūt) | Failed. After negotiations failed, Bektūt led an attack on 7 Rabīʿ I/28 April, which also failed | – |
| 26 Rabīʿ I 719/17 May 1319 | Third assault on Herat (led by Yasaʾur) | One month siege. Failed | Yasaʾur burned crops and caused mayhem in Khurasan before retreating to Garmsīr |
| 719–20/ 1319–20 | Ghiyāth al-Dīn launches "mop up" operations against collaborators | Āzāb, Bākharz, Isfizār, Kh$^{w}$āf, and Tūlak brought under control. Farāh was subjugated in Rabīʿ I 721/April 1321. Kartid kingdom consolidated | Heratis received exemptions from taxes and imposts (Chapter Four). Kartid troops secured treasures, fineries, provisions, armaments, cereals, horses, cattle, sheep, and peoples as booty from Kartid turncoats (Chapter Nine) |
| Jumādá I 720/ June 1320 | Yasaʾur killed by Kebek, khan of *ulus* Chaghatai | – | – |

Waṣṣāf and Sayfī are the earliest sources on Yasaʾur's arrival. Their reports do not align. Sayfī states that Yasaʾur had pledged allegiance to Öljeitü and requested permission to settle in Khurasan with 10,000 troops, booty, and livestock. Öljeitü's *yarlīgh* allocated to Yasaʾur tracts "from the Oxus to Mazandaran," and obliged Khurasan's *malik*s and amirs to honor and assist Yasaʾur.[75] Waṣṣāf's narrative,[76] Kempiners discerned, gives "much more the impression of Yasaʾur as a refugee who took control of an area in Shibūrghān."[77] Later, Waṣṣāf continues, a "pestilence (*wabāʾ*) called *yūt*" afflicted livestock.[78] Now one *mann* of flour could not be purchased for eight *aqcha*. Consequent to this calamity, Öljeitü allocated to Yasaʾur bivouacs and pastures around Bādghīs, Panjā, and Sarakhs.[79] In no way did the Il-Khan cede any part of Khurasan to Yasaʾur. Indeed, he dispatched his son, Abū Saʿīd, and his *atabeg*, Amir Siwinch, to govern Khurasan.[80]

After Öljeitü expired, his successor, sultan Abū Saʿīd Bahādur Khān, executed an *ʿahd-nāmah* (covenant or treaty) responsive to Yasaʾur's petition for confirmation of status. The sultan is unequivocal that Yasaʾur and his amirs were temporarily in Khurasan, with the ultimate objective of recovering their patrimonies (*ulus*) in Transoxiana with Ilkhanid logistical assistance.[81] In contemporary terminology, the Ilkhanate was assigning "safe havens" for Chaghataid "insurgents"—not permanent control or residence. As often happens with such arrangements, insurgents become nuisances for the hosts.

### *Yasaʾur's predicament*

A reconstruction of events is that Yasaʾur had been battling Kebek (r. 1318–26),[82] Esen-Buqa's brother. Yasaʾur fled to Khurasan with his booty, which included captives. Yasaʾur intended to winter in a tract between

75 al-Harawī, *Harāt*, 650.
76 Waṣṣāf, *Taḥrīr*, 338.
77 Kempiners, "Khurasan," 114.
78 *Yūt* (or *zūd*, *zhūd*): Unseasonable storm that freezes over pastures, causing animals to die of starvation and/or cold. "The term can be used broadly for natural disaster that kills a lot of animals" (Thomas J. Barfield, e-mail to author, 2 February 2020). Waṣṣāf wrote *wabāʾ*, an Arabic word for disease, assuming that *yūt* (a Mongolian word) meant veterinary disease.
79 Waṣṣāf, *Taḥrīr*, 338–39. Panjā: possibly Panjdih, an oasis on the Murghāb. See Barthold, *Geography*, 39. *Mann* and *aqcha*: see glossary.
80 Waṣṣāf, *Taḥrīr*, 339; Kempiners, "Khurasan," 114–15.
81 Ḥāfiẓ-i Abrū, *Rashīdī*, 129–33, 132; al-Harawī, *Harāt*, 670–71; Kempiners, "Khurasan," 115.
82 On the background, see Kato, "Kebek."

Shibūrghān and Murghāb; but since Kebek had followed him over the Oxus (to recover livestock and captives), Yasa'ur was forced to move captives, livestock, and loyalists from Fāryāb and Murghāb deeper into Khurasan (i.e., in the direction of Herat). Since Yasa'ur entered Khurasan in 715/1315 with Kebek in hot pursuit, *yūt* and famine, which appear to be linked disasters wrought by extreme cold and snow, probably struck that very winter (AH 715/ April 1315 to March 1316). Nearly 100,000 souls, thinly-clad (*barahna*: bare or naked) and on foot, perished from the cold (*sarmā*) and famine (*qaḥṭ*).[83] Per the standard caveat, the figure is not accepted literally. The corpus of captives and followers was substantial; a large percentage of this body died.[84]

An inherent disadvantage of live booty is that until said booty is monetized (sold or bartered), it must be fed. In the case of people captured in clement weather, they must be suitably clothed for winter.[85] Humans and animals are debilitated or destroyed by maladies, famines, and extreme temperatures. Yasa'ur was unable to expeditiously monetize slaves and livestock.[86] Winter and famine—and assuredly, human and animal diseases arising from malnutrition and cold weather—combined to *devalue* or *deplete* assets. Moreover, slaves and livestock that did not perish would have been emaciated and feeble, afflicted by (human or veterinary) diseases. They could not be readily bartered or sold. Yasa'ur was in financial straits. Being *persona non grata* in Transoxiana, he was unable to return. Yasa'ur, therefore, looked inwards—Khurasan—for bases, allies, wealth, and power.

*Yasa'ur's challenge*

Yasa'ur tried to lord over Khurasan. He liberally interpreted Öljeitü's "from the Oxus to Mazandaran" clause; and read the proviso that obliged *malik*s and amirs to honor and assist him as conveying authority *over* the foregoing classes.

Yasa'ur wrote to Ghiyāth al-Dīn Kart demanding his presence. The *malik* interpreted Öljeitü's *yarlīgh* less liberally when drafting his reply; but tried to temper the rejection with a mission to Yasa'ur comprising Sufis and scholars.

[83] Based on al-Harawī, *Harāt*, 649–50 (year given: 716/1316f.).

[84] For an estimate, see Kempiners, "Khurasan," 121–22.

[85] See Chapter 3, § "Plunder or Administer?"

[86] Alexander and Philip sold captives quickly (Chapter Three, n.125). Probably common practice.

Yasaʾur was not mollified.[87] The impasse continued, with the *malik* justifiably rejecting Yasaʾur's professed mandate: after all, he had his own mandate from the Il-Khan, which had not been revoked or amended.

Plenipotentiary Yasāʾūl's death framed a confrontation between two polar forces: Yasaʾur and Ghiyāth al-Dīn. In war, polar forces emerge that pull lesser objects—faithless *bandagān* and seditious amirs—to each pole. If Ghiyāth al-Dīn destroyed the Yasaʾur "pole," then the lesser objects in Yasaʾur's orbit will detach. This political-military debris can (1) flee the region; (2) stay and be crushed; or (3) voluntarily enter the Kartid orbit.[88]

Fickle Ilkhanid amirs and refractory Kartid *bandagān* were drawn to Yasaʾur's orbit. Bektūt performed the gymnastic feat of fighting for both sides. The Kartid state had been diminished by the upheavals of the forgoing decade and Ghiyāth al-Dīn's absence. The state stood to benefit if Ghiyāth al-Dīn eliminated Yasaʾur—the principal military power standing athwart the Kartid's path to political supremacy. If Ghiyāth al-Dīn neutralized Yasaʾur, the amirs and *malik*s supporting the Chaghataid would be attracted to (or exterminated by) the last centripetal force left standing in eastern Khurasan: the Kartid state.

Sultan Abū Saʿīd acted belatedly to suppress Yasaʾur. There was infighting within the Ilkhanate that undoubtedly distracted Amir Chūpān and vizier Tāj al-Dīn ʿAlī Shāh (like Siwinch's bid to become regent), and intrigues between Tāj al-Dīn and Rashīd al-Dīn (leading to the latter's execution in 718/1318). But by *c.* 717–18/1317–18, vizier and regent recognized the peril and advocated for military campaigns by Ghiyāth al-Dīn, to be supported by an Ilkhanid army commanded by the Jalayirid, Amir Ḥusayn (d. 722/1322).[89]

### *Yasaʾur's campaigns*

Yasāʾūl was extorting Khurasanians for the last time. The exaction was ostensibly to pay for a marriage between Yasāʾūl and a relative of Yasaʾur.

[87] al-Harawī, *Harāt*, 650–53.

[88] The analogy to orbits, planetary objects, and centripetal force is from military science.

[89] On Amir Ḥusayn, see Abu Bakr al-Qutbi Ahari, *Tarikh-i Shaikh Uwais*, tr. J.B. van Loon (Mouton, 1954), 7; Patrick Wing, *The Jalayirids: Dynastic State Formation in the Mongol Middle East* (Edinburgh: Edinburgh University Press, 2016), 65–67.

On receiving news of Öljeitü's demise, Amir Siwinch—the crown prince's *atabeg*—sprinted west with his twelve-year-old charge to try to secure the regency. Yasāʾūl had sent men into Herat to extort funds, which they did. Ghiyāth al-Dīn did not intervene, unwilling to antagonize an amir who remained Ilkhanid plenipotentiary. Moreover, the Ilkhanid court remained in flux after the accession of a malleable young prince, and political jockeying by Siwinch and Chūpān. In a delicious moment of irony, Yasāʾūl's camp was attacked by Yasaʾur's, Mubārak-Shāh's, and Bektūt's troops, and pillaged of extorted funds, livestock, and valuables. Yasāʾūl was later killed. Yasāʾūl's demise lay in a conflict with Bektūt for control of Ilkhanid forces.[90]

Bektūt and Yasaʾur confederated.[91] The struggle for supremacy in Khurasan was now between Ghiyāth al-Dīn's camp and Yasaʾur's camp. Bektūt occupied a northeast (from Andkhūd) to north (Bādghīs) corridor, which terminated above Herat. Yasaʾur roamed the region between Quhistān and Ghazni, down to Sīstān. He obtained keen support from the petty lords of Farāh and Isfizār; and sullen support from Sīstān's ruler,[92] Naṣīr al-Dīn.[93] Kartid enemies were situated to the north and the south of Herat. The Kartid stronghold—a strip running from around Jām in the west, to Ghūr and Gharjistān in the east—was sandwiched in between.[94] This strip contained the mass of the Kartid kingdom's economic production: agriculture, animal husbandry, crafts, and skilled trades. Control of economic production sustained the Kartid state and contributed to its triumph.

In 717/1317, Yasaʾur settled his army in the Herat Valley. He worshipped (*ziyārat*) at ʿAbdallah Ansari's shrine at Gazurgah. Ghiyāth al-Dīn

90 Ḥāfiẓ-i Abrū, *Rashīdī*, 123–26; al-Harawī, *Harāt*, 654–59; Waṣṣāf, *Taḥrīr*, 342–43. The dispute is analyzed in Kempiners, "Khurasan," 123–29.

91 The parties conferred at Chisht-i Sharīf in Jumādá II 718/August 1318. al-Harawī, *Harāt*, 683ff.; Ḥāfiẓ-i Abrū, *Rashīdī*, 139ff.; see also Kempiners, "Khurasan," 123–27.

92 Yasaʾur claimed that Öljeitü and Abū Saʿīd had granted him dominion "from the Oxus to Mazandaran; and Zābul and Kabul, from Shaṭṭ-i Sind to the limits of Kīj and Makrān." See Ḥāfiẓ-i Abrū, *Rashīdī*, 137–39, 137; cf. al-Harawī, *Harāt*, 677–80, 677. Sīstān's ruler (see note below) did not accept Yasaʾur's claim but was bullied into submission.

93 Possibly Muḥammad b. Muḥammad Naṣīr al-Dīn (d.*c.* 718/1318), of the Mihrabānid line of the "Maliks of Nīmrūz." See C.E. Bosworth, *The New Islamic Dynasties* (Edinburgh: Edinburgh University Press, 1996), cat. no. 106.

94 Treacherous *bandagān* at Bākharz and Khʷāf were punished by the Kartid. See al-Harawī, *Harāt*, 746–49 (Bākharz), 750–59 (Khʷāf); Kempiners, "Khurasan," 164–66.

sent a delegation to Yasaʾur led by his second son, Hāfiẓ, which included Shaykh al-Islam Shihāb al-Dīn Ismāʿīl Jāmī, Niẓām al-Dīn Nasafī, and ʿAfīf al-Dīn Muftī. Yasaʾur made his (by now) tiresome demands for submission; the delegation departed. Yasaʾur's militias plundered harvests before returning to Bādghīs. Ghiyāth al-Dīn compared Yasaʾur's activities to that of a plague of locusts (*malakh*) ravaging a region. Cereals became scarce.[95] This is when sultan Abū Saʿīd/Amir Chūpān and Yasaʾur were engaged in their diplomatic *kabuki*, and Yasaʾur was not categorized as "in rebellion." Ghiyāth al-Dīn was hindered from responding forcefully. This began to change with the Ṣafar 718/April 1318 intelligence brief from Kartid allies in Ghazni and Garmsīr informing Herat of Yasaʾur's preparations to attack Khurasan. The brief gave him ample warning to alert Kartid commanders and castellans from Ghūr to Nishapur.[96]

Ghiyāth al-Dīn was keeping the Ilkhanid court apprised, but could not gain traction moving the Ilkhanate to take firm action against the Chaghataid interlopers. Consequent to Yasaʾur's and Bektūt's invasion of Mazandaran in summer 718/1318,[97] the balance tipped in the Kartid's favor. His emissaries to Sulṭāniyya were well received by sultan Abū Saʿīd and Amir Chūpān. Yasaʾur was, at last, proclaimed "in rebellion" (*bā mā yaghī shudi-and*). Amir Ḥusayn was dispatched to confront Yasaʾur. Ghiyāth al-Dīn Kart received an open mandate to terminate threats in the eastern Ilkhanate.[98]

Özbeg Khan (r. 1312–41), leader of the Golden Horde, marched on Darband, Winter 718/1318–19, "a concerted effort by Özbeg Khan to relieve the pressure on the Čaġatayid prince Yasaʾur in Khurasan."[99] The Ilkhanate experienced military pressures on two fronts, which stretched its resources. Özbeg Khan's invasion served as an excuse for an uprising against Chūpān by a coterie of amirs. Dissenters tried to cleave him from his charge, who was resentful of his overbearing regent. The court was distracted at a critical moment. The impact of the revolt vis-à-vis events in Khurasan is unclear.

95 al-Harawī, *Harāt*, 661–62.
96 Ibid., 681–82.
97 See Kempiners, "Struggle," 138–39.
98 al-Harawī, *Harāt*, 694–95. He received a *yarlīgh*, gifts, and *khilʿat*.
99 Charles Melville, "Abū Saʿīd and the revolt of the Amirs in 1319," in *L'Iran la face à la domination mongole*, ed. Denise Aigle (Téhéran: Institut Français de Recherche en Iran, 1997), 89–120, 96, n.39.

A Mamluk historian's claim of collusion between dissident Ilkhanid amirs and Yasaʾur is plausible.[100]

Ghiyāth al-Dīn, meanwhile, took the fight to the enemy.[101] I leave the blow-by-blow recounting of the final years of the struggle to others and focus on four connected events: the siege of Turbat-i Jām and the three offensives against Herat (see Table 4.1).

After pillaging Mazandaran, Yasaʾur sent emissaries to cities of western Khurasan calling for submission—more of the bluff and bluster that had characterized his attempts to establish himself as the master of eastern Persia. Leaders of the cities rejected his demands and proclaimed their fealty to sultan Abū Saʿīd and Ghiyāth al-Dīn. They recognized that the conflict had tipped in the Kartid's favor. Sayfī writes: "no town or citadel [of Khurasan] had yielded [to Yasaʾur] and most of his army had perished in the towns, on the [campaign] trail and at the citadels, especially at Mashhad-Ṭūs."[102] Yasaʾur sent envoys to Turbat-i Jām, *c.* Shawwāl 718/December–January 1318–19, demanding Shaykh al-Islam Shihāb al-Dīn Ismāʿīl Jāmī's presence. His demand was rejected. Infuriated and desperate, Yasaʾur dispatched a *lashkar* to seize Shaykh Jāmī,[103] resulting in the extraordinary spectacle of violent resistance by the Shaykh al-Islam and his darwishes. The Jāmī Sufis fiercely defended the citadel for several days, forcing the *lashkar* to withdraw in frustration.[104] The Jāmī hagiographer, ʿAlī Būzjānī, postulated that the intent behind Yasaʾur's attempt to capture the Shaykh al-Islam of Jam is that if Jāmī were captured, the people of Khurasan would fall in line.[105] Overstated, perhaps, but illustrative of the Shaykh's importance to Khurasanians and the Kart king. Jāmī Sufis had unambiguously demonstrated their loyalties to Abū Saʿīd and Ghiyāth al-Dīn Kart, for which superlative rewards awaited them.[106]

Yasaʾur was now presented with the unenviable (to him) choices of retreating to his Garmsīr strongholds, and remaining a roving bandit (albeit

[100] Ibid., 111, n.129. Analyzed by Melville.

[101] al-Harawī, *Harāt*, 695ff.

[102] al-Harawī, *Harāt*, 692. See also Mīrkhʷānd, *Rawżat*, 4,348–49.

[103] *Lashkar*: army. It probably meant a force ranging from contemporary battalion strength (1,000 men) to brigade level (3,000 to 5,000 men).

[104] al-Harawī, *Harāt*, 692–93; Ḥāfiẓ-i Abrū, *Rashīdī*, 153–54; Mīrkhʷānd, *Rawżat*, 4,349–50.

[105] Būzjānī, *Rawżat*, 105.

[106] On the Jāmī shrine's architectural ensemble, see Mahendrarajah, *Sufi Saint*, Chapter 5.

of diminished status relative to his erstwhile lofty claims of lordship over Khurasan), or (miraculously) capturing Herat and vaulting to the top of the political pinnacle. He chose the latter. Given the fortifications of Herat, this was an incorrigible gambler's last roll of the dice. The Kartid advised his subjects in the vicinities of Herat to seek shelter, and dispatched messengers to Ghūr, Herat Valley, and Isfizār to direct people to shelter in nearby citadels. Ghiyāth al-Dīn primed Nikudari, Herati, Sistani, Ghurid, Khalaj, and Pashtun units. The first assault was led by Mubārak-Shāh b. Böjäi, in Muḥarram 719/February 1319, with 6,000 cavalry. He was trounced by a Nikudari *lashkar* and Herati warriors (*mubāriz-ān*) that sallied to fight them.[107]

The Chaghataids, led by Bektūt, returned with reinforcements and attacked on 5 Rabīʿ I 719/26 April 1319. After a brief clash, Bektūt co-opted Shaykh al-Islam Quṭb al-Dīn Aḥmad Chishtī to write to Ghiyāth al-Dīn to secure a settlement, which the Kartid rejected. Bektūt launched an assault on 7 Rabīʿ I/28 April. Another demonstration of futility: without siege equipment, besiegers had no chance. Hurling cavalry against fortifications was an exercise in animal cruelty.[108] Bektūt tried to use Shaykh al-Islam Chishtī to again negotiate with the Kartid, but Ghiyāth al-Dīn was resolute. He sensed victory was nigh.

Bektūt retreated, suddenly, when he heard that the Ilkhanid army from Iraq was approaching; however, once it was ascertained the army would not arrive for two months, Yasaʾur became emboldened.[109] On 26 Rabīʿ I 719/17 May 1319 he settled near Herat, and launched his attack thereafter, besieging the city for one month. He made no headway and retreated to Garmsīr, burning crops and causing mayhem in Khurasan.[110] The Ilkhanid army arrived, finally, but Yasaʾur was tracked and killed by Kebek Khan.[111]

[107] al-Harawī, *Harāt*, 697–98; Ḥāfiẓ-i Abrū, *Kart*, 146. See Table 4.1, *supra* (timetable).
[108] The toll on warhorses before the advent of mechanized warfare was horrendous.
[109] al-Harawī, *Harāt*, 700–09; Ḥāfiẓ-i Abrū, *Kart*, 146–48; Kempiners, "Khurasan," 145–47.
[110] al-Harawī, *Harāt*, 710–16; Ḥāfiẓ-i Abrū, *Kart*, 148–151; Mīrkhʷānd, *Rawżat*, 4,352–53.
[111] Ḥāfiẓ-i Abrū, *Rashīdī*, 158–59; Ḥāfiẓ-i Abrū, *Kart*, 163; May, "Ilkhanate," 308–09.

## Political Stability at Herat

The death of Öljeitü (d. 716/1316) was a relief for Ghiyāth al-Dīn. The malevolent Il-Khan, no friend of the Kartids, left behind a young successor and a powerful regent, both of whom proved good friends to the Kartids.

Abū Saʿīd and Chūpān were delighted by the Kartid's victories. The *malik* had the advantage, which he pressed. He dispatched his confidant, Nāṣir al-Dīn ʿUbaydallāh (n.d.), to the Ilkhanid court at Arrān (Āẕarbayjān) to tout his successes and identify to the Il-Khan those who had collaborated with Yasaʾur (namely, Quṭb al-Dīn Isfizārī, Majd al-Dīn Muḥammad Khʷāfī, and Farrukhzād b. Quṭb al-Dīn of Tūlak). Nāṣir al-Dīn ʿUbaydallāh met with Abū Saʿīd, Chūpān, Tāj al-Dīn ʿAlī Shāh, and other high officials, and promoted Ghiyāth al-Dīn Kart's cause. He received from Tāj al-Dīn and Chūpān (on behalf of Ghiyāth al-Dīn) 50,000 dinars and *yarlīgh* "exempting (*muʿāf wa musallam*) for three years Heratis from the taxes [specific to sedentary and nomadic peoples] (*qalān wa qubchūr*), and the occasional taxes (*ʿawāriż-āt*) imposed by the *dīwān* of Khurasan."[112]

Abū Saʿīd's *yarlīgh* also conveyed to Ghiyāth al-Dīn chattels and estates (*asbāb wa amlāk*) of Quṭb al-Dīn Isfizārī, Majd al-Dīn Khʷāfī, Farrukhzād Tūlakī, et al.[113] According to the Timurid era chronicler, Faṣīḥ Khʷāfī, this stipulation was annulled by Abū Saʿīd when the parties appealed.[114] Irrespective of applicablity and veracity,[115] fear of expropriation and sanction, coupled to the ascent of Ghiyāth al-Dīn's star in the Ilkhanid court, focused the minds of *bandagān*, reinforced alliances between the Kartid court and its *bandagān*. Clients drawn from every rank—officials, viziers, amirs, *ṣadrs*,

112 al-Harawī, *Harāt*, 739–41. *Qubchūr*: see I.P. Petrushevsky [Petrushevskiĭ], *Kishāwarzī wa munāsabāt-i arżī dar Īrān-i ʿahd-i Mughūl*, tr. Karīm Kishāwarz, 2 vols (Tehran: Intishārāt-i nīl, 1347/1968), 2:691–710; Ryoko Watabe, "Census-taking and the *Qubchur* taxation system in Ilkhanid Iran," *Toyo Bunko* 73 (2015):27–63. Smith, "Mongol and Nomadic Taxation," 52–60: the tax applied to nomadic peoples; but cf. A.K.S. Lambton, "Mongol Fiscal Administration in Persia," *Studia Islamica* 64 (1986):79–99, esp. 92: "a levy or additional cess, which was imposed on the population on the basis of a poll-tax in addition to the ordinary or regular (traditional) taxes, and that it was sometimes also levied on the basis of the number of flocks owned [...]."

113 al-Harawī, *Harāt*, 741.

114 Faṣīḥ, *Mujmal*, 898; see also Kempiners, "Khurasan," 163–64.

115 Returning estates or dominion over homelands is simpler than returning liquid assets (cash, grains, jewels, etc.). The Kartid had bills to pay and it is unlikely that all (or any) of the seized assets were returned. See Chapter Nine, "Herat's Economy."

*qādīs*, Sufis, *bandagān*—appreciated that they could benefit by associating *voluntarily* with the Kartid court. *Bandagān* became less inclined to pursue independent agendas or destabilize the Kartid state.

Ghiyāth al-Dīn's consolidation campaign allowed him to solidify, and even extend, Kartid political hegemony.[116] The Kartid kingdom, by my appraisal, had hitherto never been as politically unified and as thoroughly dominated by Herat as it was from the post-Yasa'ur consolidation phase (*c.* 720/1320) to Ghiyāth al-Dīn Kart's death (in 729/1329).

The Hajj of 721/1321 was an occasion for Ghiyāth al-Dīn to showcase his newfound status to the notables and commoners of his kingdom.[117] He assembled a pilgrim caravan in Herat that included high government officials,[118] like Ikhtiyār al-Dīn Muḥammad Hārūn and Ṣadr al-Dīn Khaysārī, and more than 200 notables from Herat, Ghūr, Fūshanj, and Isfizār. The caravan departed Herat in Rajab 721. On reaching Turbat-i Jām, it was joined by Shaykh al-Islam Jāmī, his grandson Mu'īn al-Dīn Jāmī (d. 783/1382),[119] and other shaykhs of Jām. In Nishapur, Quṭb al-Dīn Yaḥyá Jāmī Nīshāpūrī (d. 740/1339), Chief Justice of Nishapur,[120] and other notables from Nishapur came aboard. In this manner, the caravan acquired notables and swelled to nearly 2,000 souls on its journey to Baghdad, where they were met by Abū Sa'īd and Chūpān. The sultan honored the Kart *malik* by appointing him to the prestigious role of "commander of the Hajj caravan" (*amīr al-ḥajj*), thereby making him responsible for safeguarding the wealthy and eminent pilgrims from predators (namely, Bedouins) during the arduous trek, and delivering the Il-Khan's *maḥmal* (ceremonial palanquin) and offerings.[121] The caravan reached Mecca. Hajj rituals were performed, and *ziyārat* made at the hallowed graves of Mecca and Medina. The caravan returned to Baghdad, where it was welcomed by throngs and Abū Sa'īd, Chūpān, and Tāj al-Dīn 'Alī Shāh.[122]

[116] First observed by Kempiners, "Khurasan," 164–67.

[117] al-Harawī, *Harāt*, 770 (uses the pro-forma "aforementioned year," 720/1320); cf. Ḥāfiẓ-i Abrū, *Kart*, 165, and Faṣīḥ, *Mujmal*, 899 (Hajj year is 721/1321).

[118] Caravan (*qāfila*) here means a train of horses (for men) and camels (for baggage).

[119] Future Kartid vizier, from 735/1334f. to nearly the end of the dynasty.

[120] Zanganah, *Sarzamīn-i Jām*, 137–39 (biography).

[121] A *maḥmal* may include a *kiswa* (decorative covering for the Ka'ba) as an offering.

[122] al-Harawī, *Harāt*, 768–73; Ḥāfiẓ-i Abrū, *Kart*, 165–67; Faṣīḥ, *Mujmal*, 899–90.

In 722/1322, Ghiyāth al-Dīn and his entourage returned to Herat. He received from the Il-Khan and Chūpān fresh honors (and probably cash, too); and (by Ḥāfiẓ-i Abrū's term) a *soyūrghāl*.[123] The *soyūrghāmīshī* (royal favor) probably allowed the *malik* (in my opinion) to collect or retain taxes (for a limited time) that were otherwise due to the Ilkhanid fisc. This in order to provide him funds for public works and agriculture. The *malik* went on a spending spree (see Chapters Eight and Nine). Sadly, 722/1322 is about when our diligent and loquacious Sayf al-Harawī expired, terminating abruptly his invaluable *History of Herat*. Ghiyāth al-Dīn's reign brought prosperity to Herat, new construction projects, and the restoration of venerable institutions like Herat's Friday Mosque.

## The Perfidious Kartids

I shall conclude by rejecting the label "perfidious Kartids" that has attached to the dynasty consequent to the Hindū Noyan, Nawrūz, and Chūpān affairs. Chūpān fell out with Abū Sa'īd and took shelter in Herat,[124] but was "betrayed" by Ghiyāth al-Dīn and killed in Muḥarram 728/November 1327.[125] Scholars, medieval and modern, have been reproachful in tone or word of Kartids as being "treacherous." This view is linear.

Fahkr al-Dīn and Ghiyāth al-Dīn Kart were *bandagān* of the Il-Khan and owed him for the *tangible* and *intangible* benefits (sgl. *ni'mah*) that they received from the Il-Khan *and* his agents. This type of loyalty, Roy Mottahedeh has demonstrated, falls within the category of "acquired loyalty."[126] Jürgen Paul parsed a critical dimension of loyalty: the twinned duties of fidelity (*wafā'*) and service (*khidma*).[127]

Thus, while Ghiyāth al-Dīn owned Chūpān Suldus *wafā'* and *khidma* for benefits, he had a higher level of *wafā'* and *khidma* to Abū Sa'īd than Chūpān: the well-spring for every imperial favor is the Il-Khan, even if the

[123] Ḥāfiẓ-i Abrū, *Kart*, 167. *Soyūrghāl* is anachronistic; the term was rarely used in Ilkhanid Persia. *Soyūrghāl* (benefice) is linked to the Mongolian word, *soyūrghāmīshī* ("favor"), and used alongside the Persian auxiliary verb, *kardan*: *soyūrghāmīshī kardan* ("to show favor").

[124] See Melville, *Chupan*, 19–28.

[125] Ḥāfiẓ-i Abrū, *Rashīdī*, 177–78; Ḥāfiẓ-i Abrū, *Kart*, 167–69; Mīrkhwānd, *Rawżat*, 4,376–80.

[126] *Acquired loyalty*: Roy Mottahedeh, *Loyalty and Leadership in an Early Islamic Community* (New York: I.B. Tauris, 2001), 72–84.

[127] Paul, "*Khidma*."

favor is decreed or implemented by a vizier. Fahkr al-Dīn owed a higher level of *wafā*ʾ and *khidma* to Ghāzān than to Nawrūz. Nawrūz owed Ghāzān *wafā*ʾ and *khidma*; Chūpān owed sultan Abū Saʿīd *wafā*ʾ and *khidma*. Both breached their covenants with their respective Il-Khan. Breaches of loyalty are often forgiven, but in some instances disloyalty demands the ultimate penalty.

Nothwithstanding the above, Shaykh al-Islam Shihāb al-Dīn Ismāʿīl Jāmī's advice to Fakhr al-Dīn on the Nawrūz affair applies to the Chūpān incident: "You must do something to remedy this situation; otherwise Herat and the whole realm of Khurasan will be lost over this affair." Pragmatism prevailed.

# Prolegomenon
# The Late Period: 729–83/1329–81

Muʿizz al-Dīn (Abū al-Ḥusayn) Muḥammad Kart, Ghiyāth al-Dīn's third son, ruled the Kartid state from 24 Ramażān 732/19 June 1332 to 5 Dhū al-Qaʿda 771/31 May 1370.[1] Despite youthful mistakes, he built on his father's foundations. Following the death of the last Il-Khan, Abū Saʿīd Bahādur Khān (13 Rabīʿ II 736/30 November 1335),[2] the Kartids became one of the independent Persian kingdoms that established themselves from Balkh to Āẕarbayjān and the Persian Gulf, the most prominent being Jalayirids (Īlkā or Ilkanid), Qara-Qoyunlu (and later, Aq-Qoyunlu), Sarbadarids,[3] and Muzaffarids.[4]

Ṭaghā-Temür (d. 754/1353), the nominal Il-Khan—or "Chinggisid pretender" as Charles Melville put it—was elected at a congress held in 737/1336 at Sulṭān-Maydān (in the Nishapur Quarter). He involved himself in the post-Ilkhanate struggles transpiring in western Persia. The absence of Ṭaghā-Temür's armies, and his vizier's exactions, fostered a rebellion in the Bayhaq district of Nishapur Quarter. Tax rebels morphed into the Sarbadarid dynasty. This confessionally mixed band allied with Shaykh Ḥasan Jūrī (d. 742/1342), a charismatic "Sufi" of indeterminable Shiʿi proclivities. The joint forces marched on Herat but were defeated. They remained a menace

1 Muḥammad Ismāʿīl Mablagh Gharjistānī, "Malik Muʿizz al-Dīn Ḥusayn [Part 1]," *Āryānā* No. 198 (1337/1958f.):25–30; idem, "Malik Muʿizz al-Dīn Ḥusayn [Part 2]," *Āryānā* No. 199 (1337/1958f.):25–28.

2 Key political actors of the east on the eve of Abū Saʿīd's death are identified in Ḥāfiẓ-i Abrū, *Zubdat al-tawārīkh*, ed. Kamāl Ḥājj Sayyid Jawādī, 4 vols (Tehran: Asāṭīr, 1395/2016), 1:63.

3 J.M. Smith, *The History of the Sarbadar Dynasty, 1336–1381 A.D. and its Sources* (The Hague: Mouton, 1970); Jean Aubin, "La fin de l'État Sarbadar du Khorassan," *Journal Asiatique* CCLXII [262] (1974):95–118.

4 John Limbert, *Shiraz in the Age of Hafez* (Seattle: University of Washington Press, 2004).

until Muʿizz al-Dīn established détente with their leader, Khwājah ʿAlī Muʾayyad (r. 764–83/1363–81).

Muʿizz al-Dīn came to rule his domains like an old-fashioned Persian *Padishah*. By this I mean that he tried to hew to *idealized* Persian concepts of kingship as articulated in pre-Islamic literature as *The Letter of Tansar*; and post-Islamic mirrors for princes.[5] On, for instance, the restoration of faith, where "a man of true and upright judgment" was needed "when corruption became rife and men ceased to submit to Religion, Reason and the State, and all sense of values disappeared,"[6] are ideals reflected in the Kartid's proclamation of independence dated 19 Jumādá I 750/5 August 1349, and his letters to Sultan Muḥammad b. Tughluq-Shāh (r. 724–52/1324–51) of the Delhi Sultanate.

The economy flourished because of Muʿizz al-Dīn's engagement with agricultural and hydrological policies: "[a king] will bring to pass that which concerns the advance of civilization, such as constructing underground channels, digging main canals, building bridges [...], rehabilitating villages and farms [...]."[7] This royal duty, Abū Ḥāmid al-Ghazālī, declares, was pre-Islamic in origin: "They [pre-Islamic kings] founded villages, excavated irrigation tunnels and brought out all the waters that were being wasted to give life to the land."[8] Muʿizz al-Dīn devised a methodology for the apportionment of waters. His system, having fallen into disuse under Temür (d. 807/1405), and son, Shāh-Rukh (r. 809–50/1407–47), was revived by the Timurid ruler, Sulṭān-Abū Saʿīd Mīrzā (r. 855–73/1451–69).[9] The Kartid funded construction projects, and instituted policies that seemingly improved social and religious life. His most important contribution to Persian and Islamic histories was his steadfast maintenance of peace between

[5] On the influence of Persian advice literature on Islamic ideals, see Patricia Crone, *Medieval Islamic Political Thought* (Edinburgh: Edinburgh University Press, 2005), 148–64.

[6] *The Letter of Tansar*, tr. Mary Boyce (Rome: Istituto Italiano per il Medio ed Estremo Oriente, 1968), 26–70 (quotes are from p.37 and p.40).

[7] Niẓām al-Mulk, *Siyāsatnāmah*, eds Muḥammad Qazwīnī and M. Chahārdahī (Tehran: Kitābfurūshī-yi Zawwār, 1344/1965), 8; idem, *Book of Government*, or *Rules for Kings (The Siyāsat-nāma or Siyar al-mulūk)*, tr. H. Darke (New Haven: Yale University Press, 1960), 10.

[8] Abū Ḥāmid al-Ghazālī Ṭūsī, *Naṣīḥat al-Mulūk*, ed. Jalāl Humāʾī (Tehran: Majlis, 1315/1937), 47–48; idem, *Ghazālī's Book of Counsel for Kings*, tr. F.R.C. Bagley (Oxford: Oxford University Press, 1964), 55.

[9] "Sulṭān" or "Shāh" are components of Timurid proper names; hence the hyphenation.

the Kartid kingdom and its neighbor to the west, the nascent Twelver Shiʿa Sarbadarid polity.

Muʿizz al-Dīn's favored son, Ghiyāth al-Dīn (Pīr ʿAlī) Kart (r. 771–83/1370–81), broke the détente and inflicted sectarian conflict on the Nishapur Quarter. Temür (r. 1370–1405), then planning his invasion of Khurasan, observed the weakened state of the Kartid military. Notables (*ashrāf wa aʿyān*), alarmed by the political, military, and economic harms wrought by Pīr ʿAlī's anti-Shiʿa campaigns; and preparations to resist Temür, secretly approached Temür to establish an accommodation to protect themselves and Herat.[10] Thusly did the notables of Khurasan ensure that the Kartid era expired (to borrow T.S. Eliot's words), "not with a bang but a whimper."

[10] Shivan Mahendrarajah, "Tamerlane's conquest of Herat and the 'politics of notables'," *Studia Iranica* 46/1 (2017):49–76. On "politics of notables," see Boaz Shoshan, "The 'Politics of Notables' in Medieval Islam," *Asian and African Studies* 20/2 (1986):179–215.

# 5

# From Ilkhanate to Independent Kingdom

## The Fading Ilkhanate and the Kartids

The Kartid kingdom bequeathed by Ghiyāth al-Dīn Kart to his son and heir,[1] Shams al-Dīn Kart (III) (r.*c.* 729–30/1329–30), was stable, prosperous, and encompassed (more or less) the lands itemized in Möngke's *yarlīgh* of 649/1251.[2] Shams al-Dīn had been appointed *qā'im-i maqām* (*locum tenens*) by his father during sundry absences. He was the anointed heir despite his alcoholism.[3] Ghiyāth al-Dīn had tried to curtail the crown prince's alcoholism, but once the father died, his drinking spun out of control. He died of "ill-health," surely, alcohol abuse. During his fleeting reign, security slipped.[4] His successor was Ghiyāth al-Dīn's second son, Ḥāfiẓ Muḥammad (r.*c.* 730–32/1330–32). He was of artistic bent and averse to governing. Ghurid amirs ran roughshod over him and ultimately assassinated him inside Herat's citadel.[5]

The next successor was Ghiyāth al-Dīn's third son, Mu'izz al-Dīn. He was instated by Ghurid power brokers. He secured for himself the customary robe of honor and diploma from sultan Abū Sa'īd. The youthful *malik* worked diligently and diplomatically to pull the support of the royal retinue and Kartid army's diverse constituents to his person—namely, the army's non-Ghurid elements (Herati, Baluch, Khalaj, Sijzī, Pashtun, Nikudari, Mongol)—to balance putative Ghurid opposition. He quelled the civil

[1] Faṣīḥ, *Mujmal*, 907 (death incorrectly noticed as AH 728).

[2] Sīstān was outside of Kartid control by 732/1332; the status of *Afghānistān* is unknown.

[3] Ghiyāth al-Dīn left a testament (*waṣiyyat-nāmah*) for Shams al-Dīn (III) before making the 721/1321 Hajj. al-Harawī, *Harāt*, 769–70; 'Abd al-Ḥayy Ḥabībī, "Waṣiyyat-nāmah-yi Malik Ghiyāth al-Dīn Kart," *Āryānā* No. 66 (1327/1948):38–42. It reads as advice for a crown prince.

[4] Ḥāfiẓ-i Abrū, *Kart*, 170; Isfizārī, *Rawżāt*, 2:1–4.

[5] Faṣīḥ, *Mujmal*, 909; Ḥāfiẓ-i Abrū, *Kart*, 170; Isfizārī, *Rawżāt*, 2:5.

unrest that had gripped Herat and its environs consequent to the rebellion of Ghurid units and regicide of his brother in 732/1332. He co-opted ulama to help impose a sense of direction and normalcy within the populace, by imposing, for instance, the Islamic duty "to promote the good and forbid the reprehensible" (*al-amr bi'l ma'rūf wa'l-nahy 'an al-munkar*),[6] through the hand of Shaykh al-Islam Niẓām al-Dīn 'Abd al-Raḥīm Mābīzhān-Ābādī (Khʷāfī) (d. 738/1337f.).[7]

The fraying of the Kartid state was not entirely the result of ineffectual leadership by Shams al-Dīn (III) or Ḥāfiẓ Muḥammad Kart. The Ilkhanate had been disintegrating in the last years of sultan Abū Sa'īd's reign.[8] This impacted upon the Kartid state at a critical juncture: the phase bracketed by the death of Ghiyāth al-Dīn and accession of Mu'izz al-Dīn. As Charles Melville showed, the 719/1319 "revolt of the amirs" was quashed and order reimposed by Chūpān;[9] but with Chūpān's execution in 727/1328, simmering rivalries boiled over.[10] Khurasan was an Ilkhanid "Elba island" (of sorts), where irritants to the Il-Khan's serenity, or agitators temporarily spared the executioner's blade, were exiled. Narīn-Taghā'ī (d. 729/1329) was such a person. He had advanced within the Ilkhanid *nomenklatura* following Chūpān's death, but his personality vexed the Il-Khan. He was appointed plenipotentiary for Khurasan and shunted to Herat, where he proceeded to aggravate Kartids by impinging on their prerogatives.

The "rebellion" of Narīn-Taghā'ī (see below) was one of a series of episodes in the waning years of the Ilkhanate, where various amirs challenged the Il-Khan's authority or usurped his prerogatives. Michael Hope has argued that the decline of the Il-Khan's powers and prerogatives can be traced to Öljeitü's death, when "the military aristocracy assumed full control of the Ilkhan[id] government, relegating the [Il-]khan to the status of a mere figurehead."[11] Although some may challenge Hope's characterizations of "full

6 On the obligation, see M.A. Cook, *Commanding Right and Forbidding Wrong in Islamic Thought* (Cambridge: Cambridge University Press, 2000).

7 Ḥāfiẓ-i Abrū, *Kart*, 171; Isfizārī, *Rawżāt*, 2:7. Mābīzhān-Ābād is a district in Khʷāf; both *nisbas* are used interchangeably. On this shaykh al-Islam of Herat, see Chapters Eight and Nine.

8 See Melville, *Chupan*, 29ff.

9 See Melville, "Revolt."

10 See Melville, *Chupan*, 30; Hope, *Power*, 192–96.

11 Hope, *Power*, 183.

control" and "mere figurehead," his inquiry does reveal that the Ilkhanate was weakened by internecine intrigues; and comports with Charles Melville's thesis of an intrinsically brittle Ilkhanate in the last decade of its existence, which shattered when struck by a force: the death of Abū Saʿīd.[12] Standing athwart the "decline and fall" paradigm is David Morgan, who argues that the Ilkhanate fell without declining: the principal reason for the collapse being the inability to form a consensus on the succession to the Ilkhanid throne in the absence of a male heir from Hülegü's line. Morgan is not "convinced that the reign of Abu Saʿid was qualitatively that much worse than many previous periods in Ilkhanid history."[13]

The sources on Abū Saʿīd's reign are weighted toward describing fascinating events: the political intrigues leading to the execution of vizier Rashīd al-Dīn; the salacious tale of the Il-Khan's infatuation with the delectable Baghdād Khātūn bt. Chūpān; and the fall of the house of Chūpān. Modern journalism's aphorism, "if it bleeds it leads," may explain the foci of histories about Abū Saʿīd's reign.[14] Medieval historians' narratives presumably skewed modern historians' perspectives. Irrespective of whether the Ilkhanate declined before it fell, or fell without declining, the Ilkhanate fragmented and slipped into history.[15]

## *Narīn-Taghāʾī*

The "revolt" of Narīn-Taghāʾī is given under 729/1329, the year Ghiyāth al-Dīn Kart died. Although Ghiyāth al-Dīn's actions are described in the beginning of Mīrkhʷānd's and Ḥāfiẓ-i Abrū's chronicles,[16] with Shams al-Dīn (III) identified as his *locum tenens* at Herat, my sense is that the Kartid died midway through the events.[17]

[12] Melville, *Chupan*, esp. 2–3, 29–30, 43.
[13] David Morgan, "The Decline and Fall of the Mongol Empire," *JRAS* 19/4 (2009):427–37, 433.
[14] An example is Mustawfī's narrative, dedicated almost exclusively to events at court. al-Qazwīnī/Rawshan, *Tārīkh-i guzīda*, 2:539–50.
[15] On disintegration in the west, see Patrick Wing, "The Decline of the Ilkhanate and the Mamluk Sultanate's Eastern Frontier," *Mamluk Studies Review* 11/2 (2007):77–88.
[16] Mīrkhʷānd, *Rawżat*, 4,388–92; Ḥāfiẓ-i Abrū, *Ẕayl-i jāmiʿ al-tāwarīkh-i Rashīdī* (London: British Library, Or. 2885), f. 418ᵃ–420ᵃ; cf. Ḥāfiẓ-i Abrū, *Rashīdī*, 185–86 (Bayānī ed.). There are key textual differences between MS Or. 2885 and Bayānī's edition.
[17] Ḥāfiẓ-i Abrū, *Kart*, 169–70 (he skips over events regarding Narīn-Taghāʾī).

Narīn-Taghā'ī established winter quarters (*qishlāq*) in Mazandaran. He wanted the (Mongol?) *tümen* that had been attached to the Karts to be transferred to him. Ghiyāth al-Dīn went to him and spoke diplomatically, sought permission to leave—then dashed to Iraq and secured a *yarlīgh* from Abū Sa'īd confirming his authority over the *tümen*. Infuriated, Narīn-Taghā'ī dispatched envoys to Shams al-Dīn (III) demanding obeisance. They returned empty-handed. Narīn-Taghā'ī dispatched troops to seize Shams al-Dīn, which they failed to do. The last we read of Ghiyāth al-Dīn is of him hurrying back to Herat from Abū Sa'īd's *urdū*. Narīn-Taghā'ī sacked Nishapur and headed toward Baghdad seeking an audience with Abū Sa'īd.[18] Ultimately, his intrigues, and destructive activities in Khurasan, caught up with him. Narīn-Taghā'ī's head joined similar adornments to the ramparts of Sulṭāniyya.[19]

Ghiyāth al-Dīn apparently expired on his return to Herat.[20] Since he was devoted to Aḥmad-i Jām, the Sufis of Jām claim that Ghiyāth al-Dīn is interred in the *Kirmani Mosque*, one of the three magnificent buildings that he commissioned at the shrine-complex.[21] Since there is no inscription to the tomb shown to this author, their avowal is plausible (if he died in proximity to Turbat-i Jām), but unverifiable.

Around 729–30/1329–30, Abū Sa'īd appointed Amir Shaykh-'Alī (d. 737/1337) b. 'Alī Qūshchī as the governor of Khurasan;[22] and promoted 'Alā' al-Dīn Muḥammad Faryūmadī (d. 27 Sha'bān 742/5 February 1342) to vizier. He tasked the pair with repairing the damage wreaked by Narīn-Taghā'ī.[23] The appointments reflect a lack of confidence in Shams al-Dīn Kart (III) or Ḥāfiẓ Muḥammad (whoever was then in office). Faryūmadī was a competent administrator; whereas Ghiyāth al-Dīn's first two successors were incompetents. Faryūmadī was intimate with the Jāmī Sufis; he sponsored a seminary at Aḥmad-i Jām's shrine.

18 Mīrkhʷānd, *Rawżat*, 4,388–90.

19 Melville, *Chupan*, 33–34.

20 Ḥāfiẓ-i Abrū/London (Or. 2885), *Rashīdī*, f. 420ᵃ, says he died at Herat.

21 Mahendrarajah, *Sufi Saint*, Chapter 5.

22 On him, see Melville, *Chupan*, 31, n.85, and 32, Table 3.

23 Ḥāfiẓ-i Abrū, *Rashīdī*, 186; Mīrkhʷānd, *Rawżat*, 4,393.

David Morgan noted that in the absence of an external enemy, armies "are liable to start breaking up the furniture at home."[24] An *external foe* is ideal for roving bandits: raiding of Jochid, Chaghataid, or Mamluk lands, with the wealth—women, slaves, livestock, grains, gold, gems, etc.—ported *into* the Ilkhanate, thereby enriching local economies. However, if the external foe is powerful, and raiding cannot be conducted across frontiers, then troops will plunder *internal* targets.[25] This may explain Narīn-Taghā'ī's sack of Nishapur. His men had been denied entry into Herat—therefore its portable wealth—so he let them rape and pillage in Nishapur. An amir who did not feed his people through pillage and mayhem was unlikely to remain their amir for long. It is fairer to say that Narīn-Taghā'ī was *paying* his troops than to say he was in *rebellion* against Abū Sa'īd.

### *Chupanid-Jalayirid Struggles in the West*

The struggles for supremacy out west bear noting because Khurasanian amirs—Ṭaghā-Temür, the new "Il-Khan" of Khurasan (below); Arghūn-Shāh of the Jawni-Qurban; and Ilkhanid governor, Shaykh-'Alī b. 'Alī Qūshchī—stuck their oars into Western waters, which impacted adversely on the Nishapur Quarter. It can be argued that the Kartids and Herat Quarter benefited (to some degree) from Ṭaghā-Temür's distractions.

There was no single viable candidate for the Ilkhanid throne following Abū Sa'īd's death, that is, a consensus candidate did not emerge from among the contenders. Arpa Ke'un (r. 736/1335–36) of Tolui's line through fourth son, Arïgh Böke, stepped into the breach to confront the Golden Horde: the Horde had invaded Āẕarbayjān about two months before Abū Sa'īd died. To reinforce his claim to the throne, he married Abū Sa'īd's half-sister, Sāṭī Beg bt. Öljeitü, who was Amir Chūpān's widow. He released amirs jailed by Abū Sa'īd, but also executed amirs and princelings. However, his execution of Abū Sa'īd's principal wife, Baghdād Khātūn (d. 736/1336), on the allegation

[24] Morgan, "Decline," 431 and n.12.

[25] Cross-border raiding by Pashtun tribes propelled the Durrani confederation to power and wealth under Aḥmad Shāh Durranī (d. 1772). See Barfield, *Afghanistan*, 97–103. Their raiding was constrained in the nineteenth century when Afghanistan's frontiers with wealthier neighbors (Persia, Russia, India) became borders. Pashtun tribes resorted to *internal plunder*. This, accompanied by inter-tribal feuds and "tanistry" (to adopt Joseph Fletcher's reformulation of a Celtic institution), led to cycles of instability, chaos, and conflict.

of regicide (by poisoning); and turning his sights on Abū Saʿīd's pregnant young wife, Dilshād Khātūn (Chūpān's granddaughter), was to prove his undoing. Ḥajjī Khātūn, Abū Saʿīd's mother, opposed Arpa Keʾun; she sent her daughter-in-law to her (i.e., Ḥajjī Khātūn's) brother, ʿAlī-Pādishāh, in Diyarbakr (and there gave birth to a daughter). ʿAlī-Pādishāh installed Mūsá Khan, one of Baidū's grandsons on the throne and marched against Arpa Keʾun. Following defections and clashes, Arpa Keʾun capitulated. Vizier Ghiyāth al-Dīn Muḥammad b. Rashīd al-Dīn Fażlallāh was executed on 21 Ramażān 736/3 May 1336; Arpa Keʾun was executed on 3 Shawwāl 736/15 May 1336. ʿAlī-Pādishāh (d. Dhū al-Ḥijja 736/July 1336) briefly took control of parts of the west.[26]

The Chupanids witnessed an ephemeral revival of fortunes.[27] They had to contend with the Jalayrids, who subsequently swallowed their territories in Āẕarbayjān, Armenia, and Iraq. A sketch of the Chupanids and Jalayrids in the wake of Abū Saʿīd's death suffices to frame the political background in western Iran, which stands in contrast to the *relatively* orderly political transition in Khurasan. The Chupanids were of the Turco-Mongol Suldus tribe; the Jalayir tribe apparently originated in Mongolia.[28] Jalayirs served Il-Khans; for instance, the Amir Ḥusayn (d. 722/1322) who had been dispatched to Khurasan to assist Ghiyāth al-Dīn Kart. Ḥusayn had two distinct marital links to Öljeitü, who held him in favor, but not so at Abū Saʿīd's court, where the Chupanids dominated. Ḥusayn's son, Ḥasan, was married to Baghdād Khātūn, but had been forced to renounce her as a consequence of Abū Saʿīd's passion for her. The Chupanid-Jalayirid rivalry was between two Chupanid lines: one descending from Temürtāsh (d. 728/1328) b. Chūpān; the second descending from Dimashq Khwāja (d. 727/1327) b. Chūpān. The sons of Temürtāsh, namely, Ḥasan (d. 27 Rajab 744/15 December 1343), were pitted against the newest husband of Dilshād Khātūn bt. Dimashq Khwaja: Ḥasan Jalayir (d. Rajab 757/July 1356).[29]

[26] Faṣīḥ, *Mujmal*, 913–14; Ḥāfiẓ-i Abrū, *Rashīdī*, 191–97; Mīrkhʷānd, *Rawżat*, 4,398–405; Ahari/van Loon, *Uwais*, 59–63; Melville, *Chupan*, 44–53; Wing, *Jalayirids*, 75–77; Peter Jackson, "Arpā Khan," *EIr*, 2:518–19.

[27] Michael Hope, "The Political Configuration of Late Ilkhanid Iran: A Case Study of the Chubanid Amirate (738–758/1337–1357)," *Iran* 60 (forthcoming).

[28] See Wing, *Jalayirids*, 29ff.

[29] See genealogical figures in ibid., 66, 68, 69 (esp. Fig. 4.4), 209.

Ḥasan Jalayir raised the banner against ʿAlī-Pādishāh and his puppet, Mūsá Khan. ʿAlī-Pādishāh was killed and Mūsá Khan put to flight. Ḥasan installed Muḥammad Khan at Tabriz as his Chinggisid puppet; and married Dilshād Khātūn (who bore him Shaykh-Uways; he would lead the Jalayirid dynasty to its political apogee). Standing against Ḥasan Jalayir was Ḥasan b. Temürtāsh, who acquired the sobriquet Ḥasan-i Kūchik ("Little Ḥasan") to distinguish him from Ḥasan Jalayir, now nicknamed Ḥasan-i Buzūrg ("Big Ḥasan"). Ḥasan-i Kūchik installed Sāṭī Beg as his puppet. The Ḥasans battled for territories in Anatolia, Iraq, and western Persia.[30]

*The Congress at Sulṭān-Maydān*

The transition in Khurasan to independent kingdoms, in contrast to the events in the west, was fairly orderly. The transition manifested in a congress.[31] This consultative assembly was dubbed a *quriltai* by one medieval chronicler;[32] but whether it was convened under, and adhered to, the protocols of a Mongol *quriltai*,[33] awaits inquiry. Let us consider it a congress, where regional potentates (amirs and *maliks*); administrators and viziers; and prominent religious leaders (Sufis, judges, shaykhs al-Islam), met to discuss pressing affairs and establish political parameters. The congress was held late autumn 737/1336 at Sulṭān-Maydān in the mountains north of Nishapur.[34] It was convoked by the terminal Ilkhanid governor of Khurasan, Shaykh-ʿAlī b. ʿAlī Qūshchī.[35]

Attendees included the Jawni-Qurban, represented by Arghūn-Shāh (d. 743/1343 or 746/1345f.) b. Nawrūz (or b. Orday) b. (the *basqaq*) Arghūn

[30] Ibid., 65–94; C.P. Melville and ʿAbbas Zaryab, "Chobanids," *EIr*, 5:496–502; Peter Jackson, "Jalayerids," *EIr*, 14:415–19.

[31] Muḥammad b. ʿAlī b. Muḥammad Shabānkārāʾī, *Majmaʿ al-ansāb*, ed. Mīr-Hāshim Muḥaddis̱ (Tehran: Amīr Kabīr, 1363/1984), 306ff. Appended is Ghiyāth al-Dīn Faryūmadī's *Ẕayl*-i *Majmaʿ al-ansāb* (pp. 339–49). Hereinafter, "Faryūmadī, *Ẕayl*, __." I am indebted to Prof. Peter Jackson for his elucidations on the authorship of *Majmaʿ al-ansāb* and *Ẕayl*.

[32] See Jean Aubin, "Le Quriltai de Sultân-Maydân (1336)," *Journal Asiatique* 279 (1991):175–97, 181 and n.13 (classification as *quriltai* is by Shabānkārāʾī).

[33] Michael Hope, "The Transmission of Authority through the Quriltais of the Early Mongol Empire and the Īlkhānate of Iran (1227–1335)," *Mongolian Studies* 34 (2012):87–115.

[34] Sulṭān-Maydān: Jean Aubin, "Réseau pastoral et réseau caravanier: les grand'routes du Khorassan à l'époque mongole," in *Études sur l'Iran médiéval: géographie historique et société*, ed. Denise Aigle (Paris: Association pour l'avancement des études iraniennes, 2018), 91–113.

[35] Shabānkārāʾī, *Majmaʿ*, 306–07 (on the convocation and attendees).

Aga (d. 673/1275); other amirs of the Nawruz clan (*umarā-yi Nawrūzī*); amirs from (among other locales), Gunābād (in Khʷāf), Isfarāyn, Jām, Rayy, and Ṭūs.[36] Political elites included Muʿizz al-Dīn Muḥammad Kart;[37] the descendants of ʿAlāʾ al-Dīn Hindū (d. 722/1322f.); and ʿAlāʾ al-Dīn Muḥammad Faryūmadī (d. 742/1342) and his retinue.

The most fascinating component, which lent the congress its unique political-social flavor, was representation by five prominent Khurasanian Sufi families: Sufi shaykhs from Baḥrābad,[38] Bisṭam, Chisht-i Sharīf, Turbat-i Jām, and Mayhana/Mihna. The identity of the Baḥrābad shaykh is not disclosed: Ṣadr al-Dīn Ibrāhīm Ḥammūya (d. 722/1322) officiated at Maḥmūd Ghāzān Khan's conversion,[39] but his son, Saʿd al-Dīn Yūsuf Ḥammūya, died before the Sulṭān-Maydān congress.[40] Sharaf al-Dīn Bisṭam (n.d.) represented the line of Bāyazīd. The saint's tomb at Bisṭam was patronized by Öljeitü; probably Ghāzān, too.[41] Quṭb al-Dīn Aḥmad Chishtī (whom we have met),[42] represented the heirs of Quṭb al-Dīn Mawdūd Chishtī (d. 533/1139). Shaykh al-Islam Shihāb al-Dīn Ismāʿīl Jāmī (d.*c.* 738/1338), and Quṭb al-Dīn Yaḥyá Jāmī Nīshāpūrī (d. 740/1339), Chief Justice of Nishapur,[43] represented the Sufis of Jām. The family of Abū Saʿīd b. Abū al-Khayr (d. 440/1049) of Mayhana (in Turkmenistan), was represented by Quṭb al-Dīn Fażlallāh (d. 782/1380f.) b. Shams al-Dīn Muʾayyad.[44] The progeny of Aḥmad-i Jām and Abū Saʿīd b. Abū al-Khayr were patronized by Timurids. The two Sufi families remained intimates into the dawn of the Safawid age.

[36] Commentary on attendees is in Aubin, "Sultân-Maydân," 181–84.

[37] The *malik* was probably accompanied by vizier Muʿīn al-Dīn Jāmī (d. 783/1382). He was descended from Aḥmad-i Jām. Appointed vizier in 735/1334f. Yūsuf-i Ahl/Moayyad (ed.), *Farāʾid-i Ghīyāṣī*, 1:241–44, 241 (letter referencing his relocation from Turbat-i Jām to Herat in 735/1334–35 following his appointment to the vizierate).

[38] Jamal Elias "The Sufi Lords of Bahrabad: Saʿd al-Din and Sadr al-Din Hamuwayi," *Iranian Studies* 27/1 (1994):53–75.

[39] Melville, "Pādshāh-i Islām."

[40] Elias "Sufi," 57 (genealogy); Faṣīḥ, *Mujmal*, 916.

[41] Donald Wilber, *The Architecture of Islamic Iran: The Il Khanid Period* (Princeton: Princeton University Press, 1955), 127–28; Cat. No. 28, Plates, 32–40. Work was done at the shrine in Ghāzān's reign. Ghāzān's and Öljeitü's names appear on inscriptions.

[42] Shabānkārāʾī, *Majmaʿ*, 306: name given as Aḥmad Bust, a copyist's error. Re-arranging the dots for consonants *b-s-t* yields *ch-sh-t*, which is precisely how it is read by Jean Aubin in "Sultân-Maydân," 187–88.

[43] On Jāmī Nīshāpūrī, see Būzjānī, *Rawżat*, 115–18; Mahendrarajah, *Sufi Saint*, 112 n.61 and Appendix 1, Fig. A1.2.

[44] Faṣīḥ, *Mujmal*, 872, 978–79.

Absent from Shabānkārāʾī's list is a known representative of the family of Herat's "patron saint," ʿAbdallāh Anṣārī (d. 481/1089). This reflects either their diminished political status in pre-Timurid Khurasan, or their political quiescence. Shihāb al-Dīn Ismāʿīl Jāmī and Quṭb al-Dīn Aḥmad Chishtī had intervened to resolve political crises. There is no intimation in the sources of participation in Herat's politics by a member of the Anṣārī clan.

*Ṭaghā-Temür*

The outcome of the congress was the elevation of Ṭaghā-Temür (d. 754/1353)—a descendant of Chingiz Khan's brother, Jochi Qasar—to Ilkhanid suzerain.[45] Steppe protocols demanded that independent monarchs honor Chingiz Khan's legacy through the erection of a legal façade: the installation of a Chinggisid suzerain. Temür titled himself amir and ruled through a nominal Chinggisid, Sulṭān-Maḥmūd Khan. Ṭaghā-Temür was this sort of figurehead. His strengths lay in western Khurasan and eastern Mazandaran, with his base at Astarabad. Jawni-Qurban dominated a sliver of land formed by four points: Nishapur, Nisā, Abīward, and Mashhad-Ṭūs (but lost control of Nishapur by 749/1348f.).[46] They were sandwiched between Ṭaghā-Temür's domains and the Kartid kingdom.

Ṭaghā-Temür, not appreciating his manifold limitations, aspired for greatness. He entangled himself in the battle of the Ḥasans unfolding in the west.[47] He tried to involve himself in Kartid affairs: Ḥāfiẓ-i Abrū noted tersely that "*malik* Muʿizz al-Dīn did not allow him [Ṭaghā-Temür] to interfere with the wealth or affairs of Herat and its vicinities."[48] Ṭaghā-Temür probably assumed that as suzerain, he was entitled to a share of Kartid tax revenues; but the Kartid, apparently confident of the support of his army, rejected Ṭaghā-Temür's demand. He softened the blow by marrying Sulṭān-Khātūn (fl. 783/1381) bt. Ṭaghā-Temür. The last Kart ruler, Ghiyāth al-Dīn (Pīr ʿAlī) Kart (b.*c*. 738/1338; r. 771–83/1370–81), was the product of their marital union.

45 Ḥāfiẓ-i Abrū, *Cinq Opuscules de Ḥāfiẓ-i Abrū*, ed. Felix Tauer (Prague: l'Académie Tchécoslovaque des Sciences, 1959), 5–8 (essay on Ṭaghā-Temür).

46 Ibid., Notes, p.17 (Tauer's "Commentaire" section).

47 See Ḥāfiẓ-i Abrū, *Zubdat*, 1:65–67; Melville, *Chupan*, 53–59; Smith, *Sarbadar*, 68–71.

48 Ḥāfiẓ-i Abrū, *Kart*, 172. The Kartid may have paid nominal tribute.

Ṭaghā-Temür's involvement in Chupanid-Jalayirid struggles spared Mu'izz al-Dīn his father-in-law's interference in Kartid affairs, but the absence of his (nominal) suzerain's armies spawned a new threat to Ṭaghā-Temür, Jawni-Qurban, and Kartids.

## Emergence of the Sarbadars

Sarbadars began life as a tax revolt, *c.* 736–37/1336–37, in Bāshtīn, a dependency of Sabzavar, the largest city in Bayhaq district of Nishapur Quarter. They were resisting tax mandates by 'Alā' al-Dīn Faryūmadī, Ṭaghā-Temür's fiscal manager. The Sarbadars' origins, despite hagiological tales,[49] were profane. 'Abd al-Razzāq Bāshtīnī (d. 738/1338), scion of a landowning family, rallied Bāshtīnī tax resisters. The rebels captured Sabzavar in 738/1337, which became their base. Political disorder and deterioration of security persisted in parts of Khurasan consequent to Abū Sa'īd's death. Bāshtīnī rebels took advantage of prevailing conditions and transformed from rebels to roving bandits. "Sarbadar" refers to the band's vocation, and the fate of captured highwaymen: *sar-ba-dār*: "head-on-the [executioner's] block." Their banditry exacerbated social-political problems in parts of Nishapur Quarter. Ṭaghā-Temür was focused on the west, thereby allowing the bandits to prosper.

### *Ṭaghā-Temür's Misadventures*

Ṭaghā-Temür and Arghūn-Shāh had marched their armies in mid-737/early 1337 at the behest of Shaykh-'Alī to join the fight in Āẕarbayjān. Arghūn-Shāh, however, withdrew midway. The combined armies occupied Sulṭāniyya in spring 737/1337, but were ejected by Ḥasan-i Buzūrg in summer 737/1337. Ṭaghā-Temür and Shaykh-'Alī retreated to Khurasan, where Arghūn-Shāh was waiting. Arghūn-Shāh had not been favorably disposed to Shaykh-'Alī, now weakened by the misadventure. Arghūn-Shāh executed Shaykh-'Alī (in 737/1337); and imprisoned Ṭaghā-Temür, but re-installed him in 739/1338 at the behest of Quṭb al-Dīn Yaḥyá Jāmī Nīshāpūrī, 'Alā' al-Dīn Faryūmadī,

[49] The (lost) *Tārīkh-i Sarbadār-ān* propagated a charming Shi'i-themed story. Two brothers, Ḥasan and Ḥusayn (of course!) took umbrage at the "un-Islamic" demands of tax-collectors (for wine, women, and boys), slew the offenders and sparked a popular uprising.

et al.[50] Yaḥyá was a supporter as evinced by this report, and an anodyne advice letter from him to Ṭaghā-Temür.[51]

ʿAlāʾ al-Dīn Faryūmadī raised taxes to pay for Ṭaghā-Temür's expedition.[52] If, as Ḥāfiẓ-i Abrū has maintained, Muʿizz al-Dīn did not allow Ṭaghā-Temür a share of Herat's revenues, it is likely that Arghūn-Shāh did not share his revenues either. Why would he? He had jailed the "Il-Khan" and executed his ally, Shaykh-ʿAlī. Faryūmadī had to extract more money from a shrunken tax base (Khurasan minus Kartid domains minus Jawni-Qurban domains); hence the squeeze on Bayhaq.

### *The Sarbadars Ally with Shiʿi Extremists*

The Bāshtīnī bandits were now led by Wajīh al-Dīn Maʿsūd (r. 738–45/1338–44), who had murdered his brother, ʿAbd al-Razzāq.[53] The deceased had been disinclined to establish a polity. He had instead relentlessly pursued a vendetta against Faryūmadī, even pillaging the vizier's homeland, Faryūmad.[54] Wajīh al-Dīn Maʿsūd had ambitions that transcended banditry. He took control of the Sarbadars to furnish the band with political objectives, and thereby change its trajectory.

The Sarbadars' successes were connected to the absences of Ṭaghā-Temür's army: his participation in a campaign with Arghūn-Shāh in 738/1337 against Quhistān's ruler, Muḥammad Mawlāy;[55] and a venture in 739/1339 in support of Ḥasan-i Buzūrg. Sāṭī Beg bt. Öljeitü, a pitiful pawn in Jalayirid-Chupanid struggles,[56] was installed at Arrān in 739/1338 as Ḥasan-i Kūchik's fictional Il-Khan,[57] his counterpoise to Ṭaghā-Temür (Ḥasan-i Buzūrg's "Il-Khan"). Ṭaghā-Temür and Arghūn-Shāh, however, hastily withdrew to Khurasan in 739–40/early summer 1339 following a rift with Ḥasan-i

50 Smith, *Sarbadar*, 97–98 and n.26; Peter Jackson, "Toḡa Timur," *EIr* (online only); Ahari/van Loon, *Uwais*, 63–64; Ḥāfiẓ-i Abrū, *Rashīdī*, 200–201; Shabānkāraʾī, *Majmaʿ*, 309–10. See also al-Qazwīnī/Rawshan, *Tārīkh-i guzīda*, 2:559–64 (on Ṭaghā-Temür).

51 Yūsuf-i Ahl/Moayyad (ed.), *Farāʾid*, 1:83–85.

52 See Smith, *Sarbadars*, 94–96, 101–104 (on Faryūmadī and taxation).

53 Ḥāfiẓ-i Abrū, *Cinq*, 18; Mīrkhʷānd, *Rawżat*, 4,497; Faryūmadī, *Ẕayl*, 347.

54 Dawlatshāh al-Samarqandī, *Tadhkirat al-shuʿarāʾ*, ed. E.G. Browne (Leiden: Brill, 1900), 279; Faṣīḥ, *Mujmal*, 917. See also Smith, *Sarbadar*, 106–07.

55 Ahari/van Loon, *Uwais*, 65.

56 Wing, *Jalayirids*, 75, 85, 87–88.

57 Ahari/van Loon, *Uwais*, 67–68; Ḥāfiẓ-i Abrū, *Rashīdī*, 204–05; Wing, *Jalayirids*, 87.

Buzūrg, who was informed by Ḥasan-i Kūchik that Ṭaghā-Temür had communicated with him and promised him fealty.[58] Ḥasan-i Buzūrg was incensed by the betrayal and terminated dealings with the Khurasanians. Wajīh al-Dīn Maʿsūd recognized Ḥasan-i Kūchik's rule.

Wajīh al-Dīn Maʿsūd allied with a "Sufi" of Shiʿi proclivities, Shaykh Ḥasan Jūrī (d. 742/1342). Jūrī had traveled to Sabzavar to become an acolyte of a charismatic preacher, Shaykh Khalīfa (d. 22 Rabīʿ I 736/9 November 1335). When Khalīfa died by hanging (at the hands of persons unknown), Jūrī took charge of Khalīfa's group. Shaykh and darwishes departed Sabzavar and traveled to Nishapur Quarter. The shaykh's preaching attracted crowds and garnered him the suspicion of ulama and sayyids of Nishapur and Mashhad-Ṭūs. They complained to the political authorities, to wit, Muḥammad Bīk (d. 774/1373) b. Arghūn-Shāh, that Ḥasan Jūrī and his men were arming and preparing for war; that Jūrī had instructed his adherents thusly: "now is the time for concealment" (*waqt-i ikhfā*); live normally but when he gave the signal at the "time of the Advent" (*waqt-i ẓuhūr*), to wage war.[59] Jūrī was jailed by the Jawni-Qurban. Wajīh al-Dīn Maʿsūd, recognizing the political potential of the preacher, launched a successful operation to free him.

Around 741–42/1340–42, by John Masson Smith's estimation,[60] with which I concur, the fusion of the *Sarbadar* cluster and the *Shaykhiyya* cluster had yielded a confessionally mixed entity, about half-Shiʿi and half-Sunni. The Shiʿism espoused is unclear, but evidence of Shiʿi *ghuluww* by the Shaykhiyya is manifest.[61] The Sarbadar-Shaykhiyya amalgam had not fused conflicting ideologies, but had agreed on political objectives. In *c.* 741/1340, the Sarbadar-Shaykhiyya coalition seized Nishapur from the Jawni-Qurban, obliging Arghūn-Shāh's officials to flee to Mashhad-Ṭūs.[62] Ṭaghā-Temür belatedly recognized the threat. He dispatched an army under his brother, ʿAli Kāwūn (d. Shaʿbān 742/February 1342). They clashed at Bayhaq.

[58] Ahari/van Loon, *Uwais*, 67–68; Ḥāfiẓ-i Abrū, *Rashīdī*, 206–08; Wing, *Jalayirids*, 88.

[59] Ḥāfiẓ-i Abrū, *Cinq*, 16; Smith, *Sarbadar*, 55–60; Shivan Mahendrarajah, "The Sarbadars of Sabzavar: Re-examining their 'Shiʿa' roots and alleged goal to 'destroy Khurasanian Sunnism'," *Journal of Shiʿa Islamic Studies* 5/4 (2012):379–402, 387–90.

[60] Smith, *Sarbadar*, 119. See also I.P. Petruchevsky, *Nahżat-i Sarbadārān-i Khurāsān*, tr. Karīm Kishāwarz (Tehran: Intishārāt-i Payām, 1351/1972), 57–60.

[61] On *ghuluww* (extremism) and *ghulat* (extremists), see Moojan Momen, *An Introduction to Shiʿi Islam* (London: Yale University Press, 1985), 45, 65–71, 99–104.

[62] Ḥāfiẓ-i Abrū, *Cinq*, 19; Smith, *Sarbadar*, 114–15.

Ṭaghā-Temür's army was trounced and ʿAli Kāwūn killed. The Sarbadar-Shaykhiyya coalition pursued Ṭaghā-Temür's fighters and court officials into Mazandaran, which is how vizier ʿAlāʾ al-Dīn Faryūmadī met his demise.[63]

## The Sunni-Shiʿi Coalition Targets the Kartids

The Sarbadar-Shaykhiyya reaped dividends from their victory. Ḥāfiẓ-i Abrū wrote of their fame spreading far and wide, of notables and commoners, Turk and Tajik, submitting to their rule.[64] An exaggeration, but illustrative of the Sarbadars' vault from highwaymen to political contenders. The Sunni-Shiʿi coalition turned its sights on Herat (or so the sources claim). The western part of the Kartid realm was in danger but not the fortified city. Muʿizz al-Dīn Kart could have hunkered behind Herat's defenses, but his father had been criticized by *bandagān* for hunkering in Herat while Yasaʾur ravaged their homelands,[65] sallying only when he had the advantage. Muʿizz al-Dīn decided not to allow the Sarbadar-Shaykhiyya coalition to pillage his domains. A fair reading of Ḥāfiẓ-i Abrū's statement that Muʿizz al-Dīn had defended Herat *and* its vicinities from the Sarbadars prior to their clash at Zāwa,[66] bolsters the assessment that the *malik* ventured *c.* 180 miles/290 km from Herat to prevent harm from befalling his kingdom's agricultural regions. He sought also to protect the Sunni shrine at Turbat-i Jām from possible attack by Shiʿi extremists. The sepulcher of Aḥmad-i Jām had been significant to his ancestors (but not to him).[67] It was sacred space to notables in the Kartid court, including Muʿizz al-Dīn's vizier/nephew, Khʷājah Muʿīn al-Dīn Jāmī, who accompanied the king on the Zāwa campaign.

### *Battle of Zāwa*

In Ṣafar 743/July 1342, Muʿizz al-Dīn sortied to confront the Sarbadar-Shaykhiyya coalition at Zāwa.[68] The Kartid expeditionary army included

[63] Ḥāfiẓ-i Abrū, *Cinq*, 23–24; Mīrkhʷānd, *Rawżat*, 4,509–511; Faṣīḥ, *Mujmal*, 926; Petruchevsky, *Sarbadārān*, 67; Smith, *Sarbadar*, 114–16 and nn.47, 49, and 52.

[64] Ḥāfiẓ-i Abrū, *Cinq*, 24.

[65] Faṣīḥ, *Mujmal*, 898.

[66] Ḥāfiẓ-i Abrū, *Kart*, 172–76.

[67] Muʿizz al-Dīn was not a devotee of Aḥmad-i Jām. Mahendrarajah, *Sufi Saint*, 63–65, 109.

[68] Zāwa: see Krawulsky, *Ḫorāsān*, 1:41; Le Strange, *Lands*, 356. It is *c.* 80 miles/128 km west of Turbat-i Jām and *c.* 70 miles/112 km southeast of Nishapur. The region is known today for Turbat-i Ḥaydariyya (the "tomb of [Shaykh] Ḥaydar").

Baluch, Gharjistani, Ghurid, Khalaj, Nikudari, Sistani, and "Tajik and Turk" units.[69] Battle was joined on 13 Ṣafar 743/18 July 1342. The Sarbadar-Shaykhiyya coalition had the upper hand, initially, but Kartids emerged victorious;[70] even capturing the Sarbadars' court poet, Ibn Yamīn Faryūmadī (d. 8 Jumādá II 769/30 January 1368).[71] When the Sarbadars thought victory was near, a Sarbadar warrior intentionally killed Ḥasan Jūrī.[72] Shaykhiyya became demoralized by their shaykh's death, which allowed the Kartids to rally and triumph.

Muʿizz al-Dīn Kart had a resounding triumph to his credit, which fueled the young king's hubris and moved him into making unpropitious political choices (Chapter Six). The border between the Kartid and Sarbadarid realms settled west of the shrine city, Turbat-i Jam. The borders remained thus until Temür's invasions of Khurasan in 782–83/1380–81, when the boundaries of regional kingdoms were erased.

### *Kartid-Sarbadarid Relations, 1342–63*

"By attacking Shaykh Ḥasan too openly, the assassin made it plain that this was murder [. . .]. The dervishes consequently withdrew from further cooperation with [Wajīh al-Dīn] Maʿsūd."[73] ʿIzz al-Dīn Sūgandī (n.d.),[74] Jūrī's acolyte, became his successor. On 27 Dhū al-Qaʿda 743/23 April 1343, Sūgandī decamped for Āmul and Sārī in Mazandaran.[75] Wajīh al-Dīn Maʿsūd also went to Mazandaran, but for reasons unclear: was he raiding or pursuing Shaykhiyya? In any event, he was captured and executed in 745/1344.[76]

69 Ḥāfiẓ-i Abrū, *Kart*, 173; Ḥāfiẓ-i Abrū, *Cinq*, 32.

70 Ḥāfiẓ-i Abrū, *Kart*, 172–76; Ḥāfiẓ-i Abrū, *Cinq*, 25, 32–37; Mīrkhʷānd, *Rawżat*, 3,710–713, 4,511; Dawlatshāh, *Tadhkirat*, 281; Faṣīḥ, *Mujmal*, 928; Sharaf al-Dīn ʿAlī Yazdī, *Ẓafarnāmah*, ed. Muḥammad ʿAbbasī, 2 vols (Tehran: Amīr Kabīr, 1336/1957), 1:23–24; Rūḥallāh Munshī, *Tārīkh-i pasandīdah: Taḥrīrī az Ẓafarnāmah-yi Yazdī* [*Selected History: The Liberated Ẓafarnāmah of Yazdī*], ed. Jamshīd Kiyānfar, 2 vols (Tehran: Intishārāt-i Asāṭīr, 1389/2010), 1:18 (This is the *Ẓafarnāmah*, but shorn of Yazdī's turgid prose).

71 On him, see ʿAbd al-Ghanī Barzīn-Mihr, *Shuʿarā wa fuẓalāʾ dar bārgāh-yi mulūk-i Kart-i Harāt* (Peshawar: n.p., 1377/1998), 27–37.

72 See explanation in Smith, *Sarbadar*, 116–18.

73 Ibid., 118.

74 On him, see Mīr-Sayyid Ẓahīr al-Dīn Marʿashī, *Tārīkh-i Ṭabaristān wa Rūyān wa Māzandarān*, ed. Muḥammad Ḥusayn Tasbīhī (Tehran: Intishārāt-i sharq, 1345/1966), 171–72.

75 Faryūmadī, *Zayl*, 347–48.

76 Smith, *Sarbadar*, 119–21 and n.65. Smith's review of the sources did not clarify Maʿsūd's reasons for invading Mazandaran. Maʿsūd may have been pursuing Shaykhiyya.

Enmity between the Sarbadar and Shaykhiyya wings flowing from the murder of Ḥasan Jūrī proved problematic for Maʿsūd's successors.

The Sarbadar-Shaykhiyya coalition was volatile for two decades, from 743/1342 to 764/1363. Both dates, not coincidentally, reflect when Shaykhiyya leaders were murdered by Sarbadars: Jūrī in 743/1342; Darwish ʿAzīz in 764/1363. Factions engaged in internecine feuding. Ouster followed ouster. The general cycle being: a Sarbadarid ruler is murdered by the Shaykhiyya faction; a Shaykhiyya rules, briefly, and is murdered by the Sarbadarids. The Sarbadar-Shaykhiyya polity did not threaten the Kartids, but remained a menace to Jawni-Qurbanids and Ṭaghā-Temür. In 754/1353, the factions took a break from feuding and assassinated Ṭaghā-Temür in his own tent (Chapter Six).

ʿAlī Muʾayyad (r. 764–83/1363–81) formed a ruling condominium with a Shaykhiyya, Darwish ʿAzīz. In keeping with local customs, Muʾayyad murdered his co-regent and seized control of the Sarbadar-Shaykhiyya polity. ʿAlī Muʾayyad became the terminal ruler of the polity. He hewed to the Twelver Shiʿa interpretation of Islam; and tried to purge his realm of Shaykhiyya. He strove assiduously to dissuade his subjects of Shiʿi *ghuluww* beliefs and rituals; and to inculcate "proper" Twelver Shiʿa beliefs.

## Kartid Doctrine

The *emerging* Kartid doctrine, which *later* defined Kartid-Sarbadarid relations in the Muʿizz al-Dīn/ʿAlī Muʾayyad epoch (from 764/1363 to 771/1370), was "live and let live": Muʿizz al-Dīn did not reveal ambitions to extend his realm westward; and ʿAlī Muʾayyad (implicitly or explicitly) agreed not to threaten the east. John Masson Smith observed that "ʿAlī Muʾayyad needed peace in the east because he had to make war in the west."[77] This was said with respect to the Jawni-Qurban, but the assessment applies to the Kartids, too. Sarbadars were (implicity or explicitly) granted carte blanche to expand westward (as far as the Sarbadarid armies could advance), but any movement beyond the 59th Meridian East would be countered by the Kartids.[78]

[77] Smith, *Sarbadar*, 148.

[78] *Circa* 59° 00′ E to 59° 30′ E: line of demarcation between Sarbadarids and Kartids. Zāwa is at *c.* 59° 13′ E; Mashhad, 59° 36′ 0″ E; Turbat-i Jām, 60° 37′ 21″ E; but cf. Nishapur, 58° 47′ 45″ E, which the Jawni-Qurban ceded to the Sarbadars (see Ḥāfiẓ-i Abrū, *Cinq*, Notes, p.17).

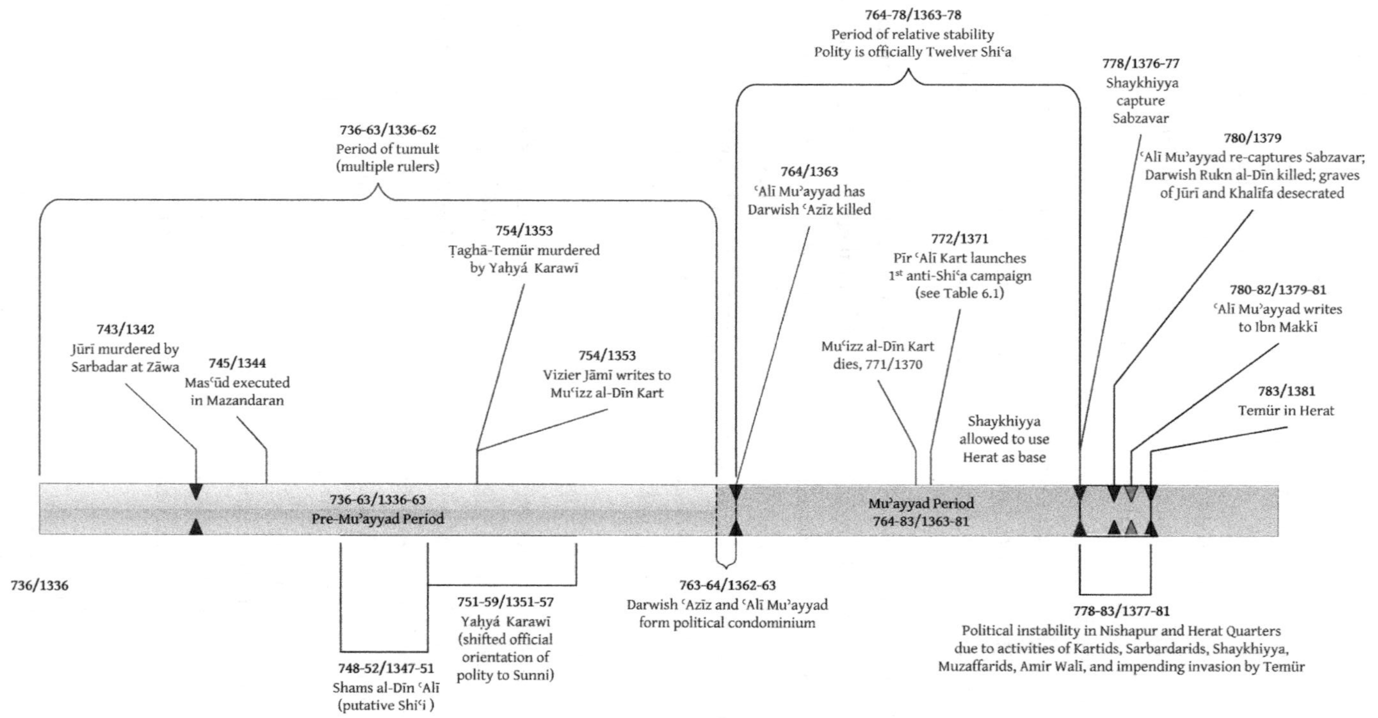


Figure 5.1 Sarbadar Dynasty, political-military timeline, 736/1336 to 783/1381.

The reign (r. 750/1349 to 754/1354)[79] or (r. 748–52/1347–51)[80] of Shams al-Dīn ʿAlī Sarbadar (occasionally, ʿAlī Shams al-Dīn) relates to the proffer on Kartid doctrine. Shams al-Dīn ʿAlī espoused indeterminate Shiʿi ideals; and as Smith noted, was probably a darwish by avocation. Shams al-Dīn ʿAlī implemented building programs that stimulated his realm's economy;[81] however his repressions and fanaticism further de-stabilized the wobbly polity. Shams al-Dīn acted to extirpate alcohol and drug consumption; and ordered prostitutes murdered.[82] He developed a network of informants; and supposedly traveled in disguise (a popular trope) to record the words and deeds of subjects. The outcome is that commoners, notables, and officials were terrified of him. The internal strife he generated climaxed with his assassination;[83] but before this transpired, Arghūn-Shāh and Muʿizz al-Dīn, allegedly "fearful" (*khāʾif*) of Shams al-Dīn ʿAlī, moved against him.[84]

It is difficult to place Mīrkhʷānd's report within an agreeable timeframe: Arghūn-Shāh died either in 743/1343 or 746/1345f.;[85] we can reliably place Shams al-Dīn ʿAlī (d. 28 Shawwāl 752/18 December 1351) in office from *c.* 748/1347 to 752/1351.[86] The involvement of Muḥammad Bīk (d. 774/1373), not his father Arghūn-Shāh, is credible. Ḥāfiẓ-i Abrū does not mention this military engagement in his *opuscule* on the Jawni-Qurban, but confirms the warm intimacy of the Kartids and Jawni-Qurbanids, which included a marital bond.[87] Muʿizz al-Dīn and Muḥammad Bīk evidently acted in unison.

The Jawni-Qurban in the Mashhad-Ṭūs region were being pressed by Shams al-Dīn ʿAlī and on the backfoot when the Sarbadars learned of the Kartid army's advance. Muʿizz al-Dīn Kart bivouacked at "Farāh-jard" (Farhād-gard). The Kartids advanced no further, but the lingering presence

[79] Faṣīḥ, *Mujmal*, 940 (from Muḥarram 750), 947 (to Shawwāl 755).

[80] Smith, *Sarbadar*, 129; cf. A.H. Morton, "The History of the Sarbadars in Light of New Numismatic Evidence," *Numismatic Chronicle* 16 (1976):255–58, 256 (regnal dates).

[81] Mīrkhʷānd, *Rawżat*, 4,515–16; Dawlatshāh, *Tadhkirat*, 282–83; Smith, *Sarbadar*, 130–31. Shams al-Dīn ʿAlī restored Sabzavar's Friday mosque and built cisterns within it.

[82] Mīrkhʷānd, *Rawżat*, 4,516; Dawlatshāh, *Tadhkirat*, 282.

[83] Smith, *Sarbadar*, 131–33.

[84] Mīrkhʷānd, *Rawżat*, 4,516.

[85] Ḥāfiẓ-i Abrū, *Cinq*, 28 (d. 746); Faṣīḥ, *Mujmal*, 929 (d. 743).

[86] Morton, "Numismatic," 256 (establishes correct regnal dates).

[87] Ḥāfiẓ-i Abrū, *Cinq*, 27–30. Pīr ʿAlī Kart married Muḥammad Bīk's daughter.

of the Kartid army within striking distance of Mashhad-Ṭus caused the Sarbadars to pause, then withdraw to Sabzavar. Muʿizz al-Dīn withdrew to Herat. The Kart king was enforcing a geo-political "red line" by prudently demonstrating military vigor and political resolve without participating in the conflict.

# 6

# From Kartid Sultanate to Tamerlane

## The Ephemeral Sultanate at Herat

Muʿizz al-Dīn's subsequent political choices, fueled by hubris, belied the strength and prudence reflected by the above episode, and precipitated his temporary deposition from office and social-political upheaval within and without Herat.

Muʿizz al-Dīn's woes stemmed from his violation of Chinggisid diplomatic protocols. The political arrangement under which the Kartids had ruled until the death of Abū Saʿīd Bahādur Khān in 736/1335 was as *banda* of the *īlkhān*; and the Il-Khan had the Grand Qaʾan as his liege-lord. (The Qaʾan's status in the later years of the Mongol Empire with respect to the Il-Khan was nearer to nominal than actual.) Hence the installation of Ṭaghā-Temür, who acknowledged submission to the Grand Qaʾan, Toghan-Temür (r. 1332–70). Protocols were publicly respected. Coinage (*sikka*), and the announcement of the ruler's name in the Friday sermon (*khuṭba*), are two symbols of legitimacy.[1] The Sarbadars found it expedient to publicly express fealty to Ṭaghā-Temür by striking coins in his name.[2]

### *Independence by* Sikka

Not so Muʿizz al-Dīn Kart. He reached for the mantle of *sulṭān*, and adapted for his circumstances the symbolic language found in Islamic and Ilkhanid coins.[3]

[1] See, e.g., A.K.S. Lambton, *State and Government in Medieval Islam* (London: Routledge, 1981), 116–17, 248–49.

[2] Smith, *Sarbadar*, 74 and n.27.

[3] On coins of the Il-Khans, including nominal Il-Khans, see Bahrām ʿAlāʾ al-Dīnī, *Sikka-hā-yi Īrān* [vol. 1]*: Dawra-yi Īlkhānān-i Mughūl* [*Coins of Iran: The Mongol Ilkhanid period*] (Tehran: Intishārāt-i Barg-i nigār, 1395/2016).

Figure 6.1 Kartid, silver "½ *tanka*" (4.97 g), Herat, no date (courtesy of Stephen Album).

He portrayed himself as the leader of (Sunni) Muslims, and "the Strengthener of the [True] Faith" (*muʿizz al-dīn*).[4] He minted coins, probably as early as 749/1348f., one year before his independence proclamation, in which he identified himself as sultan.[5] Two coins from the independence period are available, both minted at Herat.[6]

Figure 6.1 shows no date, but the inscription indicates that the coin, a "half-*tanga*,"[7] was "minted in the times (*ayyām*) of the government of the exalted *sulṭān*, the watchful king (*mālik riqāb*) of the peoples (*al-umam*),[8] [and] the Strengthener (*muʿizz*) of the Truth and the Faith (*al-ḥaqq wa al-dīn*). May God perpetuate his kingdom!"[9]

[4] On titles in coinage, see Stephen Album, "A hoard of silver coins from the time of Iskandar Qarā-Qoyūnlū," *The Numismatic Chronicle* 16 (1976):109–157, 110–111.

[5] I am indebted to numismatists par excellence, Stephen Album and Bahram ʿAlaʾ al-Dini, for their assistance in reading the inscriptions.

[6] Neither coin is listed in Bahrām ʿAlāʾ al-Dīnī, *Sikkah-hā-yi Īrān* [vol. 2]*: az inqirāż-i Īlkhānān-i Mughūl tā istīlā-yi Tīmūr Gūrkān* [*Coins of Iran: from the fall of the Mongol Ilkhanids to Tamerlane's Conquest*] (Tehran: Intishārāt-i Barg-i nigār, 1396/2017).

[7] *Tanka*: from Sanskrit; *tanga* in Khurasan (where it became a generic term for silver coins). Stephen Album, *Checklist of Islamic Coins* (Santa Rosa, CA: Stephen Album, 3rd. ed., 2011), 9; R.E. Darley-Doran, "*Tanga* and *Tanka*," *EI²*, 10:185.

[8] *Umam* (sgl. *umma*): peoples, tribes, sects, communities.

[9] Fig. 6.1: *ḍuriba fī ayyām dawlat al-sulṭān al-aʿẓam / mālik riqāb / al-umam muʿizz al-ḥaqq wa al-dīn / khallad Allāh mulkahu.*

Figure 6.2 Kartid, silver *dīnār* (5.18 g), Herat, AH 74x (AH 749?) (courtesy of Stephen Album).

Figure 6.2, a *dīnār*, bears the same inscription, but has a date, partially effaced, of "74x."[10] Muʿizz al-Dīn's choice of inscription followed Ilkhanid patterns (namely, *al-sulṭān al-aʿẓam* and *khallad Allāh mulkahu*), especially Abū Saʿīd's inscriptions.[11] The obverse has the Muslim profession of faith (*kalima*), a common feature.

*Independence by Proclamation*

At this juncture, Muʿizz al-Dīn Kart was an autonomous sovereign in all but his title. Dispensing with Ṭaghā-Temür as the suzerain—a token of respect that probably cost Muʿizz al-Dīn little or nothing financially—was gratuitous and tactless. It was bound to inflame the passions of Turco-Mongols who idealized Chingiz Khan, particularly so when provocateurs notified Turco-Mongol chiefs of this breach of protocol. Muʿizz al-Dīn elevated himself to sultan (*ʿalá sarīr al-sulṭanat bih-madīnat Harāt*) by proclamation. The date of his accession was on or before 19 Jumādá I 750/5 August 1349, the date of the proclamation, which is found in manuscripts of Yūsuf-i

10 Fig. 6.2: *ḍuriba fī ayyām dawlat al-sulṭān al-aʿẓam / ---- muʿizz al-ḥaqq wa al-dīn / khallad Allāh mulkahu* (partially effaced).

11 See Sheila Blair, "The coins of the later Ilkhanids: A typological analysis," *JESHO* 26/3 (1983):295–317, esp. 297–300, Figs 5 and 6; eadem, "The coins of the later Ilkhānids: Mint organization, regionalization, and urbanism," *Museum Notes* 27 (1982):211–30.

Ahl Jāmī's epistolary collection, *Farā'id-i Ghiyāṣī.*[12] It was penned by vizier Mu'īn al-Dīn Jāmī: the highfalutin and rhymed prose (*saj'*) is the unfortunate—for the information-seeking historian—hallmark of Jāmī's literary *oeuvre.*

The proclamation's title announces Mu'izz al-Dīn's accession and implores, "God save [the Kartid kingdom] from the dangers (*al-makhāfāt*) surrounding the Kingdom and the Province." The preamble dwells on obligations of sultans to return people to Revelation; eliminate unbelief, polytheism, innovations, and deviations in faith (*kufr wa bida' wa shirk wa ẓalālat*), and substitute them with (laudable) customs, regulations, justice, and equity (*qawā'id wa qawānīn-i 'adl wa inṣāf*). Religion and kingship are twins (*tawāmin*), conjoined (*maqrūn*) and inseparable.[13] A fragment from *Sūrat al-nisā'* (the rationale for which is self-evident) follows: "O ye who believe! Obey Allah, and obey the Messenger, *and those charged with authority among you*" (Q4:59).[14] Authority over the province of Islam (Khurasan) has been bestowed (by God) on Mu'izz al-Dīn Kart. To demonstrate that he took the obligation seriously, the proclamation continues: "Our commands and interdictions (*amr wa nahy*) were realized (*nāfiẕ*) in the hinterlands and cities (*jamī'-i bilād wa amṣār*)." The Kartid king's triumph at extinguishing infernos ignited by "world-burning" (*jahān-sūz*) "Gog and Magog" (*yājūj wa majūj*) people is recalled:[15] his victory at Zāwa over "the army of extremists and sectaries (*sipāh-i ghulāt wa ahl-i bid'at*)" and the killing of the "accursed demon (*dīw-i rajīm*) [Shaykh Ḥasan Jūrī], who was the head of the heretics (*rās al-malāḥida*) and the leader of the unbelievers (*ra'īs al-zanādiqa*)." Since

12 Yūsuf-i Ahl/Fatih, *Farā'id*, ff. 444b–445b; idem/Aya Sofya, *Farā'id*, ff. 96a–97a; idem/Berlin, *Farā'id*, ff. 287a–289a; idem/Tehran, *Farā'id*, pp. 618–20. The letter is not in the two-volume *Farā'id-i Ghiyāṣī* edited by Heshmat Moayyad. The letter was first analyzed by Jean Aubin in "Le Khanat de Čaġatai et le Khorassan (1334–1380)," *Turcica* 8/2 (1970):16–60, 31.

13 The concept in Persia of twinning kingship and religion predate Islam. See R.C. Zaehner, *The Dawn and Twilight of Zoroastrianism* (New York: Putnam, 1961), 284–85. It is eloquently explained by the Sasanian king, Ardashir I (r. AD 224–41), quoted extensively in Said Amir Arjomand, *The Turban for the Crown* (Oxford: Oxford University Press, 1988), 76–77.

14 *Those charged with authority among you*: In classic Sunni thought, this means Companions and commanders of the Prophet, ulama, and caliphs. Shi'a claim it refers to the "infallible imams." The prevalent view is that it refers to leaders of the *umma*. See, e.g., Wadad Kadi, "Authority," *EQ*, 1:188–90; cf. A.K.S. Lambton, "Concepts of Authority in Persia: Eleventh to Nineteenth Centuries A.D.," *Iran* 26 (1988):95–103.

15 Q18:94 (*Sūrat al-kahf*): "the Gog and Magog (People) do great mischief on earth [...]." See Keith Lewinstein, "Gog and Magog," *EQ*, 2:331–33.

"unbelief and oppression (*kufr wa ẓulm*) were nigh and had utterly blocked Islam's sunlight [...], we expended every effort" to resist impiety.

"Gog and Magog" is not hyperbole. The phrase will have resonated with ulama and others knowledgeable about Quranic allusions. Here, D̲h̲ū al-Qarnayn (Q18:83), identifiable with Alexander the Great,[16] is the epitome with whom Muʿizz al-Dīn wished to be identified. In Scripture, D̲h̲ū al-Qarnayn, "Possessor of the Two Horns,"[17] is begged for relief by those fearful of the Gog and Magog people. They invite him to "erect a barrier between us and them" (Q18:94). D̲h̲ū al-Qarnayn, referencing God's grace, which had granted him power, replies: "Help me therefore with strength (and labor): I will erect a stronger barrier between you and them" (Q18:95). Muʿizz al-Dīn's self-image, possibly, was that of D̲h̲ū al-Qarnayn: just and righteous; neither greedy nor selfish. In any event, Muʿizz al-Dīn was appealing for the public's cooperation in his divinely guided mission.

The above served as context and justification for self-promotion: Muʿizz al-Dīn Kart playing the venerable role of *Pādishāh-i Islām*: defender of (Sunni) Islam. The text continues. Scholars of Islam have deemed that to acquire worthily (*istiḥqāq*) the crown of kingship (*tāj-i sulṭanat*), a Padishah of Islam must command the observance of festivals and assemblies, and appoint governors and judges. Therefore, this sublime date, 19 Jumādá I 750/5 August 1349,[18] we desire that sayyids, shaykhs, ulama (etc.)—the "people who unbind and bind in this Kingdom" (*ahl-i ḥall wa ʿaqd-i īn mamlakat*)[19]—to "willingly and eagerly submit to us with an oath of allegiance" (*bih ṭawʿ wa raghbat bā mā bayʿat-i sulṭanat kardand*);[20] strengthen (our kingdom) with their covenants, documents, oaths (etc.) (*bih ʿahūd wa paymān wa mawāṣīq wa aymān muʾakkad kardānīd*). Henceforth, in order to "further the posture of the True Faith and the Word of God; [and] holy war against infidels (*jihād bā kuffār*); and 'to enjoin the good and forbid the reprehensible' [...], we decree

---

[16] Alexander, or perhaps an ancient Persian shah. ʿAbdullah Yusuf ʿAli, *The meaning of the Holy Qurʾan* (Beltsville, MD: Amana, 11th ed., 2004), 731, n.2428; pp. 738–42 (Appendix VI: "Who was D̲h̲ū al-Qarnayn?," Q18:83–98).

[17] The two horns possibly represent east and west, the limits of Alexander's domains. John Renard, "Alexander," *EQ* 1:61–62.

[18] This is the proclamation date; the convocation was sometime in 750/1349–50.

[19] *Ahl al-ḥall wa al-ʿaqd*: see Lambton, *State, et passim* (on the concept in Islamic thought).

[20] On oaths made by men with God as their witness, see Mottahedeh, *Loyalty*, esp. 42–60.

(*farmā ʾīm*) that *amr-i ma ʿrūf wa nahy-i munkar* be implemented throughout the country (*jamī ʿ-i bilād*); and infidel [Mongol] customs (*rasūm*) that persist in the domains of Islam (*bilād-i Islām*) be castoff (*bar-andāzand*)." Hereafter, all affairs should be conducted in harmony with the prescriptions of the Sharia.[21]

*Herat-Delhi Political Union?*

Mu ʿizz al-Dīn Kart dispatched two missives to sultan Muḥammad b. Tughluq-Shāh (r. 724–52/1324–51) of the Delhi Sultanate about his establishment of a sultanate at Herat. The first was transmitted after the 19 Jumādá I 750 proclamation;[22] the second after the convocation.[23] Both letters are deferential in tone and honorifics: the author is *malik*; the recipient is *sulṭān*. Since Muḥammad's self-image was that of "the warrior in the path of God" (*al-mujāhid fī sabīl ʾillāh*), a *kunya* found in his *sikka*,[24] the first epistle addresses him as *al-sulṭān al-ghāzī Abū al-mujāhid*; the second has a variant, *al-sulṭān al-ʿaẓim al-ghāzī Abū al-mujāhid*. Other honorifics, like "Shadow of God" (*ẓill Allāh*) and "Servitor of the Two Holy Cities" (*khādim al-ḥaramayn*) are liberally sprinkled in both letters.

*First letter: post-proclamation*

Mu ʿizz al-Dīn desires to become the sultan's *banda*. He explains in allegorical terms about the emergence in *Īrān-zamīn* of a miscellany of kingdoms (*mulūk-i ṭawā ʾif*),[25] that is, after the Ilkhanate fragmented; how each entity (*ṭa ʾifa*) pursued a parochial agenda; of the sea of strife (*baḥar-i fitna*) that had arisen, its waves crashing and drowning armies. Mu ʿizz al-Dīn and Khurasanians desire a faithful suzerain; therefore he pledges allegiance and petitions for a decree of confirmation.[26]

[21] Full citations to the 19 Jumādá I 750 letter in *Farā ʾid-i Ghiyāṣī* are in n.12, *supra*.

[22] Yūsuf-i Ahl/Moayyad (ed.), *Farā ʾid*, 1:146–49. Undated, but *c.* 750/1349–50.

[23] Ibid., 1:182–85. Undated, but in 750/1349–50.

[24] Jackson, *Delhi Sultanate*, 278. On *kunya* (*agnomen*), see Schimmel, *Islamic Names*, 4–8.

[25] *Mulūk-i ṭawā ʾīf*: "the kings of the territorial divisions." M. Morony, "Mulūk al-ṭawā ʾif," *EI*², 7:551–52. Vizer Jāmī's use of *mulūk al-ṭawā ʾīf* reflects its pre-Islamic Persian sense, namely, the rulers of the provinces of the fragmented empire of Alexander of Macedon.

[26] Yūsuf-i Ahl/Moayyad (ed.), *Farā ʾid*, 1:146–49. *Baḥar-i fitna*: the Sarbadars, probably.

*Second letter: post-convocation*

The second letter to Muḥammad b. Tughluq was dispatched after the convocation. It was allegedly dictated by Muʿizz al-Dīn, but the eloquent language betrays Jāmī's hand. The Kartid announces his self-promotion and delves into the underlying motives.[27]

Muʿizz al-Dīn Kart describes how since early in the year 750 (from March 1349 to March 1350), sundry distresses (*parishānī*) had reached his ears from all corners of "fearful Khurasan" (*khurāsān-i hirāsān*). The agitations stemmed from political upheaval and moral turpitude in towns and hinterlands (*amṣār wa aqṭār*) that had fallen to rebels and corruptors (*ahl-i baghī wa fasād*). Knaves and ruffians (*runūd wa awbāsh*) roamed, occasioning upheavals and abuses. A contingent of shaykhs, amirs, and ulama had appealed to the *malik* for relief from political-religious strife (*dar taskīn-i īn fitna-hā-yi gūnāgūn*).[28] After consultations it was determined by them (*ittifāq kardand*) that a pious sultan was best positioned to extinguish the fires of *fitna*, meaning he had to assume the mantle of Padishah of Islam. And so, in this year, 750/1349, people of rectitude (*ahl-i salāh*), Turk and Tajik, from near and far, heard the call and gathered at Herat. Muʿizz al-Dīn is saying (in effect), "the notables begged me to do something about the 'religious strife' (*fitna*); they believed that I should become sultan and I (reluctantly) agreed because 'the country needs me'!"

*Analysis*

It is not known what Muḥammad b. Tughluq made of the entreaty. It is possible he entertained it. Consequent to the 1329 invasion of the Sultanate by *ulus* Chaghataid under Tarmashirin (r. 1326–34), Muḥammad had sought an alliance with the Ilkhanate.[29] He had wanted to annex Chaghataid lands in "northern Afghanistan,"[30] which were integral to his "Khurasan

[27] Muʿizz al-Dīn Kart "was evidently concerned that his adoption of the style of sultan" may prejudice his relationship with Muḥammad b. Tughluq. Jackson, *Delhi Sultanate*, 235. Hence the detailed explanation.

[28] Yūsuf-i Ahl/Moayyad (ed.), *Farāʾid*, 1:182–85.

[29] Jackson, *Delhi Sultanate*, 232–33.

[30] Ibid., 263–65 ("Khurasan project"); see also ibid., 233–35, and nn.108, 114 (relations with notables of Khurasan; hopes for alliances). Michael Hope said to this author that Muʿizz al-Dīn may have encouraged sultan Muḥammad to pursue his Khurasan project.

project."[31] If so, a political-military alliance between Muḥammad and Muʿizz al-Dīn is reasonable. The Delhi-Herat connection may have been concrete, that is, not limited to cordial diplomatic relations. Sultan Muḥammad (if Ibn Battuta is correct) had granted to Muʿizz al-Dīn a Sindi city, Bakār (Bhakkār), "whose tax yield is fifty thousand silver dinars a year."[32] The bequest is plausible (even if the professed tax yield may not be) because Jāmī relationships with the Delhi Sultanate are traceable to the Mongol irruptions. This is when progeny of Shaykh al-Islam Aḥmad-i Jām migrated to India, and there fostered social and economic relationships with influential Indians.[33] These Herat Quarter–Delhi connections flourished into the early Mughal era. Jāmīs married into Indian and Turkic families. Jāmī blood flowed through the veins of emperors Humayun and Akbar the Great.[34] It is logical that Muʿizz al-Dīn, guided by his worldly vizier, Muʿīn al-Dīn Jāmī, would correspond with Delhi and expect material support from sultan Muḥammad b. Tughluq.

Why cast off the Turko-Mongol "yoke" for a Turko-Indian yoke, particularly since the Turko-Mongol yoke, personified by the inept Ṭaghā-Temür, sat so gently on Muʿizz al-Dīn Kart's shoulders? The Kartid knew that his actions would provoke a violent reaction from the Chaghataids, which indeed it did. The Chaghataids were goaded by the Kartid's enemies—Jāmī shaykhs, no less—into deposing him (see below).

[31] Geographical expanses of *ulus* Chaghatai ("Chaghataid nation") included Transoxiana, parts of Khurasan, Badakhshān, Bāghlan, and vicinities of Kabul. It incorporated diverse clusters of Turkic and Turko-Mongol peoples. The composite included the Qaraunas, who had shifted loyalties from Ilkhanids to Chaghataids. On the chief powers of *ulus* Chaghatai, see Beatrice Manz, *The Rise and Rule of Tamerlane* (Cambridge: Cambridge University Press, 1989), 154–165 (Appendix A); Map 2 (p.26) of the *ulus*, *c*.1360; eadem, "The *ulus* Chaghatai before and after Temür's rise to power: The transformation from tribal confederation to army of conquest," *CAJ* 27/1 (1983):79–100.

[32] Ibn Battuta, *The Travels of Ibn Battuta*, vol. 3., tr. H.A.R. Gibb (Cambridge: Cambridge University Press, 1971), 3:580 and n.160. I find Ibn Battuta's information on Herat, Kartids, and Aḥmad-i Jām chaotic or manifestly erroneous. His descriptions of Sultanate India, on the other hand, are quite lucid. It raises the suspicion that he had not visited certain parts of Khurasan, but had relied on interlocutors and literary sources.

[33] Mahendrarajah, *Sufi Saint*, 58–59 (Quṭb al-Dīn Muḥammad Jāmī and an Indian patron).

[34] Ibid., 47–51, 78–82. *Farāʾid-i Ghiyāṣī* has numerous letters to/from Herat and Jām to/from the Sultanate. Kartid and Jāmī political, social, and economic ties to the Muslim sultans at Delhi, from Iltutmish (d. 1236) to Firuzshah (d. 1388), await exploration.

*Organizing the Kartid Sultanate*

Before we delve into how the Chaghataids took umbrage at Muʿizz al-Dīn Kart's self-promotion and terminated his embyronic sultanate, the re-organization of the Kartid court and putative Kartid Islamization plans are noted.

The vizierate experienced a re-organization at its apex, which fashioned a political-religious triumvirate. Muʿīn al-Dīn Jāmī received a royal confirmation (*manshūr*) dated 20 Jumādá I 750/6 August 1349 for the vizierate (*wizārāt*) in Muʿizz al-Dīn's *dīwān*.[35] He would direct the triumvirate. Next to him, although of superior moral puissance and erudition, was Shaykh al-Islam Saʿd al-Dīn Masʿūd (722–93/1322–90) b. ʿUmar b. ʿAbdallāh Taftāzānī. Jamāl al-Dīn Malik Ikhtasān (n.d.), hitherto unknown,[36] became a (junior) vizier. Knowledge of this re-organization and triumvirate are from a decree dated 25 Jumādá I 750/11 August 1349,[37] empowering Taftāzānī and Jāmī with ordering the affairs of state and faith (*umūr-i dīn wa dawlat*). Jāmī is accorded the title Khʷājah-yi Jahān,[38] analogous to, say, Grand Vizier. Taftāzānī was Herat's de facto or de jure shaykh al-Islam: he is identified as Shaykh al-Islām al-Aʿẓam.[39] Their duties with respect to ordering the "affairs of state and faith" flowed from the Islamization ambitions broached by Muʿizz al-Dīn in his 19 Jumādá I 750 proclamation. Malik Ikhtasān, was responsible, presumably, for managing the day-to-day affairs of court following Jāmī's promotion.

Jāmī and Taftāzānī were intimates: the Shaykh al-Islam educated the vizier's son, Shaykh al-Islam Żiyā al-Dīn Yūsuf (d. 797/1394f.).[40] The Sufis of Jām were long-standing associates of the Taftāzānī clan. Saʿd al-Dīn Masʿūd Taftāzānī resided and taught at Turbat-i Jām in 752/1351. The Jāmī Sufis

35 Yūsuf-i Ahl/Fatih, *Farāʾid*, ff. 458ᵇ–460ᵃ; idem/Tehran, *Farāʾid*, pp. 644–46.

36 Jean Aubin suggests that Ikhtasān was a defector (*transfuge*) from, or agent of, the Delhi court. Aubin, "Khanat," 30 and n.55.

37 Yūsuf-i Ahl/Fatih, *Farāʾid*, ff. 445ᵇ–447ᵇ; idem/Aya Sofya, *Farāʾid*, ff. 97ᵃ–98ᵇ; idem/Berlin, *Farāʾid*, ff. 289ᵃ–291ᵇ; idem/Tehran, *Farāʾid*, pp. 620–23.

38 On the use of Khʷājah-yi Jahān in the Delhi Sultanate, see Ibn Battuta, *Travels*, *et passim*; Aubin, "Khanat," 32.

39 On Taftāzānī shaykhs al-Islam, see Chapter Nine; Mahendrarajah, "Shaykh al-Islam."

40 On Żiyā al-Dīn Yūsuf, see Mahendrarajah, *Sufi Saint*, 66, 145, 178; Figures A1.3 and A1.5.

and Taftāzānī shaykhs al-Islam remained close friends up to the expiration of Sunni dominance in Herat.[41]

Taftāzānī and Jāmī formed a potent political-religious battery at court and in Herat. Taftāzānī would have been central to fulfilling Muʿizz al-Dīn's ambitions of implementing *al-amr bi'l maʿrūf wa'l-nahy ʿan al-munkar*, and abandoning Mongol laws and customs (*yasāq wa yusūn*). The heated rhetoric about "the army of extremists and sectaries" may indicate interest in renewing conflict with the Sarbadars. However, the Kartid sultanate expired before Taftāzānī and Jāmī could implement Muʿizz al-Dīn's ideas.

## Chaghataids Terminate the Sultanate at Herat

Muʿizz al-Dīn Kart appears to have held the expectation that if he acknowledged Muḥammad b. Tughluq as suzerain, the sultan would militarily pressure the Chaghataids should they threaten Kartids. He possibly thought the sultan's reputation for religious zeal, his acquisition of diplomas from the pseudo-caliphs of Cairo,[42] and insertion of the caliph's name in the Friday sermon (*khuṭba*) and coins (*sikka*),[43] and the Sultanate's history of strife with *ulus* Chaghatai, would garner him support.[44] But when the Kartid wrote, he appears not to have appreciated that diplomatic relations between *ulus* Chaghatai and the Sultanate had improved; the Sultanate was sundered by internal dissent;[45] and he could not have known that Muḥammad b. Tughluq would die on 21 Muḥarram 752/20 March 1351, the *hijri* year (752) that Chaghataid militias descended on Herat.

### *The Ouster*

Muʿizz al-Dīn Kart was out of office from *c.* 752/1351f. to 753/1353. He renegotiated with the Chaghataid leader his return to Herat, where he remained

[41] Mahendrarajah, "Shaykh al-Islam," 274–75. The last Sunni Shaykh al-Islam of Herat, Sayf al-Dīn Aḥmad Taftāzānī, was executed by Shāh Ismāʿīl I, Ṣafawī, in 916/1511.

[42] For a different view of the Cairene caliphate, see Mustafa Banister, *The Abbasid Caliphate of Cairo, 1261–1517* (Edinburgh: Edinburgh University Press, 2021).

[43] Jackson, *Delhi Sultanate*, 271–72.

[44] Ibid., 217–37; see also Peter Jackson, "The Mongols and the Delhi Sultanate in the reign of Muḥammad Tughluq (1325–1351)," *CAJ* 19 (1975):118–57.

[45] Jackson, *Delhi Sultanate*, 255–77.

until his death on 5 Dhū al-Qaʿda 771/31 May 1370. The circumstances of his removal and return follow.

The early Timurid era historian, Ḥāfiẓ-i Abrū, relates that "a group of Shaykhs from Jām" (*jamʿī az mashāʾīkh-i Jām*) had traveled to Transoxiana to meet with the chiefs of *ulus* Chaghatai and complain about Muʿizz al-Dīn.[46] A later writer, Ghiyāth al-Dīn Khʷāndamīr, supplies one name from this cohort: Rażī al-Dīn Aḥmad Jāmī (d. 767/1366),[47] the custodian (*mutawallī*) of Aḥmad-i Jām's shrine.[48] Rażī al-Dīn Aḥmad's brother, Shams al-Dīn Muṭahhar (d. bet. 751–67/1350–66), was the vizier's father.[49] Lawrence Potter suggested that "[i]ntra-family jealousy" may have played a role.[50] Even if Rażī al-Dīn Aḥmad were jealous of Muʿīn al-Dīn Jāmī, I doubt rivalry was the motive. I have explained in my history of Aḥmad-i Jām's shrine-complex and saint cult that the Jāmīs have held together through nine centuries of political vicissitudes in Khurasan (Seljuqs, Khʷarazm-Shāhs, Mongols, Timurids, Safavids, Afsharids, Qajars, Pahlawis, Islamic Republic); one seismic religious shift (majority Sunni to majority Shiʿa), by not permitting inter-lineage and intra-family rivalries to spill over and inflict harm to shrine and community. I have argued that the Kartid's ouster was instigated because he had seized Jāmī estates situated in the vicinities of Herat.[51] Muʿizz al-Dīn Kart's brother and successor, Muḥammad Bāqir Kart (r.*c.* 752–53/1351–53), returned the estates to the Jāmī Sufis on 23 Ṣafar 753/10 April 1352.[52]

In any event, Chaghataid chieftains were suitably incensed by the undoubtedly hyperbolic tales told to them by Jāmīs about Muʿizz al-Dīn's hubris. Khʷāndamīr's colorful descriptions—adapted from Ḥāfiẓ-i Abrū[53]—were fluently rendered by Wheeler Thackston: "'Has the race of Genghis Khan collapsed that there is no one to destroy this shah? The vile Ghurid has

[46] Ḥāfiẓ-i Abrū, *Kart*, 179.

[47] Khʷāndamīr/Siyāqī (ed.), *Ḥabīb*, 3:381; Khʷāndamīr/Thackston (tr.), *Habib*, 221.

[48] See Mahendrarajah, *Sufi Saint*, 63–66, 109; Table 5.2; Figures A1.3 and A1.4.

[49] See ibid., 62, 66, 109; Table 8.1; Figures A1.3 and A1.5.

[50] Potter, "Kart Dynasty," 119.

[51] Shivan Mahendrarajah, "A revised history of Mongol, Kart, and Timurid patronage of the shrine of Shaykh al-Islam Ahmad-i Jam," *Iran* 54/2 (2016):107–28, 116–117.

[52] The decree is in Yūsuf-i Ahl/Berlin, *Farāʾid*, fol. $310^{b}$–$311^{b}$; idem/Fatih, *Farāʾid*, fol. $461^{b}$–$462^{a}$; idem/Tehran, *Farāʾid*, pp. 649–50; Būzjānī, *Rawżat*, 146 (edited version). Discussed in Mahendrarajah, *Sufi Saint*, 135.

[53] Ḥāfiẓ-i Abrū, *Zubdat*, 1:228; Ḥāfiẓ-i Abrū, *Karts*, 180.

become so bold that he regards no one but himself," exclaimed the leaders of the Arlat and Apardi tribes. The chief of *ulus* Chaghatai, Amir Qazghan (r.*c.* 747–59/1346–58) decried:[54] "How can this Tajik contemplate autonomy? God willing, by blow of the glittering sword will the fire of his rebelliousness be quenched, and by the cold wind of attack by warriors will the palace of his prosperity be leveled to the ground."[55] Chieftains articulated a long-standing belief that only Turkic peoples—not "lowly" Tajiks—have the "right" to kingship: "of what race (*nizhād*) is he that he claims (*daʿwá*) the sultanate? How can a Tajik assert kingship (*pādshāhī*)?"[56]

The call to arms was heard from Andkhūd to Kāshghar, although this does not mean that militias from as far afield as Kāshghar participated. In *Tawishqān-Īl*, "Year of the Hare" (AH 752/28 February 1351 to 17 February 1352), tribal *lashkar*s, some 30,000 fighters, crossed the Oxus and gathered at Balkh. Their invasion (by my estimation) transpired after the summer had passed, in late 1351/early 1352 (before *Tawishqān-Īl* expired). Muḥammad Bāqir's decree of 23 Ṣafar 753/10 April 1352 was presumably penned not long after he assumed office. Details of the invasion are in Khʷāndamīr (who follows Mīrkhʷānd, who follows Ḥāfiẓ-i Abrū—who originated the details). Thackston's translation is superb. I shall therefore not regurgitate the report. Suffice it to mention that Chaghataid umbrage was palliated by the prospect of hurling cavalry against fortifications and defensive artillery.

Muʿizz al-Dīn Kart sallied to battle the Chaghataids, with poor results for him. He retreated behind Herat's fortifications. Qazghan is said to have derided the Kartid's martial aptitude. The parties reached an impasse: the Chaghataids had no prospect of capturing Herat or breaching its fortifications without siege equipment and skilled personnel. The Chaghataids never got past the "Kartid Wall," a *c.*10 mile/16 km perimeter encompassing Herat's suburbs (see Chapter Ten). A standoff ensued: Chaghataids could not enter Herat; the Kartids could not disperse the menace lingering outside.

The presence of Chaghataid militias will have stilled social and economic exchanges between Herat and its agrarian purlieus. Amirs on both sides were dejected by the standoff and searched for an exit. Qazghan harbored doubts,

54 On Qazghan/Qazaghan, see Aubin, "Khanat," *passim*. He was Qaraunas.
55 Khʷāndamīr/Siyāqī (ed.), *Ḥabīb*, 3:381; Khʷāndamīr/Thackston (tr.), *Habib*, 221.
56 Ḥāfiẓ-i Abrū, *Cinq*, 38; Ḥāfiẓ-i Abrū, *Karts*, 180.

complaining—even if the words put in his mouth are inexact—of "self-interested persons" leading him astray. The parties talked truce and conciliation. Envoys were exchanged; the Kartid paid tribute and pledged fealty. The Chaghataids could withdraw with honor, which they did with haste.[57]

The likelihood of Muʿizz al-Dīn remaining in office distressed the "self-interested persons" that had triggered the Chaghataid incursion. Muʿizz al-Dīn's amirs, predominant among them being Ghurid commanders, soured on the Kartid and turned, forcing him to take refuge at Fort Iskilchih. Muḥammad Bāqir was installed, possibly a few days before he published the decree of 23 Ṣafar 753/10 April 1352 releasing Jāmī assets.

In 753/1352, shortly after his overthrow, Muʿizz al-Dīn fled to Transoxiana with an escort of fifty horsemen to seek asylum with Qazghan. He was welcomed by the chief of *ulus* Chaghatai, but certain Chaghataid amirs considered Muʿizz al-Dīn's presence in their midst a gift from Heaven and connived to murder him. The Kartid, however, retained Qazghan's protection. Qazghan has use for him and spared his life. Muʿizz al-Dīn regained the throne, but the "how" is not known. A report claims that he had marched into Herat's citadel and ejected his brother, which is unlikely.[58] It is all but certain that Qazghan and Muʿizz al-Dīn had negotiated with Ghurid amirs, Jāmī shaykhs, and Herat's *aʿyān*; and utilized arbitrators to facilitate the Kartid's return. These details are not known.

*The Return*

Qazghan will have seen the benefit of strong and stable leadership in Herat. He will not have wanted political disarray to weaken the region; and open it up for conquest by the Sarbadars. Although the sources do not say this, he was probably receiving tribute from Muʿizz al-Dīn. An annual tribute, which aside from pacifying Chaghataid chieftains baying for the Kartid's blood, will have defrayed the outlays for their misadventure.

57 The discussion so far is based on Ḥāfiẓ-i Abrū, *Cinq*, 38–43; Ḥāfiẓ-i Abrū, *Karts*, 179–85; Mīrkhʷānd, *Rawżat*, 3,713–716; Isfizārī, *Rawżāt*, 2:13–16; Khʷāndamīr/Siyāqī (ed.), *Ḥabīb*, 3:381–82; Khʷāndamīr/Thackston (tr.), *Habib*, 221; Yazdī/ʿAbbāsī (ed.), *Ẓafarnāmah*, 1:24–28; Yazdī/Munshī, *Tārīkh-i pasandīdah*, 1:19–22.

58 The discussion so far is based on Ḥāfiẓ-i Abrū, *Cinq*, 43–45; Ḥāfiẓ-i Abrū, *Karts*, 185–88; Mīrkhʷānd, *Rawżat*, 3,716–718; Isfizārī, *Rawżāt*, 2:17–20; Khʷāndamīr/Siyāqī (ed.), *Ḥabīb*, 3:382–83; Khʷāndamīr/Thackston (tr.), *Habib*, 221–22; Yazdī/ʿAbbāsī (ed.), *Ẓafarnāmah*, 1:28–29; Yazdī/Munshī, *Tārīkh-i pasandīdah*, 1:22–23. See also Faṣīḥ, *Mujmal*, 940–43 (AH 751–53).

What of the "conspirators"? Muḥammad Bāqir Kart was briefly jailed and released; he went to Shiraz, where he resided until his death. The fate of the amirs that had revolted is not known. It is unlikely that Muʿizz al-Dīn risked angering Ghurid amirs or their troops. An amnesty was definitely included in the agreement that returned him to office.

Saʿd al-Dīn Masʿūd Taftāzānī, an intimate of Muʿizz al-Dīn Kart, to whom he had dedicated a treatise in 748/1347, found it expedient to remove himself to Turbat-i Jām for the duration of 752/1351–52, and possibly 753/1352–53. It is unclear if he was involved in the *coup d'état*, but his confidant, the vizier, certainly was—and Muʿizz al-Dīn thought so, too. Jāmī was incarcerated *c.* 753/1352f. after Muʿizz al-Dīn regained office. On 21 Rabīʿ II 754/26 May 1353, the vizier wrote from jail to his uncle-cum-father-in-law-cum-employer begging for clemency.[59] He maintained his innocence and claimed ignorance of his other uncle's (i.e., Rażī al-Dīn Aḥmad Jāmī's) dastardly deeds. In Ramażān 754/October 1353, the vizier was released; he wrote to Muʿizz al-Dīn to express gratitude.[60] Muʿīn al-Dīn returned to the vizierate.[61] His "bad" uncle was not punished.

City of God aptly describes the shrine communities that prospered as a consequence of financial and political patronage lavished on them by sultans and viziers. The shrine at Jām was affluent and formidable. Muʿizz al-Dīn probably did not want to retaliate against an influential and popular religious institution. Nonetheless, relations between the Kartid court and Jāmī shrine were decidedly arctic until 763/1361f., when Muʿizz al-Dīn made a benefaction that cracked the ice.[62] Meanwhile, the Shaykhs of Jām had their advocate—the vizier—back inside the Kartid court.

Muʿizz al-Dīn's ego was deflated by the ouster. He was, naturally, distrustful of "self-interested persons" promoting a particular course of action. He apparently realized that he was ill advised (at best), or manipulated, by the vizier (and others) into pursuing agendas that had cost him soldiers and treasure, and nearly cost him the throne. For the balance of his reign (two decades), he exercised prudence and diplomacy. In my opinion, he realized

[59] Yūsuf-i Ahl/Moayyad (ed.), *Farāʾid*, 1:338–42.

[60] Ibid., 1:363–67.

[61] The vizier was no stranger to the Kartid gaol. See Mahendrarajah, *Sufi Saint*, 65 and n.54.

[62] See ibid., 106 (benefaction and inscription honoring Muʿizz al-Dīn) and Plates 6–7.

that he could not see every angle to propositions put before him by officials, and decided that "no further action" was the judicious path. This is illustrated by his reaction—or lack thereof—to the murder of a father-in-law, Ṭaghā-Temür, despite calls for retaliation from significant quarters (see below).

Muʿizz al-Dīn had to publicly abase himself before he could close the door on this disagreeable episode: a condition of his return was public acknowledgement of Chaghataid suzerainty. He was compelled to mint coins (possibly as early as 753/1352f.) in the name of Būyān Qulī Khān (r. 749–60/1348–59), the Chaghataids' nominal Chinggisid.

Coins reflecting Chaghataid suzerainty have surfaced.[63] Figure 6.3 is an exemplar. The obverse has the *kalima* in a square surrounded by the names of the four caliphs. The reverse: "The exalted sultan, Būyān Qulī Khān. May God perpetuate his kingdom!" (*al-sulṭān al-aʿẓam | Būyān Qulī Khān | khal-lad Allāh mulkahu*). Struck in Herat, 75x.

## Muʿizz al-Dīn Kart's Second Reign

Muʿizz al-Dīn's bombast and conceit manifest in his proclamation of 5 August 1349 and his epistle to Muḥammad b. Tughluq thereafter, lead

Figure 6.3 Kartid coin in the name of the Chaghataid, Būyān Qulī Khān, Herat, AH 75x (courtesy of Stephen Album).

[63] Album, *Checklist*, 255 (Kartid coins), 216 (coins in name of Būyān Qulī Khān, including two minted at Herat). See also O. Codrington, "Note on Musalman Coins collected by Mr. G.P. Tate in Seistan," *JRAS* (1904):681–86, 682: struck at Herat, 75x. *Kalima* in square (as above) but with variant, *al-sulṭān al-ʿādil | Būyān Qulī Khān | khallad Allāh* [---]. Cf. ʿAlāʾ al-Dīnī, *Sikka-hā-yi Īrān* [vol. 2], 51–56: Chaghataid coins, but none were minted at Herat.

to the view that he may have been preparing for fresh hostilities against the Sarbadars. But with his return in 753/1352f., the Kartid's hubris and zeal were overcome by prudence and continence. It was not just suspicion of enemies burrowed inside the Kartid court that circumscribed his actions. The *malik*'s position with respect to internal enemies appears to have been secure; however, external enemies presented him with fluid conditions that demanded vigilance. Firstly, the Sarbadars, despite being riven by strife, had to be surveilled. Secondly, he ordinarily would have secured his realm's western border through a compact with the Sarbadars, but with their leaders dying in brisk succession, détente had to await the accession of ʿAlī Muʾayyad. Thirdly, Kartid *bandagān* were inclined to rebel, necessitating action by his army. Fourthly, and doubtless the paramount source of anxiety for the Kartid court, was the intensifying threat presented by *ulus* Chaghatai.

I shall expound on the four points sketched above: prudence, détente, *bandagān*, and *ulus* Chaghatai (namely, Temür).

*Prudence: Resisting Anti-Shiʿa Conflict*

Yaḥyá Karāwī (r.*c.* 752–59/1351–57)[64] had succeeded Shams al-Dīn ʿAlī (r.*c.* 748–52/1347–1351f.) as chief of the Sarbadar-Shaykhiyya condominium. Karāwī was devious; he lulled his enemies by projecting an image of restraint and rationality. This picture, relative to his predecessor's religious fervor, was not difficult to paint. Karāwī had come to power with the backing of factions opposed to Shams al-Dīn ʿAlī, namely, Sunnis. Although not a darwish, Karāwī showed respect to the Shaykhiyya, but shifted the official orientation of the Sarbadarid state to Sunni.[65] He acknowledged Ṭaghā-Temür's suzerainty, and inflated his ego by striking coins in his name and paying tribute.[66]

[64] Morton, "Numismatic," 256 (correct regnal dates).

[65] Mīrkhʷānd/Kiyānfar (ed.), *Rawżat*, 4,518; and Muḥammad Mīrkhʷānd, *Rawżat al-ṣafā*, 10 vols (Tehran: Intishārāt-i markazī khayyam pīrūz, 1339/1960), 5:620. Smith, *Sarbadar*, 133–34, esp. n.60.

[66] See Smith, *Sarbadar*, 74–76, 133–136, and 202 (list of coins); for mints and transcriptions, see E. von Zambaur, "Contributions à la numismatique Orientale," *Numismatische Zeitschrift* 37 (1905):113–98, 181–83.

Ṭaghā-Temür had survived a tempestuous epoch through a combination of caution and good fortune. Reassured by Yaḥyá Karāwī's outward deference, he became careless. He allowed Karāwī and 300 Sarbadars to enter his winter quarters (*qishlāq*) near the Caspian Sea—ostensibly for Karāwī to pay homage to his suzerain. The Sarbadarid cohort was inexplicably permitted to remain under arms. They struck on 16 Dhū al-Qaʿda 754/13 December 1353. One of Yaḥyá Karāwī's lieutenants felled Ṭaghā-Temür inside his own tent; Karāwī decapitated him. Ṭaghā-Temür's retinue was massacred.[67] The Sarbadars sought to secure for themselves all of Ṭaghā-Temür's territories. Other than for the Jawni-Qurban enclaves of Abīward, Khabūshān, Mashhad-Ṭūs, Nisā, and Yāzir,[68] Sarbadars had control (notionally, in instances) of western Khurasan, up to the Caspian littoral.[69]

This turn of affairs presented Muʿizz al-Dīn Kart with challenges. Arguably, Būyān Qulī Khān was his new suzerain. Ṭaghā-Temür, although a former suzerain, was his father-in-law. The latter connection, surely, resulted in pressure from the harem: Sulṭān-Khātūn (fl. 783/1381) bt. Ṭaghā-Temür, one of the Kartid's wives and mother to his designated heir, Ghiyāth al-Dīn (Pīr ʿAlī) Kart, was (one senses) a formidable lady. She, not Pīr ʿAlī, came out to greet Temür when Herat capitulated in 783/1381.

Pressure to act against the Sarbadars came from Muʿīn al-Dīn Jāmī, who claimed Herat's notables backed his proposal for war.[70] The preamble in Jāmī's letter reflects his religious biases. *Fitna*, he alleges, was raging from Mazandaran to Herat, and led to Ṭaghā-Temür's murder. His passing, however, is fortuitous: "The fortunes of God were blessed by chance." A catastrophe had befallen Islam: Ṭaghā-Temür had not defended the Faith and Khurasanians (that is, he had allowed the Sarbadars to prosper).[71] The

[67] Ḥāfiẓ-i Abrū, *Cinq*, 7; Mīrkhʷānd, *Rawżat*, 4,518–519; idem/1960 ed., *Rawżat*, 5:620; Smith, *Sarbadar*, 134–39.

[68] On Jawni-Qurban territories, see Ḥāfiẓ-i Abrū, *Cinq*, 28. Nishapur was lost to the Sarbadars by *c*. 749/1348f. Ibid., Notes, p.17.

[69] They had trouble holding their domains. Smith, *Sarbadar*, 139–40.

[70] Yūsuf-i Ahl/Moayyad (ed.), *Farāʾid*, 1:354–62.

[71] Shiʿi-oriented coins struck in Ṭaghā-Temür's name reflect legends with Muḥammad's name, followed by the names of the Twelve Imams. See ʿAlāʾ al-Dīnī, *Sikka-hā-yi Īrān* [vol. 1], 536 (struck at Āmul, 738/1337f.); and 570 (Āmul, 742/1341f. This coin has the Shiʿi supplement to the *shahāda*: "[...] *ʿAlī walī Allāh*"). Āmul was a venerable center for ʿAlid beliefs and learning.

assassination was an opportunity to extirpate *fitna* and return Khurasan to Islam. The crux:

> It is often said that the faith is renewed by miracles. As one man's candle can be ignited by another [man's candle], the hope is that the candle of [God's] mandate is re-ignited [by you] [...]. If, as the triumph (*nuṣrat*) of [Sunni] Islam moves to error,[72] [...] it is no mistake that the fire of *fitna* blazes. You [Muʿizz al-Dīn Kart] are favored [by the Almighty]. The sword of [God's] servant (*āb-dār*) [...] must obliterate (*bih bād-i fanā bar dād*), without hesitation (*bī-dirīgh*), the Sarbadar outlaws (*gardankishān*)![73]

Jāmī allows himself the pleasure of unleashing his belletrist skills on his father-in-law, interspersing the missive with excerpts from hadith and Qurʾan. But if we peel away the polemics—like "sectaries" (*ahl-i bidʿat*) and "party of Satan" (*ḥizb-i shayṭān*)—a political text emerges: the vizier is not proposing war solely on the basis of anti-Shiʿa prejudice, but because he perceives advantages to the Kartid state. Benefits would stem from the Kartid annexation of western Khurasan (presumably, minus the Jawni-Qurban's enclaves). The vizier apparently believed that the Sarbadar-Shaykhiyya polity was innately unstable and would implode if struck by a powerful external force. The Kartids could then extend their domains from the southeastern Caspian Sea littoral to the Hindu Kush, Sīstān, and Indus. Kartids would pay for the war with plunder and tax revenues from acquired lands. He was not wrong about the polity's inherent instability; however, it is possible the fractious Shiʿi-Sunni hybrid polity at Sabzavar could have united for the limited purpose of defeating the Kartids—before returning to their pursuit of factionalism.

Muʿizz al-Dīn demurred. A wise decision. War would have pitted him against the Sarbadar-Shaykhiyya confederation and other contenders for Ṭaghā-Temür's erstwhile dominions.[74] Muʿizz al-Dīn may have distrusted Jāmī's motives; he possibly feared that his devious vizier was hatching another scheme.

[72] Presumably means the Sunni path is losing ground to the Shiʿi path.

[73] Yūsuf-i Ahl/Moayyad (ed.), *Farāʾid*, 1:356.

[74] The primary challenger for Ṭaghā-Temür's domains, apart from Sarbadars, was Amir Walī b. Shaykh-ʿAlī Hindū. On him, see Smith, *Sarbadar*, 142–44; Ḥāfiẓ-i Abrū, *Cinq*, 9–14.

*Kartid-Sarbadarid Détente*

ʿAlī Muʾayyad came to power as co-regent with Darwish ʿAzīz (d. 764/1363). They ruled from 763/1362 to 764/1363, when Muʾayyad had his Shaykhiyya co-regent murdered. He hunted down Shaykhiyya, and desecrated the tombs of Khalīfa and Jūrī: "one wonders whether the extreme measures taken [by Muʾayyad] does not betray more than mere political hostility toward [Shaykhiyya] [...]. ʿAlī committed outrages against the dervishes—outrages which suggest moral revulsion as well as political antagonism."[75] ʿAlī Muʾayyad was oriented to the Twelver Shiʿa, and minted coins reflecting Twelver Shiʿi formulae.[76] He tried to extirpate Shiʿi extremist concepts and rituals that had taken root in his realm, and replace them with "proper" Twelver Shiʿa concepts and rituals.[77]

ʿAlī Muʾayyad moved to secure his borders with the Kartids and Jawni-Qurban. "ʿAlī Muʾayyad needed peace in the east because he had to make war in the west."[78] There is no direct evidence of an agreement between ʿAlī Muʾayyad and Muḥammad Bīk; nor is there direct evidence of an agreement between Muʾayyad and Muʿizz al-Dīn. But there is indirect evidence. According to a document penned by Muʿīn al-Dīn Jāmī, Muʿizz al-Dīn Kart and Muḥammad Bīk had met and conferred within the sacred confines of Aḥmad-i Jām's shrine at Turbat-i Jām in Muḥarram 768/September–October 1366.[79] The meeting was held for "the security and tranquility of Muslims, and the sustainment and contentment of peoples" (*īn ijtimāʿ sabab amn wa amān-i muslimān-ān wa qūt wa salwat-i jahānī-ān gasht*).[80] Specifics are not provided. The meeting demonstrates the Kartid's willingness to parley with rivals. Muʿīn al-Dīn Jāmī includes fulsome praise for Muʿizz al-Dīn.[81]

75 Smith, *Sarbadar*, 146–47.

76 On the Shiʿi coins, see Smith, *Sarbadar*, 188–89, 197–98, 202–203 (list of coins); ʿAlāʾ al-Dīnī, *Sikka-hā-yi Īrān* [vol. 2], 31–50 (images and transcriptions); E. von Zambaur, "Contributions à la numismatique Orientale," *Numismatische Zeitschrift* 36 (1904):43–122, 99; Bedrich Augst, "A Persian coin of the 'Gallows Bird' dynasty," *Numismatic Review* 4/2–4 (1947):91–92 and Plate XXIV (excellent image).

77 See Mahendrarajah, "Sarbadars," 384, 394–96.

78 Smith, *Sarbadar*, 148. Said of the Jawni-Qurban but applies to the Kartids, too.

79 Yūsuf-i Ahl/Moayyad (ed.), *Farāʾid*, 1:275–81. Spiritual edifices serve as "safe spaces" for meetings between rivals. See Mahendrarajah, *Sufi Saint*, 161–63.

80 Yūsuf-i Ahl/Moayyad (ed.), *Farāʾid*, 1:276.

81 Ibid., 1:278–79; also Aubin, "Khanat," 45–46.

The praise by Jāmī, and the Kartid's willingness to sojourn at Jām and patronize the shrine (in 763/1361f.), indicate that the Jāmīs and the Kartid had moved on from the earlier unpleasantness and fashioned a cordial working relationship.

ʿAlī Muʾayyad occupied himself developing his Twelver Shiʿa state. He expelled Shaykhiyya, but was unsuccessful at extirpating the "unorthodox" (*ghuluww*) Shiʿi beliefs of his subjects.[82] Darwish rebels outside his realm, and Shaykhiyya adherents inside his realm, were to undermine his state. Muʿizz al-Dīn granted Shaykhiyya asylum in Herat but barred them from unsettling the Kartid-Sarbadarid détente.

*Rebellious* Bandagān

The Kartid realm was held together by a wide network of petty lords (pl. *bandagān*), a few of whom were predisposed to rebellion whenever opportunity presented itself. Muʿizz al-Dīn, like his father, had to suppress *bandagān* who yearned to establish their own kingdom. In this instance, the seditious *banda* was Satilmish Bīk (d. 759/1358) b. ʿAbdallāh Mawlāy of Quhistān, who found an ally in Muḥammad Khʷājah (d. 759/1358), Apardi amir of Shibūrghān and Andkhūd. Qazghan was probably deceased.[83] Muḥammad Khʷājah had nursed a grudge against the Kartid since the Chaghataid siege of Herat in 752/1351f. The pair, joined by Chūpān Qaraunas (n.d.), moved to seize citadels in Khʷāf, Bākharz, and Jām. Muʿizz al-Dīn (at the head of the Kartid army) met in Taybād with Zayn al-Dīn (Abū Bakr) Taybādī (d. 789/1391), a Sufi devoted to Aḥmad-i Jām. Taybādī was fond of Muʿizz al-Dīn Kart, who probably took spiritual counsel with the Sufi.

Battle was joined at Zirrah (near Lake Sistan). Satilmish Bīk and Muḥammad Khʷājah were killed.[84] Vizier Jāmī penned a letter to Muʿizz al-Dīn congratulating him for liberating Bākharz and defeating the rebels.

82 ʿAlī Muʾayyad's failure was due in part to the dearth of qualified Shiʿi ulama to educate the masses on Twelver Shiʿa beliefs. In desperation, Muʾayyad wrote to "the first martyr," Muḥammad ibn Makkī (d. 786/1384), pleading for him to come to Khurasan to educate the masses. See Mahendrarajah, "Sarbadars," 381, 395–96.

83 Faṣīḥ, *Mujmal*, 953 (Qazghan's death, AH 759/1357–58).

84 Ḥāfiẓ-i Abrū, *Cinq*, 45–47; Ḥāfiẓ-i Abrū, *Karts*, 188–90; Mīrkhʷānd, *Rawżat*, 3,719–722; Khʷāndamīr/Siyāqī (ed.), *Ḥabīb*, 3:383–84; Khʷāndamīr/Thackston (tr.), *Habib*, 222; Isfizārī, *Rawżāt*, 2:21–23.

Kartid subjects, Jāmī writes, should be grateful for their king's deeds, which fortified "the House of Kart, [the] progeny of Sultan Sanjar" (*Āl-i Kart bin Sanjar*).[85] A chronogram by Mīrkhʷānd,[86] reproduced in Khʷāndamīr,[87] has the Satilmish-Khʷājah episode terminating in the "middle of" [16th] Rabīʿ I 759/*c.* 26 February 1359.

The year is significant because the internal politics of *ulus* Chaghatai were heating up, which connects to the fourth point: the threat posed by the *ulus.* By 771/1370, after a decade of struggles, Temür was perched at the political apex of *ulus* Chaghatai. Muʿizz al-Dīn Kart died on 5 Dhū al-Qaʿda 771/31 May 1370, leaving the bulk of his kingdom to his favorite son, Pīr ʿAlī Kart (r. 771–83/1370–81), a young man intellectually ill-equipped to grasp, much less manage, the danger presented by Temür.

*Temür and the Kartids*

The politics of Transoxiana were not readily severed from the politics of Khurasan (and vice versa). Satilmish Bīk had sought an ally in Muḥammad Khʷājah (Apardi), just as Rażī al-Dīn Aḥmad Jāmī had sought an ally in the amirs of the Apardi and Arlat. The Oxus was now a notional line of demarcation between Khurasan and Transoxiana.

The Chaghatai occupied a slender strip of Khurasan, ceded to Turkic and Turco-Mongol émigrés.[88] Areas integral to the *ulus* were (west to east): Andkhūd, Shibūrghān, Balkh, Khulm, Qunduz, and Ṭāliqān, and populated by (among others), the Apardi, Arlat, and Qaraunas.

The martial spirits of the "tribes" of the *ulus* had not been harnessed and focused on attaining specific political objectives. Yasaʾur had had limited successes. Temür, however, was an astute and skilled politician. He fused discrete and fractious components of the *ulus,* and transformed the amalgamated product into an army of conquest.[89] But before Temür could

[85] Yūsuf-i Ahl/Moayyad (ed.), *Farāʾid,* 1:345–47. The biological link to Sanjar is fabricated.

[86] Mīrkhʷānd, *Rawżat,* 3,721–722; cf. Faṣīḥ, *Mujmal,* 948 (under AH 756/1355–56).

[87] Khʷāndamīr/Siyāqī (ed.), *Ḥabīb,* 3:384; Khʷāndamīr/Thackston (tr.), *Habib,* 222.

[88] This strip is today called "Afghan Turkistan." Descendants of *ulus* Chaghatai are generically-categorized "Uzbek" or "Turkmen." See Gunnar Jarring, *On the distribution of Turk tribes in Afghanistan: An attempt at a preliminary classification* (Lund: Gleerup, 1939). Familiar Turco-Mongol "tribes" (e.g., Apardi, Arlat, Kereit, Merkit, Naiman, Oirat) are now called "Uzbek" (ibid., 52–64). On "Chaghatai Turks," see ibid., 67–68.

[89] See Manz, "*ulus* Chaghatai," *et passim.*

coalesce and direct the *ulus*, he had to claw his way to its political apex.[90] The Kartids and Jawni-Qurban protected Temür's family, which allowed him to continue his struggles for supremacy without fearing for his family. Temür's son lived at the Kartid court. Other family members resided in Mākhān under the Jawni-Qurban's protection.[91]

Qazghan was succeeded by son, ʿAbdallāh (r. 759–*c*. 761/1358–60), then grandson, Amir Ḥusayn (d.*c*. 771/1369f. or 776/1375f.) b. Musalā.[92] Ḥusayn became Temür's principal opponent for supremacy over *ulus* Chaghatai. The contenders acquired allies outside the *ulus*, which in Temür's case included the Kartids.

There are two categories into which the relationship between Temür and Muʿizz al-Dīn may be fitted: a *passive alliance*, the view propounded in Shāmī's *Ẓafarnāmah* (completed *c*. 806/1404),[93] and in Yazdī's *Ẓafarnāmah* (completed *c*. 832/1427f.).[94] The second is an *active alliance*, the view propounded in *Rawżat al-ṣafā* of Mīrkhʷānd (d. 903/1498), and followed by his grandson, Khʷāndamīr (d. 941/1534f.), in *Ḥabīb al-siyar*.

First, the *Ẓafarnāmah* viewpoint, which is also in Naṭanzi (completed *c*. 816/1413f.). They are early sources and claim that Temür sought protection for his family, principally his first-born son,[95] Jahāngīr (b.*c*. 757/1356f.; d.*c*. 777/1376f.).[96] Temür's confidant, Chākū (Chekü) Barlās,[97] was dispatched to Herat, where he was graciously received by Muʿizz al-Dīn. The Kartid sought an alliance with Temür, and invited Temür to meet him at Sarakhs.

[90] See Manz, *Tamerlane*, 41–65 (Temür's rise to political apex).

[91] Mājān (Mā<u>kh</u>ān or Mā<u>ch</u>ān): western district of Marw and eponymous canal. Le Strange, *Lands*, 398–99, 403; Mahdī Sayyidī, *Jughrāfiyā-yi tārīkhī-yi Marw* (Tehran: Bunyād-i mawqūfāt-i Duktur Maḥmūd Afshār, 1386/2008), 71–73, 236–38.

[92] For their biographies, see Muʿīn al-Dīn Naṭanzī, *Muntakhab al-tawārīkh-i Muʿīnī*, ed. Parwīn Istakhrī (Tehran: Asāṭīr, 1383/2004f.), 205–14.

[93] Niẓām al-Dīn Shāmī, *Ẓafarnāmah*, eds F. Tauer and Muḥammad Aḥmad Panāhī (Tehran: Intishārāt-i Bāmdād, 1363/1984).

[94] Yazdī (d.*c*. 858/1454) follows Shāmī. "Yazdī's [*Ẓafarnāmah*] must be considered essentially a reworking of Shāmī's [*Ẓafarnāmah*]." John Woods, "The Rise of Tīmūrid Historiography," *JNES* 46/2 (1987):81–108, 102; Shāmī is the "most prominent of Yazdī's sources." İlker Evrim Binbaş, *Intellectual networks in Timurid Iran: Sharaf al-Dīn ʿAlī Yazdī and the Islamicate republic of letters* (Cambridge: Cambridge University Press, 2016), 223.

[95] ʿUmar-Shaykh (d. 793/1394) b. Temür was possibly older. See John Woods, *The Timurid Dynasty* (Bloomington, IN: RIIAS, 1990), 14 n.34.

[96] Yazdī/Munshī, *Tārīkh-i pasandīdah*, 1:184; Woods, *Timurid*, 17, 29 (Table 2).

[97] On Chikū/Chekü and the Barlās, see Manz, *Tamerlane*, *et passim*.

However, Temür distrusted the Kartids because of their history of "perfidy," which Yazdī singularly describes in detail. This, Shāmī, Yazdī, and Naṭanzi claim, is why Temür refused the Kartid's invitation to meet. Nonetheless, not wishing to be churlish, Temür entrusted Jahāngīr to Muʿizz al-Dīn Kart. (But if Kartids were so perfidious, why gift-wrap the boy for them?) Jahāngīr b. Temür came to Herat accompanied by Mubārak-Shāh Sanjarī of Mājān, while others of Temür's family were ensconced at Mājān.[98]

The *active alliance* version is that Temür met with Muʿizz al-Dīn,[99] and was granted one of the Kartid's select steeds (*asb-i khāṣa-yi khūd*); 200 *kharwār* (60,000 kg/132,000 lb) of cereals (*ghalla*) from (the silos at) Sarakhs;[100] and 10,000 *Kapakī* dinars.

The narratives are not mutually exclusive. Reconstructing events, it seems that the *active* alliance transformed into a *passive* alliance—the product of later circumstances. This is why the Timurid court stenographer, ʿAlī Yazdī,[101] spills a pint of ink to blacken the Kartid house; whereas Shāmī and Naṭanzī treat gently the allegation of Kartid duplicity.[102]

The active alliance emerged after Temür was imprisoned in Mājān by ʿAlī Bīk b. Arghūn-Shāh. He was younger brother to Muḥammad Bīk (d.*c.* 774/1373), then leading the Jawni-Qurban.[103] Muḥammad Bīk secured Temür's release. Temür then contacted Muʿizz al-Dīn Kart; they met at Sarakhs where the cereals supplied by the Kartids were stored. Temür would have needed cereals and silver to feed and pay, and thereby retain, his supporters. The meeting probably transpired between 762/1361 and 764/1363 when Temür was in tight straits. In 767/1366, with Ḥusayn ruling *ulus* Chaghatai, Temür's family was entrusted to the Sanjarī clan at Mājān; Chākū Barlās visited the Kartid court.[104]

98 Yazdī/Munshī, *Tārīkh-i pasandīdah*, 1:99–100; Yazdī/ʿAbbāsī (ed.), *Ẓafarnāmah*, 1:112–14; Shāmī, *Ẓafarnāmah*, 43–44; Naṭanzī, *Muntakhab*, 193; Manz, *Tamerlane*, 48, 52–53 (and n.45 to p.53); Aubin, "Khanat," 43–47. Jahāngīr lived in Herat for several years.

99 Khʷāndamīr/Siyāqī (ed.), *Ḥabīb*, 3:400–02; Khʷāndamīr/Thackston (tr.), *Habib*, 231–32; Mīrkhʷānd, *Rawżat*, 4,547–49; Aubin, "Khanat," 43–44.

100 Cereals of Sarakhs were supposedly of high quality. Krawulsky, *Ḫorāsān*, 1:76–77.

101 For more refined views of Yazdī's history, see Binbaş, *Intellectual*, 1–3, 217–23.

102 Yazdī/Munshī, *Tārīkh-i pasandīdah*, 1:99–100 and Yazdī/ʿAbbāsī (ed.), *Ẓafarnāmah*, 1:112–13; cf. Shāmī, *Ẓafarnāmah*, 43; Naṭanzī, *Muntakhab*, 193.

103 On ʿAlī Bīk and Jawni-Qurban, see Paul, "Zerfall und Bestehen," 713ff.

104 Yazdī/Munshī, *Tārīkh-i pasandīdah*, 1:44–46; Yazdī/ʿAbbāsī (ed.), *Ẓafarnāmah*, 1:51–53; Shāmī, *Ẓafarnāmah*, 20–21; Naṭanzī, *Muntakhab*, 172, 189–94; Ḥāfiẓ-i Abrū, *Zubdat*,

## Political Triangle: Jāmī Sufis, Kartids, and Temür

The Kart vizier, Muʿīn al-Dīn Jāmī, doubtless propelled Kartid support for Temür—although the sources make no mention of his role.

### *The Jāmī Branch in Transoxiana*

The Jāmī family had marital and affinal connections in Samarqand and Tirmiz, including with the Sayyids of Tirmiz.[105] The Tirmizi sayyids produced the holders of high religious ranks, chiefly, the *ṣadr* and *shaykh al-Islām*, who for generations dominated Transoxiana's political-religious scene. Yazdī's *Ẓafarnāmah* reports on persons titled *khān-zāda*—a rendering of *khānd-zāda*; contraction for *khudāwand-zāda*, or sayyid—including the ʿAlāʾ al-Mulk sayyids, who were Temür's intimates, and came to recognize his position.[106] Yūsuf-i Ahl's *Farāʾid-i Ghiyāṣī* contains many letters to the Jāmī branch in Samarqand and Tirmiz, including ʿAlāʾ al-Mulk sayyids.[107] The Tirmizi sayyids, apart from rebelling one time (in 773–74/1372–73),[108] a betrayal for which they were forgiven,[109] remained faithful: "[f]rom then onwards the Tirmidh sayyids remained Timur's faithful adherents [...]." In 1394, for instance, "Timur took up his quarters in Tirmidh in the house of *khudāwand-zāda* ʿAlāʾ al-Mulk."[110] The ʿAlāʾ al-Mulk Jāmī lineage assumed the stewardship of Aḥmad-i Jām's shrine from 809/1407 until (at least) 863/1459.[111]

Muʿizz al-Dīn Kart's support for Temür could be a case of "hedging bets," balanced by support for his rival, Ḥusayn. He, learning of Kartid support for Temür, tried to acquire assistance for himself. Ḥusayn came to Herat, where he was treated properly, but it is not made known if Muʿizz

1:406–07 (under AH 767); Ḥāfiẓ-i Abrū, *Cinq*, 28–29; Aubin "Khanat," 43–44; Manz, *Tamerlane*, 47–53.

105 On the sayyids of Tirmiz, see V.V. Barthold, *Four Studies on the History of Central Asia: Ulugh Beg*, tr. by V. and T. Minorsky (Leiden: Brill, 1963), 2:4–7, 19. On Jāmī marital and affinal ties to the sayyids, see Mahendrarajah, *Sufi Saint*, 67, 139–40, and Fig. A1.4.

106 See, e.g., Yazdī/ʿAbbāsī (ed.), *Ẓafarnāmah*, 1:157; Yazdī/Munshī, *Tārīkh-i pasandīdah*, 1:140; Manz, *Tamerlane*, 57 and n.62. One prominent name is ʿAlī Akbar Tirmizī (n.d.).

107 Yūsuf-i Ahl/Moayyad (ed.), *Farāʾid*, 2:314–17 (from the vizier to ʿAlī Akbar Tirmizī).

108 Yazdī/ʿAbbāsī (ed.), *Ẓafarnāmah*, 1:170–73; Yazdī/Munshī, *Tārīkh-i pasandīdah*, 1:150–53; Manz, *Tamerlane*, 60. Date established by Manz.

109 Executions were abhorred and avoided where possible. See Manz, *Tamerlane*, 64.

110 Barthold, *Four Studies*, 2:19 (the year given is 1371).

111 Mahendrarajah, *Sufi Saint*, 117; Table 5.2; Fig. A1.4.

al-Dīn gave him cash, matériel or foodstuffs.[112] Alternatively, Muʿizz al-Dīn may have decided to support only Temür because, firstly, the Tirmizi sayyids and the Transoxiana Jāmīs supported Temür; secondly, the shrewd vizier, Muʿīn al-Dīn Jāmī, had evaluated the struggle between Temür and Ḥusayn and decided the probability of success favored Temür; thirdly, Muʿizz al-Dīn was trying to protect the patrimonies of sons, Pīr ʿAlī and Muḥammad Kart, by accommodating Temür.

### *Vizier Jāmī and Statecraft*

An excursus on viziers, statecraft, and espionage may help in appreciating the roles of the Jāmī Sufis in, firstly, facilitating Muʿizz al-Dīn's interactions with Temür; secondly, facilitating the downfall of Pīr ʿAlī Kart.

One of the principal duties of any vizier in medieval Persia was that of spymaster. The paramountcy of intelligence in statecraft is under-appreciated. Ibn Battuta describes his arrival in Sind and investigation by the sultan's intelligence officers; form of the report they prepared on arrivals; the manner in which it was swiftly transmitted to the sultan.[113] Ideally, every arrival to the Kartid realm will have been investigated. Seljuq vizier Niẓām al-Mulk (d. 485/1092) on espionage and statecraft:[114]

> [The king] must have postmasters [= spymasters]. [...] In every age [before Islam and after], [Iranian] kings have had postmasters, through whom they have learnt everything that goes on, good and bad. [...] But this [espionage] is a delicate business involving some unpleasantness; it must be entrusted to [...] men who are completely above suspicion and without self-interest, for the weal or woe of the country depends on them. They must be directly responsible to the king and not to anyone else [...].[115]

Muʿīn al-Dīn Jāmī was the "Eyes and Ears" (*ʿuyūn wa jawāsīs*) of the King.[116] He was well placed to operate as the Kartid spymaster. Firstly, the *Farāʾid-i*

[112] Mīrkhʷānd, *Rawżat*, 4,548–49.

[113] Ibn Battuta, *Travels*, 3:593–95.

[114] Niẓām al-Mulk, *Book of Government*, 66–75, 78–91, 162–63.

[115] Niẓām al-Mulk, *Book of Government*, 66–67; idem, *Siyāsatnāmah*, 73–74. On the *barīd*, postal system, which included intelligence gathering and reporting, see Adam Silverstein, *Postal Systems in the Pre-Modern Islamic World* (Cambridge: Cambridge University Press, 2007).

[116] On "Eyes and Ears," see Silverstein, *Postal*, 20–23. See also Boyce (tr.), *Tansar*, 49–51.

*Ghiyāṣī* shows that he corresponded with viziers, amirs, and sultans over his long tenure (from 735/1334–35 to *c.* 780–82/1378–80;[117] d. 783/1381). Secondly, he traveled on the Hajj, and became acquainted with men of high standing; thirdly, his Sufi family had a sprawling international network of informants: family, sultans, amirs, viziers, ulama, sayyids, Sufis, darwishes, and devotees in Persia, India, and Central Asia. Niẓām al-Mulk advices: "Spies must constantly go out to the limits of the kingdom in the guise of merchants, travelers, Sufis, [medicine sellers], and mendicants (*darwīsh-ān*), and bring back reports [...]."[118] Jāmī did not have to dispatch spies in "the guise of" Sufis because his extensive Sufi family traveled far and near; and Aḥmad-i Jām's shrine, seminaries and hospices attracted pilgrims, Sufis, ulama, and notables from around the eastern Islamic world. As we witnessed with the machinations of Shihāb al-Dīn Ismāʿīl Jāmī, ʿAbd al-Raḥman Isfarāyinī, and ʿAlāʾ al-Dawla Simnānī in securing Ghiyāth al-Dīn Kart's parole from Öljeitü's court, the Sufi social-political network was influential.

The vizier was the hub through which flowed an enormous quantity of information from a bewildering array of sources. His erudition and perspicacity will have benefited him in filtering and analyzing myriads of reports, sifting fact from rumor, and identifying real nuggets. This talent would ordinarily have benefited the Kartid state, but with respect to pressing political deliberations—say, the question of "shall we stick with Pīr ʿAlī or shall we stick it to Pīr ʿAlī?"—the Jāmī clan, as the guardians of Aḥmad-i Jām's legacy, utilized a consensus approach: they consulted and acted in *their* best interests. Herein lies the chief drawback to *this* vizier functioning as chief of intelligence: Muʿīn al-Dīn was not "without self-interest." He had loyalties to his family, which was perched at the apex of a formidable Sufi *Gemeinschaft*. This will become clear momentarily.

## Muʿizz al-Dīn Kart's Last Will and Testament: A Divided Realm

Pīr ʿAlī and Muḥammad were step-brothers and rivals for the throne. Pīr ʿAlī was the son of Sulṭān-Khātūn;[119] Muḥammad was from a union (concubinage

[117] The vizier served Pīr ʿAlī, too, but possibly not to the bitter end.
[118] Niẓām al-Mulk, *Book of Government*, 78; idem, *Siyāsatnāmah*, 87.
[119] Ḥāfiẓ-i Abrū, *Cinq*, 32; Ḥāfiẓ-i Abrū, *Kart*, 172.

or marriage) with a lady from the Chaghatai's Arlat tribe.[120] Muʿīn al-Dīn Jāmī was married to Muʿizz al-Dīn's daughter from the Arlat union, that is, to Muḥammad's sister. The Jāmī-Arlāt marital and non-marital ties are too opaque to unravel: it was no coincidence (in my opinion) that Rażī al-Dīn Aḥmad Jāmī complained to the Apardi and Arlat about Muʿizz al-Dīn. Rażī al-Dīn had influential relatives in *ulus* Chaghatai. His progeny at Turbat-i Jām administered Aḥmad-i Jām's shrine until the death of his son, Shihāb al-Dīn Ismāʿīl Jāmī (d. 809/1407), when the stewardship shifted to Rażī al-Dīn Aḥmad's progeny in Transoxiana.

Intrigues in the seraglio between the first/older wife and the second/younger wife (i.e., Sulṭān-Khātūn and the Arlat lady) exacerbated the anxieties confounding the dying king's mind. He partitioned his kingdom between both sons, but not equally. Muḥammad Kart received a rump state at Sarakhs, while Pīr ʿAlī received Herat and its dominions. John Masson Smith was harsh in his assessment: "possessed of a kind of fatuity that had all too often afflicted rulers, he intended to divide his realm between the two [brothers]."[121] Muʿizz al-Dīn (in my opinion) did this to conciliate the Arlat, and forestall Muḥammad Kart (and his Arlat relatives) from fomenting strife if he were disinherited outright.

The Jāmī leadership's reaction to the accession of Pīr ʿAlī is an unknown variable, meaning it was conceivably a key factor. There is an odd phrase in Muʿizz al-Dīn's decree issued just before his death on 5 <u>Dh</u>ū al-Qaʿda 771/31 May 1370, confirming Shihāb al-Dīn Ismāʿīl Jāmī (d. 809/1407) b. Rażī al-Dīn Aḥmad as the shrine's custodian: "*I* have spoken and *I* have cast [this] off *my* neck" (*man guft-am wa az gardan-i khūd bīrūn kard-am*).[122] A personal interjection in a chancery text, and in the first-person singular (not majestic first-person plural), hints of hidden undertows.

In any event, Muʿizz al-Dīn's decision was based chiefly on hope and not reality: the hope of a dying father that the Chaghataids, now led by Temür, would not march on Herat and seize his favorite son's patrimony. His judgment, clouded by affection for Pīr ʿAlī, failed to anticipate the young heir's impetuousness and inability to accept wise counsel, which sparked defections

120 Ḥāfiẓ-i Abrū, *Cinq*, 49; Ḥāfiẓ-i Abrū, *Kart*, 192. Her name is not given.
121 Smith, *Sarbadar*, 150.
122 Yūsuf-i Ahl/Berlin, *Farāʾīd*, ff. 315$^b$–316$^b$.

of high-level *aʿyān* to Temür and contributed to the fall of the Kartid dynasty. Muʿīn al-Dīn Jāmī directed a surreptitious campaign against Pīr ʿAlī, while Jāmī ally, Zayn al-Dīn Taybādī, headed a vociferous campaign.[123]

## Downfall: the Reign of Pīr ʿAlī Kart

The last years of the Sarbadars, and their conflicts with the Kartids and interlopers in Sarbadarid-Kartid space, namely, Amir Walī of Mazandaran, have been analyzed by Jean Aubin.[124] Pīr ʿAlī, with his father barely in his grave, marched on Sarakhs in (late summer to early fall) 772/1370 to snatch his half-brother's patrimony. Muḥammad Kart allied with the Sarbadarids, who had suffered provocation from Pīr ʿAlī, which they interpreted "as a *casus belli*."[125] Pīr ʿAlī was forced to abandon his Sarakhs campaign in winter 772/1370–71. He subsequently came to a political accommodation with Muḥammad,[126] which allowed Pīr ʿAlī to disengage from Sarakhs and focus on the Sarbadars. The downfall of the Kartids was rooted in Sunni–Shiʿa sectarian conflict.

### *Ghāzī Pīr ʿAlī Kart*

Pīr ʿAlī decided to become a Sunni "warrior for God" (*ghāzī*) and wage jihad against ʿAlī Muʾayyad's Twelver Shiʿa kingdom. He acquired a fatwa from ulama at a Ḥanafī college (*Niẓāmiyya*) in Herat,[127] which proclaimed the Kartid duty-bound to defend the Sunni path against the Shiʿa.[128] John Masson Smith hypothesized that Pīr ʿAlī's animus toward the Sarbadars had genesis in "familial hatred" for the murder of his grandfather, Ṭaghā-Temür. Muʿizz al-Dīn's greatest triumph had been at Zāwa: "we may imagine the eagerness of the prince to surpass his father's exploits."[129] A further possibility is the imperative for Pīr ʿAlī to secure support in religious and military quarters (ulama, amirs, *aʿyān*). It probably did not hurt to wrap himself in the banner of (Sunni) Islam and fight the Shiʿa.

[123] On Taybādī's campaign, see Mahendrarajah, "Tamerlane's Conquest."
[124] Aubin, "Sarbadar." See also Smith, *Sarbadar*, 148–55.
[125] Smith, *Sarbadar*, 151.
[126] Ibid.; Ḥāfiẓ-i Abrū, *Cinq*, 51–52; Ḥāfiẓ-i Abrū, *Kart*, 194–95.
[127] Possibly one of the three seminaries patronized by the Kartids. See Table A3.1.
[128] Ḥāfiẓ-i Abrū, *Cinq*, 52; Ḥāfiẓ-i Abrū, *Kart*, 196.
[129] Smith, *Sarbadar*, 150.

*Ghāzī* Pīr ʿAlī forged ahead with his anti-Shiʿa campaigns, beginning in 773/1371–72. The Kartid campaigns continued annually. The Nishapur Quarter, and its cities of Nishapur and Sabzavar, bore the brunt of the conflict. The city of Nishapur, Ḥāfiẓ-i Abrū hastens to remind his readers, was a majority Sunni city but under Shiʿi rule; hence, a prize for Pīr ʿAlī, who wanted to be the "liberator" (*fātiḥ*) of Nishapur. Amir Walī took interest in the conflict. Walī, after nibbling hesitantly at the westernmost verges of the Sarbadars' realm,[130] took larger bites: western Khurasan and Sabzavar. The Shiʿi state was mauled and dismembered by Walī and Pīr ʿAlī. Muʿizz al-Dīn had granted Shaykhiyya fugitives asylum but forbade them from disquieting the détente. Pīr ʿAlī had no such compunctions; he unleashed the Shaykhiyya on ʿAlī Muʾayyad's state.[131] Shaykhiyya fugitives in Shiraz, led by one Darwish Rukn al-Dīn, were armed and pointed at Khurasan by Shāh Shujāʿ (r. 759–86/1358–84), the Muẓaffarid dynast of Fars. Add to this volatile mixture one Iskandar-Shaykhī b. Afrāsiyāb Chilāwī/Chalāwī,[132] who inveigled himself into Kartid service.[133]

The chronology and summary in Table 6.1 are based on Smith,[134] Aubin,[135] Ḥāfiẓ-i Abrū,[136] Mīrkhwānd,[137] Khwāndamīr,[138] and Isfizārī.[139]

### *Pīr ʿAlī Kart and Temür*

Pīr ʿAlī was not politically astute. By unsettling the détente that Muʿizz al-Dīn had nurtured, he set in train events that brought destruction and chaos to western Khurasan, impoverished the Kartid fisc and enfeebled his military. An observation—in a Timurid era hagiography—is on target in its evaluation of Pīr ʿAlī's path: "he eschewed his father's path in its entirety" (*ṭarīq-i pidar rā tamām az dast bāz dāsht*).[140]

130 The realm ran from Bisṭām (*c.* 55° 00′ E) to Farhād-Gard and included Nishapur

131 Smith, *Sarbadar*, 151.

132 Member of a minor Shiʿi dynasty from Āmul, Mazandaran. C.E. Bosworth, "Āl-e Afrāsīāb," *EIr*, 1:742–43. On Chilāwī/Chalāwī and Pīr ʿAlī, see Ḥāfiẓ-i Abrū, *Kart*, 198–99.

133 Smith, *Sarbadar*, 85, 152.

134 Ibid., 83–86, 151–55.

135 Aubin, "Sarbadar," 99–104.

136 Ḥāfiẓ-i Abrū, *Cinq*, 9–11, 13, 52–57; Ḥāfiẓ-i Abrū, *Kart*, 195–202.

137 Mīrkhwānd, *Rawżat*, 3,725–26.

138 Khwāndamīr/Siyāqī (ed.), *Ḥabīb*, 3:366–67; Khwāndamīr/Thackston (tr.), *Habib*, 211–12.

139 Isfizārī, *Rawżāt*, 2:29–31.

140 Anonymous, *Maqāmāt-i Tāybādī*, ed. Sayyid ʿAlāʾ al-Dīn Gūsha-Gīr (Dizfūl [Khūzistān]: Intishārāt-i afhām, 1382/2003), 89. Written in the reign of Shāh-Rukh (r. 809–50/1407–47).

*Table 6.1 Kartid-Sarbadarid Campaigns in the Nishapur Quarter, 773/1371 to 783/1381*

| Year | Event | Political/Military Impact | Social/Economic Impact |
|---|---|---|---|
| 773/1371–72 | 1st Kartid campaign for Nishapur | Failed. Kartids withdraw | Fighting in orchards outside Nishapur |
| 774/1372–73 | 2nd Kartid campaign for Nishapur | Failed. Kartids withdraw | Damage to the countryside |
| 775/1373–74 (?) | 3rd Kartid campaign for Nishapur | Failed. Kartids withdraw | Severe damage to the countryside. Kartid army plunders villages in the Quarter |
| 776/1374–75 | 4th Kartid campaign for Nishapur | Failed. Kartids withdraw | "Most" orchards and edifices destroyed; "some" *kārīzes* clogged |
| 776/1374–75 or possibly 777/1375–76 | Sabzavar under siege by Amir Walī | 1). ʿAlī Muʾayyad on defensive;<br>2). Re-deploys troops from Nishapur for the defense of Sabzavar<br>3). Walī lifts siege of Sabzavar; withdraws to Mazandaran | Not specified |
| 777/1375–76 | 5th Kartid campaign for Nishapur | 1). Muʾayyad defending Nishapur and Sabzavar<br>2). Nishapur capitulates to Kartids<br>3). Pīr ʿAlī appoints Iskandar-Shaykhī Chilāwī as Nishapur's governor | Not specified |
| Not clear | – | 1). Iskandar-Shaykhī joins forces with Darwish Rukn al-Dīn<br>2). Renounces allegiance to Kartids<br>3). Nishapur controlled by the Shiʿa (= Shaykhiyya + Chilāwī) | Not specified |

| | | | |
|---|---|---|---|
| 778/1376–77 | Iskandar-Shaykhī and Rukn al-Dīn besiege Sabzavar | 1). Shaykhiyya collaborators embedded in Sabzavar aid the besiegers<br>2). Sabzavar capitulates<br>3). Muʾayyad flees; finds refuge with Walī in Mazandaran<br>4). *Khuṭba* read in Rukn al-Dīn's name<br>5). Nishapur *and* Sabzavar under Shiʿa control (= Shaykhiyya + Chilāwī) | Severe damage to the Sabzavar region |
| 778/1376–77 (possibly later) | 6th Kartid campaign for Nishapur (to seize it from Shaykhiyya and Chilāwī) | Successful | Not specified |
| 780/1379 | ʿAlī Muʾayyad besieges Sabzavar in six month campaign; receives military support from Walī | 1). Sabzavar re-captured<br>2). Shaykhiyya appeal to Pīr ʿAlī for help<br>3). Pīr ʿAlī refuses<br>4). Rukn al-Dīn executed | Sabzavar region in ruins; famine prevails |
| 782–83/1380–81 | Temür invades Khurasan | Muʾayyad covenants with Temür; retains his kingdom as Temür's *banda* | N/A |

Pīr ʿAlī's campaigns, ostensibly to "defend" Islam from Shiʿa, weakened Sunnis and Shiʿis of Khurasan, and empowered extremist (*ghulāt*) Shiʿis. In trying to recover Nishapur from Twelver Shiʿa rule, he engaged in destructive campaigns, but after securing victory, he carelessly handed Nishapur to a putative Shiʿi (Iskandar-Shaykhī), who renounced his allegiance to the Kartids and allied with Shiʿi extremists (Shaykhiyya). This forced Pīr ʿAlī to re-conquer just "liberated" Nishapur. Ḥāfiẓ-i Abrū is harsh in his criticisms of Pīr ʿAlī. His perspectives were undoubtedly shaped by Temür's political-military acumen. It is likely (in my opinion) that Ḥāfiẓ-i Abrū's words are a paraphrase of Temür's words.

> Ghiyāth al-Dīn was an imprudent (*ghāfil*) man. He was inept (*tamām nadāsht*) at the governance and politics of [Khurasan]. He was effete (*narm-khuy*) and innocuous (*kam-āzār*). He was unable to commit to diligent efforts in warfare [...] and [in] directing the affairs of war and killing.[141]

While the Kartids and the Sarbadarids were locked in combat, Temür, who had by 771/1370 near-complete control of the *ulus* Chaghatai,[142] was looking toward Khurasan. In 778/1376f., Temür's emissary to the Kartid court was received with pacifying words by Pīr ʿAlī, who professed fealty and friendship (*banda wa khidmatgār*). He offered to have his son, Pīr Muḥammad Kart, enter Temür's service. Temür affianced his niece, Siwinj-Qutlugh Āgā (the daughter of his sister, Shīrīn-Bīk Āgā, and Temür's confidant, Amir Muʾayyad Arlat), to the Kart boy.[143] The betrothal was held in Samarqand, and the celebrants returned to Herat in 780/1378f.[144] Meanwhile, Pīr ʿAlī, consequent to Iskandar-Shaykhī's betrayal, was trying to re-capture Nishapur. ʿAlī Muʾayyad, after being ejected from his capital by Shaykhiyya, had allied with Amir Walī. Their armies besieged Sabzavar.

The impact of the long war, namely, the costs to the Kartid treasury and injuries to the agricultural and pastoral economies of the Nishapur Quarter,

141 Ḥāfiẓ-i Abrū, *Cinq*, 62; Ḥāfiẓ-i Abrū, *Kart*, 207.

142 Although Temür's rule was recognized by Ramażān 771/April 1370 (shortly before the death of Muʿizz al-Dīn Kart), it was not until 781/1379 that the last of the *ulus* tribes was brought under his control. See Manz, *Tamerlane*, 66–67.

143 Woods, *Timurid*, 17.

144 Ḥāfiẓ-i Abrū, *Cinq*, 58–59; Ḥāfiẓ-i Abrū, *Kart*, 202–03.

would have been sufficient to unsettle the amirs and *aʿyān* of the Kartid realm. They became alarmed in 780/1378f. when Pīr ʿAlī began strengthening Herat's defensive perimeter.[145]

Pīr ʿAlī's preparations to resist Temür unsettled Herat's *aʿyān* because, firstly, they, too, probably lacked confidence in his martial abilities; secondly, they feared that their city, painstakingly re-built after Elǰigidei's despoliations, would again suffer desolation. Upper-echelon notables decided to seek accommodation with Temür.[146]

A group of Khurasanian notables, led by vizier Muʿīn al-Dīn Jāmī, wrote to Temür's chief (*ṣadr*) in Samarqand, *c.* 781/1379–80, offering support. A distich makes known that the security of the people (*amān-i khalq*) of Khurasan lies within Temür's realm (*dawlat-i tū*).[147] After receiving indication of interest, Jāmī wrote directly to Temür in 782/1380.[148] Jāmī informs Temür of the ease with which Herat and Khurasan can be conquered—provided Temür had internal support in figuratively (and literally?) opening Herat's gates:

> To any king that [Khurasan] wants to give itself to,
> It will surrender itself to him.[149]

Jāmī's ally, Zayn al-Dīn Taybādī, ran a strident (indeed, insolent) campaign.[150] The essence of the story is that Taybādī had had a cordial relationship with Muʿizz al-Dīn Kart, but not with Pīr ʿAlī, which bruised the irascible Sufi's ego. Pīr ʿAlī began hardening the Kartid Wall (*shahr-band*), *c.* 780/1378f., and collared unemployed for corvée labor. This, and his preparations to defy Temür, dismayed Heratis: apprehension increased and dejection suffused the masses.[151] Taybādī wrote to him to offer unsolicited and injudicious advice, telling Pīr ʿAlī (who is depicted in the *Maqāmāt-i Tāybādī* as debauched) to return to God.[152] Pīr ʿAlī rejected the advice, and apparently scolded the Sufi.

145 Ḥāfiẓ-i Abrū, *Cinq*, 60; Ḥāfiẓ-i Abrū, *Kart*, 205; Faṣīḥ, *Mujmal*, 976.
146 Examined in Mahendrarajah, "Tamerlane's Conquest."
147 Ibid., 61; Yūsuf-i Ahl/Moayyad (ed.), *Farāʾid*, 2:556–59 (Jāmī's letter).
148 Yūsuf-i Ahl/Moayyad (ed.), *Farāʾid*, 1:173–81 (Jāmī's letter).
149 Ibid., 1:175. See Mahendrarajah, "Tamerlane's Conquest," 62; Mahendrarajah, *Sufi Saint*, 45–47 (marketing Aḥmad-i Jām to Temür).
150 See Mahendrarajah, "Tamerlane's Conquest," esp. 55–57, 59.
151 Anon./Gūsha-Gīr, *Tāybādī*, 89; Mahendrarajah, "Tamerlane's Conquest," 56.
152 Yūsuf-i Ahl/Moayyad (ed.), *Farāʾid*, 1:471–75 (Taybādī's letter).

Taybādī was overcome with rage by the denunciation. He decided to pursue Pīr ʿAlī's ouster.[153]

Pīr ʿAlī Kart was not politically tone deaf; he knew or sensed that insiders opposed him, although he probably did not fathom the extent of the scheming. In a decree from Rabīʿ II 782/5 July–2 August 1380,[154] Pīr ʿAlī appointed the vizier's illustrious son, Shaykh al-Islam Żiyā al-Dīn Yūsuf Jāmī (d. 797/1394f.),[155] as *ṣadr* of Herat. The position was designed to be powerful and "strengthen" Islam. Pīr ʿAlī was trying to appease critics in religious circles. The Kartid office of the *ṣadr* (*ṣadārat*) amounted to nothing:[156] five months after the decree was issued, Żiyā al-Dīn Yūsuf was escorting Temür on his pilgrimage to the "illuminated tomb" (*rawẓa-yi munawwar*) of Aḥmad-i Jām.

*Temür in Herat*

The fall of Herat came quickly and with minimal violence—as intended by the Jāmī-led faction.[157] Temür, on his march to Herat, stopped at Turbat-i Jām (and was hosted by Żiyā al-Dīn Yūsuf); thence to Taybād to meet with Zayn al-Dīn Taybādī. Temür and Taybādī forged a cordial bond at their meeting despite a rocky start. Taybādī had committed an act of *lèse-majesté* against Temür, which actually made him respect the Sufi. Temür explained to Ḥāfiẓ-i Abrū that in previous encounters with holy men they had betrayed their fear of him, but Taybādī had caused *him* to experience "fear and dread" (*ruʿb wa harās*).[158] Taybādī was evidently quite the character. Taybādī used his newfound leverage to help Herat. He pleaded with Temür: "do not enslave or pillage the people of Herat" (*mardum-i Harāt-rā asīr wa ghārat nakunī*).[159] Herat was spared. This was not accidental.

Herat was surrounded by Chaghtaid forces. Kartids resisted, briefly and spiritlessly. The city capitulated in Muḥarram 783/April 1381 not long after

[153] Anon./Gūsha-Gīr, *Tāybādī*, 90–91; Faṣīḥ, *Mujmal*, 976 (AH 780/1378f.).

[154] Yūsuf-i Ahl/Berlin, *Farāʾid*, ff. 303ᵇ–305ᵃ; idem/Fatih, *Farāʾid*, ff. 457ᵇ–458ᵇ; idem/Tehran, *Farāʾid*, pp. 642–44.

[155] On Żiyā al-Dīn Yūsuf, see Būzjānī, *Rawżat*, 109; Mahendrarajah, *Sufi Saint*, 66, 145, 178.

[156] On the Kartid *ṣadārat*, see Chapter 9.

[157] Mahendrarajah, "Tamerlane's Conquest," esp. 50–53, 68–72.

[158] Ibid., 65–68. Ḥāfiẓ-i Abrū, *Kart*, 206.

[159] Anon./Gūsha-Gīr, *Tāybādī*, 73; see also Faṣīḥ, *Mujmal*, 979 (AH 782/1380f.).

the Chaghataids breached the Kartid Wall and flooded the suburbs. A city that resists a conqueror like Chingiz Khan or Tamerlane was usually subjected to general massacre (*qatl-i ʿāmm*), but not Herat. Kartid soldiers were not executed and Timurid troops did not pillage or burn Herat. Temür's brutal treatment of neighboring Fūshanj just days earlier is illustrative of what could have happened at Herat.[160] Temür did, however, secure penalties from Heratis and Kartids. He dismantled Herat's fortifications at strategic points (see Chapter Ten), extracted a ransom, emptied the treasury and permitted the Kartid family to live (for now). Pīr ʿAlī's mother, Sulṭān-Khātūn, his son, Pīr Muḥammad, and Iskandar-Shaykhī, met with Temür.[161] Pīr ʿAlī later met Temür. The following day, Herat's notables queued to greet Temür and to pledge allegiance (*bandagī*) to him. About 200 eminent men (*kadkhudā-yi muʿtabar*) from Herat and its environs were deported to Shahr-i Sabz (Temür's hometown).[162] It is likely that few, probably none (in my opinion), of the deportees included *aʿyān* from the Jāmī-led bloc that had initiated dialogue with Temür.

Pīr ʿAlī Kart was incarcerated in Samarqand and executed in 785/1383. A son, Amir Ghūrī, was also killed. Pīr Muḥammad, who had married Temür's niece, Siwinj-Qutlugh Āgā, was spared, provisionally. They, and two sons, were ultimately murdered in 791/1389 by Mīrānshāh (d. 810/1408) b. Temür, acting on his father's orders.[163]

160 On Temür's subsequent campaigns and destruction wrought, see Jean Aubin, "Comment Tamerlan prenait les villes," *Studia Islamica* 19 (1963):83–122.

161 Iskandar-Shaykhī became an interlocutor for Temür and served him.

162 Based on: Ḥāfiẓ-i Abrū, *Cinq*, 60–66; Ḥāfiẓ-i Abrū, *Kart*, 204–12; Naṭanzī, *Muntakhab*, 238–39; Khʷāndamīr/Siyāqī (ed.), *Ḥabīb*, 3:388–89, 430–31; Khʷāndamīr/Thackston (tr.), *Habib*, 225, 245–46; ʿAbd al-Razzāq al-Samarqandī, *Maṭlaʿ-i saʿdayn wa majmaʿ-i baḥrayn*, ed. ʿAbd al-Ḥusayn Nawāʾī, 4 vols (Tehran: Pazhūhishgāh-i ʿulūm-i insānī wa muṭālaʿāt-i farhangī, 1372/1993; 1383/2004f.), 1.2:525–28.

163 Potter, "Kart Dynasty," 54; Muḥammad Ismāʿīl Mablagh Gharjistānī, "Suqūṭ-i sultanat-i dūdmān-i Kart [Fall of the Kart kingdom]," *Āryānā* No. 200 (1338/1959):17–24.

# Part I: Reflections and Conclusions

It was inevitable that once Chingiz Khan's armies crossed the Oxus into Persia that the Mongols would *eventually* have to administer the land. Charles Tilly discerned:

> the wielders of coercion find themselves obliged to administer the lands, goods, and people they acquire; they become involved in extraction of resources, distribution of goods, services, and income, and adjudication of disputes. But administration diverts them [Mongols] from war, and creates interests that sometimes tell against war.[1]

The obligations of administering an ancient sedentary civilization such as Persia's would have distracted the Mongols from the pursuit of portable wealth. Settling could have been perceived as sedentarization, and antithetical to steppe ethos. Pillaging and returning to Inner Asia to enjoy the social, political, and economic fruits of expeditions were possibly preferable to settling and ruling. An alternative to settling and governing is (1) to deport to Inner Asia certain captives of economic or social value (craftsmen, artisans, women, etc.); and (2) to slaughter the remaining population.[2] This calculus, conceivably, undergirded the mass deportations and exterminations perpetrated by the Mongols in Persia.

[1] Tilly, *Coercion,* 20.

[2] Mongols feared rebellion and having to again confront fortifications. John Masson Smith, "Demographic Considerations in Mongol Siege Warfare," *Archivum Ottomanicum* 13 (1993–94):329–34. Mongol armies were small; they could not garrison every town. Massacre was one solution. See Barfield, *Perilous,* 203. The rebellion in Herat after Tolui had "subjugated" it reinforced the imperative for mass murder.

The roving bandit/stationary bandit thesis as propounded in Chapter Three should be qualified for the Mongol circumstances. In its early years, Chingiz Khan's polity "was in its essence a booty distribution system." After "endemic civil war," peace came to the steppe; therefore, "the only permissible objects of plunder lay beyond the confines of Mongolia,"[3] its sedentary neighbors. Mongols, with conquests near home (bits of North China, Qara Khitai, and such), and Chingiz Khan's establishment of the structures of law and administration for his nascent polity, had become acquainted with the instruments of administration. Employment of Chinese and Persian bureaucrats in conquered lands would become the norm.[4] Mongols acquired Persia in unplanned circumstances: Chingiz Khan was compelled to conquer the Khʷārazm-Shāh's realm sooner than he would have wanted to because of the Utrār massacre. He died in 1227 without leaving a plan for Persia, which was considered joint imperial property; not part of a patrimony or princely appanage. "Joint 'satellite' administration" became the practice.[5]

In 630/1232f., Ögödei (r. 1229–41) appointed Chin-Temür (d. 633/1235f.) as the governor of Khurasan, in part due to prevailing anarchy. It had become clear that Persia could not be left unattended. Ögödei instituted revitalization efforts in east Persia; efforts that were rudimentary and hindered by Chinggisid rivalries in Mongolia and Khurasan. The Mongols were fumbling in the dark vis-à-vis Persia. Ögödei's death (1241), followed by an interregnum (1241–46), Chinggisid intrigues, elevation of Güyük (r. 1246–48), another interregnum (1248–51)—continuing struggles among Chinggisid lineages—left the Mongols with little focus or resources for the administration, much less sustained revitalization, of Persia. The Empire was also fixated on securing lands in the west.[6] Lastly, Inner Asians (Chinese, Uighurs, etc.) were familiar to the Mongols, but not predominantly Muslim

[3] Paul Buell, "Early Mongol Expansion in Western Siberia and Turkestan (1207–1219): a Reconstruction," *CAJ* 36/1 (1992):1–32, 2.

[4] A Chinese advisor to Ögödei said that the Mongols acquired China on horseback but could not rule it from that position.

[5] On this concept, see Paul Buell, "Sino-Khitan administration in Mongol Bukhara," *JAH* 13/2 (1979):121–51, esp. 147.

[6] The conquest of north China and Manchuria was completed in 1235; much of Russia and eastern Europe was in Mongol hands by 1241.

Persia, which probably confounded their interpretations of, and approaches to, Persia.

The settlement of the Persian question had to await the accession of Möngke (r. 1251–58). "Mongke recognised that the Mongols stood to benefit more in the long term through taxation rather than via short-term gains through plunder and preying on their subjects."[7] He instituted centralization policies, administrative structures, and the modes for enumerating, controlling, conscripting, and taxing subject peoples.[8] A society that is preparing for war, Tilly noted, must create an "infrastructure of taxation, supply, and administration."[9] This is what Möngke did, enabling the Mongol Empire, which had effectively paused its expansion, to continue to march. In the 750s/1250s the Empire's troops were conducting operations in Syria, Iraq, Eurasia, China, Tibet, Indochina, and Korea. Unlike Nikudars and Qaraunas, the Mongols could no longer rob and run: they had become too big. They had to administer empire, and extract economic and human resources from settled civilizations, in order to keep expanding.

Thomas Allsen has shown that the Mongol military system, which relied on, inter alia, conscription, was then a crushing burden on the Empire and subjects.[10] The limits on expansion were already manifest. The social and economic costs of expansion may exceed their overall returns. Edward Gibbon's observation encapsulates the Roman Empire's dilemma: "in the prosecution of remote wars, the undertaking became every day more difficult, the event more doubtful, and the possession more precarious and less beneficial."[11] The extent to which economic reality (costs v. benefits) contributed to the Mongol Empire's dissolution awaits exploration.

7 May, *Mongol Empire*, 85.

8 See Allsen, *Mongol Imperialism, et passim.*

9 Tilly, *Coercion*, 20.

10 Allsen, *Mongol Imperialism*, 190–210, esp. 210–16. On their manpower demands, see John Masson Smith, "Mongol Society and Military in the Middle East: Antecedents and Adaptations," in *War and Society in the Eastern Mediterranean: 7th–15th centuries*, ed. Y. Lev (Leiden: Brill, 1997), pp. 249–66.

11 Edward Gibbon, *The Decline and Fall of the Roman Empire*, vols 1–3 (unabridged) (New York: Modern Library, 1995), 58. See also R.M. Coats and G.M Pecquet, "The calculus of conquests: the decline and fall of the returns to Roman expansion," *The Independent Review* 17/4 (2013):517–40.

Once the Mongols decided to administer conquered lands and pay dividends to Chinggisid shareholders (holders of shares, *qubi*, or apportioned peoples and lands),[12] administration of empire got underway. Juwaynī: "the census of the provinces having been completed [in 1257], the World-Emperor [Möngke] apportioned them [the lands] all amongst his kinsmen and brothers."[13] The Qa'an had set in motion sundry processes whereby the Mongols:

> succeeded in creating the largest contiguous land-based empire in human history because they were able to mobilize effectively the human and material resources of the areas under their control [...]. All of their subjects—nomadic tribesmen, urban dwellers, and agriculturalists—were required to help further Mongol imperial ambitions.[14]

The Kartid state emerged in 649/1251 from this context. Hülegü was dispatched to implement, inter alia, Möngke's writ. Shams al-Dīn Kart's rejection of a Jochid's claim on Herat's *dīwān* was to demonstrate that: (1) he was the undisputed authority and had Hülegü's backing; (2) the era of haphazard administration had ended: no more arbitrary claims on the fisc; no more capricious demands by Chinggisid splinters.

Why Herat? Why did the Mongol Empire (guided by its Persian advisors) select Herat as the Kartid capital, and Herat Quarter for revitalization? Why not Balkh, Marw, or Nishapur—the other three "Quarters" of Khurasan? The eponymous capitals of the four quarters nestle in verdant oases, with natural and/or artificial channels to irrigate farms and orchards. Why Herat?

One answer lies in the geographic setting for Herat and the Herat River Valley. Not just the topography, but the latitude and longitude of the city; and Herat's rulers' capacity to access or block, and thereby control and profit from, migratory and trading routes. Balkh is farthest east (36° 46′ N/66° 54′ E); Marw, most northern (37° 39′ N/62° 11′ E); Nishapur is farthest west (36° 12′ N/58° 47′ E). But Herat (34° 20′ N/62° 12′ E), sits in the "middle":

12 See Allsen, "Sharing," esp. 176–77.
13 Juvainī/Boyle, *World-Conqueror*, 2:523. See also, Allsen, "Sharing," 176–77. On the census in Persia, see Allsen, *Mongol Imperialism*, 130–34.
14 Allsen, *Mongol Imperialism*, 7.

the long and luxuriant Herat River Valley is east of Herat, where waters from the Paropamisus and Hindu Kush nourish the Hari Rud. Another lush tract extends from the Oxus and Shibūrghān, to Murghāb (an exceptionally fertile region). It incorporates Fāryāb and Marūchāq, and encompasses farmlands and pasturelands. To Herat's west are precious agricultural areas: Bākharz, Fūshanj, Jām, and Kūsūyi. South, southwest, and southeast are *Afghānistān*, Āzāb, Bust, Farāh, Ghūr, Izfizār, Sistān, and Tūlak, also encompassing farms, pastures, and remarkable water resources (Hilmand River, Farāh River, Khāsh River, Harūd River, Lake Sistān, among others).

Möngke's patent was drafted to encompass the territories above (plus Fīrūzkūh, Gharjistān, Kābul, Tikīnābād, and Tirāh), which combine to form a contiguous mass of agricultural and pastoral regions. This mass included (1) migratory routes for pastoral nomads and livestock traversing north and south of, and through, the Hindu Kush; and (2) caravan routes: (a) east-west routes above the Hindu Kush, from Kābul and Balkh, to Mashhad, Nishapur, and Caspian Sea provinces; (b) east-west routes below the Hindu Kush, from Qandahar and Ghazni via Bust to Farāh and Zaranj (thence Herat); (c) north-south routes (Mashhad-Ṭūs to Farāh); and (d) west/south-west routes (to Bam, Kirmān, Yazd and beyond; Bam to the Persian Gulf) and south (to Sistān and Balūchistān).

One may think of Herat as a city that can be bypassed by Inner Asian caravans: caravans could travel north of Herat from Tirmiz, Balkh or Marw to Sarakhs, Mashhad-Ṭūs and beyond. However, this is to oversimplify caravan movements, and to ignore key factors like terrain and highway security. It also privileges the idea that commercial and cultural exchanges with Inner Asia were paramount, thereby diminishing the value of economic and intellectual exchanges between Persia and India.

Merchandise flowed between Indian cities like Shikapur, Multan, and Peshawar to/from: Qandahar (via the Bolan Pass and Sanghar Pass); Ghazni (Gumal Pass); Kabul (Khyber Pass); to/from cities like Zaranj, Farāh, and Kabul, to/from Ghazni, Qandahar, Balūchistān, Sistān, Kirmān, and Yazd. People and merchandise moved along the Indus on flat-bottomed boats,[15] and possibly the Hilmand, too. A trade in slaves (from Qandahar and Ghazni)

[15] There was a sea trade between Hormoz and Gujarat in the seventh/thirteenth century.

to India persisted into the Mughal era. Cotton and silk, saffron, cumin and other spices, were traded.[16] The shift of the epicenter of Chishtiyya Sufism, from Ghūr to India, is an example of the eastward movement of Persian ideas. Ibn Battuta's record of his residence in India reveals the ubiquitous influence of Persian peoples and cultures on Indian life and politics. Intellectual and cultural traffic flowed west from India. Names encountered, such as ʿAlāʾ al-Dīn Hindū, Hindū Bītikchī, and Hindū Noyan, suggest Indian origins for Khurasanian personages.

Herat, as the Kartid capital, was well situated to serve the Mongol cantonment at Bādghīs; and Mongol amirs were at hand should the Kartids stray. Another reason to select Herat is that it enjoys salubrious weather. The "120-day winds" (June to October) blow in from the Qara-Qum to Sistān, along a 140 miles/225 km wide corridor from Bākharz to the Herat Valley. The winds inflict harm to edifices, fauna, and flora, but offer respites from the summer heat. The winds are why this part of Persia has windmills. Windmills were indispensable to local economies.

Chinggisid royals were not the only ones with economic interests in Khurasan, and in particular, the Herat Quarter. ʿAṭāʾ-Malik Juwaynī, for example, had purchased one-fourth of Khabūshān village (located in the Nishapur Quarter),[17] which had been damaged by the Mongols. He enticed Hülegü to underwrite the reconstruction costs: "[a]ll the expense of re-building he met with cash from the treasury so that no charge fell upon the people" (or Juwaynī). The "Supreme Minister [...] gave 3,000 gold dinars so that the work of rebuilding and restoration might begin."[18] The bazaar was rebuilt, and the subterranean channels (*qanāt*) were repaired. Personal profit surely played decisive roles in (1) the selection of settlements to be developed; (2) the specific projects to be funded (e.g., mosques, bazaars, *qanāt*s, etc.); and (3) the sources of funds.

Consequent to the revitalization of *select* locales and *select* projects, agricultural and pastoral activities, and commercial exchanges, were expected to enrich the Kartid state, Ilkhanate, and Mongol Empire—and opportunists

[16] See, generally, J.K. Chawla, *India's overland trade with Central Asia and Persia during the thirteenth and fourteenth centuries* (New Delhi: Munshiram Manoharlal Publishers, 2006).

[17] Khabūshān: see Le Strange, *Lands*, 393.

[18] Juvainī/Boyle, *World-Conqueror*, 2:617.

like Juwaynī. However, none of the hoped for economic progress would be possible without security in the Kartid kingdom: if caravans carrying merchandise and merchants on east-west and north-south routes cannot safely traverse the highways and byways of Khurasan without being pounced on by Nikudars or Qaraunas; landlords, waterlords, and peasants had their homes, farms, villages, silos, and hydrological assets raided, robbed, or ruined by roving bandits; and vendors within bazaars and craftsmen in ateliers feared robbery, thuggery, and murder by knaves and ruffians (*runūd wa awbāsh*), then there will be little economic progress and development of infrastructure in town and country. Absent the provision of indispensable *public goods*—security for persons and property—farmers, merchants, and craftsmen will not return. This was the problem faced by the Kartids.

The political and military environment in which the Kartids had to operate was daunting. Hence the introduction of the concept of the *conflict ecosystem* as a means for the visualization of the complexities and the opacities of the political-military theater: roving bandits and prey; Turko-Mongol nomad v. sedentary Tajik and Turk; the newly arrived Central Asian nomad v. established Khurasanian nomad; land-tenure, pasture and water-usage conflicts; conflicts of religion (Shaman/Buddhist ideologies v. Perso-Islamic ideologies), and so on. Complicating the Kartids' political and economic choices were the competing Chinggisid lines, their political agents and armed loyalists; and the proxy wars (later, open conflict) between Jochids and Toluids; Chaghataids and Toluids. A quip from modern Afghanistan exemplifies the Kartids' predicament: "it's hard to do nation-building while being shot at." If these issues were not sufficient to keep Kartids occupied and off-balance, they had to contend with Il-Khans who did not subscribe to the revitalization agenda, namely Abāqā, whose clever solution to Chaghataid raids on the Herat Quarter was to obliterate Herat and deport its people.[19] There was also the baleful Il-Khan, Öljeitü, who "devoted much time to fighting with the Kart dynasty of Herat."[20] The milieux in which the Kartids had to function were brutal and shaped by fickle imperial, Jochid, Chaghataid, and Ilkhanid egos, policies, and demands.

[19] al-Harawī, *Harāt*, 352–55.
[20] Hope, *Power*, 15.

War diverts economic and intellectual capital from investing in capital projects, and engaging in socio-economic activities that benefit the *broader* populace.[21] A climate of uncertainty will affect individual and group choices: do I invest in a *qanāt* or bury my gold? Do we remain in Herat or relocate to Yazd? A fraught climate will hinder *collective action*: unity of effort and purpose of denizens in bettering their society and economy; for example, by banding to repair ruined aqueducts or cisterns, which would benefit even those Heratis that did not contribute efforts. Corvée was employed, but peasants and laborers do not stand idle waiting to be press-ganged. They tend to flee.

Kartids had to foster an environment that enticed the productive classes (*ra ʿāyā*) to migrate to Herat, and deterred Heratis from absconding to safer regions. Besides, public works require funds. It is impossible to extract agricultural taxes (*ʿushr, kharāj*) from fallow lands; commercial/sales taxes (*tamghā*) from empty bazaars; *qalān, qubchūr*, and *ʿawāriż-āt* from non-existent *ra ʿāyā*, landlords, waterlords, and pastoralists.[22] The *conditio sine qua non* for economic development was security.

This was Nawrūz's (d. 696/1297) predicament (one partly of his creation). Hence his transformation from a mobile bandit to stationary bandit and birth of the Kartid-Nawruzid union. The transitory union oversaw the revitalization of Herat and Sīstān. Fahkr al-Dīn Kart continued re-development ventures (see Part Two).

Despite the conflicts and social-political uncertainties in the decades between Shams al-Dīn Kart's investiture in 649/1251, and Ghiyāth al-Dīn's victory over Yasaʾur in 720/1320, economic progress and urban development took place. Abāqā had a point: if Herat were not an attractive target—people

[21] War benefits the bureaucrats who control the taxation and procurement processes; suppliers and manufacturers along the armaments and materiel supply chain; and the stakeholders in government. Moreover, in a booty economy, fighters, their dependents, foragers, etc. stand to profit from the acquisition of portable wealth. But war has *social costs*: by reducing economic and human capital available for agricultural production—a vital economic sector in medieval ages not just for food, but for surplus wealth, which went toward investments in *public works* (cisterns, dams, highways)—and other forms of economic and cultural production. Men compelled or paid to fight are peasants who are not farming or laborers not toiling in construction projects.

[22] On forms of taxation, see Franz Schurmann, "Mongolian Tributary Practices of the Thirteenth Century," *HJAS* 19/3 (1956):304–89; Smith, "Mongol and Nomadic Taxation" (includes revisions to Schurmann); Watabe, "*Qubchur.*"

for enslavement, livestock, cereals, etc.—Herat and its agricultural environs would not have been pillaged by the Chaghataids under Barāq in 668/1270; Nikudars in 687/1288 and 688/1289; and Yasaʾur between 718/1318 and 720/1320. The bar for attracting bandits was not high; still, it is manifest that Herat and its agricultural and pastoral purlieus had experienced infrastructure development and growth in agricultural production during this seventy-year period (1251–1320). To illustrate: Yasaʾur had hoarded stolen wheat at the Tūlak citadel of ally, Farrukhzād b. Quṭb al-Dīn (Kartid turncoat). When Ghiyāth al-Dīn captured the citadel, *c.* 720/1320, he recovered 10,000 *kharwārs* (*c.* 3 million kg/6.6 million lb) of wheat.[23] The total represented a fraction of the cereals (barley, wheat, and rice) harvested in the Kartid realm. Thus, even after taking a subtraction for inflation by Sayfī, the number suggests that wheat production had been robust.

Muʿizz al-Dīn Kart had had a tricky start to his tenure. He was not his father's legatee, and acceded to the kingship when Ḥāfiẓ Muḥammad Kart was murdered. He settled into the post. Following the death of the last Il-Khan, Abū Saʿīd Bahādur Khān, on 13 Rabīʿ II 736/30 November 1335, the Kartids effectively became an independent kingdom. Muʿizz al-Dīn led a delegation to Sulṭān-Maydān, where Ṭaghā-Temür was selected as nominal suzerain. Muʿizz al-Dīn was now strong enough to not allow Ṭaghā-Temür "to interfere with the wealth or affairs of Herat and its vicinities."[24]

Muʿizz al-Dīn triumphed at Zāwa against the Sarbadar-Shaykhiyya coalition. Conceit led him to proclaim independence, renounce Ṭaghā-Temür's suzerainty, and seek the suzerainty of Muḥammad b. Tughluq-Shāh. Muʿizz al-Dīn's enemies goaded the Chaghataids into ousting him. The Turko-Mongols came to regret their actions and re-installed Muʿizz al-Dīn. The Kartid's most important contribution to Iranian and Islamic histories was maintaining peace between the Sunni Kartid kingdom and Twelver Shiʿa Sarbadarid kingdom of ʿAlī Muʾayyad.

Pīr ʿAlī Kart "eschewed his father's path in its entirety." Possibly hyperbolic, but accurate at its pith: where it mattered, maintaining peace and prosperity in Khurasan, and in not fanning the flames of Sunni-Shiʿi sectarianism

[23] al-Harawī, *Harāt*, 764.
[24] Ḥāfiẓ-i Abrū, *Kart*, 172.

(*fitna*), he did eschew Muʿizz al-Dīn's sober policies. By donning the mantle of *ghāzī* and igniting *fitna*, he weakened the Kartid army and treasury; attracted malevolent actors (Amir Walī and Shāh Shujāʿ); and inflicted harm on the peoples and economies of Nishapur Quarter.

Vizier Muʿīn al-Dīn Jāmī, and Herati notables, helped deliver the city to Temür. Notables of Herat "were in the habit of looking after their own affairs as well as those of the city without asking whether they were legally entitled to do so,"[25] as when they first welcomed, later resisted, the Seljuqs. The story of Herat is usually the story of notables (*ashrāf wa ʿayān*), notwithstanding the toils of merchants, craftsmen, artisans, laborers, and peasants (*raʿāyā*). The sources to which historians are prisoner recount the words and deeds of *ashrāf wa ʿayān*, but not those of *raʿāyā*. Nonetheless, it is to Herat's socio-economic history that we turn.

[25] Jürgen Paul, "The Histories of Herat," *Iranian Studies* 33/1 (2000):93–115, 104–05.

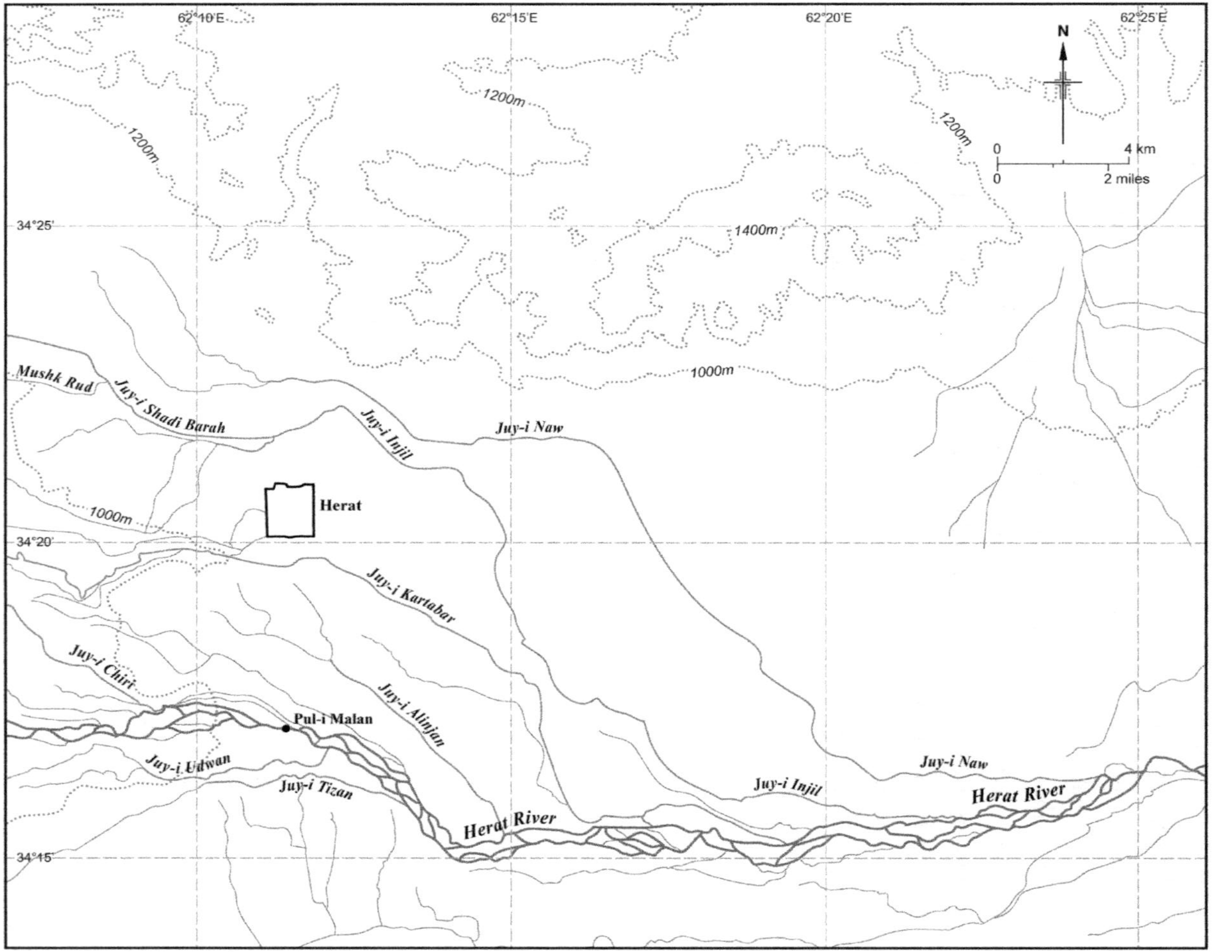


Map 4 Arterial waterways of Kartid Herat. Follows on Allen, Catalogue, Map 1.

# PART II

# SOCIAL, ECONOMIC, AND CULTURAL RENEWAL IN HERAT

# 7

# Early Efforts to Revive Agriculture and Commerce

## Khurasan and Herat

### *Geography and Topography*

"*Iran-zamin*, 'the land of Iran,' means more than a place of habitation and extends beyond the present political entity." For the multifarious peoples of Persia, this is the area where they "have maintained their special way of life through centuries of invasion, social change, and political turmoil. [It] is the birthplace and home of an unique Iranian culture—the product of an ancient relationship between diverse peoples and their homeland."[1] An integral geographical, political, cultural, and economic constituent of *Iran-zamin* is the vast geographical expanse called Khurasan.[2]

Geographical Khurasan is a long and narrow tract—somewhat like a trapezoid (the northern and southern limits are nearly parallel)—whose ill-defined boundaries stretch from the southeastern littoral of the Caspian Sea to the Hindu Kush. The limits of political-cultural Khurasan are nebulous, but generally admitted to include territories influenced by Persian culture: parcels in Turkmenistan, Uzbekistan, and Tajikistan.[3] The tract is

[1] John Limbert, *Iran: At War with History* (Boulder: Westview Press, 1987), 1. Geographical and cultural extents of *Iran-zamin/Īrānshahr* are elucidated in pp. 1–10.

[2] The finest analytical exposition on Khurasan's topography and multifarious peoples is in C.E. Bosworth, *The Ghaznavids* (Edinburgh: Edinburgh University Press, 1963), 145–52. The 73,253 word *Encyclopædia Iranica* entry, "Khorasan," *EIr*, 16:591–672 (2021), by authors M. Labbaf-Khaniki, R. Rante, C. Ceretti, M. Luce, C.E Bosworth, D.G. Tor, K. Ghereghlou, Y.M. Haghighi, A. Tarzi, and P. Oberling, is the most perceptive resource about Khurasan.

[3] On Greater Khurasan, see Rocco Rante, "'Khorasan Proper' and 'Greater Khorasan' within a politico-cultural framework," in *Greater Khorasan: History, Geography, Archaeology and Material Culture*, ed. Rocco Rante (Berlin: De Gruyter, 2015), 9–26; David Durand-Guédy, "Pre-Mongol Khurasan: A Historical Introduction," in *Greater Khorasan* (pp. 1–8).

bounded in the north by the River Oxus (*Amū Darya*, *Jayhūn*) and the Black Sands (*Qara-Qum*) desert; in the southwest/south by two salt deserts: *Dasht-i Kawīr* and *Dasht-i Lūt*. Quhistān, Sistān, Bamiyān, and Ghūr are at Khurasan's southwestern/southern limits; Qandahar and Ghazni, the southeast.[4] Khurasan's forbidding topographical features were eloquently described by Edmund Bosworth:

> [t]he mass of brown shading or hatching which a relief map displays to us, the lifeless salt deserts, the land-locked river basins, the indeterminate rivers which peter out in lakes and swamps and permit no navigation or access to the sea: all betray an uncertain water-supply, a harsh climate, an arid terrain and introspective, closed human communities.[5]

The land is ostensibly inhospitable; however, water originating in mountains, and held in underground water basins, is plentiful.[6] Three millennia ago, the ingenious Iranian mind conceived a scientific marvel,[7] the *kārīz*, which transports water from subterranean reservoirs to thirsty farmers and farmlands. It is costly and labor-intensive to excavate a *kārīz*,[8] more so the farther

[4] A dated but enjoyable narrative geography is Elisée Reclus, *The Universal Geography: Earth and its Inhabitants*, vol. 9, ed. A.H. Keane (London: J.S. Virtue, [1890?]), 16–58 (Sistān and Afghanistan). A British political agent offers keen insights in C.E. Yate, *Khurasan and Sistan* (Edinburgh: William Blackwood, 1900), esp. 1–21 (Herat and Farāh), 75–109 (Sistān), 110–24 (Hilmand). Commentary on geographical, historical and social aspects is in the travelogue, J.P. Ferrier, *Caravan Journeys and Wanderings in Persia, Afghanistan, Turkistan and Beloochistan*, tr. W. Jesse (London: John Murray, 1856).

[5] Bosworth, *Ghaznavids*, 145.

[6] On harnessing scarce resources, see Elisabeth Beazley and Michael Harverson, *Living with the Desert* (Warminster, UK: Aris & Phillips, 1982), 31–48; Abigail Schade, "Hidden Waters: Groundwater Histories of Iran and the Mediterranean" (Ph.D. diss., Columbia University, 2011), esp. 1–23, 100–124.

[7] Paul Ward English, "The Origin and Spread of Qanats in the Old World," *Proceedings of the American Philosophical Society*, 112/3 (1968):170–81; idem, *City and Village in Iran: Settlement and Economy in the Kirman Basin* (London: University of Wisconsin Press, 1966), esp. 30–39, and Figs. 6–9; H.E. Wulff, "The Qanats of Iran," *Scientific American* 218/4 (1968):94–105; idem, *The Traditional Crafts of Persia* (Cambridge: MIT Press, 1966), 249–54; Heinz Gaube, *Iranian Cities* (New York: New York University Press, 1979), 4–7; Parviz Mohebbi, *Techniques et ressources en Iran: du 7e au 19e siecle* (Teheran: Institut Français de Recherche en Iran, 1996), 77–80, Fig. 1; Anthony Smith, *Blind White Fish in Persia* (New York: E.P Dutton, 1953), esp. 56–60, 79–86, 97–101, 110–14, and 151–54.

[8] Excavating or restoring a *kārīz* requires engineers (sgl. *muqannī*); whereas cutting or clearing a *jūy* mostly involves menial labor. In Herat today, a *jūy* is often a simple overground canal.

the mother-well (*chāh-mādar*) is from the outlet.[9] A *kārīz* requires frequent maintenance to prevent silting/collapse.

The aridity of a Khurasanian region, and scarcity of surface waters, has only briefly hindered human settlement—provided the soil was suitable for agriculture. A substantial percentage of Iran's land capacity is unsuitable for sustainable crop production: *c.* 10.50% of surveyed lands are rated "very good" to "medium" for crop farming (based on topography, soil, climate); "poor" and "very poor" are 17.70%; excluded (11.9%) and unsuitable lands (59.9%) comprise the bulk.[10] Medieval agronomical treatises supplied guidance on soils and irrigation requirements by soil type; suitability of crops and their probable yields.

The precious parcels of the arid Iranian Plateau capable of sustaining agricultural enterprises, therefore, demand transportation of water if water was not nearby. Absent sensible management of Khurasan's natural resources and food insecurity will prevail. Herat's fame as a "breadbasket" is testament to the ingenuity and industry of its peoples.[11]

### *Hydrological Network of Herat*

The region's irrigation network is complex. It encompasses *kārīzs*, aqueducts (*jūy*), rivers, canals, streams (*nahr*, *rūd*, *-āb*), deep-wells (*chāh-i ʿamīq*), shallow-wells (*chāh-i nīm-i ʿamīq*); dams, dykes, and weirs (*band*, *ḥabs*, *sadd*); sluices and regulators (*jūy-bār*, *qulb*); and water control-boxes (*naṭarah*), to distribute water from natural reservoirs (*daryāʾ*, *daryā-cha*, *baḥr*) or cisterns (*ḥawż*, *āb-anbār*, *pāyāb*, etc.), subterranean basins, and arterial waterways (e.g., Harī Rūd, Farāh River, Jām River, Murghāb, Oxus) before they debouch in the deserts of Central Asia or Persia. The districts of Herat located north of the Harī Rūd are primarily irrigated through an extensive network of overground channels, which proved fortuitous after the

9 The length of a *kārīz* may vary greatly: 5–10 miles/8–16 km is not uncommon; but longer lines, 20–25 miles/32–40 km, also exist. The depth of a mother-well can range from 25–350 ft/7.62–106.7 m. See A.K.S. Lambton, "The Qanāts of Yazd," *JRAS* 2/1 (1992):21–35, 22; also Lambton, *Landlord*, 217; but cf. Beazley & Harverson, *Desert*, 34–39: they identify *kārīzs* of Gunābād (Khurasan) at a depth of 979 ft/300 m.

10 M.B. Mesgaran, et al., "Iran's Land Suitability for Agriculture," *Scientific Reports* 7, no. 7,670 (2017):1–12, Table 1, and Figures 1, 2, 4.

11 See, e.g., G.B. Malleson, *Herat: The Granary and Garden of Central Asia* (London: Allen & Co., 1880), 90–106.

Mongol depredations: there were fewer *kārīzs* for the hordes to wantonly destroy. It is easier to repair a *jūy* than a *kārīz*—especially if the *kārīz* traverses long distances and is sourced from a reservoir far beneath the surface. The recovery of Herat after Elǰigidei was expedited by Herat's dependence on *jūy* waters.

The course of an arterial waterway (*nahr, rūd, jūy*),[12] from its origins at the Harī Rūd, is instructive. The artery traverses a westerly to northwesterly course, passing either to the north or the south of Herat. Along the course it encounters natural or artificial branches, which transport water in different directions. This network parallels the structure of a leaf: a *jūy*'s or *nahr*'s branch (channel) as the *midrib*, with lateral *veins* (sub-channels, which have subordinate channels). Lying between the veins are the sown fields (sgl. *mazraʿa*), hamlets, and villages that utilize the water. Courses from a *jūy*'s channels, tributaries, and tertiary outlets confront weirs and rivulets, which block, reserve, and re-direct waters.

Irrigation of fields is governed by law and custom (*ʿurf, rawāj*). The owner of a *jūy* or *kārīz* owns the lands above a *kārīz*; and on both sides of a *jūy* for "X" hundred *gaz*; and the points where water disgorges. Boundaries (*ḥarīm*) are determined by law and custom. A waterlord ordinarily will not allow anyone without legitimate water rights (*ḥaqqāba*) to irrigate fields without permission and/or payment of fees (for the "right" to use his water: Islamic law technically bars the sale of water).[13] How legal concerns on water rights and title to lands were addressed in *early* Kartid Herat are lacunae.[14] Once Kartid shaykhs al-Islams and *qāḍīs* became involved in (formally or informally) arbitrating ownership and rights disputes, a level of order will have prevailed. Disputes over water rights persisted into the later Kartid period. One dispute

[12] Thirty waterways (*jūy, nahr, rūd*) within Herat's ten Timurid era districts are annotated in Terry Allen, *A Catalogue of the Toponyms and Monuments of Timurid Herat* (Cambridge, MA: Aga Khan Program for Islamic Architecture, 1981), 12–24, Cat. Nos. 11–40. Not all date from the pre-Mongol or Kartid era. The handlist in Terry Allen, *Timurid Herat* (Wiesbaden: Ludwig Reichert, 1983), 63–64, should be read alongside his *Catalogue*: it is annotated with putative dates of construction or the earliest mention of that toponym.

[13] Lambton, *Landlord*, 210.

[14] Documents and communal memory ordinarily help resolve legal concerns, but with the disappearance of owners and rights-holders, and emergence of forged legal documents, water rights and land ownership issues are unclear. Hence the imperatives for the legal reforms promulgated by Ghāzān and Rashīd al-Dīn; and the water-distribution system instituted by Muʿizz al-Dīn Kart (see Chapter Eight).

was arbitrated by the Shaykh al-Islam and resulted in the promulgation of the aforementioned Kartid water regulations.

Yazd's Water Museum (*Mūzi-yi āb*) records Yazd's adaptation to its desert cradle; and forms and tools of water-management. The museum's artifacts and schematics, and field research in Fars, Yazd, Kirman, and Herat, have helped me to appreciate the logic of Herat's hydrological network, and to visualize its layout. The description below of Herat's network is based on field research and my interpretation of *Risāla-i ṭarīq-i qismat.*[15]

Water exiting from a sub-channel is distributed to farmlands in a specified district through a network of cisterns, dams (*band*), sluices (*sar-qulb*; *qulb*), channels, trenches, and *naṭarahs.*[16] Although not declared in sources, a clepsydra (*tashta* or *garī*: water-clock) is used to measure shares or units of water allocated per parcel. The *sar-qulb* (the primary sluice) is at the principal point of departure from a "branch" or "vein" (in *Ṭarīq-i qismat*, six of nine *bulūk*s had *at least* one *sar-qulb* and seven of nine had *at least* one *band*); thence to a tributary sluice, and intermittently, to a tertiary sluice (*qulb-chih*).[17]

A *qulb* has the same operating principal as the heart (Ar. *qalb*). Water exiting from an arterial waterway through a flume (artificial passageway) enters an atrium; a lock allows water to flow from atrium to ventricle (reservoir; possibly formed by a dam). The reservoir (if it is a *sar-qulb*) will have multiple sluice gates (say, a gate at each main compass point).[18] A sluice gate system permits water to flow to one or more channels for a precise time limit in an irrigation cycle. When the specified time expires, the gate is re-sealed; then a gate to a channel at another compass point unlocks (and so on). Water courses from *sar-qulb* to *qulb* (if there is a *sar-qulb*), or *qulb* to *qulb-chih* (if there is a *qulb-chih*) and/or *naṭarah.*[19]

[15] Qāsim b. Yūsuf al-Harawī, *Risāla--i ṭarīq-i qismat-i āb-i qulb* [*Treatise on the Method for the Apportionment of Sluice-Waters*], ed. Māyil Harawī (Tehran, 1347/1968). For citations to studies on the author and his treatises, see Chapter Eight, n.36.

[16] See also Mohebbi, *Techniques*, 80–82.

[17] Depictions of water-distribution by *kārīz* are in ibid. 79 (Fig. 1); Michael Bonine, "From Qanāt to Kort: Traditional Irrigation Terminology and Practices in Central Iran," *Iran* 20 (1982): 145–59, 154 (Fig. 4). Figures do not depict *sar-qulb*, *qulb*, *qulb-chih*, or *naṭarah*, but an intermediary device (by whatever label) functioned as the regulator.

[18] Sluice gate: not necessarily a complex device; a mud or brick dam would suffice.

[19] *Naṭarah*: the root *n-ṭ-r* produces words like watch, guard, protection, warden, lookout.

A *naṭarah* could be the main controller/timer for distribution to parcels, with a clepsydra measuring, to seconds,[20] shares of water allocated to each parcel/sub-parcel.

Distribution is usually regulated by a human (not just the devices above). A water-manager (*mīrāb*, *mīr-ābānih*) is employed in large settlements.[21] Farmlands are irrigated once per cycle: each cycle runs for "X" days (determined by custom and practice). Each "X" is divided into twenty-four-hour blocks (*shabāna-rūz*), with each *shabāna-rūz* commencing at dawn.[22] Lands above a channel are irrigated first (usually), then parcels lateral to a channel; finally, the parcels below it. Devices like *naṭarah* and *tashta* time flows to ensure distribution is being made pursuant to the recipient's *ḥaqqāba*. For instance, a farmer's share may be 43 minutes and 20 seconds of water every ten days. This must be measured precisely.[23]

Records are ordinarily maintained by *mīrābs* and/or subordinates lest legal disputes erupt, which are often resolved by higher authorities. A degree of equity is inherent in water rights. Custom/law recognizes that if equity is not incorporated into *ḥaqqāba*, waters may be exhausted when the next rights-holder's *shabāna-rūz* arrives. A *mīrāb* may therefore adjust cycles to ensure that every rights-holder receives an equitable share. Water rights may be adjusted for soil quality, crop type, and growing season.[24]

The hydrological network of Herat includes not only those structures designed to transport, reserve, or utilize waters from disparate wellsprings, but also grain silos (*anbār*); rice-hulling mills (*āb-dang*); watermills, windmills, and animal-powered mills. The erection of mills was not contingent on state involvement. Their simple designs allowed for mills to sprout wherever economic demands and financial resources coincided.

20 Bonine, "Qanāt," 150–51; Lambton, "Qanāts," 24.

21 *Mīrāb*: a central figure in the management of hydrological systems. Lambton, *Landlord*, 123–24, 220–24; Mohebbi, *Techniques*, 84–86; Jürgen Paul, *Herrscher, Gemeinwesen, Vermittler: Ostiran und Transoxanien in vormongolischer Zeit* (Stuttgart: Franz Steiner, 1996), 56–57, 64. The post could be hereditary, with knowledge passed from generation to generation.

22 See, e.g., Lambton, "Qanāts," 23–24; A.K.S. Lambton, "The Regulation of the Waters of the Zāyande Rūd," *BSOAS* 9/3 (1938):663–73; Bonine, "Qanāt," *et passim*.

23 Bonine, "Qanāt," 151.

24 Ibid., 149.

*Watermills*

The watermills of Persia are of great antiquity.[25] Water from a nearby *jūy* or *kārīz* will power the mills (*jūy ṭāḥūna, āsiyāb*), which are often below the surface (especially *kārīz*-powered mills). The Persian watermill's (so-called Norse) design permits the harnessing of weaker flows. Water does not cascade onto a mill's blades from a drop-tower (*burj-āb*), but is delivered through a pressure nozzle. Nozzles can be changed if water pressures decline.[26] A mill's axel revolves slowly; the stones grind slowly and steadily.

Watermills were not necessarily commercial endeavors: the uncomplicated Persian design requires little maintenance and technical expertise. The Persian watermill allows for a miller to grind a few bushels of grain for his family or hamlet. The "Vitruvian" watermill, in contrast, requires mightier water flows and involves intricate mechanics. Maintenance of Vitruvian mills is therefore more complex. These mills existed in pre-modern Persia, but it is not known if Vitruvian mills were erected along the Harī Rūd. The Zāyanda Rūd, which courses through Isfahan, had stronger flows, especially after spring thaws, which justified the costs and efforts of building Vitruvian mills.

*Windmills*

A key component within the hydrological system, despite its disassociation from water, is the windmill. These are not the picturesque vertical blade designs seen in Europe; Persian windmills have horizontal blades directed north/northwest.[27] Mills operate from June to October when a corridor from Bākharz to the Herat Valley is subjected to the "one hundred and twenty day winds" (*bād-i ṣad wa bīst rūz*) that blow from the Qara-Qum desert to Sistān. This corridor is *c.* 140 miles/225 km wide and 350 miles/563 km long. Winds are said to gust 38–71.5 mph/61–115 kmph.[28] If the high-end of the range is accurate, or gales are unremitting, the winds inflict damage to dwellings. Winds injure fauna and damage flora; the colloquial epithet for the winds is "the ox-killing wind" (*bād-i kushta gāw*).

[25] Beazley & Harverson, *Desert*, 73–78; Wulff, *Traditional*, 280–83; Michael Harverson, "Watermills in Iran," *Iran* 31 (1993):149–77.

[26] Wulff, *Traditional*, 280–82.

[27] Michael Harverson, *Persian Windmills* (Sprang-Capelle: The International Molinological Society, 1991), 3–9; Beazley & Harverson, *Desert*, 89–90; Wulff, *Traditional*, 284–89.

[28] Harverson, *Windmills*, 4; Wulff, *Traditional*, 288 ($v$ = 32 m/s, or 115.2 kmph).

The winds, fortuitously, arrive during "the time of the wheat harvest." Windmills, Nancy Dupree writes, "work day and night, renting the air with the most incredible squeals and squalls."[29] The 120-day winds drive windmills in the Bākharz–Herat Valley corridor. Mills are usually not commercial, often serving the needs of a hamlet or cluster of families. Windmills complement watermills; and they may temporarily supplant watermills when water flows dwindle in summer or drought.

*Herat Province*

Maps 1–4 reflect the course of the Herat River: from its origins in the Hindu Kush, passage south of Herat city, and northwest course into the Qara-Qum, where it debouches. Since water is the essence of the Herat oasis, districts (*bulūk*; pl. *bulūkāt*) of Herat province (*wilāyat*) are defined by their primary hydrological feature: the water-channel (*jūy*). "In the immediate area of Herat, the *buluk*s are long strips, curving along the contours of the valley from the water sources [located] to the east, past the walled city, to the *dasht* (unwatered land) west of the city, where the canal water gives out."[30]

Herat *wilāyat* was divided into ten tax/administrative *bulūks* that were tied closely to the system of water sharing.[31] Seven *bulūks* are situated to the north of the Hari Rud; three to the south. The districts north of the Herat River are Tūrān wa Tūniyān, Ghūrwān wa Pāshtān, Sabaqar, Parwānah wa Hawādasht,[32] Khiyābān, Injīl, and Ālinjān. The three to the south are Kambarāq, Guẕārah, and Udwān wa Tīzān.[33] The regions north of the Hari Rud are primarily irrigated by four *jūys* traversing northwest from the Hari Rud. They are (from east to west): Jūy-i Naw (called Jūy-i Sabaqar before the

[29] Nancy Hatch Dupree [née Wolfe], *An Historical Guide to Afghanistan* (Kabul: Afghan Tourist Organization, 1977), 253. See also Nancy Hatch Wolfe, *Herat: A Pictorial Guide* (Kabul: Afghan Tourist Organization, 1966), 44.

[30] Allen, *Catalogue*, 4.

[31] The ten districts are taken from the tax registers for irrigated lands, with the exception of Bulūk-i Parwānah wa Hawādasht, which is given only by Ḥāfiẓ-i Abrū. Allen, *Catalogue*, 7, Cat. No. 4; Krawulsky, *Ḫorāsān*, 1:27–28. Allen suggests the *bulūk*'s absence from the registers is because it was tax-exempt in the Timurid era. The districts are demarcated in Krawulsky, *Ḫorāsān*, v.2, Map 2. Krawulsky's Maps 1–8, and Allen's pullout Maps 1–2 are outstanding.

[32] Parwānah wa Hawādasht encompasses or adjoins Gāzurgāh. See Krawulsky, *Ḫorāsān*, v.2, Map 2. Gāzurgāh contains numerous shrines.

[33] The districts are described, analyzed, and annotated in Allen, *Catalogue*, 6–9, Cat. Nos. 1–10; Krawulsky, *Ḫorāsān*, 2:24–28. See also Krawulsky, *Ḫorāsān*, v.2, Map 2.

middle of the Kartid era), Jūy-i Injīl, Jūy-i Kārtabār (also known as Shāh Jūy), and Jūy-i Ālinjān (Map 4).

Injīl district is to the north, northeast, east, and southeast of Herat. It encompasses fertile lands below the eponymous *jūy* and the Jūy-i Kārtabār/ Shāh Jūy. In the northwest, Jūy-i Injīl branches into Jūy-i Shādī Barah and Mushk Rūd.[34] In the Timurid era, inner Herat obtained waters from Injīl district.[35] This is logical, and probably followed earlier practices. Water entered the walled city through an aqueduct in the northeast. Fixed allotments of water were distributed thence to city wards/quarters.[36]

*Herat: The Inner City*

It is an approximate square of 1.5 × 1.5 km (2.25 km$^2$ = 0.9 mile$^2$).[37] It was enclosed by a defensive wall, which no longer exists. According to Ibn Ḥawqal (4th/10th century) there were four gates: Saray (also called Balkh) Gate (north: to Balkh); Khūsh Gate (east: to Ghūr), Firūzābād Gate (south: to Sīstān); Ziyād Gate (west: to Nishapur). Saray Gate was iron; the other three gates were of wood. The citadel (*quhandiz, ḥiṣār, qalʿa*) was in the enclosed city, to the north.[38] "Government house" was three *farsang* (or one mile per Le Strange) outside Herat on the Fūshanj road (i.e., west), in a place called Khurāsān-Ābād.[39] A Friday mosque (*masjid-i jāmiʿ*) thrived inside Herat.

Mustawfī (d.*c.* 744/1344) claims that under the Shansabānī dynasts (Ghurids), Herat was a major city, with 444,000 houses, 12,000 shops, 6,000

[34] Allen, *Catalogue*, 7, Cat. No. 27.

[35] Ibid., 7; Krawulsky, *Ḫorāsān*, 1:23; Ḥāfiẓ-i Abrū, *Jughrāfiyā-yi Ḥāfiẓ-i Abrū: qismat-i rubʿ-i Khurāsān, Harāt*, ed. Māyil Harawī (Tehran: Bunyād-i farhang-i Īrān, 1349/1970), 18.

[36] Allen, *Catalogue*, 24.

[37] Major Sanders (Bengal Engineers), in Herat after the Persian siege of 1838, measures the inner city thusly: 1,600 yards (north to south), 1,500 yards (east to west). C.M. MacGregor, *Central Asia: Part II* (Calcutta: Office of the Superintendent of Government Printing, 1871), 341; cf. Rafi Samizay, *Islamic Architecture in Herat* ([Kabul]: The Ministry of Information and Culture, 1981), 114: proffers 1,200 m × 1,200 m (= 1,312 yards by 1,312 yards).

[38] On the centrality of the *quhandiz* in Khurasan's cities, see Paul Wheatley, *The Places Where Men Pray Together* (Chicago: University of Chicago Press, 2001), 172ff. On Herat's *quhandiz*, see Allen, *Catalogue*, 33, Cat. No. 53.

[39] Ibn Ḥawqal, *Safarnāma-yi Ibn Ḥawqal*, tr. Jaʿfar Shiʿār (Tehran: Amir Kabir, 1366/1987), 171–72; Le Strange, *Lands*, 408; Muḥammad b. Aḥmad al-Muqaddasī, *The Best Divisions for Knowledge of the Regions: Aḥsan al-taqāsīm fī maʿrifat al-aqālīm*, tr. Basil Collins (Reading: Garnet, 2001), 243; Ibrahīm Iṣṭakhrī, *Masālik al-mamālik*, tr. Anon., ed. Iraj Afshar (Tehran: Bungāh-i tarjumah wa nashr-i kitāb 1340/1961), 209–10; Wheatley, *Places*, 173.

public baths, 359 colleges (sgl. *madrasa*) and Sufi lodges (sgl. *khānaqāh*), one fire-temple, caravansarays, and mills.[40]

There were five gateways (*darwāza* or *darb*) in the Kartid era. Gates were situated at the primary compass points—Khūsh Gate (east), Firūzābād Gate (south), ʿIrāq Gate (west)—except the north, where they were at the northwest (Malik Gate) and northeast (Bar-Amān Gate).[41] In the Timurid era, Malik Gate was also called Maydān Gate; Bar-Amān Gate became Qipchāq Gate (see Chapter Ten, "The Kartid Gates").

Four bazaars (Ar.: *sūq*; Per.: *bāzār*) were situated along the four thoroughfares from Khūsh (east), Firūzābād (south), ʿIrāq (west), and Malik (northwest) gates; the northeast gate (Bar-Amān) did not lead to a bazaar. Each of the four main intramuros bazaars bore the name of its respective gateway and eponymous thoroughfare.[42] Bazaars intersected at the city center, forming the central bazaar, *chahār-sūq* or *chahār-sū* ("four bazaars").[43] Ibn Ḥawqal describes the pre-Kartid bazaars, and notices the extensive suburbs lying beyond the gates.[44]

The five gates, four quarters, bazaars, and population in 1884–85 are described by the *Afghan Boundary Commission*.[45] Residing then in Herat were 589 "Afghan" families (3,043 head); 1,099 "Fārsīwān" (Persian-speaking) "Qizilbash" families (5,089 head); Jews (144 families; 640 head); Hindus (30 individuals).[46]

The inner city contains the *masjid-i jāmi*ʿ (first referenced in 4th/10th century). The mosque underwent multiple expansions over one millennium, with major work, *c.* 1200, by the Ghurids.[47] The mosque is one of

40 Mustawfī/Le Strange (ed.), *Nuzhat*, 152; cf. Mustawfī/Le Strange (tr.), *Nuzhat*, 151.

41 al-Harawī, *Harāt*, 712; see also Isfizārī, *Rawżāt*, 1:77–78. Cf. Allen, *Catalogue*, 36–38.

42 On the eponymous bazaars, see Allen, *Catalogue*, Cat. Nos. 100 (Firūzābād), 101 (ʿIrāq), 102 (Khūsh), and 103 (Malik).

43 Allen, *Catalogue*, 49–53.

44 Ibn Ḥawqal, *Safarnama*, 172; Le Strange, *Lands*, 408. On Herat's bazaar in 1845, see Ferrier, *Caravan*, 173–74; the bazaar, *c.* 1885, see C.E. Yate, *Northern Afghanistan* (Edinburgh: William Blackwood, 1888), 25–26.

45 *Afghan Boundary Commission* ("ABC"), 6 vols including index (Simla: Government Central Press, 1888–92), 2:562–70 (city), 3:52–53 (gates).

46 *ABC*, 2:562–63. It is not clear if Afghan is being used to mean Pashtun, or used generically to mean people from Afghanistan. Fārsīwān is frequently conflated with Iranian and Shiʿa (i.e., "Qizilbash"). This may be the case here. Qizilbash is a valid exonym for a Twelver Shiʿa community within Afghanistan.

47 Allen, *Catalogue*, 103–111.

the outstanding edifices of the eastern Islamic world. It is not possible to determine the layout of inner Herat at the cusp of the Mongol invasions. Nevertheless, descriptions by Ibn Ḥawqal, Iṣṭakhrī, et al., and Allen's reconstructions, help in sketching its ostensible layout. The enclosed area held madrasas, hospices, mosques, and bazaars, and was the locus of socio-economic and intellectual activities.

## Herat after Elǰigidei

### *Ögödei's Initiatives*

It was impossible for the Mongols to utterly desolate Herat and the communities that dotted the surrounding plains and the mountain ranges through which traversed the Hari Rud. Elǰigidei attacked towns on the Herat River toward Awbih (east of Herat), but it is unlikely he could attack every settlement. Inhabitants will have fled ahead of his army. In 617/1221, for example, inhabitants of Turbat-i Jām, hearing of the Mongol advance, fled to Kūh-i Bizd in the Bīnalūd range west of Mashhad.[48] Khurasanians also took shelter behind city walls, but once it became clear that city walls offered little protection against Mongol siege techniques, and instead concentrated targets by converting walls and gates into an abattoir's pen, Khurasanians will have "run for the hills." Sometime after the Mongols had departed, inhabitants will have come down from their hiding places, gradually at first, later in streams, to re-occupy their farms and homes, or to occupy the properties of the recently departed. Agricultural production, albeit in limited forms, would have resumed in the Herat River Valley. Although the Mongols assuredly tried to corral any livestock in sight, shepherds and nomads will have taken to high ground with their flocks, which is to say, meat and dairy would have been available to the fortunate few for consumption, and for economic exchanges.

A solemn tale claims that forty people survived in Herat and its environs following Elǰigidei's depredations. Under the leadership of one of the forty (a *mawlānā*, naturally), the band lived near Herat's congregational mosque (*masjid-i jāmiʿ*), subsisting on gathered foods while planting crops

[48] Būzjānī, *Rawżat*, 81–82. Bīnalūd range runs northwest to southeast, between 36° and 37° N; 59° and 60° E. It has a maximum elevation of 10,535 ft/3,211 m.

for the year ahead. They subsisted thusly for fifteen years, 619/1222 to 634/1236–37,[49] until Ögödei (r. 1229–41) dispatched agents and allocated funds to rebuild Herat, marking the first Mongol revitalization effort at Herat.

Ögödei's initiatives are presented by Sayf al-Harawī in Islamic packaging. Ögödei is depicted as just and favorably disposed toward Muslims, unlike the rest of Chingiz Khan's brood, especially Chaghatai, a morose creature wedded to steppe traditions. Ögödei proscribed Mongols from preventing Muslims in Transoxiana and Khurasan from erecting mosques, madrasas, Sufi lodges, and other Islamic buildings. He offered nearly 100,000 pure gold dinars (*dīnār-i zar-i surkh*) to anyone of his faith (Shamanist or Buddhist) inclined to honor Islam by erecting spiritual and sepulchral edifices, with a supplement of 2,000 dinars for shaykhs and ulama. The Qaʾan's logic (ventures our chronicler) paralleled the Qurʾanic exhortation, "For you is your religion and for me is my religion" (Q109: 06),[50] not an unreasonable view considering the Mongols' "firm policy of religious tolerance."[51] Chaghatai was apparently furious at Ögödei.

In 635/1237f., ʿIzz al-Dīn Muqaddam al-Harawī, a weaver deported to Turkistan by Tolui,[52] journeyed to Herat with a cohort to execute Ögödei's policies. They were welcomed by compatriots.[53] The following day, returnees and residents gathered at Herat's *masjid-i jāmiʿ*. "Everyone who was in Herat received three *mann* (≈ 9 kg/20 lb) of wheat (*gandum*)" for sowing "every fifty *kūtak* of land."[54] Since *jūys* were still clogged (*anbāshta*),[55] wells supplied water to the tilled lands.[56] Well-water will have been sufficient at this early stage in Herat's rebirth, but it is doubtful that well-water met the needs of *inner* Herat's residents in later years; hence the aqueduct identified above.

49 al-Harawī, *Harāt*, 130; Mīrkhwānd, *Rawżat*, 3,885. See also Muḥammad Ismāʿīl Mablagh Gharjistānī, "Wīrānī-hā wa ābādī-hā-yi mujaddid-i Harāt [Ruin and Revival in Herat]," *Āryānā* No. 185 (1337/1958):37–40.

50 al-Harawī, *Harāt*, 132.

51 Morgan, *Mongols*, 37. On "religious toleration" under Ögödei, and tensions between his perspectives and Chaghatai's, see May, *Mongol Empire*, 103.

52 ʿIzz al-Dīn was deported to Turkistan. Isfizārī, *Rawżāt*, 2:108–09; Faṣīḥ, *Mujmal*, 790–91. He was in the delegation that met Tolui. They apparently negotiated the city's surrender.

53 al-Harawī, *Harāt*, 145.

54 Ibid., 146. *Mann*: see glossary. *Kūtak* is evidently a measure or share of land.

55 New wells were probably excavated and existing wells cleared of blockages.

56 al-Harawī, *Harāt*, 146.

That year, Qisatay Kūr, commander (*amīr*) of Garmsīr[57] and *Afghānistān*, assumed the post of *shaḥna*. He was eloquent, exhorting everyone to cooperate in building and farming. Plebe and noble (*ważīʿ wa sharīf*) worked together to sow fields. Cotton (*panba*) was one of the crops;[58] 400 *mann* (≈ 1,188 kg/2,614 lb) of cotton was shipped to *Afghānistān* in exchange for farm implements and oxen (*darāz-dumbāl*).[59] Cotton was carried by twenty men, each bearing 20 *mann* (≈ 59.4 kg/130.7 lb) on his back.[60] Muqaddam and Qisatay imposed corvée (*ḥashar*; *bīghār*) on Heratis; for two and one-half months everyone worked assiduously to re-open Injīl channel (*jūy-i injīl*). They irrigated one farm (*mazraʿa*).[61]

ʿIzz al-Din Muqaddam al-Harawī expired in 636/1238–39; he was succeeded by his son, Shams al-Dīn Muḥammad b. ʿIzz al-Din, with the Qaʾan's approval.[62] Ögödei dispatched skilled workers to Herat, along with *shaḥna* Kharlugh and *bitikchī* Sūkū.[63] Muḥammad b. ʿIzz al-Din, Kharlugh, and Sūkū were tasked with making the region thrive.[64] The trio reached Herat in 637/1239–40. Each erected a pavilion (*kūshk*) outside the walled city near Khūsh Gate. Seven shops, including a baker, cook, butcher, blacksmith, greengrocer, haberdasher (*khabbāz wa ṭabbākh wa qaṣṣāb wa ḥaddād wa baqqāl wa bazzāz*), thrived.[65] Ögödei dispatched additional support through his emissary, Taksīnak. Batu (d.*c.* 1256), Jochi's son, dispatched builders along with his emissary, Yunūj Bīk. Labors were apportioned: Yunūj Bīk re-opened Jūy-i Sabaqar (later called Jūy-i Naw);[66] Bahādur Mālānī (Elǰigidei's appointee), re-opened Jūy-i Mālān;[67] Taksīnak labored with repairs to Jūy-i Injīl.[68] The work on

[57] On *Garmsīr* ("warm region": anglicized to "Gurmsel" and "Garmsel"), see n.120, *infra*.

[58] Cotton (*Gossypium*): requires torrid temperatures and abundant water supplies.

[59] *Darāz-dumbāl*: see glossary. On oxen in Persia, see Marco Polo/Yule (tr.), *Travels*, 1:92.

[60] al-Harawī, *Harāt*, 146. If accurate, this reveals a dearth of draft animals in Herat.

[61] Ibid. Injīl probably supplied water for the cotton field (see n.58, *supra*). If so, the sequence of events should be reversed, i.e., cotton was planted after Injīl was re-opened.

[62] Faṣīḥ, *Mujmal*, 791.

[63] al-Harawī, *Harāt*, 152–53.

[64] Ibid., 153.

[65] Ibid., 154. The seventh vendor's specialty (if different) is not clarified. On alternate meanings for *kūshk*, see Mottahedeh, "Lexicography," 470–71.

[66] Jūy-i Sabaqar: see Allen, *Catalogue*, 18, Cat. No. 29. Kartid improvements transformed it to the "New Canal." See Chapter Eight, § "Kartid Initiatives."

[67] Jūy-i Mālān: see Allen, *Catalogue*, 17, Cat. No. 26.

[68] al-Harawī, *Harāt*, 158.

Jūy-i Sabaqar and Jūy-i Mālān, which transect agricultural zones, was to develop farming.

In 638/1240–41 began the final enterprise in Herat prior to Ögödei's death in 1241. The governor, Majd al-Dīn Kālīwanī, was Batu's selectee. He had met with Batu at his *urdū* and been furnished with two golden tablets of authority (*pā'īza-yi zarīn*); he was dispatched with an emissary (*ilchī*) to Körgüz (George),[69] the Uighur administrator of eastern Khurasan (in office, 637–39/1239ff. or to 640/1242–43).[70] Then to Herat with Körgüz's *ilchī*. Kālīwanī had presumably received instructions from Batu to protect the Jochid agenda against their Chinggisid rivals, and received financial and logistical assistance from Körgüz. Muḥammad b. ʿIzz al-Din was deposed, but Kharlugh and Sūkū were retained.[71]

Despite Chinggisid conflicts and other impediments, three pavilions holding shops were erected beside Khūsh Gate, *c.* 637/1239–40. With the re-opening of arterial channels—Jūy-i Injīl (work initiated 635/1237–38; completed 638/1240–41);[72] Jūy-i Ālinjān (opened in 638/1240–41);[73] Jūy-i Mālān and Jūy-i Sabaqar (work commenced *c.* 636/1238–39)—people from "Turkistan and Khurasan" started migrating to Herat. The enumerated population of "adults and minors" stood at 6,900 in 638/1240–41.[74]

Socio-economic activities were returning to Herat and its agricultural vicinities. Shops in the pavilions erected by the Khūsh Gate served the growing population. Discrete social and economic datum interspersed by Sayfī; for instance, on population growth in the region; on restoration of irrigation channels; exchanges of cotton for oxen; and abundance of grain and fruit, show that by Möngke's accession in 1251, Herat's agricultural vicinities were recovering from Elǰigidei's depredations of 619/1222.

[69] al-Harawī, *Harāt*, 161; Faṣīḥ, *Mujmal*, 793.

[70] On Uighurs serving Mongols, see James Millward, *Eurasian Crossroads: A History of Xinjiang* (New York: Columbia University Press, 2007), 64–67. Körgüz was possibly Christian.

[71] al-Harawī, *Harāt*, 161–62; Faṣīḥ, *Mujmal*, 793.

[72] al-Harawī, *Harāt*, 162; cf. Faṣīḥ, *Mujmal*, 791 (opened 637/1239f., and "water flowed into Herat," meaning, the inner city).

[73] Jūy-i Ālinjān: In Ālinjān District. The channel courses northwest from the Herat River and approaches Jūy-i Kārtabār southwest of the inner city. Allen, *Catalogue*, 13. On its opening, see al-Harawī, *Harāt*, 162–63; Faṣīḥ, *Mujmal*, 793.

[74] al-Harawī, *Harāt*, 163.

*Möngke's Initiatives*

Möngke's principal action, in accord with his centralization policies,[75] was to order the census of Herat. Sayfī does not give details of the 653/1255 census.[76] Based on Allsen's analysis of the efficiency of Möngke's approach, the census was surely comprehensive.[77] It probably paralleled in methodology (if not in scope) the 638/1240–41 census, when people from around Herat assembled to be enumerated by agents of *malik* Majd al-Dīn Kālyūnī (d.*c.* 640/1241f.).[78] The census served to enumerate and to register people for taxation and the corvée—including military service.[79]

The four Mongol census takers are named: Lablaqā'ī (Lablaqa), Markitā'ī (Merkidaï) Khʷārizmī, Majd al-Arkān, and Shihāb Mu'ayyad.[80] Merkidaï was the chief census taker; he and Shams al-Dīn Kart established a rapport. They connived to rid themselves of Kharlugh. Merkidaï maligned him to Möngke; Kharlugh was terminated and Merkidaï was appointed *shaḥna* of Herat, with Lablaqa as his aide (*nawkar*). Merkidaï erected a pavilion to the south (possibly just beyond the gate), and encouraged his retinue to build and cultivate (*'imarāt wa zirā'at*). He built a *ṭāram* (wooden building of a circular form with a domed or vaulted roof) and *dargāh-yi 'aẓīm* (grand court or reception hall).[81]

Early reconstruction efforts involved the labors and the funds of various Chinggisid stakeholders. Arghūn Aqa had served Güyük, but was re-appointed by Möngke despite his Ögödeid ties because he "had on his staff

75 See Allsen, *Mongol Imperialism, et passim.*

76 al-Harawī, *Harāt*, 278. Sayfī's dating of the census is inaccurate. See explanation in Allsen, *Mongol Imperialism*, 132–33. I have relied on Allsen's dating.

77 On the census in Persia, see Allsen, *Mongol Imperialism*, 130–34. The Mongol imperial court probably received "an extensive summary of the results, the complete census rolls, because of their bulk, being retained at the local level." Ibid., 122 n.30.

78 al-Harawī, *Harāt*, 163. The first census in Sīstān was in 639/1241f.; *qalān* and *qubchūr* taxes were subsequently implemented. See Anon./Bahār (ed.), *Sīstān*, 367.

79 On military recruitment in Persia, see Allsen, *Mongol Imperialism*, 203–07. Shams al-Dīn Kart the Elder's domains contributed "a total of seven *tümens*." Ibid. 205, referencing al-Harawī (Calcutta ed.), *Harāt*, 189; al-Harawī, *Harāt*, 221.

80 al-Harawī, *Harāt*, 278; Allsen, *Mongol Imperialism*, 122.

81 al-Harawī, *Harāt*, 278–79. Probably in 657/1258f., the date in Faṣīḥ, *Mujmal*, 811. Since Merkidaï was a Mongol, the *ṭāram* could have been based on a *yurt*, where the lattice wall frame is termed *tarem*. On yurts, see Albert Szabo and Thomas Barfield, *Afghanistan: An Atlas of Indigenous Domestic Architecture* (Austin: University of Texas Press, 1991), 63–71.

representatives [...] from each princely line, who looked after the interests of their respective masters [...]."[82] Chinggisid intrigues adversely impacted on governance and reconstruction in Herat, with princes jostling for influence and maneuvering to install their agents. This period, nonetheless, witnessed cooperation in Herat by Chinggisid stakeholders: concerted efforts to re-open irrigation channels, which reflected shared interests in Herat's revivification, but not from altruism. Incomes from Khurasanian territories "had been assigned to specific princes—their 'shares' in the profits of empire—and therefore they had the right to monitor [...] major administrative initiatives such as census taking and tax collecting."[83]

Beyond the taxation practices of the Mongol Empire in Persia,[84] we know nothing about Möngke's initiatives to maximize revenues from Herat and its vicinities. Three taxes in force in Möngke's time (*qubchūr*, *qalān*, *kharāj*) are identified by Sayfī,[85] but applicable rules, rates, and revenues are unknown. We learn of one enforcement. Early in Shams al-Dīn Kart's reign (*c.* 653/1255), Muḥammad b. ʿIzz al-Dīn had dispatched army chiefs, tribal leaders and their followers to the far corners of *Afghānistān* and Sīstān to collect the annual taxes (*ruʾūs-i sipāh wa aʿyān-i hasham wa khidam rā bi-aṭrāf-i Afghānistān wa bih Sīstān firistād tā kharāj wa māl-i sālīyānah wa wājib-i dīwānī jamʿ kun-and*).[86]

*Economic Costs of Waging War v. Benefits from Conquest and Domination*

Resistance to demands for taxes and tributary status was practically de rigueur in parts of the *notional* Kartid realm—regions delineated in Möngke's 649/1251 *yarlīgh* but not yet under Kartid dominion. Firstly, *maliks* and *mihtars* (princes) of *Afghānistān*, Sīstān, and Khurasan did not submit because Shams al-Dīn had displayed a golden *pāʾīza* and broadcast Möngke's *yarlīgh*. For example, when Shams al-Dīn tried to enforce the *yarlīgh* in Sīstān (in 653/1255), Shams al-Dīn ʿAlī b. Masʿūd (d. 653/1255), Sīstān's ruler, resisted and was killed.[87] His nephew, Naṣīr al-Dīn Muḥammad, ruled Sīstān

[82] Allsen, *Culture and Conquest*, 19.
[83] Ibid., 19.
[84] Allsen, *Mongol Imperialism*, 144–71.
[85] al-Harawī, *Harāt*, 215, 217, 241.
[86] Ibid., 241.
[87] Anon./Bahār (ed.), *Sīstān*, 368; al-Harawī, *Harāt*, 262–72; Lane, *Mongol Rule*, 163.

for many years, but not continuously as a Kartid *banda*. He wriggled free, *c.* 1264, after petitioning Hülegü.[88] Kartids sometimes had to pitilessly grind down contumacious local lords.[89] The case of Almār, castellan of Fort Tīrī,[90] is illustrative. He refused to submit or to pay: "I refuse to serve Mongols and will never give tribute to pagans." Tīrī was invested for weeks, and when the Kartids breached it, Shams al-Din Kart inflicted terrible cruelties on Almār and his soldiers.[91]

Collecting funds, even from those who had submitted, was a problem. Collection of taxes and tribute involved losses of blood and treasure for Kartids and Mongols, which had to be weighed against revenue stream potential for the refractory regions: will the losses of today be compensated through future revenue streams: taxes payable in cash, cereals, gold, livestock, pelts, etc.; corvée labor and conscription?[92] Rulers seek to maximize revenues to the state, but they are subject to immutable realities; for example, their bargaining power, transaction costs, and discount rates (present value of future returns). Rulers must offer *some* return for the revenues that they extract; they cannot be purely exploitative.[93]

The "Swiss cheese" model of governance (Chapter Two) afforded rulers flexibility: they could dominate the "cheesy bits," while ignoring (where possible) the "holes." If people in holes became unruly,[94] punitive expeditions were launched.[95] "Pillage and enslave" (*ghārat wa asīr*) is a phrase that recurs in the sources for very good reason.[96]

[88] Malik Shāh Ḥusayn b. Malik Ghīyāth al-Dīn Sīstānī, *Iḥyā' al-mulūk*, ed. Manuchihr Sutudih (Tehran: Bungāh-i tarjumah wa nashr-i kitāb, 1344/1966), 79–81; Anon./Bahār (ed.), *Sīstān*, 368–69; Anon./Gold (tr.), *Sīstān*, 325–26; Lane, *Mongol Rule*, 166.

[89] See Lane, *Mongol Rule*, 163–67 (the Kartid's efforts at subjugating local lords).

[90] Fort Tīrī: on Tirin River (*Tīrī Rūd*), a tributary of the Hilmand. On the Hilmand River, its tributaries, volumes, and associated details, see Adamec, *Gazetteer*, 2:114–127.

[91] Lane, *Mongol Rule*, 164. See narrative in al-Harawī, *Harāt*, 238–40.

[92] See, e.g., Coats and Pecquet, "Calculus of Conquests," esp. 522ff.

[93] This is a topic that cannot be properly treated here, but see Margaret Levi, *Of Rule and Revenue* (Berkeley: University of California Press, 1988), 10–40.

[94] The mountainous Afghanistan/Pakistan borderlands had "holes" called *yāghistān*: "land of the unruly." These areas were of negligible economic utility, but since inhabitants now and again raided caravans traveling between Persia and India, they had to be punished.

[95] Booty—chattels and slaves—were monetized to defray costs of expeditions.

[96] Taybādī implored Temür: "do not enslave or pillage the people of Herat" (*mardum-i Harāt-rā asīr wa ghārat nakunī*). See Chapter Six and n.159.

## Early Ilkhanid and Kartid Efforts

The historical record is thin on early Kartid and early Ilkhanid revitalization efforts. Self-interests played pivotal roles in (1) the selection of urban settlements (quarters and wards) and the rural communities (farmlands and clusters of settlements) to be developed; (2) the specific projects to be funded (e.g., mosques, bazaars, subterranean channels, etc.);[97] and (3) the sources of funds for developments.

ʿAṭāʾ-Malik Juwaynī purchased one quarter of Khabūshān village and induced Hülegü to underwrite reconstruction costs: "[a]ll the expense of re-building he met with cash from the treasury so that no charge fell upon the people." Irrigated waters flowed, the bazaar was rebuilt, the Friday mosque was restored; "inhabitants returned [...] bringing peasants and *qanat*-diggers from Quhistan [...]. They built workshops and laid out a garden adjoining the Friday mosque."[98] Moreover, "[a]n order was given for the amirs and dignitaries of court to build houses [in Khabūshān], each in accordance with his rank and ability."[99]

Thomas Allsen doubts the Khabūshān episode was "at all typical" of development processes in Khurasan under Hülegü; whereas in Armenia, "more systematic measures are in evidence."[100] In Armenia, according to Grigor of Akancʿ, Hülegü "began to rebuild the devastated places [...] and from each inhabited village he selected householders, one from the small, and two or three from the large villages [...] and sent them to all of the destroyed places to undertake rebuilding."[101] Taxes were collected from the Armenian regions picked for rebuilding. Hülegü also ordered the rebuilding of Baghdad.[102] Reconstruction processes of Ilkhanid Khurasan—a large, wealthy province that will have generated substantial tax revenues for the Ilkhanid fisc—are unknown because historians of Persia are stuck with Juwaynī, Mustawfī,

[97] An example of this type of development is the *gunbad* (dome) erected at Turbat-i Jām in 633/1236. The benefactor is still unknown. Mahendrarajah, *Sufi Saint*, 103–06.

[98] Juvainī/Boyle, *World-Conqueror*, 2:617; cf. Rashīd al-Dīn/Thackston, *Jāmiʿ*, 3:343.

[99] Rashīd al-Dīn/Thackston, *Jāmiʿ*, 3:343.

[100] Allsen, *Mongol Imperialism*, 90 (Allsen relies on Grigor of Akancʿ for Armenia).

[101] Grigor of Akancʿ, *The History of the Nation of the Archers*, tr. R.P. Blake and R.N. Frye, *HJAS* 12/3 (1949):269–399, 345.

[102] Allsen, *Mongol Imperialism*, 90.

et al. Mustawfī, an Ilkhanid fiscal officer, submits haphazard economic and fiscal information on the provinces; his data on Khurasan is abysmal. Ilya Petrushevsky did what he could to make sense of Mustawfī's figures.

The Khabūshān episode is reflective of the centrality of self-interest. Adam Smith's observation on the function of self-interest in propelling entrepreneurship is well known: "It is not from the benevolence of the butcher, the brewer, or the baker that we expect our dinner, but from their regard to their own interest."[103] Ephemeral amirs controlled sections of Khurasan; it is reasonably presumed that they, like Juwaynī, profited by acquiring and developing lands and hydrological assets. We are in an absence of evidence situation, but that is not evidence of absence. Our understanding of human nature points to profit as motive. This does not mean that "systematic measures" were employed: even haphazard economic development is progress.

The last years of Shams al-Dīn Kart the Elder's reign were evidently prosperous. This despite his self-imposed exile at Khaysār, 669–74/1270–75, when son, *malik* Tark (n.d.) substituted for him in Herat. The year 671/1272–73 was a banner year (according to Sayfī): grain and fruit were in abundance; people from Khurasan and beyond drifted into Herat and lived comfortably.[104] A census—an opportunity to enumerate and then tax—was held in 672/1273–74. A large sum of dinars flowed into the Ilkhanid fisc.[105]

The early years of Shams al-Dīn Kart the Younger *may* have been prosperous for Herat;[106] but evidence of initiatives by him to improve agricultural production, to repair hydrological assets, and otherwise develop the economy, are unavailable. Reconstruction efforts had been ongoing in Sīstān, for instance, during the reign of Shams al-Dīn Kart the Elder, which suggests possibilities for Herat. Channels and edifices were restored in Sīstān between 663/1264f. and 675/1276f., and agriculture was thriving.[107]

Kartid control of territories had frayed. Sīstān (Sijistān), Tikīnābād, and Bustistān (Bust) had been itemized in Möngke's *yarlīgh*. They were

[103] Adam Smith, *An Inquiry into the Nature and Causes of the Wealth of Nations*, ed. Edwin Cannan (Chicago: University of Chicago Press, 1976 [2012 reprint]), 30. On profits and motives, see also Ibn Khaldun, *Muqaddimah*, vol. 2, ch. 5, §§ 1–2, 5, 9–13.

[104] al-Harawī, *Harāt*, 359.

[105] Ibid., 360. The results of the census are not disclosed.

[106] ʿAlāʾ al-Dīn, his son at Herat, quit for Khaysār, leaving the city politically adrift.

[107] Anon./Bahār (ed.), *Sīstān*, 372–73; Anon./Gold (tr.), *Sīstān*, 329.

transferred by the Il-Khan, Aḥmad Tegüder (r. 1281–84),[108] to Naṣīr al-Dīn Muḥammad (r. 653/1255 to late 8th/early 9th century). In *c.* 683/1284f., Naṣīr al-Dīn received from Aḥmad Tegüder gifts, *pāʾiza*, and patent (*farmān*) to govern Sīstān, Farāh, Qalʿa-yi Gāh, Nīh,[109] and Bust, to the Indus (*Āb-i Sind*), and the lands bordering the river (*tamāmī-yi nawāḥī-yi rūd*).[110] Aḥmad Tegüder appears not have rendered support to the Kartids.

After the Nikudari raids of 687/1288 and 688/1289, and Nawrūz's despoliations in Khurasan and Sīstān in 691/1291, Herat, and the agricultural and commercial economies of its surroundings, required resuscitation.

## Nawrūz's Revitalization of Herat and Sīstān

### *Depopulation and Destruction in Herat*

Nawrūz, to recap, was considered by the Ilkhanate to be in rebellion between early 688/1289 and early 694/late 1294. Nawrūz ruled independently, that is, politically dominated, Khurasan from *c.* 691/1291 to 694/1294f. After breaking his alliance with the Chaghataid-Ögödeid union, Nawrūz wanted Fakhr al-Dīn Kart to govern Herat; he secured his release, *c.* 693/1294, from Shams al-Dīn the Younger's jail. Fakhr al-Dīn's martial and managerial skills were employed by Nawrūz, who strove to revive the economies of Herat and Sīstān.

Sayf al-Harawī's narratives of devastation and bleakness in Herat consequent to the Nikudarid and Nawruzid pillages are slightly exaggerated, but in

108 Jackson, "Aḥmad Takūdār."

109 Nīh: An oasis west of Lake Zarah. Le Strange, *Lands*, 340.

110 Anon./Bahār (ed.), *Sīstān*, 374; Anon./Gold (tr.), *Sīstān*, 330–31; Sīstānī, *Iḥyāʾ al-mulūk*, 84–85. "Lands bordering the river" covers large extents. The Harūd, Farāh, Hilmand/Hīrmand, and Khʷāsh/Khāsh rivers flow into the Hāmūn Basin. Harūd and Farāh form *Hāmūn-i Farāh* (Lake Farāh); the Khʷāsh and Hilmand form *Hāmūn-i Sawarān*. If flows are plentiful, a third lake emerges (*Hāmūn-i Zarah*). The bodies may merge into one lake: Lake Sistan/Lake Zarah. The main city was Zaranj. Iṣṭakhrī/Afshar (ed.), *Masālik al-mamālik*, 195–96 (on waterways); Reclus, *Geography*, 9:29–31; Barthold, *Geography*, 66–70; Le Strange, *Lands*, 338–44 (Harūd, pp. 340–41; Khʷāsh, pp. 342–43); Adamec, *Gazetteer*, 2:106 (Harūd/Harūt River). *Hāmūn* means plain, but with high water volumes, a plain could transform into a marsh/lake. Adamec, *Gazetteer*, 2:97 (Gūd-i Zirrah depression), 2:103–105 (*Hāmūn*). Zaranj: Iṣṭakhrī/Afshar (ed.), *Masālik al-mamālik*, 192–94; al-Muqaddasī/Collins (tr.), *Aḥsan al-taqāsīm*, 243, 248–49; M.A. Sīstānī "Jughrāfiyā-yi tārīkhī-i Zaranj" [Historical geography of Zaranj, Part 1], *Āryānā* No. 272 (1346/1967):11–25; idem, […, Part 2], *Āryānā* No. 273 (1346/1967):15–27. Waterfowl and fish were plentiful in the Hāmūn Basin.

evaluating his reports, we should recall that he had lived through the appalling events. He will have received—apart from inflated tales—sober reports from reliable interlocutors. Herat and its agricultural environs did suffer harm in the raids, which adversely impacted on social and economic activities. Sayfī, and historians who followed his narratives, paint a rosy picture of life and renewal in Herat *after* Nawrūz's revitalization efforts; of peasants who praised the justice and foresight of Nawrūz. Thanks to Nawrūz, claims Sayfī, Herat prospered.[111]

This picture was painted to comport with the assertion advanced in chronicles that Nawrūz had been acting under Ghāzān's orders. Although the economic situation cannot be quantified, Herat and its environs recovered from Nikudarid and Nawruzid depredations; and Nawrūz was the catalyst for social and economic renewal.

### *Nawrūz's Initiatives at Herat*

In addition to Fakhr al-Dīn Kart, Nawrūz needed the support of petty lords (*maliks* and amirs) of Khurasan and Sīstān. Nawrūz dispatched amirs Nīkī Bāwarchī (n.d.) to Isfizār, and Ilātimūr (n.d.) to Sīstān. He next wrote to Naṣīr al-Dīn Muḥammad of Sīstān; Jalāl al-Dīn of Farāh; and Ḥisām al-Dīn of Isfizār. His letter, penned in the name of the nominal suzerain (Ürüng Temür/Awrang Timūr) that he had appointed, was sealed with the *Āl tamghā*.[112] The letter's *intitulatio*, which ordinarily follows the *invocatio*, was a variant of the Turkish royal maxim, *sözümiz*: "Our word."[113] The letter proclaimed that Nawrūz had been appointed—by whom shall be clarified shortly—"to return Herat to prosperity" (*shahr-i Harāt rā bih ḥāl-i ābādānī bāz-ār-am*).[114] *Raʿāyā* from the Herat region living in your domains,

[111] al-Harawī, *Harāt*, 410.

[112] *Āl tamghā*: vermillion color ink seal embossed on *recto* of Mongol imperial documents; cf. *qarā tamghā* (black seal): a personal seal that may accompany *Āl tamghā*, possibly on *verso*, where countersigns appear. For vivid exemplars of *Āl tamghā* seals owned by Iran's *National Library and Archives*, see Yasuhiro Yokkaichi, "Four Seals in Phags-pa and Arabic Scripts on Amīr Čoban's Decree of 726 AH/1326 CE," *Orient* 50 (Japan, 2015):25–33; cf. Dai Matsui, "Six Seals on the Verso of Čoban's Decree of 726 AH/1326 CE," *Orient* 50 (Japan, 2015):35–39.

[113] *Sözümiz* was commonly used in imperial documents. It is the eastern Turkish equivalent of the Mongolian "Our word" (*ügä manu*). On Nawrūz's use of *sözümiz*, see Waṣṣāf, *Taḥrīr*, 178 (*Nawrūz sūzbadīn*); Mīrkhʷānd, *Rawżat*, 4,203 (*Nawrūz sūzandīn*).

[114] al-Harawī, *Harāt*, 409; cf. Ḥāfiẓ-i Abrū, *Kart*, 78.

Nawrūz orders, must be repatriated. They were threatened with retaliation for non-compliance.

Sayf al-Harawī, and Ḥāfiẓ-i Abrū (who follows Sayfī), insist that Nawrūz's authority and *Āl tamghā* were obtained from Ghāzān, on whose behalf Nawrūz was operating.[115] This is incorrect. Waṣṣāf and Mīrkhʷānd make manifest that Nawrūz was publishing decrees under Ürüng Temür's name.[116] Moreover, the sequence of the episodes demonstrates that Nawrūz was operating independent of Ghāzān, with whom he had yet to form an alliance.

After six months, Bāwarchī and Ilātimūr returned to Herat with 5,000 prominent Herati notables (*kadkhudā-yi Harawī*) in tow. Meanwhile, petty lords, fearing repercussions, will have heeded Nawrūz's directive and expelled *raʿāyā* from their domains. Bāwarchī was appointed *shaḥna* and governed for two years.[117] Nawrūz commanded: "for two years, no person, Mongol or Muslim, shall harass or make demands of the people of Herat" (*wa ḥukm farmūd kih tā muddat-i dū sāl, hīch kasī az mughūl-ān wa muslim-ān bi-mardum-i Harāt taʾarrużī na-rasānad wa muṭālabatī na-namāʾīd*).[118] Bāwarchī barred nomads (read: predatory bands) from Herat and its surroundings. Highways were cleared of bandits (*rāh-hā-yi makhūf īman gasht*). People were no longer fearful and migrated to Herat from other areas of Khurasan (*az aṭrāf-i mamālik-i khurāsān khalq rawī bih Harāt āward*). Merchants from other provinces of Persia and foreign lands (India? Transoxiana?) visited to transact; they felt safe because the highways and byways to Herat were free from hazards (*tujjār az yamīn wa yasār-i wilāyāt wa buldān āsūda-ḥāl wa īman az makhūfāt-i turuq rawān shud-and*). Herat prospered.[119]

[115] al-Harawī, *Harāt*, 409; cf. Ḥāfiẓ-i Abrū, *Kart*, 78: his rendering is that when Arghūn died in 690/1291, his son, Ghāzān, took his place and appointed Nawrūz to govern Khurasan. Ḥāfiẓ-i Abrū erases Geikhatu's reign and Nawrūz's autonomous rule in Khurasan.

[116] Waṣṣāf, *Taḥrīr*, 178 (*wa farmān-hā bih nām-i shāhzāda Awrang Timūr bih aṭrāf mī-firistād*); Mīrkhʷānd, *Rawżat*, 4,203 (*yarlīgh-hā bih nām-i Awrang Timūr niwisht wa Nawrūz sūzandīn bar ān raqam-zada bih aṭrāf wa jawānib mī-firistād*).

[117] Nawrūz had written *c.* 691/1292 to Shams al-Dīn Kihīn demanding his presence in Herat. When he demurred, Nawrūz appointed Bāwarchī, *c.* 692/1293. Once Nawrūz secured Fakhr al-Dīn Kart's release, the younger Kartid replaced Bāwarchī in 693/1293–94.

[118] Isfizārī, *Rawżāt*, 1:428; cf. al-Harawī, *Harāt*, 409 (different wording).

[119] al-Harawī, *Harāt*, 409–10; Ḥāfiẓ-i Abrū, *Kart*, 78–79.

The *History of Sīstān* claims an army had been dispatched to *wilāyat-i Garmsīr* and outskirts (*ḥawālī*),[120] Bust, and Tikīnābād in 695/1295f.,[121] to clear out "thieves and ruffians" (*duzdān wa runūd*); highways were cleared of "wickedness and mischief" (*sharr wa fasād*).[122] If per chance this was Nawrūz's or Nīkī Bāwarchī's doing, the year should be adjusted to 692–93/1293–94. An arterial trade route from Herat to India passes through Farāh to Bust and Tikīnābād, thence to Ghazni or Qandahar, and to India.[123] Hence the imperative to secure Farāh, Bust, Tikīnābād, and Garmsīr.

*Analysis of Nawrūz's Initiatives*

Nawrūz's nascent polity needed taxes from pastoral, agricultural, and commercial activities. He therefore fostered activities that stimulated the economy.

Firstly, Nawrūz (through his *shaḥna*, Nīkī Bāwarchī) provided an invaluable *public good*: security. Absent physical security for persons and property, little economic activity will take place. Herat will have remained desolate—if not completely "empty of people" (*az mardum khālī būd*) as averred by Sayfī, then fairly close. Socio-economic activities would have been low. However, once Nawrūz instituted security and barred other predators from Herat and its purlieus, and established for himself a monopoly on theft, *ra'āyā* will have returned or migrated from other Persian provinces in search of farming or share-cropping,[124] labor, trading, and crafting opportunities.

Secondly, the prominent Herati notables (*kadkhudā-yi Harawī*) forcibly repatriated were merchants, ulama, landowners, and professionals whose physical presence in Herat, and active participation in cultural, judicial, and economic activities, were indispensable to the cultural and economic revitalization of Herat and vicinities. There can be no economic prosper-

[120] *Garmsīr*: Bellew, *Seistan*, 33–54: on journey from Qandahar to Bust to "Gurmsel" (*Garmsīr*). Adamec, *Gazetteer*, 2:85–87: modern district of Garmsīr is from *c.* 30° 15′ to 31° 15′ N; 62° 30′ to 64° 15′ E. It is *c.* 8,500 mile$^2$/22,015 km$^2$.

[121] Further on Bust, Tikīnābād, and Sīstān, see Minorsky (ed.), *Ḥudūd*, 344–46.

[122] Anon./Bahār (ed.), *Sīstān*, 376; Anon./Gold (tr.), *Sīstān*, 333.

[123] On Balūchistān, Sīstān, Hilmand, and Garmsīr; and trading centers and caravan routes in those regions, see Barthold, *Geography*, 72–86.

[124] Tenant-farmers held share-cropping contracts (*muzāra'a*) with landlords. On the division of crops and rents, see, generally, Lambton, *Landlord*, 306–29.

ity without the participation of merchants,[125] shopkeepers,[126] *ṣarrāfs*,[127] waterlords, landlords, *muqannīs* (*kārīz* engineers), *mīrābs* (water-managers), hydrologists, agronomists, and such; no cultural renaissance without sermonizers (*khaṭīb*), imams, madrasa lecturers, Sufis.[128] Essential to the furtherance of economic activities is a functioning judiciary, which necessitates the hiring of juris-consults (*muftī*), judges (*qāḍī*), bailiffs, and such.[129] The state's bureaucratic apparatus (scribes, tax-collectors, etc.) had to have expanded.

Pastoral nomads of Khurasan assuredly traded with *kadkhudās*, *raʿāyā*, and Heratis once the sedentary classes were back on their feet earning livelihoods, and had economic surpluses available. Pastoral nomads traded livestock, meat, dairy, wool, etc. for vegetables, cereals, fabrics, pottery, etc. In the absence of medieval reports on interactions between nomad and sedentary, modern studies must suffice. This in no way diminishes their value. Thomas Barfield offers keen insights on social and economic interactions between nomads and *raʿāyā* from the 1970s at the bazaar of Imam Saheb (below the Oxus; north of Qunduz). The bazaar had seven associated caravansarys and hundreds of shops. One caravansaray, "Serai Imam Khan," is examined and sketched. Imam Khan had specialty shops (haberdashers, carpenters, coppersmiths, etc.) and general vendors (tea-houses, eateries, grocers, general goods). The sheep market (*bāzār-i gūsfand*) was (from nomadic pastoralists' perspectives) a central feature. The bazaar was open daily, but on two market days (determined by custom; days are uniform for the region's bazaars), people from surrounding villages descended on Imam Saheb to transact, window-shop, socialize, and enjoy treats like hot bread. Market day was a social and commercial event.[130]

125 Merchants: wholesalers, traders (sgl. *tājir*; pl. *tujjār*; Persian: *bāzārgān*, etc.).

126 Shopkeepers: retailers, vendors, peddlers (*bāʾi*, *bāzārī*, *-farūshī*, *dast-farūsh*, etc.)

127 *Ṣarrāf* (shroff): banker, lender, moneychanger, broker of bills of exchange, insurer.

128 *Kadkhudā*: protean term with various meanings through time. Sayfī is using it to mean: landlord, waterlord; chief of a *ṭāʾifa* (guild, society, tribe); head of a village, district, or ward; ulama and Sufi shaykhs. Craft guilds (coppersmith, carpenter, weaver, etc.) and trade guilds (butcher, corpse-washer, etc.) persisted in medieval Persia.

129 *Shaḥna* (pl. *shaḥna-gān*) used for "policeman" in *c.*1315. al-Harawī, *Harāt*, 603. It is likely that watchmen patrolled bazaars and caravansarys at night to thwart thievery.

130 Thomas Barfield, *The Central Asian Arabs of Afghanistan* (Austin: The University of Texas Press, 1981), esp. 82–109, and Figure 3.

Returning to Kartid Herat. Traders from beyond Herat traveled to Herat to transact (Sayfī's *tujjār az yamīn wa yasār…*), and could do so because: (1) there was security along the byways and highways to Herat; (2) there were crafted products (e.g., metalworks, ceramics, fabrics) in Herat for visiting traders to purchase;[131] (3) there existed a large group of Heratis with surplus wealth that could afford to purchase the merchandise brought by traders.[132] Most commercial transactions were undoubtedly taxed.

Nawrūz fostered agricultural production, including initiatives for the restoration of hydrological systems. Evidence of Nawrūz's initiatives that benefited the general public and economy comes from Farāh, Sīstān, and Garmsīr/Hilmand.

*Farāh*: Jalāl al-Dīn of Farāh had rejected Nawrūz's authority. Nawrūz deposed and jailed him in Herat and imposed direct rule over Farāh. Jalāl al-Dīn's brother, Ināltikīn, pledged allegiance to Fakhr al-Dīn Kart (*har dū malik ʿahdī basta shud wa mīs̱āqī gard āmad*) and received from him assurances and cloak of honor (*khilʿat-i khāṣṣ*).[133] The corresponding report in *Tārīkh-i Sīstān* is ambiguous: Ināltikīn became *banda* of a sovereign king of Islam (*āmadan malik Ināltikīn bih bandagī-yi khudāwand malik al-Islām*)—Nawrūz? Fakhr al-Dīn?— who returned him to Farāh with grain (*ghalla*) for seed (*bih jihat-i tukhm*) and provisions (*ʿalūfa*) for the people.[134] Seed signifies support for agricultural production.

*Sīstān*: Rukn al-Dīn Maḥmūd, son of Sīstān's ruler Naṣīr al-Dīn, became the *malik* of Nīh.[135] *Tārīkh-i Sīstān* does not say he was appointed by Nawrūz; just that he went to Nīh from Nawrūz's court. But since he was Nawrūz's appointee at Zamīndāwar (see below), it is inferred that Rukn al-Dīn Maḥmūd had become Nawrūz's *banda*. He revived Nīh (*ān qaṣaba rā ābādān gardānīd*), erected a citadel and restored subterranean waterways (*kārīz-ha-yi ān rā ṣāliḥa kard*). Nīh was reliant on *kārīz* waters from mother-wells in

131 On Herati miniature paintings and metalwork, see Potter, "Kart Dynasty," 157–60.

132 Merchants need a pool of customers to justify travel expenses and risks.

133 al-Harawī, *Harāt*, 424–25.

134 Anon./Bahār (ed.), *Sīstān*, 375–76; Anon./Gold (tr.), *Sīstān*, 332. Gold translates this event thusly: "King Yenaltakin went to the court of the Sovereign King of Islam." *Banda*, a term annotated in Chapter Two, does not translate as "went to the court of…"

135 Anon./Bahār (ed.), *Sīstān*, 378; Anon./Gold (tr.), *Sīstān*, 336.

neighboring hills;[136] hence this initiative. Trees and orchards flourished in Nīh and its vicinities.

Waṣṣāf professes that Nawrūz had caused *qaṣabas* in Sīstān to prosper. Mīrkhʷānd confirms that Sīstān's villages (*qurá*) and *qaṣabas* thrived because of Nawrūz. Mīrkhʷānd and Waṣṣāf say that Nawrūz had exhorted *raʿāyā* (of Sīstān) to cultivate and to develop (*mardum rā bih zirāʿat wa ʿimārat targhīb wa taḥrīṣ mī namūd*) their homeland. Cereals became plentiful and grain prices dropped.[137]

*Hilmand*: The fortified township (*qarya-yi maḥrūsa*) of Dīwarik/Dīwarak (= Dīwālak in "Garmsel"?), in ruins since the Mongol irruptions, was irrigated and made habitable.[138]

Nawrūz captured Qalʿa-yi Dāwarī (Zamīndāwar). The castellan appointed at Qalʿa-yi Dāwarī by Nawrūz in 693/1294 was Rukn al-Dīn Maḥmūd.[139] It is not stated that Rukn al-Dīn invested in agriculture, but it is quite likely that he had. Bust, Tikīnābād, and Zamīndāwar were fertile regions, and doubled as way stations for caravans;[140] hence the importance of the citadels throughout Hilmand region.

*Herat*: Probative evidence of initiatives by Nawrūz and/or Fahkr al-Din to improve agriculture in Herat is imperfect. Sayfī is content to announce that because of Nawrūz's actions and justice, Herat recovered quickly, coming to rival Samarqand and Baghdad![141] It is fortuitous that Waṣṣāf, Mīrkhʷānd, and the anonymous authors of *History of Sīstān* left "bread crumbs" for modern historians: efforts to develop Sīstān and Hilmand; prosperity of Sīstān's *qaryas* and *qaṣabas*; of *raʿāyā* being encouraged to farm. This, combined with Sayfī's assertions of prosperity, indicates that Herat had benefited from revitalization endeavors. A critical point to appreciate is that Herat's hydrological networks had benefited from post-Mongol restorations; the network was not wrecked in the raids of 687/1288, 688/1289, and 691/1291. The network,

136 See Le Strange, *Lands*, 340.

137 Waṣṣāf, *Taḥrīr*, 177; Mīrkhʷānd, *Rawżat*, 4,202. *Qaṣaba*: see glossary.

138 Anon./Bahār (ed.), *Sīstān*, 376; Anon./Gold (tr.), *Sīstān*, 333. On Dīwālak in Garmsīr, see Adamec, *Gazetteer*, 2:66, 2:85.

139 Anon./Bahār (ed.), *Sīstān*, 375; Anon./Gold (tr.), *Sīstān*, 332.

140 On the region, see Le Strange, *Lands*, 344–46; Minorsky (ed.), *Ḥudūd*, 345; Barthold, *Geography*, 72–74; Adamec, *Gazetteer*, 2:231–42, 2:296–302.

141 al-Harawī, *Harāt*, 410.

however, would have fallen into disrepair from neglect when *ra'āyā* died or fled. Overground channels—the principal mode of irrigation in Herat—were easier to refurbish than Nīh's subterranean channels.

Exhortations alone by Nawrūz will not have fostered economic growth absent (1) tangible security for persons and property; hence, the safeguarding of highways, which encouraged and permitted people to migrate to Herat, and traders to journey with valuable merchandise; and (2) fiscal-legal incentives for landlords, waterlords, and share-cropping peasants. We do not know of such incentives, but Nawrūz's command, that "for two years, no person, Mongol or Muslim, shall harass or make demands of the people of Herat," means that Heratis were burdened only with Nawrūz's demands for taxes and corvée; but not the arbitrary and capricious impositions of Mongol and Persian amirs and *a'yān*. This reflects the monopoly on theft established by a stationary bandit.

Apropos of the criticality of fiscal/legal incentives, we turn to the Ilkhanid fiscal and legal reforms of Il-Khan Ghāzān and vizier Rashīd al-Dīn.

# 8

# Later Efforts to Revive Agriculture and Commerce

## Ilkhanid Land Reforms

It behoves us to recognize the influence of Rashīd al-Dīn (d. 718/1318),[1] an erudite and perspicacious Persian, in the crafting of Ilkhanid agricultural reforms. Between 1295 and 1312, Rashīd al-Dīn was in dialogue with a Mongolian amir, Bolad Ch'eng-Hsiang (Pūlād Chīnksānk; d. 1313), who had served Qubilai Qa'an (d. 1294) and helped to reform the Yüan government.[2] Bolad became the vizier's interlocutor on scientific knowledge from China and India. A subject on which Bolad and Rashīd al-Dīn collaborated was agronomy.[3] Rashīd al-Dīn subsequently compiled an agronomical treatise.[4]

"Revitalization of fallow lands" (*iḥyā' al-mawāt*) became a pillar of Ilkhanid policy. Although Rashīd al-Dīn gives credit for the fiscal-legal reforms to Ghāzān, the reforms vis-à-vis hydrology and agronomy, agricultural and land taxes, will have originated with the Ilkhanate's Persian bureaucrats. They will have impressed on the Il-Khan the decrepit state of hydrological systems; and the indispensability to state and society (namely, the Ilkhanid fisc) of improving agricultural production and stimulating tax inflows. The Ilkhanid camp was divided: Mongol elements wanted to continue with their pursuit of violent theft; while other elements recognized the

[1] Stefan Kamola, *Making Mongol History: Rashid al-Din and the Jami' al-tawarikh* (Edinburgh: Edinburgh University Press, 2019).

[2] Allsen, *Culture*, 72–80.

[3] Ibid., 115–26.

[4] Rashīd al-Dīn Fażlallāh, *Āthār wa Aḥyā'*, eds Manuchihr Sutudih and Iraj Afshar (Tehran: University of Tehran, 1368/1989). See A.K.S. Lambton, "The *Athar wa ahya'* of Rashid al-Din Fadl Allah and his contribution as an agronomist, arboriculturist and horticulturlist," in *The Mongol Empire and its Legacy*, eds R. Amitai and David Morgan (Leiden: Brill, 1999), 126–54.

logic of gentle theft over the long term. Ghāzān embodied the latter class.[5] He supported the Persian bureaucrats.

Rashīd al-Dīn writes, "there has never been a realm more devastated than this one was recently, particularly places visited by the Mongol army."[6] Uncertainties arising from arbitrary and capricious laws, regulations, and imposts were thwarting new investments in agriculture and hydrology: "If anyone wants to make improvements, he doesn't even begin for fear that it is state property or somebody's property [...]" and could be confiscated after "great expenses" were paid by him.[7] A reasonable fear among potential investors was that a Mongol amir or local warlord, observing the success of a project funded by an investor, would swoop down and seize the asset, or extort some portion of the project's incomes. Hence the twinned imperatives of establishing *security* and enforcing *property rights.*

*The Economic Theory*

"Property," Adam Smith wrote, is "the grand fund of all dispute":

> the age of shepherds is that where government first commences. Property makes it absolutely necessary. When once it has been agreed that a cow or a sheep shall belong to a certain person not only when actually in his possession but where ever it may have strayed, it is absolutely necessary that the hand of government should be continually held up [...] to preserve the property of the individualls.[8]

A *conditio sine qua non* for investments in farmlands, pasturelands, aqueducts, *kārīzs*, dams, watermills, windmills and such is that there must exist a *predictable* legal framework: property laws must not be opaque, fluid, and arbitrarily enforced. A level of *certainty* must be instituted within society and the economy. This allows for the measured evaluation of investment

5 See Thomas Barfield, "Turk, Persian, and Arab: Changing Relationships between tribes and state in Iran and along its frontiers," *Iran and the Surrounding World*, eds Nikke Keddie and Rudi Matthee (Seattle: University of Washington Press, 2011), 61–86, esp. 66–70.

6 Rashīd al-Dīn/Thackston, *Jāmi'*, 3:528.

7 Ibid., 3:529. See also Ibn Khaldun, *Muqaddimah*, vol. 2, ch. 3, § 41 (on protecting property).

8 Adam Smith, *Lectures on Jurisprudence*, eds R.L. Meek, et al. (Oxford: Clarendon, 1978), 208. See also John Locke, *Second Treatise on Government*, ed. C.B. Macpherson (Indianapolis: Hackett, 1980), Chapter 5 ("of Property").

decisions. "Risk" is inextricably conjoined to investment choices, but *risk* is not equal to *uncertainty*: risk is either *measurable* or *immeasurable*. A *measurable uncertainty* is a *manageable risk*. An *immeasurable uncertainty* is the persistence of *unknowable phenomena*.[9] If an uncertainty is incalculable, then it is an unmanageable risk.

Fear of unfathomable phenomena deter investors; hence the importance of turning immeasurable uncertainties into measurable uncertainties. If risk can be quantified, then it can be factored into business decisions. To illustrate, high-yield bonds ("junk bonds") offer investors a higher rate of interest than U.S. Treasury debt instruments (bonds, notes, bills). This is because they include a *risk premium*, which is high: the *default risk* for issuers of junk bonds is higher than the U.S. Government's default risk: this rate is zero because Treasury obligations are backed by "the full faith and credit" of the U.S. Government. Interest on U.S. Treasuries is low; for example, 1% on five-year Treasury notes (at no risk to capital); versus 9% for junk. The risk premium is 8% (junk rate minus risk-free rate). Junk bonds are scored by default risk ("BB+" is "best" in junk class; "C" is worst). BB+ junk may pay 5% while C may pay 11%. An investor can calculate potential return (say, 5% per annum over the five-year duration of the bond) and potential loss (say, 20% probability that he will lose some of the capital invested in BB+ bonds). Risk has been measured.

The point is that political, fiscal, and legal environments in Persia in the 7th/13th century reflected *immeasurable uncertainties*; hence, Rashīd al-Dīn's lament quoted above. Islamic institutions and wealthy individuals avoided investing charitable (waqf) and private funds in hydrological and agricultural projects because circumstances were unfathomable. To stimulate investments in fallow lands and impaired hydrological systems, the Ilkhanate had to *invert* the existing paradigm: from where immeasureable uncertainties dominated, to where *measurable* uncertainties prevailed. This is precisely what Rashīd al-Dīn and the Il-Khan *intended* through their promulgation of fiscal-legal reforms.

[9] See Frank Knight, *Risk, Uncertainty, and Profit* (Boston: Houghton Mifflin, 1921), 19–20, a seminal study that still influences the fields of economics and finance.

*The Reforms*

Rashīd al-Dīn illustrates a series of political, legal, and fiscal initiatives by the Il-Khan. Several promulgations were to eliminate (or mitigate) immeasurable uncertainties in key areas:[10] (1) streamlining the issuance of legal documents; (2) prohibiting the hearing of legal claims older than thirty years; (3) requiring sellers to prove title (ownership) prior to the sale; (4) annulling outdated property deeds; (5) abolishing extraordinary taxes; and (6) establishing guidelines for tax collection. Scholars will debate whether these edicts were enforced, and if so, their effectiveness. My focus is on *intent*, which was to seminally change the climate for investments, rebuilding, commerce, agriculture, and pastoralism. That said, implementation of Ghāzān's edicts will have been the purview of Ilkhanid representatives in Khurasan (viziers, *shaḥnas*, and such); Kartid *maliks* and bureaucrats; chief justices (*qāḍī al-quḍāt*) of Herat and the judges (*qāḍī*) working under them—not faceless and disinterested bureaucrats in Tabriz.

Parochial interests will have operated at district and province levels, and led to the implementation of *select* Ilkhanid laws and fiscal policies. Which is to say, if an Ilkhanid law benefited the economic interests of land-hungry men of stature in Khurasan, their allies at Herat (Kartid *maliks*, viziers, bureaucrats, *qāḍīs*) will have enforced it.

A reform of interest here is the amending of land usage/tenure laws by Rashīd al-Dīn and Ghāzān. They also offered incentives to anyone who restored ruined hydrological systems and revivified fallow farmlands. Their logic was impeccable: "when fallow lands are made to flourish, grain will be cheap; and when expeditions are mounted [...] provisions will be readily available. Money will also flow into the treasury and increase."[11] Nasīr al-Dīn Ṭūṣī (d. 672/1274), in his "Memorandum on Finance" for the Il-Khan (Hülegü or Abaqā), devoted sections to sources of agricultural, pastoral, and commercial taxes,[12] which served to highlight for Il-Khans the imperative to develop agriculture and commerce.

10 Rashīd al-Dīn/Thackston, *Jāmiʿ*, 3:480–99.

11 Ibid., 3:529.

12 M. Minovi and Vladimir Minorsky, "Nasīr al-Dīn Ṭūṣī on Finance," *BSOAS* 10/3 (1940): 755–89, 771–74 (§§ 6–10 on agricultural, pastoral, and commercial taxes).

An initiative in support of reviving abandoned lands was the creation of a three-tier system to bring lands and hydrological systems into operation speedily and economically. Rashīd al-Dīn describes the three-tiers:

*Tier 1*:[13] lands that had "water and irrigation canals and did not entail great expense or outlay of labor to be cultivated and irrigated" (it was not necessary to dig or clear a *kārīz* or *jūy*). *Tier 2*: "lands that needed moderate improvement, where irrigation canals [*kārīz* or *jūy*] had to be repaired or dug." *Tier 3*: lands that required "difficult" improvements, where "dams had to be made for irrigation, and the underground water channels were ruined and had to be repaired."

Regarding Tier 1 lands, the *dīwān* receives no revenues from the first harvest; but from the second harvest, revenue equal to one-third of the prevailing *dīwān* tax rate went to the *dīwān*, two-thirds to the investor "to repay his efforts." For the third harvest, three-quarters of the tax rate "customary in each province" went to the *dīwān*, one-quarter to the investor. "Over and above that, any money realized by the cultivator was his." And so on for Tiers 2 and 3. Considering the costs and labors involved with improving Tier 2 lands, in Year 3, the *dīwān* received two-thirds (not three-quarters as with Tier 1), and the investor received one-third. Since Tier 3 lands were those that required substantial improvements (i.e., larger outlays of cash by investors), the Year 3 *dīwān* rate dropped to 50% (with 50% to the investor). A crucial Tier 3 provision is that the ownership of the asset transferred to the investor and his progeny "in perpetuity."[14] The tax rate was deemed *kharāj* (land tax). The investor could sell the asset (evidently free of encumbrances); and the "divan would take the established amount of land tax from the purchaser."[15]

[13] See Rashīd al-Dīn/Thackston, *Jāmiʿ*, 3:529–31; Rashīd al-Dīn, *Jāmiʿ al-tawārīkh*, eds Muḥammad Rawshan and Muṣṭafá Mūṣawī, 4 vols (Tehran: Nashr-i Alborz, 1373/1994 [reprinted by Mīrāṡ-i maktūb, 1384/2005f.]), 1,526–33.

[14] Rashīd al-Dīn/Thackston, *Jāmiʿ*, 3:530. This comports with Ḥanafī law, which rewards revivers of fallow (*mawāt*) lands.

[15] Rashīd al-Dīn/Thackston, *Jāmiʿ*, 3:530; Rashīd al-Dīn/Rawshan (ed.), *Jāmiʿ*, 1,531. The ownership proviso is written after Tier 3 rates without a paragraph break, which is why I have stated that ownership is limited to Tier 3. However, the condition probably applied to Tier 1 and 2 investors, too, otherwise an immeasurable uncertainty exists for an investor who develops properties to which he cannot secure title; moreover, Ḥanafī law states that if *mawāt* land is cultivated, ownership attaches to the cultivator. Lambton's reading of this proviso supports my reasoning: "Anyone reclaiming dead land acquired thereby rights of ownership and rights of sale." Lambton, *Landlord*, 91.

To stimulate investments in agricultural land, Ghāzān decreed that all state-owned estates (*mawāẓiʿ-i dīwānī*) that had been untended for years,[16] and farmlands that had been uncultivated for extended periods, were to be decreed fallow lands. This freed the lands for exploitation. Any person who is desirous of making investments in state lands could do so under any of the three tiers. Any person could continue to make improvements to private lands (if their local lords permitted it); and with respect to lands that had long been fallow, "anyone who wanted could make improvements without consultation."[17]

An investor's outlays for the revivification of fallow lands (from Tier 1 to Tier 3) can be prohibitive: he has to supply money, oxen, fodder, implements, supplies, and shelter (for peasants and families). These are the "original and annual expenses"[18] frequently borne by farmers.[19] Adding to the investor's startup costs is that, in Year 1, he must advance (*taqāwī*) seed for planting, and provide foodstuffs (principally, grains) for farmers and their families because there is no stored surplus from an earlier harvest. If an investor has to overhaul, de-silt, or excavate a *kārīz* before fallow lands can be cleared, tilled, fertilized, and seeded (Tiers 2 to 3), his expenditures will be higher. It could take a series of bountiful harvests to recover even the expenses for restoring or de-silting Tier 1 or Tier 2 *kārīzs* and *jūys*. Rashīd al-Dīn and Ghāzān Khān recognized the technical complexities and financial risks involved at each tier level when devising their Tier 1, 2, and 3 income-sharing formulae. Tier 3 lands involved the highest expenditures; hence the unambiguous reward of absolute ownership and inheritance by progeny; or if held in trust (waqf), then perpetual ownership.

*Implementation of Reforms in Khurasan*

The effectiveness of the reforms, and their applicability throughout the Ilkhanate, will be debated.[20] Scholars have grumbled that Rashīd al-Dīn's

[16] Crown lands (*injü*) were distinct from state lands (*dīwānī*); but in the Mongol period, legal lines were murky. See Lambton, *Landlord*, 78.

[17] Rashīd al-Dīn/Thackston, *Jāmiʿ*, 3:529–30; Rashīd al-Dīn/Rawshan, *Jāmiʿ*, 1530, 1532.

[18] See Smith, *Wealth*, 882–83.

[19] Share-cropping peasants shouldered many burdens. See, generally, Lambton, *Peasant*, 295–329; Mahendrarajah, *Sufi Saint*, 129 and n.12.

[20] Positive views are found in Petrushevsky, *Kishawārzī*, 1:102–16 (reforms), 1:174–217 (analyses of data); idem, "Socio-Economic," esp. 5:483, 494–500.

claims about the success of the fiscal-legal reforms are self-serving. Perhaps. However, the points stressed by Rashīd al-Dīn make sense from an investor's perspective. Concerns voiced about property rights; and importance of agricultural production for economic growth and tax revenues, are reflected in intellectual discourses on economics, property rights, and human nature.[21]

The logic underlying select Ilkhanid legal reforms is inescapable. Take for example the difficulties posed by ancient property deeds and stale legal claims. Thousands fled, died, or were deported consequent to the Mongol invasions, leaving behind houses and estates that will have been occupied by squatters, real heirs, and bogus heirs. Eighty years after the Mongol invasions, that is *c.* 700/1300, how does one prove ownership of a house, watermill, *jūy*, or farm? Are there former neighbors (so-called communal memory) that can testify in court (eighty years later) that a claimant is the progeny of the decedent? His lawful heir? His *sole* heir? That he has no male agnates—not even *one* distant male cousin—with legitimate claims to some share (or to all) of the disputed property? Witnesses, if alive (decades after 619/1222), "and of sound mind and memory," will have to attest to the signatures and seals on documents. Witnesses will be difficult to locate if, say, they had fled to India or Anatolia with the Mongol irruptions; and to then be produced in a court in say, Herat.

The annulment of antiquated deeds and preclusion of claims older than thirty years were pragmatic and common sense measures. The slate was wiped clean. People with licit or illicit occupancy could no longer be evicted through legitimate or fraudulent claims, and through recourse to outdated/invalid deeds. They had *tenure security*: they held secure title to the property and could not be legally evicted.[22] Lands that had been abandoned, or for which no licit claim could be upheld, became available for investors to exploit—or they became state (*dīwānī*) or crown (*injū*) lands. An Il-Khan could distribute state and crown lands to his clients: Kartids, viziers, amirs, bureaucrats, ulama, and Sufi shaykhs.[23]

[21] See citations above to Ibn Khaldun, Locke, and Smith. See also J.B Murtazashvili and I. Murtazashvili, *Land, the State, and War* (Cambridge: Cambridge University Press, 2021), 23–37 ("A Theory of Property Rights").

[22] See, e.g., Colin Deschamps and Alan Roe, "Land Conflict in Afghanistan," in *The Rule of Law in Afghanistan*, ed. Whit Mason (Cambridge: Cambridge University Press, 2011), 205–22.

[23] Öljeitü granted land and *jūy* to Shihāb al-Dīn Ismāʿīl Jāmī, 29 Ṣafar 706/9 September 1306. See Yūsuf-i Ahl/Berlin, *Farāʾid*, f. 317$^{a}$–317$^{b}$; Mahendrarajah, *Sufi Saint*, 130–32.

The involvement of Fakhr al-Dīn Imāmī (d. bet. *c.* 698/1298f. and Rajab 699/March 1300),[24] a former Chief Justice of Herat (from 671/1272f. to?),[25] in drafting components of edicts by Ghāzān relating to obsolete deeds and stale claims,[26] lends weight to the view that the problems of old property claims and outdated deeds were of paramount importance in Herat. The Imāmī family retained Herat's chief judgeship from (at least) the reign of Mu'izz al-Dīn Kart[27] to the end of the Timurid age.[28] It is unlikely that Khurasan's judges deviated from Imāmī's guidance vis-à-vis outdated deeds/claims, not out of loyalty, but because the reforms make sense from jurisprudential and financial standpoints. Khurasan had suffered the brunt of the Mongols' wrath. There doubtless were thousands of hectares of farmlands and pasturelands, and optimal hydrological properties, which could be profitably utilized if legal impediments and political uncertainties were eliminated by fiat. Notables of Khurasan will have desired unfettered ownership of farms, pastures, *jūys*, *kārīzs*, and villages. Kartid kings, *qāḍīs*, and bureaucrats, and Ilkhanid appointees and functionaries in Khurasan, will have implemented the Il-Khan's edicts, particularly if they advanced their interests, or the interests of their allies.[29]

Ilkhanid reforms appealed to self-interests of investors.[30] Access to power centers determined access to state lands, fallow non-state lands, and hydrological assets. Rashīd al-Dīn's and Ghāzān's three-tier system came with a

[24] Fakhr al-Dīn Imāmī was contemporary with Shams al-Dīn and Bahā' al-Dīn Juwaynī, and Rashīd al-Dīn. He secured a vizierate in Kirman. Khwāndamīr/Siyāqī (ed.), *Ḥabīb*, 3:271–72; Khwāndamīr/Thackston (tr.), *Habib*, 156–57; Nāṣir al-Dīn Munshī Kirmānī, *Simṭ al-'ulá lil-ḥaḍrat al-'ulyā: Tārīkh-i Qarā-Khiṭā'iyān-i Kirmān*, ed. Maryam Mīr-Shamsī (Tehran: Intishārāt-i Duktur Maḥmūd Afshār Yazdī, 1394/2015f.), 118, 121–23.

[25] al-Harawī, *Harāt*, 359 (on his appointment at Herat).

[26] Rashīd al-Dīn/Thackston, *Jāmi'*, 3:482–83, 3:489.

[27] On the appointment of Jalāl al-Dīn Maḥmūd Imāmī (d.*c.* 780–82/1378–81), a descendant of Fakhr al-Dīn Imāmī, see Khwāndamīr/Siyāqī (ed.), *Ḥabīb*, 3:385; Khwāndamīr/Thackston (tr.), *Habib*, 223; Muḥammad Ismā'īl Mablagh Gharjistānī, "Dānishmand-ān-i mu'āṣir-i dūdmān-i Kart [Scholars Contemporary with Kartids]," *Āryānā* No. 205 (1338/1960):49–56, at 50–51; Barzīn-Mihr, *Shu'arā wa fuẓalā'*, 81.

[28] Beatrice Forbes Manz, *Power, Politics and Religion in Timurid Iran* (Cambridge: Cambridge University Press, 2007), 212. Likewise, progeny of the (putative) Shaykh al-Islam of Herat, Sa'd al-Dīn Mas'ūd Taftāzānī, held the post of Shaykh al-Islam of Herat until Shāh Ismā'īl I, Ṣafawī, captured Herat.

[29] Öljeitü's grant to Jāmī (n.23, *supra*), orders Kartids and Ilkhanids (*viz.*, 'Alā' al-Dīn Hindū and 'Alā' al-Dīn Faryūmadī) to implement the Il-Khan's will.

[30] On self interest see Smith, *Wealth*, 30; and Ibn Khaldun, *Muqaddimah*, vol. 2, ch. 5, §§ 1–2, 5, 9–13.

crucial proviso: to each province was appointed "one or two great men" who were responsible for allocating contracts to anyone desirous of securing estates; hence the creation of the *Dīwān-i Khāliṣāt* (*Chancery for Royal Demesne*).[31] We do not know how the Chancery operated in Khurasan; but we can be certain that high levels of lobbying, favoritism, and corruption were involved. Ibn Khaldun noted men of rank and status succeed in acquiring property and making a living.[32] The better the access to Il-Khans, Kartid royals, Ilkhanid and Kartid viziers, and other men in positions of authority, the more likely an investor was to secure for his institution or himself the finest agricultural tracts and hydrological assets in the Herat Quarter.

A man of wealth (say, a merchant in Herat), or the chief of an Islamic institution (say, the Sufi shrine at Jām) who had connections to the political authorities in Khurasan (say, Kartid *maliks* and viziers named Jāmī and Faryūmadī), and had investable cash (for instance, private funds, waqf funds, accumulated alms), would be foolish to not avail himself of the *injü* and *dīwānī* lands being offered *gratis* by the Ilkhanate—lands delivered free of liens, litigation, and other encumbrances. An investor (be it an individual or an institution) had to assume risks to their capital;[33] and the expenses and exertions of clearing and cultivating overgrown farmlands, and refurbishing decrepit aqueducts, cisterns, dams, and watermills; identifying, locating, and hiring competent estate managers, engineers, *mīrābs*, *muqannīs*, agronomists, hydrologists, accountants and other (skilled and unskilled) workers. For his capital and energies, he acquired legal title to the asset. His limitation—the restraint on his entrepreneurial ambitions—therefore, is *liquidity*: cash available to invest.

[31] Rashīd al-Dīn/Thackston, *Jāmi'*, 3:530; Rashīd al-Dīn/Rawshan, *Jāmi'*, 1,531–32. See also Lambton, *Landlord*, 91.

[32] Ibn Khaldun, *Muqaddimah*, vol. 2, ch. 5, §§ 5–6.

[33] The risk to capital is now measured: not even a lawful heir could take the asset. If laws on property rights and contracts are upheld by Khurasan's (Kartid-appointed) *qāḍīs*, anxieties relating to expropriation and capricious law enforcement are mitigated. Some political risk existed: loss of the asset if the old regime is supplanted by a new regime, or the beneficiary fell out favor with his (Ilkhanid or Kartid) patron; but that is par for the course.

## Kartid Initiatives

Shams al-Dīn Kihīn's initiatives toward revitalizing agriculture (as noticed) are not known. Fakhr al-Dīn Kart's agricultural initiatives are unclear (but we know much about his urban development projects, which are discussed in Chapters Nine and Ten). The principal sources on hydrological developments under Ghiyāth al-Dīn, and son Mu'izz al-Dīn Kart, are late: Ḥāfiẓ-i Abrū's *Geography*,[34] completed by 823/1420; Qāsim b. Yūsuf's treatise on hydrology, the *Risāla-i ṭarīq*, completed by 927/1521. Another late source with scattered information is *Rawżāt al-jannāt* by Isfizārī. Qāsim b. Yūsuf, and his treatises on hydrology and agronomy,[35] have been studied by Maria Subtelny.[36]

### *Ghiyāth al-Dīn Kart*

Jūy-i Naw ("New Canal") was re-opened in 637/1238f. by Shams al-Dīn Muḥammad b. 'Izz al-Dīn al-Harawī when it was known by its former name, Jūy-i Sabaqar (work began *c.* 636/1238f. under his father, 'Izz al-Dīn Muqaddam al-Harawī). The Jūy underwent major improvements under Ghiyāth al-Dīn Kart; hence the name change. The canal irrigates an extensive tract situated between Jūy-i Naw (the old Jūy-i Sabaqar) and Jūy-i Injīl. The tract runs from the Harī Rūd origins of both *jūys* (the southeast) to the northwest of the city of Herat. Jūy-i Naw also supplies water to the Khiyābān District, which is situated above inner Herat. In the Timurid period, Khiyābān was the exclusive address for Herat's affluent; it is home to numerous Timurid era sepulchral and spiritual edifices.[37] The Khiyābān enjoyed a degree of social and economic importance in the Kartid period, too.

[34] Ḥāfiẓ-i Abrū/Harawī (ed.), *Jughrāfiyā*; Krawulsky [Ḥāfiẓ-i Abrū], *Ḫorāsān*.

[35] Qāsim b. Yūsuf al-Harawī, *Irshād al-zirā'a* [*Guidance on Agriculture*], ed. Muḥammad Mushīrī (Tehran: Intishārāt-i Dānishgāh-yi Tihrān, 1346/1968).

[36] Maria Subtelny, *Timurids*, 136–45; eadem, "A Persian Agricultural Manual in Context: The *Irshad al-zira'a* in Late Timurid and Early Safavid Khorasan," *Studia Iranica* 22 (1993): 167–217; eadem, "Mirak-i Sayyid Ghiyas and the Timurid Tradition of Landscape Architecture: Further Notes to 'A Medieval Persian Agricultural Manual in Context'," *Studia Iranica* 24, no. 1 (1995):19–60; eadem, *Le monde est un jardin: aspects de l'histoire culturelle de l'Iran médiéval* (Paris: Assoc. pour l'Avancement des Études Iraniennes, 2002), ch. 1 (on irrigation).

[37] See, generally, Fikrī Saljūqī, *Khiyābān* (Kabul: Intishārāt-i anjuman-i Jāmī, 1343/1964).

Ghiyāth al-Dīn overhauled and enlarged the New Canal.[38] Reduced water flows had led farmers to abandon Jūy-i Sabaqar's agricultural expanses.[39] He transferred farmlands situated along the canal into waqf for a hospice, *Khānaqāh-yi Ghiyāth al-Dīn Kart*, which he had erected outside the walled city.[40] He built water-control boxes (sgl. *naṭarah*) to regulate flows,[41] which implies the employment of weirs (*band*) and rivulets to first block, then re-direct, water flows to farmlands pursuant to a schedule. Water distribution was supervised by water-managers appointed by the *malik*. He also conveyed seven watermills into waqf for the eponymous hospice.[42] The location of the mills is uncertain,[43] but appear to have been situated off the New Canal's northern course.

Sayf al-Harawī provides only an abstract of the *malik*'s development activities and pious deeds.[44] He claims that Ghiyāth al-Dīn's charitable benefactions were made entirely with his personal funds, "unsullied and sinless."[45] Firstly, even if he had transferred *milk* estates (private land) to mortmain (waqf), this does not preclude the possibility that he had acquired those estates from the Il-Khan's inventory of *injü* and *dīwānī* lands. Secondly, the legal prescription that principal (*aṣl*) conveyed to waqf must be the personal assets of the settlor (*wāqif*; fem., *wāqifa*), with full and legal possession, can be satisfied by transferring (in modern parlance: "laundering") the crown or state lands through middlemen ("straw") purchases. It is unlikely, however, that anyone will have litigated Ghiyāth al-Dīn's waqfs, especially not the beneficiaries who enjoyed the usufruct (*manfaʿa*), nor will a Herati *qāḍī* have entertained *hostile* challenges in his court.[46]

[38] al-Harawī, *Ṭarīq-i qismat*, 10–11.

[39] See Allen, *Catalogue*, Map 1, from Grids 7 to 12 (left-right) and F to K (top-bottom).

[40] al-Harawī, *Harāt*, 745; Allen, *Catalogue*, 149, Cat. No. 501; al-Harawī, *Ṭarīq-i qismat*, 10–11.

[41] Allen, *Catalogue*, 23 (discussion). Two water-controllers known as *Naṭarah-yi Malik* (Allen, *Catalogue*, Cat. Nos. 41 and 42) were Kartid. The second *naṭarah* (No. 42) is on the New Canal and attributed to Ghiyāth al-Dīn Kart.

[42] al-Harawī, *Ṭarīq-i qismat*, 10–11, misidentifies the beneficiaries of waqf estates and mills (Allen, *Catalogue*, 150, Cat. No. 503). Four waqf estates were identified (Allen, *Catalogue*, Nos. 149, 207, 308, 369 in Grids 9-H, 12-K, 11-J, 1-D, respectively).

[43] al-Harawī, *Ṭarīq-i qismat*, 11; Allen, *Catalogue*, 18 (on the mills), Cat. No. 369 and Grid 1-D. On the Pul-i Bābā Kamāl bridge mentioned by al-Harawī, see Allen, *Catalogue*, 44, Cat. No. 84 (it was called Pul-i Tūlakī in Kartid times but rebuilt and re-named in the Timurid era).

[44] al-Harawī, *Harāt*, 744–45; Isfizārī, *Rawżāt*, 1:507.

[45] al-Harawī, *Harāt*, 745 (*az khāliṣ-i māl bi-wabāl-i khud bar-uw waqf kard*).

[46] A waqf underwent a pro forma legal challenge in court, which results in a confirmatory judgment by the *qāḍī*. See Subtelny, *Timurids*, 182–83, 259 (on confirmatory rulings); 257–60

The *malik*'s personal wealth and the Kartid state's fiscal health were inextricably tied to his political health: a portion of his reign passed as a hostage in Öljeitü's *urdu*; and when he was in Herat, he was undermined by ʿAlāʾ al-Dīn Hindū, Böjäi, Yasāʾūl, et al. Lastly, he had Yasaʾur's aggressions to quell and wreckages to rectify. His fairest years were when he was held in high esteem by Amir Chūpān and sultan Abū Saʿīd (from *c.* 720/1320 to his death in 729/1329). This decade is when he had the funds to sponsor two major projects at the shrine of Aḥmad-i Jām.[47] The Kartid, who had to swim upstream for years, would have done his best to foster agriculture and commerce before 720/1320; but the last decade of his reign is assuredly when his most ambitious projects were launched.

Two ostensibly major hydrological projects sponsored by Ghiyāth al-Dīn are here noted. First, a cistern (*Ḥawż-yi Ghiyāth al-Dīn Kart*) near the Herat citadel.[48] This cistern possibly survives as the *Ḥawż-yi Pahlawān*, a Safawid (re)construction located in the Malik Bazaar.[49] Second, construction of the Salūmad Dam (*Band-i Salūmad*) in Khʷāf.[50]

Ghiyāth al-Dīn probably initiated the Salūmad project after he defeated Yasaʾur's ally, Majd al-Dīn Muḥammad Khʷāfī.[51] Khʷāf (when Ḥāfiẓ-i Abrū wrote *Geography*) had little river water, but irrigation by *kārīz* was prolific. Apart from the cultivation of fruit, cotton was a major cash crop. Mulberry trees (*dirakht-i tūt*) were cultivated and silk was produced (*abrīsham ḥāṣil kunand*).[52] Cotton cultivation demands abundant water supplies; hence the investment (in my opinion) by Ghiyāth al-Dīn in the Salūmad Dam. Ḥāfiẓ-i Abrū does not mention the dam, just the nearby village (Qarya-yi

(description of the waqf); 260–311 (translation); 311–12 (ruling by Herat's Chief Justice—a descendant of Fakhr al-Dīn Imāmī—followed by witnesses, seals, etc.).

47 Mahendrarajah, "Revised History," 112, 115–16; Mahendrarajah, *Sufi Saint*, Table 5.1.

48 al-Harawī, *Harāt*, 738; Isfizārī, *Rawżāt*, 1:507; Allen, *Catalogue*, 25 (Cat. No. 50).

49 Allen, *Catalogue*, 25.

50 Isfizārī, *Rawżāt*, 1:199–201. The project is not declared by Sayfī. W.M. Clevenger, "Dams in Ḫorāsān: Some Preliminary Observations," *East and West* 19/3 (1969):387–94, 393, gives the dimensions of Salūmad Dam (now Salāmī Dam) with images (Fig. 29–31). The dam's Kartid era dimensions cannot be determined. Refurbishments to the dam were authorized by the Timurid Sulṭān-Ḥusayn Bayqarā (r. 873–911/1469–1506).

51 al-Harawī, *Harāt*, 750–54 (fall of Fort Niyāz-Ābād, Khʷāf, Rabīʿ I 720/April–May 1320), 755–59 (fall of Fort Mābīẕhan-Ābād, Khʷāf, shortly thereafter); also Isfizārī, *Rawżāt*, 1:507–08.

52 Krawulsky, *Ḫorāsān*, 1:37; Mustawfī/Le Strange, *Nuzhat*, 152; Le Strange, *Lands*, 357–58. Mulberry leaves comprise the diet of silkworms.

Salāma). Salāma had a watermill of unique design.[53] Khʷāf, in the path of the "120-day winds," had a profusion of windmills.[54] The renowned windmills of Nashtifān (modern Khʷāf) still stand.

Districts west of the Herat River, even if they had more river waters than did Khʷāf (e.g., Jām and Bākharz),[55] still had to barrage, re-direct, and reserve water. The dimensions of dams were not always large (unlike the Salūmad), nor was their construction elaborate: functionality superseded style. Dams of various dimensions and designs persist throughout Khurasan; however, as Clevenger's survey makes clear, it is difficult to determine if a dam had pre-Islamic origins, much less Kartid origins.

### *Muʿizz al-Dīn Kart*

Muʿizz al-Dīn appointed Shaykh al-Islam Niẓām al-Dīn ʿAbd al-Raḥīm Khʷāfī (d. Dhū al-Qaʿda 738/May–June 1338) b. Faṣīḥ al-Dīn Muḥammad Mābīzhan-Ābādī (or Khʷāfī) just after commencing his reign (in Ramażān 732/June 1332).[56] In 733/1332f., Niẓām al-Dīn was directed with assessing the water-distribution system in Herat's *bulūks*. Prevailing rules and regulations (*qāʿida wa qānūnī*) on the distribution of water to holders of legitimate water rights (*ḥaqqāba*) became a Kartid policy imperative. Niẓām al-Dīn conducted a village-by-village survey.[57] Our knowledge of the Kartid system is based on Qāsim b. Yūsuf al-Harawī's averment that the Timurids followed the Kartid system: in every locale, water distribution by *qulb* and *naṭarah* followed protocols established by Shaykh al-Islam Niẓām al-Dīn (*bih dastūr wa qāʿida-yi qadīm basta kardih*).[58] "These distribution patterns were re-established and formally confirmed during the reign of the Timurid Sulṭān-Abū Saʿīd by Kamāl al-Dīn Shaikh-Ḥusain (d. 888/1483), the *muḥtasib* of Herat […]."[59]

Niẓām al-Dīn's assignment arose when Muʿizz al-Dīn Kart learned of disputes among farmers along the New Canal, in the Khiyābān District. The

[53] Harverson, "Watermills," 152.

[54] Harverson, *Windmills*, 5–6.

[55] See, e.g., Clevenger, "Dams in Ḫorāsān," 390, 392–93 (Figs. 7–10, 22–25, 26–28): Farīmān Dam (north of Turbat-i Jām), Kirāt Dam (Bākharz), and Pul Band (Bākharz).

[56] Faṣīḥ, *Mujmal*, 917 (date of decease); Mābīzhan-Ābād is a district within Khʷāf.

[57] al-Harawī, *Ṭarīq-i qismat*, 1–2, 12–13; Subtelny, *Timurids*, 137–38.

[58] al-Harawī, *Ṭarīq-i qismat*, 15.

[59] Subtelny, *Timurids*, 138.

dispute's specifics are unclear, but it is likely that farmers nearest to arterial channels were monopolizing flows, leaving little water for those farthest from the arteries. This happens to be a timeless problem and fount of conflict. The involvement of a shaykh al-Islam as an investigator and arbitrator of disputes was not uncommon.[60]

The outcome of Niẓām al-Dīn Khʷāfī's survey is the following distribution system. Three watermen (*mard-jūy*) were assigned at each primary (*madār*) outlet from an arterial channel (*jūy* or *nahr*). They were tasked with barraging (*qulb basta shūd*) and distributing water to eighteen households pursuant to schedule: one *mard-jūy* was responsible for four households (*khāna*) above the channel (*bālā-yi āb*); one for six *khāna* level with the channel (*miyān-i āb*); the third, eight *khāna* below the channel (*pāyān-i āb*). A timing device (*naṭarah*) may be used to measure shares. The three tracts receive water every five days.[61] The land mass encompassed per block of three watermen and eighteen households is 160 *jarībs*: 80 *jarībs* (*bālā*), 50 *jarībs* (*miyān*), and 30 *jarībs* (*pāyān*).[62]

Conditional situations noted in *Ṭarīq-i qismat* have been omitted for simplicity. To illustrate, volume/speed of flows (*gaz-mar*) from canals (pl. *anhār*) impact on the equitable distribution of water shares: a tract may receive more than its lawful entitlement if flows are strong. Therefore, flow volumes must first be measured (*gaz-mar-i anhār rā taḥqīq sāz-and*) by water-managers and adjustments applied. Customarily, tracts above channels are watered first, then the middle tract, and finally, the tract below. Flows from a *naṭarah* must be measured to comply with law and equity. In every instance, *qulb* and *naṭarah* managers have to act prudently. I have not offered a measurement for *jarīb* because it varies with farming practices, region, terrain, and such; probably due "in part to the fact that *jarīb* is not purely a surface conception but is bound up by measures of weight [...]."[63]

60 See, e.g., Mahendrarajah, "Shaykh al-Islam."

61 On intricacies of water cycles, see Lambton, "Regulation," *et passim*; Bonine, "Qanāt," 148–52. There will be changes to water cycles due to volumes, season, crop, etc.

62 al-Harawī, *Ṭarīq-i qismat*, 12–15. How uniformity of blocks—the 80–50–30 *jarīb* and 4–6–8 household spatial distribution—was determined is unclear.

63 Lambton, *Landlord*, 407. The Afghan *jarīb* came into being in the twentieth century. The Persian *jarīb* is 1 hectare/10,000 m$^2$, but that, too, is a modern measurement.

Qāsim b. Yūsuf publishes data for nine *bulūk*s, abstracted from late 9th/ early 15th century tax registers. Only Ḥāfiẓ-i Abrū identifies the tenth *bulūk*, Bulūk-i Parwānah wa Hawādasht, which led Terry Allen to suggest that it was tax-exempt during the Timurid era.[64] The data are from *c.* 150 years after the Kartid state expired. Nonetheless, *judicious* use can be made of certain facts in *Ṭarīq-i qismat* to sketch the outlines of the Kartid water system.

The data for the nine *bulūk*s of Herat (plus Fūshanj, Shāfilān, and Kurūkh) often include the waterways involved; the *gaz-mar* for a waterway (e.g., 38,000 *z̲irā*ʿ);[65] and the employment of a water-manager (*mīr-ābānih*) who was entitled to a tithe (*dih-yak*) of the harvest. Occasionally, a dam attendant (*band-bānī*) was employed (if there was a dam, of course) and entitled to, say, sixty *mann* of grain (*ghalla*); a *sar-qulbī* (manager of the primary *qulb*) was, say, entitled to twelve-and-a-half Tabrizi dinars (*dīnār-i tabrīzī*).

Taxes applicable to watermills (*ṭāḥūna*; pl. *ṭawāḥīn*) changed with a mill's location along the watercourse. A watermill paid, say, 300 Tabrizi dinars per millstone (*ḥajar*) where water flowed fastest, but 150 dinars at mid-course; 100 dinars at farther points along the *jūy* where flows—therefore nozzle pressures—weakened.[66]

The above was cherry-picked for illustrative purposes only. Every position did not exist at every *bulūk*. A few terms are opaque, like *rak̲h̲nagī*;[67] and the role of the *jawzaqih*.[68] *Rak̲h̲na* (sgl. breach or conduit) are the channels cut

[64] See Chapter 7, n.31. Whether this *bulūk* existed as a distinct administrative entity in the Kartid era, or was incorporated within a neighboring *bulūk*, is open to discussion.

[65] *Z̲irā*ʿ: see glossary. *Z̲irā*ʿ could mean (as used in *Ṭarīq-i qismat*) the extent of land watered. *Gaz-mar* is water-flow per unit of time, i.e., "X" *gaz* per *mar*. *Gaz* is a measure of length; *mar* is a computational measure, frequently fixed at 50 or 100. Thus, for e.g., 7 *gaz* × 50 *mar* = 350 *gaz-mar*. See terse entry in *Dihkhuda* 12:19, 144.

[66] See, e.g., al-Harawī, *Ṭarīq-i qismat*, 19–20, 33–34, 43–44, 53–54, 61–62, 67, 73, 77, 81, 85.

[67] Apparently an irrigation fee; for example: *rakhnagī* rate is 150 Tabrizi dinars (*rakhnagī ṣad wa panjāh dīnār-i tabrīzī bahā mī-dihad*), ibid., 44; but for lands above Naṭarah-yi Malik (Allen, *Catalogue*, 23, Cat. No. 41: Kartid reconstruction), the rate is 5,000 Tabrizi dinars (*wa dar* ʿ*auẓ-i rakhnagī-hā panj hazār dīnār-i tabrīzī*), ibid.; payment of 500 Tabrizi dinars for/per …? (*wa dastūrī az rakhnagī bi-zadān pānṣad dīnār-i tabrīzī*), ibid., 30. *Rakhna* has multiple meanings (see *Dihkhuda* 8:11, 980–82), but not as an irrigation fee or tax.

[68] *Jawzaqī* appears as a *nisba* from Nishapur. See ʿAbd al-Karīm al-Samʿānī, *Kitāb al-Ansāb*, eds ʿAbd al-Raḥman al-Yamānī, et al., 13 vols (Hyderabad: Osmania Oriental Publications Bureau, 1962–82), 3:365–67. Etymologically linked to cotton (see *Dihkhuda* 4:7, 903), but its meaning with respect to agriculture in Herat is opaque.

through legal boundaries (walls and fences) that allow water to flow from one orchard/farm to another orchard/farm. Hence the fees paid by beneficiaries of water to landlords who permit the water to flow through *rakhna-hā* (conduits) on their lands. The *jawzaqih* may have supervised those who removed the seed cotton from the bolls, leaving the dried locules.[69]

The employment of a *sar-qulbī* reflects a position subordinate to *mīr-ābānih* (*mīrāb*), but superior to waterman (*mard-jūy*). The latter was probably just a peasant who managed his patch; hence his exclusion from the compensation schemes in *Ṭarīq-i qismat*. The water-manager's (*mīrāb*) compensation varied with location: he was occasionally entitled to one-tenth of the harvest along with, say, sixty *mann* (178 kg/392 lb) of grain, which makes sense: if the *mīrāb* had farms within his aegis that primarily cultivated fruits and vegetables, then supplementing his income with cereals was crucial: grains can be stored; whereas fruits and vegetables perish and presumably generate less cash measure for measure. A share of the harvest (especially at 10%) is an incentive to improve yields and productivity.

Levies applied on mills are logical: millstones revolving at faster speeds grind more bushels of grain per hour than millstones in a lighter flow section of a *nahr* or *jūy*; hence the higher tax.[70] In some instances, watermills paid a flat tax rate, say, 100 dinars. This rate may reflect low water-flows even after the spring thaw when water volumes ordinarily increase, and the likelihood that the mills do not operate in summer.

Terminological opacities and potential anachronisms aside, the contours of Muʿizz al-Dīn Kart's system as gleaned from *Ṭarīq-i qismat* are these:

1. The primary division was the *buluk*. Each *buluk* had one or more *mīrāb*; he had subordinates (known titles are: *sar-qulbī*, *band-bānī*, *jawzaqih*).
    a. Compensation for the *mīrāb* was 10% (*dih-yak*) of the harvest. This was occasionally supplemented with cereals and dinars.
    b. Compensation for the *band-bānī* and *jawzaqih* was usually in grain, but the *sar-qulbī* was usually paid in dinars.
        i. *Sar-qulbi*: six of nine *bulūks* had at least one;

[69] I am grateful to Kamyar Abedi of the Dehkhoda Institute for the above explanation.

[70] See n.66, *supra*.

    ii. *Band-bānī*: six of nine *bulūks* had at least one;
    iii. *Jawzaqih*: five of nine *buluks* had at least one.[71]

2. Each *buluk* was subdivided into multiple 160 *jarīb* parcels. Each subdivision had three watermen (*mard-jūy*) and eighteen households.
    a. The 160 *jarībs* were irrigated every five days. Compensation (if any) for watermen is not given. Structured irrigation without disputes between neighboring farmers was the underlying imperative.
    b. Several *qulbs*, *qulb-chihs* (lesser *qulbs*), and *naṭarahs* were operational within each *buluk*.
3. Mill operators were taxed according to estimated efficiencies, that is, three tax tiers existed. A flat tax was applied to certain mills.
4. Irrigation fees (*rakhnagī*) applied in every *buluk*.[72] Higher rates indicate crops that demand high volumes of water: cotton, almonds, pistachios, walnuts, and cashews; cash crops: cotton, saffron, mulberry trees (silkworms subsist on the leaves, hence the categorization as "cash crop").

*Patronage, Waqfs, Investments*

Direct evidence that Ghiyāth al-Dīn, or Il-Khans Öljeitü, or Abū Sa'īd Bahādur Khān had distributed crown or state lands in the Herat area to individuals or Islamic institutions is not available. Mongol or Kartid decrees, like the 706/1306 *yarlīgh* by Öljeitü granting *injü* lands to Shaykh al-Islam Shihāb al-Dīn Ismā'īl Jāmī, have not surfaced. The Sufi shrine at Turbat-i Jām benefited from patronage by Ghiyāth al-Dīn, and Ilkhanid sultans (Öljeitü and Abū Sa'īd), viziers (namely, Faryūmadī), and amirs (namely, Chūpān). A tiny shrine was transformed into a major shrine-complex, and became a prominent landlord and waterlord in Bākharz, Fūshanj, Harāt-Rūd, Jām, Khʷāf, and Kūsūyi.

Mosques, hospices, shrines, prayer/festival areas (*'īdgāh, muṣallá*), and cemeteries (sgl. *maqbara*) were patronized by Fakhr al-Dīn Kart.[73] Two hospices and Herat's *Masjid-i jāmi'* were patronized by Ghiyāth al-Dīn

[71] Recall that data are given for just nine of ten *bulūks*.
[72] In the Bulūk-i Sabaqar, *rakhnagī* was applied in seven zones: five zones were charged at 250 Tabrizi dinars; two zones at 750 Tabrizi dinars.
[73] Allen, *Catalogue*, 228–31, and Cat. Nos. 414, 445, 499, 508, 558, 559, 560, 562, 573, 580, and 598; al-Harawī, *Harāt*, 462–63. See also Appendix 3, *infra*.

Kart.[74] Other Islamic institutions were patronized by Muʿizz al-Dīn Kart and Sulṭān-Khātūn. It is not known if the *Madrasa-yi ʿIzz al-Dīn ʿUmar Marghānī* and *Madrasa-yi Shams al-Dīn Kart* [I] had been patronized by any Kartid *malik*;[75] but patronage is likely considering that ʿIzz al-Dīn ʿUmar Marghānī (d. 599/1202f.) was Shams al-Dīn Kart's grand-uncle and had served the Ghurid sultan, Ghiyāth al-Dīn.[76]

Patronage is not just about erecting edifices with exquisite artistic flourishes and architectural designs, but also ensuring the institution's survival after the patron has expired. The cornerstone of patronage is the *income-producing assets* that keep edifices from crumbling and the patron's legacy from disappearing. Maria Subtelny observed that "it was the endowment [the waqf] established for their maintenance and for the support of the activities they housed that guaranteed their permanence and ensured their viability as social institutions."[77] Waqfs included income-producing assets; for example, agricultural and pastoral estates;[78] hydrological holdings (*jūy*, *kārīz*, watermill); and commercial rental properties (e.g., shops inside a bazaar). Incomes maintain the institution (daily operations, upkeep of buildings, grounds, salaries, etc.). They had to generate surpluses that could be diverted for the provision of social services: an affluent hospice or seminary was expected to provide social services within its catchment area (for instance, food for indigents).[79]

When Ghiyāth al-Dīn Kart endowed one of his hospices, Sayf al-Harawī noted, he gave it "all that is needful for a hospice."[80] By this Sayfī means the hospice's seven (income-producing) watermills and farmlands.[81]

[74] Allen, *Catalogue*, 228–31, and Nos. 428 (Herat's Friday Mosque), 501, 502, and possibly 512; al-Harawī, *Harāt*, 742–45. See also Appendix 3, *infra*.

[75] Allen, *Catalogue*, Cat. Nos. 464 and 487.

[76] See Potter, "Kart Dynasty," 33–36.

[77] M. Subtelny, "A Timurid Educational and Charitable Foundation: The Ikhlasiyya complex of ʿAli Shir Navaʾi in 15th-century Herat and its endowment," *JAOS* 111/1 (1991):38–61, 38.

[78] Estates have hamlets or villages for the share-croppers; they pay rent. Taxes were often shifted to peasants, who usually must pay the *ʿushr* (10% tax) on the harvest; they may also pay the *kharāj muqāsama* (fixed tax on land; say, 20%). Landlords paid *kharāj waẓīfa* (variable land tax). See Shivan Mahendrarajah, "The Gawhar Shad Waqf Deed: Public works and the commonweal," *JAOS* 138/4 (2018):821–57, esp. 825, 856, and nn. 32–33, 183.

[79] See Mahendrarajah, *Sufi Saint*, 143–48 ("Public Service in the Catchment Area").

[80] al-Harawī, *Harāt*, 745.

[81] See nn. 40 and 42, *supra*.

The administrator (*mutawallī*) of Ghiyāth al-Dīn's waqfs receives after-tax harvests: the state could hold the crops in the field until taxes are paid (waqfs are not inherently tax-exempt);[82] and rents from his tenant farmers (frequently paid in grain), with repayment of loans (if any) and advances (if any).[83] He will monetize a part of this income; store part of it to pay staff and feed the hospice's residents; and use one part for pious activities like "soup kitchens." Another part, *surplus cash*, is invested in capital improvements and to purchase new income-producing assets: estates, aqueducts, mills, bazaars. In the absence of debt and equity markets, the principal investment vehicles for the affluent were precious metals and immovable property. These assets also functioned as hedges against inflation.

Pre-Mongol spiritual and sepulchral buildings that stood in Herat despite Elǰigidei's actions were restored by Kartids, who also sponsored new construction projects (Appendix 3). Anecdotal evidence suggests that some, if not many, of the revitalized or newly founded institutions became landlords and waterlords. When Ghiyāth al-Dīn restored the Ghurid era *Madrasa-yi Ghiyāthiyya*,[84] and renovated Herat's venerable *Masjid-i jāmi*ʿ,[85] he probably founded waqfs to provide them with "all that is needful." He donated 10,000 dinars to the mosque for building and pious activities.[86] This suggests that institutions with surplus cash from investments, alms, and large donations (as above) will have employed cash for, inter alia, investments in new income-producing assets.

Qāsim b. Yūsuf relates a story that one can envision recurring in different locales of Herat Quarter. *Raʿāyā* approached Ghiyāth al-Dīn about the condition of Jūy-i Sabaqar and beseeched him to restore it. They offered him an ownership and revenue-sharing compact of four *dāng* (shares) to him and two *dāng* for them.[87] This is why Jūy-i Sabaqar was restored and became Jūy-i Naw. The division of ownership reflected his cash outlays and

82 See Mahendrarajah, "Gawhar Shad Waqf Deed", 825, 856. We know nothing about Kartid *kharāj* and *ʿushr* collection practices.

83 See ibid., 855. After taxes, rents, and repayment of interest-bearing loans (*musāʿada*) or advances (*taqāwī*) of seed or cash, a share-cropper and family subsisted on the remainder.

84 Allen, *Catalogue*, Cat. No. 460.

85 Ibid., Cat. No. 428.

86 al-Harawī, *Harāt*, 759.

87 al-Harawī, *Ṭarīq-i qismat*, 10 (*chahār dāng milk-i tū wa dū dāng milk-i mā bāshad*). One *dāng* is one-sixth share in real estate; hence 4 × ⅙ = ⅔ share to the *malik*; 2 × ⅙ = ⅓ share to *raʿāyā*.

(unsaid by Qāsim b. Yūsuf or Sayf al-Harawī) his hiring of skilled overseers, engineers, laborers, and elimination of red tape;[88] and the farmers' daily toils. This is a common sense bargain that married cash-rich investors to cash-poor farmers.

[88] This dovetails with Ḥanafī law on *iḥyā' al-mawāt* and Ilkhanid fiscal-legal reforms, namely, ownership attaches to the revivifier. The *malik* had two-third share of "X" hundred *gaz* of land on both sides of the *jūy*. Boundaries (*ḥarīm*) of a *jūy* are determined by local custom.

# 9

# Urban Renewal and Cultural Renaissance

## Rebuilding Herat: Mongol Initiatives

Early Ilkhanid development efforts were haphazard and rudimentary. Il-Khans also circumscribed rejuvenation efforts; for instance, there was a prohibition on construction inside Herat.[1] The Ghurid era Friday mosque remained dilapidated; inner Herat's bazaars were yet to be revamped. Three pavilions were erected near Khūsh Gate and roofed seven shops. Sometime after 653/1255, *shaḥna* Merkidaï erected a pavilion and possibly two other structures. Reconstruction was episodic until 699/1299f., when Fakhr al-Dīn Kart defied the Mongols by initiating fortification projects. He apparently employed Nikudaris to advance his political objectives, and received from them a share of the spoils. These monies allowed him to underwrite his construction projects.

An example of episodic development by the early Ilkhanids is the case of the major workshop (*kār-khānah-yi ʿālī*) erected beside the Firūzābād Gate in 663/1264 by Shams al-Dīn Kart. He also built a bazaar opposite the workshop.[2] The workshop was patronized by Abāqā and inspected by him. Architects and builders from Khurasan were engaged for the project. Shams al-Dīn's ambitions, however, were circumscribed by the Il-Khan: despite objections, Abāqā insisted that bazaar and workshop be located outside the walled city.[3]

The *kār-khānah* was imperial property, but what it produced is not publicized by Sayfī. The workshop must have profited the Empire and Ilkhanid

[1] There is just a terse mention of the ban in al-Harawī, *Harāt*, 311.

[2] al-Harawī, *Harāt*, 311–13; Faṣīḥ, *Mujmal*, 818.

[3] Although "walled city" is used, we do not know the condition of the *c*. 1.5 km x. 1.5 km walls following Eljigidei's demolition of defenses at key points, followed by years of neglect.

notables, otherwise it would not have been founded. Given the prominence of silk and cotton fabrication in Herat before the Mongol invasions, and the Empire's economic interest in gilded and embroidered fabrics, it probably produced precious textiles. The events surrounding the return of ʿIzz al-Dīn Muqaddam al-Harawī to Herat are illuminating.

ʿIzz al-Dīn Muqaddam had crafted exquisite fabrics for the Mongols during his Central Asian exile.[4] He informed Ögödei that Herat's climate was more conducive to textile production than Besh Baliq (Turkistan),[5] where the Khurasanians were being held captive; that he could annually "double" (*aẓʿāf*) revenues flowing to the Empire's treasury (*khazīna*),[6] relative to current production.[7] Consequently, a subset of the 1,000 households (*khāna-wār*) of Persian captives was released by Ögödei in 635/1237f. (ʿIzz al-Dīn's cohort); a second and larger cohort followed in 637/1239f.[8]

It should be stated upfront that Ögödei had already decided to revitalize Herat and its vicinities, principally to increase the flow of manufactured goods and revenues flowing to the Empire.[9] He was searching for a competent native of Herat who could expeditiously revitalize (*ābādān*) the region and agriculture (*zirāʿat*), and render Herat habitable (*ʿimārat*). Ögödei inquired of his (Persian?) advisors, "from the captive *raʿāyā* of that province [Herat], which [craft] guild should We appoint?" (*az raʿāyā wa usārī-yi ān wilāyat kudām ṭāʾīfa ra nām-zad gardān-īm*?).[10] The selection of ʿIzz al-Dīn to lead the first cohort, and its composition, was based on advice from Ögödei's inner circle.

[4] Khurasan's crafted textiles were renowned. See summary in R.B. Serjeant, "Material for a History of Islamic Textiles up to the Mongol Conquest," *Ars Islamica* 11 (1946):98–145, 111–20 (Khurasan and Quhistān); for Herat, see pp. 117–19. Further on textiles in Persia, see Wulff, *Traditional*, 172–230.

[5] Besh Baliq/Bīsh Bāligh/Bishbalïq: see Bregel, *Historical Atlas*, Maps 16–19.

[6] al-Harawī, *Harāt*, 143–44; Isfizārī, *Rawżāt*, 2:109. See discussion and translations of passages in Thomas Allsen, *Commodity and Exchange in the Mongol Empire: A Cultural History of Islamic Textiles* (Cambridge: Cambridge University Press, 1997), 38–40.

[7] Textiles crafted by Khurasanians in Besh Baliq have survived. J.C.Y. Watt & A.E. Wardwell, *When Silk was Gold: Central Asian and Chinese Textiles* (New York: The Metropolitan Museum of Art, 1997), esp. 132–35.

[8] al-Harawī, *Harāt*, 145 (1st wave) and 158 (2nd wave).

[9] See Allsen, *Commodity*, 39 and esp. n.56 (a Russian source).

[10] al-Harawī, *Harāt*, 141.

ʿIzz al-Dīn Muqaddam was the provost (*wālī*) of the weavers' (*jāma-i bāfān*) guild of Herat.[11] His cohort was selected to provide specific talents at Herat. Sobriquets (sgl. *laqab*) of deportees who returned with ʿIzz al-Dīn,[12] or the fabrics they crafted in exile,[13] reveal the importance to the Empire of certain skills and crafts: carpet-spreader (*farrāsh*); gold-inlaid (*zarbaft, zar-nigār*) or laced/embroidered fabrics (*jāma-yi muṭarraz*; cf. *ṭirāz*),[14] "gold brocaded garments with imperial illustrations" (*jāma-yi zarbaft-i muṣawwar-i pādshāhāna*); precious fabrics (*jāma-yi qīmatī*) of other classes.

The weavers' return was almost thirty years before the Kartid *kār-khānah-yi ʿālī* was erected. Meanwhile, we lose track of them. The workshop's output is thus speculative. But as with the revival of cotton cultivation in Herat Quarter consequent to Ögödei's initiatives (Chapter Seven), the Quarter's sericulture industry was probably resuscitated.[15] Repatriation of weavers signifies revival of Herat's textile crafts.

## Rebuilding Herat: Kartid Initiatives

The prohibition on construction was broken by Fakhr al-Dīn through the rebuilding of fortifications, but even before he launched projects in 699/1299f., there probably were refurbishments, possibly even major works, inside the city. Homes of erstwhile Heratis (deported, departed, deceased) were occupied by Mongol and Kartid officials, amirs, and squatters. Migrants to post-Īlchīgadaï Herat will have found it necessary to make their new dwellings habitable. They would have excavated or unclogged water-wells, cisterns, and sewage trenches; cleared streets and alleys of debris. Mosques, hospices, and shrines will have enjoyed clean ups and renewed activities. Once arterial channels and sub-channels, and weirs, cisterns, and water-wells were excavated, restored or built, and the population of inner Herat proliferated, the city's suburbs experienced renascence; hence the Kartid Wall (built before

[11] Ibid., 110; see also Isfizārī, *Rawżāt*, 2:59; Jūzjānī/Raverty, *Nāṣirī*, 2:1037 (n.1 from p.1,036); cf. Mīrkhwānd, *Rawżat*, 3,911. Sayfī does not state guild (*ṭāʾifa*), but a guild probably existed, of which ʿIzz al-Dīn was *wālī*. He was confirmed as *wālī* by Jalāl al-Dīn Mengübirtī.

[12] On *laqab* (cognomen, sobriquet), see Schimmel, *Islamic Names*, 12–13.

[13] al-Harawī, *Harāt*, 141–44, 145; Isfizārī, *Rawżāt*, 2:108–09.

[14] *Ṭirāz*: from Persian *ṭarāzīdan*, "to embroider." Came to refer to embroidery and caliphal apparel crafted in state-owned or regulated workshops. See R.B. Serjeant, "Material for a History of Islamic Textiles up to the Mongol Conquest," *Ars Islamica* 9 (1942):54–92.

[15] Sericulture (raising silkworms) was a feature in the Quarter before the Mongol invasions.

752/1351; see Chapter Ten), to protect the socio-economic achievements of the foregoing half-century.

Fakhr al-Dīn Kart deserves credit for resisting Mongol proscriptions. Indeed, his unconstrained spirit, which caused considerable problems for his subjects even after his demise, enriched Herat's treasury of cultural heritages: his superlative bequest to posterity is Qalʿa-yi Ikhtiyār al-Dīn, which, with later enhancements, illumes Herat's skyline.

Appendix 3, Table 1: Edifices Built/Re-Built in Herat, itemizes actual or putative sponsorship of urban development projects, from the earliest endeavors of Muḥammad b. ʿIzz al-Din, et al., to Muʿizz al-Dīn Kart's projects. Sponsorship by Pīr ʿAlī Kart is not known. Edifices itemized in the table are flagged in Figure 9.1 (if locations are known).

*Commercial Spaces*

Fakhr al-Dīn restored the Malik Bazaar,[16] an integral component of the commercial infrastructure of Herat. Ghiyāth al-Dīn expanded on Fakhr al-Dīn's project by extending the Malik Bazaar, and erecting three caravansarays and one grand pavilion. He funded a cistern (*ḥawż*) and public steam bath (*ḥammām*). The cistern was inside the bazaar complex.[17] Sayfī does not declare this, but an aqueduct—a subterranean or overground conduit from a *jūy*—supplied the cistern. The author of a history of Yazd helps in visualizing the centrality of cistern to bazaar. Water from Taft exited a channel in the middle of the bazaar complex (and supplied a cistern?); thence, one channel led to the caravansaray; a second led to the hammam.[18] Ghiyāth al-Dīn's caravansarays and hamman will have been supplied from his *ḥawż* or by sub-channels (*jūy-chih*) extending from the conduit that supplied the cistern.

During Ghiyāth al-Dīn's four-year absence, Öljeitü's plenipotentiary, Amir Yasāʾūl (d.*c.* 717/1317), and cohort Muḥammad Duldāʾī

[16] Isfizārī, *Rawżāt*, 1:78; Allen, *Catalogue*, 49–50.

[17] On its possible location and present identification, see Allen, *Catalogue*, 25. The bazaar was expanded by Timurids. Safawids built, after *c.* 1634, the large cistern near the center of the Chahār-Sūq complex. A.W. Najimi, "The Cistern at Char-Suq," *Afghanistan Journal* 9/2 (Graz, 1982):38–41 (included are diagrams of the cistern and bazaar complex).

[18] Aḥmad b. Ḥusayn b. ʿAlī Kātib, *Tārīkh-i jadīd-i Yazd*, ed. Iraj Afshar (Tehran: Intishārāt-i farhang-i Irān-zamīn, 1357/1978), 130. Mother-wells in Taft hill country, *c.* 13.5 miles/21.5 km southwest of Yazd, fed several underground channels.

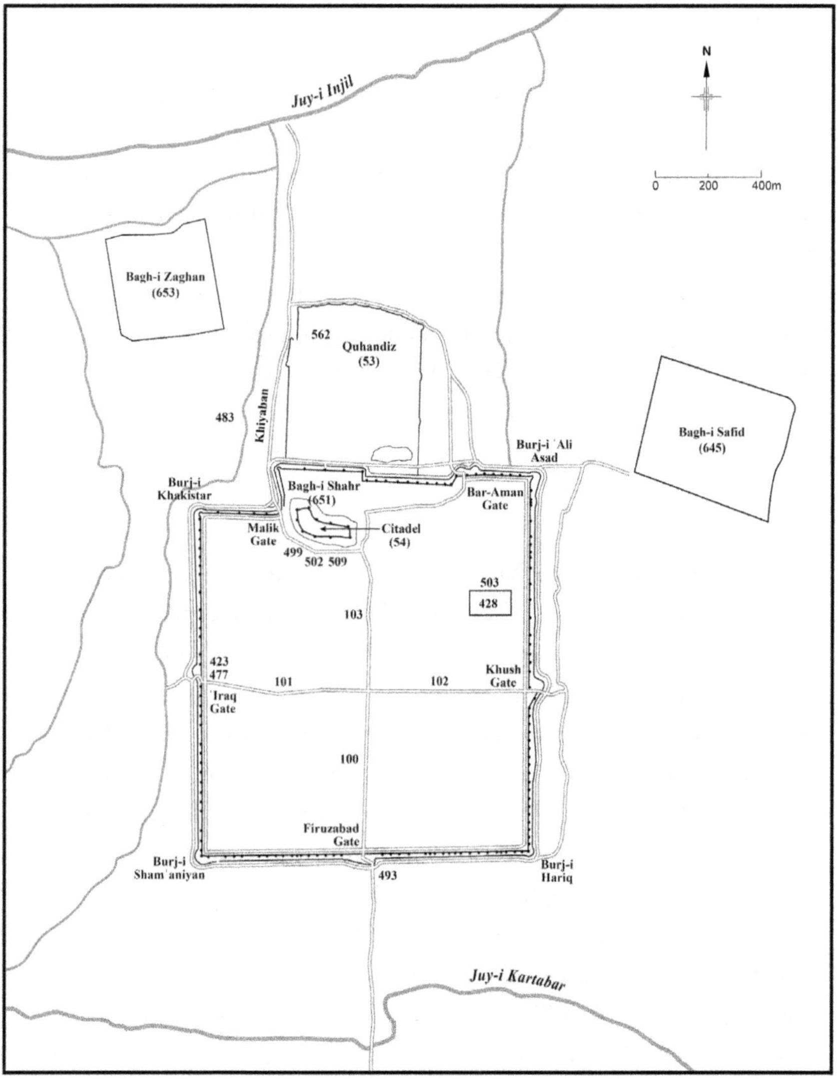


Figure 9.1 Sketch of Kartid Herat. Follows on Allen, *Catalogue*, Map 2.

(d.*c.* 715/1315) b. Danishmand Bahadur, were extorting the peoples of Herat. They both built bazaars. Duldāʾī forced vendors to relocate (from Malik Bazaar?) to his bazaar (Sūq-i Sulṭān). Given Yasāʾūl's reputation for turpitude, Sayfī insists, Yasāʾūl did not just destroy homes and gardens to clear space for his bazaar, he constructed it with the bricks and beams of mosques and seminaries. The pair appointed "'ruffians and scum" (*runūd wa awbāsh-ān*) as watchmen and policemen (*ʿasas-ān wa shaḥna-gān*), who harrassed and extorted Heratis.[19]

Economic activities were assuredly constricted during the four-year period when Yasāʾūl, Danishmand Bahadur's progeny,[20] and their allies, distressed Heratis. Yasaʾur's raids into Khurasan, and activities in Garmsīr, probably throttled trade between Herat and regions to its east (Qandahar, Ghazni, India), and south/southwest (Kirmān, Sīstān).[21] The elimination of Yasaʾur, and recalcitrant *bandagān* at Āzāb, Bākharz, Farāh, Isfizār, Khʷāf, and Tūlak, erased obstacles to trans-regional and international trade.

*Herat's economy, 719/1319 to 729/1329*

The post-Yasaʾur economy (ten-year period from final operations against Yasaʾur's allies to Ghiyāth al-Dīn's death) was, by my estimation, flourishing. Heratis benefited from Sultan Abū Saʿīd Bahādur Khān's *yarlīgh*, "exempting for three years Heratis from [itemized taxes], and the occasional taxes imposed by the *dīwān* of Khurasan."[22] The Kartid had liquid assets that he employed to stimulate the economy. Firstly, Abū Saʿīd had bestowed 50,000 dinars on the *malik*; secondly, booty enriched Kartid coffers.

Abū Saʿīd's *yarlīgh* also allocated to Ghiyāth al-Dīn the chattels and estates (*asbāb wa amlāk*) of Quṭb al-Dīn Isfizārī, Majd al-Dīn Khʷāfī, Farrukhzād Tūlakī, et al., Kartid *bandagān* that had joined Yasaʾur. Ghiyāth al-Dīn was allegedly forced to return them when Abū Saʿīd annulled this penalty. This aspect is debated below.

The term *asbāb wa amlāk* is often found in endowment (*waqf*) deeds and applied to (movable and immovable) personal assets. Abū Saʿīd's ruling may have targeted personal assets, not "state assets" (lands, livestock, cereals, slaves, arsenals, provisions, treasures, and plunder) held by an amir

19 al-Harawī, *Harāt*, 603; Allen, *Catalogue*, 53.

20 On Danishmand's progeny in Khurasan, see Chapter 4, n.34.

21 Caravans avoid unsafe highways. Marco Polo's lament, of lawlessness, murder, and risks taken by merchants, reveals the importance of safe roads. Marco Polo/Yule (tr.), *Travels*, 1:79; 1:92–93 (his experiences with Qaraunas).

22 See Chapter 4, § "Political Stability at Herat."

governing Āzāb, Bākharz, Farāh, Isfizār, Khʷāf or Tūlak as the *banda* of the Kartid *malik*. Control of personal estates and chattels, and dominion over their homelands (i.e., Isfizār, Khʷāf, and Tūlak) *may* have been restored by Ghiyāth al-Dīn; but all the confiscated assets were definitely not returned. Majd al-Dīn Khʷāfī had acquired wealth through, inter alia, banditry. He pledged fealty (*banda*) to Yasaʾur and paid him tribute. Majd al-Dīn stored treasure at Ḥiṣār-i Mābīzhan-Ābād (Khʷāf);[23] he possibly held assets at Ḥiṣār-i Niyāz-Ābād (Khʷāf).[24] Both citadels fell to Kartids. Farrukhzād Tūlakī hoarded treasures and cereals at Qalʿa-yi Tūlak (including 10,000 *kharwārs* of wheat plundered by Yasaʾur).[25] Ḥiṣār-i R-Z-H (Bākharz) was captured with its "treasures, fineries, provisions, armaments, horses, and numerous captives" (*māl wa niʿmat wa zakhīra wa asliḥa wa marākib wa barda-yi bisyār dar dast-i sipāh-i manṣūr-i Malik al-Islām Ghiyāth al-Ḥaqq wa al-Dīn uftād*).[26]

Opponents and turncoats were punished by Ghiyāth al-Dīn. The castellan of Ḥiṣār-i R-Z-H was hauled to Herat in fetters and executed; a band of robbers (*duzd-ān*) from Farāh were executed outside Firūzābād Gate; Majd al-Dīn's Sīstānī soldiers were executed. Others were bastinadoed (*chūb-zad*) or pilloried (*dū-shākhih*).[27] Majd al-Dīn signed a compact (*ʿahd-nāmah*) with the Kartid and opened his treasury (*dar-i khazīnih bih-kushād*).[28] Farrukhzād accepted arbitration by Chief Justice Quṭb al-Dīn Yaḥyá Jāmī Nīshāpūrī and lost his holdings (including the 10,000 *kharwārs*) as penalty; but his ally, Ghiyāth al-Dīn Āzābī, paid with his life.[29] In Rabīʿ I 721/April 1321, Farāh was captured by Kartids. Amir Ḥusayn (Jalayirid; d. 722/1322), as Ilkhanid plenipotentiary for Khurasan, issued a decree sealed with *Āl tamghā* directing Ināltikīn Farāhī to transfer 5,000 *kharwārs* of cereal to the Kartid army (*bih jihat-i sipāh-i Harāt*). He refused. Shams al-Dīn (III) dispatched 2,000 Nikudaris to Farāh to collect the dues. Twenty thousand head of ovines and bovines (*ghanm wa baqar*) were rounded up, the citadel taken and Farāh

23 al-Harawī, *Harāt*, 750–51. On the citadels named here, see Table 10.1, *infra*.
24 Ibid., 753. Ḥiṣār-i Niyāz-Ābād had a castellan (*kūtwāl*) and treasurer (*khazīnih-dār*).
25 Ibid., 764, 767.
26 Ibid., 748.
27 Ibid., 748. Slew of executions in Muḥarram-Ṣafar 720/March–April 1320.
28 Ibid., 757–59.
29 Ibid., 767. On Jāmī Nīshāpūrī, see Chapter 5, and below.

pillaged. Nikudaris returned to Herat with plenty of booty and countless captives (*bā ghanīmat bī-ḥadd wa asīr bī-shumār*).[30]

The summaries above make manifest that every turncoat had to pay a penalty: cash or blood. This is logical: Āzābī, Farāhī, Isfizārī, Khʷāfī, Tūlakī, et al., by allying with Yasaʾur, had cost Kartids and Khurasanians blood and treasure over five years of upheaval, violence, destruction (for instance, burned crops), and lost economic opportunities.

War is expensive and plunder is indispensable. Cicero's "endless streams of money" encapsulates this truth. Amir Ḥusayn "billed" Ināltikīn for costs, but when he refused, the Nikudaris operated as "collection agents." This episode epitomizes an economic reality. Kartids could not afford to pay troops from the fisc.[31] Yasaʾur's spoils (for instance, 10,000 *kharwārs*) became Kartid assets. Chattels returned to Majd al-Dīn and company—*if at all*—would have been reduced by (1) distributions to soldiers, dependents of deceased soldiers (families are often guaranteed payouts, if not, soldiers are reluctant to serve), and disabled veterans; (2) deductions by the Kartid treasury (*bayt al-māl*) to defray costs of the expeditions mounted over five years against Farrukhzād, Majd al-Dīn, et al.

Ghiyāth al-Dīn Kart—returning to this section's theme—was flush with liquid assets, which he employed to stimulate the economy. He spent lavishly on commercial and non-commercial building projects at Herat, Turbat-i Jām, and other parts of his realm, thereby creating employment for *raʿāyā*. The Kartid's commercial and non-commercial construction projects complemented his agricultural and hydrological projects.

Herat's economy was thriving. If Herat's economy were recessionary or moribund, why erect one pavilion and three caravansarays? Why not stick to constructing hospices and seminaries, building activities that would generate employment for *raʿāyā*, but with the bonus of burnishing the Kartid's legacy as patron of Islamic learning and culture? "Build it and they will come" is not an economic principle (much less a sound

[30] Ibid., 777–79; Faṣīḥ, *Mujmal*, 99 and n.2. Ghiyāth al-Dīn Kart was away on the Hajj.

[31] Alexander could afford to reward families of fallen (Holt, *Treasures*, 51–52); and payoff soldiers' debts worth *c.* 280 short tons of (silver) coins (ibid., 124–27; 1 ton = 907 kg/2,000 lb). On his sources of non-tax revenue, see ibid., 44–67, 181–85 (Holt's Appendix 2).

one).[32] If caravans did not detour to Herat, bazaars and caravansarays would stand empty, crumbling monuments to Ghiyāth al-Dīn's hubris. If he *anticipated* increased trade (per the "build it…" hypothesis), he would have erected one caravansaray, not three. Terry Allen was on target by noticing that by the late Timurid era, Herat's bazaars had grown *with* the city.[33] Ghiyāth al-Dīn was adding "building blocks" because Herat and its economy were expanding.

### *Building blocks*

As Herat's population and economy expanded, building blocks were methodically added. A view is that "Moslem towns grew so spontaneously and haphazardly as to prevent the development of a systematic street pattern." Herat's logical layout is attributed to the "Milesian mentality of its Greek conquerors."[34] Michael Bonine, however, has demonstrated that (surveyed) cities did not develop organically; they manifest intrinsic logic.[35] Factors like overground or subterranean channels; gradient (for water distribution and removal of sewage); and climate (windmills and wind-catchers point toward the wind), contributed to decisions on urban layout and placement of edifices. Kartids did not erect buildings willy-nilly. They appear to have followed pre-existing patterns.[36]

Caravansarays were strategically placed in the wards of Herat to meet the economic needs of that geographic sector. For example, haulers delivering raw materials or finished products to, and collecting merchandise from manufacturers, craftsmen, and merchants in the southwest quadrant of Herat, will have stayed in caravansarays in the southwest. If not, they would have to trudge across town. This arrangement allowed visitors to meet Herati merchants and producers in the same economic field. Just as

[32] Oil- and gas-rich Dubai and Doha embraced this approach. Buildings stand empty or have low tenancy; rents are declining. Foreign contractors promoted the approach and profited from designing, supplying, and completing construction projects.

[33] Allen, *Catalogue*, 89.

[34] Paul Ward English, "The Traditional City of Herat, Afghanistan," in L.C. Brown (ed.), *From Madina to Metropolis: Heritage and Change in the Near Eastern City* (Princeton: The Darwin Press, 1973), 73–90, 75, 78; cf. Gaube, *Iranian Cities*, 55–57 (origins of plan of Herat).

[35] M. Bonine, "The Morphogenesis of Iranian Cities," *Annals of the Association of American Geographers*, 69/2 (1979):208–24. Herat was not included in Bonine's study.

[36] Gaube, *Iranian Cities*, 55 (consistency in layout of inner Herat since the tenth century).

there are specialty bazaars—greengrocers' market, spices, textiles, ceramics, copperworks—caravansarays catered to a neighborhood's industries. We have no details, but merchants' guilds or craft guilds tended to determine a caravansary's economic orientation.[37] Parochial factors (ethnicity and tribe) possibly influenced which caravansarays catered to specific commercial fields, haulers, and vendors.[38] In summary, each of the three caravansarays probably accommodated certain commercial fields; and each was proximate to the bazaar that had vendors specializing in the same commercial field(s).[39]

Bazaars, "little bazaars" (*bāzār-chih*), caravansarays, "little caravansarays" (*tīm-chih*), warehouses, workshops, and shops were discrete entities scattered across Herat's wards; but they collectively comprised Herat's *bazaar network*.[40] The construction of caravansarays suggests that merchandise was flowing to *and* from Herat. That is, traders were staying in Herat to sell their wares and purchase Herati merchandise. After unloading goods at Herat, haulers are unlikely to have quit Herat without loading freight: to return without vendible goods would make their trip less profitable, even unprofitable. Traders who stay overnight in Herat to conduct business require amenities; hence caravansarays, which offer lodgings, stables (sgl. *iṣṭabl*), and latrines.[41] Cisterns and hammams are nearby.

### *Transportation hubs*

Herat was a commercial center that (1) consumed merchandise and (2) produced merchandise. Goods (including agricultural produce) of Herat not consumed locally would be shipped from Herat to purchasers located elsewhere in Persia (and beyond). But Herat was not a transportation

[37] Little that is known of early guilds is in W. Floor, "Guilds in Iran: An overview, from the earliest beginnings until 1972," *ZDMG* 125 (1975):99–116.

[38] See, e.g., Barfield, *Central Asian*, 86 (three of seven caravansarays owned by Central Asian Arabs and patronized by Arab visitors).

[39] On Timurid era bazaars and certain products, see Allen, *Catalogue*, 89–90.

[40] "Bazaar network" is adopted from Allen, *Catalogue*, 89.

[41] Sayfī does not offer these details, but historians of Yazd certainly do. See, e.g., Jaʿfar b. Muḥammad b. Ḥasan Jaʿfarī, *Tārīkh-i Yazd*, ed. Iraj Afshar (Tehran: Bungāh-i tarjumah wa nashr-i kitāb, 1343/1965), 63: caravansary with four *ṣuffa* (estrade; raised floor; covered space), 80 *wiṣāq* (chambers; lodgings), and *pāyāb* (shallow reservoir). The caravansary was located near shops, cisterns (pl. *ḥiyāż*), hammam, and mosque.

*hub*.[42] It was not along *north-south* caravan routes (e.g., Zaranj to Nishapur or Mashhad, traversing west of Herat);[43] or *east-west* caravan routes: (1) through the Hindu Kush (arduous terrain best left to nomads and locals); (2) above the Hindu Kush (via northern Khurasan); (3) below the Hindu Kush (e.g., to/from Ghazni and Qandahar via Bust to/from Zaranj and Farāh).

In order to enter Herat, caravans had to detour from hubs situated north and south of the city.[44] Zaranj was one hub south of Herat; possibly a major hub.[45] Farāh was another hub.[46] Caravansarays and forts function as transportation hubs: traders can safely remain overnight while transfering goods carried by one long-distance hauler to another, or to a short-distance hauler, for distribution along that operator's "spoke."

Herat was not an *unavoidable* way station: caravans did not have to stop at Herat—unless they had goods to off-load and load. Caravans on east-west routes would not detour 131 miles/211 km north (from Farāh to Herat) unless haulers/traders had compelling reasons to enter Herat. Caravans on north-south routes could bypass Herat by traversing west of the city. If it were a matter of delivering merchandise purchased by Herati merchants from "foreign" suppliers (India, Ghazni, Kirman, Yazd, Persian Gulf), cargo could be off-loaded at Farāh or Zaranj and transported by pack animal into Herat.

Entry into Herat was no casual affair. A caravan had to detour north from Zaranj or Farāh, cross the Mālān Bridge located *c.* 3.25 miles/5.2 km

42 Hub: akin a spoked wheel; hence "hub-and-spoke," where primary and secondary hubs distribute freight along spokes (air, water, and land routes).

43 Cf. "The north-south road along the Harirud River from Bukhara and Marv to Sistān and Kermān passed through Herat [and] the Silk Road from West Asia to China also passed through there." Arash Khazeni, "Herat I: Geography," *EIr*, 12:203–05. The Hari Rud's south-north journey begins *c.* 80 miles/128 km *northwest* of Herat; part of its northern course, *c.* 65 miles/104 km, forms the Iran-Afghanistan border. The river terminates in Turkmenistan.

44 My comments are limited to the Zaranj and Farāh hubs. For later evidence on southern routes, see Warwick Ball, *Archaeological Gazetteer of Afghanistan* (Oxford: Oxford University Press, 2019), Maps 23, 69–73, 83–98.

45 See descriptions of roads, bridges, and waterways in Barthold, *Geography*, 66–73; Adamec, *Gazetteer*, 2:220–24; Iṣṭakhrī/Afshar (ed.), *Masālik al-mamālik*, 192–201, esp. 195 (by boat from Bust to Lake Sīstān), 199 (by land from Bust to Sīstān; thence to Herat).

46 See, e.g., Barthold, *Geography*, 66 and n.14, 72; *ABC* 1:96, 108, 3:31–47 (on waters, forts, and roads in the Farāh-Juwayn-Isfizār region, along with sketch maps).

south of Herat,[47] and be subjected to searches and possibly pay taxes and tolls before advancing to Herat. The caravan must then pass through Herat's defensive circumvallations and gateways, suffer new searches, perhaps pay more tolls. Ibn Battuta describes this onerous process. On crossing an Indian river (the Ravi?), ten miles from his destination of Multān:[48]

> the goods of all who pass are subjected to a rigorous examination and their baggage searched. Their practice at the time of our arrival was to take a quarter of everything brought in by the merchants, and to exact a duty of seven dinars for every horse.

Ibn Battuta objects in terms that will resonate with modern air travelers, about the intrusiveness of the baggage search and his sense of violation.

Haulers and traders must have had financial incentives to detour to Herat to tolerate searches, indignities, delays, dangers, expenses, taxes, and tolls. The post-Yasaʾur economy of Herat probably made their efforts worthwhile; hence the erection of three caravansarays in the final decade of Ghiyāth al-Dīn's reign.

*Caravans and merchandise*

"Caravan" (Per: *kārwān*; Ar. *qāfila*) may evoke images of wheeled wagons trundling over steppe and sierra, but since early Islamic times in Persia, the wheel had been replaced by the one-humped cold-adapted camel as the principal mode of transportation for freight. Horses, camels, and mules were indispensable to moving people and merchandise. Persian and Arabian steeds were esteemed. Marco Polo observed that, "[i]n this country of Persia there is a great supply of fine horses; and people take them to India for sale[.]"[49] Herat was apparently central to the horse trade.[50] Herat's "Horse and Camel Bazaar" (*bāzār-i asb wa shutūr*) was situated "south of the citadel, in an

[47] See description penned in May 1885 by British officers of their route from Herat's south gate to Malan Bridge in *ABC*, 3:153–55.

[48] Ibn Battuta, *Travels*, 3:604–05; cf. ibid., 2:478 (double taxation of horses at Multān).

[49] Marco Polo/Yule (tr.), *Travels*, 1:79.

[50] Ali Bahrani Pour, "The Trade in Horses between Khorasan and India in the 13th–17th Centuries," *The Silk Road* 11 (2013):123–38 (the bulk of his evidence is post-Kartid). See also Simon Digby, *War-horse and Elephant in the Delhi Sultanate: A Study of Military Supplies* (Oxford: Oxford Monographs, 1971), 23–36 (land and sea trade in horses).

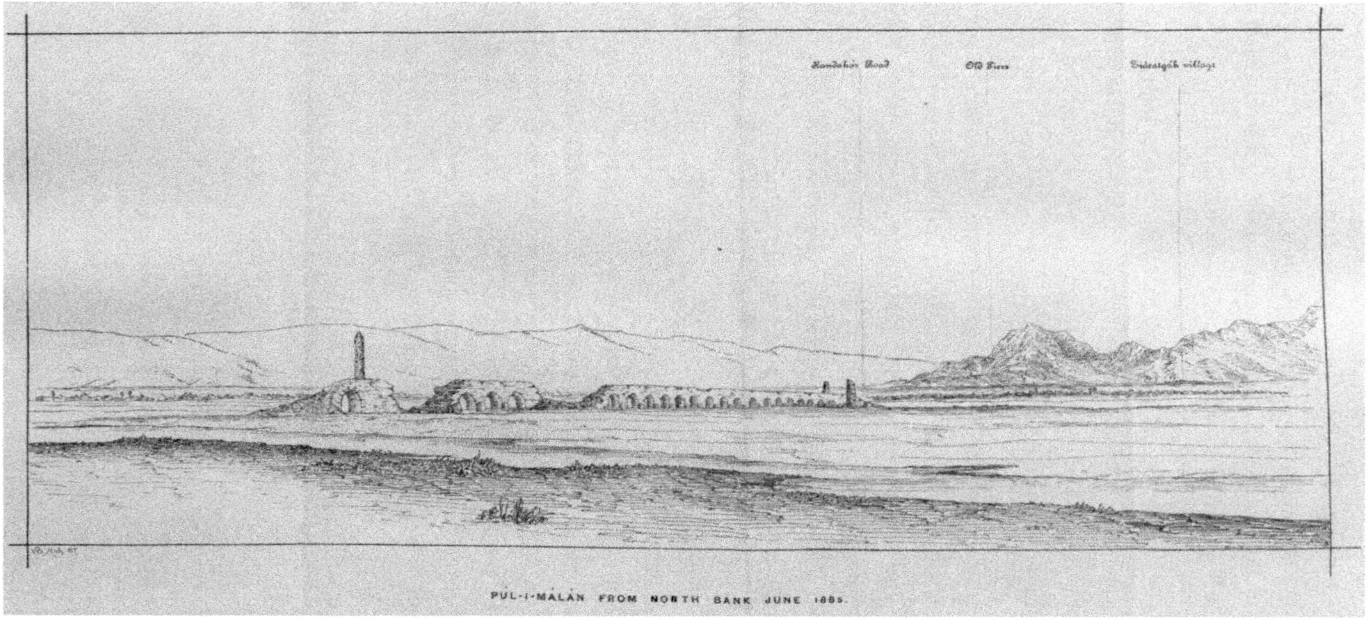


Figure 9.2 Sketch of Mālān Bridge, 1885.

unroofred area."[51] Mongols pastured horses at Bādghīs, and *c.* 750s/1350s were selling their horses in Herat's bazaar.[52]

We find hints in primary sources on trade and the types of goods valued in Persia and India: "fruits from Khurasan[,] which are regarded as great luxuries in India"; "white slaves" sold in Sind; a merchant from Iraq trading horses, camels, and arrows in Ghazni.[53] Silks and cottons were cherished. A trade in slaves thrived between India and *Afghānistān* (Ghazni and Qandahar) into the Mughal era.[54] Kartids possibly imported crucible steel from Chāhak (located at the junction of Fars, Yazd, and Kirman), a center for steel production.[55] Kirmanis were "very skilful in making harness of war; their saddles, bridles, spurs, swords, bows, quivers, and arms of every kind, are very well made indeed [...]."[56]

### *Public Spaces*

Fakhr al-Dīn Kart developed an *ʿīdgāh* (Arabic: *muṣallá*; Persian: *namāzgāh*) inside Herat.[57] This was an open area for festivals (*ʿīd*), prayers, and public assemblies. Another *ʿīdgāh*, which pre-dated the Mongols, was outside the walls, to the north:[58] Shams al-Dīn Kart the Elder summoned here the "entire population of Herat."[59] The existence of two *ʿīdgāh*s—one intramuros and one extramuros—reflects the imperative to provide for the religious needs of Herat's growing population.[60]

Fakhr al-Dīn built a Sufi convent (sgl. *khānaqāh*) and refurbished neighborhood mosques, including the Greengrocers' Mosque. He donated

[51] Allen, *Catalogue*, 51, Cat. No. 98; cf. Isfizārī, *Rawżāt*, 1:78. Possibly the location labeled "Pferdemarkt-Platz" in Oskar von Niedermayer's sketch of Herat (see Fig. 10.5).

[52] Ḥāfiẓ-i Abrū, *Kart*, 186.

[53] See Ibn Battuta, *Travels*, 3:594, 3:596; 2:478 (on horse trade).

[54] Shadab Bano, "India's overland slave trade in the medieval period," *PIHC* 58 (1997):315–21; idem, "Slave markets in medieval India," *PIHC* 61 (2000):365–73. Details are scarce.

[55] Rahil Alipour, "Persian crucible steel production: Chāhak tradition" (Ph.D. thesis, University College London, 2016). On Chāhak, see Le Strange, *Lands*, 278, 287.

[56] Marco Polo/Yule (tr.), *Travels*, 1:86.

[57] *ʿīdgāh* is an agoronym. Allen (*Catalogue*, 157) views *ʿīdgāh* as a "functional term."

[58] Allen, *Catalogue*, 157–58.

[59] al-Harawī, *Harāt*, 310 (reported under 662/1263f.).

[60] On Bukhara's pre-Mongol *ʿīdgāh*, see Abū Bakr Muḥammad b. Jaʿfar Narshakhī, *The History of Bukhara*, tr. R.N. Frye (Cambridge, MA: Mediaeval Academy of America, 1954), 52–53; idem, *Tārīkh-i Bukhārā*, eds. Muḥammad b. Zafar ibn ʿUmar and Mudarris Rażawī ([Kabul]: Intishārāt-i wizārat-i iṭṭilāʿāt wa kultūr, 1362/1983), 71–73.

substantial funds for the daily provision of 1,000 *mann* (2,970 kg/6,534 lb) of bread and ten head of sheep for *āsh* (potage), winter cloaks and such, for the indigent, infirm, orphans, and darwishes. Travelers and itinerant holy men were to be accommodated at his *khānaqāh*.[61]

Fakhr al-Dīn Kart was ostensibly pious. Every week he visited his *khānaqāh* to meet with darwishes for intellectual and spiritual exchanges (*ṣuḥbat*).[62] He may have been a Sufi by training. He patronized cemeteries, but it is not clear what this patronage entailed. The funds were possibly used to ensure that the graveyards were maintained, the landscapes manicured, and vicinities free of vagrants and addicts, so that anyone visiting the tomb of a loved one, or making a pilgrimage (sgl. *ziyārat*), was not harassed or displeased.

Herat's cemeteries hold the sanctified remains of eminent men and women. *Ziyārat* to the graves of holy persons was an ubiquitous pious activity.[63] A Timurid era hagiography depicts Herat as "the place where spirits thrive" (*arwāh-ābād*).[64] When Abāqā decreed that Herat be obliterated—an order nullified by rational minds—Sayfī ascribed the reprieve to Herat's surfeit of shaykhs, ulama, ascetics (*gūsha-nishīn-ān*; corner-sitters), and sanctified spaces.[65] Spiritual connections between Herat's ephemeral peoples and Herat's growing roster of spiritual and sepulchral sites have endured over the ages. Kings appreciated the imperative of patronizing culturally significant locales. A sepulchral landmark patronized by Fakhr al-Dīn is the tomb of Muḥammad Abū al-Walīd.[66]

61 al-Harawī, *Harāt*, 462–63.

62 In the Sufi sense, *ṣuḥbat* (*lit.*, companionship, discourse), is a complex and indispensable process in a Sufi's spiritual progress along the mystical Path.

63 A compilation of three guidebooks to sacred spaces is by Fikri Saljuqi, *Risāla-yi Mazārāt-i Harāt: Shāmil-i sih ḥiṣṣa* (Herat: Markaz-i nashrātī Fārūqī, 1379/2000), which includes, Sayyid Aṣīl al-Dīn Wā'iẓ ['Abd Allāh b. 'Abd al-Raḥmān al-Ḥusaynī], *Maqṣad al-iqbāl-i sulṭānīyah wa marṣad al-āmāl-i khāqānīyah*. Another key edition is: idem, *Maqṣad al-iqbāl*, ed. Mayīl Harawī (Tehran: Pizhūhishgāh-i 'ulūm-i insānī wa muṭāla'āt-i farhangī, 1386/2007).

64 Anon./Gūsha-Gīr, *Tāybādī*, 74.

65 al-Harawī, *Harāt*, 353. On sacred topography, see Mahendrarajah, *Sufi Saint*, 149ff.; Denise Aigle, "Among Saints and Poets: The Spiritual Topography of Shiraz," in Durand-Guedy, et al. (eds), *Medieval Iran*, pp. 142–76. On Timurid Herat's "geography of sanctity," see R.K. Salikuddin, "Sufis, Saints, and Shrine: Piety in the Timurid Period, 1370–1507" (Ph.D. diss., Harvard University, 2018), 186–233, esp. 198–217 and Figures 2, 5–7 (locations of sites).

66 See Allen, *Catalogue*, Cat. No. 573; Wā'iẓ/Harawī, *Maqṣad*, 15–16; Wā'iẓ/Saljūqī, *Maqṣad*, 45–46. A.W. Najimi, "The restored mausoleum of Abu'l-Walid in Herat: Challenges in heritage restoration in Afghanistan," *Afghanistan* 1/2 (2018):302–36.

Ghiyāth al-Dīn Kart sponsored and endowed two *khānaqāhs*. His most important project was the restoration of the Ghurid era *Masjid-i jami*ʿ, now over 800 years old. The Friday Mosque is a reconstruction of an edifice ruined by fire,[67] meaning, a mosque has stood in this space for over one millennium. It is "Ghurid" because restorations began under the terminal Shansabānī dynasts.[68] An inscription transcribed by Fikrī Saljūqī in 1967 credits sultan Ghiyāth al-Dīn Muḥammad (d. 599/1203) with constructing it in 597/1200,[69] although work was completed under his son, Ghiyāth al-Dīn Maḥmūd (d. 609/1212). Sultan Ghiyāth al-Dīn was interred inside a *gunbad/gunbad-khāna* (dome; dome-chamber) that he erected beside the mosque.[70] It was called the "Dome of the Kings" (*gunbad-i malik-ān*) in the Kartid era. Kartid *maliks* are supposedly entombed therein.

The Ghurid sultan Ghiyāth al-Dīn also sponsored the *Madrasa-yi Ghiyāthiyya* (built *c.* 597–99/1200–03),[71] to the north of the mosque. The construction of *Madrasa-yi Ghiyāthiyya* was erroneously attributed to Ghiyāth al-Dīn Muḥammad Kart by Christine Noelle-Karimi: "Apart from rebuilding the mosque 'better and stronger than before', Malik Ghiyāth al-Dīn ordered a college, the Madrasa-yi Ghiyāthīya, to be constructed along its northern side."[72] The Kartid only restored the seminary, allegedly at Öljeitü's behest;[73] but probably of his own volition since the Kartids connected their House to the Ghurids.

[67] The mosque's history is in Allen, *Catalogue*, 103–11; Lisa Golombek, "The Resilience of the Friday Mosque: the Case of Herat," *Muqarnas* 1 (1983):95–102; Bernard O'Kane, *Timurid Architecture in Khurasan* (Costa Mesa, Calif.: Mazda, 1987), 353–57, Cat. No. 58; Fikrī Saljūqī, *Bakhshī az tārikh-i Harāt-i bāstān* (Kabul: Maṭbaʿa-i dawlatī, 1362/1983), 12–34; Ḥāfiẓ-i Abrū, *Kart*, 191–92; Guya Itemadi [Gūyā ʿIttimādī], "The General Mosque of Herat," *Afghanistan* 8/2 (Kabul, 1953):40–50.

[68] C.E. Bosworth, "Ghurids," *EIr*, 10:586–90, and Table 1.

[69] Fikri Saljooqi [Fikrī Saljūqī], "The complete copy of the ancient inscription of the Ghiassuddin grand mosque in Herat," *Afghanistan* 20/3 (Kabul, 1967):78–80.

[70] Saljūqī, *Harāt-i bāstān*, 36–37; Wāʾiẓ/Harawī, *Maqṣad*, 40–41.

[71] Allen, *Catalogue*, 131, Cat. No. 460; Wāʾiẓ/Saljūqī, *Maqṣad*, 78; cf. Wāʾiẓ/Harawī, *Maqṣad*, 40–41.

[72] Noelle-Karimi, *Pearl*, 19; cf. Allen, *Catalogue*, 131: Allen flags the mistaken attribution to Khʷāndamīr/Siyāqī (ed.), *Ḥabīb*, 3:379; Khʷāndamīr/Thackston (tr.), *Habib*, 219; Ghiyāth al-Dīn Khʷāndamīr, *Faṣlī az khulāṣat al-akhbār*, ed. Gūyā ʿIttimādī ([Kabul]: Maṭbaʿa-i dawlatī, 1345/1967), 14. See also al-Samarqandī, *Maṭlaʿ-i saʿdayn*, 1.1:124.

[73] al-Harawī, *Ṭarīq-i qismat*, 6.

Returning to Kartid restorations at the *Masjid-i jami*ʿ, Terry Allen quotes extensively from Sayfī's glowing report on Ghiyāth al-Dīn's renovations to the Friday Mosque.[74] Allen's translation and commentary should be read in their entirety. The gist is that the mosque had been dilapidated for decades, having suffered damage and neglect in the post-Mongol period. It urgently needed prophylactic restorations, which it received only under Ghiyāth al-Dīn, along with aesthetic refurbishments. A forceful earthquake struck Herat, 6 Jumādá I, 765/10 February 1364,[75] which severely damaged edifices throughout the Herat region, and collapsed the Friday Mosque's *ṭāq* (arch), leaving only its two supporting pillars (*pāʾī-yi ṭāq*). Muʿizz al-Dīn Kart repaired it, along with other impaired structures.[76]

Muʿizz al-Dīn and his (evidently) favorite wife, Sulṭān-Khātūn, were supporters of Herati Sufis. The pair patronized four *khānaqāh*s;[77] but nothing is known of the spiritual or juridical orientations of the four. One hospice was erected to honor the memory of Quṭb al-Dīn (Abū Naṣr) Yaḥyá Jāmī Nīshāpūrī (d. 740/1339), Nishapur's Chief Justice.[78] Yaḥyá was one of the eminent progeny of Aḥmad-i Jām.[79] He is buried outside the Firūzābād Gate,[80] possibly in the eponymous *khānaqāh*.

Yaḥyá had attended the congress at Sulṭān-Maydān that selected Ṭaghā-Temür as the nominal suzerain. He was (as noted earlier) supportive of Ṭaghā-Temür: when Arghūn-Shāh incarcerated him, Yaḥyá advocated for his release. It is not difficult to visualize the hand of the influential Sulṭān-Khātūn behind the *malik*'s benefaction. Moreover, Yaḥyá had associated closely with ʿAlāʾ al-Dawla Simnānī (d. 735/1336) and Ṣafī al-Dīn Ardabīlī (d. 735/1334); and had influential interlocutors with whom he corresponded; for instance, the Khalji sultan of Delhi, Jalāl al-Dīn Fīrūzshāh (r. 689–95/1290–96);[81] and the Ilkhanid vizier, Ghiyāth al-Dīn

74 al-Harawī, *Harāt*, 742–43; Allen, *Catalogue*, 105.

75 Faṣīḥ, *Mujmal*, 959 (precise date); N.N. Ambraseys and C.P. Melville, *A History of Persian Earthquakes* (Cambridge: Cambridge University Press, 1982), 44.

76 Ḥāfiẓ-i Abrū, *Kart*, 191; Allen, *Catalogue*, 105–06.

77 Allen, *Catalogue*, Cat. Nos. 493, 503, 513, 520.

78 ʿAbd al-Raḥman Jāmī, *Nafaḥāt al-uns min ḥażarāt al-quds*, ed. Mihdī Tawḥīdī-Pūr (Tehran: Intishārāt-i kitābfurūshī-i Maḥmūdī, 1336/1957), 577–78; Zanganah, *Sarzamīn-i Jām*, 137–39.

79 Būzjānī, *Rawżat*, 115–18; Mahendrarajah, *Sufi Saint*, 112 and Figure A1.2.

80 Būzjānī, *Rawżat*, 117; Allen, *Catalogue*, Cat. Nos. 493.

81 Yūsuf-i Ahl/Moayyad (ed.), *Farāʾid*, 1:89–93.

Muḥammad (d. 736/1336) b. Rashīd al-Dīn Fażlallāh (d. 718/1318).[82] He is said to attended the convocation at which Öljeitü had designated Abū Saʿīd Bahādur Khān as his political heir (*walī-ʿahd*). Yaḥyá delivered the homily (*waʿẓ*) to the assembly.[83]

Muʿizz al-Dīn patronized just one seminary in Herat, *Madrasa-yi Sabz-i Fīrūzābādi*.[84] *Khānaqāhs* were more prominent than seminaries before the Timurid era, which reflects, inter alia, the interests of patrons, administrators, lecturers, and students; and the absence of clear lines demarcating curricula at seminaries from curricula at hospices. By the end of Herat's Timurid age, seminaries had attained supremacy over hospices by a ratio of about two to one.[85] Pīr ʿAlī Kart secured his anti-Shiʿa fatwa from a Ḥanafī madrasa in Herat.[86] It is possible the ulama that issued it were associated with Sabz-i Fīrūzābād college.

## Functions of Economic and Public Spaces

A false dichotomy is implied in the above classifications of commercial structures and non-commercial structures. Secondary *functions* exist for *economic spaces* (bazaars and caravansarays) and for *public spaces* (cisterns, hammams, hospices, seminaries, mosques). Economic spaces had social, cultural, and political functions; while select public spaces had economic functions.[87] The histories of Yazd are rich in social and economic information.[88] They help in understanding the logic intrinsic to building projects at Herat; for example, Ghiyāth al-Dīn's sponsorship of cistern, hammam, and caravansaray had intrinsic logic: the components are not disconnected or random choices. The constituents collectively exhibit synergies or mutualisms. Benefactions of hammam plus reservoir (or water-well or *kārīz*) for a bazaar or caravansary recurs in post-Mongol Yazd.

82 Ibid., 2:23–24, 25–30.

83 Būzjānī, *Rawżat*, 117.

84 Allen, *Catalogue*, 137, Cat. No. 484.

85 See explanation in Mahendrarajah, *Sufi Saint*, 165–67.

86 Ḥāfiẓ-i Abrū, *Kart*, 196.

87 Kimia Ghasemia, et al., "The livability of Iranian and Islamic cities considering the nature of traditional land uses in the city and the rules of their settlement," *Habitat International* 90 (August 2019):1–14. Table 1: features of physical structures (mosques, bazaars, etc.) by *space* (religious, economic, political, public, etc.) and by *function* (primary v. secondary).

88 Jaʿfarī, *Tārīkh-i Yazd*; Kātib, *Tārīkh-i jadīd-i Yazd*.

A.W. Najimi noted that early modern Herat had cisterns scattered across its wards. Larger cisterns were near, or attached to, religious and public buildings. Heratis without access to wells were usually no more than 200 meters from a cistern. Professional water-carriers and children transported water.[89] Medieval Yazd had manifold and diverse water reserves (termed *chāh*, *ḥawż*, *ḥawż-khāna*, *pāyāb*, *qullatayn*).[90] Benefactions for economic and public spaces often included water supply and/or storage. The term *siqāyah* (to supply cups of water to the public) is often found.[91] Public access to potable water was a policy goal for benefactors. We may reason that while the chief purpose of Ghiyāth al-Dīn's cistern was to sustain components of the bazaar network, the cistern will have been utilized by residents, too. There probably were water stores in every ward of Kartid Herat. Business and Islamic institutions would have shared some of their water supplies with neighbors.

Hammams were central to social and economic life in Persian cities. Public steam baths were crucial for the maintenance of hygiene; adherence to religious prescriptions on ablutions; visited before or after major life events (circumcision, birth, marriage). Barbers, shavers, beard dyers, head-shavers, and masseurs operated inside hammams.[92] Merchants transacted inside the baths; attendees shared news, rumors, and gossip.

Caravansarays were not just economic loci for merchants. They brought locals and visitors together for social/religious interactions. Mosques near bazaars offered spiritual succor: the Greengrocers' Mosque (*Masjid-i tarrah-furūshi*) was intramuros (but its location is uncertain).[93] Herat's *Masjid-i jāmiʿ* served the Khūsh Bazaar. Bazaar members (*bāzārī*; sgl. *bāzāra*; pl. *bāzārgān*) and business visitors could transact, attend prayers, *dhikr*, and lectures at nearby mosques, Sufi hospices, and Islamic colleges.

A caravansaray, warehouse, or shop is a *primary* feature of Herat's bazaar network. Mosques, hospices, madrasas, teahouses, eateries, lodgings, stables, cisterns, hammams, and latrines comprise the network's *secondary* and *tertiary*

[89] Najimi, "Cistern," 38. See also Samizay, *Islamic Architecture*, 115.
[90] *Qullatayn*: Arabic dual of *qullat*. Two large jars jointly holding *c.* 1,200 pints of water.
[91] See, e.g., Jaʿfarī, *Tārīkh-i Yazd*, 64.
[92] See, generally, W. Floor and W. Kleiss, "Bathhouses," *EIr*, 3:863–69.
[93] Allen, *Catalogue*, 117, Cat. No. 445: thought to be located in Malik Bazaar, but perhaps not.

features. As components were added to Herat's bazaar network, teahouses, eateries, lodgings, and public baths would have been inaugurated by entrepreneurs to serve visitors and residents.

## Supervision of Educational-Charitable Institutions and Public Buildings

Jalāl al-Dīn al-Qāyinī (d. 838/1435), Shāh-Rukh's *muḥtasib* (censor of morals) for Herat,[94] wrote in a didactic treatise of unknown social-political impacts, that pre-Timurid shaykhs al-Islam had supervised educational-charitable institutions (seminaries, hospices) and waqfs.[95] Irrespective of the title (*qāḍī* or shaykh) of the person doing the supervising, there had been supervision of Islamic institutions and pious endowments.

The duty is traceable to (at least) the time of Shaykh al-Islam ʿAbdallāh Anṣārī (d. 481/1089) of Herat. Anṣārī was responsible for setting in order "the affairs of darwishes, dependents, and *al-ghāliyyīn* by his own right;[96] and regulating seminaries, scholars, and hospices" (*ittisāq umūr al-murīdīn wa al-atbāʿ wa al-ghāliyyīn fī ḥaqq-hi wa intiẓām al-madāris wa al-aṣḥāb wa al-khwāniq*).[97]

### *Fakhr al-Dīn Kart*

Fakhr al-Dīn Kart, despite his sponsorship of spiritual and sepulchral spaces and execution of endowments, is not known to have appointed a *ṣadr*, *qāḍī*, or shaykh al-Islam to supervise Islamic institutions and waqfs. In 700/1300f., he appointed a *muḥtasib*, Shams al-Dīn Qādisī (fl. 700/1300f.),[98] whose

[94] On *muḥtasib*, see C. Cahen, et al., "Ḥisba," *EI*², 3:485–93, esp. 490–91 (A.K.S. Lambton on *muḥtasib* in Persia); Roy Mottahedeh and K. Stilt, "Public and private as viewed through the work of the '*Muhtasib*'," *Social Research* 70/3 (2003):735–48.

[95] Jalāl al-Dīn al-Qāyinī, *Naṣāʾiḥ-i Shāh-Rukhī* (Vienna: Nationalbibliothek, MS Cod. A.F. 112), fol. 126ᵃ–127ᵃ. On the title, see Subtelny, *Timurids*, 107–110.

[96] *Al-ghāliyyīn* (sgl. *ghālī*; usual pl. *ghulāt*): "zealots"? Given the sectarianism prevailing in Anṣārī's lifetime, quelling zealotry may have been in a Shaykh al-Islam's remit.

[97] ʿAbd al-Ghāfir b. Ismāʿīl Fārisī, *al-Mukhtaṣar min kitāb al-siyāq li-tārīkh Naysābūr*, ed. Muḥammad Kāẓim Maḥmūdī (Tehran: Mīrās-i maktūb, 1384/2005), 174–75; cf. idem, *al-Muntakhab min al-siyāq li-tārīkh Naysābūr*, eds Ibrāhīm b. Muḥammad Ṣarīfīnī and M.A. ʿAbd al-ʿAzīz (Beirut: Dār al-kutub al-ʿilmiyyah, 1989), 284–85. See Richard Bulliet, "The Shaikh al-Islām and the Evolution of Islamic Society," *Studia Islamica* 35 (1972):53–67, esp. 60–61; and Mahendrarajah, "Shaykh al-Islam," 275 and n.129.

[98] Qādis: not Spain's Cadiz. A region northeast of Herat. Adamec, *Gazetteer*, 3:213. A round-up of notables of the Kartid court is in Barzīn-Mihr, *Shuʿarā wa fuẓalāʾ*; Qādisī is not named.

mandate was the pitiless enforcement of morality laws.[99] Fakhr al-Dīn promulgated rules under the duty "to command the good and forbid the reprehensible" (*al-amr bi'l ma'rūf wa'l-nahy 'an al-munkar*). Alcohol consumption was allegedly pervasive. Qādisī enforced prohibition. Women were barred from leaving their homes alone (male relatives were punished if they failed to restrain the women). Gamblers and inebriates were severely punished (bastinado, corvée, jail, public humiliation).[100] While this—and probably worse—was being inflicted on Heratis, hedonism flourished within the Kartid court: the unbridled pursuit of the pleasures of wine, cannabis, courtesans, and catamites.[101]

These edicts apparently expired along with the legislator, although nephew Mu'izz al-Dīn tried to propagate some variant of this policy (see below). The implementation of strict morality laws was not unusual for this geographical space or epoch: Shams al-Dīn 'Alī the Sarbadarid implemented exacting ordinances (Chapter Five), presumably under *al-amr bi'l ma'rūf wa'l-nahy 'an al-munkar*. In Shiraz, Kartid contemporary Mubāriz al-Dīn Muḥammad Muẓaffar (d. 766/1364) earned the epithet *muḥtasib*, the enmity of commoners, blinding by his own son, and enduring ridicule in Hafiz's verses (for instance, "Drink not wine to the strains of the harp, for the inspector (*muḥtasib*) is awake").[102]

*Ghiyāth al-Dīn Kart*

Qāḍī Ṣadr al-Dīn b. Fakhr al-Dīn Khaysārī (fl. 721/1321f.) was appointed as the chief judge of Herat (*hukūmat-i qāḍā'-i mamālik-i Harāt*) by Ghiyāth al-Dīn Kart. Since this involved the ouster of an office-holder, a dispute followed, which Öljeitü resolved in Ghiyāth al-Dīn's favor. Khaysārī's remit

[99] On this *muḥtasib*'s activities, see Gammell, *Pearl*, 39. *Muḥtasib*s had, inter alia, oversight of public spaces, such as ensuring the cleanliness of mosques (Mottahedeh & Stilt, "Public," 744). It is unclear what Qādisī did apart from enforcing morality laws.

[100] al-Harawī, *Harāt*, 464–65. *Al-amr bi'l ma'rūf* became a blunt weapon under the Wahhabi regime in Saudi Arabia. See Cook, *Commanding Right*, 165–92. The Saudi model was adopted, with modifications, by a major Saudi client, the Taliban (1994–2001).

[101] Khwāndamīr/Siyāqī (ed.), *Ḥabīb*, 3:371–72, 376–78; Khwāndamīr/Thackston (tr.), *Habib*, 215, 218–19; Ghiyāth al-Dīn Khwāndamīr, *Rijal-i kitab-i Ḥabīb al-siyar*, ed. 'Abd al-Ḥusayn Nawā'ī (Tehran: Anjuman-i āsār wa mafākhir-i farhangī, 1379/2000), 78–81. Described in vivid prose in Gammell, *Pearl*, 40–41.

[102] Limbert, *Shiraz*, 36–37.

(based on the purported text of Öljeitü's decree) came to encompass (on paper if not in actuality) the bulk of the Kartid realm.

Authority vested in Khaysārī's office included oversight of social-religious positions such as prayer leader, sermonizer, and shaykh al-Islam; religious-political offices as inspector (*muḥtasib*) of weights and measures; supervision of mosques, seminaries, hospices, and the trustees of pious endowments (*mansab-i qāḍāʾ wa khaṭābat wa imāmat wa iḥtisāb wa shaykh al-Islāmī wa taṣarruf-i manābir wa masājid wa madāris wa khānqāh-āt wa tawliyat-i awqāf*). Sayyids, Sufis, scholars, imams, and *raʿāyā* had to assist him and defer to and obey him in all matters without exception (*sabīl-i aʾimma wa sadāt wa muʿārif wa aṣḥāb-i manāṣib wa ʿumūm-i raʿāyā* [...] *dar riʿāyat janāb-i aw hīch daqīqa az daqāʾīq-i muṭāwaʿat wa muẓāharat farū na-guzār-and*).[103]

By the middle of Ghiyāth al-Dīn Kart's reign there evidently were a number of active mosques, seminaries, hospices, and waqfs in Herat and beyond that required supervision by a senior judge or shaykh al-Islam, that is, Qāḍī Khaysārī.

*Muʿizz al-Dīn Kart*

Young and hubristic Muʿizz al-Dīn Kart claimed bombastically of waging "holy war against infidels" (*jihād bā kuffār*); implementing *al-amr biʾl maʿrūf waʾl-nahy ʿan al-munkar* "in the entire country" (*jamīʿ-i bilād*); and discarding "infidel [= Mongol] customs (*rasūm*) that persist in Islamic lands" (*bilād-i Islām*). His removal from office by the Chaghataids (from *c.* 752/1351 to 753/1353) expelled the gas from that balloon. Nonetheless, while the details of Muʿizz al-Dīn Kart's social and religious policies in Herat cannot be described, it is evident he favored an active role in furthering religious and social policies in Herat. Ḥāfiẓ-i Abrū's opinion is that the *malik* was virtuous and strived to rectify injustices and promote Islamic law and rectitude.[104] His views can be tested against information on the perspectives and activities of the Kartid's religious-political appointees.

103 al-Harawī, *Harāt*, 617–21. Faṣīḥ, *Mujmal*, 891–92 (under 715/1315f.). On Khaysarī, see also Muḥammad Ismāʿīl Mablagh Gharjistānī, "Niwīsandi-gān, Dānishmand-ān, Ṣūfī-ān muʿāṣir-i dūdmān-i Kart [Writers, Scholars, and Sufis contemporary with the Kart rulers]," *Āryānā* No. 204 (1338/1959):23–30, 27–28. Khaysarī joined the 721/1321 Hajj caravan. See al-Harawī, *Harāt*, 770.

104 See Ḥāfiẓ-i Abrū, *Kart*, 171.

The first such appointee is Shaykh al-Islam Niẓām al-Dīn ʿAbd al-Raḥīm Khʷāfī, who had assisted Muʿizz al-Dīn in devising a water-distribution system. Niẓām al-Dīn was based in Herat shortly after Muʿizz al-Dīn's reign commenced on 24 Ramażān 732/19 June 1332. He was zealous in faith and known as "the master of submission [to God]" (*pīr-i taslīm*). He implemented *al-amr biʾl maʿrūf waʾl-nahy ʿan al-munkar*. The shaykh fell afoul of Turkic tribal settlers at Bādghīs. Allegations were made that the Turks were acting unjustly and impiously. Niẓām al-Dīn anathemized (*takfīr*) them as infidels (*kufr*) in a fatwa.[105] Turkic chiefs marched on Herat in 738/1338. Muʿizz al-Dīn hunkered inside the citadel. Heratis, perhaps feeling little love for their enjoiner of the good and forbidder of the purportedly reprehensible, secured a fatwa (from someone) that said it was licit to sacrifice one life to save numerous lives. The judgment was handed to the Shaykh al-Islam, who perused it, performed his ablutions, dressed in clean clothes, and dutifully stepped outside the Malik Gate (northwest). He was killed and buried in the Khiyābān. The Turks left.[106]

It is not reported by Ḥāfiẓ-i Abrū, et al., if the late Shaykh al-Islam had oversight of hospices, seminaries, mosques, and Sufi shrines like his predecessor, Ṣadr al-Dīn Khaysārī. The foci of their reports are his polarizing opinions and dramatic demise.

An illustrious appointee of Muʿizz al-Dīn Kart is Shaykh al-Islam Saʿd al-Dīn Masʿūd (722–93/1322–90) b. ʿUmar b. ʿAbdallāh Taftāzānī. His appointment on 25 Jumādá I 750/11 August 1349,[107] to Muʿizz al-Dīn Kart's "office of the *ṣadr*" (*biʾl-ishārat al-ṣadārat ʿan ḥaḍrat al-malikiyya al-muʿizziyya*), was embodied in a royal decree (*manshūr-i humāyūn*) requiring him to work with an intimate (newly titled) Khʷājah-yi Jahān, Muʿīn al-Dīn Jāmī, to oversee the affairs of the state and faith (*umūr-i dīn wa dawlat*). The jurisprudential currents (*madhhab*) of Herat were diverse and included Twelver Shiʿa. Taftāzānī

105 *Takfīr*: *ipse dixit* labeling of Muslims as *kufr* is not used, but this is what Niẓām al-Dīn did. J.O. Hunwick, "*Takfīr*," *EI²*, 10:122. "Excommunication" by *takfīr* is used by Wahhabis against Sufis and Shiʿa; and Sunnis who disagree with their interpretations of Islam.

106 Ḥāfiẓ-i Abrū, *Kart*, 171; Khʷāndamīr/Siyāqī (ed.), *Ḥabīb*, 3:384–85; Khʷāndamīr/Thackston (tr.), *Habib*, 223; Khʷāndamīr, *Rijal*, 82–83; cf. Ibn Battuta, *Travels*, 3:577–80. See also Barzīn-Mihr, *Shuʿarā wa fuẓalā*ʾ, 79–80.

107 Yūsuf-i Ahl/Fatih, *Farāʾīd*, ff. 445ᵇ–447ᵇ; idem/Aya Sofya, *Farāʾīd*, ff. 97ᵃ–98ᵇ; idem/Berlin, *Farāʾīd*, ff. 289ᵃ–291ᵇ; idem/Tehran, *Farāʾīd*, pp. 620–23.

was proficient in Ḥanafī and Shāfiʿī jurisprudence, but "personally adhered to the Hanafi school."[108] The Ḥanafī path was presumably dominant in Herat by 750/1349, but his authority, although not specified, was assuredly not limited to oversight of just Ḥanafī or Shāfiʿī colleges. ʿAbdallāh Anṣārī, for instance, was Ḥanbalī, but supervised seminaries oriented to other *madhhabs*. In any event, Taftāzānī was designated as the *imām* (*imāmī farmāʾīm*),[109] and tasked with guiding the social classes and institutions itemized below, and ensuring that none deviated from the paths of justice and equity (*wa āz shawāriʿ-yi ʿadl wa jāda-yi inṣāf-i mā inḥirāf na-namāʾīd*).

Taftāzānī's duties included: lifting up the oppressed and striking down wrongdoers (*wa dar iʿānat-i maẓlūm-ān wa qamʿ-i ẓālim-ān*); assisting in rebuilding the provinces (*ʿimārat-i wilāyāt*); encouraging *raʿāyā* in maintaining rectitude and following the right path (*istimālat-i raʿāyā-i malālat bih-khūd rāh na-dihad*); fostering the well-being (*wa dar tarfīh*) of holy men (*arbāb-i khayr*) and welfare of mosques, seminaries, and hospices engaged in virtuous affairs (*wa rawnaq-i masājid wa madāris wa khawāniq-i masāʿī-yi jamīla*). Taftāzānī had to honor Sharia court judges (*wa dar taʿẓīm wa tawqīr-i quḍāt-i Islām*); esteem sayyids, ulama, and Sufi shaykhs (*taʿẓīm wa tabjīl-i sādāt wa mashāʾikh wa ʿulamāʾ-yi rāsikh*); and assist each (of the foregoing) in fulfilling their obligations and collecting their emoluments (*waẓāʾif wa marāsim-i ishān rā bar mawāżī-yi sahl al-ḥuṣūl marjū al-wuṣūl taʿyīn kardih bar-rasānad*). The shaykh al-Islam was to submit reports (to the *malik*) on the welfare of the state, because the oppressed should be protected from the oppressors (*wa hamagī aḥwāl-i mamālik bih ʿarż mī-rasānad tā ham maẓlūm-ān az ẓālim-ān īman bāsh-and*).[110]

It is not known for how long this political-religious battery operated in Herat. The transitory deposition of Muʿizz al-Dīn Kart followed in 752/1351. Taftāzānī went on to live peripatetically, but he remained in communication with the court.[111] Saʿd al-Dīn Masʿūd was not appointed to the office

[108] Wilferd Madelung, "Taftazani," *EI²*, 10:88–89. See also Thomas Würtz, *Islamische Theologie im 14. Jahrhundert* (Berlin: de Gruyter, 2016), 17–36; Barzīn-Mihr, *Shuʿarā wa fuẓalāʾ*, 69–77.

[109] *Imām*: guide to Muslims without the significance of the title in the Shiʿa context.

[110] Yūsuf-i Ahl/Fatih, *Farāʾid*, f. 447ᵃ; idem/Aya Sofya, *Farāʾid*, ff. 98ᵃ–98ᵇ; idem/Berlin, *Farāʾid*, ff. 291ᵃ–291ᵇ; idem/Tehran, *Farāʾid*, p. 623. I thank Saqib Baburi for help with this text.

[111] See, e.g., his letters in Yūsuf-i Ahl/Moayyad (ed.), *Farāʾid*, 1:259–61 (to Muʿizz al-Dīn Kart); and 1:463–70 and 1:490–93 (to Pīr ʿAlī Kart).

(*manṣab*) of shaykh al-Islam, but his title as given in Muʿizz al-Dīn's decree is shaykh al-Islam; moreover, Taftāzānī's duties and obligations parallel those of other shaykhs al-Islam in Islamic history.[112] It is quite likely that he was the de facto or de jure shaykh al-Islam of Herat.

Jalāl al-Dīn Maḥmūd Imāmī (d. 782/1380–81), Chief Justice (*qāḍī al-quḍāt*) of Herat, was another of Muʿizz al-Dīn Kart's enduring appointments.[113] Just as Taftāzānī's progeny held the position of Shaykh al-Islam of Herat until the implementation of Safawid rule,[114] Imāmī's progeny retained the position of Chief Justice, with one fleeting interlude, until the Safawid conquest.[115] The Chief Justice will have had close interactions with the vizier,[116] and Shaykh al-Islam and Ṣadr al-Sharīʿa of Herat.

Ṣadr al-Sharīʿa was a late Kartid era post about which little is known with respect to remit. *Ṣadr*,[117] and its intensive form, *ṣadr al-ṣudūr* ("*ṣadr* of *ṣadrs*"), represented holders of social, religious, political, and (sometimes) administrative authority in Transoxiana. Title bearers tended to be Ḥanafī. *Ṣadr al-sharīʿa* was an enduring title in Bukhara.

Ibn Battuta, in Bukhara (*c.* 733/1333?), claims, "I met on this occasion the learned and virtuous jurist Ṣadr al-Sharīʿa; he had come from Harāt and is a pious and learned man."[118] Edmund Bosworth suggested this was Ṣadr al-Sharīʿa ʿUbayd-Allāh b. Masʿūd al-Maḥbūbī (d. 747/1346).[119] This is possible: "come from" Herat could mean "returned from" Herat. There are four letters in *Farāʾid* from an unnamed Ṣadr al-Sharīʿa, each directed to an unnamed *qāḍī*;[120] the letters are tentatively dated to Muʿīn al-Dīn Jāmī's

112 Mahendrarajah, "Shaykh al-Islam," *et passim.*

113 Khʷāndamīr/Siyāqī (ed.), *Ḥabīb*, 3:385; Khʷāndamīr/Thackston (tr.), *Habib*, 223; Khʷāndamīr, *Rijal*, 83; Zanganah, *Sarzamīn-i Jām*, 141–42 (terse notice).

114 The first Shiʿi shaykh al-Islam of Herat was installed in 928/1521f. He was also Chief Justice. Khʷāndamīr/Siyāqī (ed.), *Ḥabīb*, 4:610; Khʷāndamīr/Thackston (tr.), *Habib*, 627.

115 Manz, *Timurid Iran*, 212.

116 The Jāmī, Imāmī, and Taftāzānī families remained close until the end of the Timurid era. There are letters in *Farāʾid* between the vizier and one *qāḍī* Jalāl al-Dīn in Herat, but since they lack specifics, they cannot be connected with certainty to *the* Qāḍī Imāmī. See Yūsuf-i Ahl/Moayyad (ed.), *Farāʾid*, 2:347–48 and 2:389–91.

117 C.E. Bosworth, "*Ṣadr*," *EI²*, 8:748–50; idem, "Āl-e Borhān," *EIr*, 1:753–54.

118 Ibn Battuta, *Travels*, 3:554 (misidentified in translator's n.56 as Ṣadr al-Dīn Khaysārī).

119 Bosworth, "*Ṣadr*," 8:749b. Faṣīḥ, *Mujmal*, 936 (genealogy and decease). There is a letter from Yaḥyá Jāmī Nīshāpūrī to Ṣadr al-Sharīʿa, which appears to be the ʿUbayd-Allāh of Bukhara. See Yūsuf-i Ahl/Moayyad (ed.), *Farāʾid*, 2:609–10.

120 Yūsuf-i Ahl/Moayyad (ed.), *Farāʾid*, 2:349–50, 2:351–52, 2:353–54, 2:355–56.

vizierate. There is no reason why the *ṣadārat* (office of *ṣadr*) and *ṣadr al-sharīʿa* could not have thrived in Kartid Herat. Kartids borrowed titles/offices from the Delhi Sultanate (e.g., Khʷājah-yi Jahān).[121] Why not one from Bukhara?[122] The Ṣadr al-Sharīʿa who penned a couplet (*bayt*) in praise of Muʿizz al-Dīn Kart was definitely not the Bukharan Ṣadr al-Sharīʿa: "Abū al-Fatḥ, sultan of all sultans, by whom the House of Kart, progeny of Sanjar gained glory."[123] This panegyrist lived contemporaneous with Muʿizz al-Dīn.[124] Heshmat Moayyad suspected that the Kartid Ṣadr al-Sharīʿa (or at least one of them) was Saʿd al-Dīn Kālūnī.[125] He was a contemporary of Ilkhanid vizier ʿAlāʾ al-Dīn Hindū (d. 722/1322f.), to whom he penned a missive.[126]

### *Pīr ʿAlī Kart*

In a Rabīʿ II 782/5 July–2 August 1380 decree, Pīr ʿAlī Kart appointed the vizier's son, Shaykh al-Islam Żiyā al-Dīn Yūsuf Jāmī (d. 797/1394f.),[127] as *ṣadr* of Herat. His office (*ṣadārat*) had supervisory authority over appointed religious-political positions such as *muḥtasib* and *qādī*; and (possibly appointed) religious positions such as prayer leader (imam) and sermonizer (*khaṭīb*);[128] dignitaries (for instance, sayyids and shaykhs), for Herat and its dependencies. Decisions on judicial proceedings; curricula; the Friday sermon (*khuṭba*); the office for the supervision of weights and measures (*iḥtisāb*); administration of pious endowments (pl. *awqāf*); and the inspectorship of finance (*ishrāf*) and the treasury (*bayt al-māl*), and related appointments, terminations, etc., had to be approved by him.[129]

121 There are letters in *Farāʾid* to the Indian Khʷājah-yi Jahān.
122 A title from Transoxiana, Ṣadr-i Jahān, was held by Ṣadr al-Dīn Aḥmad Zanjānī (fl. 1298), a vizier under Geikhatu (r. 1291–95).
123 Mīrkhʷānd, *Rawżat*, 3,686; Khʷāndamīr/Siyāqī (ed.), *Ḥabīb*, 3:367; Khʷāndamīr/Thackston (tr.), *Habib*, 213 (my translation in slightly different from Thackston's).
124 Barzīn-Mihr, *Shuʿarā wa fuẓalāʾ*, 83; Muḥammad Ismāʿīl Mablagh Gharjistānī, "ʿUrafāʾ [Associates]," *Āryānā* No. 206 (1338/1960):48–56, 51.
125 Yūsuf-i Ahl/Moayyad (ed.), *Farāʾid*, 2:352, n.* (Moayyad's annotations).
126 Ibid., 2:60–62. There are other letters relating to Kālūnī. See ibid., 2:58–59, 2:411–420.
127 On him, see Mahendrarajah, *Sufi Saint*, 66, 145, 178 and Fig A1.3 and Fig A1.5.
128 Imams and *khaṭībs* were ordinarily not appointed by a ruler, but candidates may have been nominated or endorsed by local notables (amirs, judges, shaykhs al-Islam).
129 Yūsuf-i Ahl/Berlin, *Farāʾid*, ff. 303b–305a; idem/Fatih, *Farāʾid*, ff. 457b–458b; idem/Tehran, *Farāʾid*, pp. 642–44. See transcription and analysis in Gottfried Herrmann, "Zur Entstehung des Ṣadr-Amtes," in *Die Islamische Welt zwischen Mittelalter und Neuzeit*, eds Ulrich Haarmann and P. Bachmann (Beirut: Franz Steiner Verlag, 1979), 278–95.

Pīr ʿAlī Kart appointed Żiyā al-Dīn Yūsuf Jāmī at a thorny moment in Herat's religious politics. Zayn al-Dīn Taybādī, for instance, was running a vociferous anti-Pīr ʿAlī campaign, which will have resonated within Herat's religious circles (see Chapter Six). Żiyā al-Dīn Yūsuf was the chief of Aḥmad-i Jām's *khānaqāh*, protégé of Saʿd al-Dīn Masʿūd Taftāzānī,[130] and ally of Taybādī. Pīr ʿAlī made the appointment to appease his critics and demonstrate his piety and devotion to an Islamic agenda. The *ṣadārat* amounted to naught: Żiyā al-Dīn Yūsuf Jāmī was escorting Temür on his pilgrimage to the shrine of Aḥmad-i Jām five months after the appointment. He later accompanied Temür on campaign as spiritual advisor.

A *ṣadr*'s obligations as detailed in Pīr ʿAlī's decree are not materially divergent from the core obligations of ʿAbdallāh Anṣārī al-Harawī, Ṣadr al-Dīn Khaysārī, Saʿd al-Dīn Masʿūd Taftāzānī, and probably other appointees (Ṣadr al-Sharīʿa and Qāḍī al-quḍāt): oversight of hospices, seminaries, mosques; supervision of religious personnel and pious endowments. From Fakhr al-Dīn to Ghiyāth al-Dīn to Muʿizz al-Dīn to Pīr ʿAlī—four reigns that spanned eighty-six years—Kartids saw fit to install *qādīs*, *muḥtasibs*, *ṣadrs*, shaykhs al-Islam and such to supervise Islamic institutions and/or to regulate social-religious life in Herat.

Certain of the ordinances promulgated by Kartids seem draconian to modern eyes; and rhetoric on protecting the oppressed from oppressors appear melodramatic. However, this type of rhetoric and legislation served to institute structure and direction to a society experiencing anomie in the wake of depredations by Mongols, Nikudaris, and Chaghataids. Legislation and religious-political positions (Ṣadr al-Sharīʿa, Shaykh al-Islam, *muḥtasib*, *qāḍī*, etc.) were intended to fashion, as the enacting Kartid *malik* interpreted His Message, a just and equitable society under God.

[130] Taftāzānī educated Żiyā al-Dīn. Mahendrarajah, *Sufi Saint*, 178.

# 10

# Fortified Landscape of Herat and its Environs

> We shall make him climb the town walls, which are as high as mountains[,] until the nails of his ten fingers are worn away [...]. We shall make him climb the town walls[,] which are made of hard-pounded earth.[1]

## The Fortified City

Herein lies the Mongols' fear of sedentary peoples and their fortifications; fear born of bitter experiences in China,[2] which cost Mongols blood and treasure. The Mongols came to excel at siege warfare with the benefit of Chinese siege engineers and technologies; and by using sedentary people against their own fortifications ("arrow-fodder" as John Masson Smith put it). The Mongols' fears, however, were well rooted. Hence their opposition to the rebuilding of Herat's fortifications.

Fahkr al-Dīn launched projects in 699/1299–1300 to fortify Herat.[3] Nikudari raids and Mongol threats to his power lent urgency to his fortification ventures. In so doing he was defying the Mongols and their opposition to rebuilding in Herat, much less rebuilding fortifications. A central project was Herat's citadel, Qalʿa-yi Ikhtiyār al-Dīn, which is named after commander (*sālār*) Ikhtiyār al-Dīn Muḥammad Hārūn (fl. 721/1321).[4] Development of trenches, walls, bastions, and gateways was Fahkr al-Dīn's related project.

[1] de Rachewiltz, *Secret History*, § 276; quoted in Smith, "Demographic Considerations."

[2] Analysis of the Mongols' travails in Asia is in Stephen Pow, "Fortresses that shatter empires: A look at Möngke Khan's failed campaign against the Song Dynasty, 1258–1259," *Annual of Medieval Studies at CEU* 23 (2017):96–107.

[3] al-Harawī, *Harāt*, 462–63; Ḥāfiẓ-i Abrū, *Kart*, 101; Mīrkhʷānd, *Rawżat*, 4,229; Isfizārī, *Rawżāt*, 1:437–38; Allen, *Catalogue*, 34, 228–31.

[4] *Sālār* Ikhtiyār al-Dīn (fl. 655/1257f.) served Shams al-Din Kart, but he is not the *sālār* that served Fakhr al-Dīn and Ghiyāth al-Dīn. It is unclear when the citadel acquired its name.

The dialectic of offense v. defense determines the character and physiognomy of fortifications.

*Offense and Defense*

Offense and defense are complementary facets in warfare: offensive strategies and tactics shift and shape defensive strategies and tactics. It applies not only to warfare, but also, for example, to American football, where the defensive team adapts to the offensive team's unfolding play. A maxim is that an attacker's/defender's methods *evolve* (based on lessons learned in combat—warfare is Darwinian), compelling the other side to *adapt*. The side that must adapt is (in theory) a step behind the evolved enemy; for example, if a new artillery piece can penetrate a two meter-thick rampart, then the wall must be thickened. Herat resisted Elǰigidei for over six months; but certain cities of Transoxiana and Khurasan fell to the Mongols relatively quickly. Nishapur's defenses had been weakened by Ghuzz attacks in the twelfth century;[5] hence Tolui's fairly swift breach of Nishapur's walls.

Öljeitü brought a range of ballistae, scaffolds, and scaling paraphernalia to besiege Herat in 698/1298f. Fakhr al-Dīn was cognizant of the latest in Ilkhanid siege equipment, arms, armor, and martial techniques: it is the atypical soldier who is not enthralled by, or envious of, the "toys" possessed by friends and foes. Enhancing fortifications to address new technical challenges is achieved by, inter alia, elevating towers, thickening ramparts, reinforcing embankments, and deepening and widening moats. Enhancing and repairing are continual processes: defenses that withstood mangonel strikes in 1300 may collapse in 1320 from strikes by newer artillery. Fortifications of city and citadel (in theory) would have been engineered by Kartid sappers/counter-sappers to resist the latest generation (*c.* 699/1299f.) in Ilkhanid siege technologies and techniques. "Latest generation," however, unveils a conundrum. How do we determine who held the qualitative edge in the offense-defense dialectic: Persians or Mongols? Where was the line between Ilkhanid technologies and techniques, and the Empire's military technologies and techniques? The line between indigenous (Ghurid, Herati, etc.) military innovations and Ilkhanid innovations? Although there were scientific exchanges between

[5] I owe this insight to Jürgen Paul.

Yüan China and Ilkhanid Persia, this was no one-way street. Inner Asians embraced Persian and Arab technologies and proficiencies.[6]

On the offense-defense dialectic, we can be certain of this: by 720/1320, Ghiyāth al-Dīn Kart's army was adept at siege warfare. Sayfī claims that the citadel at Mābīzhan-Ābād (Khʷāf) was the strongest in Khurasan and Iraq. Yet, after a siege of less than one week, it was surrendered out of respect for the Kartids' siege skills and willingness to employ them.[7] Given the inverse nature of siege/counter-siege, the report shows that Kartid army engineers had the expertise to design and develop robust fortifications.

### *Diffusion of Knowledge*

Diffusion of military technologies is assumed. Certain technologies and techniques were universal by 700/1300. Any qualified military engineer of medieval Persia will have known if square bastions were better suited for a circumstance than hemi-circular bastions; or if a trench should be trapezoidal or rectilinear. Arabic literature on the military sciences is extensive.[8] Asian and non-Asian manuals incorporate Persian, Greek, Roman, Arab, Turk, Indian, Mongol, Chinese, and Crusader technologies and techniques.

Any civilized society—Persia and its ingenious peoples qualify—had the intellectual wherewithal to design and erect continuous closed barriers (*enceinte*), trenches, gateways, and citadels. A ruler, however, had to have "the managerial and organizational skills and resources, and the ability to put thousands and even tens of thousands of men to work in a purposeful, coordinated fashion while simultaneously keeping then fed, clothed, housed and policed."[9] This is just what Fahkr al-Dīn did: he marshalled and directed intellectual, economic, and human resources.

A Euro-centric perspective is that Oriental peoples (namely, Persians) learned from "civilized" peoples (namely, Greeks and Romans), but even

6 Allsen, "Circulation of Military Technology," 265–93.

7 al-Harawī, *Harāt*, 755–57; Kempiners, "Struggle," 166. Majd al-Dīn Muḥammad Khʷāfī, the rebellious Kartid *banda*, probably realized that the defenses would eventually be breached; if the cost to the Kartids was too high, reprisals would be harsher.

8 George Scanlon, *A Muslim Manual of War* (New York: American University in Cairo Press, 2012), 6–20 (titles surveyed). The glossary contains mostly Arabic military terms.

9 Martin van Creveld, *Technology and War* (New York: The Free Press, 1991), 34. On fortress warfare and its technological foundations, see ibid., 33–43.

Alexander the Great borrowed from Persian generals.[10] If the tactics employed by the Sasanian shah, Khusraw I, Anushirvan (r. AD 531–79), as reported by Procopius (d.*c.* 560 AD) in *The Persian Wars* are indicative, Persians had much to teach the Romans; for example, bridging the Euphrates and catching Romans off-guard; and siege tactics against the fortified city of Edessa.[11] Persians and their military tactics were in the minds of Byzantine emperors if Procopius's book on Justinian's buildings is indicative.[12] Persians assuredly studied Byzantine manuals like *Strategikon* considering that their empires were in conflict—as when the book was composed (Book XI, § 1, is titled "Dealing with the Persians"!).[13]

Directly related to diffusion of knowledge are the roles of Ghurids in shaping Herat's defenses.[14] Ghaznavid sultan Masʿūd employed Ghurids as siege specialists.[15] Ghurids—the dominant force in the Kartid army—had the technical expertise and combat experiences from defending redoubts against Mongols. Ghurids, and Khurasanians, in general, will have introduced innovative defense strategies; molded the defensive arsenal arrayed, and tactics employed, along the citadel's battlements and city's perimeter defenses.

## Evidence on Herat's Fortifications

A reconstruction of Kartid era defenses is proffered below. Two notes: firstly, the evidence supplied by medieval historians is occluded in instances by terminological confusion (explained below). Secondly, I supply European terminologies if the Arabic or Persian word is generic; for example, *burj* (tower), where *barbican* (bastioned gateway) is the technical term. *Rukn* (pl. *arkān*; pillar or corner-stone) is properly, *bastion.*

10 A siege tactic used at Gaza (elucidated below).

11 Procopius, *History of the Wars*, tr. H.B. Dewing (London: Heinemann, 1914–19), Book II, § 21 (Euphrates), §§ 26–27 (Edessa). For context, see Daryaee, *Sasanian*, 30–31.

12 Procopius, *Buildings*, tr. H.B. Dewing (London: Heinemann, 1940), *et passim.*

13 Maurice, *Maurice's Strategikon*, tr. G.T. Dennis (Philadelphia: Univ. of Penn. Press, 1984).

14 Not just Ghurid but Khurasanian acumen. Khurasanian sappers specialized in mining Crusader castles. Ibn Munqidh, *An Arab-Syrian Gentleman and Warrior in the Period of the Crusades*, tr. P.K. Hitti (New York: Columbia University Press, 1929), 102–03, 188.

15 Bosworth, *Ghaznavids*, 121. On Ghūr as locus for armaments manufacturing and martial skills, see C.E. Bosworth, "Early Islamic History of Ghūr," *CAJ* 6/2 (1961):116–33.

### *The Physical Evidence*

The archaeological and architectural evidence is not entirely illuminating vis-à-vis Kartid defenses. This is not criticism of the fields, but rather, a commentary on the nature of materials: a trench circumvallating Herat was excavated; the earth removed was stacked for a second circumvallation: the embankment. The trench was reinforced in sections with stones, but stones, bricks, and beams are pilfered by denizens to build houses; trenches fill with rubbish and disappear. The defensive walls and the citadel were constructed of clay-and-straw plaster (*kāh-gil*),[16] gypsum mortar, and mud, materials that require maintenance, especially after storms and earthquakes. The archaeological evidence disappears over time. Herat was besieged in 1838 and 1857 by Persian armies. British military engineers seminally altered Herat's fortifications to withstand shelling by modern artillery.

### *The Historical Evidence*

Fakhr al-Dīn Kart enlisted *raʿāyā* from Āzāb, Bākharz, Fūshanj, Gharjistān, Ghūr, Harāt-Rūd, Herat, Isfizār, Kharih (Kurūkh), and Kūsūyi. Sayfī does not use *ḥashar* or *bīghār*, but the corvée is implied:[17] the diggers of trenches, haulers of stone, kneaders of clay, and stackers of earth—among other crucial but menial toils—will have been drawn from the ranks of peasants and laborers. However, *raʿāyā* is a broad term that includes specialists: Fakhr al-Dīn needed cooperative architects, engineers, carpenters, armorers, smiths, etc. Specialists are paid.[18] Development of a citadel complex and perimeter is expensive. Fakhr al-Dīn assuredly spared no expense in fortifying the city, his residence and court: Kartids (unlike Timurids) lived inside Qalʿa-yi Ikhtiyār al-Dīn.

It is necessary to sort out Sayfī's reports on Fakhr al-Dīn's projects. Sayfī has created ambiguities through four distinct reports. Did the Kartid even erect a citadel? It is not clear whether Fahkr al-Dīn erected the citadel from

[16] On building materials, see Beazley & Harverson, *Desert*, 11–22.
[17] Isfizārī, *Rawżāt*, 1:437, supplies the term *iḥẓār* (summoned or ordered).
[18] On the *malik*'s sources of funds, see Chapter 4, § "Reign of Fakhr al-Dīn Kart."

the foundations up; restored the pre-Mongol citadel;[19] or if someone else had done it, namely, Bulabān (r. 669–70/1270–71), the Ilkhanid governor appointed by Abāqā when Shams al-Dīn Kart the Elder fled to Khaysār following his ill-fated interactions with Baraq. Ḥāfiẓ-i Abrū says that Fakhr al-Dīn built the citadel in the reign of Il-Khan Ghāzān (d. 703/1304).[20] If so, it was standing by 703/1304.

Eljigidei had commanded that all major buildings be demolished (but not all were); the blocking of the trench (*khandaq*); destruction of merlons (solid intervals after crenels in battlements), towers, and ramparts (*shurafāt wa abrāj wa bārū rā kharāb kard-and*).[21] His order (pursuant to universal military practices) targeted the vitals of Herat's defenses: barbicans, bastions, towers, gateways. Breaches were struck in city walls at strategic points; however, the entire (*c.* 6 km) perimeter wall was not flattened (Temür followed the pattern depicted). A stump of the citadel (minus ramparts and towers) stood.

Sayfī's four reports:

1. "Governor Bulabān restored Ikhtiyār al-Dīn citadel" (*malik* Bulabān *ḥiṣār-i Ikhtiyār al-Dīn rā bih ḥāl-i ʿimārat bāz āward*);[22]
2. "The late *malik* Fahkr al-Dawla wa al-Dīn (may his grave be fragrant!), ordered the construction of the *burj* (towers, turrets, barbicans, bartizans), *bārū* (ramparts, battlements), and *khāk-rīz* (embankment, mound, glacis); and breastwall (*band-i khandaq*)[23] of the city of Herat" (*bih-farmūd tā burj wa bārū wa khāk-rīz wa band-i khandaq-i shahr-i Harāt rā ʿimārat kard-and*);[24]
3. *after* the aforementioned project (*baʿd az ān kih*), Fahkr al-Dīn Kart revamped the "embankment and trench" (*band wa khandaq maʿmūr gasht*),[25] and he completely constructed the *burj* (towers, etc.), *bārū*

[19] On the pre-Mongol citadel, see Ibn Ḥawqal/Shiʿār (tr.), *Safarnāma*, 172; Iṣṭakhrī/Afshar (ed.), *Masālik al-mamālik*, 209–10.
[20] Ḥāfiẓ-i Abrū/Harawī (ed.), *Jughrāfiyā*, 13; Krawulsky, *Ḫorāsān*, 1:19.
[21] al-Harawī, *Harāt*, 118.
[22] al-Harawī, *Harāt*, 355; al-Harawī (Calcutta ed.), *Harāt*, 335 (same wording).
[23] *Band-i khandaq*: breastwall (or possibly revetment). Elucidated below.
[24] al-Harawī, *Harāt*, 462; al-Harawī (Calcutta ed.), *Harāt*, 439–40.
[25] *Khandaq*: trench (synonyms: ditch, moat, foss/fosse); dry and/or wet per circumstance (it is difficult to flood a trench against gravity; hence a mix of dry and wet trenches).

(ramparts, etc.), curtain wall (*faṣīl*),[26] and *khāk-rīz* (embankment, etc.) (*burj wa bārū wa faṣīl wa khāk-rīz ʿimārat tamām girift*);[27]

4. Fakhr al-Dīn constructed "at the foot of the citadel, inside the city, two large trenches" and "an enormous *fīl-band*"[28] (*dar pā-yi ḥiṣār dar andarūn-i shahr dū khandaq-i ʿaẓīm bih-kunad wa fīl-bandī bas buzurgh bih-sākht*).[29]

"Bulabān restored the Ikhtiyār al-Dīn citadel" is explicit, but the literal may not be accurate. Firstly, Abāqā did not allow construction within city limits; his first choice was to flatten Herat and depopulate it.[30] Thus, permitting construction inside Herat—of a citadel no less—is uncharacteristic. Secondly, the use of "Ikhtiyār al-Dīn" is anachronistic: a scribe living in a later age interpolated the label because "Ikhtiyār al-Dīn" was the name by which *he* knew the citadel.[31] Thirdly, Sayfī usually does not supply a name for Herat's citadel, just *ḥiṣār* or *qalʿa*; for instance, "the citadel to the north" (*dar ḥiṣār bar ṭarf-i shumāl*).[32] If it had a popular appellation, Sayfī would have used it (just as he identified Fort Iskilchih).

The report *may* be referring to the construction at Fort Iskilchih by Bulabān,[33] which (1) did not just materialize; (2) was outside Herat's limits (southwest); and (3) was standing during Öljeitü's 698/1298f. siege. It is Iskilchih that Öljeitü had invested. Once Fahkr al-Dīn vacated Iskilchih for Khaysār, Öljeitü turned his sights on Herat *city*.[34]

Turning to Sayfī's three reports relating to Fahkr al-Dīn's initiatives.

Sayfī does not specify the citadel as the subject of any project, or even if the *malik* had erected a citadel. Ḥāfiẓ-i Abrū uses a verb for "repair" in his abstract of the Kartid's fortifications.[35] Sayfī's reports refer to the overhaul of

[26] *Faṣīl*: two meanings: (i) distance between two curtain walls; (ii) the *inner* curtain wall (cf. *outer* curtain wall) in defensive circumvallations. Elucidated below.

[27] al-Harawī, *Harāt*, 462; al-Harawī (Calcutta ed.), *Harāt*, 440.

[28] *Fīl-band*: "elephantine" (*fīl, pīl*) earthen mound/embankment?

[29] al-Harawī, *Harāt*, 463; al-Harawī (Calcutta ed.), *Harāt*, 440.

[30] al-Harawī, *Harāt*, 352–53.

[31] See, e.g., ibid., 405: erroneous claim that "Ḥiṣār-i Ikhtiyār al-Dīn" existed in 688/1289.

[32] al-Harawī, *Harāt*, 743. See comments by Allen, *Catalogue*, 34.

[33] Ḥāfiẓ-i Abrū, *Kart*, 186: that Iskilchih was erected by Muʿizz al-Dīn Kart's progenitors.

[34] al-Harawī, *Harāt*, 456–59; Ḥāfiẓ-i Abrū, *Kart*, 99–100.

[35] Ḥāfiẓ-i Abrū, *Kart*, 101 (*marammat nīk kard-and*).

the pre-Mongol citadel *and* Herat's defensive perimeter; but it is not possible to delineate which project is which. Since Sayfī uses *burj wa bārū*, etc., then again *burj wa bārū*, etc.—after *baʿd az ān kih*—it is certain that he is referring to two distinct but connected projects. Imprecise terms foster confusion: *khāk-rīz* has multiple meanings: embankment, earthworks, mound, glacis; *burj* could, in a martial context, stand for tower, turret, barbican, bartizan; *bārū*, ramparts, could mean bulwark, tower, fort, battlement, and embrasure (*sūrākh-i tīr-kish*); while *burj wa bārū* in conjunction may mean fortress or barbican.

The clincher that the *malik* overhauled the pre-Mongol citadel is that he had built his *fīl-band* and two *khandaq*s at the "foot of the citadel" (*pā-yi ḥiṣār*), *ipso facto*, there was a *ḥiṣār*. The citadel (Qalʿa-yi Ikhtiyār al-Dīn), where Danishmand Bahadur and his squadron were massacred, was standing by 706/1307.

Sayfī:[36] Pursuant to Fahkr al-Dīn's directives, ramparts were constructed, and interrupted at strategic points for towers that soared to fourteen *gaz*; the spacing (*faṣīl*) between the two curtain walls was six *gaz*: "six *gaz* of earth (*khāk*) lay between the [first] wall (*dīwār-i bārū*) and the [second] wall" (*dīwār-i faṣīl*).[37]

Isfizārī:[38] "in 699 [1299f.]," the *malik* "fortified (*istakhām dād*) the towers (pl. *burūj*), wall (sgl. *bārū*), trench, and *khāk-rīz* of Herat (the *dīwār-i bārū* was made of *kāh-gil*); and the towers elevated (*buland kard*) to fourteen *gaz*; and (there was six *gaz* of *khāk* between the two *faṣīl* (*az miyān-i har dū faṣīl*); the *khāk-rīz* was made strong and high (*tund wa buland gardānīd*) and the *raʿāyā* of Herat [were enlisted for the projects])."

Mīrkhwānd:[39] he confirms the revamping of *burj* and *bārū*, and elevation of towers; that six *gaz* lay between *faṣīl* and *khāk-rīz* (i.e., between first and second walls).

Ḥāfiẓ-i Abrū:[40] elevation of towers by four *gaz* (i.e., from ten *gaz* to fourteen *gaz*); six *gaz faṣīl* space. He adds that the base of the trench (*tah-i*

36 al-Harawī, *Harāt*, 462; al-Harawī (Calcutta ed.), *Harāt*, 440.

37 *Dīwār-i bārū* and *dīwār-i faṣīl*: clarified below; for now, "first wall" and "second wall."

38 Isfizārī, *Rawżāt*, 1:437; cf. ibid 1:78 (by the Timurid era the *faṣīl* space had expanded to ten *gaz*). My parentheses reflect the editor's insertions in square brackets.

39 Mīrkhwānd, *Rawżat*, 4,229; cf. ibid., 6,312 (ten *gaz faṣīl* space in Timurid era).

40 Ḥāfiẓ-i Abrū, *Kart*, 101.

*khandaq*) was overhauled; meaning that it was cleaned of debris and probably deepened.

Elevation of towers from ten *gaz* to fourteen *gaz* (+40%) by Kartids; and expansion of the *faṣīl* space from six *gaz* to ten *gaz* (+66.67%) in the Timurid era, means that the embankment's crown and base expanded: engineering proportions had to be maintained. Ramparts will have been thickened accordingly. An aspect that is simple to grasp but too detailed to treat here is the math involved. The implications of elevating towers include forcing the enemy to move offensive artillery farther back to adjust for trajectories or to stay out of range of defensive artillery, results in the reduction of their missiles' force (a function of mass and acceleration) and kinetic energy.

The unending dialectic of offense-defense is reflected in the above reinforcements. Sources do not explain how the towers were built or utilized, which is regrettable, not just from architectural curiosity, but military perspectives. Defenders launched—apart from arrows and bolts from handheld weapons—stones and bolts from assorted classes of torsion artillery. Artillery pieces are fitted in the *faṣīl* space; others are placed on towers. Defensive artillery is employed not only against personnel, but also against enemy siege equipment—the equivalent of modern counter-battery fire.

## Kartid Fortifications

### *The Citadel*

Opaque terminologies aside, we can stipulate, first, that by the time of Danishmand Bahadur's demise a citadel existed *inside* Herat; second, Herat was well fortified and able to withstand Böjäi's siege, from Shaʿbān 706/ February 1307 to late <u>Dh</u>ū al-Ḥijja 706/June 1307. Herat's gates were reluctantly opened to Böjäi, which indicates that *strategic equilibrium* had been reached: when the power of offensive weapons is offset by fortifications and defensive weapons. Hence the blockade—a besieger's ace—that starved Herat into capitulation.

The citadel's layout in the Kartid era; number of towers, heights, design; extent and height of ramparts; technical features (crenellations, merlons, embrasures),[41] are lacunae. Descriptions and schematics below relate to later iterations.

The citadel rests on a motte, about 3,117 ft/950 m above sea level. A UNESCO team performed restorative work in 1976–79.[42] The Soviet invasion and its aftermath prevented further work. Post-war restorations were conducted by the *Aga Khan Trust for Culture* (2008–12) following excavations by the *German-Afghan Archaeological Mission to Afghanistan* (2005–09). The citadel complex has an upper- and lower-section: the upper citadel is the fortress proper, aptly "fort" (*arg*: a neologism). Consequent to the addition of the Timurid Gateway and Tower,[43] a third level emerged, an elevated extension to the Tower.

The Arg held the treasury, dungeons, officers' quarters, and arsenal. Fortifications of the Arg were paramount. Eighteen semi-circular or circular towers of sundry dimensions were erected (Fig. 10.1, Fig. 10.2; three towers do not exist). Eleven towers fortify the upper citadel, reaching maximum height, *c.* 103.2 ft/31.40 m (above street level). Enclosure walls reflect average height of *c.* 52.49 ft/16 m and maximum thickness of *c.* 6.56 ft/2 m.[44] The complex extends *c.* 820–53 ft/250–60 m (east-west), *c.* 197–263 ft/60–80 m (north-south), and covers an approximate area of 21,528 yd$^2$/18,000 m$^2$ (*c.* 4.4478 acres).[45]

Ghiyāth al-Dīn Kart sponsored improvements to the citadel: the construction of a *bārgāh* (audience hall, grand court), which was decorated to reflect his 720/1320 victory: the western wall depicted sultan Abū Saʿīd Bahādur Khān's victorious armies; the eastern wall, Yasaʾur's dead, wounded, defeated, and dejected forces, with the Kartid's and sultan's forlorn nemesis dismounted (to symbolize defeat and humiliation).[46] The work

41 On technical features, see Sidney Toy, *The Strongholds of India* (London: Heinemann, 1957). Further on the citadel's history, see Saljūqī, *Harāt-i bāstān*, 8–11; Lisa Golombek and Don Wilber, *The Timurid Architecture of Iran and Turan*, 2 vols (Princeton: Princeton University Press, 1988), 1:301–02, Cat. No. 68.

42 Andrea Bruno, et al., *Restoration of Monuments in Herat* (UNESCO Technical Report, UNDP/AFG/75/022, 31 December 1981).

43 On the Timurid addition, see Ute Franke, et al., *Ancient Herat: Excavations and Explorations in Herat City* (Berlin: Staatliche Museen zu Berlin, 2017), 367–463; Allen, *Catalogue*, 34–35, Cat. No. 54; on Timurid inscriptions, see O'Kane, *Architecture*, 115–18, Cat. No. 1.

44 Bruno, et al., *Monuments*, 11; Franke, et al., *Ancient*, 24.

45 Franke, et al., *Ancient*, 24.

46 al-Harawī, *Harāt*, 743–44; Isfizārī, *Rawżāt*, 1:506.

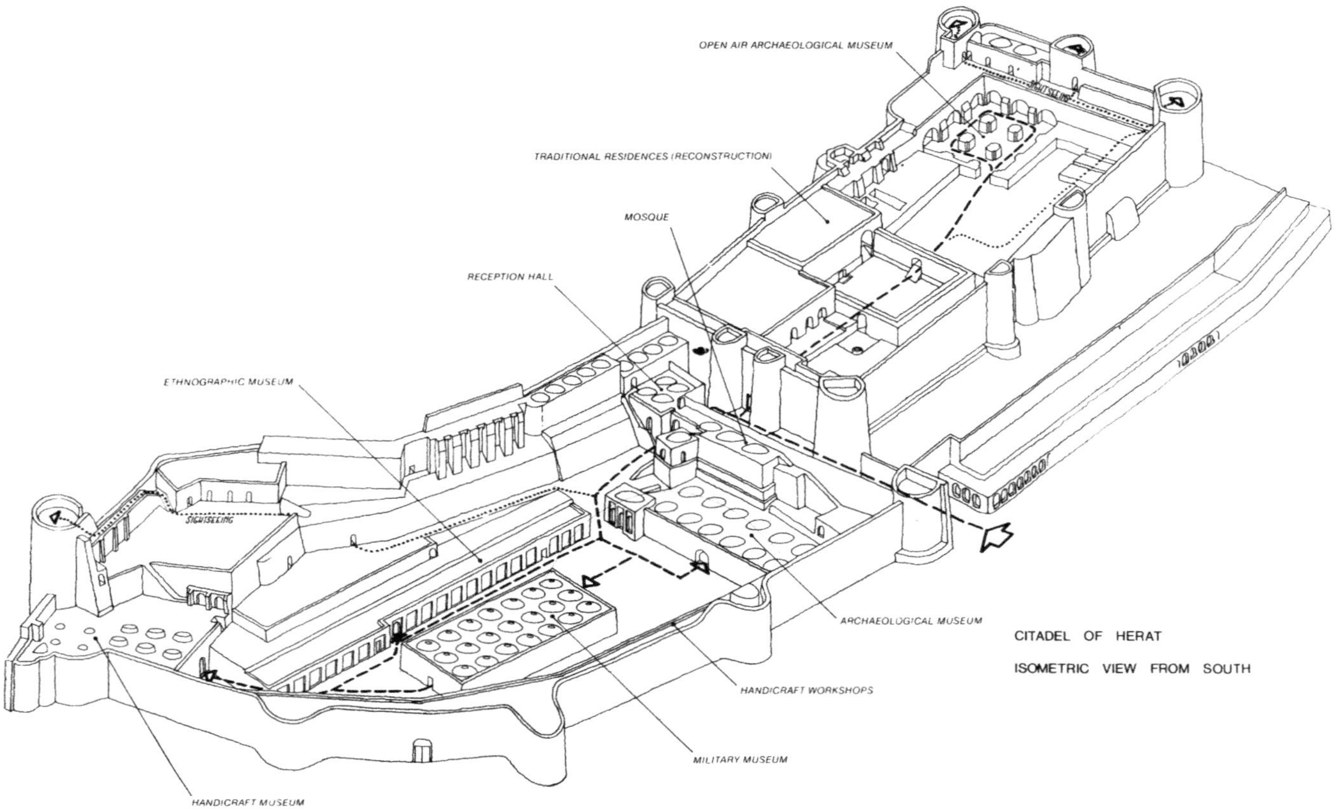


Figure 10.1 Schematic of citadel by UNESCO, 1976–79 (courtesy of UNESCO).

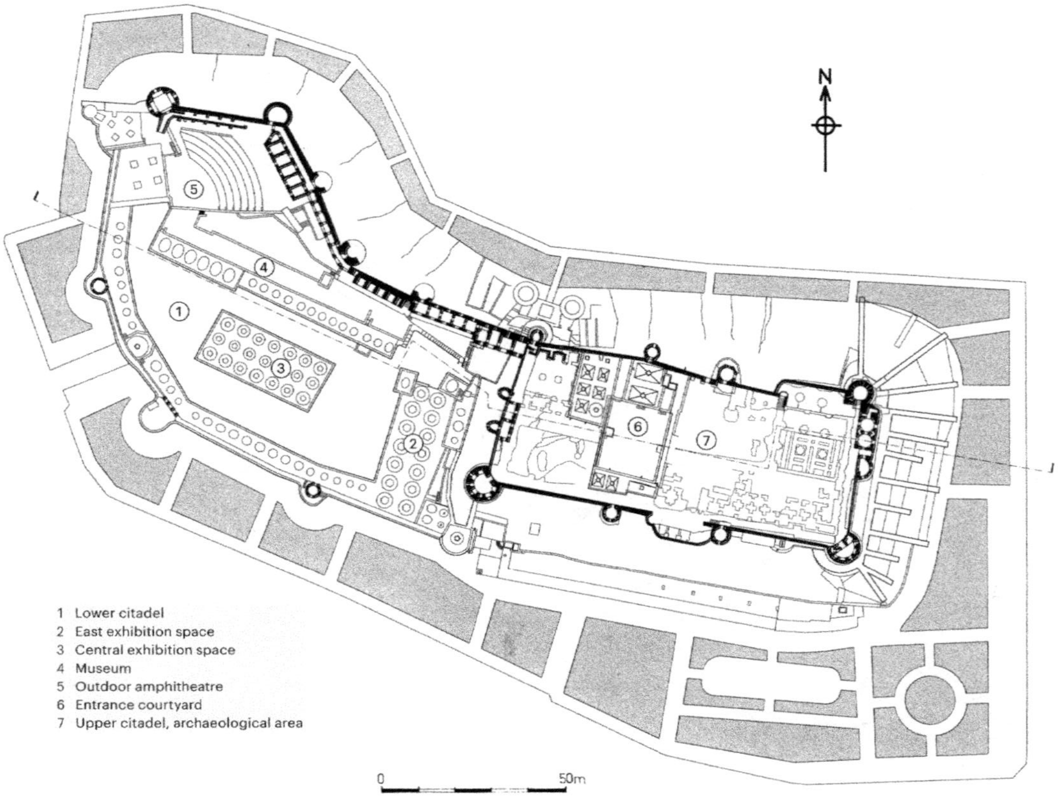


Figure 10.2 Schematic of citadel by AKTC, 2008–12 (courtesy of Aga Khan Trust for Culture).

served also to restore damage inflicted by Böjäi's supporters from Isfizār and Farāh.[47]

The citadel's gateways will have been fortified when the city gateways were rebuilt, although Sayfī does not confirm this. The citadel had two principal gateways. One led north (Isfizārī wrongly claims), to the "Horse [and Camel] Bazaar"; one, south to a plain.[48] Isfizārī's directions must be reversed: the Horse and Camel Bazaar was located *south* of the citadel.[49] The North Gate led to City Garden (*Bāgh-i shahr*),[50] thence the plains.

The North Gate allowed king, cavalry, and Kartid officials to depart without being observed or impeded in Herat's narrow streets, or trapped in the city. There probably were tunnels and/or posterns. Fakhr al-Dīn esteemed the value of sneaking away at night, which is how he slipped the noose during Öljeitü's cordon of Fort Iskilchih in 698/1298f.[51]

There is no mention of enhancements to Fort Iskilchih. The last we hear of Iskilchih is when Temür occupied Herat in Muḥarram 783/April 1381. Pīr ʿAlī's youngest son, Amir Ghūrī, the castellan, had refused to surrender the Fort. He relented when his father visited with him and insisted.[52]

Another fort, Shamīrān, allegedy existed beyond the north wall.[53] Fort Shamīrān, which has legendary origins, was active in the Samanid, Ghaznavid, and Seljuq periods,[54] but whether it was active, or even standing, in the Kartid period is doubtful. Mustawfī, who completed *Nuzhat c.* 741/1340, refers to it in the present tense. Shamīrān was supposedly in the area called the "Mound of the Bang Smokers" (*tal-i bangiyān*).[55] It is possibly identifiable with the ruined *quhandiz*.[56] Rafi Samizay, however, pinpoints Shamīrān

[47] al-Harawī, *Harāt*, 554. Kartid renegades from Isfizār and Farāh.

[48] Isfizārī, *Rawżāt*, 1:78.

[49] Allen, *Catalogue*, 51, Cat. No. 98: Horse and Camel Bazaar (*bāzār-i asb wa shutūr*).

[50] Ibid., 209, Cat. No. 651. The Bāgh was built by Fakhr al-Dīn Kart.

[51] al-Harawī, *Harāt*, 458; Ḥāfiẓ-i Abrū, *Kart*, 99.

[52] Ḥāfiẓ-i Abrū, *Kart*, 211.

[53] Mustawfī, *Nuzhat* 152; Mustawfī/Le Strange (tr.), *Nuzhat*, 150; cf. Le Strange, *Lands*, 409. Mustawfī apparently relied on outdated literature.

[54] Isfizārī, *Rawżāt*, 1:61, 69, 77, 98–99, 386, 388; 2:50, 54–55; ʿAbd al-Raḥman Fāmī Harawī, *Tārīkh-i Harāt* (Tehran: Mīrās̱-i maktūb, 1387/2008), f. 67[b] (terse mention).

[55] *Bang*: see glossary.

[56] Allen, *Catalogue*, 33, Cat. No. 53 (written *quhandiz-i M-Ṣ-R-Kh* or *M-Ṣ-R-Q*); M. Shokoohy, "The Monuments at the Quhandiz of Herat, Afghanistan," *JRAS* 1 (1983):7–31; for recent excavations at the *quhandiz*, see Franke, et al., *Ancient*, 689–731.

to where Qalʿa-yi Ikhtiyār al-Dīn stands,[57] that is, beneath it. Resolving the two possibilities is that there had been two citadels: Qalʿa-yi Shamīrān and Quhandiz-i M-Ṣ-R-Kh.[58]

### *Trench*

Construction techniques for circumvallating trenches date to antiquity.[59] Herat's trenches were (based on the underlying science) probably trapezoidal or rectilinear: the two designs are favored by military engineers.[60] An Indian manual, *Kautilya's Arthasastra*, recommends that wet trenches be trapezoidal.[61] In places where terrain or soil disallowed wide (that is, trapezoidal or rectilinear) trenches, a deep V-shaped trench (*fossa fastigata*) is cut instead. Herat's trench was possibly dry in peacetime but filled in preparation for a siege (if topography and water-supply permitted flooding). From a fluke that preserved a vital fact, we learn that the trench, or section of it, was dry during Tolui's siege (see below).

British officers noted that the trench was supplied by a conduit entering from the north.[62] We do not know if this is a modern innovation or reflective of pre-modern practices. A terrain's slope, and water supply, pose problems with respect to flooding trenches. Terry Allen postulated that Herat's trenches were meant to be used as "a dry moat."[63] Trenches, even if not filled with river water due to supply or topography, can be filled with polluted waters and linked to sewage trenches.[64] A subterranean drainage system had "brought the waste water outside to the fields,"[65] but it is unclear if this applied to the Kartid era. Sumps, sewage, and drainage trenches may have been linked to the *khandaq*. Polluted moats would have deterred all but the most intrepid attacker.

57 Samizay, *Islamic Architecture*, 112–13.

58 On putative locations, see Franke, et al., *Ancient*, 744–45, Figs. 797 and 798.

59 On trenches, with schematics and commentary on trench types, see L.H. Keeley, et al., "Baffles and Bastions: The Universal Features of Fortifications," *Journal of Archaeological Research* 15/1 (2007):55–95, 58–62, and Fig. 1. See also Vegetius, *Epitome of Military Science*, tr. N.P. Milner (Liverpool: Liverpool University Press, 2d rev. ed., 2001), Book IV, Chap. 5.

60 See Keeley, et al., "Baffles," 58–62 and Figures 1–2.

61 *Kautilya's Arthasastra*, tr. R. Shamasastry (Mysore: Sri Raghuveer, 5th ed., 1956), 50.

62 *ABC*, 3:53 (from 1885). Water originated in the Hari Rud. See comments by Major Sanders (from 1839–40) in MacGregor, *Central Asia*, 345–46.

63 Allen, *Catalogue*, 27.

64 Gaube, *Iranian Cities*, 48–50; illustration No. 33 on p.45 (sewage system in Herat, 1970s).

65 Samizay, *Islamic Architecture*, 115.

### *City Walls*

Raids by Nikudaris and sieges by Ilkhanid expeditions impressed on Fakhr al-Dīn the importance of having a solid primary defensive perimeter. This is the rough square (1.5 km by 1.5 km) walls of inner Herat. These walls were erected on an embankment. Along part of the northern course of the citadel complex was the perimeter bulwark identified by Terry Allen as Fakhr al-Dīn's *fīl-band*.[66] The *fīl-band* was probably an "elephantine" mound that merged (in an indeterminable manner) with the encircling embankment.

In 783/1381, Temür ordered the demolition of key Kartid defenses: he "ordered the fortifications (*bārū*) of the old city destroyed, and [multiple] breaches (*rakhna-hā*) made to the walls (*diwār-hā*). In keeping with this order, the [five] gates were extracted (*bar-kandad*), and trenches (*khandaq-hā*) opposite [the gates] were blocked (*rīkht-and*) and breaches struck in the wall."[67] Kartid era dimensions of circumvallations cannot be determined. We have to utilize Timurid era figures and reports by British military officers.

#### *The embankment*

Major Henry Raverty's military eye recorded and described the embankment as it stood in the nineteenth century.[68] The embankment was an artificial earthen mound, 50–60 ft (*c.* 15–18 m) in height, with walls 30 ft (*c.* 9 m) higher. The mound encircled the inner city. The slope of the mound (from base to ramparts) was angled 40° to 45°. The trench was *c.* 30 ft wide, deep, and wet. Major Edward Sanders (writing *c.* 1839–40), says the "walls of the city are 25 to 30 feet in height, and are erected on a large rampart or mound of earth varying from 40 to 60 feet in height. On the outside of all is a deep wet ditch."[69]

Ḥāfiẓ-i Abrū (writing *c.* 823/1420), describes Herat's (Timurid era) embankment (*khāk-rīz*) and curtain walls (*dīwār-i shahr*). The embankment was sixty *gaz* in width (by width he probably means the base; but could mean

[66] Allen, *Catalogue*, 34, 228.
[67] Ḥāfiẓ-i Abrū, *Kart*, 211.
[68] Jūzjānī/Raverty, *Nāṣirī*, 2:1,039, n.9 (by Raverty). See comments by Sanders in MacGregor, *Central Asia*, 341ff.; by British officers (in 1884), in *ABC* 3:52. See also Gaube, *Iranian Cities*, 34–36, 48, 50, 51–55; illustration nos. 21–23, 33, 36, 41–42.
[69] MacGregor, *Central Asia*, 338.

the crown). The embankment's height was thirty *gaz*. The trench (*khandaq*) was opposite the embankment (*khāk-rīz*), and bridged at every gateway.[70] There were two curtain walls: "thereafter, the *faṣīl* and the *muqātala* of the *khāk-rīz* were separated; each of the two walls being 2,000 *gaz* [...]" (*b'ad az ān faṣīl wa muqātala āz khāk-rīz judā kardih, har dū dīwārī dū hazār gaz* [...]).

Ḥāfiẓ-i Abrū's depiction suggests: (1) *diwār-i shahr* (city wall) referred collectively to *two* curtain walls; (2) one wall was the "battle [wall]" (*muqātala*); (3) the other was "the *faṣīl* [wall]." As Terry Allen explains, "[t]he square walls were frequently repaired and assaulted, strengthened and undermined. By the Timurid age, and probably long before, the walls had grown to an enormous embankment [...], and a curtain wall was erected along the crest of the embankment."[71] The curtain walls, not the embankment itself, are wrecked at strategic points by victors. This is more efficient than demolishing every circumvallation and filling in the entire trench (six km perimeter of walls, trenches, and mounds). Elǰigidei and Temür took this path of expediency.

Curtain walls and embankment, as they stood during Tolui's siege, were described by a defender who fell from atop the curtain wall (*sar-i bārah-yi shahr-i Harāt*) and rolled down the embankment (*khāk-rīz*) into the trench (*khandaq*). He was dressed in the "battle-rattle" of his epoch, helmet and cuirass, which, along with the incline of the counterscarp and trench, saved his life. The fall from the top of the wall to edge of the trench was twenty *gaz*; thence forty *gaz* to the trench's nadir (if accurate, the trench was quite deep). He was captured by Mongols who had descended into the (dry) trench (*bih miyān-i khandaq*) and advanced to the foot of the counterscarp (*dar pā-yi faṣīl*).[72]

Ḥāfiẓ-i Abrū's and Raverty's comments help in visualizing the defensive perimeter of Kartid Herat. Their reports are elaborated below.

The embankment was called *band* or *khāk-rīz*. It was constructed of stacked earth. Earth excavated to create the trench, which tracked the

[70] Ḥāfiẓ-i Abrū/Harawī (ed.), *Jughrāfiyā*, 12–13; Krawulsky, *Ḫorāsān*, 1:18–19. Allen, *Catalogue*, 27–28; cf. Mīrkhʷānd, *Rawżat*, 6,312 and Mīrkhʷānd/1960 ed., *Rawżat*, 7:517.

[71] Allen, *Catalogue*, 26. On curtain walls, see Keeley, et al., "Baffles," 57–58; Sidney Toy, *A History of Fortification: From 3000 BC to AD 1700* (London: Heinemann, 1955), 195–99.

[72] Jūzjānī/Raverty, *Nāṣirī*, 2:1039; Minhāj al-Dīn Jūzjānī, *Ṭabaqāt-i Nāṣirī*, 2 vols, ed. ʿAbd al-Ḥayy Ḥabībī (Kabul: Anjuman-i tārīkh-i Afghānistān, 1342–43/1963–64), 2:123; cf. Allen, *Catalogue*, 27.

embankment's base, was stacked and compressed, layer by layer, to form a solidified earthen mound. The embankment, from crown to base, was 50–60 ft (per Raverty). The 30 *gaz* height (per Ḥāfiẓ-i Abrū), say, 60–70 ft, suggests that Ḥāfiẓ-i Abrū's measurements and Raverty's do not materially diverge. The embankment merged with the *fīl-band* (the how and where are lacunae). The *glacis* (outer slope), was inclined from 40° to 45° (angles sufficient to impede escalades). Ḥāfiẓ-i Abrū's width of 60 *gaz* (*c.* 120–140 ft?) is probably the base of the embankment. The *outer* slope (glacis) of the embankment (here called *counterscarp*) sometimes had a *berm* at the base—possibly with a short wall at the edge (the defender who fell would not have rolled into the trench if there had been a wall). The *scarp* (*inner* wall) of a trench (counterscarp is now the *outer* wall) is often reinforced by a *revetment*: this is a stone wall, which minimizes damage to the embankment by the (usually toxic) liquid in the *khandaq*. There could be a *breastwall* (Sayfī's *band-i khandaq*?) circumvallating the trench.

An exercise to illustrate the above. If the embankment is an isosceles trapezoid with congruent angles of 45° (Raverty's 40°–45° slope); height (H) = 30 *gaz*; base (B) = 60 *gaz*; then crown (C) = 30 *gaz*. Dimensions are, say, 60′ (H) × 60′ (C) × 120′ (B). But uniformity in height, base, crown, and incline is impossible due to immutable factors: topography and geology.[73] An isosceles trapezoid is the theoretical layout not the final structure. Reports by Sanders, Ferrier, et al. makes manifest that the physiognomy of Herat's defenses in the nineteenth century was not uniform.[74] The interior side (*scarp*) of the embankment, for example, was not sloped in places; and homes were built along or against the scarp. In short, the physiognomy of the Kartid era embankment and trench was also heterogeneous.

Figure 10.3 is for informational purposes. It shows, inter alia: (1) the circumvallations of Juwayn (1884) comprising: (a) embankment; (b) ramparts; (c) trench; (d) breastwall; (e) *chemin de ronde* (the patrol path); (2) two breastwall designs (parapet and mini-mound); (3) dimensions and layouts of curtain walls; (4) towers; and (5) two different types of trenches. The physiognomy does not exhibit heterogeneity.

[73] Ferrier, *Caravan*, 171 (on soil quality); MacGregor, *Central Asia*, 349 (on terrain).

[74] Ferrier, *Caravan*, 170–71; MacGregor, *Central Asia*, 341–46; *ABC*, 52–53.

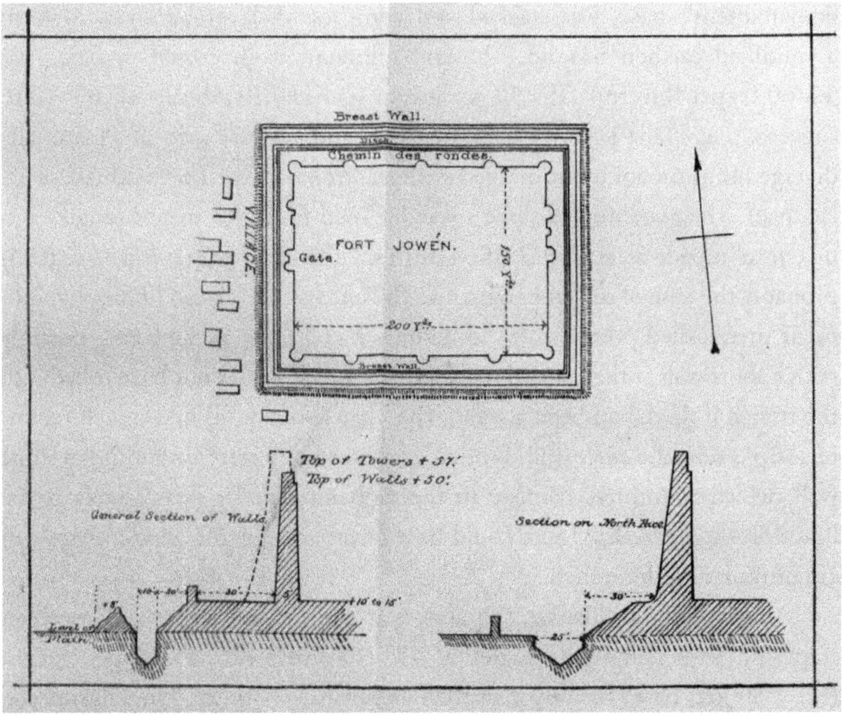


Figure 10.3 Defensive posture of Fort Juwayn, 1884 (for illustrative purposes only).

*The curtain walls* (diwār-i shahr)

The embankment's crown was the platform for *diwār-i shahr.* The crown is flattened and hardened to accommodate construction. *Diwār-i shahr* has two distinct but interwoven components: the *inner* curtain wall (with its back to the city of Herat); the *outer* curtain wall (parapet; possibly breast high) erected at the crest of the embankment. The inner wall was known as *dīwār-i faṣīl*; the outer wall was called *dīwār-i bārū.* Ḥāfiẓ-i Abrū's expression (*faṣīl wa muqātala*) bolsters the analysis that the inner wall was the *faṣīl* wall; the outer wall, the *muqātala* (battle) wall. Since fighting customarily transpires along the outer wall, "battle wall" is apropos. Sayfī refers to the pair as *dīwār-i faṣīl* and *dīwār-i bārū.*[75] Respectively, inner wall and battle wall; collectively, *diwār-i shahr.*

[75] al-Harawī, *Harāt,* 462. See also n.37, *supra.*

The *diwār-i shahr* sprouted numerous *burjs*,[76] and exhibited *bārūs*.[77] It is not possible to determine how the Kartid era *burjs* were constructed; for example, whether they were semi-circular or U-shaped; how far they protruded;[78] designs of crenels, embrasures, arrow-loops; whether galleries (*hourdes*) extended beyond the ramparts. Military architectural choices are manifold, and adaptable to the building materials, terrain, and imperatives of the environment. Timurids undoubtedly followed select Kartid patterns.

Mīrkhʷānd claims there were 149 *burjs* in 899/1493f.[79] Since the square walls are *c.*1.5 km × 1.5 km, the perimeter is *c.* 6 km. One tower every 40 m/131 ft, "a bowshot apart," is reasonable. The total of 149 apparently includes the five gateway towers (*barbican*) and the four corner towers (*bastion*): 140 towers along the ramparts plus nine dedicated towers (five barbicaned gateways and four bastions).[80] Edward Sanders, who sojourned at Herat to prepare a battle damage assessment consequent to the Persian siege of 1838, claims there were "numerous towers of half oval plan; these are generally 100 feet apart, and the [total] number [of towers] on the four sides exceeds 150 [...]."[81]

The elevation of towers and battlements was not merely to improve visibility and accuracy, but to harness gravity ($g = 9.80\ m/s^2$): firstly, to *increase* the force ($F = m\mathbf{a}$),[82] and kinetic energy ($E = MV^2$),[83] of defenders' projectiles; secondly, to *decrease* the lethality of the attackers' projectiles. The Persian tactic adopted by Alexander at Gaza was to construct a mound opposite Gaza's citadel and emplace thereon his siege machines,[84] thereby reducing the negative action of gravity. Citadels that command heights are harder to subdue, which contributed to the Mongols' travails in Ghūr and Gharjistān.

76 *Burj*: towers; barbicans (reinforced gateways; gateway towers); bartizans (overhanging turrets); turrets (small tower atop big tower, including movable turrets).

77 *Bārū*: fortified walls, with battlements (crenels, merlons, embrasures, arrow-loops).

78 See descriptions in MacGregor, *Central Asia*, 342.

79 Mīrkhʷānd, *Rawżat*, 6,312; Mīrkhʷānd/1960 ed., *Rawżat*, 7:517–18.

80 It is not clear if gateway towers count as two discrete units or one integrated unit. If the former, or combinations, the 140 total will change. The citadel's Timurid Gateway has two distinct towers. See Franke, et al., *Ancient*, 367–94.

81 MacGregor, *Central Asia*, 342. Dimensions of some towers are noted.

82 *Force = mass × acceleration*: F (in Newtons) = kg × ($m/s^2$).

83 *Energy = mass × velocity squared*: E (in Joules) = kg × $(m/s)^2$. At impact, $E = \frac{1}{2} MV^2$. See, e.g., Marsden, *Greek*, 89–90 and Figure 1 (on missile trajectory and impact).

84 Fox, *Alexander*, 192; Marsden, *Greek*, 104. Simple in theory but difficult in practice.

The accuracy and lethality of enemy projectiles are debilitated by (1) distance from target; (2) gravity; (3) drag—air resistance opposite to direction of missiles; (4) crosswinds. When erecting fortifications and excavating trenches, defenders seek to force attackers to emplace their artillery as far back as possible, thereby reducing effectiveness. Open spaces circumvallating the embankment and the trench serve to deny shelter to the enemy, and push them farther back. Kartids probably demolished structures surrounding *diwār-i shahr* when preparing for a siege. The sources do not express this, but it was common practice.[85] Defensive artillery then has clear fields of fire.[86]

The battle wall has crenellations, merlons, and embrasures. It is from behind this wall that archers discharged arrows and crossbow bolts, and javelineers hurled javelins.[87] The battle wall was pivotal: it protected defenders; concealed their strength or weakness; and allowed the defenders to monitor attempts by besiegers to bridge the trench, sap the embankment, or scale the glacis. Defenders launched arrows, bolts, javelins, and boulders directly onto foes. The *muqātala* wall improved defenders' visibility and accuracy, while exploiting gravity to amplify the acceleration and force of their projectiles.

The spacing (*faṣīl*) between the two curtain walls in the Kartid era was six *gaz*. The *faṣīl* space is created by packing several *gaz* of earth to create a solid earthen base, thereby solidifying both walls. Hypothetically, if the outer curtain wall is twelve ft high (the inner wall is higher), then seven ft of earth will be stacked to create the *faṣīl*. This leaves a battle wall of five ft. A solid earthen base reinforces both walls, which makes the battle wall harder to destroy with missile strikes. A *faṣīl* space facilitated the movement of warriors during combat; and flow of reinforcements, weapons, ammunition, and provisions. Steps constructed at various points permitted movement from city level to the top of the embankment.[88]

85 See, e.g., Herbert Franke, "Siege and defense of towns in medieval China," in *Chinese Ways in Warfare*, eds F.A. Kierman and J.K. Fairbank (Cambridge, MA: Harvard University Press, 1974), pp. 151–201, 152–53. Cf. MacGregor, *Central Asia*, 348 (cover used by attackers).

86 On defensive artillery, see Marsden, *Greek*, 116–63 (includes diagrams).

87 Javelins (*rimāḥ*; sgl. *rumḥ*) noted in al-Harawī, *Harāt*, 712. On the armaments utilized in early medieval Khurasan, see Bosworth, *Ghaznavids*, 119–22; see also W.F. Paterson, "The Archers of Islam," *JESHO* 9/1 (1966):69–87.

88 On curtain walls and inter-linked elements, see M. Philippides and W.K. Hanak, *The Siege and the Fall of Constantinople in 1453* (Burlington, VT: Ashgate, 2011), 297–357, and plates and maps at beginning of Part Two. See also Toy, *Fortifications*, 195–99.

The parallel curtain walls continue: they are bisected by the three gateways in the middle of the east, south, and west walls, but not the north, where there were two gates (NE and NW). The walls merge seamlessly with the bastions (*arkān*) at each corner. Fakhr al-Dīn will have reinforced the four bastions; but this is not stated in any source. The bastions' Timurid era names (clockwise): Burj-i ʿAlī Asad (northeast), Burj-i Ḥarīq (southeast), Burj-i Shamʿāniyān (southwest), Burj-i Khākistar (northwest).[89] The hemi-circular shape visible in Gaube possibly reflects an earlier pattern for bastions.[90]

Kartid defenses followed contours instituted in the hazy past. Persians did not need Vitruvius to advise them on how to develop defenses; however, his words are enlightening with respect to towers and bastions. Towers must project beyond the wall and be placed no more than a bowshot apart,[91] such that if one tower is attacked, defenders in neighboring towers can rain arrows on besiegers. The thickness of the ramparts (read: *faṣīl*) should be such that defenders may pass one another without interference. Steps and walkways must be constructed to allow for movement of reinforcements and supplies from city level to the defenders. Square cities are disfavored: right angles where walls join can be pounded down by battering rams. Round towers are more resistant to battering rams and mangonel strikes than are square towers.[92] Hence the hemi-circular towers and bastions at Herat referenced in reports by British officers (like Major Edward Sanders, Bengal Engineers).

Fakhr al-Dīn Kart's fortifications astounded Danishmand Bahadur. The Mongol amir, on entering Herat through the Khūsh Gate, was astonished by the magnificence (*shikūh*) of the *khāk-riz* (here, counterscarp), the strength and height of the *dīwār-i bārū*, the sturdiness (*muḥkamī*) of the mound

[89] Ḥāfiẓ-i Abrū/Harawī (ed.), *Jughrāfiyā*, 13; Krawulsky, *Ḫorāsān*, 1:19; Allen, *Catalogue*, 28; cf. al-Harawī, *Harāt*, 118: *Burj-i Khāk bar sar* is the proper name; *Khākistar* is a colloquialism; and Shamʿāniyān is given by Ḥāfiẓ-i Abrū. *Shamʿ-sāz* and *shammāʿ* mean chandler.

[90] Gaube, *Iranian Cities*, 34, illustration No. 21 (image from 1916). On bastions, see Keeley, et al., "Baffles," 67–72 and Fig. 7 and Fig. 8A.

[91] The range of an arrow or crossbow bolt varies, but generally, an arrow or bolt can pierce body armor at under 50 m. A longer range, 300 ft/91.44 m, for arrow/bolt penetration of mail or armor, is proffered in Paterson, "Archers of Islam," 86.

[92] Vitruvius Pollio, *The Ten Books on Architecture*, tr. M.H. Morgan (Cambridge, MA: Harvard University Press, 1914), Book 1, Chap. 5, esp. ¶ 2 ("Towns should be laid out not as an exact square nor with salient angles, but in circular form [...]") and ¶ 5; see also Vegetius/Milner (tr.), *Epitome*, Book IV, Chap. 2 (disfavoring of straight lines).

(*band*), and the ingresses and egresses of the gateway (*darwāza*). He ordered them destroyed.[93] His directive was not executed (but he was).

Herat's fortifications, however, did not remain unscathed. After Herat capitulated to Böjäi b. Danishmand in Dhū al-Ḥijja 706/June 1307, battlements and towers were destroyed by the Mongols (*dīwār-hā-yi burj wa bārū wa faṣīl-i shahr kharāb kunad*).[94] The damage caused was reversible. A complaint was submitted by ʿAlāʾ al-Dīn Hindū and Böjäi to Öljeitü against Ghiyāth al-Dīn Kart.[95] They alleged, inter alia, that the Kartid was repairing Herat's "portals and towers" (*durūb wa burūj-i shahr*).[96] The wording suggests that gateways and barbicans had been wrecked by Böjäi's troops. By disabling gateways and barbicans, the Mongols had unimpeded access to inner Herat. It is logical that Ghiyāth al-Dīn would repair the portals and attendant barbicans as quickly as possible.

Muʿizz al-Dīn Kart repaired the curtain walls after an earthquake struck Herat on 6 Jumādá I, 765/10 February 1364.[97] It is not known if he did further work on the citadel or defenses, but he did develop a second major circumvallation, the "Kartid Wall."

### *The Kartid wall* (shahr-band)

Muʿizz al-Dīn erected a second perimeter wall (*shahr-band*).[98] The contours of this wall are difficult to trace because Temür demolished them. Terry Allen offers a descriptive reconstruction of the contours of the second perimeter wall.[99] Based primarily on a proffer by Heinz Gaube,[100] the putative perimeter was outlined on a map.[101] The "Kartid Wall" (after Franke, et al.) is a square, *c.* 3.80–4 km × 3.80–4 km. If we simplify this to 4 × 4 km, the perimeter is 16 km/10 miles. The area encompassed is *c.* 16 km$^2$ (*c.* 6.2 mile$^2$).

93 Ḥāfiẓ-i Abrū, *Rashīdī*, 84.
94 al-Harawī, *Harāt*, 551; Ḥāfiẓ-i Abrū, *Kart*, 113.
95 See Chapter 4, § "Ghiyāth al-Dīn Kart: Undermined at Herat."
96 al-Harawī, *Harāt*, 584; Ḥāfiẓ-i Abrū, *Kart*, 121.
97 Ḥāfiẓ-i Abrū, *Kart*, 191; Faṣīḥ, *Mujmal*, 959.
98 Isfizārī, *Rawżāt*, 1:81–82, 2:14.
99 Allen, *Catalogue*, 31–32.
100 Heinz Gaube, "Innenstadt und Vorstadt. Kontinuität und Wandel im Stadtbild von Herat zwischen dem 10. und 15. Jahrhundert," in *Beiträge zur Geographie orientalischer Städte und Märkte*, ed. Günther Schweizer (Wiesbaden: Reichert Verlag, 1977), pp. 213–40.
101 See Franke, et al., *Ancient*, 742 (aerial photograph and sketch).

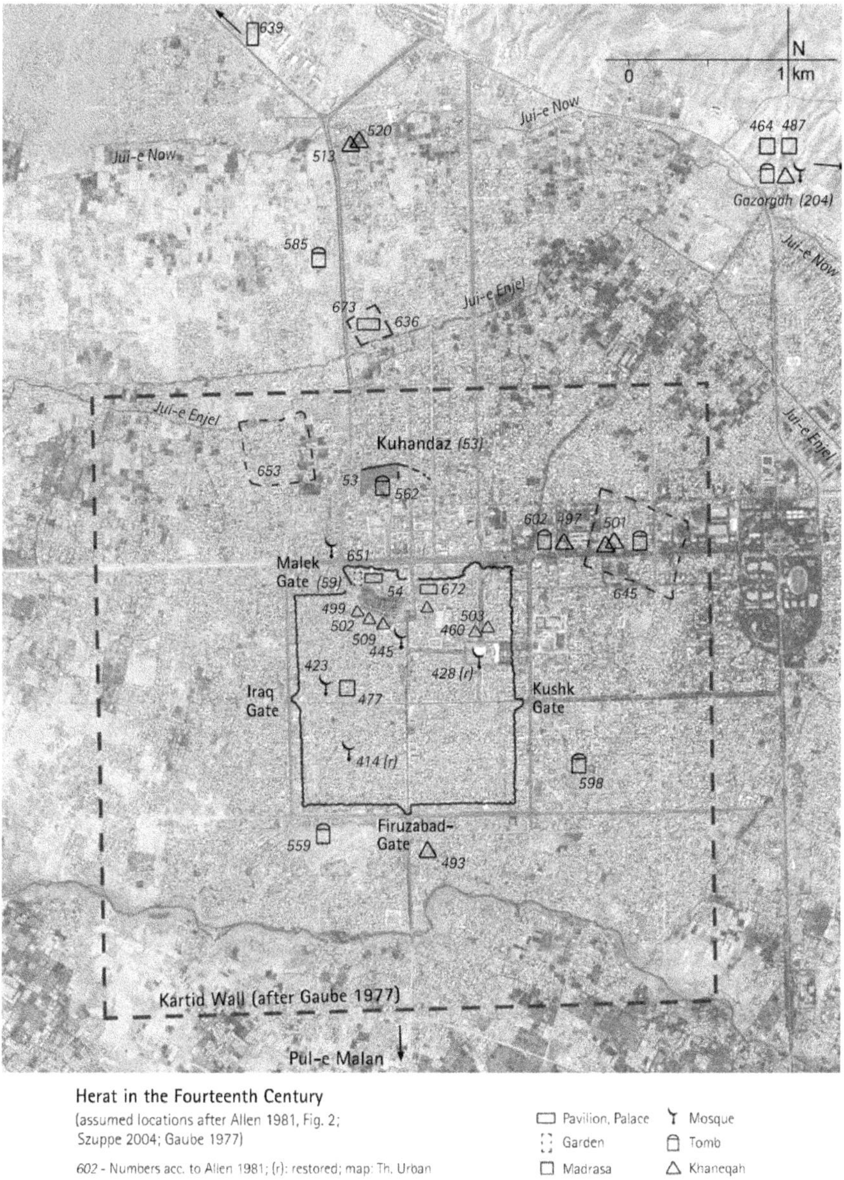


Figure 10.4 Aerial photograph of Herat with depiction of Kartid Wall (courtesy of Thomas Urban, ©Ancient Herat).

Khʷāndamīr and Isfizārī, based on their interpretations of Ḥāfiẓ-i Abrū, claim the Kartid Wall was built to defend against Amir Qazghan's invasion.[102] Mīrkhʷānd and Isfizārī elsewhere proffer the extents of the Kartid Wall.[103] None of them saw the wall, which was demolished before the first of the three, Mīrkhʷānd, was born. They are conflating details and relating anecdotes. They describe the northern and eastern limits of the wall, but fail to recognize that this means, illogically, that there were no western or southern limits.[104] Ḥāfiẓ-i Abrū, who saw the Kartid Wall, does not delve into limits.[105] The mention of *a* wall in his report on the invasion was redacted by Khʷāndamīr and Isfizārī.

The hypothesis below is based on the adjective (*chapar*) to the noun *dīwār*. *Dīwār-hā-*[*yi*] *chapar* (palisade; wooden hide; screen of wattle-and-daub construction) is referenced by Ḥāfiẓ-i Abrū in his report on Muʿizz al-Dīn's war council. In succeeding sentences, only the noun *dīwār* appears. Khʷāndamīr and Isfizārī skip war council discussions and write: after the king "took counsel with his amirs and notables," he "ordered that a wide wall (*dīwār-i pahnāwarī*) be constructed from [Point X] to [Point Y]."[106]

The wall constructed ahead of the Chaghataid invasion was not the stout 10 mile/16 km Kartid Wall, but a (temporary) protective screen with rudimentary parapets for Kartid infantrymen. The *chapar* appears to have been attached to the interior side of the wall. The hypothesis resolves the mystery of the missing western and southern limits. Ḥāfiẓ-i Abrū gives just the northern and eastern limits.[107] This is where the *chapar* was erected. Kartids knew the enemy would take the high ground in the north to northeast,[108] which they did. Chaghataids had 30,000 cavalry. The Kartids had 4,000 cavalry; and 10,000–12,000 or 10,000–15,000 infantry. A *chapar* was ideal for a commanding officer with a supply of infantrymen that could be deployed

102 Khʷāndamīr/Siyāqī (ed.), *Ḥabīb*, 3:381; Khʷāndamīr/Thackston (tr.), *Habib*, 221; Isfizārī, *Rawżāt*, 2:14; cf. Ḥāfiẓ-i Abrū, *Zubdat*, 1:230–31 and Ḥāfiẓ-i Abrū, *Kart*, 181–82.

103 Mīrkhʷānd, *Rawżat*, 6,311–12; Mīrkhʷānd/1960 ed., *Rawżat*, 7:517; Isfizārī, *Rawżāt*, 1:81–82,

104 See the cogent analysis in Allen, *Catalogue*, 31–32.

105 Ḥāfiẓ-i Abrū, *Zubdat*, 1:230–31; Ḥāfiẓ-i Abrū, *Kart*, 181–82 (preparations for Qazghan); 208–09 (breached by Temür); Ḥāfiẓ-i Abrū, *Cinq*, 40.

106 Khʷāndamīr/Siyāqī (ed.), *Ḥabīb*, 3:381; cf. Isfizārī, *Rawżāt*, 2:14 (different wording); but cf. Ḥāfiẓ-i Abrū's language: he does not qualify *dīwār* or use *pahnāwarī*.

107 On the limits, see Ḥāfiẓ-i Abrū, *Zubdat*, 1:231; Allen, *Catalogue*, 31.

108 See Map 4 and Figure 10.4. British officers also noticed the high ground. *ABC*, 3:53.

along the northern and eastern limits of the Kartid Wall. Defenders could rain arrows, bolts, and javelins on Chaghataid cavalry while obtaining concealment and protection behind the (solid) Kartid Wall and (temporary) *chapar*.

The Kartid Wall was constructed *before* 752/1351. A *c.* 16 km/10 mile perimeter takes time, money, and labor to construct. Given Herat's painful history with roving bandits, my thesis is that the Kartid Wall was designed to protect Herat's environs from bandits, not an army bearing with it siege technologies and techniques. Father and son, however, tried to use the wall to defend Herat against Chaghataid armies. Muʿizz al-Dīn was successful; Pīr ʿAlī Kart was not. Qazghan's cavalrymen were not equipped for siege warfare but Temur's army certainly was. The wall encompassed affluent neighborhoods like Khiyābān (north). The contexts for Bukhara's "Wall of Kanpirak" (*Dīwār-i Ka[m]pirak*; *Kampīr-Dīwāl*: "the old woman"), and Constantinople's "long wall of Anastasios," help in elucidating my thesis.

The Wall of Kanpirak's perimeter was more than 250 km.[109] The reason for its existence is instructive. The *History of Bukhara* relates how Bukharan notables had complained to the governor of Khurasan in *c.* 166/782f., about infidel Turks plundering villages and dragging Muslims into captivity. He ordered the amir of Bukhara:[110]

> to build walls for Bukhara so that all of the villages of Bukhara would be inside those walls, similar to Samarqand,[111] so the Turks could not enter the district of Bukhara [...]. It was completed in the year 215/830.

Constantinople's "long wall of Anastasios" (after Anastasios I; d. 518) was 65 km from Constantinople: it was *c.* 45 km long, 5 m high, 3.3 m thick.[112] It was intended to thwart attacks by "barbarians" (Huns and Avars), but proved inadequate against them. It offered little security in the age of awesome siege engines.

[109] Kanpirak Wall encircled the Bukharan oasis. R.N. Frye, *Bukhara: The Medieval Achievement* (Norman, OK: University of Oklahoma Press, 1965), 10, 26.

[110] Narshakhī/Frye (tr.), *History of Bukhara*, 33–34 and n.146 (Tehran MS reads Kanpirak for Kampirak); Narshakhī (Kabul ed.), *Tārīkh-i Bukhārā*, 46–48, 47–48 (quote).

[111] On Samarqand's walls, see Bregel, *Historical Atlas*, 82.

[112] Philippides and Hanak, *Constantinople*, 298; A. van Millingen, *Byzantine Constantinople: The Walls of the City and Adjoining Historical Sites* (London: John Murray, 1899), 342–43.

The long walls of Constantinople, Bukhara, and Samarqand, which enclosed suburbs and hinterlands, proved useful—up to a point. With the diffusion of siege technologies and techniques, even barbarians had the technological and intellectual capacities to breach city walls. The transformation of the Mongols is the example: from roving bandits on horseback to conquerors who acquired and applied Asian military sciences.

The Kartid Wall was not rebuilt by the Timurids because it was deemed indefensible. Rightly so. If the perimeter was as depicted in Fig. 10.4 it was indefensible against a force bearing with it siege technologies and techniques. Long walls also force defenders to divide their forces. Attackers launch diversions that further divide defenders' forces, and then breach at another point. Defending a *nucleus*—a dry/wet trenched and walled/palisaded settlement organized round/square—is a timeless practice from Africa, Asia, Near East, and Europe.[113] Weaknesses multiply as the perimeter extends.

The Kartid Wall was probably a robust earthen mound with sturdy mud/clay walls and four gates. One gate is known: Darwāza-yi Anṣārī—the north gate, to the highway to Gāzurgāh. There will have been a series of intervaled watchtowers. This defensive posture would have been sufficient to monitor hinterlands, villages, hamlets, granaries, watermills, and such lying beyond Herat's enclosed suburbs; and to defend the suburbs against surprise attack by raiders. If a threat is detected, alarms are raised and reinforcements surged to secure the threatened sector. Unlike the faraway wall of Anastasios, the Kartid Wall was not far removed from garrisons in Herat, Qalʿa-yi Ikhtiyār al-Dīn, and Fort Iskilchih.

Constantinople's landward "Theodosian Walls," *c.* 6 km, extended northwest from the Sea of Marmara, and terminated below the Golden Horn. It was *the* defensive perimeter; comprising earthworks, curtain walls, battlements, towers, and trenches. It developed over nine centuries and cost Byzantium manifold fortunes.

There is no intimation that Kartids expended the resources to construct a 10 mile/16 km wall replete with battlements and towers. Furthermore, maintaining, garrisoning, and securing this perimeter would have exhausted finances and strained logistics. Assuming *arguendo* that the wall mimicked

[113] See Keeley, et al., "Baffles," Figure 6 (schematic of an African village's defenses).

the physiognomy of the 1.5. × 1.5 km inner wall, a 16 km wall would have required a *burj* every 40 m/131 ft, or 400 *burjs*; plus barbicans, bastions, gateways, guardhouses, and thousands of trained, equipped, victualled, and remunerated soldiers to garrison, 24/7, every gatehouse, barbican, bastion, tower, and parapet. Even Byzantium struggled to pay their bills in this respect, particularly in the waning years of the Empire when Constantinople's finances were parlous.

Temür's nimble breach of the Kartid Wall supports the thesis that the wall was not designed to withstand an army equipped with siege equipment and scientific training.

Ḥāfiẓ-i Abrū writes that with Temür's invasion looming, Pīr ʿAlī Kart "built" Herat's city wall (*shahr-bandī bunyād kardih būd*).[114] However, "repaired" and "reinforced" Muʿizz al-Dīn's wall are accurate. Terry Allen wrote: "[t]hese considerations [raised by Allen] suggest strongly that Ghiyath al-Din's wall followed the line of Muʿizz al-Din's [wall]."[115] Pīr ʿAlī was hoping that a reinforced *shahr-band* would keep the Chaghataid army out of Herat.

Temür inspected the defenses and ordered the construction of contravallations. These are trenches and mounds excavated or erected by army engineers opposite to the defensive circumvallations. Contravallations protect besiegers while they furrow forward. Temür circulated his battle plan. Chaghataid soldiers swarmed the wall—ordinarily under protective fire from archers—forcing Kartid soldiers to duck or flee. Chaghataids reached the *faṣīl-i shahr-band* (the wall's counterscarp), where scaling ladders (*nardubān-hā*) were emplaced along the base (*pā-yi dīwār*). They clambered over. Meanwhile, a flaw in the wall was identified (assuredly by scouts reconnoitering and probing the defenses for weaknesses). They found an inlet for an aqueduct leading from the Jūy-i Injīl into Herat. Chaghataids penetrated at the inlet and flooded Herat's suburbs. Defenders abandoned the Kartid Wall and withdrew behind the square walls.

Siege engines that had been transported by Chaghataids were not employed against the Kartid Wall: it was demonstrably scalable and porous.

114 Ḥāfiẓ-i Abrū, *Kart*, 205; Faṣīḥ, *Mujmal*, 976.
115 Allen, *Catalogue*, 32.

There was no need to waste the ammunition (stones) they carted. Temür's soldiers, having now infiltrated and engulfed the suburbs, encircled the walled city.[116] Herat capitulated.

*The Five Gateways*

Fakhr al-Dīn Kart reinforced Herat's primary gateways (*bar har darb bandī buzurg bih-bast*).[117] Gateways in pre-cannon times were the most vulnerable points in a citadel or city, a point confirmed by Sayfi: he says that Herat was impenetrable in light of its solid defenses; but recognized that the city's defenses can be penetrated through the gateways, especially during the heavier ebb-and-flow of traffic at harvest times.[118] Gateways were apparently kept open and barriers withdrawn at daytime for harvest season. A timeless practice was to eject outsiders from the city at dusk and lock the gates. Travelers arriving at night stayed outside. This is one reason why a caravansaray may be built outside a main gate.

There were barbicans (reinforced and protruding towers) attached to gateways in the Timurid era; each had wooden turrets that accommodated four to five archers.[119] This design is logical. The architectural forms of Kartid gateways and barbicans are unknown; however, scientific realities cannot be ignored by military engineers:[120] barbicans tend to be hemi-circular. Since Qal'a-yi Ikhtiyār al-Dīn's towers were hemi-circular, this design was probably extended to other towers. Barbicans must merge with perimeter walls whereby fissures do not develop and weaken the adjoining walls; they must accommodate multiple defenders; towers must enhance the defenders' field of vision, field of fire, create kill zones and eliminate dead zones (areas that enfilades from battle walls and towers cannot reach, which would allow besiegers to advance with impunity).[121]

116 Ḥāfiẓ-i Abrū, *Kart*, 209; Isfizārī, *Rawżāt*, 2:40; Shāmī, *Ẓafarnāmah*, 83–84; Yazdī/Munshī, *Taḥrīrī az Ẓafarnāmah*, 1:218–21; Yazdī/'Abbāsī (ed.), *Ẓafarnāmah*, 1:232–34; Mīrkhʷānd, *Rawżat*, 4,672–73 (Mīrkhʷānd follows Ḥāfiẓ-i Abrū but muddles critical details).

117 al-Harawī, *Harāt*, 462. On gateways/gatehouses, see Toy, *Fortifications*, 199–209.

118 al-Harawī, *Harāt*, 684.

119 Isfizārī, *Rawżāt*, 2:253 (*bar bālā-yi darwāza-hā khāna-hā az chūb bih-misal-i ṣandūq-hā sākhta būd-and*). The wooden turrets resembled chests (*bih-misal-i ṣandūq*). On Herat's gates, see Allen, *Catalogue*, 36–38, Cat. Nos., 56–60.

120 On barbicans, see Keeley, et al., "Baffles," 67–79; Toy, *Fortifications*, 120–25.

121 See Keeley, et al., "Baffles," Figure 8 (schematic of dead zones/kill zones).

Gateways had machicolations (called "murder holes" in Europe; "killing holes" in Persian: *sūrākh-hā-yi muqātala*). These are openings between corbels of an overhanging parapet or crests of parapets (for instance, the *muqātala* wall), or holes drilled into the ceiling of the gateway. Defenders in the guard-room (located above the gateway) used the machicolations to drop missiles onto attackers.[122]

*Bridges*

Bridges over the *khandaq* connected to every primary gateway.[123] Non-retractable bridges were customarily destroyed by defenders at the commencement of a siege. There was a drawbridge (*pul-i rawān*) at the Malik Gate in the Timurid era.[124] We cannot determine if there were drawbridges in Kartid Herat.[125]

*Baffles and redans*

Gateways are universally designed to hinder penetration by an enemy when gates are open for military or civilian purposes. Rather than permitting incoming traffic direct access to the thoroughfares of Herat, baffles and/or redans are installed after the bridge; possibly before the bridge, too.[126] Redans are outer barricades to hinder incoming traffic. Gabions—gunnysacks or baskets filled with sand/gravel—have been used for centuries to protect entryways. A purpose for redans, gabions, and baffles was to prevent the entry en masse (*coup de main*, in military jargon) of enemy cavalry and/or infantry.

Baffles take manifold forms, from "simple" zigzag designs (bent-axis, oblique, etc.), to labyrinthine designs of great complexity.[127] Bent-axis (Ar. *bāshūra*) portals were features of Muslim fortifications in Aleppo, Baghdad,

[122] Toy, *Strongholds*, 4–5 (on machicholations generally, and in Sultanate India).
[123] Ḥāfiẓ-i Abrū/Harawī (ed.), *Jughrāfiyā*, 12; Krawulsky, *Ḫorāsān*, 1:19. Obviously (perhaps) this applies to the Kartid era, too,
[124] Isfizārī, *Rawżāt*, 2:200.
[125] A Mamluk drawbridge is noted in Kate Raphael, *Muslim Fortresses in the Levant* (London: Routledge, 2011), 150. Drawbridges were common in India (see Toy, *Strongholds*, *et passim*), but dating their construction is difficult.
[126] On redans (two projecting parapets forming a V-shape) at Herat, but dateable to 1839–40, see MacGregor, *Central Asia*, 341. See sketch of redans in Toy, *Strongholds*, 21.
[127] Keeley, et al., "Baffles," 62–67, and Figs. 3–5. See also Toy, *Fortification*, 199–209.

Damascus, and Cairo; possibly introduced from Khurasan.[128] Ḥāfiẓ-i Abrū states that the portals had several iron barrier gates (portcullis?) along a zigzig passageway akin to a "camel's neck" (*ushtur gardan*; vernacular for twisted defiles).[129] Zigzag passageways forced attackers to twist and turn inside of an enclosed area flanked by defenders, exposing them to fire along the route; and sealing them in, front and back, with iron gates. Attackers trapped between iron gates are butchered.

If Oskar von Niedermayer's sketch of Herat's perimeter is reflective of pre-modern patterns,[130] a simple baffle was employed after the bridge that forced the enemy to turn left then right—the preferred mode. Shields were held on the left arm and weapon in the right hand; unshielded right flanks and rears were exposed to defenders. Cavalry then turn right and pass around a barrier before entering a thoroughfare.[131] This arrangement, a practice from antiquity, is manifest in Figure 10.5 for south gate. A left-right entry (Ḥāfiẓ-i Abrū's "camel's neck" passageway) flanked by defenders, interior iron gates, barbicans, turrets, and guardrooms, combined to minimize the vulnerability of Herat's principal portals.

*Dedicated portals*

Barriers impede mundane daily traffic—camels, horses, and pedestrians; carts and peddlers' pushcarts; shepherds with flocks of fat-tailed sheep—the charming tableaux that continue to characterize daily life in Herat. It is unwise, however, to leave the gates open or to withdraw barriers. Hence the imperative for dedicated portals to manage daily traffic at non-harvest times. Isfizārī claims there were three ports (*bāb*) at each gateway, except for Malik Gate, which had two ports.[132] This implies dedicated portals of dissimilar dimensions and functions. Posterns possibly existed. Side gates were often built into the wall adjoining a bastion's base. They served to, inter alia, regulate daily pedestrian traffic.

[128] K.A.C. Creswel, "Bāb," *EI²*, 1:830–32 (quoting al-Maqrīzī); cf. Raphael, *Muslim Fortresses*, 21–22, 28, 148–49 (on *bāshūra*).

[129] Ḥāfiẓ-i Abrū/Harawī (ed.), *Jughrāfiyā*, 12; Krawulsky, *Ḫorāsān*, 1:19.

[130] Oskar von Niedermayer, *Afganistan* (Leipzig: Hiersemann, 1924), Figure 3. Niedermayer's eagle eye caught minutiae not reflected in British military sketches.

[131] On left-turn baffles, see Keeley, et al., "Baffles," 63–64, Fig. 4.

[132] Isfizārī, *Rawżāt*, 1:78. He is referring to Timurid era designs.

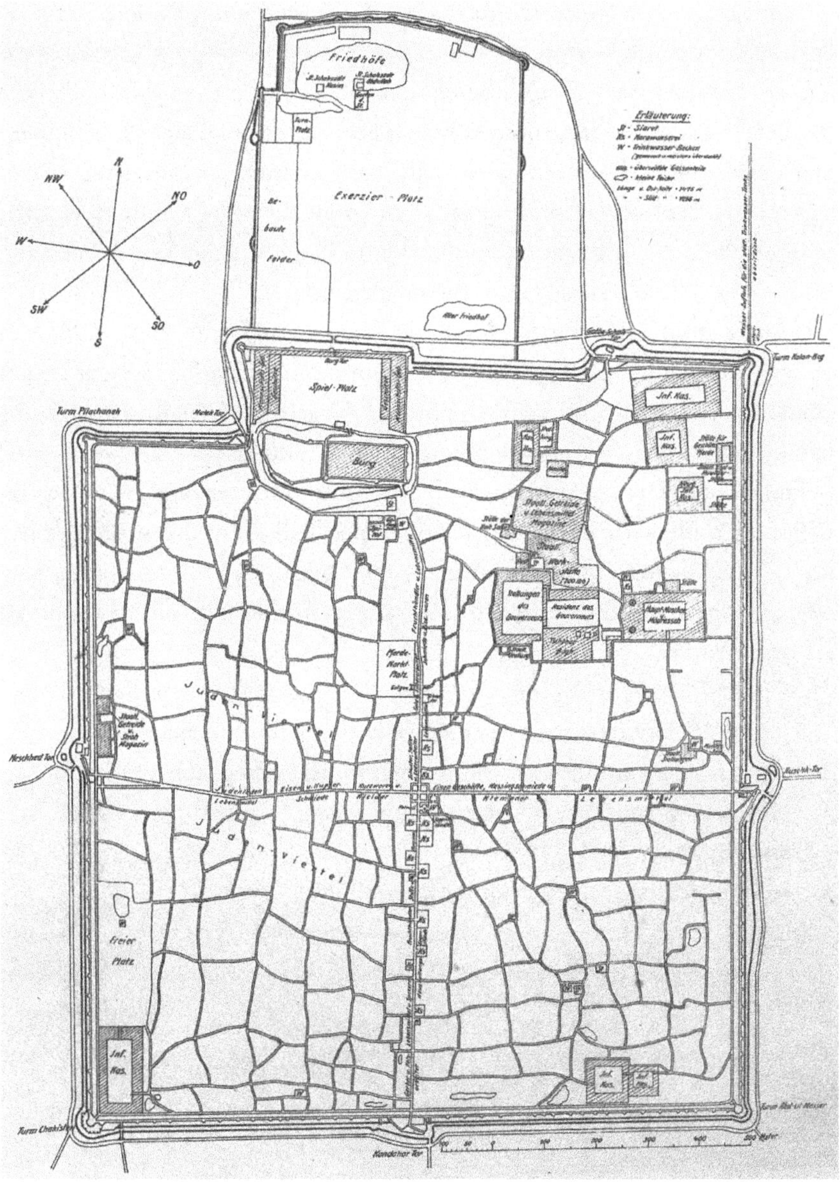


Figure 10.5 Sketch map of Herat by Oskar von Niedermayer, 1915.

Sorties via sally ports and/or main gateways are indispensable tactics in defense. Sorties are mounted, for instance, to surprise (indeed, terrorize) the enemy, as they try to set up siege equipment, pontoon the moat, or sap the mound.[133] There may have been sally ports concealed in Herat's embankment or citadel walls;[134] however, since walls, bastions, and embankment do not survive, we shall never know. A sally port only has to be a slim crevice cut obliquely into the fortification's wall, wide and high enough for a cavalier and his charger.[135] It is re-sealed after the riders exit.

Apart from sally ports, portals designed to regulate daily traffic can be engineered for dual-functions. Sally ports must have barriers to thwart penetration when open. Sayfī's reports of Ghiyāth al-Dīn Kart taking the battle to Yasa'ur's *lashkars* are telling: about 1,000 armor-clad (*āhan-pūsh*) Nikudari and Harawi cavalry sortied.[136] In another engagement, Kartids sallied to clash with Yasa'ur's cavalry, which had arrayed outside the five gates.[137] Sayfī's reports suggest that (1) sally ports existed; or (2) entryways were of sophisticated designs. Portals (sally ports and multi-function ports) are designed to:

1. permit cavalry to sortie as a cohesive body (défilé or échelon);
2. allow friendly troops to withdraw methodically from the battlefield;
3. hinder penetration by the enemy when opened for sallies and withdrawals;[138]
4. to be obscured from view of the enemy.[139]

[133] On sorties against siege engineers, see Ibn al-Qalanisi, *Damascus Chronicle of the Crusades*, tr. H.A.R. Gibb (London: Luzac, 1932), 121–22.

[134] On the design of a Seleucid-Sasanid sally port at Marw, see Georgina Herrmann, et al., "The International Merv Project. Preliminary Report on the Eighth Season (1999)," *Iran* 38 (2000):1–31, 13. On sally ports, see Toy, *Fortification*, 31.

[135] N.C. Loader, "A Possible East Sally Port in the North-East Extension at Mycenae? A Brief Note," *The Annual of the British School at Athens* 91 (1996):191–96 and Fig. 1.

[136] al-Harawī, *Harāt*, 698.

[137] Ibid., 713.

[138] Not just the enemy, but desperate civilians. Following a sortie, "[t]he gate could not be shut [...] because the pressure of the crowd trying to enter was so great. Consequently, the enemy, intermingling with the townspeople, entered in such numbers that the town was taken by force." William of Tyre, *A History of Deeds Done Beyond the Sea*, trs. E.A. Babcock and A.C. Krey, 2 vols (New York: Columbia University Press, 1943), 2:258.

[139] If not obscured, enemy bowmen and artillerymen will concentrate fire on the portal and on exiting/returning cavalry.

Returning cavalry must not expose unguarded flanks to the enemy. Portals are designed to permit cavalry to return whereby the squadron's shielded (left) side is exposed to the enemy. A clockwise return process is a timeless practice. To illustrate, cavalry sally out of the Bar-Amān Gate (northeast) to engage the enemy, but return single file parallel to the east wall. They receive protective fire from compatriots along the battle wall; they are shielded by the breastwall to their left (if *band-i khandaq* means breastwall). They turn into the Khūsh Gate's *return gate*. Whereas cavalry exiting Khūsh Gate (east) return parallel to the south wall and enter Herat through Firūzābād Gate (and so on).

## The Kartid Gates

The Kartid gates were made from iron (*darwāza-hā-yi āhanīn*) and proclaimed the epithets of the House of Kart (*alqāb-i mulūk*). The gates were expropriated by Temür.[140] A debate persists on which and how many Kartid gates were made of iron.[141] Ibn Ḥawqal's report described four gates: one of iron; three of wood (Chapter Seven). This is the basis for the belief that the Kartid era Malik Gate (which possibly stood where Saray Gate had stood) was cast from iron, and the remaining Kartid gates were of wood. Ibn Ḥawqal's narrative is from the 4th/10th century; quite a lot happened in Herat since. Elǰigidei is unlikely to have left the gates intact: vanquishers destroy, inter alia, the vanquished's gates, which is what Böjäi and Temür did. If by miracle Elǰigidei's soldiers had overlooked this fundamental task, the timber will have been scavenged for firewood in the post-Elǰigidei period. The Kartid gates were not the pre-Mongol gates of Herat.

Wood rots; wood burns.[142] In the Mongol epoch, when naphtha was delivered to doorsteps by launchers (*naft-andāz*), wooden gates were not just useless, they were deadly. A secondary function for machicolations is in extinguishing fires.[143] A switch from wooden doors/exterior coverings to

140 Ḥāfiẓ-i Abrū, *Kart*, 211. The Kartid gates were taken to Shahr-i Sabz, Temür's birthplace.
141 See Noelle-Karimi, *Pearl*, 23 and nn.58–59.
142 See, e.g., Vegetius/Milner (tr.), *Epitome*, Book IV, Chap. 4 (protecting gates from fire).
143 Toy, *Fortification*, 120.

non-combustible materials was crucial.[144] Moreover, timber is scarce in the Iranian plateau,[145] and used sparingly. Wood was favored for non-retractable bridges,[146] which were burned to frustrate the enemy; hence, another martial context for the maxim "to burn one's bridges."

Sayfī's report on Yasa'ur's forces besieging Herat helps in labeling the five Kartid gates. Yasa'ur's army had penetrated the suburbs, surrounded the walls, and were arrayed before the five gates (*darwāza*):[147] Darwāza-yi Khūsh (E), Darwāza-yi Fīrūzābād (S), Darwāza-yi ʿIrāq (W), Darwāza-yi Malik (NW), and Darwāza-yi Bar-Amān (NE).

There is confusion about the appellations for the NE and NW gates.[148] Ḥāfiẓ-i Abrū claims the Malik Gate was also called Bar-Amān Gate or Maydān Gate.[149] However, it is clear from Sayfī's report that both Bar-Amān and Malik existed coterminously. The problem is in identifying which is NE and which is NW. A fount of confusion is the existence of Bar-Amān village, northwest of Malik Gate;[150] hence the supposition that it had "lent its name" to the NW gate.[151] A Malik Gate had existed—probably since Fakhr al-Dīn Kart's reign.[152] Shaykh al-Islam Niẓām al-Dīn ʿAbd al-Raḥīm Khʷāfī was seized at the Malik Gate in 738/1338.[153] Malik Gate lasted to modern times. It is situated in the NW by Isfizārī,[154] by Niedermayer (see Fig. 10.5), and by a British army engineer.[155] The four principal intramuros bazaars acquire their appellations from four gates and their eponymous boulevards: Khūsh,

[144] A British officer noted that the absence of wood-covered buildings in Herat would have enabled it to survive shelling better than a European city. *ABC* 3:53; cf. Golombek & Wilber, *Timurid Architecture*, 1:27 (cypress and pistachio use in Timurid Herat). Timber was probably imported from the Caspian regions. See Wulff, *Traditional*, 74–78 (timbers of Persia).

[145] Beazley & Harverson, *Desert*, 6–7, 22.

[146] Bridges over the trench in the nineteenth century were constructed of wood. *ABC*, 1:53.

[147] al-Harawī, *Harāt*, 712 (compass points supplied by me); cf. Allen, *Catalogue*, 36–38.

[148] See Noelle-Karimi, *Pearl*, 22–23 and nn.57–58. Malik Gate (NE) and Bar-Amān Gate (NW) in the Kartid era (see ibid., 23 n.58).

[149] Ḥāfiẓ-i Abrū/Harawī (ed.), *Jughrāfiyā*, 12; Krawulsky, *Ḫorāsān*, 1:18.

[150] *Qarya-yi Bar-Amān*: see Saljūqī, *Khiyābān*, 105–06; Allen, *Catalogue*, 62, Cat. No. 158.

[151] Allen, *Catalogue*, 62.

[152] Malik Gate & Malik Bazaar: both are thought to have acquired their appellations to honor the *malik* because he developed the bazaar (see Fig. 9.1, #103). *Khānaqāh-yi Fakhr al-Dīn Kart* was near Malik Gate (Fig. 9.1, #499).

[153] See Chapter 9, n.106.

[154] Isfizārī, *Rawżāt*, 1:77: Malik Gate is north; Qipchāq Gate is NE; *ergo*, Malik Gate is NW.

[155] MacGregor, *Central Asia*, 342. See also Yate, *Northern Afghanistan*, 26.

Firūzābād, ʿIrāq, and Malik.[156] Malik Bazaar was in the NW quarter, and ran along the north-south axis, from the citadel's plaza (*pā-yi ḥiṣār*) to the intersection (*chahār-sū*).[157]

It is doubtful the name for the NE gate (the so-called Malik Gate) was transferred to the NW gate, thereby altering its name from Bar-Amān Gate to Malik Gate. Since "Amān" conveys the sense of "security," "Bar-Amān" may have been a colloquialism for "security gate," a postern near the NE bastion.[158] It made sense to have a postern here: NE gate did not connect to a bazaar,[159] but led to the *Masjid-i jāmiʿ*. In later centuries, the NE quadrant and NE gate were developed.[160] When Ḥāfiẓ-i Abrū completed *Geography* (*c.* 823/1420), the NE gate had shed its Kartid era label and assumed its Timurid name (Qipchāq Gate); hence Ḥāfiẓ-i Abrū's putative slip. Firūzābād was renamed Qandahar Gate after Herat shifted to Pashtun control. "Qipchāq" has political-military resonances to Temür and the Timurids. Bar-Amān Gate apparently became Qipchāq Gate after Temür's conquest.

Sayfī's report on Yasaʾur's encirclement does not help settle which gate is NE/NW. Kartids, writes Sayfī,[161] sallied to battle Yasaʾur's forces. They clashed in the:

North: from Bar-Āmān Gate to the Injīl Bridge and the vicinities of the old citadel (*jiwār-i quhandiz*).[162]

North: from Malik Gate, in the alley of the *quhandiz* (*dar kūchih-yi quhandiz*) and the orchards and streets (*shāriʿ*) of the White Garden (*Bāgh-i Safīd*).[163]

East: from Khūsh Gate to Rīkinah Bridge and "Markitāʾī's Courtyard."[164]

[156] On bazaars and boulevards, see Allen, *Catalogue*, 49, 51–52, Cat. Nos. 100, 101, 102, 103.

[157] Isfizārī, *Rawżāt*, 1:78. See also al-Harawī, *Harāt*, 74 n. 3.

[158] Bar-Amān: Alternatively, it could refer to a neighborhood (*maḥalla*). In later years, the NE quarter became known as "Kutub Chāq" (Quṭbīchāq) after the NE gate. See *ABC*, 2:562.

[159] Isfizārī, *Rawżāt*, 1:78; Allen, *Catalogue*, 38 and Cat. No. 60.

[160] Samizay, *Islamic Architecture*, 117–20.

[161] al-Harawī, *Harāt*, 713; cf. Ḥāfiẓ-i Abrū, *Kart*, 150 (variation in toponyms).

[162] Pul-i Injīl: Allen, *Catalogue*, 40, Cat. No. 68: carried Khiyabān throughfare over Jūy-i Injīl.

[163] Bāgh-i Safīd: Ibid., 205–07, Cat. No. 645 (built by Ghiyāth al-Dīn Kart). Kūchih-yi Quhandiz and Shāriʿ-i Bāgh-i Safīd: see ibid., 48 and Cat. No. 96.

[164] Pul-i Rīkinah: Ibid., 43, Cat. No. 81: bridge over unnamed *jūy*. *Ḥayāṭ-i markitāy* (Markitāʾī's or Merkidaï's courtyard) is unknown. Merkidaï was the chief Mongol census taker.

South: from Firūzābād Gate to Darqarā Bridge and the vicinities of Kārtabār.[165]

West: from ʿIrāq Gate, to the orchards and farms of Sīnān.[166]

Since White Garden was in the NE (see Fig. 9.1), Sayfī may have meant City Garden (*Bāgh-i Shahr*), which was north of, and adjacent to, the citadel.[167]

Ḥāfiẓ-i Abrū's Kartid history has an abstract of Sayfī's report, with several revised details. The edited text reads "ʿAydān" (for Maydān) and "Qutūchāq" (for Qipchāq), errors in the manuscripts that were not annotated by the editor. "Quṭbīchāq" is the modern label for the NE gate;[168] therefore, a copyist's interpolation. The report substitutes Maydān Gate for Sayfī's Bar-Aman Gate (thus: "from Maydān Gate [to] *jiwār-i quhandiz*"); Qipchāq Gate for Sayfī's Malik Gate (thus: "*dar kūchih-yi quhandiz* [to] *Bāgh-i Safīd*).[169]

## The Fortified Landscape of the Kartid Kingdom

The fortified topography of the Kartid kingdom within which nestled Herat, and therefore the Kartid court, military, and government, is elucidated below.

A nucleus with *enceintes* was generally sufficient to guarantee the safety of kings and subjects ensconced within. Herat, nonetheless, could not be entirely independent of its vicinities during a military crisis. Herat was dependent on water conveyed from Jūy-i Injīl (we know this because Temür's scouts located the inlet to an aqueduct). Secondly, Herat's agricultural vicinities had to be productive for rulers to extract agricultural taxes; and for farmers and pastoralists to engage in economic exchanges with burghers.

### *Food and Water*

Firstly, on potable water inside walled Herat.

Major Edward Sanders observed (1839–40): "A raised aqueduct of earth [...]" in the northeast, supplied by a source high in the north, "now brings a supply of water for the use of the city."[170] There were also "numerous

[165] Pul-i Darqarā: Ibid., 39, Cat. No. 64: bridge over Jūy-i Alinjān on Farāh Road.
[166] Sīnān: western district. Ibid., 81, Cat. No. 343 (village of Sīnān).
[167] Bāgh-i Shahr: Ibid., 209, Cat. No. 651 (built by Fakhr al-Dīn Kart). See Figure 9.1.
[168] See Saljūqī, *Harāt-i bāstān*, 5 (modern spelling).
[169] Ḥāfiẓ-i Abrū, *Kart*, 150; cf. al-Harawī, *Harāt*, 713.
[170] MacGregor, *Central Asia*, 348.

public reservoirs," which had been "carefully and strongly built of brick and mortar." Water "is found in abundance at a depth of less than 30 feet below the general level of the soil, and wells are very numerous."[171] But wells were apparently not ubiquitous before the eighteenth century because underground water was said to be "salty."[172]

It is not clear therefore if the supply from cisterns and wells of Kartid Herat was sufficient to sustain the city if the aqueduct from Jūy-i Injīl was destroyed. It was a common practice—since antiquity—for hidden aqueducts to be excavated. These conduits passed beneath the trench and embankment, and could not be readily located and destroyed by the enemy. Considering the prolific usage of subterranean waterways in Persia, one may reasonably expect there to have been hidden aqueducts in Herat.

Secondly, on comestibles (especially cereals and fodder) stored inside Herat.

Storing food was crucial because "armies are more often destroyed by starvation than battle, and hunger is more savage than the sword."[173] Grain was stored in state silos, educational-charitable institutions (shrines, mosques, madrasas, hospices), in homes, and on the hoof. In order for there to be an agricultural surplus (for consumption by burghers), hinterlands had to be prosperous. Silos inside the citadel, and elsewhere, held quantities of cereals (barley, wheat, sorghum, rice).[174] The stocking of silos was not merely to prepare for sieges and periods of drought and dearth, but because *raʿāyā* paid their taxes in cash and/or cereals. A silo was a state treasury. Salaries of officials and soldiers were paid in cash and grain. Grain could be retained in silos for extended periods without significant risk of ruin (some loss to vermin is expected).[175] Non-farming *raʿāyā* (craftsmen, artisans, laborers, etc.) accepted remuneration in grain and/or coin. Waqfs stipulated payments in cash and grain. Cereals would have been plentiful (in theory); but cereals are depletable assets: protracted sieges frequently lead to famine, disease, and capitulation.

[171] Ibid., 350. al-Harawī, *Harāt*, 407: confirms the existence of wells in 7th/13th century.
[172] Najimi, "Cistern," 39.
[173] Vegetius/Milner (tr.), *Epitome*, Book III, Chapter 4.
[174] al-Harawī, *Harāt*, 407: confirms the existence of hidden grain stocks in 7th/13th century.
[175] On grain storage in Sultanate Delhi, see Ibn Battuta, *Travels*, 3:621.

Starvation was a weapon in the blockader's arsenal; indeed, his most potent one if offense and defense were at strategic equilibrium. Böjäi, on determining that the breach of Herat's fortifications would prove difficult, elected to blockade Herat.[176] According to Sayfī, 100 *mann* of wheat sold for 80 dinars inside Herat, but "in Böjäi's bazaar,"[177] 100 *mann* sold for 2 dinars.[178] The blockade was successful. Muḥammad Sām surely feared surrendering to Danishmand's son, but with cereal stocks dwindling, famine intensifying, and people dying of starvation, Heratis begged for relief.[179] Muḥammad Sām surrendered the city.

*People and Livestock*

Residents of inner Herat and its suburbs, therefore, were relatively safe, and had food and water. But what of their compatriots in the hinterlands?

A just king should not leave his subjects adrift to be raped, pillaged, and murdered. The twinned duties of fidelity (*wafā*ʾ) and service (*khidma*), insightfully analyzed by Jürgen Paul,[180] in my view, extend also to *malik-raʿāyā* relations: *raʿāyā* owe their *malik* fidelity and service; and he must advance the commonweal. This includes protecting *raʿāyā*. The claim by faithless *bandagān*—Majd al-Dīn Khʷāfī, Farrukhzād Tūlakī, et al.—who had defected to Yasaʾur, illustrates a Kartid's predicament. They petitioned sultan Abū Saʿīd, arguing that they had no choice but to yield to Yasaʾur, because, unlike Ghiyāth al-Dīn, they could not hunker behind fortifications; and by yielding, had prevented the spoliation of the sultan's domains.[181] Supplicants were incorrigibles whose treachery was fueled by ambition, but they made valid points: a ruler should not sit behind fortifications while his subjects are being raped and butchered, and the realm pillaged. Muʿizz al-Dīn Kart had marched from Herat to Zāwa—*c.* 180 miles/290 km—to

[176] al-Harawī, *Harāt*, 526, 547 (five-month siege; from mid-706/Feb. to late 706/June 1307).

[177] Böjäi's bazaar: If besiegers are not wantonly robbing, raping, and murdering locals, *raʿāyā* emerge to transact with besiegers. Apart from "camp followers" (scavengers, prostitutes, etc.)—a phenomenon common to invading armies—bazaars (*agora* and *forum* in the Greek and Roman contexts) sprouted alongside enemy cantonments.

[178] al-Harawī, *Harāt*, 548.

[179] Ibid. Narratives of beleaguered resorting to *ḥarām* sources for nourishment (cannibalism; domestic animals) are not apocryphal. See, e.g., ʿAlī Kātib, *Tārīkh-i jadīd-i Yazd*, 141.

[180] Paul, "*Khidma*," *et passim*.

[181] Faṣīḥ, *Mujmal*, 898.

fight the Sarbadar-Shaykhiyya coalition. He could have remained inside fortified Herat, but his kingdom would have been despoiled by Shaykh Ḥasan's and Wajīh al-Dīn Maʿsūd's coalition.

The importance of the Kartid network of fortifications in town and country under the control of *bandagān* and castellans is manifest from Sayfī's reports on Yasaʾur. Ghiyāth al-Dīn Kart received intelligence briefs in Ṣafar 718/April 1318 from governors in Ghazni and Garmsīr. Yasaʾur had been fattening horses and training men for forty days; an attack on Khurasan was forthcoming in the next month or two. Ghiyāth al-Dīn had time to apprise commanders and *bandagān* that Yasaʾur intended to march on Herat from Zamīndāwar, thence to Ṭūs and Nishapur. He emphasized in a communiqué (to loyalists) the imperative of coordinating defense. He ordered heightened vigilance by spies and sentinels (*qarāwul wa dīdabān*); for highways to be protected; for people in highlands and lowlands to shelter in redoubts (*ʿimārat-i ḥuṣun-i bilād wa qilāʿ-i jibāl*).[182] He stressed the importance of clearing the countryside of peoples and quadrupeds (*ḥawāshī wa mawāshī*). Messengers sped from Herat to sundry destinations bearing the Kartid's communiqué. He also dispatched 100 horsemen (to coordinate the defense, apparently). The *malik* sent a homing pigeon (*kabūtar*) to the shrine of Shaykh al-Islam Aḥmad-i Jām to alert his Sufi preceptor.[183]

The policy of evacuating livestock and *raʿāyā* from the countryside did not emerge from altruism.[184] The security of Herat, and its ability to survive a siege, was contingent on denying the enemy access to the resources that it needed. Comestibles and potable water were not imperatives exclusive to the besieged.[185] A military axiom is that: "amateurs talk about strategy and tactics. Professionals talk about logistics and sustainability in warfare." Water from *jūy*s, streams, wells, and cisterns;[186] fruits, nuts, vegetables, and wild game, will have sustained invaders. Meadows and pastures fed their horses, but whether grasslands were sufficient to satisfy the requirements of horses

182 On terms for strongholds, see Mottahedeh, "Lexicography," 470–71.
183 al-Harawī, *Harāt*, 681–82. See also p.697: Muḥarram 719/Feb.–Mar. 1319 warning to *raʿāyā* to seek shelter in redoubts. This was also the product of timely intelligence.
184 On Chinese siege preparations, see Franke, "Siege," 152–61.
185 On military logistics, see Engels, *Alexander, et passim.*
186 Defenders drop carcasses into cisterns and wells to pollute the water.

and draft animals is open to inquiry.[187] Access by an enemy to livestock (fowl, oxen, goats, sheep, donkeys, horses, camels), fodder, and cereals, had to be foiled by Kartids and their *bandagān*.

*Raʿāyā* were sheltered because, if captured, they could be forced to excavate/build contravallations, scrounge for provender and firewood, forge armaments, haul stones, and used as arrow-fodder. *Raʿāyā* may voluntarily support the enemy: they had to be policed.[188] Factionalism contributed to Herat's capitulation to Tolui; Kartid *malik*s were undermined by notables in Herat (Mawlānā Wajīh al-Dīn Nasafī, for example, had advised Danishmand Bahadur on besieging Herat); ʿAlī Muʾayyad's defense of Sabzavar was undermined by Shaykhiyya partisans entrenched in Sabzavar.[189]

Physical geography hinders armies. The Hindu Kush and citadels impeded Chingiz Khan's advance, obliging him, for instance, to strike a bargain with Rukn al-Dīn Muḥammad Marghanī, castellan of Fort Khaysār. Soldiers and animals cannot traverse deserts without water, which Alexander discovered on his march through the "Gedrosian Desert" (Makrān). The Macedonian army, forced to eat their horses and pack animals, "'burned the loot for which they had harassed the farthest reaches of the Orient'."[190] Astute soldiers like Fakhr al-Dīn and Ghiyāth al-Dīn assuredly exploited the obstacles erected by nature.

The fortified landscape of the Kartid kingdom served to harness a range of resources (economic, military, political, geographical, cultural, ideological) for Herat's benefit, hinder its enemies, and control the *raʿāyā*.

### *Highways, Strongholds, and Caravansarays*

The fortifications of the Kartid realm are given in Table 10.1. These are the fortified (*maḥrūsa*) townships and citadels (*ḥiṣār*, *qalʿa*, etc.) referenced by Sayfī, et al., for Ilkhanid-Kartid Khurasan. It is not known if every given fortification continued to thrive; whether the Kartid *banda*

[187] On pasturing, see Smith, "Mongol Society," 265–66; Smith, "Mongol Manpower," esp. 280–81, 297–98; John Masson Smith, "From Pasture to Manger: The Evolution of Mongol Cavalry Logistics in Yuan China and its Consequences," in *Pferde in Asien*, eds B.G. Fragner, et al. (Vienna: Österreichischen Akademie der Wissenschaften, 2009), pp. 63–73.

[188] Franke, "Siege," 156–58 (policing potential enemies inside a city).

[189] Smith, *Sarbadar*, 152.

[190] Holt, *Treasures*, 122.

*Table 10.1 Fortified Landscape of the Kartid Realm*

| Province (District) | *Ḥiṣār, Qalʿa*, etc. | Active | Source(s) | Comments |
|---|---|---|---|---|
| Āzāb | Āzāb | *c.* 720/1320 | n/a | Implied |
| Bākharz | Ḥiṣār-i R-Z-H [Razah] | 720/1320 | al-Harawī, *Harāt*, 746–49, 751 | Captured by Ghiyāth al-Dīn Kart. Given in sources incorrectly as Z-R-H (Zarah of Sīstān) and Ḥiṣār-i Zarah |
| Farāh | Ḥiṣār (not named) | Rabīʿ I 721 / April 1321 | al-Harawī, *Harāt*, 778 | Ināltikīn Farāhī's stronghold. Captured by Nikudaris on behalf of the Kartids |
| Fūshanj | Qalʿa-yi Fūshanj | 782/1381 | Ḥāfiẓ-i Abrū, Kart, 207;<br>Yazdī/Munshī, *Pasandīdah*, 1:216–18;<br>Faṣīḥ, *Mujmal*, 979 | Attacked by Temür before surrounding Herat. Strong citadel with wet moat |
| Gharjistān | Not specified | *c.* 823/1420 | Krawulsky, *Ḫorāsān*, 1:33, but cf. ibid., 1:34–35 (no specification) | Mentioned generally by Ḥāfiẓ-i Abrū in the notice on Ghūr (see below) |
| Ghūr | Khaysār | From before 618/1221 to 783/1381 | al-Harawī, *Harāt, et passim*; Ḥāfiẓ-i Abrū, *Kart, et passim* | Citadel was active from Chingiz Khan's time to Temür's invasion |
| Ghūr | "There are strong citadels in Ghūr" | *c.* 823/1420 | Krawulsky, *Ḫorāsān*, 1:33 (no details); cf. Krawulsky, *Ḫorāsān*, 1:30 (note on Qarya-yi Fīrūzkūh) | A series of citadels may be constructed to protect the principal citadel (here, Fort Khaysār). This is a likely scenario for Ghūr and Gharjistān |
| Herat | Iskilchih (a/k/a Amān Kūh) | From before 698/1298 to 783/1381 | al-Harawī, *Harāt*, 457;<br>Ḥāfiẓ-i Abrū, *Kart*, 211<br>Yazdī/Munshī, *Pasandīdah*, 1:224 | First mentioned by Sayfī for the events of 698/1298–99 (Öljeitü v. Kartids); last mention is when Herat fell to Temür |

*Table 10.1* *(Continued)*

| Province (District) | *Ḥiṣār*, *Qalʿa*, etc. | Active | Source(s) | Comments |
|---|---|---|---|---|
| Herat | Qalʿa-yi Ikhtiyār al-Dīn | 700–83/1300–81 | al-Harawī, *Harāt*, *et passim*; Ḥāfiẓ-i Abrū, *Kart*, *et passim* | Erected by Fakhr al-Dīn Kart |
| Harāt-Rūd | Possible (pre-Mongol citadel was Ḥiṣār-i Fīrūzkūh) | Kartid era? | Krawulsky, *Ḫorāsān*, 1:30–31, 2:28–29;<br>al-Harawī, *Harāt*, 114<br>Le Strange, *Lands*, 417 | Citadel not mentioned. Qarya-i Ḥiṣārik ("mini-citadel") an agglomeration with 16 dependencies, is mentioned |
| Isfizār (Badr-Ābād) | Qalʿa-yi Badr-Ābād | 782–83/1380–81 | Krawulsky, *Ḫorāsān*, 1:36, 2:33<br>Faṣīḥ, *Mujmal*, 985<br>Yazdī/Munshī, *Pasandīdah*, 1:252 | Existed when Temür invaded Khurasan |
| Isfizār (not known) | Qalʿa-yi Muẓaffar Kūh | *c.* 823/1420 | Krawulsky, *Ḫorāsān*, 1:36, 2:33<br>Isfizārī, *Rawżat*, 1:107–110 | Citadel in the mountains (*kūh*). Zamchī Isfizārī (d.*c.* 915/1510) gives this name |
| Isfizār (Isfizār) | Qalʿa (not named) | *c.* 823/1420 | Krawulsky, *Ḫorāsān*, 1:36, 2:33 | Ḥāfiẓ-i Abrū: a citadel of clay existed in the *qaṣaba* of Isfizār |
| Jām (Turbat-i Jām; or Maʿd-Ābād-i Jām) | Ḥiṣār-i Jām | 718/1318–19 (existed into 19th century) | al-Harawī, *Harāt*, 692–93;<br>Ḥāfiẓ-i Abrū, *Rashīdī*, 153–54; Mīrkh$^{w}$ānd, *Rawżat*, 4,349–50<br>Krawulsky, *Ḫorāsān*, 1:40<br>Būzjānī, *Rawżat*, 83 | The citadel at Maʿd-Ābād-i Jām was invested by Tolui in 618/1221. Maʿd-Ābād village and Turbat-i Jām merged. Probably just one citadel |
| Jām (Būzjān) | Būzjān | *c.* 823/1420 | Krawulsky, *Ḫorāsān*, 1:40 | Būzjān was a major *qaṣaba* in the *wilāyat* of Jām since pre-Mongol times |

| | | | | |
|---|---|---|---|---|
| Jām (Farhād-Gard) | Qalʿa-yi Farhād-Gard (a/k/a Farhād-Jird) | *c.* 772/1370–71 | Ḥāfiẓ-i Abrū, *Kart*, 196<br>Faṣīḥ, *Mujmal*, 967 | This redoubt was on the Sarbadarid-Kartid border (Smith, *Sarbadars*, 151) |
| Jām (H-W-Ā-R-W) | Unknown | *c.* 823/1420 | Krawulsky, *Ḫorāsān*, 1:40, 2:36 | Noted only by Ḥāfiẓ-i Abrū |
| Kūsūyi | Ḥiṣār | *c.* 720/1320 | n/a | Implied (no specific references) |
| Khwāf | Ḥiṣār-i Kāriyān | *c.* 720/1320 | al-Harawī, *Harāt*, 750; cf. Krawulsky, *Ḫorāsān*, 1:37 | Not clear if captured by Ghiyāth al-Dīn Kart. It was reinforced by Majd al-Dīn Khwāfī. Ḥāfiẓ-i Abrū: *qarya* by name of Kāriyān, but no mention of citadel |
| Khwāf (Mābīzhan-Ābād) | Ḥiṣār-i Mābīzhan-Ābād | 720/1320 | al-Harawī, *Harāt*, 755–59<br>Faṣīḥ, *Mujmal*, 899 | Majd al-Dīn Khwāfī's main redoubt |
| Khwāf (Niyāz-Ābād | Ḥiṣār-i Niyāz-Ābād | 720/1320 | al-Harawī, *Harāt*, 750–54 | Majd al-Dīn Khwāfī's other redoubt |
| Quhistān (Turshīz) | Qalʿa-yi Turshīz | *c.* 784/1382f. | Yazdī/ʿAbbāsī, *Ẓafarnāmah*, 1:252–54<br>Yazdī/Munshī, *Pasandīdah*, 1:240–43<br>Naṭanzī, *Muntakhab*, 242–43 | Controlled by a Ghurid faction installed by Pīr ʿAlī Kart. Captured by Temür. The citadel's defenses, and how they were breached, are described |
| Sarakhs | Qalʿa-yi Sarakhs | 823/1420 | Krawulsky, *Ḫorāsān*, 1:76 (unnamed); cf. Yazdī/Munshī, *Pasandīdah*, 1:215 | Ancient citadel, built from clay. Sarakhs was the patrimony of Muḥammad Kart b. Muʿizz al-Dīn Kart |
| Tūlak | Qalʿa-yi Tūlak | 720/1320 (to *c.* 823/1420?) | al-Harawī, *Harāt*, 764–67; Faṣīḥ, *Mujmal*, 899; cf. Krawulsky, *Ḫorāsān*, 1:35 | Mountain redoubt of Farrukhzād b. Quṭb al-Dīn Tūlakī. Ḥāfiẓ-i Abrū writes of a strong citadel at "Sākhar & Tūlak" |

controlling it continuously served the Kartids. Often, toponyms become known incidentally or in a negative context; for example, when a citadel is invested because a governor or castellan refused to subordinate himself to the Kartids. The Kartid network was not static: *bandagān* at Āzāb, Bākharz, Farāh, Isfizār, Khʷāf, and Tūlak withdrew from the network when opportunity presented itself. The network of fortifications, ideally if not consistently, protected highways and byways and facilitated the movement of caravans; and flow of agricultural products from farms to markets; meats, dairy, pelts, and wool from pastures to markets. Āzāb, Farāh, Isfizār, and Tūlak were way stations or hubs in the multi-directional flow of merchandise and intellectual capital. The withdrawal of *bandagān* from the Kartid security network would have throttled (possibly stifled) Herat's socio-economic interactions with Yazd, Kirmān, Sistān, Qandahar, Ghazni, and India.

It is easier to identify citadels closer to the Kartid center, Herat, than at the edges of the Kartid realm: Sīstān, Kabul, Qandahar, Ghazni, in Garmsīr and Hilmand, and north along the Oxus. Since Sayfī, Ḥāfiẓ-i Abrū, Isfizārī, et al., focus on the center not the periphery, we, too, are trapped in the center. This is reflected in Table 10.1. Sīstān, a province itemized in Möngke's *yarlīgh* of 649/1251,[191] had drifted away from Herat's orbit. Shortly after acceding, Muʿizz al-Dīn Kart had tried to subjugate it but failed.[192] Sīstān appears not to have returned to the Kartid fold. Sīstān held major citadels, like Qalʿa-yi Ṭāq,[193] Ḥiṣār-i Zarah,[194] Ḥiṣār-i Nīh,[195] Qalʿa-yi Kāh/Gāh,[196] and Qalʿa-yi Safīd-Diz,[197] to name the few *known* to have flourished in the late 7th/13th to late 8th/14th centuries.

[191] Sīstān is interpreted narrowly today, but once extended to both banks of the Hilmand.

[192] Sīstānī, *Iḥyāʾ al-mulūk*, 95. Year: 734/1333–34.

[193] Key fortress west of Lake Sīstān since reign of Maḥmūd of Ghazna. Barthold, *Geography*, 71; Le Strange, *Lands*, 343–44. See also Anon./Bahār (ed.), *Sīstān*, 374.

[194] Le Strange, *Lands*, 337–38.

[195] Anon./Bahār (ed.), *Sīstān*, 378. Built/re-built by Nawrūz's governor in 693/1294.

[196] On the location, see G.P. Tate, *Seistan* (Quetta: Nisa, n.d. [1979; reprint of 1910–12 Calcutta ed.]), 31, 37, 67–69; Oliver St. John, et al., *Eastern Persia: An Account of the Journeys of the Persian Boundary Commission, 1870–71–72*, 2 vols (London: Macmillan, 1876), 1:325–27; *ABC*, 3:38–40.

[197] Anon./Bahār (ed.), *Sīstān*, 373; Anon./Gold (ed.), *Sīstān*, 329. Qalʿa-yi Safīd-Diz was at Lāsh, on one bank of Farāh River, with Juwayn on the opposite bank. Fort Lāsh, sketched in *ABC*, v.3 (between pp. 34–35) could be where Safīd-Diz had stood.

A network of citadels protected highways and byways. Merchandise and produce flowing to/from Herat from/to Balūchistān, Sīstān, Kirman, Yazd, Bam, Qandahar, and Ghazni passed through hubs Farāh[198] and Zaranj;[199] mini-hubs/way stations like Juwayn.[200] An example of the importance of a network of forts to which travelers can hasten is in Ibn Battuta's reports: his caravan was attacked by Pashtun bandits in a defile east of Ghazni shortly before it could reach the safety of a fortress.[201]

Caravansarays were integral to this global trade and security network; they often doubled as fortresses.[202] Caravans had schedules that would be interrupted by hazardous weather or highway conditions. For instance, caravans traveling to Bam, thence the Persian Gulf, departed once per year in winter due to extreme heat. If an annual trek is canceled, that caravan may not travel until the next year—or later if conditions have not improved. Hence the urgency to implement security through a network of caravansarys and forts, failing which, trade and travel dwindle or cease.

The eastern peripheries, Kabul, Qandahar, and Ghazni receive occasional mentions; for instance, the intelligence brief of Ṣafar 718/April 1318, which suggests loyalty to Kartids by the lords of Ghazni and Garmsīr. Qalʿa-yi Qandahār was captured in 680/1281 by Shams al-Dīn the Younger,[203] but its status since is unknown. Citadels in the Hilmand and Garmsīr regions included Qalʿa-yi Bust;[204] Qalʿa-yi Fatḥ;[205] Qalʿa-yi Dāwarī (Zamīndāwar),[206] among countless other fortifications of miscellaneous classes on both banks of the Hilmand.[207]

198 Adamec, *Gazetteer*, 2:76–80. Had a large fort.

199 Ibid., 2:220–24, 2:302. Had many forts.

200 Ibid., 2:182–93; Le Strange, *Lands*, 341–42. Had a large fort.

201 Ibn Battuta, *Travels*, 3:591 and n.210.

202 Ferrier, *Caravan*, 74 (security at caravansary). See, generally, Mohammad-Yusuf Kiani and Wolfram Kleiss, "Caravansary," *EIr* 4:798–802.

203 al-Harawī, *Harāt*, 390–93; Faṣīḥ, *Mujmal*, 835.

204 Barthold, *Geography*, 71; Adamec, *Gazetteer*, 2:135–37; Tate, *Seistan, et passim*; Terry Allen, "Notes on Bust," *Iran* 26 (1988):55–68. The name Bust/Bist is thought to derive from the twenty (*bīst*) forts that had thrived in the vicinity.

205 Barthold, *Geography*, 73; *ABC*, 3:19–22; Adamec, *Gazetteer*, 2:137–40. A large caravansaray thrived outside Qalʿa-yi Fatḥ.

206 Anon./Bahār (ed.), *Sīstān*, 375. Le Strange, *Lands*, 344–46; Minorsky (ed.), *Ḥudūd*, 345; Barthold, *Geography*, 72–74. Zamīndāwar is a large fertile tract fed by several water sources. See Adamec, *Gazetteer*, 2:231–42, 2:296–302.

207 British intelligence officers traveling northwest toward Hāmūn Basin through Garmsīr and Hilmand in 1884 recorded and mapped many fortresses, most in ruins. See *ABC*, 3:15–60.

The manifold forts constructed along the Hilmand River existed not only to protect agricultural settlements, which covered about one to two miles on both banks of the river (depending on irrigation facilities), but also overland traffic and river traffic. Joseph Ferrier (1811–86) observed (in the 1840s) that the Hilmand River coursed rapidly, and if Europeans controlled the Hilmand region, "steamboats would soon navigate it, and the supply of wood on its banks would remedy the want of coal."[208] The Hilmand originates in the northeast, traverses southwest, and flows into the Hāmūn/Sīstān Basin. The Farāh, Harūd/Harūt, and Kh$^{w}$āsh/Khāsh rivers also flow into this Basin.[209] Citadels were not accidentally placed along the Hilmand's course: Qalʿa-yi Bust was constructed by the confluence of the Hilmand and Arghandāb River,[210] which flows southwest from Qandahar. Flat-bottomed boats traveled the Indus River. It is conceivable that in the Kartid period flat-bottomed boats transported merchandise and agricultural produce from Bust to the Basin, for offloading and transport by camel and mule to Zaranj, Farāh, Juwayn, and Herat.

Yazdī/Munshī, *Pasandīdah*, 1:258–61: citadels attacked by Temür, *c.* 785/1383–84, including Qalʿa-yi Kūkah and Qalʿa-yi Surkh, which are identified in Tate, *Seistan*, 62.

208 Ferrier, *Caravan*, 429.

209 See ibid., 429–31 (observations on the Sīstān Basin); Yate, *Khurasan*, 110–24 (Hilmand); Bellew, *Mission*, 34–57 (travels from Qandahar to Bust, Gurmsel, and "*hamoon*").

210 Allen, "Bust," 55.

# Part II: Reflections and Conclusions

It is imprudent to venture into the winding alleys of Karl Wittfogel's theses on hydraulic and hydro-agricultural societies,[1] especially since he did not examine Persia; but a comment on bureaucracy and centralized control of water is unavoidable. There is no evidence the Mongol Empire, Ilkhanids or Kartids created a bureaucracy—a water authority (*dīwān-i āb*)—to manage Herat's hydrological network.[2] Kartids occasionally engaged in excavating canals (Jūy-i Naw), constructing dams (Band-i Salūmad), cisterns (Ḥawż-yi Ghiyāth al-Dīn Kart), and water-control boxes (Naṭarah-i Malik), but could not offer sustained financing. Bureaucracies and large-scale infrastructure projects demand cash, which Kartids infrequently possessed.

Ilkhanids could not afford to throw money at infrastructure projects either. The policy established by Ghāzān and Rashīd al-Dīn was to seminally change the fiscal and legal environment that had deterred potential investors. They aimed to foster a climate where individual and institutional investors had incentives to reclaim fallow lands and restore derelict hydrological assets. Il-Khan and vizier were appealing to economic self-interests of investors.[3] The pair transformed the *immeasurable uncertainties* that had deterred potential investors into *measurable uncertainties* (that is, manageable risks). Fiscal-legal reforms eliminated by fiat all legal claims over thirty years, and nullified ancient property deeds. The occupiers of farmlands and pastures, and possessors of watermills, *kārīzs*, and *jūys* in Herat and its purlieus, irrespective

1 K.A. Wittfogel, *Oriental Despotism* (New Haven: Yale University Press, 1957).

2 Kartids probably monitored the hydrological network for tax purposes. The network was monitored in the Timurid era. See Subtelny, *Timurids*, 139 and nn.176–177.

3 Self-interest is denigrated, but it motivates merchants to undertake arduous caravan journeys and *kārīz*-diggers to excavate despite the risk of cave-in. On the respect held by Iranians for *kārīz*-diggers, see Smith, *Blind White Fish*, 58.

of whether their tenancy was legal or illegal, no longer feared eviction or loss of capital improvements to farms and hydrological assets. State and private lands were declared fallow by fiat and available for cultivation, which permitted institutional and individual investors with political networks to acquire the best lands and hydrological properties.

Leaders of Islamic institutions will have taken advantage of Ilkhanid fiscal and legal reforms to secure for their institutions—and for themselves—prime real estate and hydrological assets. Moreover, institutions would have received farmlands, aqueducts, watermills, income-producing properties (rent-paying tenants; shops in the bazaars) and cash as waqf. Surplus cash is frequently invested in agricultural and hydrological projects. Islamic institutions—more than Kartid policies and officials—were responsible (by my estimation) for the revivification of agriculture in Kartid Herat. In the Timurid era, the indispensability of Islamic institutions as agro- and hydro-managers is evident;[4] however, the evidence for agro- and hydro-management by Islamic institutions in the Kartid era is not incontrovertible.

Investments in estates and irrigation by Kartids (rulers and officials), Islamic institutions (mosques, shrines, hospices), and wealthy individuals, will have resulted in legal arrangements like that between Ghiyāth al-Dīn Kart and farmers along Jūy-i Naw (formerly Jūy-i Sabaqar): he received four *dāng* (shares) in the land, while they retained two *dāng*. The bargain reflected his cash outlays and their toils.

Another model is where villagers jointly constructed and repaired hydrological assets, and managed water distribution.[5] This form of communal industry is reflected in the efforts of ʿIzz al-Dīn Muqaddam and Qisatay Kūr (Chapter Seven). Was it unique? Or did this model persist in other farming communities around Herat?

Technicians who managed Herat's hydrological network (*mīrāb, sar-qulbī, band-bānī, mard-jūy*)—if *Ṭarīq-i qismat* is indicative of Kartid

4 By the end of the Timurid period, the shrine of Imam Riza (at Mashhad), Aḥmad-i Jām (Turbat-i Jām), Abū Saʿīd b. Abū al-Khayr (at Mayhana), and ʿAbdallāh Anṣārī (at Herat), to name four institutions, had become major agro- and hydro-managers in Khurasan. The shrine of Imam ʿAli (Mazar-i Sharif), founded in 1480 by the last Timurid sultan at Herat, became a major agro- and hydro-manager.

5 See, e.g., Jürgen Paul, "Le village en Asie centrale aux XVe et XVIe siècles," *Cahiers du Monde russe et soviétique* 32/1 (1991):9–15.

praxis[6]—were not compensated from the Kartid fisc, but by individual/institutional landowners and/or tenant-farmers. Private investment in, and control of, water resources prevailed.

Kartids provided indispensable *public goods*. Security was the *conditio sine qua non* for Herat's renaissance.

Firstly, there could be no material and sustained prosperity in Herat if the threat of attacks by predators persisted. Newly constructed or refurbished hydrological assets could be destroyed and human settlements despoiled and de-populated. Fortifying the city of Herat was an imperative for the Kartids, but thwarted by Il-Khans until Fakhr al-Dīn defied them. Absent citadels bristling with manned ramparts and towers, defensive circumvallations, and well-equipped and well-trained garrisons, any prosperity being enjoyed by Heratis could quickly evaporate.

Secondly, farmers, artisans, craftsmen, merchants, ulama, and their families would not remain in, or migrate to, Herat and its purlieus if they faced persistent risk of robbery, rape, murder, mayhem, and enslavement.

Thirdly, once security had been firmly instituted and Kartids had established a monopoly on theft and violence, property rights and contract laws had to be enforced to entice migrants and to retain residents. Although the implementation of *al-amr bi'l ma'rūf wa'l-nahy 'an al-munkar* may be viewed as draconian, promulgation of morality laws sent a message to residents and potential migrants that the ruler was attempting to establish a just and equitable society. This was an important message to broadcast to an audience living in a violent and de-humanized post-Mongol world. Appointments of judges, chief justices, *muḥtasib*s, *ṣadr*s; the putative appointments of *ṣadr al-sharī'a* (Sa'd al-Dīn Kālūnī?) and shaykh al-Islam (Sa'd al-Dīn Mas'ūd Taftāzānī), served not only to reinforce this message, but to devise an enduring regulatory framework and judicial system. The Timurids built on Kartid foundations: office of *ṣadr* (*ṣadārat*); retained the Taftāzānī and Imāmī families as, respectively, the shaykhs al-Islam and chief justices of Herat down to the Safawid age. This is the Kartid legacy.

An appraisal of Kartid security postures is as follows.

[6] al-Harawī, *Ṭarīq-i qismat*, 15 (Timurids followed Kartid methodology).

The security posture of the Kartid kingdom is visualized as comprising four concentric defensive (R)ings: (R1) the walled inner city; (R2) the *bulūks* (districts) of Herat; (R3) the provinces neighboring Wilāyat-i Harāt (e.g., Fūshanj, Jām, Ghūr, etc.); and (R4) the rest of the realm (to Kabul, Murghāb, and Sind). Protecting the core (R1) was critical: lose the capital, lose the kingdom. From this core, the rings push outward and diminish in importance. At the height of Yasaʾur's activities, the outermost ring (R4) had collapsed, but the Kartids retained most of R2 and all of R1, while security was poor in R3 (for instance, when Turbat-i Jām was besieged by Chaghataids).

Carl von Clausewitz noted that "war and its forms result from ideas, emotions, and conditions prevailing *at the time*."[7] A defender/attacker will *evolve*; his mirror, an attacker/defender, must *adapt*. The adage, however, that "generals fight the last war," remains valid: defenses may not be capable of meeting fresh challenges because rulers had failed to prepare. Kartids, from Fakhr al-Dīn to Muʿizz al-Dīn, maintained Herat's qualitative edge in the offense-defense dialectic. Pīr ʿAlī's situation is difficult to judge: internal opposition (vizier Jāmī and allies), and lacklustre combat by Kartid defenders, led to quick surrender. Heratis never doggedly resisted Temür.[8]

Missile launchers—arcuballistae, ballistae, etc.—the panoply of stone-, arrow-, and bolt-launching weapons subsumed by the generic phrase *ʿarrāda wa manjanīq*, were utilized as defensive artillery.[9] The potency of defensive artillery is known and feared. Alexander was wounded at Gaza by a bolt that pierced shield and breastplate.[10] Chingiz Khan was wounded at a siege in China by an arrow that had probably penetrated body armor.[11] The most riveting story—in the literal, metaphorical, and droll senses—on the lethality and the terror-inducing potential of defensive artillery is by Procopius, in the *Gothic Wars* (AD 535–54):[12]

[7] Clausewitz, *On War*, 580 (emphasis added).

[8] Böjäi blockaded Herat because strategic equilibrium had been reached. Once Ghiyath al-Dīn's hands were untied by Sultan Abū Saʿīd and Amir Chūpān, Herat's defenses were not breached. Pīr ʿAlī opened Herat's gates to Temür.

[9] Defensive artillery was a central field in military sciences. Marsden, *Greek*, 116–63.

[10] Ibid., 95–96; Fox, *Alexander*, 192.

[11] Smith, "Demographic," 333.

[12] Procopius, *History*, Book V, § 23.

> And at the Salarian Gate a Goth of goodly stature and a capable warrior, wearing a corselet and having a helmet on his head. [He] refused to remain in the ranks with his comrades, but stood by a tree and kept shooting many missiles at the parapet. But this man by some chance was hit by a missile from an [arrow-shooting ballista] on a tower at his left. And passing through the corselet and the body of the man, the missile sank more than half its length into the tree [...] pinning him to the spot where it entered the tree, it suspended him there a corpse. And when this was seen by the Goths they fell into great fear, [and moved] outside the range of missiles [...].

Balūch, Gharjistānī, Ghurid, Herati, Khalaj, Nikudari, Pashtun (Afghan), and Sijzī (Sīstānī) units served in the Kartid army. Given the outsized roles of Ghurids in Kartid Herat, Ghurid officers probably had decisive roles in devising offensive and defensive postures. Ghurids made for superb commanders and brave warriors. Beyhaqi writes of a Ghurid officer charged with defending Tirmiz in 426/1035: he single-handedly pulled back the cords of a ballista to launch a stone weighing five or six *mann* (*c.* 26–33 lb/12–15 kg) against besiegers.[13] This to say, arcuballistae of sundry military classes would have been deployed along the ramparts of forts Ikhtiyār al-Dīn and Iskilchih; in the *faṣīl* space; and along the Kartid Wall. Lookouts (*dīdbān*) posted atop Herat's *Masjid-i jāmi*ʿ surveyed the battlefield for their comrades below.[14]

Defenders at Bukhara and Nishapur employed (inter alia) ballistae against the Mongols.[15] Defensive artillery was assuredly employed against Öljeitü's, Danishmand's, Yasaʾur's, and Böjäi's besiegers, but details are unavailable. Weapons that launched heavy projectiles (say, 55–132 lb/25–60 kg), were probably not used. These formidable machines, apart from requiring heavy stones (a scarcity on the Iranian Plateau), require large operating crews; furthermore, counter forces damage foundations and ramparts (Newton's Third Law). Weapons that launched smaller stones (say, 11–44 lb/5–20 kg), ballistae that fired single bolts or fusillades of bolts, and could be operated by one man or small crews, were used to launch assorted types of missiles into the attackers' midst to kill, maim, terrify, disorientate, demoralize, and scatter.

[13] Beyhaqi/Bosworth (tr.), *History*, 2:125–26.
[14] al-Harawī, *Harāt*, 698. Posted on the *ṭāq* (*lit.* arch; probably atop the minarets).
[15] Juvainī/Boyle, *World-Conqueror*, 1:106 (against Chingiz) and 1:176 (against Tolui).

The fortified city could endure a protracted siege. Heratis survived Böjäi's siege (from Shaʿbān 706/February 1307 to late Dhū al-Ḥijja 706/June 1307). Herat's aqueducts, cisterns, silos, and food stores sustained denizens. Well-water, although insufficient (at the period) and brackish,[16] supplied residents and livestock.

Heratis living outside the square walls would have tried to cram into inner Herat when an attack became imminent. It is sensible from a military point of view that shops and dwellings in the vicinities of the trench be leveled to deny shelter to the enemy and to allow for clear lines of fire from ramparts,[17] but sources do not express this as fact. Refugees are housed in mosques, hospices, caravansarays, and other buildings. For the duration of a siege, staff at the Friday Mosque and other institutions probably served *āsh* (vegetable potage, perhaps with scraps of meat). *Āsh* is stewed in cauldrons—not unlike the one bequeathed to the Friday Mosque by Pīr ʿAlī that stands in a protective case in the courtyard.[18] Fakhr al-Dīn donated funds for the daily provision (to indigents and such) of 1,000 *mann* (*c.* 6,534 lb/2,970 kg) of bread; ten head of sheep for *āsh*.[19] Even after taking the standard deduction for hyperbole, significant amounts of money, labor, and logistics were involved.

Two take aways from the above. Firstly, during a siege, a *malik* was obliged to feed subjects, if not morally, then to curtail disgruntlement and factionalism. During Tolui's siege, factionalism had gripped defenders and contributed to downfall. During sieges there will be one faction that wants to fight and one that wants to negotiate. The latter gains support as hunger and disease proliferate. Internal dissent, even food riots, will precipitate capitulation. Secondly, staff at Islamic institutions had the wherewithal to feed multitudes. Food stocks determined how long Herat could hold out.

Intelligence was central to the security of the Kartid realm.[20]

16 Najimi, "Cistern," 39 (well-water was "salty").

17 Franke, "Siege," 152 ("scorched earth" around city). Pashtun defenders of Herat did not clear surroundings ahead of the 1838 siege. MacGregor, *Central Asia: Part II*, 348.

18 Wolfe, *Herat*, 18 (image on p.19). Pīr ʿAlī's bronze cauldron (16 ft round; 5 ft in depth) is elaborately decorated, and used on feast days to serve a syrupy dessert. The cauldron is evidence of the superlative quality of bronzework from late Kartid Herat.

19 al-Harawī, *Harāt*, 463; Isfizārī, *Rawżāt*, 1:438.

20 On the criticality of "knowledge of the enemy," from Julius Caesar to modern times, see essay in John Keegan, *Intelligence in War* (New York: Knopf, 2003), 20–38; Silverstein, *Postal Systems*,

Fragments of the Kartid intelligence system have survived. Ghiyāth al-Dīn Kart received intelligence from as far away as Ghazni, allowing him time to prepare a multi-layered defense against Yasaʾur. Another fragment is the use of messengers (sgl. *qāṣid*). Messengers on horseback, possibly runners, too, were elements in the intelligence relay system (*barīd*) utilized to communicate with garrisons and loyalists. Homing pigeons were also employed.[21] Hence the importance of the Kartid network of "loyal servants" (pl. *bandagān*), with each *banda* controlling a redoubt in his homeland (*waṭan*, *manteqa*). A system of *bandagān*, fortresses, and outposts to hold together a kingdom is not an unusual arrangement in the Middle East (or Europe). A network of *bandagān* (or feudal lords in Europe) obviated the need for, and cost of, maintaining a standing army.

As the population grew, the Kartid Wall was erected to envelop the suburbs. The Nikudaris, Qaraunas, Pashtuns, and others remained threats to Herat's residents and its agricultural dependencies. Prosperity, especially visible evidence of affluence, will attract predators. It was doubtless appreciated by Muʿizz al-Dīn Kart that the wall provided Heratis with a sense of security, allowing them to sleep knowing that knaves and ruffians (*runūd wa awbāsh*) would not slit their throats while they slept. The threats of Muʿizz al-Dīn's time were not existential: Sarbadarids did not pose a threat, especially after they were trounced at Zāwa in 743/1342. The pre-Temür Chaghataids remained a menace, but evidently a manageable one: when the Chaghataids invaded in 752/1351f. they could not breach the wall because they did not have with them siege equipment; hence the stalemate and resolution that allowed the Chaghataids to withdraw with honor. Pīr ʿAlī's fortification project of 780/1378f. was intended to reinforce the wall against Temür's well-equipped and well-trained army.

The Kartid Wall encompassed most of R2. It had an estimated perimeter of 16 km/10 miles. Absent probative information about a wall's physical characteristics and the objective behind its construction, one cannot assume its defensive character, or that it can protect the enclosed space against an

7–28 (pre-Islamic Persia), 141–64 (Mongol era). Beyhaqi/Bosworth (tr.), *History*, 1:28–29 (evidence in *Tārīkh-i Masʿūdī* of the Ghaznavid intelligence system).

[21] Homing pigeons are not fail-safe, especially in bad weather.

*army*. Walls exist for myriad reasons.[22] Walls are erected to confine people (for instance, the Berlin Wall). The customs gates and Farmers'-General wall of pre-revolutionary Paris were designed to regulate ingress and egress, and to levy taxes and tolls:

> [C]rowds at the northern end of [Paris] set about destroying the hated symbol of their confinement: the Farmers'-General wall and its fifty-four *barrières*. The *enceinte* had been Lavoisier's last technical masterpiece, ten feet high, eighteen miles in circumference, [and] punctuated at intervals by Claude Ledoux's extraordinary customs posts.[23]

The Kartid Wall, like the Farmers'-General wall, may have been used to regulate and tax goods flowing into Herat's *bazaar network*. Denizens of Herat and its suburbs depended on the hinterlands and beyond—provided highways were passable—for the majority of their cereals, vegetables, fruits, and nuts;[24] cane/beet sugar, spices, and salt; fish, meat, and dairy; horses, camels, and oxen; raw materials (cotton, pelts, wool, oils, tallow, copper, tin, iron, etc.); firewood; select crafted products. A *shahr-band* doubling as customs barrier is logical. Tariffs on goods and tolls on traffic would defray the wall's construction costs and underwrite operating expenses.

The Kartid Wall speaks more to *population growth* and the *affluence* of Herat than it does to Herat's security posture. A perimeter of *c.* 16 km/10 miles yields an area of 16 km$^2$/6.25 miles$^2$ (or *c.* 1,618 hectares). The population had increased tremendously since the census of 638/1240f., which enumerated 6,900 people. Walled, garrisoned, and prospering urban centers attract immigrants (inflows from outside Persia) and migrants (inflows from within Persia). The 1,618 hectare space cannot inform with respect to indispensable but unavailable metrics: population density, household size, square footage of living space, hectares occupied by avenues, alleys, mosques, hospices, shrines, cemeteries, caravansarays, bazaars, waterways, and gardens. Kartid Herat's population cannot be determined.[25] It is evident, however, that the suburbs of Herat were well populated and worth protecting from predators.

[22] David Frye, *Walls: A History of Civilization in Blood and Brick* (New York: Scribner, 2018).
[23] Simon Schama, *Citizens: A Chronicle of the French Revolution* (New York: Penguin, 1989), 327.
[24] See Appendix 2, Table 1: on "Cultivation and Land Use" in Herat Quarter.
[25] See Appendix 4: "Settlements and Population."

Herat prospered from the last decade of Ghiyāth al-Dīn's reign to the early part of Pīr ʿAlī's reign. This period included intermittent phases of instability and malaise: the desultory reigns of Shams al-Dīn Muḥammad (III) and brother, Ḥāfiẓ Muḥammad; the transitory deposition of Muʿizz al-Dīn (*c.* 752–53/1351–53). Following his return to office, Muʿizz al-Dīn was more careful. He instituted détente with the Sarbadars and prohibited Shaykhiyya asylees in Herat from unsettling the peace. Muʿizz al-Dīn, with help from Shaykh al-Islam Niẓām al-Dīn, devised a method for apportioning waters. Pīr ʿAlī upset the political balance and unleashed forces beyond his ken. He brought death and decline to the Nishapur Quarter, impoverished the Kartid fisc, and weakened the Kartid army. Hence the genesis of the stratagem advanced by vizier Jāmī to arrange with Temür a controlled political transition for Herat.

Prosperity in Herat and its agricultural purlieus cannot be quantified through modern metrics. The data are not available. Herat's renaissance, however, is manifest through other indicators of social and economic progress: building or refurbishing of bazaars, pavilions, caravansarays, cisterns, hammams, mosques, seminaries, hospices; development of a complex system of fortifications to protect the seat of power and population; by the staffing of religious and religious-political offices (*muḥtasib*, *ṣadr*, *ṣadr al-sharīʿa*, *qāḍī*, *qāḍī al-quḍāt*, shaykh al-Islam) to regulate daily life in Herat, its bazaars (e.g., weights and measures), and its sepulchral and spiritual heritages (shrines, cemeteries, mosques, *gunbads*).

The labors and initiatives of Kartid *malik*s and bureaucrats in providing public goods were indispensable to socio-economic progress in Herat. But the *raʿāyā* were the backbone of efforts to revitalize post-Eljigidei Herat; for instance, when consequent to Ögödei's initiatives, plebe and noble labored to sow fields and restore waterways. Fakhr al-Dīn employed *raʿāyā* to develop Herat's fortifications. Fakhr al-Dīn's, Ghiyāth al-Dīn's, and Muʿizz al-Dīn's urban construction or restoration projects employed *raʿāyā*. *Raʿāyā* farmed, crafted, produced, traded, and developed Herat's economy. Their contributions are barely mentioned by Sayfī, Ḥāfiẓ-i Abrū, et al., but should not pass unnoticed.

# Glossary

| | |
|---|---|
| *Āb-dang* | Rice hulling by water power |
| *Āl tamghā* | Red seal (Turkish): supreme seal of the Il-Khans (qq.v. *qarā tamghā*: black seal; *altūn tamghā*: golden seal) |
| *altūn tamghā* | Golden seal: used almost exclusively for fiscal edicts |
| *ʿalūfa* | Provender |
| *aqcha* | Monetary unit (Ottoman *akçe*) |
| *ʿarrāda* | Ballistae |
| *āsiyāb-i bādī*; *āsiyā-yi bādī* | Windmill |
| *āsyā*; *āsiyāb* | Watermill (q.v. *jūy ṭāḥūna*) |
| *ʿawāriż* (pl. *ʿawāriż-āt*) | *Dīwān* taxes and tolls |
| *aylāq* | Summer quarters (nomadic peoples); (q.v. *qishlāq*) |
| *band* | Dam. Martial context: *band* or *fil-band* means earthen mound |
| *band-i khandaq* | Breastwall (probably); revetment (possibly) |
| *banda* (pl. *bandagan*) | Loyal servant, with mutual obligations of service (*khidma*) and fidelity (*wafāʾ*). Old Persian: *bandaka* (pl. *bandakā*) |
| *bang* | *Cannabis sativa* or *Cannabis indica* of hemp family *Cannabaceae*. Hashish in modern Persian |
| *bārū* | Wall, rampart, bulwark, tower, battlement, etc. |
| *basqaq* | Overseer, governor (q.v. *shaḥna*) |
| *bitikchī* | Secretary-registrar in financial administration |

| | |
|---|---|
| *bulūk* | Administrative/tax district (q.v. *wilāyat*) |
| *burj* | Tower, barbican, bartizan, bastion (q.v. *rukn*) |
| *burj-āb* | Water-tower |
| *chahār-sūq*; *chahār-sū* | Four bazaars (intersection) |
| *chapar* | Palisade; wattle-and-daub screen; wooden hide |
| *charkh-andāz* | Siege crossbows |
| *dāng* | One-sixth share in land |
| *darāz-dumbāl* | Buffalo (*gāw-mīsh*) or oxen (*darāz-dum*); Indian humped ox, Zebu (*Bos taurus indicus*) |
| *dayma, daymī* | Dry farming (no irrigation; rain fed) |
| *dīnār-i zar-i surkh* | "Red gold" (pure gold) coins |
| *dīwār-i bārū* | Outer wall facing enemy (q.v. *dīwār-i muqātala*) |
| *dīwār-i muqātala* | Battle wall (q.v. *dīwār-i bārū*) |
| *dīwār-i faṣīl* | Inner wall with back to city |
| *faṣīl* | Space between two curtain walls |
| *garī* | Water-clock (clepsydra); (q.v. *tashta*) |
| *gaz* | *c.* 1 m/1 yd.?; 1 cubit?; 24″ to 40″? (q.v. *zirāʿ*; Ar. *dhirāʿ*) |
| *gaz-mar* | A measure of water-flow (e.g. 10 *gaz* × 50 *mar*) |
| *ḥaqqāba* | Water rights |
| *ḥarīm* | Boundaries of a property |
| *ḥashar* | Corvée (levies of people) |
| *ḥawż* | Cistern |
| *iḥyāʾ al-mawāt* | Revitalization (*iḥyāʾ*) of fallow land |
| *ilchī* | Emissary (Mongolian term) |
| *injü* | Dowry for Mongolian princes (q.v. *yurt*); later, crown land |
| *jawzaqih* | Related to cotton; possibly a supervisor of cotton pickers |
| *jūy* | Aqueduct, channel, rivulet, canal |
| *jūy ṭāḥūna* | Watermill (q.v. *āsyā*; *āsiyāb*); also *ṭāḥūna* (pl. *ṭawāḥīn*) |
| *jūy-bār* | Sluice, regulator, feeder channel |
| *kadkhudā* | Protean term for leader (e.g., chief of village or city quarter) |
| *Kapakī/Kepekī dīnār* | ≈ 8 grams of silver |

| | |
|---|---|
| *kārīz* | Subterranean water-channel (Arabic: *qanāt*) |
| *khāk-rīz* | Embankment, earthworks, mound, glacis |
| *khandaq* | Dry/wet trench; *tah-i khandaq*: base of trench |
| *kharāj* | Agricultural/land tax (see below) |
| *kharāj muqāsama* | Tax on the crop (fixed at, say, 20%) |
| *kharāj waẓīfa* | Variable tax on land |
| *kharak* | Scaffolds to protect sappers |
| *kharwār* | In Khurasan, ≈ 297 kg/653.40 lb (≈ 100 Herati *mann*; q.v. *mann*) |
| *kūshk* | Pavilion (modern kiosk) |
| *kūtak* | Based on context: measure of land or shares in land |
| *māl-i sālīyānah* | Annual tax obligation |
| *manfaʿa* | Usufruct, usufruct rights, rights of disposal |
| *manjanīq* (*manganon*) | Broadly describes "any model of trebuchet" |
| *mann* | Herati *mann*, ≈ 2.97 kg/6.534 lb (q.v. *kharwār*) |
| *manshūr* | Royal decree or diploma indicating royal assent |
| *minṭaqah*, *manteqa* | Social-geographical zone to which a person's social identities are fused (q.v. *waṭan*) |
| *mazraʿa* (pl. *mazāriʿ*) | Sown field or hamlet; peasants lived by the fields |
| *mīrāb*; *mīr-ābānih* | Water-manager |
| *muʿāf wa musallam* | Exempt from taxes, tolls, levies, corvée |
| *muḥtasib* | Market inspector: responsible for weights and measures and fair dealing in the bazaar; also inspector of public morals |
| *muqannī* | Engineer who repairs/excavates a *qanāt* |
| *muzāraʿa* | Share-cropping contract |
| *muzāriʿ* (pl. *muzāriʿūn*) | Share-cropper |
| *nafṭ* | Naphtha; also chemical-based incendiaries of sundry types |
| *nafṭ-andāz* | Naphtha-hurlers |
| *nahr* | Large canal or even a river (like the Oxus) |
| *nardubān* | Scaling ladders used in siege warfare |

| | |
|---|---|
| *naṭarah* | Water-timer; regulates water-flow to fields |
| *pāʾiza* | Chinese: *pʾai-tzu*; Mongolian: *gerege*: tablet of authority |
| *pīshkish* (or *pīshkash*) | Gift from an inferior to superior; dues extracted as a present |
| *pul-i rawān* | Drawbridge |
| *qaḥṭ* | Famine |
| *qalān* (pl. *qalān-āt*) | Taxes specific to sedentary peoples (q.v. *qubchūr*); could also mean the corvée |
| *qanāt* | Subterranean water-channel (q.v. *kārīz*) |
| *qarā tamghā* | Black seal. Personal seal; affixed alongside other seals |
| *qarya* (pl. *qurá*) | Village; but could mean small town (cf. *dih*: village, hamlet) |
| *qaṣaba* (pl. *qaṣabāt*) | Protean term: hamlet, large village, even township |
| *qishlāq* | Winter quarters (nomadic peoples); (q.v. *aylāq*) |
| *qubchūr* | Taxes specific to nomadic peoples (q.v. *qalān*) |
| *qubi* | Shares in the income and/or wealth of the Mongol empire |
| *qulb* | Sluice. Primary sluice: *sar-qulb* (q.v. *naṭarah*). |
| *qullatayn* (dual of *qullat*) | Two large jars jointly holding *c.* 1,200 pints of water |
| *quriltai* | Mongol congress, which has unique protocols and rituals |
| *raʿāyā* | Sedentary classes: peasants, artisans, craftsmen, merchants |
| *rakhna* | Conduit/channel cut between walls/fences |
| *rakhnagī* | Irrigation fee |
| *rukn* (pl. *arkān*) | Bastion |
| *ṣadr*, *ṣadārat* | Kartid position and office (originated in Transoxiana) |
| *sahm* | Share, portion |
| *ṣarrāf* | "Shroff." Money-lender, broker of bills of exchange, insurer |

| | |
|---|---|
| *shabāna-rūz* | 24-hour water-flow; governed by local customs (*ʿurf, rawāj*) |
| *shaḥna* | Overseer (variously, *dārūġachī, dārūġa, basqaq*) |
| *shurfa* (pl. *shurufāt, shurafāt*) | Merlon (cf. crenel) in battlements |
| *sūrākh-hā-yi muqātala* | Machicolations ("murder holes") |
| *sūrākh-i tīr-kish* | Embrasure, arrow-loop, machicolation |
| *tamghā* | Brand, sign, seal; later tariff (akin "Goods and Services Tax") on sales and exchanges of goods and services |
| *tanka* or *tanga* | Monetary unit; also generic term for silver coins |
| *taqāwī* | Advance of cash and/or seed to peasants |
| *tashta* | Water-clock (clepsydra); (q.v. *garī*) |
| *tukhm* | Seed |
| *ulāgh* (also *ulāq*) | Steeds, remounts; also donkey/ass |
| *ulus, ūlūs, ulūs* | "Nation"; distinct peoples/tribes; originally tribes/peoples granted to a Mongol royal |
| *ʿushr* | 10% tax on agricultural revenue |
| *wabāʾ* | Pestilence (q.v. *yūt*) |
| *wājib-i dīwānī* | Obligations due to the treasury |
| *waṭan* | Homeland (q.v. *minṭaqah*) |
| *wilāyat* | Province (q.v. *bulūk*) |
| *yarlīgh* | Imperial decree, patent, diploma (Mongolian) |
| *yasāq wa yusūn* (or *yasā*) | Mongol laws and customs |
| *yurt* | Territorial appanage for Mongol royals (q.v. *injü*) |
| *yūt* (also *zūd, zhūd*) | Mongolian term. Unseasonable storm that freezes pastures, causing animals to die of starvation and/or cold. Used broadly for a natural disaster that kills a lot of animals |
| *zirāʿ* | Arabic *dhirāʿ*, *c.* 1 m/1 yd? (q.v. *gaz*). One of many terms in use for land/water measurement (*kaff, qafīz, jarīb*, etc.). |

# Appendix 1
# Genealogical and Dynastic Charts

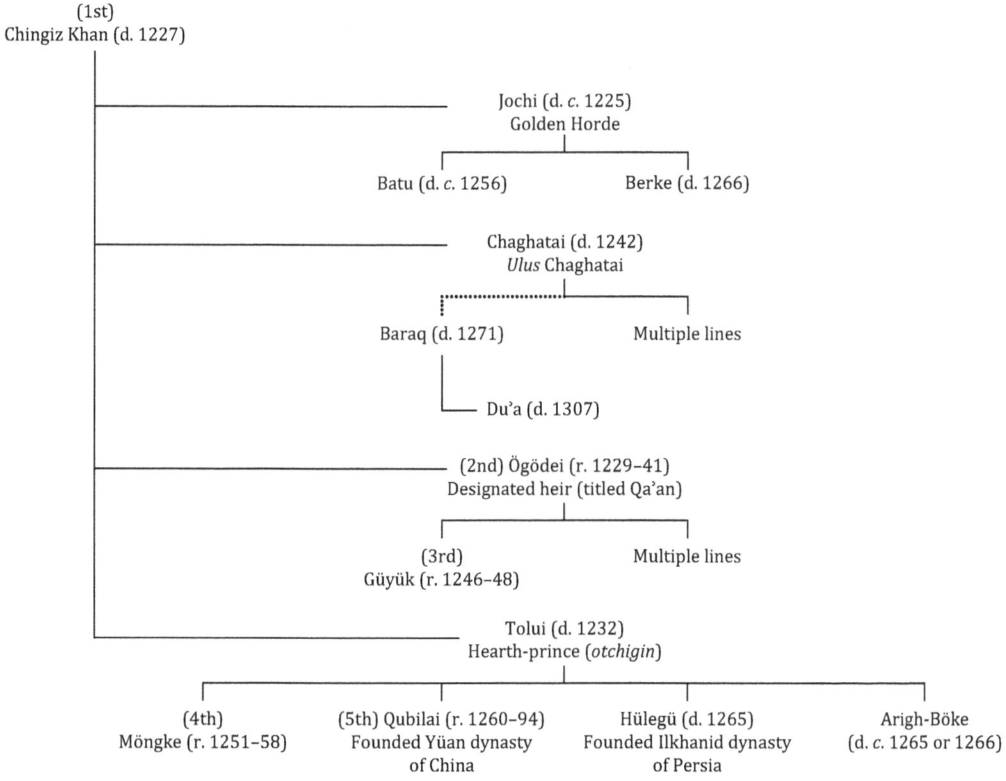


Figure A1.1 The Mongols.

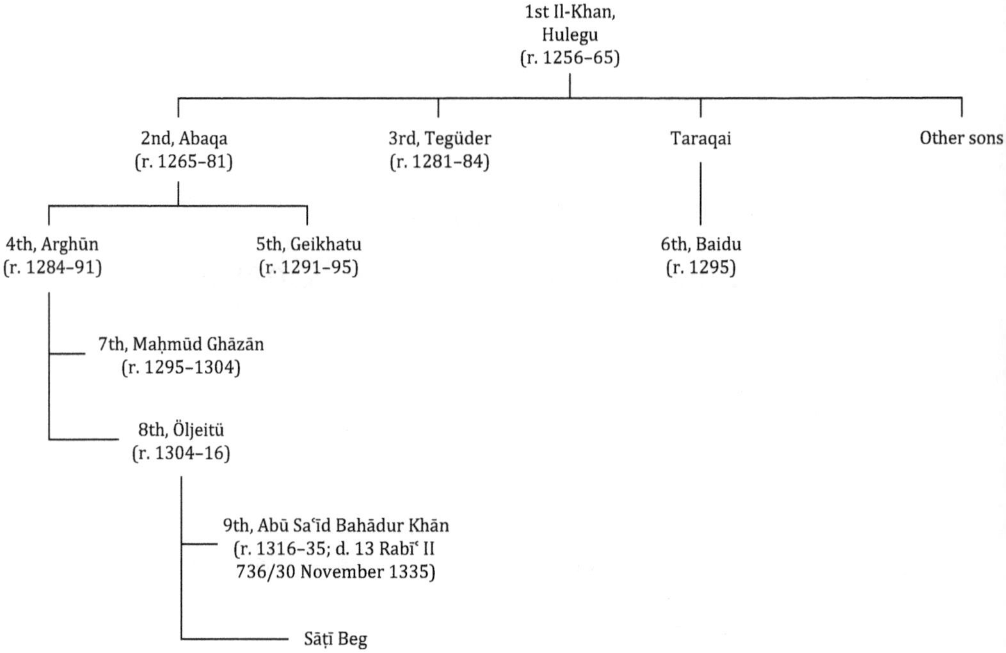


Figure A1.2 The Il-Khans of Persia.

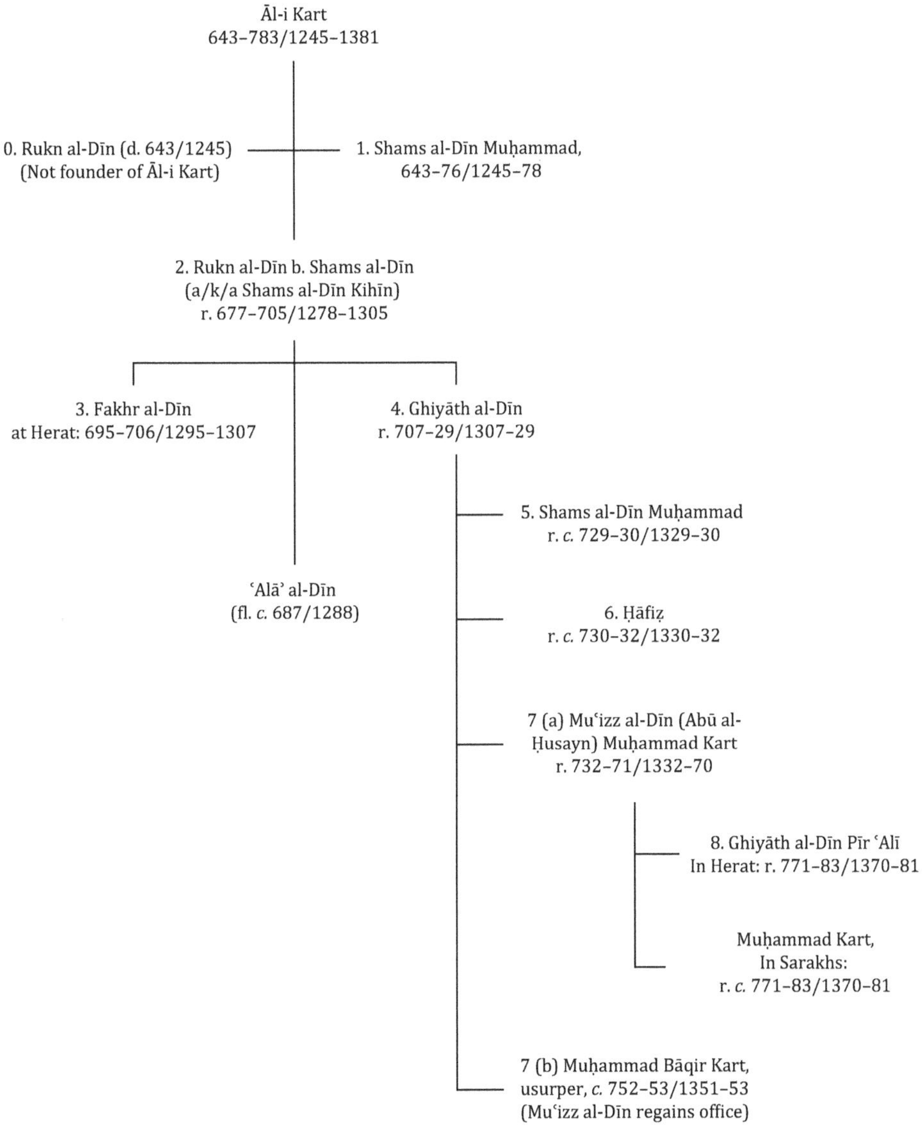


Figure A1.3 The Kart Dynasty of Herat.

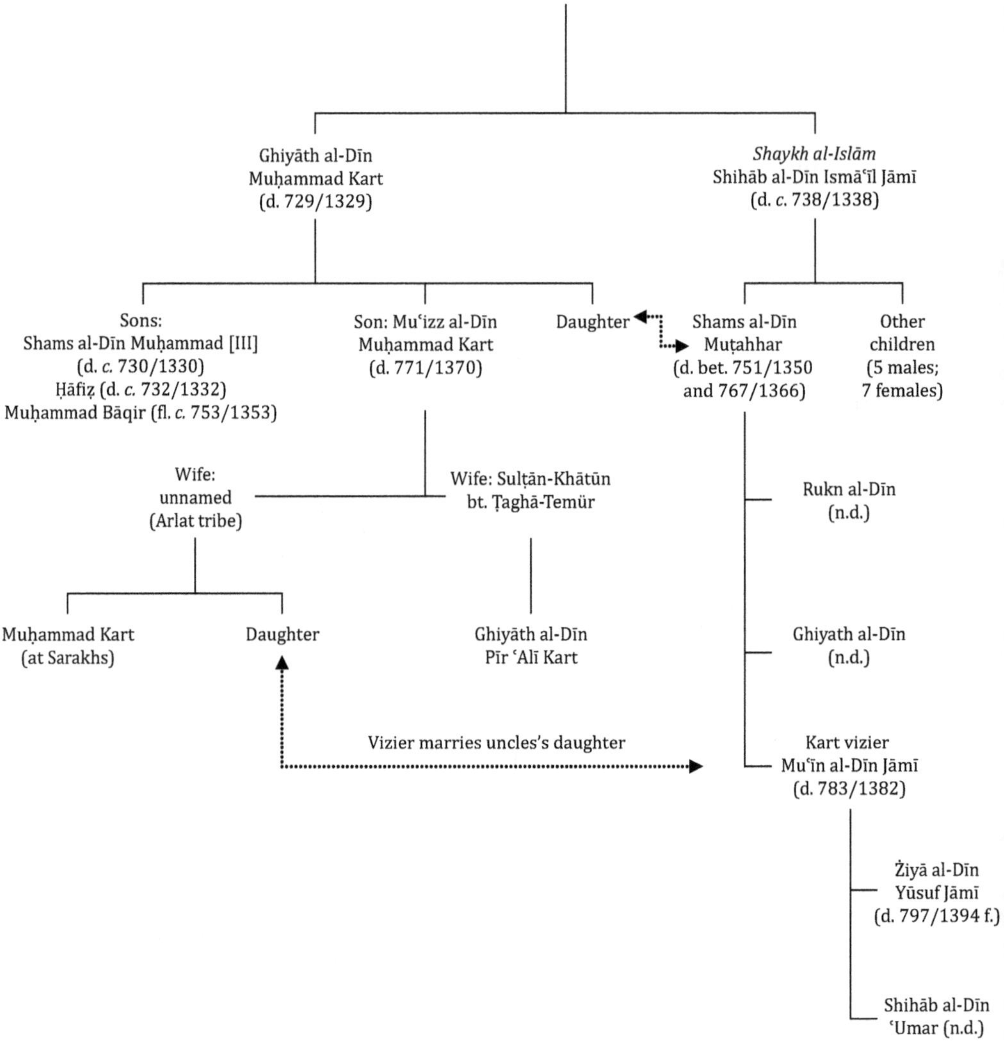


Figure A1.4 Kart-Jami marriages.

# Appendix 2
# Land and Water Use

Direct and circumstantial evidence exists on the uses of agricultural land; sources of irrigation (above or below ground); cultivation without irrigation (*dayma*, *daymī*; rain-fed: hence "dry farming"); and agricultural products of the Herat Quarter in the post-Mongol age. Related socio-economic data (for instance, on mining or wood crafts) can be extracted from the sources. Table A2.1 is a composite of information from Mustawfī and Ḥāfiẓ-i Abrū, and includes insightful commentaries by Dorothea Krawulsky (editor of Ḥāfiẓ-i Abrū's *Geography*).[1] Ḥāfiẓ-i Abrū provides only select data for the ten *bulūks* of Herat and does not specify land use. Ḥāfiẓ-i Abrū's data are not evidence of Kartid era land use; just suggestive.

Rashīd al-Dīn provides generic information on mulberries, cotton, and saffron, two of the three cash crops known to have been cultivated in the Herat Quarter in the Kartid period (see table below). Wheat (*gandum*) and barley (*jū*), says Rashīd al-Dīn, were farmed wherever possible (that is, subject to soil quality and availability of water). Millet (*gāwars*) was cultivated, along with *zurrat* (*sorghum durra*). Many species of rice were cultivated in sundry regions of Persia; the finest rice came from the Caspian Sea littoral.[2] This information is not specific to the Herat Quarter, but the cultivation of

1 Mustawfī/Le Strange (ed.), *Nuzhat*, 151–55; idem/Le Strange (tr.), *Nuzhat*, 150–52; Krawulsky, *Ḫorāsān*, 1:29–41, 2:28–37. Denoted as (M) Mustawfī; (HA) Ḥāfiẓ-i Abrū (Krawulsky ed., vol. 1); (K) Krawulsky (vol., 2: annotations). Table reflects the organization of Herat Quarter under Shāh-Rukh b. Temür (r. 807–50/1405–47). Suggestive only of Kartid era organization. See caveat on *Bulūk-i Parwānah wa Hawādasht* in Chapter 8, n.64.

2 Rashīd al-Dīn, *Āthār wa Aḥyā'*, 30–39 (mulberry), 131–42 (wheat & barley), 143–45 (millet), 146–49 (rice), 150–54 (*zurrat*), 163–64 (cotton), 203 (saffron). Corn (*zurrat* of modern Persian) was not known at the period.

cereals, cotton, and mulberries in the Quarter is confirmed by Mustawfī and/or Ḥāfiẓ-i Abrū.

Rashīd al-Dīn gives scientific guidance on the cultivation of an assortment of fruits (e.g., apple, apricot, citrus, fig, grape, melon, peach, pear, pomegranate, quince); legumes (beans, chickpeas); vegetables (e.g., beet, cabbage, carrot, cauliflower, eggplant, lettuce); and herbs (e.g., coriander, garlic, leek, onion). It is not possible to prove that these crops were cultivated in Kartid times; however, a walk through one of Herat's thriving bazaars will reveal the abundance of these fruits, vegetables, and herbs. Doubtless, many, possibly most, were also cultivated in the Kartid era.

*Table A2.1 Cultivation and Land Use in Herat Quarter*

| Province (*wilāyat*) | Produce/Products | Water Resources | Sources | Commentary |
|---|---|---|---|---|
| Āzāb | Cereals (*ghalla*) | Not given (but rain & streams are plentiful) | HA, K | HA: a contiguous region listed as "Shāfilān & Āzāb." Shāfilān: 6–7 *dih* and 30–40 *mazraʿa*; Āzāb: 7–8 *dih* and 50–60 *mazraʿa*; plus three other districts, which have dozens of villages and 100-plus *mazraʿa* |
| Bādghīs | Pistachios (M)<br>Not given (HA) | *kārīz* and *rūd* (HA) | M, HA | M: comments on abundance and quality of pistachios<br>HA: livestock plentiful (due to the excellence of meadows in the region); many flourishing villages and *c.* 200 *mazraʿa* |
| Bākharz | Fruits, primarily, grapes (*angūr*), melons (M).<br>Every variety of fruit; high-quality grape syrup (*dūsh-āb*) (HA) | Mostly *kārīz*, some river water (HA) | M<br>HA, K | M: No data<br>HA: Gives 15 toponyms (Bāghand, Kārīz, Mālīn, Razah, and Tāybād are well known); apart from them, there are many *mazraʿas* |
| Fūshanj | Fruits, mainly, grapes (> 100 varieties), melons esp. the Persian melon (*kharbuza*) (M). Many fruit types; grapes dried for raisins and currants (*ma-wīz wa kishmish*); juniper (*ʿarʿar*) and pine (*nāzhū*) are plentiful (HA) | Herat River | M, HA, K | M: "all the mills here are worked by wind"<br>HA: Fūshanj is largest *qaṣaba*, has bazaar; HA lists several toponyms but no mention of *mazraʿa*; but area has many orchards (*bāghistān*). |
| Gharjistān | Not given (HA) | Not given (but rain & streams are plentiful) | M, HA | M: no data re produce<br>HA: Mountainous and inaccessible to camels. Gold was mined in earlier times<br>Bosworth ("History of Ghūr," 120): region "metalliferous" |

*Table A2.1 (Continued)*

| Province (*wilāyat*) | Produce/Products | Water Resources | Sources | Commentary |
|---|---|---|---|---|
| Ghūr | Not given (M) | Murghāb; rain, streams, springs (*chashma-sār*); no *kārīz* use | M | M: no data; just that Ghurids are "very stupid" |
| | Grains (*ghalla*); figs (*anjīr*), pears (*amrūd*), *dūlāna* (*Mespilus germanica*), nuts (*jawz*) (HA) | | HA | HA: dry farming (*dayma*) of cereals along hillsides; fruit and nut trees, many growing wild; *c*. 100 *qarya* and 200–300 *mazāriʿ* |
| | | | | Bosworth ("History of Ghūr," 120): region "metalliferous" |
| Harāt-Rūd | "White apple" (*sīb safīd*); other fruits; crops (not specified) (M) | - | M | M: only gives information for Chīsht, which Ḥāfiẓ-i Abrū includes under Harāt-Rūd |
| | Varieties of fruit; known for quality grapes; assorted nuts (especially almonds); *shīrkhisht* trees (*Acacia arabica*?) (HA) | Herat River | HA, K | HA: Water-rich region with many farms and orchards. Main *qaṣaba*, Awbih; thriving *qaryas* and *mazraʿas*. Lead and iron mines operated; antimony (*sang-i surma*) produced here. There is thick forest cover throughout the region |
| Isfizār | Fruits, mainly, pomegranates (*anār*), and grapes; rosewood (*dirakht-i binafshih*) | *kārīz* and *rūd* (plentiful overground sources) | M, HA, K | M: Shāfiʿi redoubt and "very bigoted" |
| | | | | HA: five *qaṣabas*, each a *maḥalla* (district); and *c*. 30–40 *qarya* and 50 *mazraʿa* dependencies of (town of) Isfizār; wood crafting. |
| Jām | Fruits (M, HA) | *kārīz* (M) | M, HA, K | M: 200 dependent villages |
| | | Mostly *kārīz*, but some river sources (HA) | | HA: apart from *qaṣabas* of Būzjān, Turbat-i Jām (shrine and bazaar), Zūr-Ābād, Zirishk, etc., and *qurá* and *-ābāds*, there were over 200 *mazraʿa*. Citadels at Būzjān, Maʿd-Ābād-i Jām (and at Farhād-Gard) |

| | | | | |
|---|---|---|---|---|
| Khʷāf | Silk; madder (*Rubia tinctorum*); pomegranates, grapes, melons, and figs (M)<br>Many fruits, mainly pomegranates. Silk and cotton grown in large quantities (HA) | Mostly *kārīz*, minimal river sources (HA) | M, HA, K | M: staunch and pious Ḥanafīs<br>HA: only famous *qaṣabas* and *qaryas* listed; apart from them, there are many *qaryas* and *mazraʿas*; iron mines in operation.<br>See Chapter Eight on Salūmad Dam and windmills in Khʷāf |
| Kurūkh | Not specified | *kārīz* and *rūd* | HA, K | 89 *qarya* and *mazraʿa* in tax register (*c.* AD 1420) |
| Kūsūyi | Fruits, mainly, grapes, melons (M)<br>Fruits, esp. grapes; cereals (*ghalla*) (HA) | Water from Herat River but also by *kārīz* | M<br>HA | M: lists Kūsūyi under Fūshanj<br>HA: Many orchards, windmills (*āsiyā-hā-yi bād*), and hamlets; sown fields are irrigated by *kārīz* |
| Murghāb | Orchards and cereals (*ghalla*) | Overground sources | HA | Temür developed the region (many new canals and settlements). HA: most *mazraʿa* grew cereals; ranching was extensive (probably sheep and cattle; waters and pastures said to be excellent). Panjdih and Marūchāq are the *qaṣabas*. |
| Tūlak | Not given | Not given (but rain & streams are plentiful) | HA | HA: a contiguous region listed as "Sākhar & Tūlak"; it had *c.* 30–40 *dih* and *c.* 500 *mazraʿa*, and many strong fortresses |
| Zāwa | Silk and cotton; corn, grapes, other fruit (M)<br>Fruits are plentiful | *kārīz* and *rūd* | M, HA | HA: *qaṣaba* is Zāwa, with 39 *mazraʿa*. Turbat-i Ḥaydariyya (shrine) is identified as a *qarya*. Apart from *qaryas* listed by HA, there are numerous *mazraʿas* and *bāghistāns* |

# Appendix 3
# Urban Development in the Kartid Period

The table is derived primarily but not exclusively from Terry Allen's *Catalogue* (1981). The column "Cat. N°." refers to Allen's catalogue numbers; and since his sources are in the corresponding entry in *Catalogue*, they are not reproduced. Only supplemental references are supplied. Allen's *Timurid Herat* (1983) should be read alongside *Catalogue* for his amendations and clarifications.

In addition to Kartid projects for which evidence exists, tentative sponsorships are included and identified by the letter "T"; for example, *Madrasa-yi ʿIzz al-Dīn ʿUmar Marghānī* is listed because if it had survived the Mongol attacks, it would have been patronized by the Kartids: Marghānī was an ancestor of Rukn al-Dīn Marghanī (d. 643/1245), the castellan of Khaysār. *Madrasa-yi Niẓāmiyya* was sponsored by Seljuq vizier, Niẓām al-Mulk (d. 485/1092). It survived into the Timurid era and was refurbished by ʿAlī Shīr Nawāʾī (d. 906/1501). It was probably not neglected in the Kartid era.

The table is not dispositive or exhaustive.

*Table A3.1 Edifices Built/Re-Built in Herat*

| Cat. N°. | Category | Name | Sponsor | Comments |
|---|---|---|---|---|
| n/a | Citadel | *Qalʿa-yi Amān Kūh* (Fort Iskilchih) | Mongol | Iskilchih was not within immediate vicinities of Herat; but had line of sight to Qalʿa-yi Ikhtiyār al-Dīn |
| n/a | Commercial | Three pavilions (sgl. *kūshk*) | Mongol | Built near Khūsh Gate, *c.* 637/1239f., by Muḥammad b. ʿIzz al-Din, et al. (al-Harawī, *Harāt*, 154). |
| n/a | Commercial | Pavilion | Mongol | Built *c.* 657/1258f., outside Firūzābād Gate by the *shaḥna* Merkidaï (al-Harawī, *Harāt*, 278–79; Faṣīḥ, *Mujmal*, 811) |
| n/a | Commercial | *Bāzār* (name unknown) | Kartid | Built in 663/1264 by Shams al-Dīn Kart (I) outside Firūzābād Gate (al-Harawī, *Harāt*, 311–13) |
| n/a | Commercial | Workshop (*kār-khānah-yi ʿālī*) | Ilkhanid<br>Kartid | Built in 663/1264 by Shams al-Dīn Kart (I) outside Firūzābād Gate (al-Harawī, *Harāt*, 311–13) |
| n/a | Commercial | *Bāzār* (name not given) | Ilkhanid | Built *c.* 711f./1311f. by plenipotentiary Yasāʾūl outside Khūsh Gate (al-Harawī, *Harāt*, 603) |
| n/a | Commercial | *Bāzār-i Malik* (extension to Chahār-Sū) | Kartid | Built *c.* 719f./1319f. by Ghiyāth al-Dīn Kart (al-Harawī, *Harāt*, 745; listed by Sayfī under AH 719) |
| n/a | Commercial | Grand pavilion (*kūshk-i ʿālī*) | Kartid | Built *c.* 719f./1319f. by Ghiyāth al-Dīn Kart. East of citadel (al-Harawī, *Harāt*, 745; Allen, *Catalogue*, Cat. No. 672) |
| n/a | Commercial | Three caravansarays (sgl. *kārwānsarāʾy*; or *tīm*; diminutive, *tīm-chih*) | Kartid | *c.* 719/1319f., Ghiyāth al-Dīn Kart. Two caravansarays at *pā-yi ḥiṣār*, integrated with bazaar. Third caravansaray was near his *khānaqāh*, Cat. No. 502 (see also al-Harawī, *Harāt*, 745) |
| n/a | Public | *Ḥammām* (public baths) | Kartid | Ghiyāth al-Dīn Kart. Built near the citadel's *khandaq* (al-Harawī, *Harāt*, 744) |
| n/a | Public | *ʿĪdgāh-i dīwārī* ("walled *muṣallā*") | Kartid | Intramuros. By Fakhr al-Dīn Kart. Walled plaza (*maydān*) at *pā-yi ḥiṣār* (al-Harawī, *Harāt*, 462) |

*Table A3.1 (Continued)*

| Cat. N°. | Category | Name | Sponsor | Comments |
|---|---|---|---|---|
| 50 | Public | Cistern (*ḥawż-yi aʿẓīm*) | Kartid | Ghiyāth al-Dīn Kart (al-Harawī, *Harāt*, 745) |
| 54 | Citadel | *Qalʿa-yi Ikhtiyār al-Dīn* | Kartid | Intramuros |
| 103 | Commercial | *Bāzār-i Malik* | Kartid | Built in 699/1299f. by Fakhr al-Dīn Kart. Restoration of the pre-Mongol bazaar |
| 106 | Commercial | *Sūq-i Sulṭān* (reconstruction of pre-Mongol *Bāzār-i ʿIrāq*?) | Ilkhanid | Built *c.* 712/1312f. by Muḥammad Duldāʾī b. Danishmand during Ghiyāth al-Dīn Kart's absence (al-Harawī, *Harāt*, 603) |
| 414 | Public | *Masjid-i ʿAbdāllah ʿĀmr* | Kartid | Intramuros. Built or re-built by Fakhr al-Dīn Kart |
| 423 | Public | *Masjid-i Falak al-Dīn* | Seljuq<br>Kartid (T) | Existed in Kartid era (al-Harawī, *Harāt*, 603); stood at least until 844/1440f. Possibly Kartid supported |
| 428 | Public | *Masjid-i jāmiʿ* [Herat's Friday Mosque] | Ghurid<br>Kartid | Ghurid built. Ghiyāth al-Dīn Kart funded restorations and donated large sums. Muʿizz al-Dīn Kart restored it after the earthquake of 765/1364 |
| 445 | Public | *Masjid-i Tarrah-furūsh* (The Green-Grocers' Mosque) | Kartid | Intramuros. Refurbished by Fakhr al-Dīn Kart. Possibly located in NE quadrant (cf. Allen: in Malik Bazaar) |
| 460 | Seminary | *Madrasa-yi Ghiyāthiyya* | Ghurid<br>Kartid | Built *c.* 597–99/1200–03 by Ghurid sultan Ghiyāth al-Dīn; patronized by Ghiyāth al-Dīn Kart (possibly successors, too) |
| 463 | Seminary | *Madrasa-yi ʿIzz al-Dīn ʿUmar Marghanī* | Ghurid<br>Kartid (T) | ʿIzz al-Dīn (d. 599/1203) was an ancestor of Rukn al-Dīn Marghanī (d. 643/1245), castellan of Khaysār. Kartid status is unclear; site unlocated by Allen |
| 477 | Seminary | *Madrasa-yi Niẓāmiyya* | Seljuq<br>Kartid (T) | Built by the vizier, Niẓām al-Mulk (d. 485/1092). Survived into Timurid era. Kartid status unclear |
| 483 | Seminary | *Madrasa-yi Sabz-i Bar-Āmān* | Kartid (T) | See Allen, *Timurid Herat*, 47 n.99 |
| 484 | Seminary | *Madrasa-yi Sabz-i Fīrūzābād* | Kartid | Sponsored by Muʿizz al-Dīn Kart |

| | | | | |
|---|---|---|---|---|
| 487 | Seminary | *Madrasa-yi Shams al-Dīn Muḥammad Kart* | Kartid | Gāzurgāh region but otherwise unlocated |
| 493 | Hospice | *Khānaqāh-yi Shaykh Abū Naṣr Yaḥyá Jāmī* | Kartid | Quṭb al-Dīn Yaḥyá Jāmī Nīshāpūrī (d. 740/1339), Nishapur's Chief Justice. Built by Muʿizz al-Dīn Kart. Wāʾiẓ, *Maqṣad*, 44–45; Faṣīḥ, *Mujmal*, 924 (under AH 741) |
| 499 | Hospice | *Khānaqāh-yi Fakhr al-Dīn Kart* | Kartid | Damaged by Kartid renegades from Isfizār and Farāh during Muḥammad Duldāʾī's time (al-Harawī, *Harāt*, 554) |
| 500 | Hospice | *Khānaqāh-yi Khʷājah Ghalwah* | Kartid (T) | Shaykh al-Islam Ghalwah was favored by Shams al-Dīn Kart (I) (al-Harawī, *Harāt*, 197) |
| 501 | Hospice | *Khānaqāh-yi Ghiyāth al-Dīn Kart (I)* | Kartid | Extramuros. Endowed with seven watermills (al-Harawī, *Harāt*, 745; cf. al-Harawī, *Ṭarīq-i qismat*, 10–11: misidentified frequently as *Madrasa-yi Ghiyāthiyya*) |
| 502 | Hospice | *Khānaqāh-yi Ghiyāth al-Dīn Kart (II)* | Kartid | Intramuros. One of Ghiyāth al-Dīn Kart's caravansarays was near the *khānaqāh* (al-Harawī, *Harāt*, 745) |
| 503 | Hospice | *Khānaqāh-yi Jadīdī* | Kartid | Intramuros. Sponsored by Muʿizz al-Dīn Kart |
| 508 | Hospice | *Khānaqāh-yi Shaykh Majd al-Dīn Ṭālibah* | Kartid | Sponsored by Fakhr al-Dīn Kart. Possibly had a sepulchral component (see al-Harawī, *Harāt*, 463) and dome (*gunbad*) |
| 509 | Hospice | *Khānaqāh-yi Muʿizz al-Dīn Ḥusayn Kart* | Kartid | Intramuros. Built by Muʿizz al-Dīn Kart |
| 510 | Hospice | *Khānaqāh-yi Niẓām al-Dīn Awbahī* | Self | After 649/1251. Political appointee terminated by Shams al-Dīn Kart. Converted home and endowed it (as waqf) to avoid confiscation (al-Harawī, *Harāt*, 217–18) |
| 512 | Hospice | *Khānaqāh-yi Pul-i Darqarāh* | Kartid (T) | Extramuros. By Ṣadr al-Dīn Khaysārī (fl. 721/1321–22). He was appointed Chief Justice of Herat by Ghiyāth al-Dīn Kart (al-Harawī, *Harāt*, 617–21) |
| 513 | Hospice | *Khānaqāh-yi Sabz-i Khiyābān* | Kartid | Intramuros. Sponsored by Muʿizz al-Dīn Kart |
| 520 | Hospice | *Khānaqāh-yi Sulṭān-Khāṭūn* | Kartid | Intramuros. Sponsored by Sulṭān-Khātūn bt. Ṭaghā-Temür |
| 521 | Hospice | *Khānaqāh al-Zaynī al-Māstarī* | Kartid (T) | Intramuros. Sponsorship status is unclear. Noted in Faṣīḥ, *Mujmal*, 915–16 (year AH 736) |

*Table A3.1 (Continued)*

| Cat. N°. | Category | Name | Sponsor | Comments |
|---|---|---|---|---|
| 532 | Public | *ʿĪdgāh* (a/k/a *muṣallā*) | Kartid | Extramuros. Open prayer space for festivals, funerals, and assemblies. Existed in Shams al-Dīn Kart the Elder's time (al-Harawī, *Harāt*, 310, events of 662/1263f.) |
| 558 | Public | *Maqbarah-yi Khiyābān* | Kartid | One of seven *maqbarah* (pl. *maqābir*) or shrines (sgl. *mazār*) sponsored by Fakhr al-Dīn Kart (al-Harawī, *Harāt*, 463). Large cemetery, north and northeast of Herat. Spelled *Khiyādwān* in both editions of *Tarīkhnāmah-yi Harāt* |
| 559 | Public | *Maqbarah-yi Khʷānchahābād* | Kartid | Same as above but to the south and southwest |
| 560 | Public | *Maqbarah-yi M-Ṣ-R-<u>Kh</u>* or *M-Ṣ-R-Q* | Kartid | Cemetery by the *quhandiz* (al-Harawī/Calcutta ed., *Harāt*, 441; No. 560 is missing in Tehran ed.). By Fakhr al-Dīn Kart |
| 562 | Sepulchral | *Gunbad-i ʿAbdāllah b. Muʿāwiyah b. ʿAbdāllah b. Jaʿfar Ṭayyar* | Kartid | By the *quhandiz*. *Gunbad* erected in 706/1306f. by Fakhr al-Dīn Kart (Wāʾiẓ, *Maqṣad*, 12–13) |
| 573 | Sepulchral | *Gunbad-i Khʷājah Muḥammad Abū al-Walīd* | Kartid | A venerable shrine. Developed and funded by Fakhr al-Dīn Kart (see Wāʾiẓ, *Maqṣad*, 15; al-Harawī, *Harāt*, 463) |
| 580 | Sepulchral | *Ḥaẓīrah-yi Khʷājah ʿAbdāllah Anṣārī* | Kartid | See entry for *Qarya-yi Gāzurgāh* in Allen, *Catalogue*, Cat. No. 204. Patronized by Fakhr al-Dīn Kart |
| 598 | Sepulchral | *Mazār-i Khʷājah ʿAbdāllah Ṭāqī* | Kartid | Contemporary of ʿAbdāllah Anṣārī. Sponsored by Fakhr al-Dīn Kart |
| 645 | Public | *Bāgh-i Safīd* (White Garden) | Kartid | Extramuros. Northeast. Probably by Ghiyāth al-Dīn Kart. Existed in his time (al-Harawī, *Harāt*, 745). Not clear if public had full or limited access to Herat's *Bāghs* |
| 651 | Public | *Bāgh-i Shahr* (City Garden) | Kartid | Intramuros. North of citadel. Fakhr al-Dīn Kart |
| 653 | Public | *Bāgh-i Zāghān* (Ravens' Garden) | Kartid | Extramuros. Northwest. Temür stayed here after breaching the Kartid Wall |

# Appendix 4
# Settlements and Population

## Settlements

One evidentiary marker proffered to demonstrate economic decline in Herat after the Mongols is that the number of villages in Herat province (*wilāyat*) had declined from *c.* 400 in *c.* 290/903, to *c.* 215 in Herat's ten districts (*bulūks*) by *c.* 823/1420.[1] There are flaws with this data. The population of Khurasan declined with the Mongol invasions, but the data points—two blurry snapshots (400 v. 215 villages) captured 517 years apart—are not prima facie evidence of socio-economic decline.

The geography encompassed in Ibn Rusta's estimate (400 villages great and small),[2] and *bulūks* in Ḥāfiẓ-i Abrū (*c.* 215 villages),[3] materially diverge. Ibn Rusta's estimate is for greater Herat and its unspecified environs. Ḥāfiẓ-i Abrū specifies Herat's environs: the ten *bulūks*,[4] plus the *wilāyats* that are contiguous with, or beyond, the *bulūks*. The *wilāyats* are Herat's dependencies (*wilāyāt kih āz tawābiʿ-yi Harāt ast*): Bādghīs, Bākharz, Fūshanj, "Ghūr, Gharjistān, Sākhar, and Tulāk," Harāt-Rūd, Isfizār, Jām, Khʷāf, Kurūkh, Kūsūyi, "Shāfilān, Azāb, and Dāman Kūh," Murghāb, and "Zāwa and Maḥwilāt."[5]

[1] Potter, "Kart Dynasty," 153 and nn. 2–3, 214–15 (Potter's Appendix 3, "Demographic Considerations"). He relies in part on Petrushevsky, "Socio-Economic," *CHI* 5:483–537, 496.

[2] Ibn ʿAlī Aḥmad b. ʿUmar b. Rusta [Ibn Rusta], *Kitāb al-aʿlāq al-nafīsa*, vol. 7, ed. M.J de Goeje (Leiden: Brill, 1891), 173 (*wa madinat Harat ʿaẓīma wa ḥawālī-hā dūr wa fī rasāṭīq-hā arbaʿ māʾit qarya kibār wa ṣighār*). Ibn Rusta died after 290/903.

[3] Krawulsky, *Ḫorāsān*, 1:22–29; Ḥāfiẓ-i Abrū/Harawī (ed.), *Jughrāfiyā*, 16–27.

[4] *Bulūk-i Parwānah wa Hawādasht*: its administrative status in the Kartid era is unclear. The *bulūk*'s human settlements, nonetheless, must be enumerated.

[5] Krawulsky, *Ḫorāsān*, 1:29–41; Ḥāfiẓ-i Abrū/Harawī (ed.), *Jughrāfiyā*, 28–45. *Wilāyats* reflect the organization of Herat Quarter under Shāh-Rukh (r. 807–50/1405–47).

Estimates of *active* settlements must include the ten *bulūks*, plus any settlements in sections of *wilāyats* abutting Herat. If *bulūks* are Herat's "suburbs," the abutting areas are "Greater Herat." Bādghīs and Zāwa can be excluded from the census because they were not under Kartid rule; Azāb, Tulāk, Murghāb, etc. are far from Herat. But settlements in Greater Herat, like bits of Fūshanj or Harāt-Rūd, probably should be counted. It is evident from this exercise that the locales ascribed to Herat shift with political, administrative, and fiscal vicissitudes. Can Ibn Rusta's nebulous surroundings of Herat even be replicated?

Ḥāfiẓ-i Abrū identifies only the *principal* villages (*qarya*; pl. *qurá*) and *qaṣabas* (town, township) of *bulūk* and *wilāyat*. It is from this specification in his listing of *bulūks* that *c*. 215 villages was derived.[6] Ḥāfiẓ-i Abrū, however, frequently notes the existence of *mazraʿas* (pl. *mazāriʿ*: sown field; hamlet) and orchards (sgl. *bāghistān*). These details cannot be ignored. To illustrate, after naming (some or all) of the villages in Injīl *bulūk*, Ḥāfiẓ-i Abrū writes, "apart from these villages, there are many *mazāriʿ*."[7] Ālinjān *bulūk* adjoins the north bank of the Herat River for five *farsangs*; it had many *mazāriʿ* apart from the *c*. 44 *qurá* he named.[8] The *wilāyat* of Kurūkh had 500 *qaryas* and *mazraʿas*.[9] Qarya-yi Diraq of Harāt-Rūd *wilāyat* had 20 *mazraʿa* that were its dependencies; and Qarya-yi Dartakht had 30 *mazraʿa* dependencies, "each one the size of a village."[10] Ḥāfiẓ-i Abrū's *Geography* was finalized forty years after the Kartids. The data are not dispositive of settlements in Herat Quarter under the Kartids, but are suggestive of the breadth and configuration of settlements.

Counting *qaṣabas*, *dihs*, and *qaryas* is only part of the process of enumerating human settlements. *Mazraʿas* and *bāghistāns* were also inhabited. Orchards were often large-scale enterprises that sprawled over several hectares, and like *mazāriʿ*, contained dwellings for peasants. Harvest seasons vary by fruit and by region; populations of *bāghistāns* fluctuate as peasants

6 Potter, "Kart Dynasty," 215 and n.2.

7 Krawulsky, *Ḫorāsān*, 1:23–24, 2:25.

8 Ibid., 1:25, 2:25. South bank is *Bulūk-i Udwān wa Tīzān* (ibid., v.2, Map 2). These are fecund lands; there will have been farmsteads/hamlets along both banks.

9 Ibid., 1:29, 2:28. Krawulsky translates *mazraʿa* as Weiler (hamlet) and *qarya* as Dorf (village); both are agreeable.

10 Ibid., 1:30–31, 2:28–29.

migrate from region to region to pick fruit. No definitions of household size per *mazraʿa*, *qarya* or *qaṣaba* exist for the post-Mongol period.[11] How do we determine when a *mazraʿa* morphs into *qarya*, or *qarya* to *qaṣaba*?[12] Or when a settlement shrinks? Populations increase/decrease; therefore "average" population per settlement will increase/decrease. To assign an average number of inhabitants per active settlement (*shahr*, *qaṣaba*, *dih*, *qarya*, *mazraʿa*, *bāghistān*, *bāgh-āt*) at a specific point in time and space is a mathematical process with myriad variables—a computational game that can be played to infinity.

Every abandoned settlement cannot be blamed on the Mongol invasions. There were mass homicides, deportations, and exoduses consequent to the invasions, but apart from this cataclysmic event—and its aftershocks—abandonments of settlements transpire piecemeal over the course of time and for disparate reasons. Abandoned settlements exist all over the world. Syria's "Dead Cities" (*c.* 700 deserted settlements) are well known.[13] Data from 1365/1986 showed 614 inactive (*khālī*) settlements and 834 active (*dārāʾī*) settlements in the province of Jām.[14] Deserted settlements result from shifts in agriculture, pastoralism, ownership of land, climate, trading practices, and human pursuits.[15] A village may split and become "New Fūlān-Ābād" and "Old Fūlān-Ābād" without any loss of population. A "village could be abandoned entirely, and replaced by wholly dispersed farmsteads, without [...] any apparent reduction [from the previous] population."[16]

Changes wrought by climate and the physical environment trigger abandonment of settlements. When water-flows dwindle due to drought, depletion, or silted *kārīz*, villagers relocate. It may be cheaper to excavate a new *kārīz* than to restore the old *kārīz*. Exploitative farming practices leave soils

[11] Cf. Potter, "Kart Dynasty," 214 and n.6 (his methodology).

[12] On terminological problems (hamlet or village?), see Richard Jones, "Contrasting patterns of village and hamlet desertion in England," in *Deserted Villages Revisited*, eds C. Dyer and R. Jones (Hatfield: University of Hertfordshire Press, 2010), 8–27, esp. 11–16.

[13] Warwick Ball, *Syria: A Historical and Architectural Guide* (Northampton, MA: Interlink, 2007), 167–89.

[14] Zanganah, *Sarzamīn-i Jām*, 19. Modern provincial boundaries differ from medieval ones.

[15] For scenarios, see Christopher Dyer, "Villages in crisis: social dislocation and desertion, 1370–1520," in *Deserted Villages*, pp. 28–45.

[16] Stuart Wrathmell, "The desertion of Wharram Percy village and its wider context," in *Deserted Villages*, 109–120, 118. "Fūlān" is a placeholder for any proper name.

depleted of nutrients, forcing farmers to relocate. Farming in medieval times was harsh existence; exacerbated by the abusive practices of landlords and taxmen. Peasants vacated farms and migrated to *qaṣabas* and *shahrs* to find work. Skilled *raʿāyā* quit *qaryas* for *qaṣabas* and *shahrs*, where purchasers for their products or employers for their skills can be found. Educated men prefer professions—government, academia, clergy—to breaking their backs for over fifteen hours per day.

Lastly, nomads. They did not randomly travel hither-and-yon; they had established migratory patterns (such as summering in mountains and wintering in lowlands). Nomadic camps are mobile settlements.

## Population

Lawrence G. Potter made this proffer:

> we conclude that in times of prosperity Herat city contained 45,500 to 60,000 people, Herat velāyat 140,000 to 160,000, and the Herat quarter of Khorāsān 300,000 to 400,000. At the time of the later Karts these numbers would have been much reduced, and I suggest figures of 25,000, 60,000, and 130,000 for the city, velāyat, and quarter, respectively.[17]

This advice is apropos: "At the present state of our knowledge attempts at estimates of population sizes in the countries of medieval Islam should be postponed [...]."[18]

With respect to Herat Quarter, we can reasonably say that:

1. there was severe de-population consequent to the Mongol invasions;
2. but the population in Herat Quarter (Herat city, its *bulūks* and *wilāyats*) increased between the late 7th/13th century and Temür's invasions;
3. there were manifold settlements (termed *shahr*, *qaṣaba*, *dih*, *qarya*, *mazraʿa*, *bāghistān*, *bāgh-āt*, among others) in Herat Quarter;
4. the population fluctuated with political and economic vicissitudes;
5. the population of Herat Quarter in the Kartid era cannot be determined.

[17] Potter, "Kart Dynasty," 216. He follows Bulliet, "Medieval Nishapur," 88–89.

[18] David Ayalon, "Regarding Population Estimates in the Countries of Medieval Islam," *JESHO* 28/1 (1985):1–19, 18.

## Economic Welfare

Population decline does not equate with economic decline. In the wake of the Black Death, *c.* 1347–50, with manifold recurrences over centuries, England experienced a protracted decline in population (*c.* six million to three million by 1500). But this is not indicative of economic malaise or decline.

> Economic conditions in the fifteenth century were without doubt conducive to an expansion of population: land and food were cheap and abundant, while *labour was scarce and well-rewarded.* Conditions such as these [...] should have led to a rising birth-rate and a falling death-rate.[19]

Low population, low rents, low land prices, low food prices, and higher wages were a boon. Once England's population started rising in the early sixteenth century, real wages started falling.[20]

Stuart Borsch demonstrated the positive and negative socio-economic impacts of the Black Death in England and Egypt. Population declines were comparable in both lands; agriculture declined and hydrological assets fell into disrepair. At the risk of simplifying his analyses, English landlords lived on the lands and took interest in developments; however, in Mamluk Egypt, peasants were undermined for the benefit of absentee landlords, and to ensure that Cairenes did not experience food shortages.[21] English craftsmen earned higher wages (between +75% and +80% per year, calculated in pence);[22] for example, a carpenter's income increased (+80%); some tradesmen earned more (+222%).[23] Egyptian tradesmen, on the other hand, suffered wage declines (from -52% to -65%).[24] Higher agricultural output coupled to lower demand reduced wheat prices in England (-49%). In Egypt, for the same period, wheat prices

[19] John Hatcher, *Plague, Population and the English Economy 1348–1530* (London: Macmillan, 1977), 55 (emphasis added).

[20] See ibid., 71, Figures 1–2.

[21] Stuart Borsch, *The Black Death in Egypt and England* (Austin: University of Texas Press, 2005), esp. 24–66, 91–117. On cereals and unrest, see Ira Lapidus, "The Grain Economy of Mamluk Egypt," *JESHO* 12/1 (1969):1–15; Boaz Shoshan, *Popular Culture in Medieval Cairo* (Cambridge: Cambridge University Press, 1993), 58–66.

[22] Borsch, *Black Death*, 104, Table 6.8.

[23] Ibid., 105, Table 6.9 (thatcher's helper's wages, in pence per year).

[24] Ibid., 106, Table 6.10 and Table 6.11 (in dinars per year).

rose (+56%).[25] English workers enjoyed lower food prices and higher wages, whereas Egyptian workers suffered higher food prices and lower wages.

It is crucial to distinguish between the *short-term* effects of population declines and *long-term* effects. With respect to the Mongol invasions of Persia, the short-term social and economic impacts of homicides, deportations, and migrations will have been catastrophic. In the short- and intermediate-terms, people assuredly struggled to survive. The possible long-term economic outcomes, however, are three: recovery, stagnation, or decline.[26] The thesis propounded here is that Herat enjoyed socio-economic recovery.

Disasters are not wholly negative. They may compel positive changes; for instance, Nishapur's ruin by earthquake could have led to a better-planned Nishapur. Culls by nature (famine, epidemic, flood), while unfortunate for the doomed, are not entirely detrimental from socio-economic standpoints. Quality of life can improve: population densities in town and country decrease; housing expenses decline; infrastructure requirements (for instance, demand for water, sanitation, housing, and transport) stagnate, shrink, or increase slowly; marginal farmlands are abandoned and squatters acquire the best or better lands (mineral-rich soils; nearer to water). Erstwhile share-croppers become landlords (and hire migrants as share-cropping tenants). Fewer farmers farm lands with mineral-poor soils or farther from water; agricultural zones become compact,[27] and possibly yield more produce per acre.

Food production—crops and yields—is the crucial (but missing) metric.

If, hypothetically, each of Ibn Rusta's 400 villages cultivated ten acres, producing, say, ten bushels of wheat per acre, production equals 40,000 bushels (400 × 10 × 10).[28] If each of Ḥāfiẓ-i Abrū's 215 villages cultivated ten acres and produced, say, ten bushels of wheat per acre, production is 21,500

[25] Ibid., 100, Table 6.7 and graph; see also pp. 95–99: Tables 6.3, 6.4, and three graphs.

[26] See discussion in Bas van Bavel, et al., *Disasters and History: The Vulnerability and Resilience of Past Societies* (Cambridge: Cambridge University Press, 2020), 145–58.

[27] The demand for long canals is reduced when farming zones are compact. See extents of *jūys* in Map 4. Difficulties and costs of excavating and maintaining *jūys* decline.

[28] Bushels are hypothetical. For comparative purposes, see Bruce Campbell & Mark Overton, "A New Perspective on Medieval and Early Modern Agriculture: Six Centuries of Norfolk Farming *c.*1250–*c.*1850," *Past & Present* 141 (1993):38–105, 66–76.

bushels (215 × 10 × 10), ostensibly a large decline but no real change to each village's harvest. Population per village—data that are unavailable—is vital because it determines the number of peasants available to farm; therefore the acreage each family can cultivate; the per family share of a harvest. Variables influencing yields per acre per village include: plowing v. hoeing,[29] fertilizers, soil quality, replenishment of nitrogen, irrigation-fed v. rain-fed farming,[30] crop types, geographical/climatic zone (sub-tropical, wet, dry, temperate), and farming season (summer, winter, both).[31]

Agricultural techniques and technologies were not static between Ibn Rusta and Ḥāfiẓ-i Abrū.[32] Superior fertilizers; higher quality seed; cultivation of drought-evasive crops (e.g., barley) and drought-resistant crops (e.g., sorghum), combine to expand the extent of cultivated lands and increase yields. Yields per acre surely improved between 290/903 and 823/1420.[33] If, hypothetically, villages were producing more wheat per acre than before the Mongols, but population per village was lower after the Mongols, and surpluses persisted, a village's socio-economic health will improve. Surpluses tend to lower food prices. Farmers exchange cereals, fruits, vegetables, and cotton for mutton, dairy, oxen, pottery, textiles, and such, thereby improving nutrition and lifestyles; profiting the economy by injecting currency (cereals and coin) into the purses of pastoralists, craftsmen, and merchants; and swelling state coffers when sales and/or commercial taxes are levied.

[29] The Iroquois natives of North America enjoyed higher yields per acre than Europeans by employing ecologically friendlier practices like hoeing. Jane Mt. Pleasant, "The Paradox of Plows and Productivity," *Agricultural History* 85/4 (2011):460–92.

[30] Dry-farming may yield lower harvests, but quality could be higher. Mousavi, *Hazaras*, 99. Better quality grains earn higher prices at market.

[31] See, e.g., al-Harawī, *Irshād al-zirāʿa*, 79–87, on cultivation of cereals: seed types; seeding (in *mann*) per *jarīb*; soil preparation; alternating crops to replenish soils.

[32] Rashīd al-Dīn's *Āthār wa Aḥyāʾ*, and later Qāsim b. Yūsuf's *Irshād al-zirāʿa*, demonstrate the acquisition and transmission of scientific knowledge on seeds, soils, crops, and techniques. For a survey of agriculture, see Petrushevsky, "Socio-Economic," *CHI* 5:483–537, 500–505; for detail, see Petrushevsky, *Kishawārzī*, 2:125–217.

[33] Rashīd al-Dīn, *Āthār wa Aḥyāʾ*, 135, claims 200 *mann* (*c.* 594 kg/16.86 bushels) of wheat per *mann* of seed. Cf. Bruce Campbell, "Arable Productivity in Medieval England: Some Evidence from Norfolk," *The Journal of Economic History* 43/2 (1983): 379–404, Table 1: mean yield ratio of 4.6 to 1 for wheat (pre-1350 AD); Campbell & Overton, "New Perspective," Table 5: wheat yields of 13.2 to 15.6 bushels/acre (years 1250–1349).

We have no worthwhile quantitative data on the Herat Quarter that would allow us to assert that the *long-term* socio-economic health of people had *declined* consequent to the Mongols. The opposite—that over the long term socio-economic conditions had *improved*—is plausible. Decline is a bridge constructed on wobbly pillars.

# Bibliography

## Primary Sources

*Afghan Boundary Commission*, 6 vols. Simla: Government Central Press, 1888–92.

Ahari, Abu Bakr al-Qutbi. *Tarikh-i Shaikh Uwais*, tr. J.B. van Loon. Mouton, 1954.

ʿAlāʾ al-Dīnī, Bahrām. *Sikkah-hā-yi Īrān [vol. 1]: Dawra-yi Īlkhānān-i Mughūl [Coins of Iran: The Mongol Ilkhanid period]*. Tehran: Intishārāt-i Barg-i nigār, 1395/2016.

ʿAlāʾ al-Dīnī, Bahrām. *Sikka-hā-yi Īrān [vol. 2]: az inqirāz-i Īlkhānān-i Mughūl tā istīlā-yi Tīmūr Gūrkān [Coins of Iran: from the fall of the Mongol Ilkhanids to Tamerlane's Conquest]*. Tehran: Intishārāt-i Barg-i Nigār, 1396/2017.

Anon. *Ḥudūd al-ʿĀlam*, ed. and tr. Vladimir Minorsky. Cambridge: E.J.W. Gibb Memorial Trust, 1937 [1982 reprint].

Anon. *Maqāmāt-i Tāybādī*, ed. Sayyid ʿAlāʾ al-Dīn Gūsha-Gīr. Dizfūl [Khūzistān]: Intishārāt-i afhām, 1382/2003.

Anon. *Tārīkh-i Sīstān*, ed. Malik al-Shuʿarāʾ Muḥammad Taqī Bahār. Tehran: Intishārāt-i Muʿīn, 1381/2002 [reprint of 1314/1935 ed.].

Anon. *The Tārīkh-e Sīstān*, tr. Milton Gold. Rome: Istituto italiano per il Medio ed Estremo Oriente, 1976.

Augustine, Aurelius (of Hippo). *City of God*, tr. M. Dods. New York: Modern Library, 2000.

Beyhaqi, Abuʾl-Fazl. *The History of Beyhaqi*, tr. C.E. Bosworth, rev. M. Ashtiany, 3 vols. Boston: Ilex, 2011.

Būzjānī, ʿAlī. *Rawżat al-riyāḥīn*, ed. Heshmat Moayyad. Tehran: Bungāh-i tarjuma wa nashr-i kitāb, 1345/1966.

Clausewitz, Carl von. *On War*, trs and eds Michael Howard and Peter Paret. Princeton: Princeton University Press, 1976.

de Rachewiltz, Igor. *The Secret History of the Mongols [Yüan chʾao pi-shih or Mongqol-un niuča to(b)čaʾan]*, 3 vols. Leiden: Brill, 2004–13.

Fāmī Harawī, ʿAbd al-Raḥman. *Tārīkh-i Harāt.* Tehran: Mīrās̱-i maktūb, 1387/2008.

Fārisī, ʿAbd al-Ghāfir b. Ismāʿīl. *al-Mukhtaṣar min kitāb al-siyāq li-tārīkh Naysābūr*, ed. Muḥammad Kāẓim Maḥmūdī. Tehran: Mīrās̱-i maktūb, 1384/2005.

Fārisī, ʿAbd al-Ghāfir b. Ismāʿīl. *al-Muntakhab min al-siyāq li-tārīkh Naysābūr*, eds Ibrāhīm b. Muḥammad Ṣarīfīnī and M.A. ʿAbd al-ʿAzīz. Beirut: Dār al-kutub al-ʿilmiyyah, 1989.

Faryūmadī, Ghiyāth al-Dīn. *Zayl-i Majmaʿ al-ansāb* (see Shabānkārāʾī, *Majmaʿ al-ansāb*).

Flavius Josephus. *The Wars of the Jews*, tr. William Whiston. n.p., n.d.; [London: J.M. Dent, 1928?].

al-Ghazālī Ṭūsī, Abū Ḥāmid. *Ghazālī's Book of Counsel for Kings*, tr. F.R.C. Bagley. Oxford: Oxford University Press, 1964.

al-Ghazālī Ṭūsī, Abū Ḥāmid. *Naṣīḥat al-Mulūk*, ed. Jalāl Humāʾī. Tehran: Majlis, 1315/1937.

Grigor of Akancʿ. *The History of the Nation of the Archers*, tr. R.P. Blake and R.N. Frye. *HJAS* 12/3 (1949):269–399.

Ḥāfiẓ-i Abrū. *Cinq Opuscules de Ḥāfiẓ-i Abrū*, ed. Felix Tauer. Prague: l'Académie Tchécoslovaque des Sciences, 1959.

Ḥāfiẓ-i Abrū. *Jughrāfiyā-yi Ḥāfiẓ-i Abrū*, ed. Ṣādiq Sajjādī, 3 vols. Tehran: Mīrās̱-i maktūb, 1375–78/1997–99.

Ḥāfiẓ-i Abrū. *Jughrāfiyā-yi Ḥāfiẓ-i Abrū: qismat-i rubʿ-i Khurāsān, Harāt*, ed. Māyil Harawī. Tehran: Bunyād-i farhang-i Īrān, 1349/1970.

Ḥāfiẓ-i Abrū. *Tārīkh-i salāṭīn-i Kart*, ed. Mīr-Hāshim Muḥaddis. Tehran: Markaz-i pizhūhishī-i mīras̱-i maktūb, 1389/2010.

Ḥāfiẓ-i Abrū. *Zayl-i jāmiʿ al-tāwarīkh-i Rashīdī*, ed. Khān-Bābā Bayānī. Tehran: Anjumān-i ās̱ār-i millī, 2nd ed., 1350/1971.

Ḥāfiẓ-i Abrū. *Zayl-i jāmiʿ al-tāwarīkh-i Rashīdī.* London: British Library, Or. 2885.

Ḥāfiẓ-i Abrū. *Zubdat al-tawārīkh*, ed. Kamāl Ḥājj Sayyid Jawādī, 4 vols. Tehran: Asāṭīr, 1395/2016.

al-Harawī, Qāsim b. Yūsuf. *Irshād al-zirāʿa*, ed. Muḥammad Mushīrī. Tehran: Intishārāt-i Dānishgāh-yi Tihrān, 1346/1968.

al-Harawī, Qāsim b. Yūsuf. *Risāla-i ṭarīq-i qismat-i āb-i qulb*, ed. Māyil Harawī. Tehran: Intishārāt-i bunyād-i farhang-i Īrān, 1347/1968.

al-Harawī, Sayf b. Muªammad b. Yaʿqūb. *Tarīkhnāmah-yi Harāt*, ed. Ghulām-Riżā Ṭabāṭabāʾi-Majd. Tehran: Intishārāt-i Asāṭīr, 1383/2004.

al-Harawī, Sayf b. Muḥammad b. Yaʿqūb. *Tarīkhnāmah-yi Harāt*, ed. Muḥammad Zubayr al-Ṣiddīqī. Calcutta: Baptist Mission Press, 1944.

Ibn Battuta. *The Travels of Ibn Battuta*, vol. 3, tr. H.A.R. Gibb. Cambridge: Cambridge University Press, 1971.

Ibn Ḥawqal. *Safarnāma-yi Ibn Ḥawqal*, tr. Ja'far Shi'ār. Tehran: Amir Kabir, 1366/1987.

Ibn Khaldun. *The Muqaddimah*, ed. F. Rosenthal, 3 vols. Princeton: Princeton University Press, 1958.

Ibn Khaldun. *The Muqaddimah*, ed. Franz Rosenthal. Princeton: Princeton University Press, 2005.

Ibn Munqidh. *An Arab-Syrian Gentleman and Warrior in the Period of the Crusades*, tr. Philip Hitti. New York: Columbia University Press, 1929.

Ibn al-Qalanisi. *Damascus Chronicle of the Crusades*, tr. H.A.R. Gibb (London: Luzac, 1932).

Ibn Rusta. Ibn 'Alī Aḥmad b. 'Umar b. Rusta. *Kitāb al-a'lāq al-nafisa*, vol. 7, ed. M.J de Goeje. Leiden: Brill, 1891.

Isfizārī, Mu'īn al-Dīn Zamchī. *Rawżāt al-jannāt fi awṣāf-i madīnat-i Harāt*, ed. Muḥammad Kāẓim Imām, 2 vols. Tehran: Dānishgāh-i Tihrān, 1338/1959.

Iṣṭakhrī, Ibrahīm. *Masālik al-mamālik*, tr. Anon, ed. Iraj Afshar. Tehran: Bungāh-i tarjumah wa nashr-i kitāb 1340/1961.

Ja'farī, Ja'far b. Muḥammad b. Ḥasan. *Tārīkh-i Yazd*, ed. Iraj Afshar. Tehran: Bungāh-i tarjumah wa nashr-i kitāb, 1343/1965.

Jāmī, 'Abd al-Raḥman. *Nafaḥāt al-uns min hażarāt al-quds*, ed. Mihdī Tawḥīdī-Pūr. Tehran: Intishārāt-i kitābfurūshī-i Maḥmūdī, 1336/1957.

Jāmī, Jalāl al-Dīn Yūsuf-i Ahl. *Farā'id-i Ghiyāsī*, ed. Heshmat Moayyad, 2 vols. Tehran: Intishārāt-i bunyād-i farhang-i Īrān, vol. I, 1356/1977; vol. II, 1358/1979.

Jāmī, Jalāl al-Dīn Yūsuf-i Ahl. *Farā'id-i Ghiyāsī*. Berlin: Staatsbibliothek zu Berlin, Ms. Orient. Fol.110.

Jāmī, Jalāl al-Dīn Yūsuf-i Ahl. *Farā'id-i Ghiyāsī*. Istanbul: Süleymaniye Kütüphanesi, Fatih 4012.

Jāmī, Jalāl al-Dīn Yūsuf-i Ahl. *Farā'id-i Ghiyāsī*. Istanbul: Süleymaniye Kütüphanesi, Aya Sofya 4155.

Jāmī, Jalāl al-Dīn Yūsuf-i Ahl. *Farā'id-i Ghiyāsī*. Tehran: Central Library of the University of Tehran, 4756.

Juvainī, 'Ala' al-Dīn 'Ata-Malik. *The History of the World-Conqueror*, tr. J.A. Boyle, 2 vols. Manchester: Manchester University Press, 1958.

Jūzjānī, Minhāj al-Dīn. *Ṭabaqāt-i Nāṣirī*, ed. 'Abd al-Ḥayy Ḥabībī, 2 vols. Kabul: Anjuman-i tārīkh-i Afghānistān, 1342–43/1963–64.

Jūzjānī, Minhāj al-Dīn. *Ṭabaqāt-i Nāṣirī*, tr. H.G. Raverty, 2 vols. London: Gilbert & Rivington, 1881.

Kātib, Aḥmad b. Ḥusayn b. ʿAlī. *Tārīkh-i jadīd-i Yazd*, ed. Iraj Afshar. Tehran: Intishārāt-i farhang-i Irān-zamīn, 1357/1978.

*Kautilya's Arthasastra*, tr. R. Shamasastry. Mysore: Sri Raghuveer, 5th ed., 1956.

Khʷāfī, Faṣīḥ. *Mujmal-i Faṣīḥī*, ed. Muḥammad Farrukh, 3 vols. Mashhad: Intishārāt-i bāstān, 1339/1960.

Khʷāfī, Faṣīḥ. *Mujmal-i Faṣīḥī*, ed. Muḥsin Nājī Naṣrābādī, 3 vols. Tehran: Intishārāt-i Asāṭīr, 1386/2007f.

Khʷāndamīr, Ghiyāth al-Dīn. *Faṣlī az khulāṣat al-akhbār*, ed. Gūyā ʿIttimādī. ([Kabul]: Maṭbaʿa-i dawlatī, 1345/1967).

Khʷāndamīr, Ghiyāth al-Dīn. *Ḥabīb al-siyar*, ed. Muḥammad Dabīr Siyāqī, 4 vols. Tehran: Intishārāt-i markazī khayyam pīrūz, 1333/1954.

Khʷāndamīr, Ghiyāth al-Dīn. *Ḥabīb al-siyar*, tr. Wheeler M. Thackston, 2 vols. Cambridge: Sources of Oriental Languages and Literatures, 1994.

Khʷāndamīr, Ghiyāth al-Dīn. *Rijal-i kitab-i Ḥabīb al-siyar*, ed. ʿAbd al-Ḥusayn Nawāʾī. Tehran: Anjuman-i āsār wa mafākhir-i farhangī, 1379/2000.

Kirmānī, Nāṣir al-Dīn Munshī. *Simṭ al-ʿulá lil-ḥaḍrat al-ʿulyā: Tārīkh-i Qarā-Khiṭāʾiyān-i Kirmān*, ed. Maryam Mīr-Shamsī. Tehran: Intishārāt-i Duktur Maḥmūd Afshār Yazdī, 1394/2015–16.

Krawulsky, Dorothea. *Ḫorāsān zur Timuridenzeit [Tārīkh-i Ḥāfiẓ-i Abrū: Bakhsh-i jughrāfiyā-yi Khurāsān]*, 2 vols. Wiesbaden: Ludwig Reichert, 1982–84.

Kutbī, Maḥmūd. *Tārīkh-i Āl-i Muẓaffar*, ed. ʿAbd al-Ḥusayn Nawāʾi. Tehran: Amīr Kabīr, 1364/1985.

al-Muqaddasī, Muḥammad b. Aḥmad. *The Best Divisions for Knowledge of the Regions: Aḥsan al-taqāsīm fī maʿrifat al-aqālīm*, tr. Basil Collins. Reading: Garnet, 2001.

al-Qāyinī, Jalāl al-Dīn. *Naṣāʾih-i Shāh-Rukhī*. Vienna: Nationalbibliothek, MS Cod. A.F. 112.

Polo, Marco. *The Book of Ser Marco Polo* [*Travels*], tr. Henry Yule, 2 vols. London: John Murray, 1871.

Polo, Marco. *The Descriptions of the World*, trs. A.C. Moule and P. Pelliot, 2 vols. London: Routledge, 1938.

Marʿashī, Mīr-Sayyid Ẓahīr al-Dīn. *Tārīkh-i Ṭabaristān wa Rūyān wa Māzandarān*. ed. Muḥammad Ḥusayn Tasbīhī. Tehran: Intishārāt-i sharq, 1345/1966.

Maurice. *Maurice's Strategikon*, tr. G.T. Dennis. Philadelphia: University of Pennsylvania Press, 1984.

Mīrkhʷānd, Muḥammad b. Khāwandshāh b. Maḥmūd. *Tārīkh-i rawżat al-ṣafā fī sīrat al-anbiyā' wa al-mulūk wa al-khulafā'*, ed. Jamshīd Kiyānfar, 15 vols. Tehran: Intishārāt-i Asāṭīr, 1380/2001.

Mīrkhʷānd, Muḥammad b. Khāwandshāh b. Maḥmūd. *Tārīkh-i rawżat al-ṣafā fī sīrat al-anbiyā' wa al-mulūk wa al-khulafā'*, 10 vols. Tehran: Intishārāt-i markazī khayyam pīrūz, 1339/1960.

Munshī, Rūḥallāh. *Tārīkh-i pasandīdah: Taḥrīrī az Ẓafarnāmah-yi Yazdī [Selected History: The Liberated Ẓafarnāmah of Yazdī]*, ed. Jamshīd Kiyānfar, 2 vols. Tehran: Intishārāt-i Asāṭīr, 1389/2010.

Mustawfī, Ḥamd-Allāh. *Nuzhat al-Qulūb*, ed. Guy Le Strange. London: Luzac & Co., 1915.

Mustawfī, Ḥamd-Allāh. *Nuzhat al-Qulūb*, tr. Guy Le Strange. London: Luzac & Co., 1919.

Mustawfī, Ḥamd-Allāh. *Tārīkh-i guzīda*, ed. Muḥammad Rawshan, 2 vols. Tehran: Bunyad-i mawqūfāt-i Dr. Maḥmūd Afshār, 1394/2015.

Narshakhī, Abū Bakr Muḥammad b. Ja'far. *Tārīkh-i Bukhārā*, eds Muḥammad b. Zafar ibn 'Umar and Mudarris Rażawī. [Kabul]: Intishārāt-i wizārat-i iṭṭilā'āt wa kultūr, 1362/1983.

Narshakhī, Abū Bakr Muḥammad b. Ja'far. *The History of Bukhara*, tr. R.N. Frye. Cambridge, MA: Mediaeval Academy of America, 1954.

Nasawī, Muḥammad b. Aḥmad. *Sīrat-i Jalāl al-Dīn Mīnkubirnī*, tr. Mujtabá Mīnuwī. Tehran: Bungāh-i tarjumah wa nashr-i kitāb, 1344/1965.

Naṭanzī, Mu'īn al-Dīn. *Muntakhab al-tawārīkh-i Mu'īnī*, ed. Parwīn Istakhrī. Tehran: Asāṭīr, 1383/2004f.

Niẓām al-Mulk. *Book of Government, or Rules for Kings (The Siyāsat-nāma or Siyar al-mulūk)*, tr. Hubert Darke. New Haven: Yale University Press, 1960.

Niẓām al-Mulk. *Siyāsatnāmah*, eds Muḥammad Qazwīnī and M. Chahārdahī. Tehran: Kitābfurūshī-yi Zawwār, 1344/1965.

Procopius. *Buildings*, tr. H.B. Dewing. London: Heinemann, 1940.

Procopius. *History of the Wars*, tr. H.B. Dewing. London: Heinemann, 1914.

Qāshānī, Abū al-Qāsim 'Abdallāh b. Muḥammad. *Tārīkh-i Ūljaytū*, ed. Mahīn Hambly. Tehran: Bungāh-i tarjuma wa nashr-i kitāb, 1348/1969.

Rashīd al-Dīn Fażl-Allāh. *Āthār wa Aḥyā'*, eds Manuchihr Sutudih and Iraj Afshar. Tehran: University of Tehran, 1368/1989.

Rashīd al-Dīn Fażl-Allāh, *Kitāb-i tārīkh-i mubārak-i Ghāzānī: dāstān-i Ghāzān Khān*, ed. Karl Jahn. Ābādān: Nashr-i pursish, 1388/2009 [reprint of 1940 Luzac ed.].

Rashīd al-Dīn Fażl-Allāh. *Jāmiʿ al-tawārīkh*, ed. Bahman Karīmī, 2 vols. Tehran: Iqbāl, 1338/1959.

Rashīd al-Dīn Fażl-Allāh. *Jāmiʿ al-tawārīkh*, eds Muḥammad Rawshan and Muṣṭafá Mūṣawī, 4 vols. Tehran: Nashr-i Alborz, 1373/1994 [reprinted by Mīrās-i maktūb, 1384/2005f.].

Rashīd al-Dīn Fażl-Allāh. *Jāmiʿ al-tawārīkh*, in *Classical Writings of the Medieval Islamic World*, Vol. 3, ed. and tr. Wheeler Thackston. London: I.B. Tauris, 2012.

Saljuqi, Fikri. *Risāla-yi Mazārāt-i Harāt: Shāmil-i sih ḥiṣṣa*, Herat: Markaz-i nashrātī Fārūqī, 1379/2000.

al-Samʿānī, ʿAbd al-Karīm. *Kitāb al-Ansāb*, eds ʿAbd al-Raḥman al-Yamānī, et al, 13 vols. Hyderabad: Osmania Oriental Publications Bureau, 1962–82.

al-Samarqandī, ʿAbd al-Razzāq. *Maṭlaʿ-i saʿdayn wa majmaʿ-i baḥrayn*, ed. ʿAbd al-Ḥusayn Nawāʾī, 4 vols. Tehran: Pazhūhishgāh-i ʿulūm-i insānī wa muṭālaʿāt-i farhangī, 1372/1993; 1383/2004f.

al-Samarqandī, Dawlatshāh. *Tadhkirat al-shuʿarāʾ*, ed. E.G. Browne. Leiden: Brill, 1900.

Scanlon, George T. *A Muslim Manual of War*. New York: American University in Cairo Press, 2012.

Shabānkārāʾī, Muḥammad b. ʿAlī b. Muḥammad. *Majmaʿ al-ansāb*, ed. Mīr-Hāshim Muḥaddis. Tehran: Amīr Kabīr, 1363/1984.

Shāmī, Niẓām al-Dīn. *Ẓafarnāmah*, eds F. Tauer and Muḥammad Aḥmad Panāhī. Tehran: Intishārāt-i bāmdād 1363/1984.

Sīstānī, Malik Shāh Ḥusayn b. Malik Ghīyāth al-Dīn. *Iḥyāʾ al-mulūk*, ed. Manuchihr Sutudih. Tehran: Bungāh-i tarjumah wa nashr-i kitāb, 1344/1966.

al-Utbi, Muhammad. *Kitab-i Yamini*. tr. J. Reynolds. London: Oriental Translation Fund, 1858.

Vegetius. *Epitome of Military Science*, tr. N.P. Milner. Liverpool: Liverpool University Press, 2d rev. ed., 2001.

Vitruvius Pollio. *The Ten Books on Architecture*, tr. M.H. Morgan. Cambridge, MA: Harvard University Press, 1914.

Wāʾiẓ, Sayyid Aṣīl al-Dīn [ʿAbd Allāh b. ʿAbd al-Raḥmān al-Ḥusaynī]. *Maqṣad al-iqbāl-i sulṭānīyah wa marṣad al-āmāl-i khāqānīyah*, ed. Mayīl Harawī. Tehran: Pizhūhishgāh-i ʿulūm-i insānī wa muṭālaʿāt-i farhangī, 1386/2007.

Waṣṣāf, ʿAbdallāh b. Fażlallāh. *Taḥrīr-i tārīkh-i Waṣṣāf*, ed. ʿAbd al-Muḥammad Āyatī. Tehran: Pizhūhishgāh-i ʿulūm-i insānī wa muṭālaʿāt-i farhangī, 1383/2004 [reprint of 1346/1967 Bunyād-i farhang-i Īrān edition].

William of Tyre. *A History of Deeds Done Beyond the Sea*, trs E.A. Babcock and A.C. Krey, 2 vols. New York: Columbia University Press, 1943.

Yazdī, Sharaf al-Dīn ʿAlī. *Ẓafarnāmah*, ed. Muḥammad ʿAbbasī, 2 vols. Tehran: Amīr Kabīr, 1336/1957.

## Secondary Sources

Adamec, Ludwig W. (ed.). *Historical and Political Gazetteer of Afghanistan*, 6 vols. Graz, Austria: Akademische Druck und Verlagsanstalt, 1972–1985.

Aigle, Denise. "Among Saints and Poets: The Spiritual Topography of Shiraz." In *Cities of Medieval Iran*, eds David Durand-Guedy, et al. Leiden: Brill, 2020, pp. 142–76.

Album, Stephen. "A hoard of silver coins from the time of Iskandar Qarā-Qoyūnlū." *The Numismatic Chronicle* 16 (1976): 109–157.

Album, Stephen. *Checklist of Islamic Coins*. Santa Rosa, CA: Stephen Album, 3rd. ed., 2011.

Allen, Terry. *A Catalogue of the Toponyms and Monuments of Timurid Herat*. Cambridge, MA: Aga Khan Program for Islamic Architecture, 1981.

Allen, Terry. "Notes on Bust." *Iran* 26 (1988): 55–68.

Allen, Terry. *Timurid Herat*. Wiesbaden: Ludwig Reichert, 1983.

Allsen, Thomas. "Sharing out the Empire: Apportioned Lands under the Mongols." In *Nomads in the Sedentary World*, eds Anatoly Khazanov and André Wink. Richmond: Curzon, 2001, pp. 172–90.

Allsen, Thomas. "The Circulation of Military Technology in the Mongolian Empire." In *Warfare in Inner Asian History (500–1800)*, ed. Nicolo Di Cosmo. Leiden: Brill, 2002, pp. 265–93.

Allsen, Thomas. *Commodity and Exchange in the Mongol Empire: A Cultural History of Islamic Textiles*. Cambridge: Cambridge University Press, 1997.

Allsen, Thomas. *Culture and Conquest in Mongol Eurasia*. Cambridge: Cambridge University Press, 2001.

Allsen, Thomas. *Mongol Imperialism: the Policies of the Grand Qan Möngke in China, Russia, and the Islamic Lands, 1251–1259*. Berkeley: University of California Press, 1987.

Allsen, Thomas. *The Royal Hunt in Eurasian History*. Philadelphia: University of Pennsylvania Press, 2006.

Ambraseys, N.N. and C.P. Melville. *A History of Persian Earthquakes*. Cambridge: Cambridge University Press, 1982.

Amitai-Preiss, Reuven. "Ghazan, Islam and Mongol tradition: A view from the Mamlūk sultanate." *BSOAS* 59/1 (1996): 1–10.

Amitai-Preiss, Reuven. *Mongols and Mamluks: The Mamluk-Īlkhānid War, 1260–1281*. Cambridge: Cambridge University Press, 1995.

Arjomand, Said Amir. *The Turban for the Crown*. Oxford: Oxford University Press, 1988.

Ashby, S.P. "What really caused the Viking Age? The social content of raiding and exploration." *Archaeological Dialogues* 22/1 (2015): 89–106.

Aubin, Jean. "Comment Tamerlan prenait les villes." *Studia Islamica* 19 (1963): 83–122.

Aubin, Jean. "Elements for the Study of Urban Agglomerations in Medieval Iran." In *Cities of Medieval Iran*, eds David Durand-Guedy, et al. Leiden: Brill, 2020, pp. 27–38.

Aubin, Jean. "L'ethnogénèse des Qaraunas." *Turcica* 1 (1969): 65–94.

Aubin, Jean. "La fin de l'État Sarbadar du Khorassan." *Journal Asiatique* CCLXII [262] (1974): 95–118.

Aubin, Jean. "Le Khanat de Čaġatai et le Khorassan (1334–1380)." *Turcica* 8/2 (1970): 16–60.

Aubin, Jean. "Le Quriltai de Sultân-Maydân (1336)." *Journal Asiatique* 279 (1991): 175–97.

Aubin, Jean. "Réseau pastoral et réseau caravanier: les grand'routes du Khorassan à l'époque mongole." In *Études sur l'Iran médiéval: géographie historique et société*, ed. Denise Aigle. Paris: Association pour l'avancement des études iraniennes, 2018, pp. 91–113.

Augst, Bedrich. "A Persian coin of the 'Gallows Bird' dynasty." *Numismatic Review* 4, Nos. 2–4 (1947): 91–92.

Ayalon, David. "Regarding Population Estimates in the Countries of Medieval Islam." *JESHO* 28/1 (1985): 1–19.

Ball, Warwick. *Archaeological Gazetteer of Afghanistan*. Oxford: Oxford University Press, 2019.

Ball, Warwick. *Syria: A Historical and Architectural Guide*. Northampton, MA: Interlink, 2007.

Banister, Mustafa. *The Abbasid Caliphate of Cairo, 1261–1517*. Edinburgh: Edinburgh University Press, 2021.

Bano, Shadab. "India's overland slave trade in the medieval period." *PIHC* 58 (1997): 315–21.

Bano, Shadab. "Slave markets in medieval India." *PIHC* 61 (2000): 365–73.

Barfield, Thomas J. *Afghanistan*. Princeton: Princeton University Press, 2010.

Barfield, Thomas J. *The Central Asian Arabs of Afghanistan*. Austin: The University of Texas Press, 1981.

Barfield, Thomas J. *The Perilous Frontier*. Cambridge, MA: Blackwell, 1989.

Barfield, Thomas J. "Turk, Persian, and Arab: Changing Relationships between tribes and state in Iran and along its frontiers." In *Iran and the Surrounding World*, eds. Nikke Keddie and Rudi Matthee. Seattle: University of Washington Press, 2011, pp. 61–86.

Barthold, V.V. *Four Studies on the History of Central Asia: Ulugh Beg*, trs V. and T. Minorsky. Leiden: Brill, 1963.

Barthold, V.V. *An Historical Geography of Iran*, tr. Svat Soucek. Princeton: Princeton University Press, 1984.

Barthold, V.V. *Turkestan Down to the Mongol Invasion*. Cambridge: E.J.W. Gibb Memorial Trust, 4th ed., 1977.

Barzīn-Mihr, ʿAbd al-Ghanī. *Shuʿarā wa fuẓalāʾ dar bārgāh-yi mulūk-i Kart-i Harāt*. Peshawar: n.p., 1377/1998.

Beazley, Elisabeth and Michael Harverson. *Living with the Desert*. Warminster, UK: Aris & Phillips, 1982.

Bellew, H.W. *Record of the March of the Mission to Seistan*. Calcutta: Foreign Department Press, 1873.

Binbaş, İlker Evrim. *Intellectual networks in Timurid Iran: Sharaf al-Dīn ʿAlī Yazdī and the Islamicate republic of letters*. Cambridge: Cambridge University Press, 2016.

Biran, Michal. "The Battle for Herat (1270): A case of inter-Mongol warfare." In *Warfare in Inner Asian History (500–1800)*, ed. Nicolo Di Cosmo. Leiden: Brill, 2002, pp. 175–219.

Biran, Michal. *Chinggis Khan*. Oxford: Oneworld, 2007.

Biran, Michal. *The Empire of the Qara Khitai in Eurasian History*. Cambridge: Cambridge University Press, 2005.

Biran, Michal. *Qaidu and the Rise of the Independent Mongol State in Central Asia*. Richmond: Curzon, 1997.

Blair, Sheila. "The coins of the later Ilkhanids: A typological analysis." *JESHO* 26/3 (1983): 295–317.

Blair, Sheila. "The coins of the later Ilkhānids: Mint organization, regionalization, and urbanism." *Museum Notes* 27 (1982): 211–30.

Bonine, Michael. "From Qanāt to Kort: Traditional Irrigation Terminology and Practices in Central Iran." *Iran* 20 (1982): 145–59.

Bosworth, C.E. "Early Islamic History of Ghūr." *CAJ* 6/2 (1961): 116–33.

Bosworth, C.E. "Sistan and its Local Histories." *Iranian Studies* 33/1 (2000): 31–43.

Bosworth, C.E. *The Ghaznavids*. Edinburgh: Edinburgh University Press, 1963.

Bosworth, C.E. *The New Islamic Dynasties*. Edinburgh: Edinburgh University Press, 1996.

Boyce, Mary (tr.). *The Letter of Tansar*. Rome: Istituto Italiano per il Medio ed Estremo Oriente, 1968.

Brauer, R.W. "Boundaries and frontiers in medieval Muslim geography." *Transactions of the American Philosophical Society* 85/6 (1995): 1–73.

Bregel, Yuri. *An Historical Atlas of Central Asia*. Leiden: Brill, 2003.

Broadbridge, Anne F. *Women and the Making of the Mongol Empire*. Cambridge: Cambridge University Press, 2018.

Brockelmann, Carl. *History of the Arabic Written Tradition*, tr. Joep Lameer, 2 vols, 3 supp. vols. Leiden: Brill, 2017–19.

Bruno, Andrea, et al. *Restoration of Monuments in Herat*. UNESCO Technical Report, UNDP/AFG/75/022, 31 December 1981.

Buchanan, J.M. and D.R. Lee. "Politics, Time, and the Laffer Curve." *Journal of Political Economy* 90/4 (1982): 816–19.

Buell, Paul D. "Early Mongol Expansion in Western Siberia and Turkestan (1207–1219): a Reconstruction." *CAJ* 36/1 (1992): 1–32.

Buell, Paul D. "Sino-Khitan administration in Mongol Bukhara." *JAH* 13/2 (1979): 121–51.

Bulliet, Richard W. "Medieval Nishapur: A Topographic and Demographic Reconstruction." *Studia Iranica* 5 (1976): 67–89.

Bulliet, Richard W. "The Shaikh al-Islām and the Evolution of Islamic Society." *Studia Islamica* 35 (1972): 53–67.

Bulliet, Richard W. *Islam: The View from the Edge*. New York: Columbia University Press, 1994.

Campbell, Bruce. "Arable Productivity in Medieval England: Some Evidence from Norfolk." *The Journal of Economic History* 43/2 (1983): 379–404.

Campbell, Bruce and Mark Overton. "A New Perspective on Medieval and Early Modern Agriculture: Six Centuries of Norfolk Farming *c.*1250–*c.*1850." *Past & Present* 141 (1993): 38–105.

Chawla, J.K. *India's Overland trade with Central Asia and Persia during the thirteenth and fourteenth centuries*. New Delhi: Munshiram Manoharlal Publishers, 2006.

Chevedden, Paul. "The Invention of the Counterweight Trebuchet: A Study in Cultural Diffusion." *Dumbarton Oaks Papers* 54 (2000): 71–116.

Clevenger, W.M. "Dams in Ḫorāsān: Some Preliminary Observations." *East and West* 19/3 (1969): 387–94.

Coats, R.M. and G.M Pecquet. "The calculus of conquests: The decline and fall of the returns to Roman expansion." *The Independent Review* 17/4 (2013): 517–40.

Codrington, O. "Note on Musalman Coins collected by Mr. G.P. Tate in Seistan." *JRAS* (1904): 681–86.

Cook, M.A. *Commanding Right and Forbidding Wrong in Islamic Thought.* Cambridge: Cambridge University Press, 2000.

Crone, Patricia. *Medieval Islamic Political Thought.* Edinburgh: Edinburgh University Press, 2005.

d'Ohsson, Constantin. *Histoire des Mongols.* Amsterdam: Frederik Muller, 1852.

Daryaee, Touraj. *Šahrestānīhā i Ērānšahr [Cities of Iranshahr].* Costa Mesa, CA: Mazda, 2002.

Daryaee, Touraj. *Sasanian Persia.* London: I.B. Tauris, 2009.

Deschamps, Colin and Alan Roe. "Land Conflict in Afghanistan." In *The Rule of Law in Afghanistan*, ed. Whit Mason. Cambridge: Cambridge University Press, 2011, pp. 205–22.

Digby, Simon. *War-horse and Elephant in the Delhi Sultanate: A Study of Military Supplies.* Oxford: Oxford Monographs, 1971.

Dodkhudoeva, Lola. "Translating and copying in pre-Timurid Herat: A Persian translation of the *Iḥya' 'ulūm al-dīn*, 725–726/1325." In *Écrit et culture en Asie centrale et dans le monde turco-iranien Xe-XIXe siècles*, eds Francis Richard and Maria Szuppe. Paris: Studia Iranica Cahier 40, 2010, pp. 165–93.

Dupree, Nancy Hatch. *An Historical Guide to Afghanistan.* Kabul: Afghan Tourist Organization, 1977.

Durand-Guédy, David. "Pre-Mongol Khurasan: A Historical Introduction." In *Greater Khorasan: History, Geography, Archaeology and Material Culture*, ed. Rocco Rante. Berlin: De Gruyter, 2015, pp. 1–8.

Dyer, Christopher. "Villages in crisis: social dislocation and desertion, 1370–1520." In *Deserted Villages Revisited*, eds C. Dyer and R. Jones. Hatfield: University of Hertfordshire Press, 2010, pp. 28–45.

Elias, Jamal J. "The Sufi Lords of Bahrabad: Sa'd al-Din and Sadr al-Din Hamuwayi." *Iranian Studies* 27/1 (1994): 53–75.

Elias, Jamal J. *The Throne Carrier of God.* Albany, NY: SUNY Press, 1985.

Engels, D.W. *Alexander the Great and the Logistics of the Macedonian Army.* Berkeley: University of California Press, 1978.

English, Paul Ward. "The Origin and Spread of Qanats in the Old World." *Proceedings of the American Philosophical Society*, 112/3 (1968): 170–81.

English, Paul Ward. *City and Village in Iran: Settlement and Economy in the Kirman Basin*. London: University of Wisconsin Press, 1966.

Ferrier, J.P. *Caravan Journeys and Wanderings in Persia, Afghanistan, Turkistan and Beloochistan*, tr. W. Jesse. London: John Murray, 1856.

Floor, Willem. "Guilds in Iran: An overview, from the earliest beginnings until 1972." *ZDMG* 125 (1975):99–116.

Fox, Robin Lane. *Alexander the Great*. New York: Penguin, 1986.

Franke, Herbert. "Siege and defense of towns in medieval China." In *Chinese Ways in Warfare*, eds Frank Kierman and John Fairbank. Cambridge, MA: Harvard University Press, 1974, pp. 151–201.

Franke, U., et al. *Ancient Herat: Excavations and Explorations in Herat City*. Berlin: Staatliche Museen zu Berlin, 2017.

Frye, David. *Walls: A History of Civilization in Blood and Brick*. New York: Scribner, 2018.

Frye, R.N. *Bukhara: The Medieval Achievement*. Norman, OK: University of Oklahoma Press, 1965.

Gammel, C.P.W. *The Pearl of Khorasan*. London: Hurst, 2016.

Gaube, Heinz. "Innenstadt und Vorstadt. Kontinuität und Wandel im Stadtbild von Herat zwischen dem 10. und 15. Jahrhundert." In *Beiträge zur Geographie orientalischer Städte und Märkte*, ed. Günther Schweizer. Wiesbaden: Reichert Verlag, 1977, pp. 213–40.

Gaube, Heinz. *Iranian Cities*. New York: New York University Press, 1979.

Gharjistānī, Muḥammad Ismāʿīl Mablagh. "Dānishmand-ān-i muʿāṣir-i dūdmān-i Kart [Scholars Contemporary with the Kartids]." *Āryānā* No. 205 (1338/1960): 49–56.

Gharjistānī, Muḥammad Ismāʿīl Mablagh. "Farmānrawāʾān-i Khaysār [The Castellans of Khaysār]." *Āryānā* No. 182 (1336/1957f.): 29–36.

Gharjistānī, Muḥammad Ismāʿīl Mablagh. "Malik Ghiyāth al-Dīn." *Āryānā* No. 193 (1337/1958f.): 33–41.

Gharjistānī, Muḥammad Ismāʿīl Mablagh. "Malik Muʿizz al-Dīn Ḥusayn [Part 1]." *Āryānā* No. 198 (1337/1958f.): 25–30.

Gharjistānī, Muḥammad Ismāʿīl Mablagh. "Malik Muʿizz al-Dīn Ḥusayn [Part 2]." *Āryānā* No. 199 (1337/1958f.): 25–28.

Gharjistānī, Muḥammad Ismāʿīl Mablagh. "Niwīsandi-gān, Dānishmand-an, Ṣūfī-ān muʿāṣir-i dūdmān-i Kart [Writers, Scholars, and Sufis contemporary with the Kart rulers]." *Āryānā* No. 204 (1338/1959): 23–30.

Gharjistānī, Muḥammad Ismāʿīl Mablagh. "Shams al-Dīn Muḥammad wa Shams al-Dīn Kihīn." *Āryānā* No. 191 (1336/1957f.): 33–35.

Gharjistānī, Muḥammad Ismā'īl Mablagh. "Suqūṭ-i sultanat-i dūdmān-i Kart [Fall of the Kart kingdom]." *Āryānā* No. 200 (1338/1959): 17–24.

Gharjistānī, Muḥammad Ismā'īl Mablagh. "'Urafā' [Associates]." *Āryānā* No. 206 (1338/1960): 48–56.

Gharjistānī, Muḥammad Ismā'īl Mablagh. "Wīrānī-hā wa ābādī-hā-yi mujaddid-i Harāt [Ruin and Revival in Herat]." *Āryānā* No. 185 (1337/1958): 37–40.

Ghasemia, Kimia, Mahdi Hamzenejadb, and Abolfazl Meshkinia. "The livability of Iranian and Islamic cities considering the nature of traditional land uses in the city and the rules of their settlement." *Habitat International* 90 (August 2019): 1–14.

Gibbon, Edward. *The Decline and Fall of the Roman Empire*, vols 1–3 (unabridged). New York: Modern Library, 1995.

Glatzer, Bernt. "War and Boundaries in Afghanistan: Significance and Relativity of Local and Social Boundaries." *Die Welt des Islams* 41/3 (2001): 379–99.

Golombek, Lisa. "The Resilience of the Friday Mosque: the Case of Herat." *Muqarnas* 1 (1983): 95–102.

Golombek, Lisa and Don Wilber. *The Timurid Architecture of Iran and Turan*, 2 vols. Princeton: Princeton University Press, 1988.

Goodrich L.C. and Feng Chia-sheng. "The Early Development of Firearms in China." *Isis* 36/2 (1946): 114–23.

Gregorian, Vartan. *The Emergence of Modern Afghanistan*. Stanford, CA: Stanford University Press, 1969.

Grousset, René. *Empire of the Steppes*. New Brunswick, NJ: Rutgers University Press, 1970.

Ḥabībī, 'Abd al-Ḥayy. "Ta'dīl dar nasab-nāmah-yi Āl-i Kart [Adjustment to the genealogy of the House of Kart]." *Āryānā* No. 68 (1327/1948): 1–8.

Ḥabībī, 'Abd al-Ḥayy. "Waṣiyyat-nāmah-yi malik Ghiyāth al-Dīn Kart." *Āryānā* No. 66 (1327/1948): 38–42.

Harverson, Michael. "Watermills in Iran." *Iran* 31 (1993): 149–77.

Harverson, Michael. *Persian Windmills*. Sprang-Capelle, Netherlands: The International Molinological Society, 1991.

Haw, S.G. "The Mongol Empire: the first 'gunpowder empire'?." *JRAS* 23/3 (2013): 441–69.

Hemming, R. and J.A. Kay. "The Laffer Curve." *Fiscal Studies* 1/2 (1980): 83–90.

Herrmann, Georgina, et al. "The International Merv Project. Preliminary Report on the Eighth Season (1999)." *Iran* 38 (2000): 1–31.

Herrmann, Gottfried. "Zur Entstehung des Ṣadr-Amtes." In *Die Islamische Welt zwischen Mittelalter und Neuzeit*, eds Ulrich Haarmann and P. Bachmann. Beirut: Franz Steiner Verlag, 1979, pp. 278–95.

Holt, F.L. *The Treasures of Alexander the Great*. Oxford: Oxford University Press, 2016.

Hope, Michael. "The 'Nawrūz King': the rebellion of Amir Nawrūz in Khurasan (688–694/1289–94) and its implications for the Ilkhan polity at the end of the thirteenth century." *BSOAS* 78/3 (2015): 451–73.

Hope, Michael. "The Political Configuration of Late Ilkhanid Iran: A Case Study of the Chubanid Amirate (738–758/1337–1357)." *Iran* 60 (forthcoming).

Hope, Michael. "Some Notes on Revenge and Justice in the Mongol Empire and the Īl-Khānate of Iran." *JAOS* 136/3 (2016): 551–66.

Hope, Michael. "The Transmission of Authority through the Quriltais of the Early Mongol Empire and the Īlkhānate of Iran (1227–1335)." *Mongolian Studies* 34 (2012): 87–115.

Hope, Michael. *Power, Politics, and Tradition in the Mongol Empire and the Īlkhānate of Iran*. Oxford: Oxford University Press, 2016.

Hsiao, Ch'i-Ch'ing. *The Military Establishment of the Yuan Dynasty*. London and Cambridge, MA: Harvard University Press, 1978.

Hume, David. *A Treatise of Human Nature*, ed. L.A. Selby-Bigge. Oxford: Clarendon, 1888.

Itemadi, Guya [Gūyā 'Ittimādī]. "The General Mosque of Herat." *Afghanistan* 8/2 (Kabul, 1953): 40–50.

'Ittimādī, Gūyā. "Darbār-i mulūk-i Kart." *Āryānā* No. 2/16 (1323/1944): 46–54.

Jackson, Peter. "The Dissolution of the Mongol Empire." *CAJ* 22/3 (1978): 186–244.

Jackson, Peter. "Jalāl al-Dīn, the Mongols, and the Khwarazmian Conquest of the Panjāb and Sind." *Iran* 29 (1990): 45–54.

Jackson, Peter. "Marco Polo and His 'Travels'." *BSOAS* 61/1 (1998): 82–101.

Jackson, Peter. "The Mongols and the Delhi Sultanate in the reign of Muḥammad Tughluq (1325–1351)." *CAJ* 19 (1975): 118–57.

Jackson, Peter. *The Delhi Sultanate*. Cambridge: Cambridge University Press, 1999.

Jackson, Peter. *The Mongols and the Islamic World*. London and New Haven: Yale University Press, 2017.

Jarring, Gunnar. "A Note on Qarauna." *Orientalia Suecana* 40 (1991): 146–48.

Jarring, Gunnar. *On the distribution of Turk tribes in Afghanistan: An attempt at a preliminary classification*. Lund: Gleerup, 1939.

Jones, Richard. "Contrasting patterns of village and hamlet desertion in England." In *Deserted Villages Revisited*, eds C. Dyer and R. Jones. Hatfield: University of Hertfordshire Press, 2010, pp. 8–27.

Kamola, Stefan. *Making Mongol History: Rashid al-Din and the Jami' al-tawarikh*. Edinburgh: Edinburgh University Press, 2019.

Kato, Kazuhide. "Kebek and Yasawr: the Establishment of the Chaghatai Khanate." *Memoirs of the Research Department of the Toyo Bunko* 49 (1991): 97–118.

Keegan, John. *Intelligence in War*. New York: Knopf, 2003.

Keeley, L.H., et al. "Baffles and Bastions: The Universal Features of Fortifications." *Journal of Archaeological Research* 15/1 (2007): 55–95.

Kempiners, Russell. "The Struggle for Khurasan: Aspects of Political, Military, and Socio-economic Interaction in the Early 8th/14th Century." Ph.D. diss., University of Chicago, 1985.

Kitson, Frank. *Low Intensity Operations*. London: Faber & Faber, 1971.

Knight, Frank. *Risk, Uncertainty, and Profit*. Boston: Houghton Mifflin, 1921.

Kurrild-Klitgaard, Peter and Gert Tinggaard Svendsen. "Rational bandits: Plunder, public goods, and the Vikings." *Public Choice* 117 (2003): 255–72.

Lacey, J. *Gold, Blood, and Power: Finance and War through the Ages*. Carlisle Barracks, PA: U.S. Army War College Press, 2015.

Lambton, A.K.S. "The *Athar wa ahya'* of Rashid al-Din Fadl Allah and his contribution as an agronomist, arboriculturist and horticulturlist." In *The Mongol Empire and its Legacy*, eds. R. Amitai and David Morgan. Leiden: Brill, 1999, pp. 126–54.

Lambton, A.K.S. "Concepts of Authority in Persia: Eleventh to Nineteenth Centuries A.D." *Iran* 26 (1988): 95–103.

Lambton, A.K.S. "Mongol Fiscal Administration in Persia." *Studia Islamica* 64 (1986): 79–99.

Lambton, A.K.S. "'Pīshkash': Present or Tribute?" *BSOAS* 57/1 (1994): 145–58.

Lambton, A.K.S. "The Qanāts of Yazd." *JRAS* 2/1 (1992): 21–35.

Lambton, A.K.S. "The Regulation of the Waters of the Zāyande Rūd." *BSOAS* 9/3 (1938): 663–73.

Lambton, A.K.S. *Landlord and Peasant*. London: I.B. Tauris, 1991.

Lambton, A.K.S. *State and Government in Medieval Islam*. London: Routledge, 1981.

Lane, George. "Arghun Aqa: Mongol Bureaucrat." *Iranian Studies* 32/4 (1999): 459–82.

Lane, George. *Early Mongol Rule in Thirteenth-Century Iran*. London: RoutledgeCurzon, 2003.

Lane, George. *The Mongols in Iran: Quṭb al-Dīn Shīrāzī's Akhbār-i Moghūlān*. New York: Routledge, 2018.

Lapidus, Ira M. "The Grain Economy of Mamluk Egypt." *JESHO* 12/1 (1969): 1–15.

Le Strange, Guy. *The Lands of the Eastern Caliphate*. New York: Barnes & Noble, 1966.

Levi, Margaret. "The Predatory Theory of Rule." *Politics & Society* 10/4 (1981): 431–65.

Levi, Margaret. *Of Rule and Revenue*. Berkeley: University of California Press, 1988.

Limbert, John. *Iran: At War with History*. Boulder: Westview Press, 1987.

Limbert, John. *Shiraz in the Age of Hafez*. Seattle: University of Washington Press, 2004.

Lindisfarne-Tapper, Nancy. "The advent of Pashtūn 'Māldārs' in north-western Afghanistan." *BSOAS* 36/1 (1973): 55–79.

Ling, Wang. "On the invention and use of Gunpowder and Firearms in China." *Isis* 37/3 (1947): 160–78.

Loader, N.C. "A Possible East Sally-Port in the North-East Extension at Mycenae? A Brief Note." *The Annual of the British School at Athens* 91 (1996): 191–96.

Locke, John. *Second Treatise on Government*, ed. C.B. Macpherson. Indianapolis: Hackett, 1980.

MacGregor, C.M. *Central Asia: Part II*. Calcutta: Office of the Superintendent of Government Printing, 1871.

McGuire, M.C. and Mancur Olson. "The economics of autocracy and majority rule: the invisible hand and the use of force." *Journal of Economic Literature* 34/1 (1996): 72–96.

McNally, David. *Blood and Money: War, Slavery, Finance, and Empire*. Chicago: Haymarket, 2020.

Mahendrarajah, Shivan. "A revised history of Mongol, Kart, and Timurid patronage of the shrine of Shaykh al-Islam Ahmad-i Jam." *Iran* 54/2 (2016): 107–28.

Mahendrarajah, Shivan. "The Sarbadars of Sabzavar: Re-examining their 'Shiʿa' roots and alleged goal to 'destroy Khurasanian Sunnism'." *Journal of Shiʿa Islamic Studies* 5/4 (2012): 379–402.

Mahendrarajah, Shivan. "The Shaykh al-Islam in Medieval Khurasan." *Afghanistan* 1/2 (2018): 257–81.

Mahendrarajah, Shivan. "Tamerlane's conquest of Herat and the 'politics of notables'." *Studia Iranica* 46/1 (2017): 49–76.

Mahendrarajah, Shivan. *The Sufi Saint of Jam: History, Religion, and Politics of a Sunni Shrine in Shiʿi Iran.* Cambridge: Cambridge University Press, 2021.

Malleson, G.B. *Herat: The Granary and Garden of Central Asia.* London: Allen & Co., 1880.

Manz, Beatrice Forbes. "The ulus Chaghatai before and after Temür's rise to power: The transformation from tribal confederation to army of conquest," *CAJ* 27/1 (1983):79–100.

Manz, Beatrice Forbes. *Power, Politics and Religion in Timurid Iran.* Cambridge: Cambridge University Press, 2007.

Manz, Beatrice Forbes. *The Rise and Rule of Tamerlane.* Cambridge: Cambridge University Press, 1989.

Marsden, E.W. *Greek and Roman Artillery: Historical Development.* Oxford: Clarendon, 1969.

Martini, G.M. *ʿAlaʾ al-Dawla al-Simnani between spiritual authority and political power.* Leiden: Brill, 2018.

Matsui, Dai. "Six Seals on the Verso of Čoban's Decree of 726 AH/1326 CE." *Orient* 50 (Japan, 2015):35–39.

May, Timothy. "Military Integration in Mongol Warfare: The development of Combined Arms Warfare in the Mongol Empire." *Acta Mongolica* (2019): 41–51.

May, Timothy. *The Mongol Art of War.* Barnsley, UK: Pen & Sword, 2007.

May, Timothy. *The Mongol Empire.* Edinburgh: Edinburgh University Press, 2018.

May, Timothy. "The Ilkhanate and Afghanistan." In *New Approaches to Ilkhanid History*, eds T. May, et al. Leiden: Brill, 2020, pp. 272–320.

Melville, C.P. "Abū Saʿīd and the revolt of the Amirs in 1319." In *L'Iran la face à la domination mongole*, ed. Denise Aigle. Téhéran: Institut Français de Recherche en Iran, 1997, pp. 89–120.

Melville, C.P. "The Itineraries of Sultan Öljeitü, 1304–16." *Iran* 28 (1990): 55–70.

Melville, C.P. "Pādshāh-i Islām: The Conversion of Sultan Maḥmūd Ghāzān Khān." *Pembroke Papers* 1 (1990): 159–77.

Melville, C.P. "Persian Local Histories: Views from the Wings." *Iranian Studies* 33/1 (2000): 7–14.

Melville, C.P. *The Fall of Amir Chupan and the Decline of the Ilkhanate, 1327–37: A Decade of Discord in Mongol Iran.* Bloomington, IN: Research Institute for Inner Asian Studies, 1999.

Melville, C.P. "The Mongol and Timurid Periods, 1250–1500." In *Persian Historiography*, ed. C.P. Melville. London: I.B. Tauris, 2012, pp. 155–208.

Mesgaran, M.B., et al. "Iran's Land Suitability for Agriculture." *Scientific Reports* 7, no. 7670 (2017): 1–12.

Millward, James. *Eurasian Crossroads: A History of Xinjiang*. New York: Columbia University Press, 2007.

Minovi, M. and Vladimir Minorsky. "Naṣīr al-Dīn Ṭūṣī on Finance." *BSOAS* 10/3 (1940): 755–89.

Mohebbi, Parviz. *Techniques et ressources en Iran: du 7e au 19e siecle*. Teheran: Institut Français de Recherche en Iran, 1996.

Momen, Moojan. *An Introduction to Shi'i Islam*. London: Yale University Press, 1985.

Monsutti, Alessandro. *War and Migration: Social Networks and Economic Strategies of Hazaras of Afghanistan*. New York: Routledge, 2005.

Morgan, David O. "The Decline and Fall of the Mongol Empire." *JRAS* 19/4 (2009): 427–37.

Morgan, David O. "The 'Great "*yāsā*" of Chingiz Khān' and Mongol Law in the Īlkhānate." *BSOAS* 49/1 (1986):163–76.

Morgan, David O. "The Mongol Armies in Persia." *Der Islam* 56/1 (1979): 81–96.

Morgan, David O. *The Mongols*. Oxford: Blackwell, 2d ed., 2007.

Morton, A.H. "The History of the Sarbadars in Light of New Numismatic Evidence," *Numismatic Chronicle* 16 (1976): 255–58.

Mottahedeh, Roy. *Loyalty and Leadership in an Early Islamic Community*. New York: I.B. Tauris, 2001.

Mottahedeh, Roy. "Medieval Lexicography on Arabic and Persian terms for City and Countryside." In *Cities of Medieval Iran*, eds David Durand-Guedy, et al. Leiden: Brill, 2020, pp. 465–78.

Mottahedeh, Roy. and K. Stilt. "Public and private as viewed through the work of the 'Muhtasib'." *Social Research* 70/3 (2003): 735–48.

Mouhammed, A. H. "Ibn Khaldun and the neo-liberal model." *History of Economic Ideas* 12/3 (2004):85–109.

Mousavi, Sayed A. *The Hazaras of Afghanistan*. Richmond: Curzon, 1998.

Mt. Pleasant, Jane. "The Paradox of Plows and Productivity." *Agricultural History* 85/4 (2011): 460–92.

Murtazashvili, J.B. and I. Murtazashvili. *Land, the State, and War*. Cambridge: Cambridge University Press, 2021.

Najimi, A.W. "The Cistern at Char-Suq." *Afghanistan Journal* 9/2 (Graz, 1982): 38–41.

Najimi, A.W. "The restored mausoleum of Abu'l-Walid in Herat: Challenges in heritage restoration in Afghanistan." *Afghanistan* 1/2 (2018): 302–36.

Needham, Joseph and Robin Yates. *Science and Civilization in China*, vol. 5. Cambridge: Cambridge University Press, 2002.

Nicolle, David. "Medieval Warfare: The Unfriendly Interface." *The Journal of Military History* 63/3 (1999): 579–99.

Niedermayer, Oskar von. *Afghanistan*. Leipzig: Hiersemann, 1924.

Noelle-Karimi, Christine. *The Pearl in its Midst: Herat and the Mapping of Khurasan (15th–19th centuries)*. Vienna: Österreichischen Akademie der Wissenschaften, 2014.

O'Kane, Bernard. *Timurid Architecture in Khurasan*. Costa Mesa, CA: Mazda, 1987.

Olson, Mancur. "Dictatorship, democracy, and development." *American Political Science Review* 87/3 (1993): 567–76.

Olson, Mancur. *The Logic of Collective Action: Public Goods and the Theory of Groups*. Cambridge: Harvard University Press, 1971.

Olson, Mancur. *Power and Prosperity*. New York: Basic, 2000.

Partington, J.R. *A History of Greek Fire and Gunpowder*. Baltimore: Johns Hopkins University Press, 1999.

Paterson, W.F. "The Archers of Islam." *JESHO* 9/1 (1966): 69–87.

Paul, Jürgen. "The Histories of Herat." *Iranian Studies* 33/1 (2000): 93–115.

Paul, Jürgen. "Le village en asie centrale aux XVe et XVIe siècles," *Cahiers du Monde russe et soviétique* 32, no. 1 (1991): 9–15.

Paul, Jürgen. "Local Lords or Rural Notables: Some Remarks on the *ra'īs* in Twelfth-Century Eastern Iran." In *Medieval Central Asia and the PersianateWorld*, eds A.C.S. Peacock and D.G. Tor. London: I.B. Tauris, 2015, pp. 174–209.

Paul, Jürgen. "Zerfall und Bestehen: Die Ǧaun-i qurban im 14. Jahrhundert." *Asiatische Studien/Études Asiatiques* 65/3 (2011): 695–733.

Paul, Jürgen. *Herrscher, Gemeinwesen, Vermittler: Ostiran und Transoxanien in vormongolischer Zeit*. Stuttgart: Franz Steiner, 1996.

Petrushevsky [Petrushevskiĭ], I.P. "The Socio-Economic Conditions of Iran under the Il-Khans." *CHI* 5: 483–537.

Petrushevsky [Petrushevskiĭ], I.P. *Kishāwarzī wa munāsabāt-i arżī dar Īrān-i ʿahd-i Mughūl*, tr. Karīm Kishāwarz, 2 vols. Tehran: Intishārāt-i nīl, 1347/1968.

Petrushevsky [Petrushevskiĭ], I.P. *Nahżat-i Sarbadārān-i Khurāsān*, tr. Karīm Kishāwarz. Tehran: Intishārāt-i Payām, 1351/1972.

Philippides, M. and W.K. Hanak. *The Siege and the Fall of Constantinople in 1453*. Burlington, VT: Ashgate, 2011.

Pizhwāk, ʿAtīq-Allāh. *Ghūriyān.* [Kabul]: Anjuman-i tārīkh-i Afghānistān, 1345/1967.

Potter, Lawrence. "The Kart Dynasty of Herat: Religion and Politics in Medieval Iran." Ph.D. diss., Columbia University, 1992.

Pour, Ali Bahrani. "The Trade in Horses between Khorasan and India in the 13th–17th Centuries." *The Silk Road* 11 (2013): 123–38.

Pow, Stephen. "Fortresses that shatter empires: A look at Möngke Khan's failed campaign against the Song Dynasty, 1258–1259." *Annual of Medieval Studies at CEU*, 23 (2017): 96–107.

Pow, Stephen. "The last campaign and death of Jebe Noyan." *JRAS* 27/1 (2017): 31–51.

Purton, Peter. *A History of the Late Medieval Siege, 1200–1500.* Woodbridge: Boydell, 2010.

Rante, Rocco. "'Khorasan Proper' and 'Greater Khorasan' within a politico-cultural framework." In *Greater Khorasan: History, Geography, Archaeology and Material Culture*, ed. Rocco Rante. Berlin: De Gruyter, 2015, pp. 9–26.

Raphael, Kate. "Mongol Siege Warfare on the Banks of the Euphrates and the Question of Gunpowder (1260–1312)." *JRAS* 19/3 (2009): 355–70.

Raphael, Kate. *Muslim Fortresses in the Levant.* London: Routledge, 2011.

Ratchnevsky, Paul. *Genghis Khan.* Oxford: Blackwell, 2003.

Reclus, Elisée. *The Universal Geography: Earth and its Inhabitants*, vol. 9, ed. A.H. Keane. London: J.S. Virtue, [1890?].

Reid, James. "The Je'ün-i Qurbān Oirat Clan in the Fourteenth Century." *JAH* 18/2 (1984): 189–200.

St John, Oliver, B. Lovett, E. Smith, et al. *Eastern Persia: An Account of the Journeys of the Persian Boundary Commission, 1870–71–72*, 2 vols. London: Macmillan, 1876.

Salikuddin, R.K. "Sufis, Saints, and Shrine: Piety in the Timurid Period, 1370–1507." Ph.D. diss., Harvard University, 2018.

Saljooqi, Fikri. "The complete copy of the ancient inscription of the Ghiassuddin grand mosque in Herat." *Afghanistan* 20/3 (Kabul, 1967): 78–80.

Saljūqī, Fikrī. *Bakhshī az tārikh-i Harāt-i bāstān.* Kabul: Maṭbaʿa-i dawlatī, 1362/1983.

Saljūqī, Fikrī. *Khiyābān.* Kabul: Intishārāt-i anjuman-i Jāmī, 1343/1964.

Samizay, Rafi. *Islamic Architecture in Herat.* [Kabul]: The Ministry of Information and Culture, 1981.

Sayyidī, Mahdī. *Jughrāfiyā-yi tārīkhī-yi Marw.* Tehran: Bunyād-i mawqūfāt-i Duktur Maḥmūd Afshār, 1386/2008.

Schade, Abigail E. "Hidden Waters: Groundwater Histories of Iran and the Mediterranean." Ph.D. diss., Columbia University, 2011.

Schama, Simon. *Citizens: A Chronicle of the French Revolution.* New York: Penguin, 1989.

Schimmel, Annemarie. *Islamic Names.* Edinburgh: Edinburgh University Press, 1989.

Schmitt, Rüdiger. *The Bisitun Inscriptions of Darius the Great.* London: Corpus Inscriptionum Iranicarum, 1991.

Schurmann, Franz. "Mongolian Tributary Practices of the Thirteenth Century." *HJAS* 19/3 (1956): 304–89.

Serjeant, R.B. "Material for a History of Islamic Textiles up to the Mongol Conquest." *Ars Islamica* 9 (1942): 54–92.

Serjeant, R.B. "Material for a History of Islamic Textiles up to the Mongol Conquest." *Ars Islamica* 11 (1946): 98–145.

Sheridan, James. *Chinese Warlord: the Career of Feng Yü-hsiang.* Stanford, CA: Stanford University Press, 1966.

Shimo, Hirotoshi. "The Qarāūnās in the Historical Materials of the Īlkhanate." *Memoirs of the Research Department of the Toyo Bunko* 35 (1977): 131–81.

Shokoohy, M. "The Monuments at the Quhandiz of Herat, Afghanistan." *JRAS* 1 (1983): 7–31.

Shoshan, Boaz. "The 'Politics of Notables' in Medieval Islam." *Asian and African Studies* 20/2 (1986): 179–215.

Shoshan, Boaz. *Popular Culture in Medieval Cairo.* Cambridge: Cambridge University Press, 1993.

Silverstein, Adam. *Postal Systems in the Pre-Modern Islamic World.* Cambridge: Cambridge University Press, 2007.

Sīstānī, M.A. "Jughrāfiyā-yi tārīkhī-i Zaranj" [Part 1]. *Āryānā* No. 272 (1346/1967): 11–25.

Sīstānī, M.A. "Jughrāfiyā-yi tārīkhī-i Zaranj" [Part 2]. *Āryānā* No. 273 (1346/1967): 15–27.

Smith, Adam. *An Inquiry into the Nature and Causes of the Wealth of Nations*, ed. Edwin Cannan. Chicago: University of Chicago Press, 1976 [2012 reprint].

Smith, Adam. *Lectures on Jurisprudence*, eds R.L. Meek, et al. Oxford: Clarendon, 1978.

Smith, Anthony. *Blind White Fish in Persia.* New York: E.P Dutton, 1953.

Smith, Jr., John Masson. "Demographic Considerations in Mongol Siege Warfare." *Archivum Ottomanicum* 13 (1993–94): 329–34.

Smith, Jr., John Masson. "From Pasture to Manger: The Evolution of Mongol Cavalry Logistics in Yuan China and its Consequences." In *Pferde in Asien*, eds B.G. Fragner, et al. Vienna: Österreichischen Akademie der Wissenschaften, 2009, pp. 63–73.

Smith, Jr., John Masson. "Mongol Manpower and Persian Population." *JESHO* 18 (1975): 271–99.

Smith, Jr., John Masson. "Mongol and Nomadic Taxation." *HJAS* 30 (1970): 46–85.

Smith, Jr., John Masson. "Mongol Society and Military in the Middle East: Antecedents and Adaptations." In *War and Society in the Eastern Mediterranean: 7th–15th centuries*, ed. Yaacov Lev. Leiden: Brill, 1997, pp. 249–66.

Smith, Jr., John Masson. "Mongol Warfare with Chinese Weapons: Catapults—and Rockets?" In *Tsentral'naia Aziia ot Akhemenidov do Timuridov*, ed. V.P. Nikonorov. St Petersburg: In-t istorii material'noĭ kul'tury RAN, 2005), pp. 320–22.

Smith, Jr., John Masson. *The History of the Sarbadar Dynasty, 1336–1381 A. and its Sources*. The Hague and Paris: Mouton, 1970.

Soucek, Svat. *Inner Asia*. Cambridge: Cambridge University Press, 2000.

Subtelny, Maria. "Mirak-i Sayyid Ghiyas and the Timurid Tradition of Landscape Architecture: Further Notes to 'A Medieval Persian Agricultural Manual in Context'." *Studia Iranica* 24, no. 1 (1995): 19–60.

Subtelny, Maria. "A Persian Agricultural Manual in Context: The *Irshad al-zira'a* in Late Timurid and Early Safavid Khorasan." *Studia Iranica* 22 (1993): 167–217.

Subtelny, Maria. "A Timurid Educational and Charitable Foundation: The Ikhlasiyya complex of 'Ali Shir Nava'i in 15th-century Herat and its endowment." *JAOS* 111/1 (1991): 38–61.

Subtelny, Maria. *Le Monde est un Jardin: Aspects de l'histoire culturelle de l'Iran médiéval*. Paris: Association pour l'avancement des études iraniennes, 2002.

Subtelny, Maria. *Timurids in Transition*. Leiden: Brill, 2007.

Szabo, Albert and Thomas J. Barfield. *Afghanistan: An Atlas of Indigenous Domestic Architecture*. Austin: University of Texas Press, 1991.

Tarver, W.T.S. "The Traction Trebuchet: A Reconstruction of an Early Medieval Siege Engine." *Technology and Culture* 36/1 (1995): 136–67.

Tate, G.P. *Seistan*. Quetta: Nisa, n.d. [1979]. Reprint of 1910–12 Calcutta edition.

Tent, Jan. "Approaches to Research in Toponymy." *Names* 63/2 (2015): 65–74.

Tilly, Charles. *Coercion, Capital, and European States, AD 990–1990*. Cambridge, MA: Basil Blackwell, 1990.

Toy, Sidney. *A History of Fortification: From 3000 BC to AD 1700*. London: Heinemann, 1955.

Toy, Sidney. *Strongholds of India*. London: Heinemann, 1957.

Tumanovich, Natalia Nikolaevna. *Gerat v XVI–XVIII vekakh*. Moscow: Nauka, Glaunaja Redakcija Vostochos, 1989.

Van Creveld, Martin. *Technology and War*. New York: The Free Press, 1991.

Van Millingen, A. *Byzantine Constantinople: The Walls of the City and Adjoining Historical Sites*. London: John Murray, 1899.

Watabe, Ryoko. "Census-taking and the Qubchur taxation system in Ilkhanid Iran." *Memoirs of the Research Department of the Toyo Bunko* 73 (2015): 27–63.

Watt, J.C.Y. and A.E. Wardwell. *When Silk was Gold: Central Asian and Chinese Textiles*. New York: The Metropolitan Museum of Art, 1997.

Wheatley, Paul. *The Places Where Men Pray Together*. Chicago: University of Chicago Press, 2001.

Wilber, Donald. *Afghanistan*. New Haven: HRAF Press, 1962.

Wilber, Donald. *The Architecture of Islamic Iran: The Il Khanid Period*. Princeton: Princeton University Press, 1955.

Wily, Liz Alden. "The battle over pastures: The hidden war in Afghanistan." *Revue des mondes musulmans et de la Méditerranée* 133 (2013): 95–113.

Wing, Patrick. "The Decline of the Ilkhanate and the Mamluk Sultanate's Eastern Frontier." *Mamluk Studies Review* 11/2 (2007): 77–88.

Wing, Patrick. *The Jalayirids: Dynastic State Formation in the Mongol Middle East*. Edinburgh: Edinburgh University Press, 2016.

Wittfogel, K.A. *Oriental Despotism*. New Haven: Yale University Press, 1957.

Wolfe, Nancy Hatch. *Herat: A Pictorial Guide*. Kabul: Afghan Tourist Organization, 1966.

Woods, John E. "The Rise of Tīmūrid Historiography." *JNES* 46/2 (1987): 81–108.

Woods, John E. *The Timurid Dynasty*. Bloomington: Research Institute for Inner Asian Studies, 1990.

Wrathmell, Stuart. "The desertion of Wharram Percy village and its wider context." In *Deserted Villages Revisited*, eds C. Dyer and R. Jones. Hatfield: University of Hertfordshire Press, 2010, pp. 109–120.

Wulff, H.E. "The Qanats of Iran." *Scientific American* 218/4 (1968): 94–105.

Wulff, H.E. *The Traditional Crafts of Persia*. Cambridge, MA: MIT Press, 1966.

Würtz, Thomas. *Islamische Theologie im 14. Jahrhundert*. Berlin: de Gruyter, 2016.

Yate, C.E. *Khurasan and Sistan*. Edinburgh: William Blackwood, 1900.

Yate, C.E. *Northern Afghanistan*. Edinburgh: William Blackwood, 1888.

Yokkaichi, Yasuhiro. "Four Seals in Phags-pa and Arabic Scripts on Amīr Čoban's Decree of 726 AH/1326 CE." *Orient* 50 (Japan, 2015): 25–33.

Young, Andrew. "What does it take for a roving bandit to settle down?: Theory and an illustrative history of the Visigoths." *Public Choice* 168 (2016): 75–102.

Yusuf ʿAli, ʿAbdullah. *The Meaning of the Holy Qurʾan.* Beltsville, MD: Amana, 11th ed., 2004.

Zaehner, R.C. *The Dawn and Twilight of Zoroastrianism.* New York: Putnam, 1961.

Zambaur, Eric von. "Contributions à la numismatique Orientale." *Numismatische Zeitschrift* 36 (1904): 43–122.

Zambaur, Eric von. "Contributions à la numismatique Orientale." *Numismatische Zeitschrift* 37 (1905): 113–98.

Zanganah, Ibrāhīm. *Sarzamīn-i Jām wa rijāl-ān [Jām Region and its Eminent Men].* Turbat-i Jām: Intishārāt-i Shaykh al-Islām Aḥmad-i Jām, 1384/2006.

## Encyclopaedia Articles

Bosworth, C.E. "Āl-e Afrāsīāb." *EIr*, 1:742–43.

Bosworth, C.E. "Āl-e Borhān." *EIr*, 1:753–54.

Bosworth, C.E. "Ghurids." *EIr*, 10:586–90.

Cahen, C., et al., "Ḥisba," *EI²*, 3:485–93.

Creswel, K.A.C. "Bāb." *EI²*, 1:830–32.

Darley-Doran, R.E. "Tanga and Tanka." *EI²*, 10:185.

Doerfer, F. "Āl tamghā." *EIr*, 1:766–68.

Eilers, W. and C. Herrenschmidt. "Banda." *EIr*, 3: 682–85.

Floor, W. and W. Kleiss. "Bathhouses." *EIr*, 3: 863–69.

Hunwick, J.O. "Takfīr." *EI²*, 10:122.

Jackson, Peter. "Aḥmad Takūdār." *EIr*, 1:661–62.

Jackson, Peter. "Arpā Khan." *EIr*, 2:518–19.

Jackson, Peter. "Jalayerids." *EIr*, 14:415–19.

Jackson, Peter. "Toḡa Timur." *EIr* (online only).

Kadi, Wadad. "Authority." *EQ*, 1:188–90.

Khazeni, Arash. "Herat i: Geography." *EIr*, 12:203–05.

Kiani, Mohammad-Yusuf and Wolfram Kleiss. "Caravansary." *EIr* 4:798–802.

Labbaf-Khaniki, M., R. Rante, C. Ceretti, M. Luce, C.E. Bosworth, D.G. Tor, K. Ghereghlou, Y.M. Haghighi, A. Tarzi, and P. Oberling, "Khorasan." *EIr*, 16:591–672.

Lewinstein, Keith. "Gog and Magog." *EQ*, 2:331–33.

Madelung, Wilferd. “Taftazani.” *EI*$^{2}$, 10:88–89.
Melville, C.P. and ʿAbbas Zaryab, “Chobanids.” *EIr*, 5:496–502.
Morony, M. “Mulūk al-ṭawāʾīf.” *EI*$^{2}$, 7:551–52.
Oberling, Pierre. “Khalaj.” *EIr*, 15:363–64.
Renard, John. “Alexander.” *EQ* 1: 61–62.
Wing, Patrick. *EI*$^{3}$, “Bāydū.” 2015–04 (online only), 52–54.

# Index

EU representative:
Easy Access System Europe
Mustamäe tee 50, 10621 Tallinn, Estonia
Gpsr.requests@easproject.com

www.ingramcontent.com/pod-product-compliance
Lightning Source LLC
Chambersburg PA
CBHW072236070126
37904CB00019B/226
* 9 7 8 1 4 7 4 4 9 9 3 5 4 *